TOP BIRDING SPOTS of Southern Africa

TOP BIRDING SPOTS
of Southern Africa

compiled by
Hugh Chittenden

Line drawings by
Tony Clarkson

SOUTHERN
BOOK PUBLISHERS

ISBN 1 86812 419 3

First edition, first impression 1992
First edition, second impression 1993

Published by
Southern Book Publishers (Pty) Ltd
PO Box 3103, Halfway House, 1685

Cover design by D+R Designs
Cover photograph Nico Myburgh
Maps by Rina Coetzee
Set in 8 on 10 pt Times Roman
by Rina Coetzee
Printed and bound by Sigma Press, Pretoria

Preface

The localities covered in this book represent many of the prime and pristine habitats left in southern Africa. This book is published at a time when world focus and awareness are centred on global habitat destruction and pollution. Africa's magnificent forests and woodland are still disappearing at an alarming rate, a direct result of soaring population numbers. May we in South Africa preserve what is left of our natural habitats and strive to manage them in such a way that we can honestly hand them over to our children in a better state than they were left to us. Changes to bird population and diversity in these areas will reflect the effectiveness of our land management in years to come.

This book is affectionately dedicated to my wife, Loueen, who has for many years encouraged me in my pursuit of amateur ornithology in my spare time.

Acknowledgements

As can be seen from the long list of contributors, this book is the culmination of many hours of work by interested birders throughout southern Africa. I would especially like to thank Digby Cyrus for his help and encouragement from the start and for reviewing some of the local draft manuscripts. John McAllister, co-ordinator for the Transvaal, did more than his share to maintain a high standard in that region. I am indebted to his enthusiasm and was privileged to work with someone who has such a vast knowledge of the Transvaal birds.

I sincerely thank those who co-ordinated each region (in order geographically from north to south): Kit Hustler - Zimbabwe, John Mendelsohn - Namibia, Dave Bishop - Botswana, John McAllister - Transvaal, Corné Anderson - Northern Cape, Vincent Parker - Swaziland, Deon du Plessis - Orange Free State, Nigel Robson - Natal Midlands, Dave Brown - Eastern Cape and Phil Hockey - South-western Cape. I thank Derek Solomon for his time and assistance in helping with the Zimbabwean region. In addition to those mentioned above, draft manuscripts were also improved by David Johnson. To all of them, I am indebted. I would also like to thank P.A. Clancey for his assistance and for allowing me to use his list of southern African endemics. Ken Newman, who gave willingly of his time, I thank not only for his contributions but also for his advice and encouragement. Rob Martin, Peter Ginn and Pete Outhwaite are thanked for their help and for improving some of the original drafts.

The following are thanked for their assistance in various ways: Hu Berry, Aldo Berutti, Bophuthatswana National Parks Board, Richard Boon, Chris Brown, G. Brumme, Peter Caldwell-Barr, Mike Damp, Gary Davies, Kobus de Kok, Klaas Devenish, Liz Fraser, J.H. Grobler, Richard Hurt, Neville Hoets, Peter Lawson, Gordon Maclean, John McGowan, Peter Moore, Colin Saunders, Warwick Tarboton, Marie Timpany, Rita van Dyk, Helen Valentine, Elaine Volbrecht, Dave White and John Wyatt. A special thanks to Craig Thomassen for his help with records from Itala, and to Tony Clarkson for doing the line drawings.

I wish to thank my parents, who from an early age gave me the encouragement and the opportunity (especially during my high school days) to enjoy and appreciate outdoor life, particularly the avifauna of southern Africa. To my three good friends and partners in the forest, who have accompanied me on many hours of forest birding - thank you Barry Emberton, Hamish McLaggan and Derek Coley.

My warm thanks go to Janet Kloke who diligently helped with the typing, often long after the sun had gone down! To our children, Clair, Jinty, Gareth, Hayley and Jonathan, we thank them not only for their help, but also for their patience with busy parents, often too busy to give them time over weekends!

My wife, Loueen, who put in as many hours towards this book as I did, deserves all the praise (and more) that I can give. Without her continual inspiration, motivation and tremendous support, this book would not have become a reality.

Hugh Chittenden

Contents

Introduction

As has been the trend overseas, birding has become an extremely popular pastime here in the southern African subregion too.

This book has been designed to be used in the field, a book in which notes can be made and checklists ticked, crossed and marked. For those who do not like making lists or keeping records, it will be a useful fieldguide, both to the common species one should find during a short visit and as a guide to the more uncommon species in a particular locality.

The production of this book was a team effort. I was priviliged to work with and get contributions from about 70 different people throughout southern Africa and I believe that the pooling of their knowledge and expertise has been a tremendously worthwhile effort. The regional co-ordinators, in conjunction with many of the contributors, were responsible for choosing their localities.

This is the first fieldguide to include locality checklists. The inclusion of complete checklists would have taken up too much space in a book of this nature, which in any case would then have become more like a distribution atlas for the various localities, which was not the intention. Space restraints meant that not every single good birding spot in the subregion could be included. Southern Mozambique also regrettably had to be left out, for different reasons; hopefully in years to come this region will again become more accessible to those not wielding a gun! Though many farm properties offer excellent birding opportunities, access is not only difficult for most but the farmers' privacy should be respected and permission must be sought before entering private land.

Each region and the chosen localities have been placed in order from north to south. This means that Mana Pools (northern Zimbabwe) is the first locality to be described and Salmonsdam Nature Reserve (southern Cape) the last.

The bird information supplied comprises three main categories:

- The checklists give a guide to the most common species likely to be seen during a short visit (2-4 days).
- The species in bold print generally represent the more uncommon or interesting birds to look for in the locality, and are discussed in the SPECIAL AND INTERESTING SPECIES section.
- Those mentioned under the title ALSO RECORDED are the rare or vagrant species that have been recorded, but are not likely to be seen during a short visit.

Most checklists have been restricted to about 150 species, but some of the larger popular localities have longer lists and the smaller localities are represented by their full complement of species (i.e. 100%). These lists reflect recent records, mostly recorded during the 1980s and early 1990s. For even the most experienced birder, it would be almost impossible to see all the species listed for one locality during one short visit.

The "*specials*" were chosen for a number of reasons: generally they are *uncommon* birds whether in southern Africa as a whole or within that particular locality. A number of species frequently re-appear as "*specials*", for example Peregrine Falcon and Violeteared Waxbill. Both are widely distributed species, but everywhere uncommon or even rare. Other birds listed as special could be species that are common elsewhere, but in that particular locality are uncommon because they occur on the fringe of their normal distribution range. A good example of this would be Larklike Bunting, which is an extremely abundant bird of the western drier regions, but may be regarded as special within one of the more eastern localities. For an eastern birder it would certainly be an interesting species and possibly even a "lifer"! Other species, such as European Swallow, have been singled out as special to point out, for example, a large roosting site in the locality. For the sake of consistency, all birds mentioned in the text under SPECIAL AND INTERESTING SPECIES have been highlighted in *bold* print.

With the present surge in birding interest, and new records coming to light every year, a publication such as this soon becomes outdated. As new information and records become available it would be in the interests of southern African ornithology for new editions to improve wherever possible on the present data supplied. To this end, any new records for further use would be welcomed.

Hugh Chittenden
P.O. Box 360
Eshowe
3813

Endemicity

A book of this nature, which includes checklists, gives an ideal opportunity to "show off " southern African endemics. These comprise two categories, as recognised by P.A. Clancey in *Endemicity in the Southern African Avifauna* (Durban Museum, Novitates Vol. 13 1986) and *Four Additional Species of Southern African Endemic Birds* (Durban Museum, Novitates Vol. 14 1989). Eighty four species in the checklists (marked with two asterisks) are considered true endemics, meaning their distribution remains within the limits of the normally accepted boundaries of the southern African zoogeographic region, the Cunene and Zambezi rivers. A further 86 species (marked with one asterisk) extend marginally beyond these borders, especially from the drier western austral arid zone into desertic south-western Angola, and are considered near endemics. About two-thirds of the 170 endemic or near endemic species are to be found in the south-western arid zone.

Endemics = **
Near endemics = *

How to use this book

As already stated, this book has been designed to be used in the field and for keeping records.

Sightings can be recorded on the supplied checklists in several ways. The following are suggestions for recording data on a number of visits to one locality. A tick can be used for the first visit, the tick crossed for the second, the cross circled for the third, the species number underlined for the fourth and the species name underlined for the fifth visit. Highlighting pens can also be used.

1 213 Black Crake ☑
2 213 Black Crake ☒
3 213 Black Crake ⊗
4 <u>213</u> Black Crake ⊗
5 <u>213</u> <u>Black Crake</u> ⊗

During recent years private birding safari companies have mushroomed throughout the southern African subregion. Those interested in going on birding safaris or pelagic trips should contact their nearest Ornithological Society Branch or Bird Club for information and relevant telephone numbers.

Southern African Ornithological Society
P.O. Box 87234
Houghton
2041 Johannesburg
(011) 782 1547

Cape Bird Club
P.O. Box 5022
6000 Cape Town

Eastern Cape Wild Bird Society
P.O. Box 27454
Greenacres
6057 Port Elizabeth

Goldfields Bird Club
P.O. Box 580
Virginia
9430 OFS

Lowveld Bird Club
P.O. Box 4113
Nelspruit
1200 Transvaal

Namibia Bird Club
P.O. Box 67
Windhoek
Namibia

Natal Bird Club
P.O. Box 1218
4000 Durban

Natal Midlands Bird Club
P.O. Box 2772
3200 Pietermaritzburg

North-eastern Bird Club
P.O. Box 6007
Pietersburg North
0750 Transvaal

Northern Transvaal Ornithological Society
P.O. Box 4158
0001 Pretoria

OFS Ornithological Society
P.O. Box 6614
9300 Bloemfontein

Rand Barbets Bird Club
135 Oxford Road
2193 Saxonwold

Sandton Bird Club
P.O. Box 650890
2010 Benmore

Vaal Reefs Bird Club
P.O. Box 5129
2621 Vaal Reefs

Wesvaal Bird Club
P.O. Box 2413
2520 Potchefstroom

Witwatersrand Bird Club
P.O. Box 72091
Parkview
2122 Johannesburg

Black Sparrowhawk

1 Zimbabwe

Co-ordinator Kit Hustler

1 Mana Pools
2 Kariba
3 Kazungula
4 Victoria Falls
5 McIllwaine Recreational Park
6 Nyanga Area
7 Hwange National Park
8 Vumba Area
9 Haroni Rusitu (Lusitu)
10 Aisleby Sewage Farm, Bulawayo
11 Lake Mutirikwe (Kyle) and Great Zimbabwe
12 Matobo Hills
13 Gonarezhou National Park

Cutthroat Finches

MANA POOLS

approximately 388 species recorded to date

Mana Pools National Park is the only proclaimed national park on the south bank of the middle-Zambezi valley. It is unique in that visitors are not restricted to their vehicles and can walk freely. Caution is advised as dangerous game like elephant and buffalo occur throughout the park. The park is open in the dry season from May to October and bookings are made through the National Parks Central Booking Office in Harare.

SPECIAL AND INTERESTING SPECIES

The oxbow lake supports large numbers of storks, ducks and wading birds. Along the river the sand banks support a number of waders. Watch out for **African Skimmer** on the sand banks. Other interesting birds on the river include **Carmine**, **Whitefronted** and **Bluecheeked Bee-eaters**. A close look at the flocks of swallows could produce **Brownthroated Martin** and **Mottled** or **Böhm's Spinetails**. **Whitecrowned Plovers** are common on the river and a look in the backwaters could produce **Longtoed Plover**, **Rufousbellied Heron** or **Little Bittern**. In the shady spots with overhanging vegetation look for **Whitebacked Night Heron** and **Pel's Fishing Owl**. In the thickets along the water's edge watch for **Collared Palm Thrush**, **Redthroated Twinspot**, **Sombre Bulbul** and where there are tall trees, **Wattle-eyed** and **Livingstone's Flycatchers**. In the Mopane

ALSO RECORDED

The epiphytes that grow in the *Acacia* trees around the camp are worth investigating, particularly when they are in flower, as seven different species of sunbird, including Shelley's Sunbird, can be seen. A Barred Cuckoo has also been recorded.

Kit Hustler

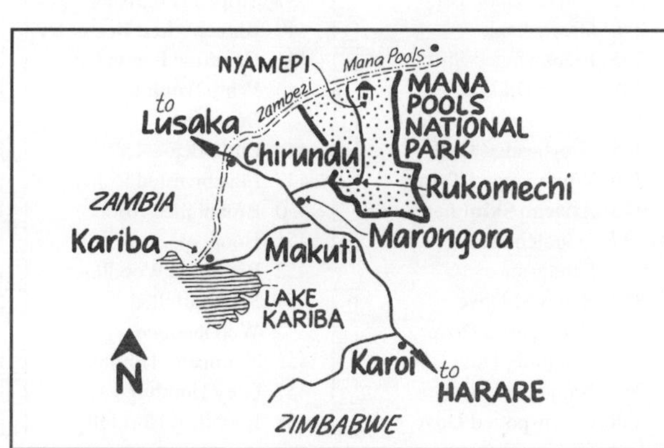

Access to the park is from the Harare-Chirundu road and is by permit only. Permits are issued at Marongora on the main Harare-Chirundu road, north of Makuti. There are two luxury lodges and all other accommodation is camping only. There is no petrol or provisions on sale in the park and visitors must take all their own requirements.

woodland on the way to the camp watch for **Redbilled Helmetshrike**, **Lilian's Lovebird** and **Arnot's Chat**. The dense Combretum thicket through which the road passes is a good place for **Crested Guineafowl** and **Yellowspotted Nicator**.

47% OF SPECIES

055 Whitebreasted Cormorant ☐
058 Reed Cormorant ☐
060 Darter ☐
062 Grey Heron ☐
064 Goliath Heron ☐
066 Great White Egret ☐
067 Little Egret ☐
071 Cattle Egret ☐
074 Greenbacked Heron ☐
075 **Rufousbellied Heron** ☐
077 **Whitebacked Night Heron** ☐
078 **Little Bittern** ☐
081 Hamerkop ☐
086 Woollynecked Stork ☐
087 Openbilled Stork ☐
088 Saddlebilled Stork ☐
090 Yellowbilled Stork ☐
091 Sacred Ibis ☐
094 Hadeda Ibis ☐
099 Whitefaced Duck ☐
102 Egyptian Goose ☐
115 Knobbilled Duck ☐
116 Spurwinged Goose ☐
121 Hooded Vulture ☐
123 Whitebacked Vulture ☐
124 Lappetfaced Vulture ☐
125 Whiteheaded Vulture ☐
126a Yellowbilled Kite ☐
132 Tawny Eagle ☐
137 African Hawk Eagle ☐
140 Martial Eagle ☐
142 Brown Snake Eagle ☐
143 Blackbreasted Snake Eagle ☐
145 Western Banded Snake Eagle ☐
146 Bateleur ☐
148 African Fish Eagle ☐
154 Lizard Buzzard ☐
157 Little Sparrowhawk ☐
159 Little Banded Goshawk ☐
161 Gabar Goshawk ☐
169 Gymnogene ☐
171 Peregrine Falcon ☐
173 Hobby Falcon ☐
189 **Crested Francolin** ☐
196 Natal Francolin* ☐
199 Swainson's Francolin* ☐
203 Helmeted Guineafowl ☐
204 Crested Guineafowl ☐
213 Black Crake ☐
240 African Jacana ☐
246 Whitefronted Plover ☐
248 Kittlitz's Plover ☐
249 Threebanded Plover ☐
258 Blacksmith Plover ☐
259 **Whitecrowned Plover** ☐
261 **Longtoed Plover** ☐
264 Common Sandpiper ☐
266 Wood Sandpiper ☐
269 Marsh Sandpiper ☐
270 Greenshank ☐
295 Blackwinged Stilt ☐
298 Water Dikkop ☐
304 Redwinged Pratincole ☐
315 Greyheaded Gull ☐
339 Whitewinged Tern ☐
343 **African Skimmer** ☐
347 Doublebanded Sandgrouse* ☐
352 Redeyed Dove ☐
354 Cape Turtle Dove ☐
355 Laughing Dove ☐
356 Namaqua Dove ☐
358 Greenspotted Dove ☐
362 Cape Parrot ☐
364 Meyer's Parrot ☐
368 **Lilian's Lovebird** ☐
371 Purplecrested Lourie ☐
373 Grey Lourie ☐
381 Striped Cuckoo ☐
382 Jacobin Cuckoo ☐
386 Diederik Cuckoo ☐
391a Whitebrowed Coucal ☐
396 Scops Owl ☐
398 Pearlspotted Owl ☐
402 Giant Eagle Owl ☐
403 **Pel's Fishing Owl** ☐
409 Mozambique Nightjar ☐
422 **Mottled Spinetail** ☐
423 **Böhm's Spinetail** ☐
426 Redfaced Mousebird ☐
428 Pied Kingfisher ☐
429 Giant Kingfisher ☐
431 Malachite Kingfisher ☐
433 Woodland Kingfisher ☐
435 Brownhooded Kingfisher ☐
436 Greyhooded Kingfisher ☐
437 Striped Kingfisher ☐
440 **Bluecheeked Bee-eater** ☐
441 **Carmine Bee-eater** ☐
443 **Whitefronted Bee-eater** ☐
444 Little Bee-eater ☐
447 Lilacbreasted Roller ☐
450 Broadbilled Roller ☐
451 Hoopoe ☐
452 Redbilled Woodhoopoe ☐
454 Scimitarbilled Woodhoopoe ☐
455 Trumpeter Hornbill ☐
457 Grey Hornbill ☐
458 Redbilled Hornbill ☐

460 Crowned Hornbill
463 Ground Hornbill
473 Crested Barbet
474 Greater Honeyguide
486 Cardinal Woodpecker
487 Bearded Woodpecker
518 European Swallow
522 Wiretailed Swallow
533 **Brownthroated Martin**
537 Eastern Sawwing Swallow
541 Forktailed Drongo
544 African Golden Oriole
545 Blackheaded Oriole
550 Whitenecked Raven
554 Southern Black Tit*
560 Arrowmarked Babbler
568 Blackeyed Bulbul
569 Terrestrial Bulbul
572 **Sombre Bulbul**
574 Yellowbellied Bulbul
575 **Yellowspotted Nicator**
576 Kurrichane Thrush
594 **Arnot's Chat**
599 Heuglin's Robin
603 **Collared Palm Thrush**
643 Willow Warbler
648 Yellowbreasted Apalis
664 Fantailed Cisticola
672 Rattling Cisticola
674 Redfaced Cisticola
683 Tawnyflanked Prinia
691 Bluegrey Flycatcher
694 Black Flycatcher
701 Chinspot Batis
705 **Wattle-eyed Flycatcher**
707 **Livingstone's Flycatcher**
710 Paradise Flycatcher
711 African Pied Wagtail
716 Grassveld Pipit
737 Tropical Boubou
740 Puffback
741 Brubru
743 Threestreaked Tchagra
744 Blackcrowned Tchagra
748 Orangebreasted Bush Shrike
751 Greyheaded Bush Shrike
753 White Helmetshrike
754 **Redbilled Helmetshrike**
761 Plumcoloured Starling
763 Longtailed Starling*
772 Redbilled Oxpecker
780 Purplebanded Sunbird
781 **Shelley's Sunbird**
787 Whitebellied Sunbird
791 Scarletchested Sunbird
793 Collared Sunbird
797 Yellow White-eye
799 Whitebrowed Sparrowweaver
801 House Sparrow
804 Greyheaded Sparrow
810 Spectacled Weaver
811 Spottedbacked Weaver
814 Masked Weaver
815 Lesser Masked Weaver
819 Redheaded Weaver
821 Redbilled Quelea
824 Red Bishop
834 Melba Finch
839 **Redthroated Twinspot**
842 Redbilled Firefinch
844 Blue Waxbill
862 Paradise Whydah
867 Steelblue Widowfinch
869 Yelloweyed Canary
884 Goldenbreasted Bunting
886 Rock Bunting

Redbreasted Swallow

KARIBA

approximately 361 species recorded to date

Lake Kariba, one of the largest man-made lakes in the world, is 260 km long. This account deals with the easternmost basins which are the most developed for tourists.

SPECIAL AND INTERESTING SPECIES

On the shoreline a vast array of wading birds can be seen including **Black Egret** and **Longtoed Plover**. **African Fish Eagle** abounds and **Osprey** is regular all year round. **Redwinged Pratincoles** occur on shorelines with gravel beaches in winter and breed on the lake's edge. The grasslands along the shore provide habitat for **Stanley's Bustard** and **Pinkthroated Longclaw**. **Fantailed** and **Desert Cisticolas** can be found in the adjacent grassland. **Reed Cormorant** and **Darter** are abundant on the lake; look out for **Whitebreasted Cormorant** whose numbers are increasing. A boat ride on the lake could produce **Greyheaded Gulls** close to fishing villages, **Whitewinged Terns** in a variety of plumage types depending on the time of the year and **Lesser Blackbacked Gull**. While in town watch for the **Crowned Eagle** that frequently displays overhead. A visit to the dam wall could produce **Peregrine Falcon**. Remember to take some form of identification with you when you go to the wall. Use a telescope from the observation point above the gorge and search the rocks downstream of the wall, as between July and January a small group of **Rock Pratincoles** takes up resi-

ALSO RECORDED

Fülleborn's Longclaw is a possibility as it occurs on the Zambian shoreline of the lake, so careful attention should be paid to any yellow longclaws seen on the shore.
Kit Hustler

There is a daily return flight between Harare and Kariba and a tarred road from Harare services the town. There are numerous resorts in the town of Kariba and on the islands and mainland some distance from the town.

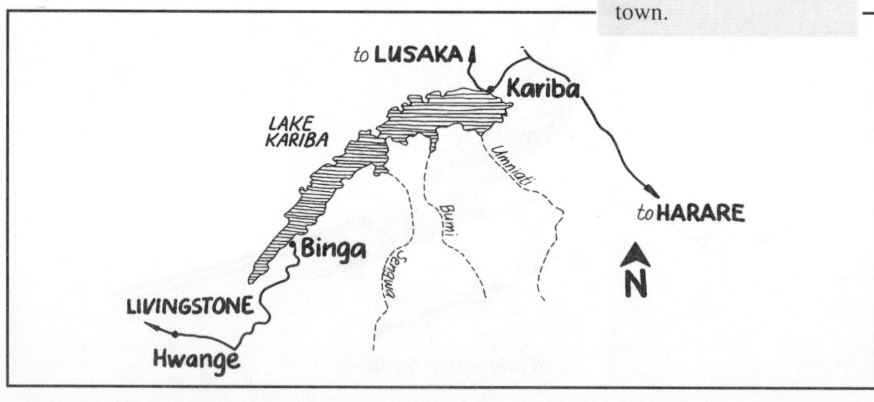

dence. At the wall, scan any feeding "swallow" flocks for **Mottled** and **Böhm's Spinetails. Mosque Swallows** are regular at the lookout point on top of Kariba Heights, which gives the best view of the lake. **Livingstone's Flycatcher** and **Redthroated Twinspot** occur in the well-wooded valley below the town. Clearance from the local National Parks Office is advisable before walking in the valley where elephant and buffalo occur regularly. **Yellowspotted Nicator** and **Natal Robin** are regular in the thick vegetation. **Angola Pittas** have been recorded at Kariba and if you are there in November watch out for them - you may be lucky! Take a careful look at the flocks of "Melba Finches" as you may be overlooking **Goldenbacked Pytilia**, which is quite regular in the town and in the thick vegetation some distance from the shoreline. During summer Combretum thickets may produce not only Angola Pitta, but also **Thrush Nightingale** and **Great Reed Warbler**, but beware of dangerous game when searching for these.

52% OF SPECIES

055 **Whitebreasted Cormorant** ☐
058 **Reed Cormorant** ☐
060 **Darter** ☐
062 Grey Heron ☐
064 Goliath Heron ☐
066 Great White Egret ☐
067 Little Egret ☐
069 **Black Egret** ☐
071 Cattle Egret ☐
074 Greenbacked Heron ☐
081 Hamerkop ☐
088 Saddlebilled Stork ☐
089 Marabou Stork ☐
099 Whitefaced Duck ☐
102 Egyptian Goose ☐
115 Knobbilled Duck ☐
116 Spurwinged Goose ☐
121 Hooded Vulture ☐
123 Whitebacked Vulture ☐
124 Lappetfaced Vulture ☐
125 Whiteheaded Vulture ☐
126a Yellowbilled Kite ☐
132 Tawny Eagle ☐
137 African Hawk Eagle ☐
141 **Crowned Eagle** ☐
142 Brown Snake Eagle ☐
146 Bateleur ☐
148 **African Fish Eagle** ☐
153 Augur Buzzard ☐
154 Lizard Buzzard ☐
157 Little Sparrowhawk ☐
159 Little Banded Goshawk ☐
169 Gymnogene ☐
170 **Osprey** ☐
171 **Peregrine Falcon** ☐
185 Dickinson's Kestrel ☐
189 Crested Francolin ☐
196 Natal Francolin* ☐
199 Swainson's Francolin* ☐
203 Helmeted Guineafowl ☐
213 Black Crake ☐
231 **Stanley's Bustard** ☐
238 Blackbellied Korhaan ☐
240 African Jacana ☐
248 Kittlitz's Plover ☐
249 Threebanded Plover ☐
258 Blacksmith Plover ☐
259 Whitecrowned Plover ☐
261 **Longtoed Plover** ☐
264 Common Sandpiper ☐
266 Wood Sandpiper ☐
270 Greenshank ☐
295 Blackwinged Stilt ☐
298 Water Dikkop ☐
300 Temminck's Courser ☐
303 Bronzewinged Courser ☐
304 **Redwinged Pratincole** ☐
313 **Lesser Blackbacked Gull** ☐
315 **Greyheaded Gull** ☐
339 **Whitewinged Tern** ☐
347 Doublebanded Sandgrouse* ☐
352 Redeyed Dove ☐
354 Cape Turtle Dove ☐
355 Laughing Dove ☐
356 Namaqua Dove ☐
358 Greenspotted Dove ☐
362 Cape Parrot ☐
364 Meyer's Parrot ☐
368 Lilian's Lovebird ☐
371 Purplecrested Lourie ☐
373 Grey Lourie ☐
377 Redchested Cuckoo ☐
381 Striped Cuckoo ☐
382 Jacobin Cuckoo ☐

6 Zimbabwe

386 Diederik Cuckoo
390 Senegal Coucal
391a Whitebrowed Coucal
396 Scops Owl
398 Pearlspotted Owl
399 Barred Owl
409 Mozambique Nightjar
421 Palm Swift
422 **Mottled Spinetail**
423 **Böhm's Spinetail**
428 Pied Kingfisher
429 Giant Kingfisher
431 Malachite Kingfisher
433 Woodland Kingfisher
435 Brownhooded Kingfisher
436 Greyhooded Kingfisher
437 Striped Kingfisher
441 Carmine Bee-eater
444 Little Bee-eater
447 Lilacbreasted Roller
449 Purple Roller
450 Broadbilled Roller
451 Hoopoe
452 Redbilled Woodhoopoe
454 Scimitarbilled Woodhoopoe
455 Trumpeter Hornbill
457 Grey Hornbill
458 Redbilled Hornbill
460 Crowned Hornbill
463 Ground Hornbill
464 Blackcollared Barbet
470 Yellowfronted Tinker Barbet
473 Crested Barbet
474 Greater Honeyguide
476 Lesser Honeyguide
481 Bennett's Woodpecker
483 Goldentailed Woodpecker
486 Cardinal Woodpecker
487 Bearded Woodpecker
491 **Angola Pitta**
496 Flappet Lark
515 Chestnutbacked Finchlark
518 European Swallow
522 Wiretailed Swallow
525 **Mosque Swallow**
529 Rock Martin
541 Forktailed Drongo
544 African Golden Oriole
545 Blackheaded Oriole
548 Pied Crow
554 Southern Black Tit*
560 Arrowmarked Babbler
568 Blackeyed Bulbul
569 Terrestrial Bulbul
574 Yellowbellied Bulbul
575 **Yellowspotted Nicator**
594 Arnot's Chat
600 **Natal Robin**
609 **Thrush Nightingale**
613 Whitebrowed Robin
628 **Great Reed Warbler**
651 Longbilled Crombec
657a Greybacked Bleating Warbler
664 **Fantailed Cisticola**
665 **Desert Cisticola**
672 Rattling Cisticola
681 Neddicky
683 Tawnyflanked Prinia
701 Chinspot Batis
707 **Livingstone's Flycatcher**
710 Paradise Flycatcher
711 African Pied Wagtail
716 Grassveld Pipit
730 **Pinkthroated Longclaw**
737 Tropical Boubou
740 Puffback
741 Brubru
743 Threestreaked Tchagra
744 Blackcrowned Tchagra
751 Greyheaded Bush Shrike
753 White Helmetshrike
754 Redbilled Helmetshrike
763 Longtailed Starling*
769 Redwinged Starling
772 Redbilled Oxpecker
787 Whitebellied Sunbird
791 Scarletchested Sunbird
799 Whitebrowed Sparrowweaver
801 House Sparrow
804 Greyheaded Sparrow
811 Spottedbacked Weaver
814 Masked Weaver
815 Lesser Masked Weaver
819 Redheaded Weaver
821 Redbilled Quelea
824 Red Bishop
829 Whitewinged Widow
833 **Goldenbacked Pytilia**
834 Melba Finch
839 **Redthroated Twinspot**
841 Jameson's Firefinch
842 Redbilled Firefinch
844 Blue Waxbill
846 Common Waxbill
855 Cutthroat Finch
857 Bronze Mannikin
860 Pintailed Whydah
862 Paradise Whydah
867 Steelblue Widowfinch
869 Yelloweyed Canary
884 Goldenbreasted Bunting
886 Rock Bunting

KAZUNGULA

approximately 300 species recorded to date

The Kazungula swamps and floodplain, within the Matetsi safari area west of Victoria Falls, are leased by the Imbabala Safari Lodge.

SPECIAL AND INTERESTING SPECIES

Waterbirds such as **Yellowbilled** and **Black Egrets, Squacco** and **Rufousbellied Herons, Pygmy Goose, Lesser Gallinule, Painted** and **Ethiopian Snipes, Whitecrowned** and **Longtoed Plovers** and **Redwinged Pratincole** may be found. **Slaty Egret** is often seen, while **Bateleur, Hooded** and **Whitebacked Vultures** are common. There is an extensive breeding area of the latter close to Kazungula. **Redbilled Francolins** are found in the fringing scrub, as is **Bradfield's Hornbill. Pearlspotted** and **Barred Owls** are usually present in the camp area. **Natal Nightjar** breeds on the floodplain. **Bluecheeked Bee-eater** can be seen hawking from the Papyrus reeds, and **Brownthroated Weaver** breeds in the reeds during February and March. **Whiterumped Babblers** are found in the reedbeds or in the fringing scrub and **Redshouldered Widow** is common. The similar **Blackbacked** and **Chirping Cisticolas** are present in reedbeds, but can easily be separated on call. **Tropical Boubou** can be very light coloured below and is then easily confused with **Swamp Boubou,** which is rare on the riverine islands.

ALSO RECORDED

Little Bittern is found in dense reedbeds, Secretarybird, Kori Bustard and Pinkthroated Longclaw on the floodplain, Longcrested Eagle and Western Banded Snake Eagle overhead, African Marsh Harrier over the reeded islands, Copperytailed Coucal in the Papyrus, Thrush Nightingale in the fringing bush and Brown Firefinch on the river's edge. Burchell's Starling and Cuckoo Finch have also been recorded. Yellowbilled Ducks have bred in the swamp.

C.J.W. Pollard

From the Victoria Falls-Kazungula road, turn off 1 km before the Kazungula-Botswana border post. The camp is not signposted as casual visits are not encouraged. Bookings to visit the camp, which is run by a fishing and game or bird viewing safari operation, can be made at Imbabala Safari Lodge. Guests are taken by boat, vehicle or on foot with an experienced and armed guide. The area abounds with dangerous animals and it is illegal to leave the tar road without permission.

8 Zimbabwe

50% OF SPECIES

058 Reed Cormorant ☐
060 Darter ☐
065 Purple Heron ☐
066 Great White Egret ☐
067 Little Egret ☐
068 **Yellowbilled Egret** ☐
069 **Black Egret** ☐
070 **Slaty Egret** ☐
071 Cattle Egret ☐
072 **Squacco Heron** ☐
074 Greenbacked Heron ☐
075 **Rufousbellied Heron** ☐
081 Hamerkop ☐
087 Openbilled Stork ☐
091 Sacred Ibis ☐
095 African Spoonbill ☐
099 Whitefaced Duck ☐
102 Egyptian Goose ☐
114 **Pygmy Goose** ☐
115 Knobbilled Duck ☐
116 Spurwinged Goose ☐
121 **Hooded Vulture** ☐
123 **Whitebacked Vulture** ☐
124 Lappetfaced Vulture ☐
125 Whiteheaded Vulture ☐
143 Blackbreasted Snake Eagle ☐
146 **Bateleur** ☐
148 African Fish Eagle ☐
161 Gabar Goshawk ☐
194 **Redbilled Francolin*** ☐
199 Swainson's Francolin* ☐
203 Helmeted Guineafowl ☐
213 Black Crake ☐
224 **Lesser Gallinule** ☐
240 African Jacana ☐
242 **Painted Snipe** ☐
248 Kittlitz's Plover ☐
258 Blacksmith Plover ☐
259 **Whitecrowned Plover** ☐
260 Wattled Plover ☐
261 **Longtoed Plover** ☐
264 Common Sandpiper ☐
266 Wood Sandpiper ☐
284 Ruff ☐
286 **Ethiopian Snipe** ☐
295 Blackwinged Stilt ☐
298 Water Dikkop ☐
304 **Redwinged Pratincole** ☐
339 Whitewinged Tern ☐
343 African Skimmer ☐
352 Redeyed Dove ☐
354 Cape Turtle Dove ☐
355 Laughing Dove ☐
358 Greenspotted Dove ☐
373 Grey Lourie ☐
377 Redchested Cuckoo ☐
381 Striped Cuckoo ☐
382 Jacobin Cuckoo ☐
386 Diederik Cuckoo ☐
390 Senegal Coucal ☐
391a Whitebrowed Coucal ☐
396 Scops Owl ☐
398 **Pearlspotted Owl** ☐
399 **Barred Owl** ☐
401 Spotted Eagle Owl ☐
405 Fierynecked Nightjar ☐
407 **Natal Nightjar** ☐
428 Pied Kingfisher ☐
429 Giant Kingfisher ☐
430 Halfcollared Kingfisher ☐
431 Malachite Kingfisher ☐
435 Brownhooded Kingfisher ☐
436 Greyhooded Kingfisher ☐
437 Striped Kingfisher ☐
438 European Bee-eater ☐
440 **Bluecheeked Bee-eater** ☐
443 Whitefronted Bee-eater ☐
444 Little Bee-eater ☐
447 Lilacbreasted Roller ☐
450 Broadbilled Roller ☐
451 Hoopoe ☐
452 Redbilled Woodhoopoe ☐
454 Scimitarbilled Woodhoopoe ☐
457 Grey Hornbill ☐
458 Redbilled Hornbill ☐
461 **Bradfield's Hornbill*** ☐
463 Ground Hornbill ☐
464 Blackcollared Barbet ☐
473 Crested Barbet ☐
486 Cardinal Woodpecker ☐
487 Bearded Woodpecker ☐
518 European Swallow ☐
522 Wiretailed Swallow ☐
527 Lesser Striped Swallow ☐
533 Brownthroated Martin ☐
541 Forktailed Drongo ☐
544 African Golden Oriole ☐
554 Southern Black Tit* ☐
560 Arrowmarked Babbler ☐
562 **Whiterumped Babbler** ☐
568 Blackeyed Bulbul ☐
576 Kurrichane Thrush ☐
596 Stonechat ☐
599 Heuglin's Robin ☐
628 Great Reed Warbler ☐
634 European Sedge Warbler ☐
635 Cape Reed Warbler ☐
643 Willow Warbler ☐
657a Greybacked Bleating Warbler ☐
672 Rattling Cisticola ☐
675 **Blackbacked Cisticola** ☐
676 **Chirping Cisticola** ☐
683 Tawnyflanked Prinia ☐
689 Spotted Flycatcher ☐
701 Chinspot Batis ☐
710 Paradise Flycatcher ☐
713 Cape Wagtail ☐
716 Grassveld Pipit ☐
719 Buffy Pipit ☐
733 Redbacked Shrike ☐
737 **Tropical Boubou** ☐
738 **Swamp Boubou** ☐
740 Puffback ☐

748 Orangebreasted Bush Shrike ☐
753 White Helmetshrike ☐
754 Redbilled Helmetshrike ☐
761 Plumcoloured Starling ☐
765 Greater Blue-eared Starling ☐
772 Redbilled Oxpecker ☐
780 Purplebanded Sunbird ☐
787 Whitebellied Sunbird ☐
791 Scarletchested Sunbird ☐
792 Black Sunbird ☐
804 Greyheaded Sparrow ☐
805 Yellowthroated Sparrow ☐
807 Thickbilled Weaver ☐
811 Spottedbacked Weaver ☐
818 **Brownthroated Weaver** ☐
821 Redbilled Quelea ☐
824 Red Bishop ☐
826 Golden Bishop ☐
828 **Redshouldered Widow** ☐
834 Melba Finch ☐
842 Redbilled Firefinch ☐
844 Blue Waxbill ☐
846 Common Waxbill ☐
865 Purple Widowfinch ☐
867 Steelblue Widowfinch ☐
869 Yelloweyed Canary ☐
870 Blackthroated Canary ☐
884 Goldenbreasted Bunting ☐
☐
☐
☐
☐
☐

VICTORIA FALLS

approximately 320 species recorded to date

The Victoria Falls village area (outside the Zambezi National Park) is bordered by about 4 km of Zambezi River, 3 km of gorges and extensive teak forests on the ridge above the village. Care must be taken while walking in the forest and away from paths in bush areas as buffalo, lion and elephant may be encountered. Areas fenced and identified as minefields must not be entered even if the fences are broken.

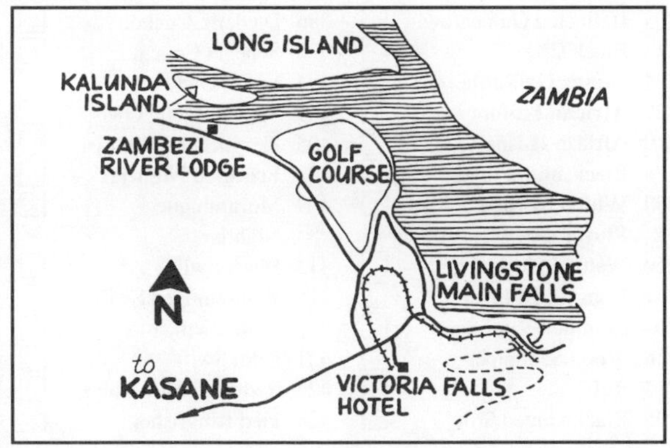

ALSO RECORDED

Bat Hawk and Pel's Fishing Owl are seen very occasionally on the river. Redthroated Twinspot and Black Stork are found in the gorges (the latter breeding September-October), Rackettailed Roller and Miombo Rock Thrush in the teak forest. Listen for Thrush Nightingale in the gorges or on the islands in areas with heavy *Lantana* scrub. Bluemantled Flycatcher has been recorded twice, as have the following waterbirds: Ringed and Grey Plovers, Turnstone, Blacktailed Godwit, Caspian Tern, Yellowbilled Duck and Green Sandpiper (the latter on the golf course). Blackcheeked Lovebird used to be found in this area but has not been recorded since the 1960s. Recent releases of this species (possibly hybridised) are found in the village area.

C.J.W. Pollard

10 Zimbabwe

SPECIAL AND INTERESTING SPECIES

Near the river **Black Egret**, **Goliath**, **Squacco** and **Rufousbellied Herons**, **Whitebacked Night Heron**, **Little Bittern**, **Pygmy Goose**, **Western Banded Snake Eagle**, **Osprey**, **Rednecked Falcon**, **Lesser Gallinule**, **African Finfoot**, **Whitecrowned** and **Longtoed Plovers** and **Halfcollared Kingfisher** may be found. **Rock Pratincole** and **African Skimmer** nest on the river from August to November but are gone by January. On the river walk look for **Collared Palm Thrush** and **Bearded Robin**. **Brown Firefinch** may be found among parties of **Blue Waxbill**. In the gorges there are two to four resident **Peregrine**, **Lanner** and **Taita Falcons**. **Freckled Nightjar** and **Longtailed Wagtail** are present.

52% OF SPECIES

058 Reed Cormorant ☐
060 Darter ☐
064 **Goliath Heron** ☐
065 Purple Heron ☐
066 Great White Egret ☐
067 Little Egret ☐
068 Yellowbilled Egret ☐
069 **Black Egret** ☐
071 Cattle Egret ☐
072 **Squacco Heron** ☐
074 Greenbacked Heron ☐
075 **Rufousbellied Heron** ☐
077 **Whitebacked Night Heron** ☐
078 **Little Bittern** ☐
081 Hamerkop ☐
087 Openbilled Stork ☐
094 Hadeda Ibis ☐
099 Whitefaced Duck ☐
102 Egyptian Goose ☐
108 Redbilled Teal ☐
114 **Pygmy Goose** ☐
115 Knobbilled Duck ☐
116 Spurwinged Goose ☐
121 Hooded Vulture ☐
123 Whitebacked Vulture ☐
126a Yellowbilled Kite ☐
132 Tawny Eagle ☐
145 **Western Banded Snake Eagle** ☐
146 Bateleur ☐
148 African Fish Eagle ☐
156 Ovambo Sparrowhawk ☐
157 Little Sparrowhawk ☐
159 Little Banded Goshawk ☐
161 Gabar Goshawk ☐
170 **Osprey** ☐
171 **Peregrine Falcon** ☐
172 **Lanner Falcon** ☐
176 **Taita Falcon** ☐
178 **Rednecked Falcon** ☐
196 Natal Francolin* ☐
199 Swainson's Francolin* ☐
203 Helmeted Guineafowl ☐
213 Black Crake ☐
224 **Lesser Gallinule** ☐
229 **African Finfoot** ☐
240 African Jacana ☐
258 Blacksmith Plover ☐
259 **Whitecrowned Plover** ☐
260 Wattled Plover ☐
261 **Longtoed Plover** ☐
264 Common Sandpiper ☐
266 Wood Sandpiper ☐
284 Ruff ☐
295 Blackwinged Stilt ☐
298 Water Dikkop ☐
306 **Rock Pratincole** ☐
339 Whitewinged Tern ☐
343 **African Skimmer** ☐
347 Doublebanded Sandgrouse* ☐
352 Redeyed Dove ☐
354 Cape Turtle Dove ☐
355 Laughing Dove ☐
358 Greenspotted Dove ☐
364 Meyer's Parrot ☐
370a Livingstone's Lourie ☐
373 Grey Lourie ☐
377 Redchested Cuckoo ☐
381 Striped Cuckoo ☐
382 Jacobin Cuckoo ☐
386 Diederik Cuckoo ☐
390 Senegal Coucal ☐
394 Wood Owl ☐
401 Spotted Eagle Owl ☐
405 Fierynecked Nightjar ☐
408 **Freckled Nightjar** ☐
409 Mozambique Nightjar ☐
412 Black Swift ☐
415 Whiterumped Swift ☐
417 Little Swift ☐
421 Palm Swift ☐
426 Redfaced Mousebird ☐
428 Pied Kingfisher ☐

Zimbabwe

430 **Halfcollared Kingfisher** ☐
431 Malachite Kingfisher ☐
435 Brownhooded Kingfisher ☐
437 Striped Kingfisher ☐
438 European Bee-eater ☐
443 Whitefronted Bee-eater ☐
444 Little Bee-eater ☐
447 Lilacbreasted Roller ☐
450 Broadbilled Roller ☐
451 Hoopoe ☐
452 Redbilled Woodhoopoe ☐
454 Scimitarbilled Woodhoopoe ☐
455 Trumpeter Hornbill ☐
457 Grey Hornbill ☐
458 Redbilled Hornbill ☐
464 Blackcollared Barbet ☐
473 Crested Barbet ☐
486 Cardinal Woodpecker ☐
487 Bearded Woodpecker ☐
496 Flappet Lark ☐
518 European Swallow ☐
522 Wiretailed Swallow ☐
527 Lesser Striped Swallow ☐
533 Brownthroated Martin ☐
538 Black Cuckooshrike ☐
541 Forktailed Drongo ☐
544 African Golden Oriole ☐
548 Pied Crow ☐
554 Southern Black Tit* ☐
560 Arrowmarked Babbler ☐
568 Blackeyed Bulbul ☐
569 Terrestrial Bulbul ☐
574 Yellowbellied Bulbul ☐
576 Kurrichane Thrush ☐
599 Heuglin's Robin ☐
603 **Collared Palm Thrush** ☐
617 **Bearded Robin** ☐
635 Cape Reed Warbler ☐
643 Willow Warbler ☐
651 Longbilled Crombec ☐
657a Greybacked Bleating Warbler ☐
672 Rattling Cisticola ☐
683 Tawnyflanked Prinia ☐
689 Spotted Flycatcher ☐
691 Bluegrey Flycatcher ☐
701 Chinspot Batis ☐
710 Paradise Flycatcher ☐
711 African Pied Wagtail ☐
712 **Longtailed Wagtail** ☐
737 Tropical Boubou ☐
740 Puffback ☐
743 Threestreaked Tchagra ☐
748 Orangebreasted Bush Shrike ☐
751 Greyheaded Bush Shrike ☐
753 White Helmetshrike ☐
754 Redbilled Helmetshrike ☐
761 Plumcoloured Starling ☐
769 Redwinged Starling ☐
772 Redbilled Oxpecker ☐
787 Whitebellied Sunbird ☐
791 Scarletchested Sunbird ☐
792 Black Sunbird ☐
793 Collared Sunbird ☐
799 Whitebrowed Sparrowweaver ☐
804 Greyheaded Sparrow ☐
805 Yellowthroated Sparrow ☐
810 Spectacled Weaver ☐
811 Spottedbacked Weaver ☐
816 Golden Weaver ☐
821 Redbilled Quelea ☐
824 Red Bishop ☐
834 Melba Finch ☐
842 Redbilled Firefinch ☐
843 **Brown Firefinch** ☐
844 **Blue Waxbill** ☐
857 Bronze Mannikin ☐
860 Pintailed Whydah ☐
862 Paradise Whydah ☐
863 Broadtailed Paradise Whydah ☐
865 Purple Widowfinch ☐
867 Steelblue Widowfinch ☐
869 Yelloweyed Canary ☐
884 Goldenbreasted Bunting ☐
886 Rock Bunting ☐
☐
☐
☐
☐
☐

McILLWAINE RECREATIONAL PARK

approximately 326 species recorded to date

Lake McIllwaine is approximately 20 km from Harare and is the main source of water for the city. The lake is 16 km long and the land around the lake forms part of the Department of National Parks Wildlife Estate. On the southern shore is a game park with a well-situated rest camp. On the northern side are a wide range of recreational facilities as well as the bird sanctuary. The National Parks camp has lodges and chalets and this accommodation must be booked through the National Parks Central Booking Office in Harare. The dominant vegetation in the game park and the bird sanctuary is Miombo woodland represented by species such as *Brachystegia spiciformis* (Musasa), *Brachystegia boehmii* (Mfuti), *Brachystegia glaucescens* (Mountain Acacia) and the Muhondo, *Jubernardia globiflora*. Depending on the water level, muddy edges to the lake often create ideal habitat for waders. Many stretches of the shoreline are covered with sedges and reeds. In several areas open grassy vleis hold a variety of birds.

SPECIAL AND INTERESTING SPECIES

A large variety of waterbirds are found along the lake shore. **Whitebreasted** and **Reed Cormorants**, **Darter** and a variety of herons breed regularly on the lake. **Cape Teal** and **Cape Shoveller** have been recorded and ten other species of

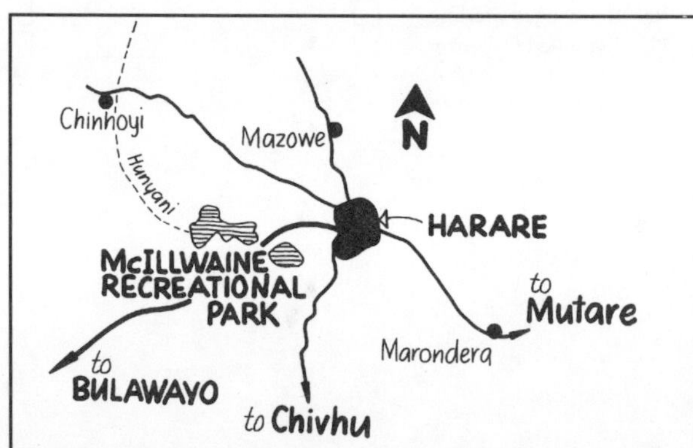

ALSO RECORDED

Grey Plover, Turnstone and Blacktailed Godwit are some of the rare waders that have been recorded. Lesser Blackbacked Gull has been seen occasionally. Lesser Flamingos sometimes spend several days on the lake.

Derek Solomon and Jacko Williams (Mrs)

The bird sanctuary can be reached by turning off at Lake Service Station on the main Harare-Bulawayo road. The same turnoff takes you to Larvon Bird Gardens. Follow the tar road for approximately 7 km, turn left into Glen Roy Road (gravel) and proceed to the lake shore. Turn left again and proceed for about 700 m to the sanctuary signpost. To reach the game park, continue along the Harare-Bulawayo road past Turnpike Service Station, and after you cross the Hunyani River bridge, turn left. Follow the signs and take the right-hand fork to the park entrance. All visitors must pay a small entrance fee.

waterfowl are common. Flocks of **Eastern Redfooted Kestrels** are common, especially along the main road to the park. **Western Redfooted Kestrel** and **Hobby Falcon** can be seen among these flocks. **Purple** and **Lesser Gallinules** and **Lesser Moorhen** are found in the reedbeds together with a variety of crakes and rails. Large numbers of waders are found on the muddy edges of the lake when the conditions are suitable. **Greyheaded Gull** and **Whitewinged Tern** are regularly seen. Seven species of cuckoo are common in the woodland, as is a variety of owls and nightjars. **Bennett's**, **Goldentailed**, **Cardinal** and **Bearded Woodpeckers** are recorded. Woodland specials include **Whyte's Barbet**, **Northern Grey Tit**, **Spotted Creeper**, **Arnot's Chat**, **Mashona Hyliota** and **Stierling's Barred Warbler. Mocking** and **Boulder Chats** can be found in the rocky outcrops around the camp. **Rufousnaped**, **Flappet** and **Redcapped Larks** are common in the open grassland. Eleven species of cisticola have been recorded, including **Ayres'** and **Palecrowned Cisticolas. Yellow Warbler** can be found in the sedges and reeds along the lake shore. **Orange**, **Yellow** and **Pinkthroated Longclaws** occur in the open grassy areas. **Greater** and **Lesser Blue-eared Starlings** are common and **Violetbacked Sunbird** has been recorded on several occasions.

46% OF SPECIES

008 Dabchick ☐
055 **Whitebreasted Cormorant** ☐
058 **Reed Cormorant** ☐
060 **Darter** ☐
062 Grey Heron ☐
064 Goliath Heron ☐
065 Purple Heron ☐
066 Great White Egret ☐
067 Little Egret ☐
071 Cattle Egret ☐
072 Squacco Heron ☐
081 Hamerkop ☐
099 Whitefaced Duck ☐
102 Egyptian Goose ☐
106 **Cape Teal** ☐
112 **Cape Shoveller*** ☐
116 Spurwinged Goose ☐
127 Blackshouldered Kite ☐
135 Wahlberg's Eagle ☐
143 Blackbreasted Snake Eagle ☐
148 African Fish Eagle ☐
154 Lizard Buzzard ☐
173 **Hobby Falcon** ☐
179 **Western Redfooted Kestrel** ☐
180 **Eastern Redfooted Kestrel** ☐
196 Natal Francolin* ☐
199 Swainson's Francolin* ☐
203 Helmeted Guineafowl ☐
213 Black Crake ☐
223 **Purple Gallinule** ☐
224 **Lesser Gallinule** ☐
227 **Lesser Moorhen** ☐
228 Redknobbed Coot ☐
240 African Jacana ☐
249 Threebanded Plover ☐
258 Blacksmith Plover ☐
260 Wattled Plover ☐
264 Common Sandpiper ☐
266 Wood Sandpiper ☐
269 Marsh Sandpiper ☐
270 Greenshank ☐
274 Little Stint ☐
284 Ruff ☐
315 **Greyheaded Gull** ☐
339 **Whitewinged Tern** ☐
352 Redeyed Dove ☐
354 Cape Turtle Dove ☐
355 Laughing Dove ☐
356 Namaqua Dove ☐
358 Greenspotted Dove ☐
361 Green Pigeon ☐
364 Meyer's Parrot ☐
373 Grey Lourie ☐
377 Redchested Cuckoo ☐
378 Black Cuckoo ☐
381 Striped Cuckoo ☐
386 Diederik Cuckoo ☐
390 Senegal Coucal ☐
396 Scops Owl ☐
405 Fierynecked Nightjar ☐
417 Little Swift ☐
421 Palm Swift ☐

Zimbabwe

426 Redfaced Mousebird ☐
428 Pied Kingfisher ☐
429 Giant Kingfisher ☐
431 Malachite Kingfisher ☐
435 Brownhooded Kingfisher ☐
436 Greyhooded Kingfisher ☐
437 Striped Kingfisher ☐
438 European Bee-eater ☐
444 Little Bee-eater ☐
447 Lilacbreasted Roller ☐
451 Hoopoe ☐
452 Redbilled Woodhoopoe ☐
454 Scimitarbilled Woodhoopoe ☐
457 Grey Hornbill ☐
464 Blackcollared Barbet ☐
467 **Whyte's Barbet** ☐
470 Yellowfronted Tinker Barbet ☐
473 Crested Barbet ☐
481 **Bennett's Woodpecker** ☐
483 **Goldentailed Woodpecker** ☐
486 **Cardinal Woodpecker** ☐
487 **Bearded Woodpecker** ☐
494 **Rufousnaped Lark** ☐
496 **Flappet Lark** ☐
507 **Redcapped Lark** ☐
518 European Swallow ☐
527 Lesser Striped Swallow ☐
538 Black Cuckooshrike ☐
541 Forktailed Drongo ☐
544 African Golden Oriole ☐
545 Blackheaded Oriole ☐
553 **Northern Grey Tit** ☐
554 Southern Black Tit* ☐
559 **Spotted Creeper** ☐
560 Arrowmarked Babbler ☐
568 Blackeyed Bulbul ☐
576 Kurrichane Thrush ☐
580 Groundscraper Thrush ☐
593 **Mocking Chat** ☐
594 **Arnot's Chat** ☐
596 Stonechat ☐
599 Heuglin's Robin ☐
602 Whitethroated Robin** ☐
610 **Boulder Chat*** ☐
613 Whitebrowed Robin ☐
624 **Mashona Hyliota** ☐
635 Cape Reed Warbler ☐
637 Yellow Warbler ☐
638 African Sedge Warbler ☐
643 **Willow Warbler** ☐
645 Barthroated Apalis ☐
653 Yellowbellied Eremomela ☐
655 Greencapped Eremomela ☐
657a Greybacked Bleating Warbler ☐
659 **Stierling's Barred Warbler** ☐
664 Fantailed Cisticola ☐
667 **Ayres' Cisticola** ☐
668 **Palecrowned Cisticola** ☐
672 Rattling Cisticola ☐
674 Redfaced Cisticola ☐
677 Levaillant's Cisticola ☐
681 Neddicky ☐
683 Tawnyflanked Prinia ☐
689 Spotted Flycatcher ☐
694 Black Flycatcher ☐
701 Chinspot Batis ☐
710 Paradise Flycatcher ☐
711 African Pied Wagtail ☐
716 Grassveld Pipit ☐
727 **Orangethroated Longclaw**** ☐
728 **Yellowthroated Longclaw** ☐
730 **Pinkthroated Longclaw** ☐
737 Tropical Boubou ☐
740 Puffback ☐
741 Brubru ☐
744 Blackcrowned Tchagra ☐
748 Orangebreasted Bush Shrike ☐
761 Plumcoloured Starling ☐
765 **Greater Blue-eared Starling** ☐
766 **Lesser Blue-eared Starling** ☐
784 Miombo Double-collared Sunbird ☐
787 Whitebellied Sunbird ☐
791 Scarletchested Sunbird ☐
795 **Violetbacked Sunbird** ☐
797 Yellow White-eye ☐
804 Greyheaded Sparrow ☐
805 Yellowthroated Sparrow ☐
810 Spectacled Weaver ☐
811 Spottedbacked Weaver ☐
814 Masked Weaver ☐
816 Golden Weaver ☐
819 Redheaded Weaver ☐
821 Redbilled Quelea ☐
824 Red Bishop ☐
827 Yellowrumped Widow ☐
841 Jameson's Firefinch ☐
842 Redbilled Firefinch ☐
844 Blue Waxbill ☐
846 Common Waxbill ☐
854 Orangebreasted Waxbill ☐
857 Bronze Mannikin ☐
860 Pintailed Whydah ☐
869 Yelloweyed Canary ☐
870 Blackthroated Canary ☐
877 Bully Canary ☐
881 Streakyheaded Canary ☐

NYANGA AREA

approximately 311 species recorded to date

This northern section of Zimbabwe's eastern highlands encompasses two national parks, Rhodes Nyanga (the largest) and M'tarazi Falls Park. On the eastern side of Rhodes Nyanga Park is Mount Nyangani (2 592 m), the highest mountain in Zimbabwe. M'tarazi Falls is Zimbabwe's highest waterfall, dropping 762 m down an escarpment to the Honde Valley. Much of the area is covered with montane forest and remnants of evergreen forest are found in the valleys. Extensive areas are now under exotic plantations. There are also very large areas of open grassland.

SPECIAL AND INTERESTING SPECIES

Black Eagles are often seen flying along the cliffs. **Longcrested Eagle** and **Augur Buzzard** are the most common raptors. **Redbreasted Sparrowhawk** can be found in the exotic plantations. **Rednecked Francolin** occurs in the area and look for **Common Quail** in the open grasslands. **Bluespotted** and **Tambourine Doves** inhabit evergreen forest in the valleys. Look for **Scarce Swift** around World's View and Nyangani. Sometimes **Mottled Swift** can also be seen there. **Blue Swallows** breed in the open grassland areas. **Eastern Sawwing Swallows** are common along the forest edges; **Barratt's Warbler** and **Roberts's Prinia** can also be found here. **Gurney's Sugarbird, Malachite, Bronze** and **Olive Sunbirds** occur around concentrations of proteas. **Redfaced Crimsonwing** and **East African Swee** are found in the forest areas.

ALSO RECORDED

Yellowbilled Ducks have been recorded on the dam at Claremont Estate. Look out for red phase immature Ovambo Sparrowhawks which can be confused with Redbreasted Sparrowhawk. Sharpbilled Honeyguide occurs in the wattle plantations around Troutbeck and Redbacked Mannikins are worth looking for in the indigenous forest. Look for Moustached Warbler lower down in the Honde Valley.

Derek Solomon and Jacko Williams (Mrs)

From Harare travel to Rusape where the turnoff to Juliasdale and Nyanga is found. The distance from Harare to Nyanga is approximately 275 km. There are several good hotels around Juliasdale and Nyanga. National Parks lodges are available at Mare, Rhodes and Udu camps, and caravan and camping sites are available locally. Bookings must be made through the National Parks Booking Office in Harare.

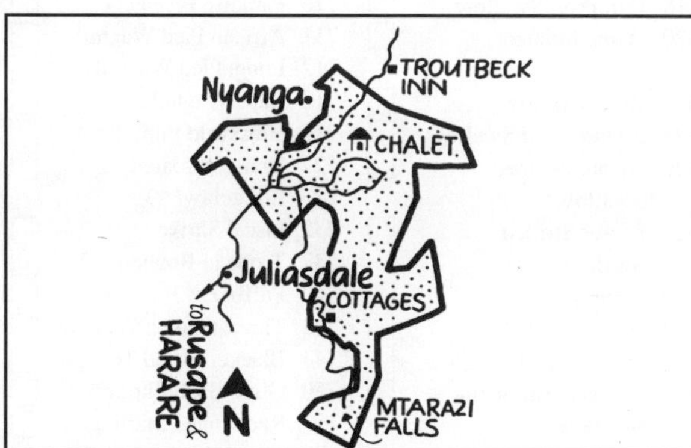

Zimbabwe

48% OF SPECIES

008 Dabchick
055 Whitebreasted Cormorant
058 Reed Cormorant
062 Grey Heron
063 Blackheaded Heron
071 Cattle Egret
081 Hamerkop
104 Yellowbilled Duck
105 African Black Duck
108 Redbilled Teal
118 Secretarybird
127 Blackshouldered Kite
131 **Black Eagle**
135 Wahlberg's Eagle
139 **Longcrested Eagle**
143 Blackbreasted Snake Eagle
149 Steppe Buzzard
153 **Augur Buzzard**
154 Lizard Buzzard
155 **Redbreasted Sparrowhawk**
160 African Goshawk
169 Gymnogene
173 Hobby Falcon
181 Rock Kestrel
196 Natal Francolin*
198 **Rednecked Francolin**
200 **Common Quail**
203 Helmeted Guineafowl
207 Wattled Crane
213 Black Crake
226 Moorhen
228 Redknobbed Coot
240 African Jacana
260 Wattled Plover
264 Common Sandpiper
266 Wood Sandpiper
349 Rock Pigeon
350 Rameron Pigeon
352 Redeyed Dove
354 Cape Turtle Dove
357 **Bluespotted Dove**
359 **Tambourine Dove**
360 Cinnamon Dove
370a Livingstone's Lourie
371 Purplecrested Lourie
375 African Cuckoo
377 Redchested Cuckoo
386 Diederik Cuckoo
391 Burchell's Coucal*
394 Wood Owl
401 Spotted Eagle Owl
412 Black Swift
415 Whiterumped Swift
416 Horus Swift
419 **Mottled Swift**
420 **Scarce Swift**
424 Speckled Mousebird
429 Giant Kingfisher
431 Malachite Kingfisher
435 Brownhooded Kingfisher
438 European Bee-eater
443 Whitefronted Bee-eater
451 Hoopoe
464 Blackcollared Barbet
467 Whyte's Barbet
470 Yellowfronted Tinker Barbet
486 Cardinal Woodpecker
494 Rufousnaped Lark
496 Flappet Lark
507 Redcapped Lark
518 European Swallow
520 Whitethroated Swallow
521 **Blue Swallow**
524 Redbreasted Swallow
526 Greater Striped Swallow*
527 Lesser Striped Swallow
529 Rock Martin
530 House Martin
531 Greyrumped Swallow
537 **Eastern Sawwing Swallow**
545 Blackheaded Oriole
547 Black Crow
548 Pied Crow
550 Whitenecked Raven
568 Blackeyed Bulbul
573 Stripecheeked Bulbul
576 Kurrichane Thrush
577 Olive Thrush
596 Stonechat
599 Heuglin's Robin
601 Cape Robin
606 Starred Robin
635 Cape Reed Warbler
637 Yellow Warbler
638 African Sedge Warbler
639 **Barratt's Warbler****
642 Broadtailed Warbler
643 Willow Warbler
645 Barthroated Apalis
661 Grassbird**
667 Ayres' Cisticola
670 Wailing Cisticola
673 Singing Cisticola
677 Levaillant's Cisticola
681 Neddicky
683 Tawnyflanked Prinia
684 **Roberts's Prinia****
690 Dusky Flycatcher
700 Cape Batis**
701 Chinspot Batis
709 Whitetailed Flycatcher
710 Paradise Flycatcher
711 African Pied Wagtail
712 Longtailed Wagtail
713 Cape Wagtail
716 Grassveld Pipit
727 Orangethroated Longclaw**
732 Fiscal Shrike
737 Tropical Boubou
740 Puffback
743 Threestreaked Tchagra
744 Blackcrowned Tchagra
750 Olive Bush Shrike*
769 Redwinged Starling

774 **Gurney's Sugarbird****	☐	807 Thickbilled Weaver	☐	851 **East African Swee**	☐
775 **Malachite Sunbird**	☐	810 Spectacled Weaver	☐	857 Bronze Mannikin	☐
776 **Bronze Sunbird**	☐	814 Masked Weaver	☐	860 Pintailed Whydah	☐
784 Miombo Double-collared Sunbird	☐	816 Golden Weaver	☐	870 Blackthroated Canary	☐
786 Yellowbellied Sunbird	☐	824 Red Bishop	☐	872 Cape Canary	☐
790 **Olive Sunbird**	☐	827 Yellowrumped Widow	☐	877 Bully Canary	☐
792 Black Sunbird	☐	831 Redcollared Widow	☐	881 Streakyheaded Canary	☐
793 Collared Sunbird	☐	836 **Redfaced Crimsonwing**	☐	884 Goldenbreasted Bunting	☐
804 Greyheaded Sparrow	☐	840 Bluebilled Firefinch	☐		
		846 Common Waxbill	☐		

HWANGE NATIONAL PARK (ROBINS AND SINAMATELLA)

approximately 365 species recorded to date

This account deals with the northern basalt area of Hwange National Park. Both rest camps have stores and petrol, but Robins is closed during the wet season (November-April). Accommodation can be booked through the National Parks Central Booking Office in Harare. There are three exclusive camps in this area (Deka, Bumboosie and Lukosi) where walking is permitted with an armed scout. The Deka Camp is in the Robins area and the main habitat type is vleis and open grassland with some broadleafed woodland. The other two camps are on the Bumboosie and Lukosi rivers respectively with riparian forest and mopane woodland away from the river.

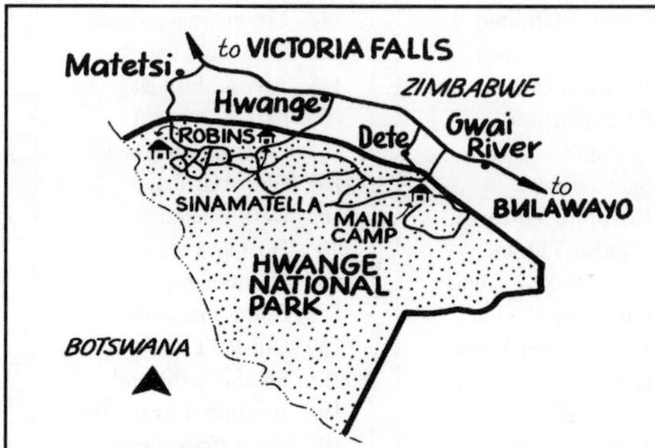

Access to the area is through the park from Main Camp, or from the main Bulawayo-Victoria Falls road at Hwange (to Sinamatella and then to Robins), or via the Pandamatenga turnoff (to Robins) some 50 km north of Hwange town. The roads in this section of the park are all gravel.

18 Zimbabwe

SPECIAL AND INTERESTING SPECIES

This area supports healthy populations of the large diurnal birds of prey, and six species of vulture (including **Egyptian**) have been recorded. Twelve large eagles have been recorded, **Tawny Eagle** being the most numerous. Mandavu Dam in the Sinamatella area is worth a visit and a number of wading birds can be seen there, including a resident pair of **Goliath Herons**. **African Skimmers** are occasional winter visitors to the dam. Salt Pan in the Robins area is the best birding spot and the slightly saline waters of the dam attract both **Lesser** and **Greater Flamingos**. Also recorded at Salt Pan are both **Pinkbacked** and **White Pelicans**, and both **Redwinged** and **Blackwinged Pratincoles**. Adjacent to the vleis at Robins numerous **Blackbellied Korhaans** are found. The mopane woodland close to the turnoff to Robins Camp holds **Arnot's Chat**, **African Golden**, **European Golden** and **Blackheaded Orioles**. Shumba picnic site is an excellent birding spot at all times of the year. **Redeyed Bulbuls** and **Redbilled Francolins** can be seen here fairly regularly, while after adequate rains **Whiskered Terns** are a common sight over the flooded pans. **Dwarf Bittern** are plentiful when the pans are full and a close look at the water's edge could reveal both **Purple** and **Lesser Gallinules**, **Moorhen** and **Lesser Moorhen** and **African** and **Lesser Jacanas**. Both **Redbilled** and **Yellowbilled Oxpeckers** occur regularly on the large mammals in all sections of the park.

Kit Hustler

52% OF SPECIES

008 Dabchick ☐
049 **White Pelican** ☐
050 **Pinkbacked Pelican** ☐
060 Darter ☐
062 Grey Heron ☐
064 **Goliath Heron** ☐
066 Great White Egret ☐
067 Little Egret ☐
071 Cattle Egret ☐
074 Greenbacked Heron ☐
079 **Dwarf Bittern** ☐
081 Hamerkop ☐
084 Black Stork ☐
086 Woollynecked Stork ☐
088 Saddlebill Stork ☐
089 Marabou Stork ☐
090 Yellowbilled Stork ☐
091 Sacred Ibis ☐
095 African Spoonbill ☐
096 **Greater Flamingo** ☐
097 **Lesser Flamingo** ☐
099 Whitefaced Duck ☐
102 Egyptian Goose ☐
108 Redbilled Teal ☐
115 Knobbilled Duck ☐
118 Secretarybird ☐
120 **Egyptian Vulture** ☐
121 Hooded Vulture ☐
123 Whitebacked Vulture ☐
124 Lappetfaced Vulture ☐
125 Whiteheaded Vulture ☐
126 Black Kite ☐
126a Yellowbilled Kite ☐
132 **Tawny Eagle** ☐
135 Wahlberg's Eagle ☐
137 African Hawk Eagle ☐
140 Martial Eagle ☐
142 Brown Snake Eagle ☐
146 Bateleur ☐
148 African Fish Eagle ☐
154 Lizard Buzzard ☐
157 Little Sparrowhawk ☐
161 Gabar Goshawk ☐
163 Dark Chanting Goshawk ☐
169 Gymnogene ☐
188 Coqui Francolin ☐
189 Crested Francolin ☐
191 Shelley's Francolin ☐
194 **Redbilled Francolin*** ☐
196 Natal Francolin* ☐

Zimbabwe

199 Swainson's Francolin* ☐
203 Helmeted Guineafowl ☐
209 Crowned Crane ☐
213 Black Crake ☐
223 **Purple Gallinule** ☐
224 **Lesser Gallinule** ☐
226 **Moorhen** ☐
227 **Lesser Moorhen** ☐
238 **Blackbellied Korhaan** ☐
240 **African Jacana** ☐
241 **Lesser Jacana** ☐
242 Painted Snipe ☐
249 Threebanded Plover ☐
255 Crowned Plover ☐
258 Blacksmith Plover ☐
260 Wattled Plover ☐
264 Common Sandpiper ☐
266 Wood Sandpiper ☐
270 Greenshank ☐
295 Blackwinged Stilt ☐
298 Water Dikkop ☐
304 **Redwinged Pratincole** ☐
305 **Blackwinged Pratincole** ☐
338 **Whiskered Tern** ☐
339 Whitewinged Black Tern ☐
343 **African Skimmer** ☐
347 Doublebanded Sandgrouse* ☐
352 Redeyed Dove ☐
354 Cape Turtle Dove ☐
355 Laughing Dove ☐
356 Namaqua Dove ☐
358 Greenspotted Dove ☐
364 Meyer's Parrot ☐
373 Grey Lourie ☐
381 Striped Cuckoo ☐
390 Senegal Coucal ☐
392 Barn Owl ☐
396 Scops Owl ☐
397 Whitefaced Owl ☐
398 Pearlspotted Owl ☐
399 Barred Owl ☐
417 Little Swift ☐
421 Palm Swift ☐
428 Pied Kingfisher ☐
429 Giant Kingfisher ☐
435 Brownhooded Kingfisher ☐
437 Striped Kingfisher ☐
438 European Bee-eater ☐
441 Carmine Bee-eater ☐
444 Little Bee-eater ☐
446 European Roller ☐
447 Lilacbreasted Roller ☐
449 Purple Roller ☐
451 Hoopoe ☐
452 Redbilled Woodhoopoe ☐
454 Scimitarbilled Woodhoopoe ☐
457 Grey Hornbill ☐
458 Redbilled Hornbill ☐
459 Southern Yellowbilled Hornbill* ☐
460 Crowned Hornbill ☐
463 Ground Hornbill ☐
464 Blackcollared Barbet ☐
473 Crested Barbet ☐
474 Greater Honeyguide ☐
483 Goldentailed Woodpecker ☐
486 Cardinal Woodpecker ☐
494 Rufousnaped Lark ☐
496 Flappet Lark ☐
498 Sabota Lark ☐
515 Chestnutbacked Finch-lark ☐
518 European Swallow ☐
524 Redbreasted Swallow ☐
527 Lesser Striped Swallow ☐
538 Black Cuckooshrike ☐
541 Forktailed Drongo ☐
543 **European Golden Oriole** ☐
544 **African Golden Oriole** ☐
545 **Blackheaded Oriole** ☐
554 Southern Black Tit* ☐
560 Arrowmarked Babbler ☐
567 **Redeyed Bulbul** ☐
568 Blackeyed Bulbul ☐
569 Terrestrial Bulbul ☐
574 Yellowbellied Bulbul ☐
576 Kurrichane Thrush ☐
580 Groundscraper Thrush ☐
587 Capped Wheatear ☐
594 **Arnot's Chat** ☐
613 Whitebrowed Robin ☐
615 Kalahari Robin* ☐
657a Greybacked Bleating Warbler ☐
664 Fantailed Cisticola ☐
672 Rattling Cisticola ☐
683 Tawnyflanked Prinia ☐
701 Chinspot Batis ☐
710 Paradise Flycatcher ☐
711 African Pied Wagtail ☐
735 Longtailed Shrike ☐
737 Tropical Boubou ☐
739 Crimsonbreasted Boubou* ☐
740 Puffback ☐
741 Brubru ☐
743 Threestreaked Tchagra ☐
744 Blackcrowned Tchagra ☐
748 Orangebreasted Bush Shrike ☐
751 Greyheaded Bush Shrike ☐
753 White Helmetshrike ☐
754 Redbilled Helmetshrike ☐
756 Whitecrowned Shrike* ☐
763 Longtailed Starling* ☐
765 Greater Blue-eared Starling ☐
769 Redwinged Starling ☐
771 **Yellowbilled Oxpecker** ☐
772 **Redbilled Oxpecker** ☐
787 Whitebellied Sunbird ☐
791 Scarletchested Sunbird ☐
798 Redbilled Buffalo Weaver ☐

799 Whitebrowed Sparrowweaver
804 Greyheaded Sparrow
811 Spottedbacked Weaver
814 Masked Weaver
816 Golden Weaver
819 Redheaded Weaver
821 Redbilled Quelea
824 Red Bishop
829 Whitewinged Widow
834 Melba Finch
841 Jameson's Firefinch
842 Redbilled Firefinch
844 Blue Waxbill
845 Violeteared Waxbill*
852 Quail Finch
855 Cutthroat Finch
861 Shafttailed Whydah*
862 Paradise Whydah
867 Steelblue Widowfinch
869 Yelloweyed Canary
870 Blackthroated Canary
884 Goldenbreasted Bunting
886 Rock Bunting

HWANGE NATIONAL PARK (MAIN CAMP)

approximately 351 species recorded to date

This account deals with the southern Kalahari sand area of Hwange National Park in the vicinity of Main Camp.

SPECIAL AND INTERESTING SPECIES

It is worth stopping at the bridge over the Gwayi River. Watch for kingfishers and herons on the shore; the reedbeds hold a variety of weavers and widow-birds. In summer, **Thrush Nightingales** occur in some of the thickets and **Emerald Cuckoos** can be heard regularly as they call from the riparian forest. **African Finfoot** is known to occur in the pools along the river and **Western Banded Snake Eagles** have been discovered in this area recently. At the turnoff from the main Bulawayo-Victoria Falls road and extending for at least 10 km is a magnificent stretch of Brachystegia woodland. A number of miombo specials occur in this woodland, including **Redfaced Crombec**, **Miombo Rock Thrush**, **Mashona Hyliota**, **Slenderbilled** and **Sharpbilled Honeyguides** and **Stierling's Barred Warbler**. If one is lucky, a flock of **Redbilled**

The turnoff to the park is about 265 km from Bulawayo on the Victoria Falls road. Main Camp is 25 km from the main road. Hwange National Park is serviced by a daily flight to and from Harare, Kariba and Victoria Falls. There are a number of safari operators who offer luxury accommodation and drives into the park, and there is a hotel close to the park.

Helmetshrikes may be seen - **Thickbilled Cuckoo** is known to parasitise this species here. **Greencapped Eremomela** and **Yellow White-eye** regularly occur in mixed bird parties in this woodland. **Broadtailed Paradise Whydah**, **Stierling's Barred Warbler** and **Blackeared Canary** can be seen in the teak woodland, as can **Bradfield's Hornbill** which occurs all year round but is more common in the drier months. Other dry-country birds include **Redeyed Bulbul**, **Redbilled Francolin**, **Pied Babbler** and, more recently, **Doublebanded Courser**. **Redcrested Korhaans** are a feature of the scrub habitats while the grassy areas hold numbers of **Kori Bustards** and **Ostriches**. **Doublebanded** and **Burchell's Sandgrouse** are regular in this area and **Yellowthroated Sandgrouse** are seen occasionally. Both **Redbilled** and **Yellowbilled Oxpeckers** occur on the large ungulates which are a feature of this national park. During the rains and when the pans are full, a large variety of waterfowl can be seen, including **Maccoa** and **Whitebacked Ducks** and **Pygmy Geese**. **Purple** and **Lesser Gallinules**, **Moorhen** and **African Jacana** are present on the pans, which are also suitable habitat for a number of crakes, including **Spotted** and **Striped**. After rain the emerging termite alates attract large numbers of **Steppe Eagles** and up to five **Lesser Spotted Eagles** have been seen in a group. **European Hobbies** are regular at these alate irruptions, as are **Eastern Redfooted**, **Western Redfooted** and **Lesser Kestrels**. **African Hobby Falcons** also feed in these flocks and can be seen regularly in the vicinity of Main Camp.

Kit Hustler

61% OF SPECIES

- 001 **Ostrich** ☐
- 060 Darter ☐
- 062 Grey Heron ☐
- 066 Great White Egret ☐
- 074 Greenbacked Heron ☐
- 081 Hamerkop ☐
- 083 White Stork ☐
- 086 Woollynecked Stork ☐
- 089 Marabou Stork ☐
- 091 Sacred Ibis ☐
- 099 Whitefaced Duck ☐
- 101 **Whitebacked Duck** ☐
- 102 Egyptian Goose ☐
- 108 Redbilled Teal ☐
- 114 **Pygmy Goose** ☐
- 115 Knobbilled Duck ☐
- 116 Spurwinged Goose ☐
- 117 **Maccoa Duck** ☐
- 118 Secretarybird ☐
- 121 Hooded Vulture ☐
- 123 Whitebacked Vulture ☐
- 124 Lappetfaced Vulture ☐
- 125 Whiteheaded Vulture ☐
- 126a Yellowbilled Kite ☐
- 127 Blackshouldered Kite ☐
- 132 Tawny Eagle ☐
- 133 **Steppe Eagle** ☐
- 134 **Lesser Spotted Eagle** ☐
- 135 Wahlberg's Eagle ☐
- 137 African Hawk Eagle ☐
- 140 Martial Eagle ☐
- 142 Brown Snake Eagle ☐
- 143 Blackbreasted Snake Eagle ☐
- 145 **Western Banded Snake Eagle** ☐
- 146 Bateleur ☐
- 154 Lizard Buzzard ☐
- 157 Little Sparrowhawk ☐
- 159 Little Banded Goshawk ☐
- 163 Dark Chanting Goshawk ☐
- 169 Gymnogene ☐
- 173 **Hobby Falcon** ☐
- 174 **African Hobby Falcon** ☐

Zimbabwe

179 **Western Redfooted Kestrel** ☐
180 **Eastern Redfooted Kestrel** ☐
183 **Lesser Kestrel** ☐
188 Coqui Francolin ☐
189 Crested Francolin ☐
194 **Redbilled Francolin*** ☐
196 Natal Francolin* ☐
199 Swainson's Francolin* ☐
203 Helmeted Guineafowl ☐
209 Crowned Crane ☐
213 Black Crake ☐
214 **Spotted Crake** ☐
216 **Striped Crake** ☐
223 **Purple Gallinule** ☐
224 **Lesser Gallinule** ☐
229 **African Finfoot** ☐
230 **Kori Bustard** ☐
237 **Redcrested Korhaan*** ☐
240 **African Jacana** ☐
248 Kittlitz's Plover ☐
249 Threebanded Plover ☐
255 Crowned Plover ☐
258 Blacksmith Plover ☐
264 Common Sandpiper ☐
266 Wood Sandpiper ☐
269 Marsh Sandpiper ☐
270 Greenshank ☐
274 Little Stint ☐
284 Ruff ☐
295 Blackwinged Stilt ☐
301 **Doublebanded Courser** ☐
345 **Burchell's Sandgrouse*** ☐
346 **Yellowthroated Sandgrouse** ☐
347 **Doublebanded Sandgrouse*** ☐
352 Redeyed Dove ☐
354 Cape Turtle Dove ☐
355 Laughing Dove ☐
356 Namaqua Dove ☐
358 Greenspotted Dove ☐
364 Meyer's Parrot ☐
373 Grey Lourie ☐
377 Redchested Cuckoo ☐
378 Black Cuckoo ☐
381 Striped Cuckoo ☐
382 Jacobin Cuckoo ☐
383 **Thickbilled Cuckoo** ☐
384 **Emerald Cuckoo** ☐
385 Klaas's Cuckoo ☐
386 Diederik Cuckoo ☐
390 Senegal Coucal ☐
396 Scops Owl ☐
398 Pearlspotted Owl ☐
399 Barred Owl ☐
401 Spotted Eagle Owl ☐
402 Giant Eagle Owl ☐
405 Fierynecked Nightjar ☐
432 Pygmy Kingfisher ☐
433 Woodland Kingfisher ☐
435 Brownhooded Kingfisher ☐
436 Greyhooded Kingfisher ☐
437 Striped Kingfisher ☐
438 European Bee-eater ☐
441 Carmine Bee-eater ☐
444 Little Bee-eater ☐
445 Swallowtailed Bee-eater ☐
446 European Roller ☐
447 Lilacbreasted Roller ☐
448 Rackettailed Roller ☐
449 Purple Roller ☐
450 Broadbilled Roller ☐
451 Hoopoe ☐
452 Redbilled Woodhoopoe ☐
454 Scimitarbilled Woodhoopoe ☐
457 Grey Hornbill ☐
459 Southern Yellowbilled Hornbill* ☐
461 **Bradfield's Hornbill*** ☐
463 Ground Hornbill ☐
470 Yellowfronted Tinker Barbet ☐
473 Crested Barbet ☐
474 Greater Honeyguide ☐
478 **Sharpbilled Honeyguide** ☐
479 **Slenderbilled Honeyguide** ☐
486 Cardinal Woodpecker ☐
487 Bearded Woodpecker ☐
494 Rufousnaped Lark ☐
496 Flappet Lark ☐
518 European Swallow ☐
524 Redbreasted Swallow ☐
527 Lesser Striped Swallow ☐
538 Black Cuckooshrike ☐
541 Forktailed Drongo ☐
543 European Golden Oriole ☐
544 African Golden Oriole ☐
545 Blackheaded Oriole ☐
548 Pied Crow ☐
554 Southern Black Tit* ☐
560 Arrowmarked Babbler ☐
563 **Pied Babbler**** ☐
567 **Redeyed Bulbul*** ☐
568 Blackeyed Bulbul ☐
576 Kurrichane Thrush ☐
580 Groundscraper Thrush ☐
584 **Miombo Rock Thrush** ☐
609 **Thrush Nightingale** ☐
613 Whitebrowed Robin ☐
615 Kalahari Robin* ☐
621 Titbabbler* ☐
624 **Mashona Hyliota** ☐
643 Willow Warbler ☐
650 **Redfaced Crombec** ☐
651 Longbilled Crombec ☐
653 Yellowbellied Eremomela ☐
655 **Greencapped Eremomela** ☐
656 Burntnecked Eremomela ☐
657a Greybacked Bleating Warbler ☐

659 **Stierling's Barred Warbler** ☐
664 Fantailed Cisticola ☐
672 Rattling Cisticola ☐
683 Tawnyflanked Prinia ☐
685 Blackchested Prinia* ☐
689 Spotted Flycatcher ☐
694 Black Flycatcher ☐
695 Marico Flycatcher* ☐
701 Chinspot Batis ☐
710 Paradise Flycatcher ☐
716 Grassveld Pipit ☐
719 Buffy Pipit ☐
733 Redbacked Shrike ☐
735 Longtailed Shrike ☐
739 Crimsonbreasted Boubou* ☐
740 Puffback ☐
741 Brubru ☐
743 Threestreaked Tchagra ☐
748 Orangebreasted Bush Shrike ☐
751 Greyheaded Bush Shrike ☐
753 White Helmetshrike ☐
754 **Redbilled Helmetshrike** ☐
756 Whitecrowned Shrike* ☐
760 Wattled Starling ☐
763 Longtailed Starling* ☐
764 Glossy Starling* ☐
765 Greater Blue-eared Starling ☐
771 **Yellowbilled Oxpecker** ☐
772 **Redbilled Oxpecker** ☐
779 Marico Sunbird ☐
787 Whitebellied Sunbird ☐
791 Scarletchested Sunbird ☐
792 Black Sunbird ☐
797 Yellow White-eye ☐
798 Redbilled Buffalo Weaver ☐
799 Whitebrowed Sparrowweaver ☐
801 House Sparrow ☐
804 Greyheaded Sparrow ☐
806 Scalyfeathered Finch* ☐
811 Spottedbacked Weaver ☐
814 Masked Weaver ☐
826 Golden Bishop ☐
829 Whitewinged Widow ☐
834 Melba Finch ☐
841 Jameson's Firefinch ☐
842 Redbilled Firefinch ☐
844 Blue Waxbill ☐
845 Violeteared Waxbill* ☐
861 Shafttailed Whydah* ☐
862 Paradise Whydah ☐
863 **Broadtailed Paradise Whydah** ☐
865 Purple Widowfinch ☐
867 Steelblue Widowfinch ☐
869 Yelloweyed Canary ☐
870 Blackthroated Canary ☐
882 **Blackeared Canary**** ☐
884 Goldenbreasted Bunting ☐
886 Rock Bunting ☐
☐
☐
☐

Pygmy Geese

VUMBA AREA

approximately 160 species recorded to date

The steep Vumba Mountains, well wooded with indigenous forest, lie to the south-east of Mutare. The Vumba Botanical Garden, 28 km from Mutare, is a landscaped garden created around a series of small streams with a huge variety of indigenous and exotic plants. The garden and the adjoining Bunga Forest Botanical Reserve are controlled by the Department of National Parks. The Bunga Forest is an area of dense indigenous trees with a network of footpaths to enable visitors to wander through the forest. Extensive forest, mainly privately owned, occurs throughout the rest of the area and extends as far as Leopard Rock Hotel.

SPECIAL AND INTERESTING SPECIES

Although only a relatively small number of species have been recorded, the area offers an excellent variety of forest specials. **Crowned Eagle** and **African Goshawk** are frequently seen. **Buffspotted Flufftail** can be heard at night, particularly around Leopard Rock Hotel. Forest specials include **Cinnamon Dove**, **Narina Trogon**, **White-eared Barbet**, **Goldenrumped Tinker Barbet**, **Scalythroated Honeyguide** and **Stripecheeked** and **Yellowstreaked Bulbuls**. **Swynnerton's Robin** is common and can be seen regularly at Seldomseen. **Starred Robin** and **Whitetailed Flycatcher** are also found in the forest, as well as **Olive** and **Orange Thrushes**. **Squaretailed Drongo** is also common. Seldomseen is a good place to look for **Chirinda Apalis; Roberts's Prinia** is not

ALSO RECORDED

Redchested and Striped Flufftails and Little Spotted Woodpecker have been found in the low-lying areas. Black Widowfinch is also worth looking for in this region and Shortwinged Cisticola has been recorded calling from the top of dead trees in the miombo and other woodland. Look for Blue Swallow during the summer months.

Derek Solomon and Jacko Williams

The route to the Vumba area from Mutare is well signposted. Accommodation is available in Mutare in the form of hotels, motels and a caravan and camping site. Hotel accommodation is available in Vumba and there is a caravan and camping site in the Vumba Botanical Garden. Seldomseen Field Study Centre (highly recommended), on the left before one reaches the Bunga Forest, offers excellent self-catering accommodation and birding, where the known territories of most of the Vumba endemic specials can be shown to guests if required.

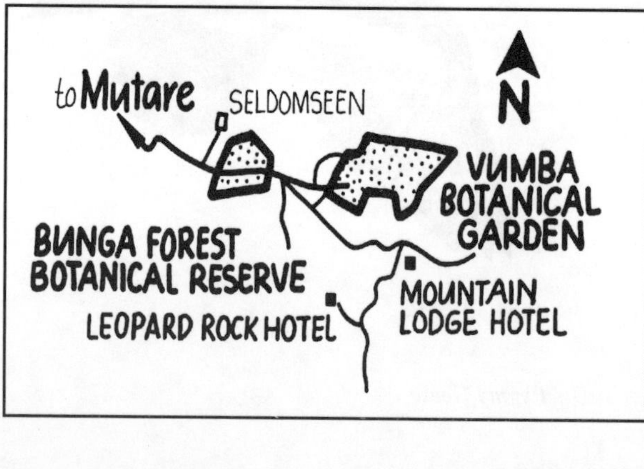

uncommon in the mid-stratum, but is generally a shy species. **Olive** and **Blackfronted Bush Shrikes** are found in the forest canopy, as is **Silverycheeked Hornbill**. Look for **Redfaced Crimsonwing** in forest clearings. Vumba Botanical Garden attracts a large number of sunbirds and **Gurney's Sugarbird** can be found in the protea plantations. Both **Thickbilled** and **Forest Weavers** should be looked for. In the open grassland look for **Grassbird** and **Singing Cisticola**.

69% OF SPECIES

- 081 Hamerkop ☐
- 137 African Hawk Eagle ☐
- 139 Longcrested Eagle ☐
- 141 **Crowned Eagle** ☐
- 149 Steppe Buzzard ☐
- 153 Augur Buzzard ☐
- 154 Lizard Buzzard ☐
- 160 **African Goshawk** ☐
- 198 Rednecked Francolin ☐
- 203 Helmeted Guineafowl ☐
- 218 **Buffspotted Flufftail** ☐
- 349 Rock Pigeon ☐
- 350 Rameron Pigeon ☐
- 352 Redeyed Dove ☐
- 357 Bluespotted Dove ☐
- 359 Tambourine Dove ☐
- 360 **Cinnamon Dove** ☐
- 370a **Livingstone's Lourie** ☐
- 377 Redchested Cuckoo ☐
- 384 Emerald Cuckoo ☐
- 385 Klaas's Cuckoo ☐
- 391 Burchell's Coucal* ☐
- 394 Wood Owl ☐
- 415 Whiterumped Swift ☐
- 419 Mottled Swift ☐
- 424 Speckled Mousebird ☐
- 427 **Narina Trogon** ☐
- 435 Brownhooded Kingfisher ☐
- 438 European Bee-eater ☐
- 456 **Silverycheeked Hornbill** ☐
- 460 Crowned Hornbill ☐
- 466 **White-eared Barbet** ☐
- 471 **Goldenrumped Tinker Barbet** ☐
- 475 **Scalythroated Honeyguide** ☐
- 476 Lesser Honeyguide ☐
- 483 Goldentailed Woodpecker ☐
- 486 Cardinal Woodpecker ☐
- 518 European Swallow ☐
- 527 Lesser Striped Swallow ☐
- 537 Eastern Sawwing Swallow ☐
- 542 **Squaretailed Drongo** ☐
- 544 African Golden Oriole ☐
- 545 Blackheaded Oriole ☐
- 550 Whitenecked Raven ☐
- 568 Blackeyed Bulbul ☐
- 569 Terrestrial Bulbul ☐
- 570 **Yellowstreaked Bulbul** ☐
- 573 **Stripecheeked Bulbul** ☐
- 576 Kurrichane Thrush ☐
- 577 **Olive Thrush** ☐
- 579 **Orange Thrush** ☐
- 596 Stonechat ☐
- 599 Heuglin's Robin ☐
- 600 Natal Robin ☐
- 601 Cape Robin ☐
- 606 **Starred Robin** ☐
- 607 **Swynnerton's Robin** ☐
- 637 Yellow Warbler ☐
- 639 Barratt's Warbler** ☐
- 644 Yellowthroated Warbler ☐
- 645 Barthroated Apalis ☐
- 646 **Chirinda Apalis**** ☐
- 661 **Grassbird**** ☐
- 670 Wailing Cisticola ☐
- 673 **Singing Cisticola** ☐
- 683 Tawnyflanked Prinia ☐
- 684 **Roberts's Prinia**** ☐
- 690 Dusky Flycatcher ☐
- 691 Bluegrey Flycatcher ☐
- 700 Cape Batis** ☐
- 709 **Whitetailed Flycatcher** ☐
- 710 Paradise Flycatcher ☐
- 712 Longtailed Wagtail ☐
- 722 Tree Pipit ☐
- 728 Yellowthroated Longclaw ☐
- 732 Fiscal Shrike ☐
- 737 Tropical Boubou ☐
- 740 Puffback ☐
- 747 Gorgeous Bush Shrike ☐
- 749 **Blackfronted Bush Shrike** ☐
- 750 **Olive Bush Shrike*** ☐
- 769 Redwinged Starling ☐
- 774 **Gurney's Sugarbird**** ☐
- 775 Malachite Sunbird ☐
- 776 Bronze Sunbird ☐
- 784 Miombo Double-collared Sunbird ☐

786 Yellowbellied Sunbird ☐	831 Redcollared Widow ☐	860 Pintailed Whydah ☐
790 Olive Sunbird ☐	835 Green Twinspot ☐	864 Black Widowfinch ☐
791 Scarletchested Sunbird ☐	836 **Redfaced Crimsonwing** ☐	869 Yelloweyed Canary ☐
792 Black Sunbird ☐	839 Redthroated Twinspot ☐	872 Cape Canary ☐
793 Collared Sunbird ☐	840 Bluebilled Firefinch ☐	877 Bully Canary ☐
797 Yellow White-eye ☐	846 Common Waxbill ☐	881 Streakyheaded Canary ☐
807 **Thickbilled Weaver** ☐	851 East African Swee ☐	☐
808 **Forest Weaver** ☐	857 Bronze Mannikin ☐	☐
810 Spectacled Weaver ☐	858 Redbacked Mannikin ☐	☐
827 Yellowrumped Widow ☐		☐

HARONI RUSITU (LUSITU)

approximately 255 species recorded to date

The area adjacent to the junction of the Haroni and Rusitu rivers provides very varied vegetation, including two protected lowland forests: the wet evergreen Vimba Forest and the dry Haroni Forest (sometimes called Makurupini Forest). The two rivers, for the most part, form the national boundary with Mozambique. The area of approximately 10 square km immediately south of the Chimanimani mountain range varies in habitat from natural riverine vegetation to wet and dry brachystegia forests, steep montane forest and grassy slopes. The area ranges in height from about 312 m to 800 m above sea level. Although the protected Vumba Forest retains its virgin status the neighbouring woodland has been greatly modified by peasant agriculture.

This is one of the more difficult localities to reach in Zimbabwe and it is advisable to inform army or police personnel encountered on reaching the area of your presence and intentions. North of Chipinge turn right onto the Chimanimani road. Travel for 4 km then turn right onto the gravel Rusitu road. Proceed along the rough and winding road in the general direction of the Rusitu River, crossing the Gata Rest Camp bridge over the Nyahode River near its juntion with the Rusitu

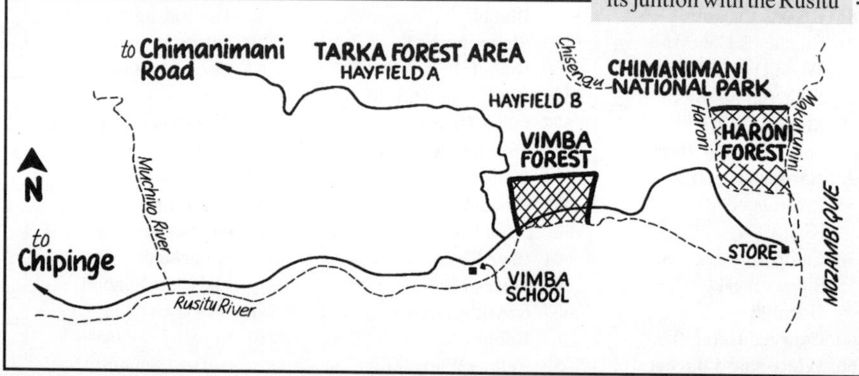

SPECIAL AND INTERESTING SPECIES

The wet Vimba Forest is the main focus of interest in this prime birding area: the dry Haroni Forest is almost devoid of birds in winter but better in summer. Forest species abound in Vimba, with great numbers of honeyguides, bulbuls, flycatchers, batises and shrikes. Several of these are skulkers or forest canopy birds which require careful observation or the use of tapes. Unusual raptors are **Ayres'** and **Crowned Eagles** and **Southern Banded Snake Eagle**. **Pel's Fishing Owl** may be seen in large trees fringing the river and **Halfcollared Kingfisher** on a twig over the water. The forest canopy may yield **Emerald Cuckoo**, characteristically calling "pretty georgie", **Delegorgue's Pigeon** and **Green Coucal** (best located by playing its taped call). **Lesser**, **Barred** and **Thickbilled Cuckoos** may also show up. Knowledge of the calls of **Narina Trogon**, **African Broadbill** and **Yellowspotted Nicator** should enable you to locate these secretive species. **Silverycheeked Hornbill** may call or be seen flying over the valley or canopy. **White-eared Barbet** should be easily seen high up on dead branches. **Scalythroated**, **Eastern** and **Slenderbilled Honeyguides** occur and **Little Spotted Woodpecker** is resident. **Angola Pitta** is present, with breeding recorded in December. **Grey Cuckooshrike** and **Rufousbellied Tit** may be found in bird parties, with **Squaretailed Drongo** in noisy attendance. Of the many bulbul species the **Yellowstreaked**, **Slender** and **Stripecheeked** are exciting to locate. **Barratt's Warbler** and **Chirinda Apalis** are probably winter visitors only. **Blackheaded Apalis** can easily be located by "spishing". Of the numerous flycatchers and batises, the **Vanga** and **Whitetailed Flycatchers** (winter) and **Mozambique** and **Woodwards' Batises** are most noteworthy. The colourful but shy **Gorgeous** and **Blackfronted Bush Shrikes** are worth locating, probably by call and with the use of a tape. **Chestnutfronted Helmetshrike** may be absent in winter. Several sunbirds occur: look for **Purplebanded**, **Yellow-bellied**, **Olive**, **Violetbacked** and **Bluethroated Sunbirds** as well as for **Forest** and **Thickbilled Weavers**. Among grassbirds and seedeating birds **Firecrowned Bishop**, **Nyasa Seed-cracker**, **Green Twinspot**, **Bluebilled Firefinch**, **Grey** and **Swee Waxbills** and **Cabanis's Bunting** justify stalking the tracks and road verges or forest and field edges.

River south of Rusitu Mission. Avoid all side roads climbing out of the valley. On reaching the Ndima road there is a community from whom directions can be obtained to the Vimba Forest. This road is impassable after rains and should not be attempted without a four-wheel drive vehicle. Allow approximately two hours' travelling time to cover the 40 km gravel road to the Vimba Forest area. Camping equipment should not be left unattended while you are out birding.

ALSO RECORDED

Crested Guineafowl and Redchested and Buffspotted Flufftails have been recorded in their respective habitats. Not well known to the area are Cuckoo and Bat Hawks and Taita Falcon. African Black Duck may be found on the river. Bluespotted Dove replaces Greenspotted Dove here. Blackbellied Starling and Redwinged Warbler may be present. Sightings of Blackshouldered Kite and Fiscal Shrike result from encroaching human settlements.

Nigel Fernsby and Pete Outhwaite

Zimbabwe

59% OF SPECIES

058 Reed Cormorant ☐
081 Hamerkop ☐
094 Hadeda Ibis ☐
105 African Black Duck ☐
127 Blackshouldered Kite ☐
138 **Ayres' Eagle** ☐
139 Longcrested Eagle ☐
141 **Crowned Eagle** ☐
144 **Southern Banded Snake Eagle** ☐
153 Augur Buzzard ☐
158 Black Sparrowhawk ☐
160 African Goshawk ☐
172 Lanner Falcon ☐
185 Dickinson's Kestrel ☐
198 Rednecked Francolin ☐
203 Helmeted Guineafowl ☐
204 Crested Guineafowl ☐
217 Redchested Flufftail ☐
218 Buffspotted Flufftail ☐
229 African Finfoot ☐
351 **Delegorgue's Pigeon** ☐
352 Redeyed Dove ☐
357 **Bluespotted Dove** ☐
359 Tambourine Dove ☐
360 Cinnamon Dove ☐
370a **Livingstone's Lourie** ☐
378 Black Cuckoo ☐
379 **Barred Cuckoo** ☐
383 **Thickbilled Cuckoo** ☐
384 Emerald Cuckoo ☐
387 **Green Coucal** ☐
391 Burchell's Coucal* ☐
394 Wood Owl ☐
399 Barred Owl ☐
403 **Pel's Fishing Owl** ☐
405 Fierynecked Nightjar ☐
419 Mottled Swift ☐
421 Palm Swift ☐
422 Mottled Spinetail ☐
423 Böhm's Spinetail ☐
424 Speckled Mousebird ☐
427 **Narina Trogon** ☐
429 Giant Kingfisher ☐
430 **Halfcollared Kingfisher** ☐
432 Pygmy Kingfisher ☐
445 Swallowtailed Bee-eater ☐
450 Broadbilled Roller ☐
456 **Silverycheeked Hornbill** ☐
460 Crowned Hornbill ☐
466 **White-eared Barbet** ☐
471 Goldenrumped Tinker Barbet ☐
475 **Scalythroated Honeyguide** ☐
476 Lesser Honeyguide ☐
477 **Eastern Honeyguide** ☐
479 **Slenderbilled Honeyguide** ☐
483 Goldentailed Woodpecker ☐
485 **Little Spotted Woodpecker** ☐
490 **African Broadbill** ☐
522 Wiretailed Swallow ☐
527 Lesser Striped Swallow ☐
537 Eastern Sawwing Swallow ☐
538 Black Cuckooshrike ☐
540 **Grey Cuckooshrike** ☐
542 **Squaretailed Drongo** ☐
544 African Golden Oriole ☐
545 Blackheaded Oriole ☐
556 **Rufousbellied Tit** ☐
560 Arrowmarked Babbler ☐
568 Blackeyed Bulbul ☐
569 Terrestrial Bulbul ☐
570 **Yellowstreaked Bulbul** ☐
571 **Slender Bulbul** ☐
572 Sombre Bulbul ☐
573 **Stripecheeked Bulbul** ☐
575 Yellowspotted Nicator ☐
577 Olive Thrush ☐
579 Orange Thrush ☐
599 Heuglin's Robin ☐
600 Natal Robin ☐
603 **Collared Palm Thrush** ☐
606 Starred Robin ☐
617 Bearded Robin ☐
638 African Sedge Warbler ☐
639 **Barratt's Warbler**** ☐
646 **Chirinda Apalis**** ☐
647 **Blackheaded Apalis** ☐
648 Yellowbreasted Apalis ☐
650 Redfaced Crombec ☐
657a Greybacked Bleating Warbler ☐
673 Singing Cisticola ☐
674 Redfaced Cisticola ☐
678 Croaking Cisticola ☐
680 **Shortwinged Cisticola** ☐
682 **Redwinged Warbler** ☐
683 Tawnyflanked Prinia ☐
691 Bluegrey Flycatcher ☐
693 Fantailed Flycatcher ☐
699 **Vanga Flycatcher** ☐
700 Cape Batis** ☐
702 **Mozambique Batis** ☐
704 **Woodwards' Batis*** ☐
705 Wattle-eyed Flycatcher ☐
708 Bluemantled Flycatcher ☐
709 **Whitetailed Flycatcher** ☐
712 **Longtailed Wagtail** ☐
720 Striped Pipit ☐
732 Fiscal Shrike ☐
737 Tropical Boubou ☐
743 Threestreaked Tchagra ☐
747 Gorgeous Bush Shrike ☐
748 Orangebreasted Bush Shrike ☐
749 **Blackfronted Bush Shrike** ☐

754 Redbilled Helmetshrike ☐
755 **Chestnutfronted Helmetshrike** ☐
768 Blackbellied Starling ☐
769 Redwinged Starling ☐
780 Purplebanded Sunbird ☐
784 Miombo Double-collared Sunbird ☐
786 Yellowbellied Sunbird ☐
790 Olive Sunbird ☐
793 Collared Sunbird ☐
795 **Violetbacked Sunbird** ☐
797 Yellow White-eye ☐
804 Greyheaded Sparrow ☐
807 Thickbilled Weaver ☐
808 Forest Weaver ☐
810 Spectacled Weaver ☐
816 Golden Weaver ☐
825 **Firecrowned Bishop** ☐
834 Melba Finch ☐
835 Green Twinspot ☐
837 **Nyasa Seedcracker** ☐
839 **Redthroated Twinspot** ☐
840 Bluebilled Firefinch ☐
846 Common Waxbill ☐
848 Grey Waxbill ☐
850 Swee Waxbill* ☐
851 East African Swee ☐
857 Bronze Mannikin ☐
858 Redbacked Mannikin ☐
864 Black Widowfinch ☐
869 Yelloweyed Canary ☐
877 Bully Canary ☐
882 **Blackeared Canary**** ☐
883 **Cabanis's Bunting** ☐
☐

AISLEBY SEWAGE FARM, BULAWAYO

approximately 410 species recorded to date

SPECIAL AND INTERESTING SPECIES

Pinkbacked Pelicans are regular at Ibis Dam where they perch in the trees with **Whitebreasted** and **Reed Cormorants**. In summer the reedbeds are full of **European Sedge** and **Great Reed Warblers**; the resident **Cape Reed** and **African Sedge Warblers** are present all year round. The

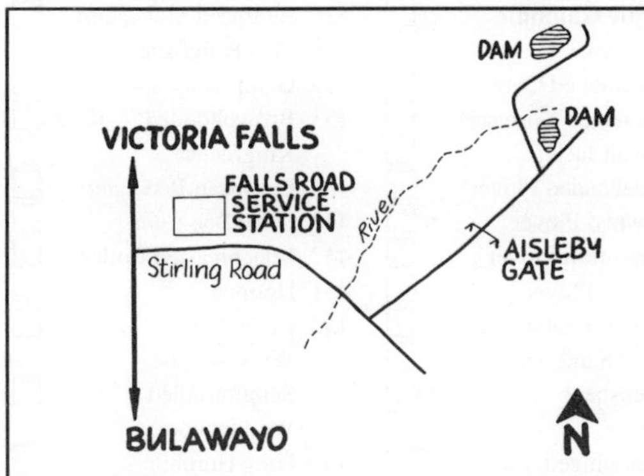

From the main Victoria Falls road, turn right just before the Falls Road Service Station and travel for about 2 km. Immediately after a small river crossing turn left along the fence to the security gate. The best birding area extends from just beyond the gate. Waterbirds and waders are numerous at the various dams.

number of ibises and herons varies daily, dependent on the water level, as does the number of ducks on the dam. **Cape Shoveller**, **Hottentot** and **Redbilled Teals** and **Southern Pochard** are regularly seen. **Purple Gallinules** are common in the reedbeds. Until recently **Redchested Flufftail** was unknown in this area, but it is probably a common resident and can be heard calling from the reedbeds. Since 1987 **European Marsh Harriers** have been a regular feature of the avifauna in summer and Aisleby is a good place to compare the difference between them and **African Marsh Harriers**.

Kit Hustler

45% OF SPECIES

008 Dabchick ☐
050 **Pinkbacked Pelican** ☐
055 **Whitebreasted Cormorant** ☐
058 **Reed Cormorant** ☐
060 Darter ☐
062 Grey Heron ☐
063 Blackheaded Heron ☐
066 Great White Egret ☐
067 Little Egret ☐
071 Cattle Egret ☐
074 Greenbacked Heron ☐
081 Hamerkop ☐
085 Abdim's Stork ☐
091 Sacred Ibis ☐
093 Glossy Ibis ☐
095 African Spoonbill ☐
099 Whitefaced Duck ☐
102 Egyptian Goose ☐
107 **Hottentot Teal** ☐
108 **Redbilled Teal** ☐
112 **Cape Shoveller*** ☐
113 **Southern Pochard** ☐
115 Knobbilled Duck ☐
118 Secretarybird ☐
126a Yellowbilled Kite ☐
127 Blackshouldered Kite ☐
135 Wahlberg's Eagle ☐
137 African Hawk Eagle ☐
143 Blackbreasted Snake Eagle ☐
157 Little Sparrowhawk ☐
161 Gabar Goshawk ☐
163 Dark Chanting Goshawk ☐
164 **European Marsh Harrier** ☐
165 **African Marsh Harrier** ☐
169 Gymnogene ☐
172 Lanner Falcon ☐
188 Coqui Francolin ☐
189 Crested Francolin ☐
191 Shelley's Francolin ☐
196 Natal Francolin* ☐
199 Swainson's Francolin* ☐
203 Helmeted Guineafowl ☐
209 Crowned Crane ☐
213 Black Crake ☐
217 **Redchested Flufftail** ☐
223 **Purple Gallinule** ☐
226 Moorhen ☐
228 Redknobbed Coot ☐
237 Redcrested Korhaan* ☐
240 African Jacana ☐
249 Threebanded Plover ☐
255 Crowned Plover ☐
258 Blacksmith Plover ☐
260 Wattled Plover ☐
264 Common Sandpiper ☐
266 Wood Sandpiper ☐
270 Greenshank ☐
294 Avocet ☐
295 Blackwinged Stilt ☐
297 Spotted Dikkop ☐
352 Redeyed Dove ☐
354 Cape Turtle Dove ☐
355 Laughing Dove ☐
356 Namaqua Dove ☐
358 Greenspotted Dove ☐
373 Grey Lourie ☐
377 Redchested Cuckoo ☐
378 Black Cuckoo ☐
382 Jacobin Cuckoo ☐
386 Diederik Cuckoo ☐
390 Senegal Coucal ☐
392 Barn Owl ☐
401 Spotted Eagle Owl ☐
415 Whiterumped Swift ☐
416 Horus Swift ☐
417 Little Swift ☐
421 Palm Swift ☐
426 Redfaced Mousebird ☐
428 Pied Kingfisher ☐
429 Giant Kingfisher ☐
435 Brownhooded Kingfisher ☐
438 European Bee-eater ☐
444 Little Bee-eater ☐
447 Lilacbreasted Roller ☐
451 Hoopoe ☐
452 Redbilled Woodhoopoe ☐
454 Scimitarbilled Woodhoopoe ☐
457 Grey Hornbill ☐

459 Southern Yellowbilled Hornbill* ☐
464 Blackcollared Barbet ☐
465 Pied Barbet* ☐
473 Crested Barbet ☐
486 Cardinal Woodpecker ☐
487 Bearded Woodpecker ☐
494 Rufousnaped Lark ☐
496 Flappet Lark ☐
498 Sabota Lark* ☐
518 European Swallow ☐
524 Redbreasted Swallow ☐
527 Lesser Striped Swallow ☐
538 Black Cuckooshrike ☐
541 Forktailed Drongo ☐
545 Blackheaded Oriole ☐
548 Pied Crow ☐
552 Ashy Tit* ☐
554 Southern Black Tit* ☐
560 Arrowmarked Babbler ☐
568 Blackeyed Bulbul ☐
574 Yellowbellied Bulbul ☐
576 Kurrichane Thrush ☐
580 Groundscraper Thrush ☐
599 Heuglin's Robin ☐
602 Whitethroated Robin** ☐
613 Whitebrowed Robin ☐
621 Titbabbler* ☐
628 **Great Reed Warbler** ☐
634 **European Sedge Warbler** ☐
635 **Cape Reed Warber** ☐
638 **African Sedge Warbler** ☐
651 Longbilled Crombec ☐
653 Yellowbellied Eremomela ☐

657a Greybacked Bleating Warbler ☐
664 Fantailed Cisticola ☐
672 Rattling Cisticola ☐
681 Neddicky ☐
683 Tawnyflanked Prinia ☐
689 Spotted Flycatcher ☐
694 Black Flycatcher ☐
695 Marico Flycatcher* ☐
701 Chinspot Batis ☐
710 Paradise Flycatcher ☐
711 African Pied Wagtail ☐
713 Cape Wagtail ☐
716 Grassveld Pipit ☐
732 Fiscal Shrike ☐
735 Longtailed Shrike ☐
737 Tropical Boubou ☐
739 Crimsonbreasted Boubou* ☐
740 Puffback ☐
741 Brubru ☐
743 Threestreaked Tchagra ☐
744 Blackcrowned Tchagra ☐
748 Orangebreasted Bush Shrike ☐
751 Greyheaded Bush Shrike ☐
753 White Helmetshrike ☐
756 Whitecrowned Shrike* ☐
761 Plumcoloured Starling ☐
763 Longtailed Starling* ☐
765 Greater Blue-eared Starling ☐
769 Redwinged Starling ☐
779 Marico Sunbird ☐

784 Miombo Double-collared Sunbird ☐
787 Whitebellied Sunbird ☐
791 Scarletchested Sunbird ☐
797 Yellow White-eye ☐
799 Whitebrowed Sparrowweaver ☐
801 House Sparrow ☐
804 Greyheaded Sparrow ☐
806 Scalyfeathered Finch* ☐
811 Spottedbacked Weaver ☐
814 Masked Weaver ☐
816 Golden Weaver ☐
819 Redheaded Weaver ☐
821 Redbilled Quelea ☐
824 Red Bishop ☐
827 Yellowrumped Widow ☐
829 Whitewinged Widow ☐
834 Melba Finch ☐
841 Jameson's Firefinch ☐
842 Redbilled Firefinch ☐
844 Blue Waxbill ☐
845 Violeteared Waxbill* ☐
846 Common Waxbill ☐
852 Quail Finch ☐
855 Cutthroat Finch ☐
861 Shafttailed Whydah* ☐
862 Paradise Whydah ☐
867 Steelblue Widowfinch ☐
869 Yelloweyed Canary ☐
870 Blackthroated Canary ☐
877 Bully Canary ☐
881 Streakyheaded Canary ☐
884 Goldenbreasted Bunting ☐
886 Rock Bunting ☐
☐
☐

LAKE MUTIRIKWE (KYLE) AND GREAT ZIMBABWE

approximately 269 species recorded to date

Kyle Recreational Park, part of the Zimbabwe Parks and Wildlife Estate, covers approximately 16 900 ha around the shoreline of Lake Mutirikwe (formerly known as Lake Kyle). The park includes the lake and a game park of 4 800 ha on the north bank. It offers a diversity of habitats including shoreline, mixed miombo woodland, Acacia thorn scrub and woodland, open vleis, grassland and exposed granite dwalas and koppies. Accommodation comprises chalets, lodges and campsites that can be booked through the National Parks Central Booking Office in Harare. Horse trails have been laid out and walking is permitted within defined areas. The dominant vegetation within the game park is miombo woodland with areas of thornveld encroaching northwards. The Great Zimbabwe National Monument is maintained by National Museums and Monuments and is well worth visiting for both its historical and birding attractions. The vegetation is unique for this area of Masvingo Province, containing patches of dense evergreen forest and riparian woodland. The Great Zimbabwe Hotel near the monument offers good accommodation and camping facilities. The Masvingo Publicity Association will provide details of private accommodation along the lake shore.

ALSO RECORDED

Both Slenderbilled and Sharpbilled Honeyguides as well as Spotted Creeper have been recorded, but are difficult to locate in the woodland canopy. The presence of Thrush Nightingale can be quite erratic from year to year. Narina Trogon, which is known to occur in miombo woodland, has not been recorded in this area for many years. Thickbilled Cuckoo parasitise Redbilled Helmetshrike nests.

Cathy Sharp

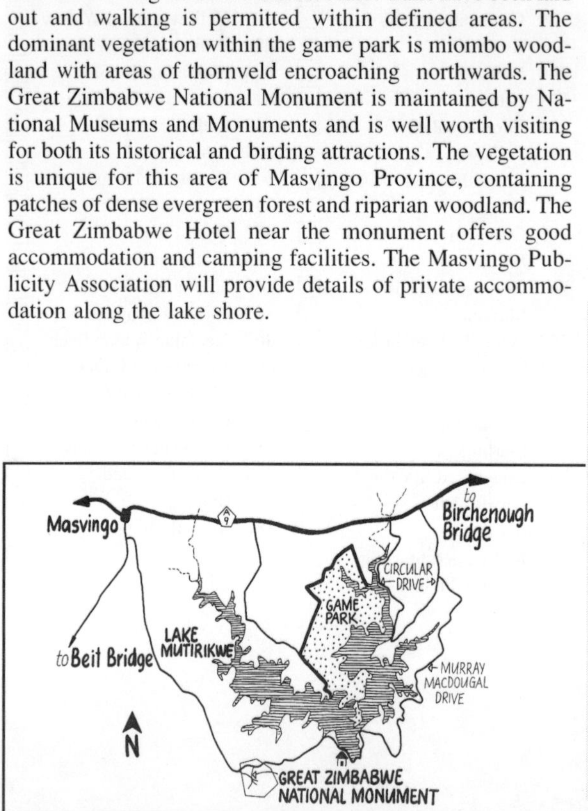

To enter the game park take the Masvingo-Birchenough Bridge road: 13 km from Masvingo town centre take a tarred road leading to the entrance of the park. Access to Great Zimbabwe and the dam wall is off the Masvingo-Beit Bridge road with the turnoff 1,5 km from Masvingo. Great Zimbabwe is 26 km from the turnoff. The road continues to the dam wall and on to the scenic Murray MacDougall Drive leading to the eastern basin.

SPECIAL AND INTERESTING SPECIES

The birdlife encountered within close proximity to one's accommodation is very rewarding. Miombo woodland specials include **Whitebreasted Cuckooshrike**, **Miombo Rock Thrush**, **Mashona Hyliota**, **Blackeared Canary**, **Northern Grey Tit**, **Redbilled Helmetshrike** and **Goldenbacked Pytilia**. **Yellowbacked Widow** is restricted to the marshy grassland and vleis, with **Yellowthroated Longclaw** occurring towards the vlei edges. **Rednecked Francolin** occurs on the forest floor with **Yellowbreasted Apalis** and **Collared Sunbird** foraging in the canopy. **Greyheaded Gull** has become more common with the establishment of small fishing fleets on the lake. The granite dwalas and the ruins themselves provide suitable habitat for **Rock Pigeon** and the elusive **Lanner Falcon**. Four nightjars are recorded: **Fierynecked**, **Rufouscheeked**, **Freckled** and **Mozambique**. These and the owls are particularly vociferous during full moon, the common owls being **Scops**, **Pearlspotted** and **Barred Owls** and **Giant** and **Spotted Eagle Owls**. Migrants include **Emerald Cuckoo** with its distinctive call. **Tambourine Dove**, **Speckled Mousebird** and **Augur Buzzard** are worth looking out for.

63% OF SPECIES

001 Ostrich ☐
008 Dabchick ☐
055 Whitebreasted Cormorant ☐
058 Reed Cormorant ☐
060 Darter ☐
062 Grey Heron ☐
063 Blackheaded Heron ☐
066 Great White Egret ☐
071 Cattle Egret ☐
081 Hamerkop ☐
083 White Stork ☐
085 Abdim's Stork ☐
099 Whitefaced Duck ☐
102 Egyptian Goose ☐
108 Redbilled Teal ☐
115 Knobbilled Duck ☐
116 Spurwinged Goose ☐
118 Secretarybird ☐
126a Yellowbilled Kite ☐
135 Wahlberg's Eagle ☐
137 African Hawk Eagle ☐
146 Bateleur ☐
148 African Fish Eagle ☐
153 **Augur Buzzard** ☐
154 Lizard Buzzard ☐
163 Dark Chanting Goshawk ☐
169 Gymnogene ☐
172 **Lanner Falcon** ☐
198 **Rednecked Francolin** ☐
199 Swainson's Francolin* ☐
203 Helmeted Guineafowl ☐
240 African Jacana ☐
249 Threebanded Plover ☐
255 Crowned Plover ☐
258 Blacksmith Plover ☐
260 Wattled Plover ☐
264 Common Sandpiper ☐
270 Greenshank ☐
298 Water Dikkop ☐
315 **Greyheaded Gull** ☐
349 **Rock Pigeon** ☐
352 Redeyed Dove ☐
354 Cape Turtle Dove ☐
355 Laughing Dove ☐
356 Namaqua Dove ☐
358 Greenspotted Dove ☐
359 **Tambourine Dove** ☐
361 Green Pigeon ☐
364 Meyer's Parrot ☐
371 Purplecrested Lourie ☐
373 Grey Lourie ☐
377 Redchested Cuckoo ☐
384 **Emerald Cuckoo** ☐
385 Klaas's Cuckoo ☐
386 Diederik Cuckoo ☐
390 Senegal Coucal ☐
396 **Scops Owl** ☐
398 **Pearlspotted Owl** ☐
399 **Barred Owl** ☐
401 **Spotted Eagle Owl** ☐
402 **Giant Eagle Owl** ☐
405 **Fierynecked Nightjar** ☐
406 **Rufouscheeked Nightjar** ☐

Zimbabwe

408 **Freckled Nightjar** ☐
409 **Mozambique Nightjar** ☐
417 Little Swift ☐
421 Palm Swift ☐
424 **Speckled Mousebird** ☐
426 Redfaced Mousebird ☐
428 Pied Kingfisher ☐
431 Malachite Kingfisher ☐
435 Brownhooded Kingfisher ☐
437 Striped Kingfisher ☐
438 European Bee-eater ☐
441 Carmine Bee-eater ☐
443 Whitefronted Bee-eater ☐
444 Little Bee-eater ☐
447 Lilacbreasted Roller ☐
450 Broadbilled Roller ☐
451 Hoopoe ☐
452 Redbilled Woodhoopoe ☐
455 Trumpeter Hornbill ☐
457 Grey Hornbill ☐
459 Southern Yellowbilled Hornbill* ☐
464 Blackcollared Barbet ☐
470 Yellowfronted Tinker Barbet ☐
473 Crested Barbet ☐
483 Goldentailed Woodpecker ☐
486 Cardinal Woodpecker ☐
487 Bearded Woodpecker ☐
494 Rufousnaped Lark ☐
496 Flappet Lark ☐
518 European Swallow ☐
524 Redbreasted Swallow ☐
527 Lesser Striped Swallow ☐
536 Black Sawwing Swallow ☐
538 Black Cuckooshrike ☐
539 **Whitebreasted Cuckooshrike** ☐
541 Forktailed Drongo ☐
545 Blackheaded Oriole ☐
548 Pied Crow ☐
550 Whitenecked Raven ☐
553 **Northern Grey Tit** ☐
554 Southern Black Tit* ☐
560 Arrowmarked Babbler ☐
568 Blackeyed Bulbul ☐
569 Terrestrial Bulbul ☐
574 Yellowbellied Bulbul ☐
576 Kurrichane Thrush ☐
580 Groundscraper Thrush ☐
584 **Miombo Rock Thrush** ☐
593 Mocking Chat ☐
596 Stonechat ☐
599 Heuglin's Robin ☐
602 Whitethroated Robin** ☐
613 Whitebrowed Robin ☐
624 **Mashona Hyliota** ☐
645 Barthroated Apalis ☐
648 **Yellowbreasted Apalis** ☐
651 Longbilled Crombec ☐
672 Rattling Cisticola ☐
679 Lazy Cisticola ☐
689 Spotted Flycatcher ☐
691 Bluegrey Flycatcher ☐
694 Black Flycatcher ☐
701 Chinspot Batis ☐
710 Paradise Flycatcher ☐
711 African Pied Wagtail ☐
728 **Yellowthroated Longclaw** ☐
732 Fiscal Shrike ☐
733 Redbacked Shrike ☐
735 Longtailed Shrike ☐
737 Tropical Boubou ☐
740 Puffback ☐
741 Brubru ☐
743 Threestreaked Tchagra ☐
744 Blackcrowned Tchagra ☐
748 Orangebreasted Bush Shrike ☐
753 White Helmetshrike ☐
754 **Redbilled Helmetshrike** ☐
761 Plumcoloured Starling ☐
769 Redwinged Starling ☐
784 Miombo Double-collared Sunbird ☐
791 Scarletchested Sunbird ☐
792 Black Sunbird ☐
793 **Collared Sunbird** ☐
797 Yellow White-eye ☐
799 Whitebrowed Sparrowweaver ☐
801 House Sparrow ☐
804 Greyheaded Sparrow ☐
805 Yellowthroated Sparrow ☐
810 Spectacled Weaver ☐
811 Spottedbacked Weaver ☐
819 Redheaded Weaver ☐
821 Redbilled Quelea ☐
824 Red Bishop ☐
827 Yellowrumped Widow ☐
830 **Yellowbacked Widow** ☐
831 Redcollared Widow ☐
833 **Goldenbacked Pytilia** ☐
834 Melba Finch ☐
841 Jameson's Firefinch ☐
844 Blue Waxbill ☐
846 Common Waxbill ☐
857 Bronze Mannikin ☐
860 Pintailed Whydah ☐
869 Yelloweyed Canary ☐
882 **Blackeared Canary**** ☐
884 Goldenbreasted Bunting ☐
886 Rock Bunting ☐
☐
☐
☐
☐

MATOBO HILLS

approximately 332 species recorded to date

These hills encompass a number of habitats, which include seasonally wet vleis in the valleys, well-wooded valleys and large open expanses of granite.

SPECIAL AND INTERESTING SPECIES

The Matobo Hills are famous for their **Black Eagles**, which have been extensively studied. A number of large raptors, including **Crowned Eagle** and **Augur Buzzard**, can be encountered in the hills. This is also the haunt of Mackinder's Eagle Owl, a large race of the **Cape Eagle Owl**. A careful look around a number of boulders will reveal **Boulder** and **Mocking Chats**. A small patch of miombo holds a number of **Miombo Rock Thrushes.** Careful observation of bird parties could reveal **Fantailed Flycatcher** and **Cape Batis**. Large swifts are worth a second look as **Mottled Swifts** are regular in the hills. **Yellowbilled Oxpeckers** were reintroduced into the area in the late 1970s and have done very well.

Kit Hustler

There is a good tarred road from Bulawayo. The only accommodation in the hills is at the National Parks rest camp at Maleme Dam. Walking is permitted everywhere in the area, except in the specially fenced game park in the western part of Matobo National Park.

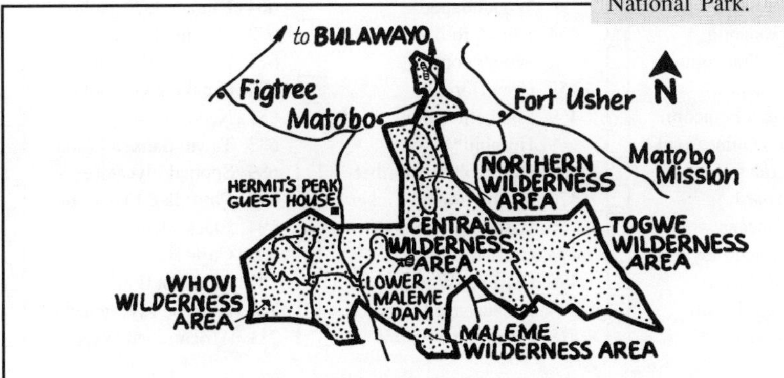

Zimbabwe

50% OF SPECIES

008 Dabchick ☐
055 Whitebreasted Cormorant ☐
058 Reed Cormorant ☐
060 Darter ☐
062 Grey Heron ☐
066 Great White Egret ☐
074 Greenbacked Heron ☐
081 Hamerkop ☐
084 Black Stork ☐
099 Whitefaced Duck ☐
102 Egyptian Goose ☐
105 African Black Duck ☐
108 Redbilled Teal ☐
114 Pygmy Goose ☐
115 Knobbilled Duck ☐
118 Secretarybird ☐
126a Yellowbilled Kite ☐
127 Blackshouldered Kite ☐
131 **Black Eagle** ☐
135 Wahlberg's Eagle ☐
137 African Hawk Eagle ☐
141 **Crowned Eagle** ☐
142 Brown Snake Eagle ☐
143 Blackbreasted Snake Eagle ☐
148 African Fish Eagle ☐
153 **Augur Buzzard** ☐
163 Dark Chanting Goshawk ☐
169 Gymnogene ☐
188 Coqui Francolin ☐
191 Shelley's Francolin ☐
196 Natal Francolin* ☐
199 Swainson's Francolin* ☐
203 Helmeted Guineafowl ☐
213 Black Crake ☐
230 Kori Bustard ☐
240 African Jacana ☐
249 Threebanded Plover ☐
255 Crowned Plover ☐
258 Blacksmith Plover ☐
260 Wattled Plover ☐
264 Common Sandpiper ☐
266 Wood Sandpiper ☐
270 Greenshank ☐
298 Water Dikkop ☐
349 Rock Pigeon ☐
352 Redeyed Dove ☐
354 Cape Turtle Dove ☐
355 Laughing Dove ☐
356 Namaqua Dove ☐
358 Greenspotted Dove ☐
361 Green Pigeon ☐
371 Purplecrested Lourie ☐
373 Grey Lourie ☐
377 Redchested Cuckoo ☐
390 Senegal Coucal ☐
392 Barn Owl ☐
398 Pearlspotted Owl ☐
400 **Cape Eagle Owl** ☐
401 Spotted Eagle Owl ☐
408 Freckled Nightjar ☐
419 **Mottled Swift** ☐
428 Pied Kingfisher ☐
429 Giant Kingfisher ☐
435 Brownhooded Kingfisher ☐
438 European Bee-eater ☐
444 Little Bee-eater ☐
447 Lilacbreasted Roller ☐
449 Purple Roller ☐
451 Hoopoe ☐
452 Redbilled Woodhoopoe ☐
454 Scimitarbilled Woodhoopoe ☐
457 Grey Hornbill ☐
459 Southern Yellowbilled Hornbill** ☐
464 Blackcollared Barbet ☐
470 Yellowfronted Tinker Barbet ☐
473 Crested Barbet ☐
486 Cardinal Woodpecker ☐
494 Rufousnaped Lark ☐
518 European Swallow ☐
524 Redbreasted Swallow ☐
527 Lesser Striped Swallow ☐
529 Rock Martin ☐
538 Black Cuckooshrike ☐
541 Forktailed Drongo ☐
545 Blackheaded Oriole ☐
548 Pied Crow ☐
550 Whitenecked Raven ☐
554 Southern Black Tit* ☐
560 Arrowmarked Babbler ☐
568 Blackeyed Bulbul ☐
574 Yellowbellied Bulbul ☐
576 Kurrichane Thrush ☐
580 Groundscraper Thrush ☐
584 **Miombo Rock Thrush** ☐
589 Familiar Chat ☐
593 **Mocking Chat** ☐
596 Stonechat ☐
599 Heuglin's Robin ☐
602 Whitethroated Robin** ☐
610 **Boulder Chat*** ☐
613 Whitebrowed Robin ☐
645 Barthroated Apalis ☐
651 Longbilled Crombec ☐
653 Yellowbellied Eremomela ☐
657a Greybacked Bleating Warbler ☐
664 Fantailed Cisticola ☐
672 Rattling Cisticola ☐
677 Levaillant's Cisticola ☐
678 Croaking Cisticola ☐
681 Neddicky ☐
683 Tawnyflanked Prinia ☐
689 Spotted Flycatcher ☐
693 **Fantailed Flycatcher** ☐
694 Black Flycatcher ☐
700 **Cape Batis** ☐
701 Chinspot Batis ☐
710 Paradise Flycatcher ☐
711 African Pied Wagtail ☐

732 Fiscal Shrike
733 Redbacked Shrike
737 Tropical Boubou
740 Puffback
743 Threestreaked Tchagra
744 Blackcrowned Tchagra
748 Orangebreasted Bush Shrike
753 White Helmetshrike
756 Whitecrowned Shrike*
761 Plumcoloured Starling
765 Greater Blue-eared Starling
769 Redwinged Starling
771 **Yellowbilled Oxpecker**
784 Miombo Double-collared Sunbird
787 Whitebellied Sunbird
791 Scarletchested Sunbird
797 Yellow White-eye
799 Whitebrowed Sparrowweaver
801 House Sparrow
804 Greyheaded Sparrow
806 Scalyfeathered Finch*
814 Masked Weaver
816 Golden Weaver
819 Redheaded Weaver
821 Redbilled Quelea
824 Red Bishop
827 Yellowrumped Widow
829 Whitewinged Widow
834 Melba Finch
841 Jameson's Firefinch
844 Blue Waxbill
846 Common Waxbill
852 Quail Finch
855 Cutthroat Finch
857 Bronze Mannikin
860 Pintailed Whydah
861 Shafttailed Whydah*
862 Paradise Whydah
867 Steelblue Widowfinch
869 Yelloweyed Canary
870 Blackthroated Canary
881 Streakyheaded Canary
884 Goldenbreasted Bunting
886 Rock Bunting

Cutthroat Finches

GONAREZHOU NATIONAL PARK

approximately 400 species recorded to date

Gonarezhou is a unique and spectacular national park: the two large river systems, the Save and the Runde, coupled with several large pans, support a wide variety of bird life. This park, the second largest in Zimbabwe, extends over 500 000 ha. Aesthetically Gonarezhou has much to offer, from the broad alluvial plains at the junction of the rivers to the eroded, cretaceous sandstone escarpment that forms the majestic Chilojo Cliffs.

Take the Tanganda road from Chiredzi for 18 km, then turn right onto the Gonarezhou road. Follow this for 38 km to the National Parks registration office at Chipinda Pools. Although many of the roads are rough, the park is accessible by two-wheel drive vehicles. The park is open from 1 April to 31 October and bookings must be made with the National Parks Central Reservations Office in Harare. Camping facilities are available at Chipinda Pools in the northern section and there is a small rest camp and camping site in the southern Mabalauta area. There are also two bush camps, Chitove and Pokwe, on the south bank of the Runde River. There are no facilities other than braai areas and long drop toilets at these two camps but they are very good sites for birding. The park is not open to non-Zimbabwe residents but hopefully this will change; tourists must therefore confirm with the central booking office whether the park is accessible or not.

SPECIAL AND INTERESTING SPECIES

Raptors are well represented and include a large breeding population of **Lappetfaced Vultures**. **Bat Hawk** can be seen in the riverine woodland where **Pel's Fishing Owl** may also be found. The pans support large numbers of waterbirds including storks, egrets and ducks. Along the rivers **Rufousbellied Heron**, **Little Bittern** and **Whitecrowned Plover** can be found. Both **Cape** and **Brownheaded Parrots** are common in the park. **Mottled Spinetails** breed in the baobabs next to the warden's accommodation at Chipinda Pools. Also look for **Böhm's Spinetail**. The baobabs also provide breeding sites for **Mosque Swallow**. In the thickets along the riverbanks look for **Yellowspotted Nicator**, **Sombre Bulbul** and **Wattle-eyed Flycatcher**. **Arnot's Chat** and **Redbilled Helmetshrike** occur in the mopane woodland.

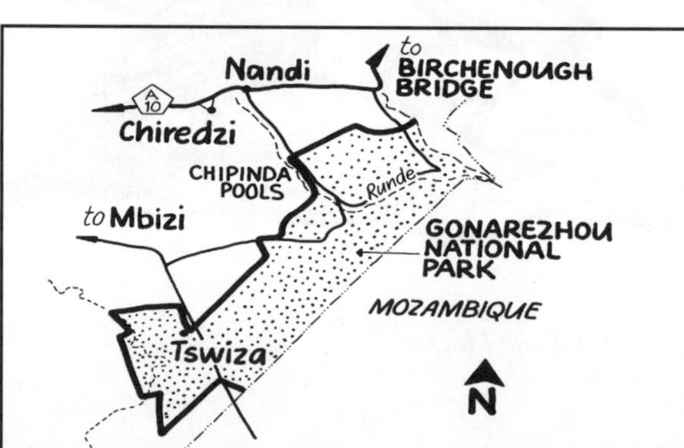

Keep a close lookout for **Thickbilled Cuckoo**, which parasitises Redbilled Helmetshrikes. Both **Redbilled** and **Yellowbilled Oxpeckers** feed on the large game.

ALSO RECORDED

This is one of the few areas where Lesser Blackwinged Plover can be found in Zimbabwe. Crested Guineafowl and Narina Trogon occur in the thickets. Several species of cuckoo, including the rare Barred Cuckoo, can be found around the Save-Runde junction. Green Coucal has also been recorded in this area. Peregrine Falcon has been recorded at Chilojo Cliffs.

Clive Stockil and Derek Solomon

46% OF SPECIES

062 Grey Heron ☐
064 Goliath Heron ☐
066 Great White Egret ☐
071 Cattle Egret ☐
072 Squacco Heron ☐
075 **Rufousbellied Heron** ☐
078 **Little Bittern** ☐
081 Hamerkop ☐
084 Black Stork ☐
086 Woollynecked Stork ☐
087 Openbilled Stork ☐
088 Saddlebilled Stork ☐
089 Marabou Stork ☐
090 Yellowbilled Stork ☐
094 Hadeda Ibis ☐
095 African Spoonbill ☐
102 Egyptian Goose ☐
115 Knobbilled Duck ☐
116 Spurwinged Goose ☐
121 Hooded Vulture ☐
123 Whitebacked Vulture ☐
124 **Lappetfaced Vulture** ☐
125 Whiteheaded Vulture ☐
126a Yellowbilled Kite ☐
129 **Bat Hawk** ☐
132 Tawny Eagle ☐
135 Wahlberg's Eagle ☐
137 African Hawk Eagle ☐
140 Martial Eagle ☐
141 Crowned Eagle ☐
142 Brown Snake Eagle ☐
146 Bateleur ☐
148 African Fish Eagle ☐
154 Lizard Buzzard ☐
157 Little Sparrowhawk ☐
159 Little Banded Goshawk ☐
161 Gabar Goshawk ☐
163 Dark Chanting Goshawk ☐
169 Gymnogene ☐
185 Dickinson's Kestrel ☐
188 Coqui Francolin ☐
189 Crested Francolin ☐
196 Natal Francolin* ☐
198 Rednecked Francolin ☐
199 Swainson's Francolin* ☐
203 Helmeted Guineafowl ☐
237 Redcrested Korhaan* ☐
240 African Jacana ☐
242 Painted Snipe ☐
246 Whitefronted Plover ☐
248 Kittlitz's Plover ☐
249 Threebanded Plover ☐
255 Crowned Plover ☐
258 Blacksmith Plover ☐
259 **Whitecrowned Plover** ☐
264 Common Sandpiper ☐
266 Wood Sandpiper ☐
298 Water Dikkop ☐
303 Bronzewinged Courser ☐
304 Redwinged Pratincole ☐
347 Doublebanded Sandgrouse* ☐
352 Redeyed Dove ☐
354 Cape Turtle Dove ☐
355 Laughing Dove ☐
356 Namaqua Dove ☐
358 Greenspotted Dove ☐
361 Green Pigeon ☐
362 **Cape Parrot** ☐
363 **Brownheaded Parrot** ☐
371 Purplecrested Lourie ☐
373 Grey Lourie ☐
375 African Cuckoo ☐
377 Redchested Cuckoo ☐
378 Black Cuckoo ☐
380 Great Spotted Cuckoo ☐
381 Striped Cuckoo ☐
382 Jacobin Cuckoo ☐
383 **Thickbilled Cuckoo** ☐

385 Klaas's Cuckoo ☐
386 Diederik Cuckoo ☐
391 Burchell's Coucal ☐
392 Barn Owl ☐
394 Wood Owl ☐
396 Scops Owl ☐
397 Whitefaced Owl ☐
398 Pearlspotted Owl ☐
399 Barred Owl ☐
401 Spotted Eagle Owl ☐
402 Giant Eagle Owl ☐
403 **Pel's Fishing Owl** ☐
405 Fierynecked Nightjar ☐
408 Freckled Nightjar ☐
409 Mozambique Nightjar ☐
415 Whiterumped Swift ☐
416 Horus Swift ☐
421 Palm Swift ☐
422 **Mottled Spinetail** ☐
423 **Böhm's Spinetail** ☐
426 Redfaced Mousebird ☐
431 Malachite Kingfisher ☐
433 Woodland Kingfisher ☐
435 Brownhooded Kingfisher ☐
436 Greyhooded Kingfisher ☐
437 Striped Kingfisher ☐
438 European Bee-eater ☐
440 Bluecheeked Bee-eater ☐
441 Carmine Bee-eater ☐
443 Whitefronted Bee-eater ☐
444 Little Bee-eater ☐
446 European Roller ☐
447 Lilacbreasted Roller ☐
449 Purple Roller ☐
450 Broadbilled Roller ☐
451 Hoopoe ☐
452 Redbilled Woodhoopoe ☐
454 Scimitarbilled Woodhoopoe ☐
455 Trumpeter Hornbill ☐
457 Grey Hornbill ☐
459 Southern Yellowbilled Hornbill* ☐
463 Ground Hornbill ☐
464 Blackcollared Barbet ☐
473 Crested Barbet ☐
474 Greater Honeyguide ☐
481 Bennett's Woodpecker ☐
483 Goldentailed Woodpecker ☐
486 Cardinal Woodpecker ☐
487 Bearded Woodpecker ☐
518 European Swallow ☐
525 **Mosque Swallow** ☐
538 Black Cuckooshrike ☐
541 Forktailed Drongo ☐
554 Southern Black Tit* ☐
560 Arrowmarked Babbler ☐
568 Blackeyed Bulbul ☐
569 Terrestrial Bulbul ☐
572 **Sombre Bulbul** ☐
574 Yellowbellied Bulbul ☐
575 **Yellowspotted Nicator** ☐
576 Kurrichane Thrush ☐
580 Groundscraper Thrush ☐
594 **Arnot's Chat** ☐
599 Heuglin's Robin ☐
643 Willow Warbler ☐
651 Longbilled Crombec ☐
655 Greencapped Eremomela ☐
664 Fantailed Cisticola ☐
672 Rattling Cisticola ☐
681 Neddicky ☐
689 Spotted Flycatcher ☐
701 Chinspot Batis ☐
705 **Wattle-eyed Flycatcher** ☐
710 Paradise Flycatcher ☐
733 Redbacked Shrike ☐
737 Tropical Boubou ☐
740 Puffback ☐
741 Brubru ☐
744 Blackcrowned Tchagra ☐
751 Greyheaded Bush Shrike ☐
753 White Helmetshrike ☐
754 **Redbilled Helmetshrike** ☐
761 Plumcoloured Starling ☐
763 Longtailed Starling* ☐
771 **Yellowbilled Oxpecker** ☐
772 **Redbilled Oxpecker** ☐
791 Scarletchested Sunbird ☐
792 Black Sunbird ☐
793 Collared Sunbird ☐
797 Yellow White-eye ☐
798 Redbilled Buffalo Weaver ☐
804 Greyheaded Sparrow ☐
805 Yellowthroated Sparrow ☐
810 Spectacled Weaver ☐
811 Spottedbacked Weaver ☐
815 Lesser Masked Weaver ☐
819 Redheaded Weaver ☐
824 Red Bishop ☐
834 Melba Finch ☐
841 Jameson's Firefinch ☐
842 Redbilled Firefinch ☐
844 Blue Waxbill ☐
857 Bronze Mannikin ☐
862 Paradise Whydah ☐
869 Yelloweyed Canary ☐
884 Goldenbreasted Bunting ☐

OTHER BIRDING SPOTS WORTH VISITING

MASHONALAND PLATEAU

Mukuvisi Woodland, Harare
This woodland, controlled by the Wildlife Society of Zimbabwe, lies just outside the city centre and is open daily to the public. The excellent Miombo woodland in the park supports many species, including Miombo endemics such as Spotted Creeper and Miombo Rock Thrush. Further information can be obtained from the Wildlife Society Shop, 3rd Floor, Monomatapa Hotel, Harare.

National Botanical Gardens, Harare
A wide range of indigenous and exotic habitats have been created in the gardens which are open daily from 06h00 to 18h00. The Department of National Parks and Wildlife Management Offices, including the Central Booking Office, are situated in the gardens.

Ewanrigg Botanical Garden, Harare District
Internationally known for its extensive displays of aloes and cycads, Ewanrigg is an excellent place to look for sunbirds, among others, particularly during the peak flowering season from late June to early August. There are no overnight facilities but there are excellent picnic sites and toilet facilities. Open daily from 07h00 to 18h00. A small entry fee is payable at the gate and firewood can be purchased from the attendant.

Marondera
The Marondera area is one of the wetter areas of Zimbabwe and boasts all the Brachystegia bird specials. It is an important agricultural area, but there are still extensive areas of well developed Miombo woodland in the area available for birding. Many farmers have developed game sections and some farms offer accommodation for birders.

Larvon Bird Garden
A visit to these gardens, on the outskirts of Harare on the road to McIllwaine, should not be missed. This bird garden has an excellent collection of over 230 birds indigenous to Zimbabwe. The large walk-in aviary gives one the opportunity to have a close-up look at many of the species one can expect to see on a trip around Zimbabwe. An entry fee is payable at the gate.

Mutepatepa
A commercial farming area north of Harare which offers excellent birding. The Hippo Pools north of Shamva is an excellent area. Accommodation is available on farms.

Dichwe Lemon Forest
Lying north-west of Harare, this forest offers some interesting birding for those who take the trouble to go there.

MATABELELAND

Tshabalala Sanctuary, Bulawayo
Situated on the road to Matobo National Park, this sanctuary is controlled by the Wildlife

Society of Zimbabwe. It consists of 1 200 ha of Acacia woodland which is home to a wide variety of birds. A small entrance fee is payable and the sanctuary is open all day. Visitors may walk throughout the area but no camping is permitted.

EASTERN DISTRICTS

Honde Valley

The turnoff is on the Juliasdale/Mutare road about 22 km from Juliasdale. Follow the road for 60 km to Aberfoyle Club. The area is best known for Moustached Warblers, but other possibilities include Delegorgue's Pigeon, Little Spotted Woodpecker, Chirinda Apalis, Shortwinged Cisticola, Firecrowned Bishop, Nyasa Seedcracker, Bluespotted Dove, Mozambique Batis, Marsh Tchagra and Redwinged Warbler. Accommodation is available at Aberfoyle Club.

Chimanimani National Park

Situated in the eastern highlands, this park includes most of the Chimanimani mountain range. Access is by foot only and food must be carried in by the visitor. The mountains should be treated with respect and visitors should take care: the region is subject to sudden storms and mist. Camping sites are available and there is a mountain hut which can be used as a communal refuge. The park is open throughout the year. Address enquiries to the Department of National Parks and Wildlife Management Central Booking Office in Harare.

Burma Valley

An interesting day's birding can be had in this hot, semi-tropical valley which lies south of Vumba.

ZAMBEZI VALLEY

Chizarira National Park

In this remote and mainly undeveloped park on the steep Zambezi escarpment, a wide variety of game and birds can be seen in the well-wooded and rugged country. There are a few special bush camps. The park is open throughout the year but during the rains a four-wheel drive vehicle is essential. Address enquiries to the Department of National Parks and Wildlife Management Central Booking Office in Harare.

Matusadona National Park

This park stretches from the shoreline of Lake Kariba back into the wild escarpment area. Only a third of the park has bush roads and entry by road is only recommended during the dry season. Generally, access by boat is recommended. Three exclusive camps are spaced along the shoreline, with more camping facilities in other areas. Address enquiries to the Department of National Parks and Wildlife Management in Harare.

Mlibizi

Situated at the top of Lake Kariba where the ferry stops, the area is noted for waterbirds and birds of dry woodland.

USEFUL TELEPHONE NUMBERS

1 *FIRMS AND SOCIETIES SPECIALISING IN BIRDING*

Birds of a Feather (Derek Solomon)
PO Box BW594, Borrowdale, Harare
(09263) 4-88 2478

Peter Ginn Birding Safaris
PO Box 44, Marondera
(09263) 79-4543
Telex: 81016 Chel
Fax: (09263) 79-3340 or
(09263) 79-4119

Ornithological Society of Zimbabwe
PO Box 8382, Causeway, Harare

Seldomseen Bird Study Centre
PO Box 812, Mutare
(09263) 20-21-5125

Larvon Bird Garden
PO Box 8312, Causeway, Harare
(09263) 4-72-4745

2 *GENERAL WILDLIFE*

National Parks
Central Booking Office
PO Box 8151, Causeway, Harare
Telegrams: Parklife Harare
(09263) 4-70-6077

Bulawayo Booking Agency
PO Box 2283, Bulawayo
Telegrams: Parklife Bulawayo
(09263) 9-6-3646

Safari Promotions
PO Box BW96, Borrowdale, Harare
(09263) 4-72-9029

Wildlife Society of Zimbabwe
PO Box 3497, Harare
(09263) 4-70-0451

Senuko Wildlife &
Environmental Safaris
PO Box 170, Chiredzi
(09263) 31-25-2924

Cresta Hotel Central
Reservations
PO Box 2833, Harare
Fax: (09263) 4-79-4655
(09263) 4-70-3131

Zimbabwe Sun Central Reservations
PO Box 8221, Causeway, Harare
Fax: (09263) 4-73-6646
(09263) 4-73-6644

Natural History Museum
PO Box 240, Bulawayo
(09263) 9-6-0045

Aberfoyle Club
Honde Valley
(09263) 4-70-8239

3 *VISAS*

Zimbabwe Trade Mission
10th Floor, Sanlam Building
cnr Commissioner & Sauer Sts,
Johannesburg, 2001
PO Box 61736, Marshalltown
(011) 838-2156

Zimbabwe Visa Service
703 Essenby House,
175 Jeppe St, Johannesburg
PO Box 8029, Johannesburg, 2000
(011) 333-1717

2 Namibia

Co-ordinator John Mendelsohn

1 Katima Mulilo
2 Mahango Game Reserve, Popa Falls and Andara Mission
3 Etosha National Park
4 Hobatere
5 Waterberg Plateau Park
6 Brandberg and Spitzkoppe
7 Daan Viljoen Nature Reserve
8 Swakopmund and Surrounding Area
9 Walvis Bay
10 Naukluft Mountains
11 Hardap

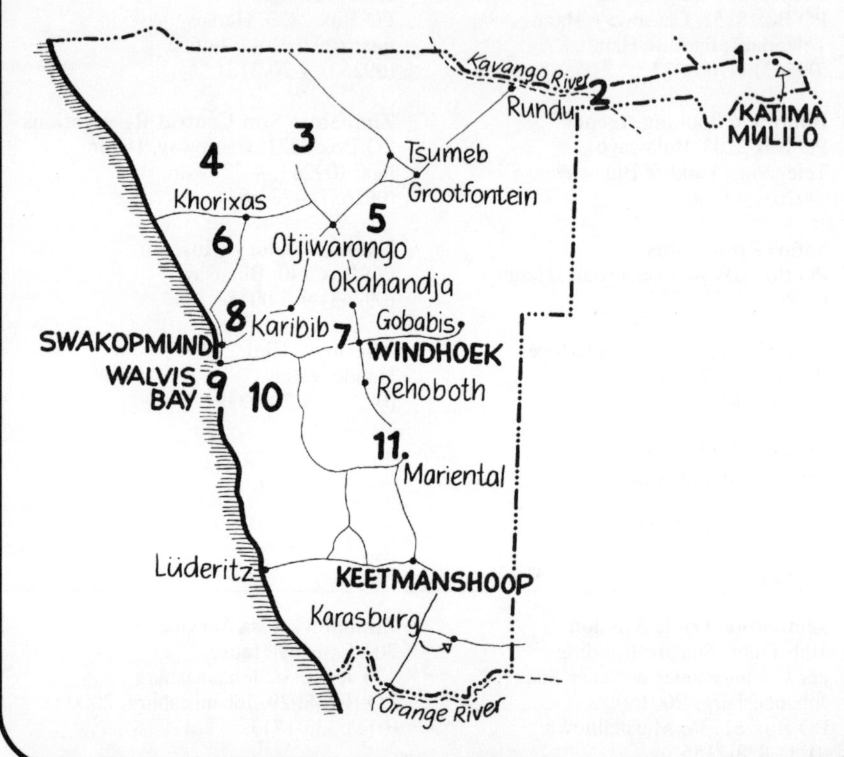

KATIMA MULILO

approximately 330 species recorded to date

Katima Mulilo, the administrative centre for the eastern Caprivi, is situated on the banks of the Zambezi River. The Zambezi River Lodge in Katima has excellent facilities as well as a neighbouring campsite. This site is highly recommended: the immediate surroundings offer excellent birding. Hippo Lodge, about 8 km east of Katima, offers rustic accommodation and is also a good area for birding. Kalizo Safari Camp is situated 40 km east of Katima, and any birder wanting to do boat trips or canoe safaris is recommended to stay at this site, which is also a good birding spot.

SPECIAL AND INTERESTING SPECIES

The Zambezi Lodge environs offer good local birding. **Livingstone's Lourie** is resident in the grounds and **African Skimmers** may be seen skimming along the river. Look out for these in the early morning and late afternoon. **Whitecrowned Plovers** are numerous along the riverbanks, and often in association with **Wattled Plovers** on the adjoining golf course. This locality is also good **Bat Hawk** terrain: they may be seen after dusk. Look out around the floodlights where bats are attracted to insects. **Wood** and **Barred Owls** are plentiful, and in summer **Pennantwinged Nightjar** may be found. The area east of the lodge towards the nature conservation offices also offers good birding, with the following frequently seen or heard: **Emerald Cuckoo**, **Redbilled Helmetshrike**, **Greyheaded** and **Orangebreasted Bush**

Katima Mulilo is easily accessible by vehicle either from the east via Victoria Falls and Kasane in Botswana, or from the west via Popa Falls or Rundu. Namib Air have a scheduled flight to Mpacha airport 20 km from Katima. Car hire is available from Zambezi Lodge, and boat trips can be arranged. Kalizo specialises in fishing and photographic trips and can guide you to most localities in the area.

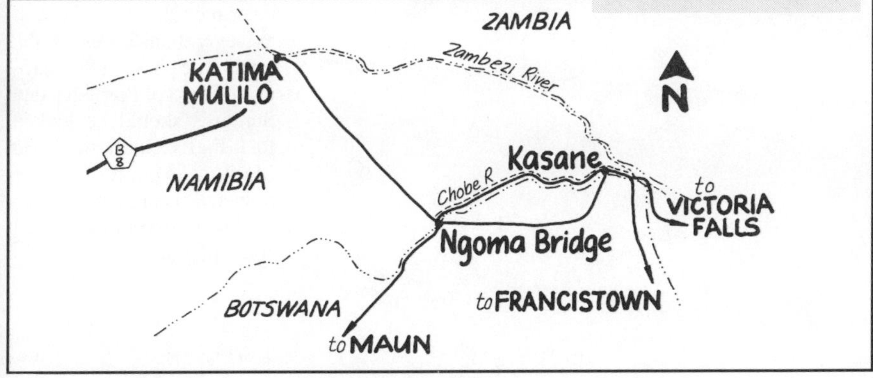

Shrikes, **Black Cuckooshrike**, **Heuglin's** and **Natal Robins**, **Yellowbellied Bulbul**, **Redbilled** and **Brown Firefinches**. The next locality not to be missed is the Katima sewage ponds. These are situated on the left of the main road when entering Katima from the west, opposite the broadcasting tower. Like most sewage works this one offers excellent birding with many waders and waterfowl. **Hottentot Teal**, **Whitebacked** and **Fulvous Ducks**, **Pygmy Goose**, **Painted Snipe**, **Black** and **Baillon's Crakes**, **Lesser Jacana**, **Lesser Gallinule**, **Rufousbellied Heron** and occassionally **Black** and **Slaty Egrets** are seen here, plus many more interesting species. The main water extraction tower to the west of Zambezi Lodge offers good views of **Rock Pratincoles** which roost on the exposed rocks when river levels are low. This site is also good for **Trumpeter Hornbill** and **Cape Parrot**, which should be looked for early morning. Look out for the resident pair of **Western Banded Snake Eagles** in this vicinity. To find **Arnot's Chat** and other woodland species, travel for approximately 8-10 km along the Ngoma road until reaching the well-developed mopane woodland. **Coppery Sunbird** can be found in urban Katima or along the riverbanks, especially when the woodland waterberry trees *Syzygium guineense* are in flower. **Pel's Fishing Owl** is resident at Maningi Manzi, 12-14 km east of Katima. This area has good backwaters but because of flooding is unfortunately not always accessible. Look for **African Finfoot** in the quiet backwaters and search through the grassy floodplains between the forest areas for **Copperytailed** and **Black Coucals**; also keep a lookout for **Pinkthroated Longclaw**. The riverine bush in this area is a good locality for **Pygmy Kingfisher** and **African Goshawk**.

Steve Braine

ALSO RECORDED

Sightings of Honey Buzzard and Osprey have been made east of Zambezi Lodge, as well as smaller species such as Collared Sunbird, Green-capped Eremomela, European Reed and European Marsh Warblers. The latter two species are extremely difficult to tell apart unless in the hand. The Katima farm area to the west of the town is a good locality for White-winged Widow, Golden Bishop, Redbilled Francolin, Helmeted Guineafowl and Dusky Lark. The woodland area surrounding the farmlands is rich in raptors, especially if one is fortunate enough to be there when termite alates emerge after the first rains. From November through to April many Hobby Falcons, Western and Eastern Redfooted Kestrels, Lesser Spotted Eagles and other raptors have been recorded. Coqui Francolin, Racket-tailed Roller and African Hobby Falcons have also been recorded here, as well as several instances of the erythristic phase of the European Cuckoo. Purplebanded Sunbirds should be looked for in the riverine bush around Maningi Manzi. Böhm's Spinetail occurs in the baobab trees within the mopane forest south of Katima.

46% OF SPECIES

- 058 Reed Cormorant
- 060 Darter
- 062 Grey Heron
- 069 **Black Egret**
- 070 **Slaty Egret***
- 071 Cattle Egret
- 072 Squacco Heron
- 074 Greenbacked Heron
- 075 **Rufousbellied Heron**
- 081 Hamerkop
- 087 Openbilled Stork
- 094 Hadeda Ibis
- 100 **Fulvous Duck**
- 101 **Whitebacked Duck**
- 107 **Hottentot Teal**
- 113 Southern Pochard
- 114 Pygmy Goose
- 115 Knobbilled Duck
- 121 Hooded Vulture
- 125 Whiteheaded Vulture
- 129 **Bat Hawk**
- 132 Tawny Eagle
- 135 Wahlberg's Eagle
- 139 Longcrested Eagle
- 142 Brown Snake Eagle
- 145 **Western Banded Snake Eagle**
- 146 Bateleur
- 148 African Fish Eagle
- 154 Lizard Buzzard
- 156 Ovambo Sparrowhawk
- 159 Little Banded Goshawk
- 160 **African Goshawk**
- 161 Gabar Goshawk
- 163 Dark Chanting Goshawk
- 169 Gymnogene
- 185 Dickinson's Kestrel
- 189 Crested Francolin
- 194 Redbilled Francolin*
- 199 Swainson's Francolin*
- 205 Kurrichane Buttonquail
- 212 African Crake
- 213 **Black Crake**
- 215 **Baillon's Crake**
- 224 **Lesser Gallinule**
- 227 Lesser Moorhen
- 229 **African Finfoot**
- 240 African Jacana
- 241 **Lesser Jacana**
- 242 **Painted Snipe**
- 249 Threebanded Plover
- 259 **Whitecrowned Plover**
- 260 **Wattled Plover**
- 264 Common Sandpiper
- 266 Wood Sandpiper
- 274 Little Stint
- 284 Ruff
- 298 Water Dikkop
- 303 Bronzewinged Courser
- 306 **Rock Pratincole**
- 338 Whiskered Tern
- 339 Whitewinged Tern
- 343 **African Skimmer**
- 352 Redeyed Dove
- 353 Mourning Dove
- 358 Greenspotted Dove
- 361 Green Pigeon
- 362 **Cape Parrot**
- 364 Meyer's Parrot
- 370a **Livingstone's Lourie**
- 378 Black Cuckoo
- 380 Great Spotted Cuckoo
- 381 Striped Cuckoo
- 382 Jacobin Cuckoo
- 384 **Emerald Cuckoo**
- 385 Klaas's Cuckoo
- 386 Diederik Cuckoo
- 388 **Black Coucal**
- 389 **Copperytailed Coucal**
- 394 **Wood Owl**
- 398 Pearlspotted Owl
- 399 **Barred Owl**
- 403 **Pel's Fishing Owl**
- 410 **Pennantwinged Nightjar**
- 416 Horus Swift
- 426 Redfaced Mousebird
- 428 Pied Kingfisher
- 429 Giant Kingfisher
- 431 Malachite Kingfisher
- 432 **Pygmy Kingfisher**
- 433 Woodland Kingfisher
- 435 Brownhooded Kingfisher
- 436 Greyhooded Kingfisher
- 441 Carmine Bee-eater
- 443 Whitefronted Bee-eater
- 444 Little Bee-eater
- 450 Broadbilled Roller
- 455 **Trumpeter Hornbill**
- 464 Blackcollared Barbet
- 470 Yellowfronted Tinker Barbet
- 525 Mosque Swallow
- 538 **Black Cuckooshrike**
- 541 Forktailed Drongo
- 544 African Golden Oriole
- 554 Southern Black Tit*
- 560 Arrowmarked Babbler
- 568 Blackeyed Bulbul
- 574 **Yellowbellied Bulbul**
- 594 **Arnot's Chat**
- 599 **Heuglin's Robin**
- 600 **Natal Robin**
- 631 African Marsh Warbler
- 643 Willow Warbler
- 657a Greybacked Bleating Warbler
- 683 Tawnyflanked Prinia
- 691 Bluegrey Flycatcher
- 694 Black Flycatcher
- 701 Chinspot Batis
- 710 Paradise Flycatcher
- 711 African Pied Wagtail
- 730 **Pinkthroated Longclaw**
- 735 Longtailed Shrike

737 Tropical Boubou ☐
738 Swamp Boubou ☐
740 Puffback ☐
743 Threestreaked Tchagra ☐
744 Blackcrowned Tchagra ☐
748 **Orangebreasted Bush Shrike** ☐
751 **Greyheaded Bush Shrike** ☐
753 White Helmetshrike ☐
754 **Redbilled Helmetshrike** ☐
778 **Coppery Sunbird** ☐
791 Scarletchested Sunbird ☐
793 Collared Sunbird ☐
804 Greyheaded Sparrow ☐
811 Spottedbacked Weaver ☐
818 Brownthroated Weaver ☐
824 Red Bishop ☐
828 Redshouldered Widow ☐
834 Melba Finch ☐
841 Jameson's Firefinch ☐
842 **Redbilled Firefinch** ☐
843 **Brown Firefinch** ☐
844 Blue Waxbill ☐
846 Common Waxbill ☐
855 Cutthroat Finch ☐
860 Pintailed Whydah ☐
861 Shafttailed Whydah* ☐
862 Paradise Whydah ☐
867 Steelblue Widowfinch ☐
869 Yelloweyed Canary ☐
870 Blackthroated Canary ☐
884 Goldenbreasted Bunting ☐
☐
☐
☐

MAHANGO GAME RESERVE, POPA FALLS AND ANDARA MISSION

approximately 390 species recorded to date

Only about 20 km of the Kavango River's 450 km length in Namibia is afforded any sort of protection and most of this falls within the three sites described here. The Mahango Game Reserve (MGR) comprises some 25 000 ha of riverine forest, floodplain and dry deciduous woodland on the Botswana border. Fifteen kilometres upstream is the Popa Falls

All three areas are marked on standard tourist road maps. The best accommodation is at Popa Falls, where pleasant hutted accommodation and camping are available. Please ask permission of the Mission authorities to visit the AM area. Some of the islands in the area are burial gounds and as such are sacred sites – ASK where you may go. MGR is one of the few reserves in Namibia where you can get out of your car and walk around – but beware – there is plenty of large game around, including lion, elephant and buffalo.

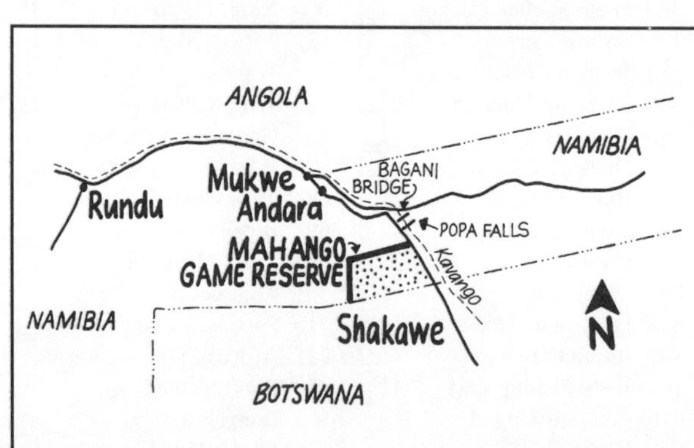

Rest Camp (PF), a small area of riverine forest, island and rocky outcrops. Both the MGR and PF are controlled by the Ministry of Wildlife and Tourism. Andara Mission (AM), established nearly a century ago, is run by the Catholic Church. It is situated where extensive quartzites have broken up the main course of the river and the area is a mass of small rocky islands and river channels. The key to the rich birdlife of these three areas is the variety of vegetation ranging from permanent aquatic habitats to dry deciduous woodlands and Acacia thickets.

SPECIAL AND INTERESTING SPECIES

The specials can be broadly divided into those species associated with the riverine habitats and those associated with the dry deciduous woodlands. MGR is the best place to see waterbirds and a walk along the floodplain margin north of Kwetche (the main picnic site) will usually produce **Wattled Crane**, **Slaty Egret**, **Rufousbellied Heron**, **Longtoed Plover**, **Pygmy Goose**, **Redwinged Pratincole** and several species of bee-eaters, kingfishers and swallows. **Copperytailed Coucals** are best seen early in the morning, and are regularly found in the papyrus beds around PF. The papyrus beds are the best place to look for **Greater Swamp Warbler** and **Chirping Cisticola**. The open-water habitats south of Kwetche are the best place to look out for **African Skimmer**; these birds are however highly seasonal (normally July-December), as are **Rock Pratincoles**, which are common on the rock outcrops in the river around PF and AM. The tall reed beds and riverine forest in all three of these areas have a variety of specials including **Tropical** and **Swamp Boubou**, **Brown Firefinch**, **Whiterumped Babbler**, **Golden** and **Brownthroated Weaver**. The forests south of Kwetche are best for **Barred Owl**, **Pel's Fishing Owl** and **Western Banded Snake Eagle**. The dry woodland specials are best seen in the MGR – these include **Rufousbellied Tit**, **Sharptailed Starling, Whitebreasted Cuckooshrike**, **African Golden Oriole**, **Dickinson's Kestrel**, **Bradfield's Hornbill** and **Blackfaced Babbler**.

ALSO RECORDED

Whitebacked Night Heron, Pennantwinged Nightjar, Bat Hawk and Marsh Owl have all been recorded in the area, but are seldom seen. In the riverine forests and thickets African Goshawk, Sharpbilled Honeyguide, Coppery Sunbird, Cuckoo Hawk, Crowned Hornbill, Natal Robin, Great Reed Warbler and Thrush Nightingale have been recorded. African Hobby Falcon, Steppe Eagle, Lesser Spotted Eagle, Rackettailed Roller, Arnot's Chat, Greyhooded Kingfisher and Stierling's Barred Warbler are regularly recorded in the drier parts of the MGR. Emerald Cuckoo, Narina Trogon, Freckled Nightjar and Wood Owl seem to be restricted to the AM area.

Christopher Hines

43% OF SPECIES

001 Ostrich
058 Reed Cormorant
060 Darter
064 Goliath Heron
066 Great White Egret
067 Little Egret
070 **Slaty Egret***
072 Squacco Heron
074 Greenbacked Heron
075 **Rufousbellied Heron**
081 Hamerkop
087 Openbilled Stork
093 Glossy Ibis
114 **Pygmy Goose**
115 Knobbilled Duck
116 Spurwinged Goose
118 Secretarybird
123 Whitebacked Vulture
124 Lappetfaced Vulture
125 Whiteheaded Vulture
126a Yellowbilled Kite
132 Tawny Eagle
135 Wahlberg's Eagle
142 Brown Snake Eagle
145 **Western Banded Snake Eagle**
146 Bateleur
148 African Fish Eagle
154 Lizard Buzzard
159 Little Banded Goshawk
161 Gabar Goshawk
163 Dark Chanting Goshawk
165 African Marsh Harrier
169 Gymnogene
185 **Dickinson's Kestrel**
194 Redbilled Francolin*
199 Swainson's Francolin*
203 Helmeted Guineafowl
207 **Wattled Crane**
213 Black Crake
223 Purple Gallinule
226 Moorhen
237 Redcrested Korhaan*
240 African Jacana
249 Threebanded Plover
260 Wattled Plover
261 **Longtoed Plover**
264 Common Sandpiper
298 Water Dikkop
304 **Redwinged Pratincole**
306 **Rock Pratincole**
343 **African Skimmer**
347 Doublebanded Sandgrouse*
352 Redeyed Dove
354 Cape Turtle Dove
356 Namaqua Dove
358 Greenspotted Dove
361 Green Pigeon
364 Meyer's Parrot
373 Grey Lourie
378 Black Cuckoo
381 Striped Cuckoo
386 Diederik Cuckoo
389 **Copperytailed Coucal**
399 **Barred Owl**
401 Spotted Eagle Owl
402 Giant Eagle Owl
403 **Pel's Fishing Owl**
426 Redfaced Mousebird
428 Pied Kingfisher
429 Giant Kingfisher
431 Malachite Kingfisher
437 Striped Kingfisher
438 European Bee-eater
440 Bluecheeked Bee-eater
441 Carmine Bee-eater
443 Whitefronted Bee-eater
444 Little Bee-eater
447 Lilacbreasted Roller
449 Purple Roller
451 Hoopoe
452 Redbilled Woodhoopoe
454 Scimitarbilled Woodhoopoe
457 Grey Hornbill
459 Southern Yellowbilled Hornbill*
461 **Bradfield's Hornbill***
464 Blackcollared Barbet
465 Pied Barbet*
483 Goldentailed Woodpecker
487 Bearded Woodpecker
494 Rufousnaped Lark
496 Flappet Lark
518 European Swallow
522 Wiretailed Swallow
524 Redbreasted Swallow
525 Mosque Swallow
527 Lesser Striped Swallow
531 Greyrumped Swallow
533 Brownthroated Martin
538 Black Cuckooshrike
539 **Whitebreasted Cuckooshrike**
541 Forktailed Drongo
544 **African Golden Oriole**
545 Blackheaded Oriole
554 Southern Black Tit*
556 **Rufousbellied Tit**
560 Arrowmarked Babbler
561 **Blackfaced Babbler***
562 **Whiterumped Babbler**
568 Blackeyed Bulbul
569 Terrestrial Bulbul
574 Yellowbellied Bulbul
580 Groundscraper Thrush
596 Stonechat
599 Heuglin's Robin
613 Whitebrowed Robin
621 Titbabbler*
635 Cape Reed Warbler
636 **Greater Swamp Warbler**

651 Longbilled Crombec ☐
657a Greybacked Bleating Warbler ☐
671 Tinkling Cisticola ☐
675 Blackbacked Cisticola ☐
676 **Chirping Cisticola** ☐
683 Tawnyflanked Prinia ☐
695 Marico Flycatcher* ☐
696 Mousecoloured Flycatcher ☐
701 Chinspot Batis ☐
710 Paradise Flycatcher ☐
711 African Pied Wagtail ☐
733 Redbacked Shrike ☐
735 Longtailed Shrike ☐
737 **Tropical Boubou** ☐
738 **Swamp Boubou** ☐
739 Crimsonbreasted Boubou* ☐
740 Puffback ☐
743 Threestreaked Tchagra ☐
744 Blackcrowned Tchagra ☐
753 White Helmetshrike ☐
762 Burchell's Starling* ☐
763 Longtailed Starling* ☐
767 **Sharptailed Starling** ☐
772 Redbilled Oxpecker ☐
779 Marico Sunbird ☐
787 Whitebellied Sunbird ☐
793 Collared Sunbird ☐
797 Yellow White-eye ☐
798 Redbilled Buffalo Weaver ☐
799 Whitebrowed Sparrowweaver ☐
804 Greyheaded Sparrow ☐
806 Scalyfeathered Finch* ☐
811 Spottedbacked Weaver ☐
816 **Golden Weaver** ☐
818 **Brownthroated Weaver** ☐
834 Melba Finch ☐
841 Jameson's Firefinch ☐
842 Redbilled Firefinch ☐
843 **Brown Firefinch** ☐
844 Blue Waxbill ☐
845 Violeteared Waxbill* ☐
846 Common Waxbill ☐
847 Blackcheeked Waxbill ☐
852 Quail Finch ☐
861 Shafttailed Whydah* ☐
862 Paradise Whydah ☐
867 Steelblue Widowfinch ☐
869 Yelloweyed Canary ☐
870 Blackthroated Canary ☐
884 Goldenbreasted Bunting ☐

Halfcollared Kingfishers

ETOSHA NATIONAL PARK

approximately 392 species recorded to date

Etosha National Park (2,27 million hectares) was proclaimed in 1907. The Etosha Pan is about 150 km long and 70 km wide, dry for most of the year, and has numerous saline seepages along the southern edges as well as non-saline seepages and artesian waterholes mostly along the eastern, southern and western sides. There are two major river inlets into the pan, the Ekuma River in the north-west and the Ovambo and Omutiya rivers in the east, which feed Fischer's Pan before overflowing into Etosha Pan. Even in years of good rainfall, Etosha Pan is only approximately 40% full and nowhere deeper than one metre, which offers ideal feeding and breeding habitats for large numbers of waders and waterbirds. Most access roads within the park are on the southern edge of the pan where waterpoints have been established, which attract mammals and birds in great numbers. The Namutoni region in the east has mixed *Spirostachys africana* (tamboti) and *Terminalia prunioides* (Lowveld cluster-leaf) woodland, interspersed with open grassy plains and palms. The central section (Halali) is predominantly mopane woodland, interspersed with mixed *Combretum imberbe* (leadwood) and *Spirostachys africana* (tamboti) areas. Grassy plains stretch along the pan's edge. The Okaukuejo region in the west comprises mainly open grassy areas with patches of mopane/leadwood woodland. Accommodation ranges from chalets to camping facilities.

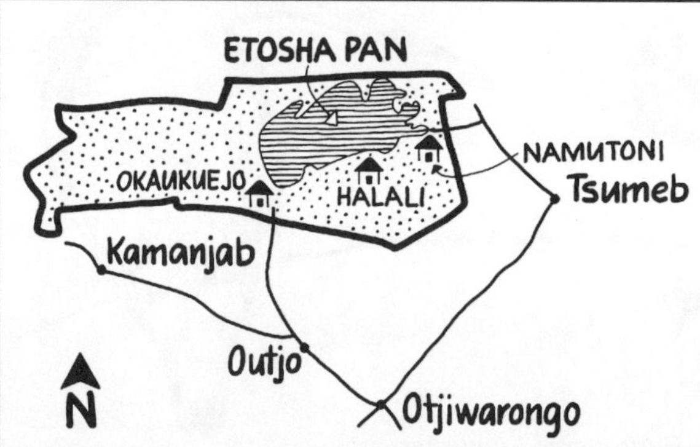

There are two entrance gates into the park; the Ombika gate (via Outjo), which is tarred to Okaukuejo Camp, and von Lindequist gate (via Tsumeb), tarred to Namutoni Camp. Internal roads are well-maintained gravel surfaces.

EASTERN ETOSHA

SPECIAL AND INTERESTING SPECIES

This area has the highest average annual rainfall (435 mm). Fischer's Pan is normally the first to hold water and the last to dry up at the end of the rainy season. Both **Great Crested** and **Blacknecked Grebes**, as well as about 12 different ducks, including **Whitebacked Duck**, **Hottentot Teal** and **Spurwinged Goose**, can be seen on Fischer's Pan. Both **Lesser** and **Greater Flamingos** and occasional visitors such as **Saddlebilled**, **Openbilled** and **Yellowbilled Storks** are present on the pan verges during the wetter months. Large flocks of **Curlew Sandpiper**, **Little Stint**, **Ruff** and feeding groups of **Avocet** and **Greenshank** can be recorded. The occasional **African Fish Eagle** and **Marabou Stork** seasonally take up residence and **Whiskered Terns** are common. North of Namutoni, on the Andoni Plains, **Clapper Larks** are evident and both **Blue** and **Crowned Cranes** can be recorded. The sandier soils are home to **Burchell's Sandgrouse**. In the woodland areas, look for **Greenspotted Dove**, **Crimsonbreasted Boubou** and, on Bloubokkie draai, **Blackfaced Babbler**. A pair of **Giant Eagle Owls** are resident at Klein Namutoni. At the camp itself, look for **Palm Swift** and in the evenings **Rufouscheeked Nightjar**, while the reedbeds adjacent to the fort are a favourite roosting site for weavers. **Redbilled**, **Swainson's** and **Crested Francolins** are common in eastern Etosha where one has an ideal opportunity to see the difference between the female **Redcrested Korhaan** and the **Whitequilled Korhaan** (further west in Etosha) by the colour of their legs.

ALSO RECORDED

Little and Dwarf Bitterns, Black and Slaty Egrets as well as Wattled Plovers are occasionally recorded around Fischer's Pan. Other unusual records include Black Stork, Spotted and Baillon's Crakes, Lesser Moorhen, Painted Snipe, Ringed and Whitefronted Plovers, Turnstone, Redshank, Knot, Ethiopian Snipe, Bartailed Godwit, Grey Phalarope and Redwinged and Blackwinged Pratincoles.

CENTRAL AND WESTERN ETOSHA

The central region around Halali is dominated by mopane woodland, which supports a limited variety of birdlife but is a good area to see **Redbilled Hornbill**, **White Helmetshrike**, **Whitecrowned Shrike**, **Violet Woodhoopoe** and **Carp's Black Tit**. One of the best places to see **Barecheeked Babbler** in southern Africa is at Halali Camp, where a flock have become quite tame; they may also be seen on the koppie behind the camp. **Little Banded Goshawk**, **Meyer's Parrot**, **Greybacked Bleating Warbler** and **Familiar Chat** should

ALSO RECORDED

Uncommon raptor records include Peregrine Falcon and Booted Eagle (migrants). During years of good rainfall, large concentrations of Harlequin and Common Quail gather in the grass cover but are unfortunately seldom seen by visitors. Both African Crake and Little Bittern have been recorded

also be looked for. The scrub mopane areas support both **Monotonous** and **Fawncoloured Larks**. A number of birds breed on the island at Okerfontein when the pan is flooded, including **Greyheaded Gull**, **Blackheaded** and **Grey Herons**, **White Pelican** and **African Spoonbill**. When conditions are suitable, both **Lesser** and **Greater Flamingos** breed on the pan, but are not visible from the access roads south of the pan. Species that are widespread in the park but more evident in the west are **Ostrich**, **Whitequilled Korhaan** and **Pale Chanting Goshawk**. Anthrax accounts for many game deaths which attract high populations of vultures. Up to 400 **Whitebacked** as well as the less common **Whiteheaded** and **Lappetfaced Vultures** can be seen. Large raptors include **Martial** and **Tawny Eagles**, **Bateleur** and when termite alates emerge, especially during October/November, **Lesser Spotted** and **Steppe Eagles**. Among the smaller raptors, **Lanner** and **Rednecked Falcons** and **Gabar Goshawks** are common. The latter are very evident at Okaukuejo Camp where they daily harass the flocks of seedeaters and other species such as **Wattled Starlings**. In all three camps, **Scops** and **Pearlspotted Owls** can be heard at night. **Whitefaced Owl** is less common but resident at Halali Camp. The Charitsaub and Salvadora plains offer good opportunities of seeing **Blue Cranes** and **Caspian Plovers** in small groups during the wetter summer months. Lark and courser species abound in the west, where **Greybacked Finchlark**, **Spikeheeled** and **Sabota Larks** and **Doublebanded Courser** are common. In the shrub areas look for **Rufouseared Warbler**. The trees in Okaukuejo Camp are good places to find **Pied Babbler**, **Wattled Starling**, **Crimsonbreasted Boubou** and **Burntnecked Eremomela**. Do not miss being at the floodlit waterhole in the evenings when large flocks of **Namaqua** and **Doublebanded Sandgrouse** come to drink. **Grey Lourie** and **Anteating Chat** are found in both the Okaukuejo and Namutoni areas, but not in the central mopane-dominated Halali region. **Pygmy Falcon** is found from Okaukuejo westwards where numerous **Sociable Weaver** nests offer breeding sites.

from Halali Camp. Other unusual records from the central region include Hamerkop, Woollynecked Stork, Sacred Ibis, Lizard Buzzard and Egyptian Vulture. Both Freckled Nightjar and Shorttoed Rock Thrush occur on rocky outcrops, unfortunately away from public roads. Bronzewinged Coursers are frequently seen on the roads after sundown. In the south and west of the park, dolomitic outcrops provide territories for Black Eagle.

Mark Paxton

60% OF SPECIES

001 **Ostrich** ☐
006 **Great Crested Grebe** ☐
007 **Blacknecked Grebe** ☐
049 **White Pelican** ☐
060 Darter ☐
062 **Grey Heron** ☐
063 **Blackheaded Heron** ☐
065 Purple Heron ☐
066 Great White Egret ☐
067 Little Egret ☐
068 Yellowbilled Egret ☐
076 Blackcrowned Night Heron ☐
083 White Stork ☐
085 Abdim's Stork ☐
087 **Openbilled Stork** ☐
088 **Saddlebilled Stork** ☐

089 **Marabou Stork** ☐
090 **Yellowbilled Stork** ☐
093 Glossy Ibis ☐
095 **African Spoonbill** ☐
096 **Greater Flamingo** ☐
097 **Lesser Flamingo** ☐
099 Whitefaced Duck ☐
101 **Whitebacked Duck** ☐
102 Egyptian Goose ☐
103 South African Shelduck** ☐
106 Cape Teal ☐
107 **Hottentot Teal** ☐
108 Redbilled Teal ☐
112 Cape Shoveller* ☐
113 Southern Pochard ☐
115 Knobbilled Duck ☐
116 **Spurwinged Goose** ☐
117 Maccoa Duck ☐
118 Secretarybird ☐
123 **Whitebacked Vulture** ☐
124 **Lappetfaced Vulture** ☐
125 **Whiteheaded Vulture** ☐
126 Black Kite ☐
126a Yellowbilled Kite ☐
132 **Tawny Eagle** ☐
133 **Steppe Eagle** ☐
134 **Lesser Spotted Eagle** ☐
135 Wahlberg's Eagle ☐
140 **Martial Eagle** ☐
142 Brown Snake Eagle ☐
143 Blackbreasted Snake Eagle ☐
146 **Bateleur** ☐
148 **African Fish Eagle** ☐
149 Steppe Buzzard ☐
159 **Little Banded Goshawk** ☐
161 **Gabar Goshawk** ☐
162 Pale Chanting Goshawk* ☐
172 **Lanner Falcon** ☐
173 Hobby Falcon ☐
178 **Rednecked Falcon** ☐
179 Western Redfooted Kestrel ☐
181 Rock Kestrel ☐
182 Greater Kestrel ☐
186 **Pygmy Falcon** ☐
189 **Crested Francolin** ☐
194 **Redbilled Francolin*** ☐
199 **Swainson's Francolin*** ☐
203 Helmeted Guineafowl ☐
205 Kurrichane Buttonquail ☐
208 **Blue Crane**** ☐
209 **Crowned Crane** ☐
213 Black Crake ☐
226 Moorhen ☐
228 Redknobbed Coot ☐
230 Kori Bustard ☐
237 **Redcrested Korhaan*** ☐
239a **Whitequilled Korhaan**** ☐
240 African Jacana ☐
247 Chestnutbanded Plover ☐
248 Kittlitz's Plover ☐
249 Threebanded Plover ☐
252 **Caspian Plover** ☐
255 Crowned Plover ☐
258 Blacksmith Plover ☐
264 Common Sandpiper ☐
266 Wood Sandpiper ☐
270 **Greenshank** ☐
272 **Curlew Sandpiper** ☐
274 **Little Stint** ☐
284 **Ruff** ☐
294 **Avocet** ☐
295 Blackwinged Stilt ☐
297 Spotted Dikkop ☐
301 **Doublebanded Courser** ☐
315 **Greyheaded Gull** ☐
338 **Whiskered Tern** ☐
339 Whitewinged Tern ☐
344 **Namaqua Sandgrouse*** ☐
345 **Burchell's Sandgrouse*** ☐
347 **Doublebanded Sandgrouse*** ☐
354 Cape Turtle Dove ☐
355 Laughing Dove ☐
356 Namaqua Dove ☐
358 **Greenspotted Dove** ☐
364 **Meyer's Parrot** ☐
365 Rüppell's Parrot* ☐
367 Rosyfaced Lovebird* ☐
373 **Grey Lourie** ☐
374 European Cuckoo ☐
377 Redchested Cuckoo ☐
378 Black Cuckoo ☐
380 Great Spotted Cuckoo ☐
382 Jacobin Cuckoo ☐
385 Klaas's Cuckoo ☐
386 Diederik Cuckoo ☐
396 **Scops Owl** ☐
397 **Whitefaced Owl** ☐
398 **Pearlspotted Owl** ☐
401 Spotted Eagle Owl ☐
402 **Giant Eagle Owl** ☐
405 Fierynecked Nightjar ☐
406 **Rufouscheeked Nightjar** ☐
412 Black Swift ☐
413 Bradfield's Swift* ☐
415 Whiterumped Swift ☐
418 Alpine Swift ☐
421 **Palm Swift** ☐
425 Whitebacked Mousebird** ☐
426 Redfaced Mousebird ☐
428 Pied Kingfisher ☐
429 Giant Kingfisher ☐
431 Malachite Kingfisher ☐
437 Striped Kingfisher ☐
438 European Bee-eater ☐
445 Swallowtailed Bee-eater ☐
446 European Roller ☐
447 Lilacbreasted Roller ☐
449 Purple Roller ☐
451 Hoopoe ☐

452 Redbilled Woodhoopoe ☐
453 **Violet Woodhoopoe*** ☐
454 Scimitarbilled Woodhoopoe ☐
457 Grey Hornbill ☐
458 **Redbilled Hornbill** ☐
459 Southern Yellowbilled Hornbill* ☐
465 Pied Barbet* ☐
474 Greater Honeyguide ☐
481 Bennett's Woodpecker ☐
483 Goldentailed Woodpecker ☐
486 Cardinal Woodpecker ☐
487 Bearded Woodpecker ☐
493 **Monotonous Lark*** ☐
494 Rufousnaped Lark ☐
495 **Clapper Lark**** ☐
497 **Fawncoloured Lark** ☐
498 **Sabota Lark*** ☐
505 Dusky Lark ☐
506 **Spikeheeled Lark*** ☐
507 Redcapped Lark ☐
508 Pinkbilled Lark* ☐
511 Stark's Lark* ☐
515 Chestnutbacked Finchlark ☐
516 **Greybacked Finchlark*** ☐
518 European Swallow ☐
523 Pearlbreasted Swallow ☐
524 Redbreasted Swallow ☐
526 Greater Striped Swallow* ☐
541 Forktailed Drongo ☐
547 Black Crow ☐
548 Pied Crow ☐
552 Ashy Tit* ☐
555 **Carp's Black Tit*** ☐
557 Cape Penduline Tit* ☐

561 **Blackfaced Babbler*** ☐
563 **Pied Babbler**** ☐
564 **Barecheeked Babbler*** ☐
567 Redeyed Bulbul* ☐
580 Groundscraper Thrush ☐
587 Capped Wheatear ☐
589 **Familiar Chat** ☐
595 **Anteating Chat**** ☐
596 Stonechat ☐
613 Whitebrowed Robin ☐
615 Kalahari Robin* ☐
621 Titbabbler* ☐
643 Willow Warbler ☐
651 Longbilled Crombec ☐
653 Yellowbellied Eremomela ☐
656 **Burntnecked Eremomela** ☐
657a **Greybacked Bleating Warbler** ☐
665 Desert Cisticola ☐
671 Tinkling Cisticola ☐
672 Rattling Cisticola ☐
685 Blackchested Prinia* ☐
688 **Rufouseared Warbler**** ☐
695 Marico Flycatcher* ☐
697 Chat Flycatcher* ☐
703 Pririt Batis* ☐
713 Cape Wagtail ☐
716 Grassveld Pipit ☐
731 Lesser Grey Shrike ☐
732 Fiscal Shrike ☐
739 **Crimsonbreasted Boubou*** ☐
743 Threestreaked Tchagra ☐
753 **White Helmetshrike** ☐
756 **Whitecrowned Shrike*** ☐

760 **Wattled Starling** ☐
761 Plumcoloured Starling ☐
762 Burchell's Starling* ☐
764 Glossy Starling* ☐
770 Palewinged Starling* ☐
779 Marico Sunbird ☐
788 Dusky Sunbird* ☐
791 Scarletchested Sunbird ☐
798 Redbilled Buffalo Weaver ☐
799 Whitebrowed Sparrowweaver ☐
800 **Sociable Weaver**** ☐
801 House Sparrow ☐
802 Great Sparrow* ☐
804 Greyheaded Sparrow ☐
806 Scalyfeathered Finch* ☐
812 Chestnut Weaver ☐
814 Masked Weaver ☐
821 Redbilled Quelea ☐
824 Red Bishop ☐
844 Blue Waxbill ☐
845 Violeteared Waxbill* ☐
846 Common Waxbill ☐
847 Blackcheeked Waxbill ☐
861 Shafttailed Whydah* ☐
870 Blackthroated Canary ☐
878 Yellow Canary* ☐
879 Whitethroated Canary* ☐
884 Goldenbreasted Bunting ☐
886 Rock Bunting ☐
887 Larklike Bunting* ☐
☐
☐
☐
☐
☐
☐
☐

HOBATERE

approximately 177 species recorded to date

Hobatere is state owned, 35 000 ha in extent, and borders on the western side of the Etosha National Park. It is run as a game reserve and incorporates a three-star lodge with good facilities and a campsite. The area is characterised by granite hills and outcrops, dominated by mopane woodland and scrub. In this semi-arid environment many species are regulated by rainfall and are only found here after good rains. The best time to visit the area is between January and May when many of the migrants can still be seen, as well as the breeding resident species.

SPECIAL AND INTERESTING SPECIES

Hobatere offers a number of Namibian specials which can normally be seen without too much effort. **Violet Woodhoopoe** and **Carp's Black Tit** should be searched for in any of the well-developed mopane woodland close to the lodge. **Whitetailed Shrike**, **Rüppell's Parrot** and **Barecheecked Babbler** are normally found within the lodge grounds. With time and patience the granite outcrops south of the lodge offer **Hartlaub's Francolin** and **Rockrunner**. April to August is the best time for accipiters, which may be seen daily harassing passerines at the lodge's bird bath, or at any of the artificial waterpoints on the grounds. These include **Gabar** and **Little Banded Goshawks**, **Little Sparrowhawk**, and with some luck, **Ovambo Sparrowhawk**. **Booted Eagle** and **Augur Buzzard** are also frequently

Hobatere Lodge is easily accessible by road, six hours' drive from Windhoek. From Windhoek travel to Otjiwarongo, from there on to Outjo. Just north of Outjo take the Kamanjab road. At Kamanjab the tar road ends and this is the last petrol stop before Opuwa, so it is advisable to refuel here. From Kamanjab you then take the main Opuwa/Ruacana road northwards for 65 km before turning off westwards on a farm track before reaching the lodge. Care must be taken during rains, as there are several dips and rivers which flow during this period. Hobatere has a good all-weather airfield 1 600 m long. Reservations should be made prior to visiting the area.

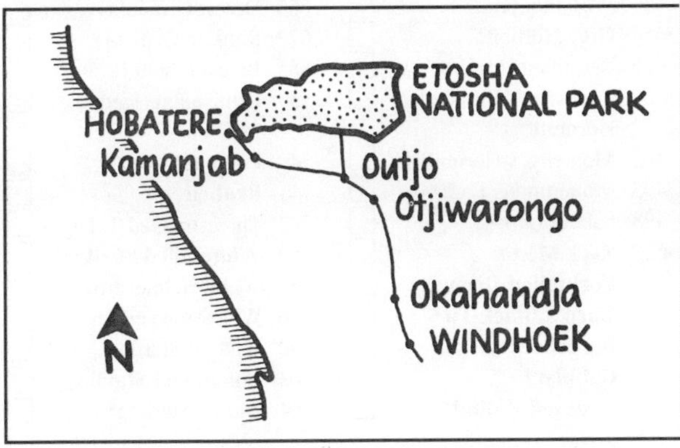

observed at these sites. Other species frequently seen are **Longtailed Starling, Forktailed Drongo, Puffback, Brubru, Redeyed Bulbul, Larklike Bunting, Groundscraper Thrush, Redheaded Finch** and **Chestnut Weaver**, the latter in breeding plumage from January to May. A walk down the dry riverbed below the lodge can produce **Giant Eagle Owl** and **Pearlspotted Owl**. At night **Scops Owls** are frequently heard as well as the occasional **Whitefaced Owl. Bradfield's Swift**, although resident, is not always encountered. Other species that can be seen are **Redbilled Buffalo Weaver, Rosyfaced Lovebird, Goldenbreasted** and **Rock Buntings** as well as **Grey Lourie, Rock Pigeon** and **Kori Bustard. Olive Bee-eaters** are evident around the lodge from November to February.

ALSO RECORDED

After good rains from March to June/July, Harlequin and Common Quail and Kurrichane Buttonquail are commonly flushed, while Rednecked and Lanner Falcons are also frequently seen. When there is open water Dabchick, Grey and Blackheaded Herons, Blacksmith Plover, Wood Sandpiper and Little Stint may be seen. Other species that occur are Ludwig's Bustard, Gymnogene, African, Black and Klaas's Cuckoo. From February to May drives at night offer Mozambique and Rufouscheeked Nightjars as well as Bronzewinged Courser and Marsh Owl.

Steve Braine

46% OF SPECIES

001 Ostrich ☐
118 Secretarybird ☐
132 Tawny Eagle ☐
135 Wahlberg's Eagle ☐
136 **Booted Eagle** ☐
142 Brown Snake Eagle ☐
143 Blackbreasted Snake Eagle ☐
153 **Augur Buzzard** ☐
156 **Ovambo Sparrowhawk** ☐
157 **Little Sparrowhawk** ☐
159 **Little Banded Goshawk** ☐
161 Gabar Goshawk ☐
162 Pale Chanting Goshawk* ☐
181 Rock Kestrel ☐
186 Pygmy Falcon ☐
194 Redbilled Francolin* ☐
197 **Hartlaub's Francolin*** ☐
203 Helmeted Guineafowl ☐
230 **Kori Bustard** ☐
237 Redcrested Korhaan* ☐
255 Crowned Plover ☐
344 Namaqua Sandgrouse* ☐
347 Doublebanded Sandgrouse* ☐
349 **Rock Pigeon** ☐
354 Cape Turtle Dove ☐
355 Laughing Dove ☐
356 Namaqua Dove ☐
365 **Rüppell's Parrot*** ☐
367 **Rosyfaced Lovebird*** ☐
373 **Grey Lourie** ☐
396 **Scops Owl** ☐
397 **Whitefaced Owl** ☐
398 **Pearlspotted Owl** ☐
402 **Giant Eagle Owl** ☐
413 **Bradfield's Swift*** ☐
439 **Olive Bee-eater** ☐
447 Lilacbreasted Roller ☐
449 Purple Roller ☐
451 Hoopoe ☐
453 **Violet Woodhoopoe*** ☐
454 Scimitarbilled Woodhoopoe ☐
457 Grey Hornbill ☐
458 Redbilled Hornbill ☐
459 Southern Yellowbilled Hornbill* ☐
462 Monteiro's Hornbill* ☐
493 Monotonous Lark* ☐
498 Sabota Lark* ☐
529 Rock Martin ☐
541 **Forktailed Drongo** ☐
555 **Carp's Black Tit*** ☐
564 **Barecheeked Babbler*** ☐
567 **Redeyed Bulbul*** ☐
580 **Groundscraper Thrush** ☐
595 Anteating Chat** ☐
615 Kalahari Robin* ☐
662 **Rockrunner*** ☐
665 Desert Cisticola ☐
672 Rattling Cisticola ☐
685 Blackchested Prinia* ☐
739 Crimsonbreasted Boubou* ☐
740 **Puffback** ☐
741 **Brubru** ☐
743 Threestreaked Tchagra ☐
752 **Whitetailed Shrike*** ☐
753 White Helmetshrike ☐
756 Whitecrowned Shrike* ☐
760 Wattled Starling ☐
763 **Longtailed Starling*** ☐
764 Glossy Starling* ☐

770 Palewinged Starling* ☐
798 **Redbilled Buffalo Weaver** ☐
799 Whitebrowed Sparrowweaver ☐
802 Great Sparrow* ☐
804 Greyheaded Sparrow ☐
812 **Chestnut Weaver** ☐
821 Redbilled Quelea ☐
834 Melba Finch ☐
847 Blackcheeked Waxbill ☐
856 **Redheaded Finch*** ☐
870 Blackthroated Canary ☐
884 **Goldenbreasted Bunting** ☐
886 **Rock Bunting** ☐
887 **Larklike Bunting*** ☐
☐
☐
☐

WATERBERG PLATEAU PARK

approximately 250 species recorded to date

The Waterberg Plateau Park (40 550 ha, 1 500 m above sea level) is situated about 60 km east of Otjiwarongo and is administered by the Ministry of Wildlife, Conservation and Tourism. The Waterberg Plateau rises about 420 m above the surrounding plains on the south-western and northern sides, and slopes gently down into the surrounding area to the north-east. The plateau is circumscribed by sandstone cliffs up to 120 m high. Below the cliffs the ground slopes steeply but evenly away to the base of the mountain. The slopes are covered with sandstone rocks weathered from the summit. The high diversity of birdlife in this semi-arid region (460 mm annual rainfall) is due to the location of the Waterberg at the meeting point of broadleafed woodland on northern Kalahari sandveld on top of the plateau and mixed thornbush savanna below. A third habitat is provided by the cliffs and scree slopes.

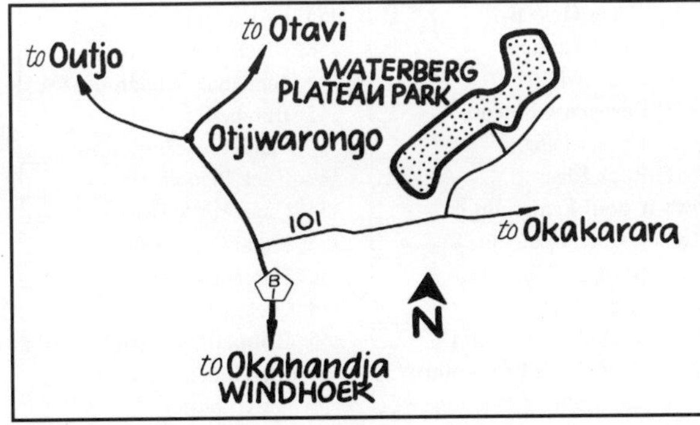

Turn off the main north road (B1) 22 km south of Otjiwarongo on to the tar road to Okakarara (C22). After about 41 km turn north onto a gravel district road D2512. The entrance to the park is clearly marked and is reached after about 35 km. Care should be taken on the district road which has a few sharp bends and a number of dips.

SPECIAL AND INTERESTING SPECIES

The Karakuwisa cliffs of the Waterberg support the most northern breeding colony of **Cape Vultures** in southern Africa, and the only surviving colony in Namibia. A hide and vulture restaurant have been established to help save this population. More than 100 vultures of four species regularly gather. These cliffs are the only known breeding site for **Booted Eagles** in Namibia and support a relatively large population of **Peregrine Falcons**. **Rosyfaced Lovebirds** roost and nest in potholes and crevices on the cliffs and descend in noisy flocks early each morning to feed in the *Acacia* savanna below. Dense flocks of **Bradfield's**, **Alpine** and smaller **Swifts** gather each morning above the cliffs before dispersing for the day. These form the main prey of the Peregrines. A number of trails above the main camp traverse the scree slopes and rocky outcrops where **Hartlaub's Francolin**, **Monteiro's Hornbill**, **Freckled Nightjar**, **Rockrunner** and **Shorttoed Rock Thrush** can be seen. The thornveld savanna below the plateau is particularly well developed in the valleys draining the escarpment. These are the best places to look for **Rüppell's Parrot**, **Violet Woodhoopoe** and **Carp's Black Tit**. Bookings can be made in the camp for a four-wheel-drive tour of the plateau. Species to look for in this open woodland are **Coqui Francolin**, **Barred Owl** (both this and Freckled Nightjar can be heard from the camp), **Bradfield's Hornbill** and **White Helmetshrike**.

ALSO RECORDED

Whiteheaded, Hooded and Egyptian Vultures have been recorded at the vulture restaurant. Steppe and Lesser Spotted Eagles and Western Redfooted and Lesser Kestrels are regular summer migrants. Ovambo Sparrowhawk, Bennett's Woodpecker, Rufousbellied Tit and Blackcrowned Tchagra are uncommon residents while Green Pigeon and Chestnut Weaver are seasonal visitors.

C.J. Brown

60% OF SPECIES

089 Marabou Stork ☐
118 Secretarybird ☐
122 **Cape Vulture**** ☐
123 Whitebacked Vulture ☐
124 Lappetfaced Vulture ☐
126 Black Kite ☐
126a Yellowbilled Kite ☐
127 Blackshouldered Kite ☐
131 Black Eagle ☐
132 Tawny Eagle ☐
135 Wahlberg's Eagle ☐
136 **Booted Eagle** ☐
137 African Hawk Eagle ☐
140 Martial Eagle ☐
142 Brown Snake Eagle ☐
143 Blackbreasted Snake Eagle ☐
146 Bateleur ☐
149 Steppe Buzzard ☐
157 Little Sparrowhawk ☐
159 Little Banded Goshawk ☐
161 Gabar Goshawk ☐
162 Pale Chanting Goshawk* ☐
171 **Peregrine Falcon** ☐
172 Lanner Falcon ☐
181 Rock Kestrel ☐
188 **Coqui Francolin** ☐
189 Crested Francolin ☐
193 Orange River Francolin* ☐
194 Redbilled Francolin* ☐
197 **Hartlaub's Francolin*** ☐
199 Swainson's Francolin* ☐
203 Helmeted Guineafowl ☐
237 Redcrested Korhaan* ☐
239a Whitequilled Korhaan** ☐
255 Crowned Plover ☐
258 Blacksmith Plover ☐
344 Namaqua Sandgrouse* ☐
345 Burchell's Sandgrouse* ☐
349 Rock Pigeon ☐
354 Cape Turtle Dove ☐
355 Laughing Dove ☐
356 Namaqua Dove ☐
358 Greenspotted Dove ☐
365 **Rüppell's Parrot*** ☐
367 **Rosyfaced Lovebird*** ☐
373 Grey Lourie ☐

375 African Cuckoo ☐
378 Black Cuckoo ☐
380 Great Spotted Cuckoo ☐
385 Klaas's Cuckoo ☐
386 Diederik Cuckoo ☐
392 Barn Owl ☐
396 Scops Owl ☐
397 Whitefaced Owl ☐
398 Pearlspotted Owl ☐
399 **Barred Owl** ☐
401 Spotted Eagle Owl ☐
402 Giant Eagle Owl ☐
405 Fierynecked Nightjar ☐
406 Rufouscheeked Nightjar ☐
408 **Freckled Nightjar** ☐
413 **Bradfield's Swift*** ☐
415 Whiterumped Swift ☐
418 **Alpine Swift** ☐
437 Striped Kingfisher ☐
438 European Bee-eater ☐
445 Swallowtailed Bee-eater ☐
447 Lilacbreasted Roller ☐
449 Purple Roller ☐
451 Hoopoe ☐
452 Redbilled Woodhoopoe ☐
453 **Violet Woodhoopoe*** ☐
454 Scimitarbilled Woodhoopoe ☐
457 Grey Hornbill ☐
458 Redbilled Hornbill ☐
459 Southern Yellow-billed Hornbill* ☐
461 **Bradfield's Hornbill*** ☐
462 **Monteiro's Hornbill*** ☐
465 Pied Barbet* ☐
483 Goldentailed Woodpecker ☐
486 Cardinal Woodpecker ☐
487 Bearded Woodpecker ☐
494 Rufousnaped Lark ☐
495 Clapper Lark** ☐
497 Fawncoloured Lark ☐
498 Sabota Lark* ☐
518 European Swallow ☐
526 Greater Striped Swallow* ☐
529 Rock Martin ☐
541 Forktailed Drongo ☐
544 African Golden Oriole ☐
552 Ashy Tit* ☐
555 **Carp's Black Tit*** ☐
557 Cape Penduline Tit* ☐
563 Pied Babbler** ☐
567 Redeyed Bulbul* ☐
580 Groundscraper Thrush ☐
583 **Shorttoed Rock Thrush*** ☐
589 Familiar Chat ☐
595 Anteating Chat** ☐
613 Whitebrowed Robin ☐
615 Kalahari Robin* ☐
621 Titbabbler* ☐
625 Icterine Warbler ☐
643 Willow Warbler ☐
651 Longbilled Crombec ☐
653 Yellowbellied Eremomela ☐
656 Burntnecked Eremomela ☐
657a Greybacked Bleating Warbler ☐
658 Barred Warbler* ☐
662 **Rockrunner*** ☐
665 Desert Cisticola ☐
671 Tinkling Cisticola ☐
672 Rattling Cisticola ☐
685 Blackchested Prinia* ☐
695 Marico Flycatcher* ☐
697 Chat Flycatcher* ☐
703 Pririt Batis* ☐
710 Paradise Flycatcher ☐
731 Lesser Grey Shrike ☐
733 Redbacked Shrike ☐
739 Crimsonbreasted Boubou* ☐
740 Puffback ☐
741 Brubru ☐
743 Threestreaked Tchagra ☐
753 **White Helmetshrike** ☐
756 Whitecrowned Shrike* ☐
762 Burchell's Starling* ☐
764 Glossy Starling* ☐
770 Palewinged Starling* ☐
779 Marico Sunbird ☐
787 Whitebellied Sunbird ☐
788 Dusky Sunbird* ☐
791 Scarletchested Sunbird ☐
798 Redbilled Buffalo Weaver ☐
799 Whitebrowed Sparrowweaver ☐
804 Greyheaded Sparrow ☐
806 Scalyfeathered Finch* ☐
814 Masked Weaver ☐
821 Redbilled Quelea ☐
834 Melba Finch ☐
844 Blue Waxbill ☐
845 Violeteared Waxbill* ☐
847 Blackcheeked Waxbill ☐
861 Shafttailed Whydah* ☐
862 Paradise Whydah ☐
870 Blackthroated Canary ☐
878 Yellow Canary* ☐
884 Goldenbreasted Bunting ☐
885 Cape Bunting ☐
886 Rock Bunting ☐
☐
☐
☐
☐
☐

BRANDBERG AND SPITZKOPPE

approximately 118 and 150 species respectively recorded to date

The Brandberg and Spitzkoppe are both large granite inselbergs, about 90 km apart, that rise out of the Namib coastal plain in Damaraland. The Brandberg, some 70 km inland from the Atlantic, is the highest mountain in Namibia (2 573 m above sea level) and rises 2 000 m above the surrounding plains. It receives about 100 mm of rain per year as well as occasional coastal fog. The Spitzkoppe is about 100 km east of the coast and lies on the 150 mm rainfall isohyet. Both mountains fall within the pro-Namib or savanna transition zone. The surrouding regions are sparsely vegetated, flat to rolling gravel and rocky plains, intersected by drainage lines supporting *Acacia* species. Characteristic vegetation consists of *Welwitchia, Euphorbia, Cyphostemma, Moringa* and *Commiphora* spp. Because of the run-off from the mountains after rainfall, these areas are more mesic than the pro-Namib generally. More than twice as many bird species are recorded for the Brandberg and Spitzkoppe as for the pro-Namib in general.

SPECIAL AND INTERESTING SPECIES

More bird species have been recorded at the Spitzkoppe than at the Brandberg because the former has been better studied and possibly because it receives slightly more rain. Arid regions are characterised by rainfall being not only low, but also highly variable (e.g. the range of annual rainfall in the

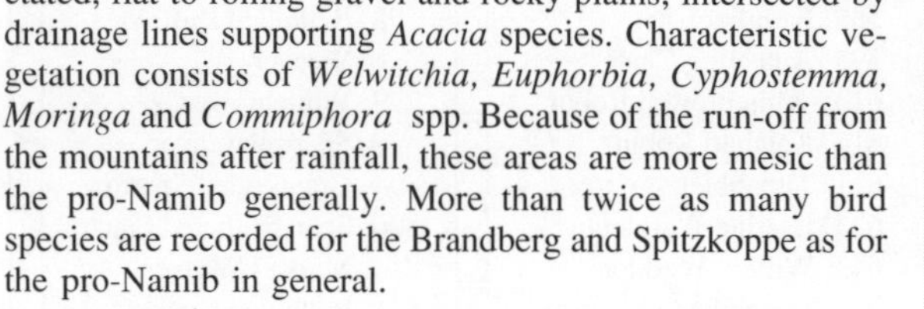

The Brandberg is reached by taking the gravel road C35 between Uis and Khorixas. Turn west 14 km north of Uis (105 km south of Khorixas) on district road 2359. The road runs to the base of the Brandberg (28 km) where there is an informal picnic/camping site. Spitzkoppe is best reached from the tar road (B2) linking Swakopmund and Okahandja. Twenty-three km west of Usakos turn north onto the Henties Bay district road (1918) and after 1 km turn north again onto district road 1930 to Uis. After 28 km turn west onto road 3716, which goes past the base of the Spitzkoppe (10 km) and then joins the Henties Bay road. The routes to both sites are suitable for two-wheel drive vehicles with reasonable road clearance. Water should be carried.

pro-Namib is 9-374 mm). In dry years Namib birds such as **Gray's Lark** extend their range eastwards, while in wet years savanna species such as **Carp's Black Tit** extend westwards. Species typical of the escarpment transition zone, which can be seen on the lower slopes of the mountains and in the wooded drainage lines, are **Hartlaub's Francolin**, **Rüppell's Parrot**, **Rosyfaced Lovebird**, **Monteiro's Hornbill**, **Herero Chat**, **Rockrunner** and **Whitetailed Shrike**. **Barecheeked Babblers** occur in similar habitat around the Brandberg, but do not extend as far south as the Spitzkoppe. The stony and rocky plains surrounding the two inselbergs support **Ludwig's Bustard**, **Rüppell's Korhaan** and **Stark's Lark**. **Augur Buzzards**, **Black Eagles**, **Lanner Falcons**, **Rock Kestrels** and owls nest on ledges on the granite cliffs, while **Bradfield's Swifts** breed and roost in the rock crevices and fissures.

ALSO RECORDED

In years of above average rainfall the following species have been recorded: Hamerkop, Lesser Honeyguide, Greater Striped Swallow, European Golden Oriole and Cape White-eye. Greater Flamingos have been recorded flying overhead to inland wetlands and two records of Redcapped Lark have been confirmed.

C.J. Brown

95% OF SPECIES

001 Ostrich
085 Abdim's Stork
102 Egyptian Goose
123 Whitebacked Vulture
124 Lappetfaced Vulture
126 Black Kite
126a Yellowbilled Kite
127 Blackshouldered Kite
131 **Black Eagle**
132 Tawny Eagle
136 Booted Eagle
137 African Hawk Eagle
140 Martial Eagle
143 Blackbreasted Snake Eagle
149 Steppe Buzzard
153 **Augur Buzzard**
161 Gabar Goshawk
162 Pale Chanting Goshawk*
172 **Lanner Falcon**
181 **Rock Kestrel**
182 Greater Kestrel
194 Redbilled Francolin*
197 **Hartlaub's Francolin***
200 Common Quail
203 Helmeted Guineafowl
205 Kurrichane Buttonquail
230 Kori Bustard
232 **Ludwig's Bustard***
236 **Rüppell's Korhaan***
239a Whitequilled Korhaan**
249 Threebanded Plover
255 Crowned Plover
258 Blacksmith Plover
297 Spotted Dikkop
299 Burchell's Courser*
301 Doublebanded Courser
344 Namaqua Sandgrouse*
345 Burchell's Sandgrouse*
347 Doublebanded Sandgrouse*
349 Rock Pigeon
354 Cape Turtle Dove
355 Laughing Dove
356 Namaqua Dove
365 **Rüppell's Parrot***
367 **Rosyfaced Lovebird***
373 Grey Lourie
385 Klaas's Cuckoo
386 Diederik Cuckoo
392 Barn Owl
396 Scops Owl
397 Whitefaced Owl
398 Pearlspotted Owl
401 Spotted Eagle Owl
406 Rufouscheeked Nightjar
411 European Swift
412 Black Swift
413 **Bradfield's Swift***
415 Whiterumped Swift
417 Little Swift
418 Alpine Swift
425 Whitebacked Mousebird**
426 Redfaced Mousebird
445 Swallowtailed Bee-eater
449 Purple Roller
451 Hoopoe
454 Scimitarbilled Woodhoopoe
457 Grey Hornbill
458 Redbilled Hornbill
459 Southern Yellow-billed Hornbill*
462 **Monteiro's Hornbill***

465 Pied Barbet* ☐
483 Goldentailed Woodpecker ☐
486 Cardinal Woodpecker ☐
487 Bearded Woodpecker ☐
498 Sabota Lark* ☐
500 Longbilled Lark* ☐
506 Spikeheeled Lark* ☐
511 **Stark's Lark*** ☐
514 **Gray's Lark*** ☐
516 Greybacked Finchlark* ☐
518 European Swallow ☐
529 Rock Martin ☐
541 Forktailed Drongo ☐
547 Black Crow ☐
548 Pied Crow ☐
552 Ashy Tit* ☐
555 **Carp's Black Tit*** ☐
557 Cape Penduline Tit* ☐
563 Pied Babbler** ☐
564 **Barecheeked Babbler*** ☐
567 Redeyed Bulbul* ☐
583 Shorttoed Rock Thrush* ☐
586 Mountain Chat* ☐
587 Capped Wheatear ☐
589 Familiar Chat ☐
590 Tractrac Chat* ☐
592 Karoo Chat* ☐
595 Anteating Chat** ☐
615 Kalahari Robin* ☐
618 **Herero Chat*** ☐
621 Titbabbler* ☐
622 Layard's Titbabbler** ☐
643 Willow Warbler ☐
651 Longbilled Crombec ☐
653 Yellowbellied Eremomela ☐
657a Greybacked Bleating Warbler ☐
662 **Rockrunner*** ☐
669 Greybacked Cisticola* ☐
685 Blackchested Prinia* ☐
688 Rufouseared Warbler** ☐
689 Spotted Flycatcher ☐
695 Marico Flycatcher* ☐
697 Chat Flycatcher* ☐
703 Pririt Batis* ☐
713 Cape Wagtail ☐
731 Lesser Grey Shrike ☐
732 Fiscal Shrike ☐
733 Redbacked Shrike ☐
739 Crimsonbreasted Boubou* ☐
741 Brubru ☐
743 Threestreaked Tchagra ☐
746 Bokmakierie* ☐
752 **Whitetailed Shrike*** ☐
761 Plumcoloured Starling ☐
764 Glossy Starling* ☐
770 Palewinged Starling* ☐
779 Marico Sunbird ☐
788 Dusky Sunbird* ☐
791 Scarletchested Sunbird ☐
799 Whitebrowed Sparrowweaver ☐
802 Great Sparrow* ☐
803 Cape Sparrow* ☐
806 Scalyfeathered Finch* ☐
814 Masked Weaver ☐
821 Redbilled Quelea ☐
834 Melba Finch ☐
845 Violeteared Waxbill* ☐
846 Common Waxbill ☐
847 Blackcheeked Waxbill ☐
856 Redheaded Finch* ☐
861 Shafttailed Whydah* ☐
870 Blackthroated Canary ☐
878 Yellow Canary* ☐
879 Whitethroated Canary* ☐
884 Goldenbreasted Bunting ☐
885 Cape Bunting ☐
886 Rock Bunting ☐
887 Larklike Bunting* ☐
☐
☐
☐
☐
☐
☐
☐
☐

Monteiro's Hornbill

DAAN VILJOEN NATURE RESERVE

approximately 260 species recorded to date

The Daan Viljoen is one of the small public nature reserves administered by the Ministry of Wildlife, Conservation and Tourism in Namibia. The greater part of the reserve covers the rolling hills of the Khomas Hochland, which overlooks the rift valley in which Windhoek lies. The area is semi-arid; the vegetation consists largely of grassland and small trees scattered across the hills, with denser and taller tree cover in the valleys along the watercourses. The tree communities are dominated by various species of *Acacia*, especially *A. hereroensis*, *mellifera*, *erioloba* and *erubescens*. Bird life is dominated by a variety of seedeaters, which exploit the rich crop of grass seeds, and a range of arboreal insectivores. After heavy rain many of the watercourses flow, some filling a number of small dams that attract a range of waterbirds. The dam at the main public resort holds water perenially and many of the waterbirds are extremely tame. Although vehicle access to the Augeigas River is prohibited, this is one of the few perennial rivers in central Namibia; the water drains continuously from the Goreangab Dam and sewage works. The many cliffs overlooking the deep river valleys are home to a good selection of cliff-dwelling birds. Visitors are free to walk around and may drive along a number of roads in the western sector of the reserve. Bookings for accommodation should be made at the Windhoek offices of the Ministry of Wildlife, Conservation and Tourism.

ALSO RECORDED

African Black Duck are regular visitors to the small dams and the Augeigas River, as are a variety of other waterbirds that sporadically arrive to take advantage of standing water. Black Storks are an unusual, though fairly regular, species. This very dry area is also home to several species that are normally associated with moist woodland in the eastern half of southern Africa, including Purple Roller, Greyhooded Kingfisher, Little Sparrowhawk, Bearded Woodpecker and Scarletchested Sunbird. Among the aerial insectivores, Bradfield's Swift is special to the "dry west". European Swifts can be abundant after good summer rains.

John Mendelsohn

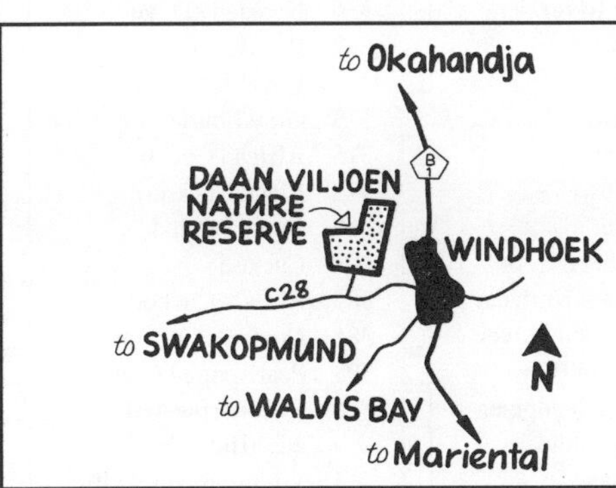

Situated about 15 km west of Windhoek, Daan Viljoen Nature Reserve is easily reached along the Khomas Hochland road (C28) leading west out of Windhoek; proceed until you find the signposted entrance on your right.

SPECIAL AND INTERESTING SPECIES

Being in the central Namibian highlands, the reserve holds many of the specials to this biome. The visitor will readily see **Monteiro's Hornbill**, **Rockrunners** and **Whitetailed Shrikes**. Rockrunners are particularly common on steep slopes covered by grass, scattered shrubs and large rocks. Similar habitat is occupied by **Longbilled Pipits**, the only common pipit in the reserve – so identification should not be a problem. **Shorttoed Rock Thrush** and **Mountain Chat** are also common in this habitat. Along the valleys, either in the riverine woodland or on the cliffs above, Monteiro's along with **Redbilled**, **Grey** and **Southern Yellowbilled Hornbills** will be seen, in addition to **Pririt Batis**, **Palewinged Starling**, **Redbilled Francolin**, **Swallowtailed Bee-eater**, **Crimsonbreasted Boubou**, **Rosyfaced Lovebird** and **Cape** and **Rock Buntings**. The open hills are home to **Orange River Francolin**, **Great Sparrow**, **Whitethroated Canary** and **Rufouscheeked Nightjar**. Both **Yellowbellied** and **Burntnecked Eremomelas** are reasonably abundant, although hard to see. A rich assemblage of seven cuckoo species is found in summer. Impressive raptors to be seen include **Black Eagle**, **Blackbreasted** and **Brown Snake Eagles**, **African Hawk Eagle** and **Lappetfaced Vulture**.

50% OF SPECIES

No.	Species	
001	Ostrich	☐
008	Dabchick	☐
055	Whitebreasted Cormorant	☐
058	Reed Cormorant	☐
060	Darter	☐
062	Grey Heron	☐
076	Blackcrowned Night Heron	☐
081	Hamerkop	☐
084	Black Stork	☐
102	Egyptian Goose	☐
103	South African Shelduck**	☐
106	Cape Teal	☐
108	Redbilled Teal	☐
124	**Lappetfaced Vulture**	☐
127	Blackshouldered Kite	☐
131	**Black Eagle**	☐
137	**African Hawk Eagle**	☐
140	Martial Eagle	☐
142	**Brown Snake Eagle**	☐
143	**Blackbreasted Snake Eagle**	☐
161	Gabar Goshawk	☐
162	Pale Chanting Goshawk*	☐
181	Rock Kestrel	☐
193	**Orange River Francolin***	☐
194	**Redbilled Francolin***	☐
203	Helmeted Guineafowl	☐
226	Moorhen	☐
228	Redknobbed Coot	☐
237	Redcrested Korhaan*	☐
249	Threebanded Plover	☐
258	Blacksmith Plover	☐
264	Common Sandpiper	☐
266	Wood Sandpiper	☐
270	Greenshank	☐
274	Little Stint	☐
284	Ruff	☐
295	Blackwinged Stilt	☐
297	Spotted Dikkop	☐
349	Rock Pigeon	☐
354	Cape Turtle Dove	☐
355	Laughing Dove	☐
356	Namaqua Dove	☐
367	**Rosyfaced Lovebird***	☐
373	Grey Lourie	☐
375	African Cuckoo	☐
378	Black Cuckoo	☐
380	Great Spotted Cuckoo	☐
385	Klaas's Cuckoo	☐
386	Diederik Cuckoo	☐
398	Pearlspotted Owl	☐
406	**Rufouscheeked Nightjar**	☐
415	Whiterumped Swift	☐

417 Little Swift ☐
421 Palm Swift ☐
425 Whitebacked Mousebird** ☐
426 Redfaced Mousebird ☐
438 European Bee-eater ☐
445 **Swallowtailed Bee-eater** ☐
447 Lilacbreasted Roller ☐
451 Hoopoe ☐
454 Scimitarbilled Woodhoopoe ☐
457 **Grey Hornbill** ☐
458 **Redbilled Hornbill** ☐
459 **Southern Yellow-billed Hornbill*** ☐
462 **Monteiro's Hornbill*** ☐
465 Pied Barbet* ☐
481 Bennett's Woodpecker ☐
483 Goldentailed Woodpecker ☐
486 Cardinal Woodpecker ☐
494 Rufousnaped Lark ☐
498 Sabota Lark* ☐
518 European Swallow ☐
526 Greater Striped Swallow* ☐
529 Rock Martin ☐
541 Forktailed Drongo ☐
552 Ashy Tit* ☐
554 Carp's Black Tit* ☐
557 Cape Penduline Tit* ☐
563 Pied Babbler** ☐
567 Redeyed Bulbul* ☐
580 Groundscraper Thrush ☐
583 **Shorttoed Rock Thrush*** ☐
586 **Mountain Chat*** ☐
589 Familiar Chat ☐
615 Kalahari Robin* ☐
621 Titbabbler* ☐
643 Willow Warbler ☐
651 Longbilled Crombec ☐
653 **Yellowbellied Eremomela** ☐
654 Karoo Eremomela** ☐
656 **Burntnecked Eremomela** ☐
657a Greybacked Bleating Warbler ☐
658 Barred Warbler* ☐
662 **Rockrunner*** ☐
685 Blackchested Prinia* ☐
689 Spotted Flycatcher ☐
695 Marico Flycatcher* ☐
703 **Pririt Batis** * ☐
713 Cape Wagtail ☐
717 **Longbilled Pipit** ☐
731 Lesser Grey Shrike ☐
732 Fiscal Shrike ☐
733 Redbacked Shrike ☐
739 **Crimsonbreasted Boubou*** ☐
741 Brubru ☐
743 Threestreaked Tchagra ☐
752 **Whitetailed Shrike*** ☐
760 Wattled Starling ☐
764 Glossy Starling* ☐
770 **Palewinged Starling *** ☐
788 Dusky Sunbird* ☐
791 Scarletchested Sunbird ☐
798 Redbilled Buffalo Weaver ☐
799 Whitebrowed Sparrowweaver ☐
801 House Sparrow ☐
802 **Great Sparrow*** ☐
804 Greyheaded Sparrow ☐
806 Scalyfeathered Finch* ☐
814 Masked Weaver ☐
821 Redbilled Quelea ☐
834 Melba Finch ☐
845 Violeteared Waxbill* ☐
847 Blackcheeked Waxbill ☐
856 Redheaded ☐
861 Shafttailed Whydah* ☐
870 **Blackthroated Canary** ☐
879 Whitethroated Canary* ☐
884 Goldenbreasted Bunting ☐
885 **Cape Bunting** ☐
886 **Rock Bunting** ☐
887 Larklike Bunting* ☐
☐
☐
☐

Whitetailed Shrikes

SWAKOPMUND AND SURROUNDING AREA

approximately 220 species recorded to date

Swakopmund has no harbour but is Namibia's seaside resort. The best birding is done at the Swakop River Mouth, the sewage works and at the Swakopmund Saltworks.

SPECIAL AND INTERESTING SPECIES

At the Swakop River Mouth **Bank** and **Crowned Cormorants** occur alongside **Cape Cormorants** on the concrete structures in the lagoon. The area is good for flamingos, waders, seabirds and other wetland species. The sewage works support waders and wetland species including **Hartlaub's Gulls.** Before reaching the gate at the saltworks take one of the gravel roads that follow the edge of the pans. Huge numbers of Cape Cormorants breed on the guano platform. **Damara Terns** breed nearby and fish over the pans. The oyster-bed pan has recently been the only regular locality for **Great Crested Grebe** in Namibia. Pans of intermediate salinity in the south-western corner of the saltworks support hundreds of **Blacknecked Grebes** and sometimes phalaropes. **Gray's Lark** occurs on the adjacent gravel plains. In the valley below Nonidas Hotel (request permission for access), there are vegetated pools that support local bush birds and wetland species including **Purple Heron**.

ALSO RECORDED

The vegetated wetland areas are attractive to vagrant American waders; Broad-billed Sandpiper, Lesser Golden Plover and White-rumped Sandpiper have been recorded.

Tony Williams

To reach the river mouth follow the seafront road to the bushes at the southern edge of town. A lagoon occurs here in years when the Swakop River has flowed. Municipal permission is required to visit the sewage works. The Swakopmund Saltworks can be reached from Terrace Bay road. Approximately 6 km north of town, turn left onto a road marked "private". Drive towards the prominent salt heaps. To Nonidas Hotel follow the Windhoek road for about 10 km.

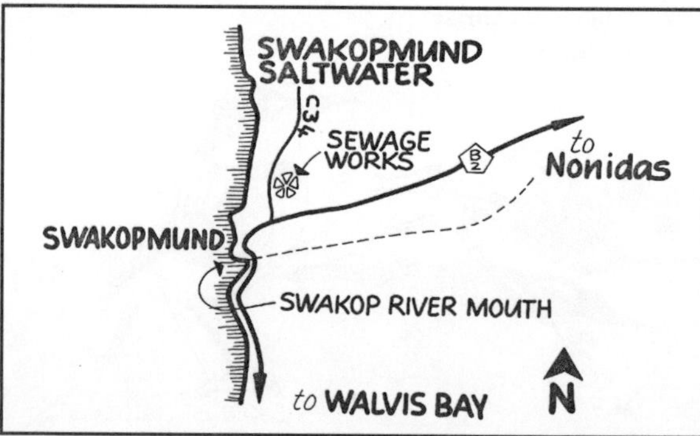

42% OF SPECIES

- 006 **Great Crested Grebe** ☐
- 007 **Blacknecked Grebe** ☐
- 008 Dabchick ☐
- 032 Whitechinned Petrel ☐
- 049 White Pelican ☐
- 053 Cape Gannet* ☐
- 055 Whitebreasted Cormorant ☐
- 056 **Cape Cormorant*** ☐
- 057 **Bank Cormorant**** ☐
- 059 **Crowned Cormorant*** ☐
- 062 Grey Heron ☐
- 065 **Purple Heron** ☐
- 067 Little Egret ☐
- 096 Greater Flamingo ☐
- 097 Lesser Flamingo ☐
- 106 Cape Teal ☐
- 112 Cape Shoveller* ☐
- 117 Maccoa Duck ☐
- 181 Rock Kestrel ☐
- 226 Moorhen ☐
- 228 Redknobbed Coot ☐
- 244 African Black Oystercatcher** ☐
- 245 Ringed Plover ☐
- 246 Whitefronted Plover ☐
- 247 Chestnutbanded Plover ☐
- 248 Kittlitz's Plover ☐
- 249 Threebanded Plover ☐
- 254 Grey Plover ☐
- 255 Crowned Plover ☐
- 258 Blacksmith Plover ☐
- 262 Turnstone ☐
- 264 Common Sandpiper ☐
- 266 Wood Sandpiper ☐
- 269 Marsh Sandpiper ☐
- 270 Greenshank ☐
- 271 Knot ☐
- 272 Curlew Sandpiper ☐
- 274 Little Stint ☐
- 281 Sanderling ☐
- 284 Ruff ☐
- 288 Bartailed Godwit ☐
- 290 Whimbrel ☐
- 294 Avocet ☐
- 295 Blackwinged Stilt ☐
- 297 Spotted Dikkop ☐
- 307 Arctic Skua ☐
- 312 Kelp Gull ☐
- 315 Greyheaded Gull ☐
- 316 **Hartlaub's Gull**** ☐
- 322 Caspian Tern ☐
- 324 Swift Tern ☐
- 326 Sandwich Tern ☐
- 327 Common Tern ☐
- 334 **Damara Tern*** ☐
- 339 Whitewinged Tern ☐
- 348 Feral Pigeon ☐
- 354 Cape Turtle Dove ☐
- 355 Laughing Dove ☐
- 367 Rosyfaced Lovebird* ☐
- 413 Bradf eld's Swift* ☐
- 415 Whiterumped Swift ☐
- 417 Little Swift ☐
- 418 Alpine Swift ☐
- 425 Whitebacked Mousebird** ☐
- 426 Redfaced Mousebird ☐
- 445 Swallowtailed Bee-eater ☐
- 454 Scimitarbilled Woodhoopoe ☐
- 507 Redcapped Lark ☐
- 514 **Gray's Lark*** ☐
- 518 European Swallow ☐
- 520 Whitethroated Swallow ☐
- 529 Rock Martin ☐
- 567 Redeyed Bulbul* ☐
- 587 Capped Wheatear ☐
- 589 Familiar Chat ☐
- 590 Tractrac Chat* ☐
- 621 Titbabbler* ☐
- 631 African Marsh Warbler ☐
- 651 Longbilled Crombec ☐
- 665 Desert Cisticola ☐
- 685 Blackchested Prinia* ☐
- 703 Pririt Batis* ☐
- 713 Cape Wagtail ☐
- 732 Fiscal Shrike ☐
- 741 Brubru ☐
- 760 Wattled Starling ☐
- 770 Palewinged Starling* ☐
- 788 Dusky Sunbird* ☐
- 796 Cape White-eye** ☐
- 801 House Sparrow ☐
- 803 Cape Sparrow* ☐
- 814 Masked Weaver ☐
- 846 Common Waxbill ☐
- 870 Blackthroated Canary ☐

☐

☐

☐

☐

☐

☐

WALVIS BAY

approximately 178 species recorded to date

The Walvis Bay lagoon and saltworks together form the most extensive shallow coastal wetland in southern Africa and rank within the top ten coastal wetlands in Africa in terms of numbers of birds.

SPECIAL AND INTERESTING SPECIES

Walvis Bay is arguably the best southern African locality for **Greater** and **Lesser Flamingos**, **Chestnutbanded Plover**, **Black Tern**, **European Oystercatcher** and **Rednecked Phalarope**. Huge numbers of waders can be seen in the lagoon and saltworks, especially at certain times of the year. Most waders and terns, including **Sand Plover** and, at times, **European Oystercatcher** (maximum 7), plus **Damara** and **Black Terns** can be seen at low tide between the cottages and the wooden jetty. There is road access and good birding is possible along the entire southern bank of the lagoon. Most records of Rednecked Phalarope (maximum 25) are from the pools to the south of the road that crosses a small bridge within the saltpans, which is where Lesser Flamingo and Chestnutbanded Plover are most common. The road ends at Paaltjies car park (and toilets), which offers the best sea gazing for those without four-wheel drive vehicles. Species such as **Whitechinned Petrel** and **Sooty Shearwater** can be found here. Bird Paradise with its ready "freshwater" pools supports various wetland species including **Maccoa Duck**, and is worth searching for vagrants, especially after strong

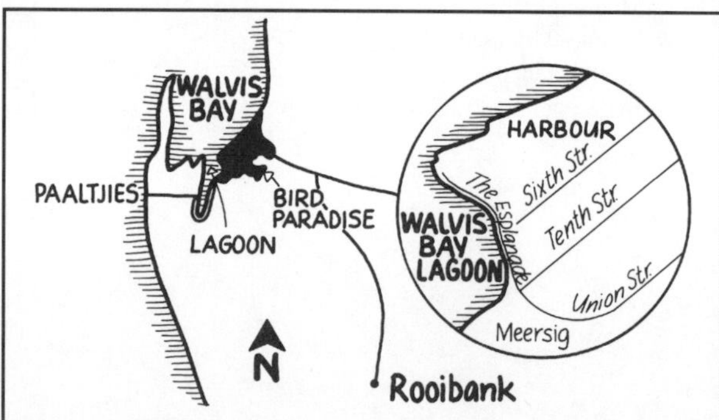

ALSO RECORDED

One or two Redshanks occur almost annually within the restricted area of the saltworks. There have been two records of Franklin's Gull, one of Antarctic Tern and one of Sabine's Gull in areas adjacent to the town.

Tony Williams

To reach the lagoon drive through the town on 10th Street or Union Street to the thatched cottages. Turn north along the lagoon. To find the saltworks and for sea gazing, follow the road signs at the edge of the lagoon to Paaltjies. Bird Paradise can be found by turning to the town centre from the arrival circle, then first left at the graveyard and first left again into Bird Paradise. To reach Rooibank leave town on the airport road. Turn south onto the gravel for approximately 10 km almost to the trees and houses. Take the small gravel road to the right, which becomes the top of a flood embankment. Follow this onto the low dunes. The Kuisel Valley is signposted on the airport road.

east winds. The low dunes at Rooibank are ideal habitat for the resident **Dune Lark**. The road towards the Kuisel Valley should yield **Gray's Lark** and **Rüppell's Korhaan**.

50% OF SPECIES

007 Blacknecked Grebe ☐
008 Dabchick ☐
032 **Whitechinned Petrel** ☐
037 **Sooty Shearwater** ☐
049 White Pelican ☐
053 Cape Gannet* ☐
055 Whitebreasted Cormorant ☐
056 Cape Cormorant* ☐
059 Crowned Cormorant* ☐
062 Grey Heron ☐
067 Little Egret ☐
071 Cattle Egret ☐
096 **Greater Flamingo** ☐
097 **Lesser Flamingo** ☐
102 Egyptian Goose ☐
103 South African Shelduck** ☐
106 Cape Teal ☐
112 Cape Shoveller* ☐
117 Maccoa Duck ☐
162 Pale Chanting Goshawk* ☐
181 Rock Kestrel ☐
223 Purple Gallinule ☐
226 Moorhen ☐
228 Redknobbed Coot ☐
236 **Rüppell's Korhaan*** ☐
243 **European Oystercatcher** ☐
244 African Black Oystercatcher** ☐
245 Ringed Plover ☐
246 Whitefronted Plover ☐
247 **Chestnutbanded Plover** ☐
248 Kittlitz's Plover ☐
249 Threebanded Plover ☐
251 **Sand Plover** ☐
254 Grey Plover ☐
258 Blacksmith Plover ☐
262 Turnstone ☐
264 Common Sandpiper ☐
266 Wood Sandpiper ☐
269 Marsh Sandpiper ☐
270 Greenshank ☐
271 Knot ☐
272 Curlew Sandpiper ☐
274 Little Stint ☐
281 Sanderling ☐
284 Ruff ☐
288 Bartailed Godwit ☐
290 Whimbrel ☐
292 **Rednecked Phalarope** ☐
294 Avocet ☐
295 Blackwinged Stilt ☐
307 Arctic Skua ☐
312 Kelp Gull ☐
315 Greyheaded Gull ☐
316 Hartlaub's Gull** ☐
322 Caspian Tern ☐
324 Swift Tern ☐
326 Sandwich Tern ☐
327 Common Tern ☐
334 **Damara Tern*** ☐
337 **Black Tern** ☐
339 Whitewinged Tern ☐
348 Feral Pigeon ☐
354 Cape Turtle Dove ☐
355 Laughing Dove ☐
415 Whiterumped Swift ☐
417 Little Swift ☐
425 Whitebacked Mousebird** ☐
426 Redfaced Mousebird ☐
503 **Dune Lark**** ☐
514 **Gray's Lark*** ☐
518 European Swallow ☐
529 Rock Martin ☐
548 Pied Crow ☐
567 Redeyed Bulbul* ☐
589 Familiar Chat ☐
590 Tractrac Chat* ☐
621 Titbabbler* ☐
631 African Marsh Warbler ☐
664 Fantailed Cisticola ☐
713 Cape Wagtail ☐
732 Fiscal Shrike ☐
741 Brubru ☐
760 Wattled Starling ☐
788 Dusky Sunbird* ☐
796 Cape White-eye** ☐
801 House Sparrow ☐
803 Cape Sparrow* ☐
814 Masked Weaver ☐
846 Common Waxbill ☐
☐
☐
☐
☐
☐
☐

NAUKLUFT MOUNTAINS

approximately 204 species recorded to date

The Naukluft Mountains are situated on the eastern edge of the Namib-Naukluft Park (4,9 million ha), within the semi-desert transition zone. Rainfall is highly variable, ranging from 51 mm to 532 mm, averaging 165 mm. The mountains consist primarily of dolomite and limestone rocks which contain large natural underground water reservoirs. These reservoirs supply numerous perennial springs in an otherwise dry region. The plains below the mountains are at about 1 000 m above sea level, while the highest peak is at about 1 965 m. Six major habitats are recognised: gravel plains, dry valleys, valley sides and mountain slopes, riverine valleys with perennial water, cliffs and gorges and the mountain plateau.

SPECIAL AND INTERESTING SPECIES

The Naukluft Mountains are situated at the junction of the Damaraland and the Karoo zoogeographic regions. The area is the southern limit of distribution of many Damaraland species such as **Whitetailed Shrike**, **Herero Chat**, **Rüppell's Korhaan**, **Rockrunner** and **Monteiro's Hornbill**, and the northern limit of Karoo species such as **Karoo Robin** and **Cinnamonbreasted Warbler**. The gravel plains support **Ostrich**, **Secretarybird**, **Lappetfaced Vulture**, **Greater Kestrel**, **Ludwig's Bustard**, **Rüppell's Korhaan**, a number of larks including **Stark's Lark**, and **Tractrac Chat**. On the rocky hillsides are found **Monteiro's Hornbill**, **Longbilled Lark**, **Shorttoed Rock Thrush**, **Mountain Chat**, **Herero Chat**, **Rockrunner** and **Whitetailed Shrike**. The cliffs pro-

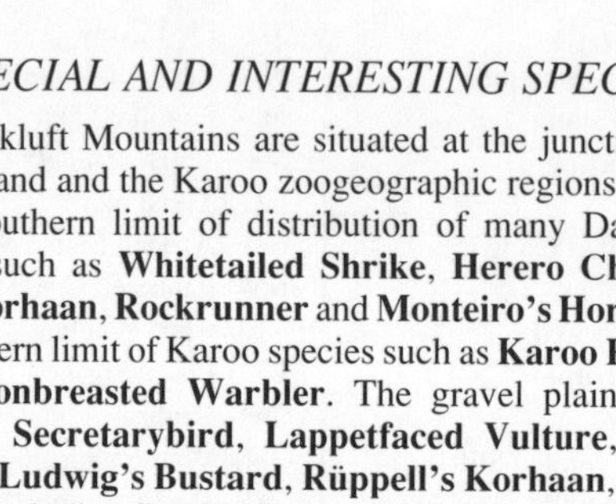

From the north, turn west off the B1 highway at Rehoboth onto district road 47. After 125 km it forms a T-junction with road C14. Turn right (north) and travel for about 16 km. The entrance to the Naukluft is on the left. From the south, turn off the B1 highway at Mariental, onto the C19 to Maltahöhe. At Maltahöhe take the C14 north for about 102 km. The entrance to the Naukluft is on the left. From the coast, take the C14 from Walvis Bay via Solitaire towards Maltahöhe. The turnoff to Naukluft is about 55 km beyond (south of) Solitaire, on the right. The Naukluft has camping facilities and a number of self-guided hiking trails, ranging from half-day walks to eight-day expeditions.

vide breeding sites for **Black Eagle**, **Augur** and **Jackal Buzzards**, **Peregrine** and **Lanner Falcons**, **Rock Kestrel**, **Cape Eagle Owl**, **Rock Pigeon**, **Rosyfaced Lovebird**, **Bradfield's Swift** and **Palewinged Starling**. Birds typical of the plateau include **Pale Chanting Goshawk**, **Doublebanded Courser**, **Namaqua Sandgrouse**, **Swallowtailed Bee-eater**, **Sabota Lark**, **Karoo Chat**, **Chat Flycatcher** and **Bokmakierie**. The valleys with perennial streams support **Hamerkop**, **African Black Duck**, a few species of waders, owls and cuckoos, **Scimitarbilled Woodhoopoe**, **Lesser Honeyguide**, **Goldentailed** and **Cardinal Woodpeckers**, **Ashy Tit**, **Cape Wagtail**, **Brubru** and **Common Waxbill**.

74% OF SPECIES

001	**Ostrich**	☐	194	Redbilled Francolin*	☐
062	Grey Heron	☐	203	Helmeted Guineafowl	☐
071	Cattle Egret	☐	230	Kori Bustard	☐
081	**Hamerkop**	☐	232	**Ludwig's Bustard***	☐
084	Black Stork	☐	236	**Rüppell's Korhaan***	☐
102	Egyptian Goose	☐	239a	Whitequilled Korhaan**	☐
103	South African Shelduck**	☐	249	Threebanded Plover	☐
105	**African Black Duck**	☐	255	Crowned Plover	☐
118	**Secretarybird**	☐	258	Blacksmith Plover	☐
123	Whitebacked Vulture	☐	264	Common Sandpiper	☐
124	**Lappetfaced Vulture**	☐	270	Greenshank	☐
126	Black Kite	☐	272	Curlew Sandpiper	☐
126a	Yellowbilled Kite	☐	295	Blackwinged Stilt	☐
127	Blackshouldered Kite	☐	297	Spotted Dikkop	☐
131	**Black Eagle**	☐	301	**Doublebanded Courser**	☐
136	Booted Eagle	☐			
137	African Hawk Eagle	☐	344	**Namaqua Sandgrouse***	☐
140	Martial Eagle	☐			
143	Blackbreasted Snake Eagle	☐	347	Doublebanded Sandgrouse*	☐
152	**Jackal Buzzard****	☐	349	**Rock Pigeon**	☐
153	**Augur Buzzard**	☐	354	Cape Turtle Dove	☐
161	Gabar Goshawk	☐	355	Laughing Dove	☐
162	**Pale Chanting Goshawk***	☐	356	Namaqua Dove	☐
			367	**Rosyfaced Lovebird***	☐
171	**Peregrine Falcon**	☐	373	Grey Lourie	☐
172	**Lanner Falcon**	☐	378	Black Cuckoo	☐
178	Rednecked Falcon	☐	385	Klaas's Cuckoo	☐
181	**Rock Kestrel**	☐	386	Diederik Cuckoo	☐
182	**Greater Kestrel**	☐	392	Barn Owl	☐
186	Pygmy Falcon	☐	397	Whitefaced Owl	☐

ALSO RECORDED

Cape Vultures used to breed in the vicinity on Rostock Mountain, but are now extinct there. Egyptian Vultures have been recorded infrequently as have White and Marabou Storks. In exceptionally wet years, Blackheaded Herons, Little and Yellowbilled Egrets, Little Bitterns and African Fish Eagles have been recorded. Other unusual records include Baillon's Crake, Purple Gallinule, African Jacana, European and African Orioles, Tree Pipit and Red Bishop. During particularly dry periods, Dune and Gray's Larks spread eastwards from the Namib into the Naukluft region.

Chris Brown

398 Pearlspotted Owl
400 **Cape Eagle Owl**
401 Spotted Eagle Owl
411 European Swift
412 Black Swift
413 **Bradfield's Swift***
415 Whiterumped Swift
418 Alpine Swift
425 Whitebacked Mousebird**
426 Redfaced Mousebird
438 European Bee-eater
445 **Swallowtailed Bee-eater**
449 Purple Roller
451 Hoopoe
454 **Scimitarbilled Woodhoopoe**
462 **Monteiro's Hornbill***
465 Pied Barbet*
476 **Lesser Honeyguide**
483 **Goldentailed Woodpecker**
486 **Cardinal Woodpecker**
498 **Sabota Lark***
500 **Longbilled Lark***
506 Spikeheeled Lark*
511 **Stark's Lark***
516 Greybacked Finchlark*
518 European Swallow
526 Greater Striped Swallow*
529 Rock Martin
541 Forktailed Drongo
547 Black Crow
548 Pied Crow
552 **Ashy Tit***
557 Cape Penduline Tit*
567 Redeyed Bulbul*
580 Groundscraper Thrush
583 **Shorttoed Rock Thrush***
586 **Mountain Chat***
587 Capped Wheatear
589 Familiar Chat
590 **Tractrac Chat***
592 **Karoo Chat***
614 **Karoo Robin****
618 **Herero Chat***
621 Titbabbler*
622 Layard's Titbabbler**
631 African Marsh Warbler
643 Willow Warbler
651 Longbilled Crombec
653 Yellowbellied Eremomela
660 **Cinnamonbreasted Warbler****
662 **Rockrunner***
669 Greybacked Cisticola*
675 Blackbacked Cisticola
689 Spotted Flycatcher
695 Marico Flycatcher*
697 **Chat Flycatcher***
703 Pririt Batis*
713 **Cape Wagtail**
731 Lesser Grey Shrike
732 Fiscal Shrike
733 Redbacked Shrike
739 Crimsonbreasted Boubou*
741 **Brubru**
746 **Bokmakierie***
752 **Whitetailed Shrike***
760 Wattled Starling
761 Plumcoloured Starling
764 Glossy Starling*
770 **Palewinged Starling***
788 Dusky Sunbird*
791 Scarletchested Sunbird
799 Whitebrowed Sparrowweaver
800 Sociable Weaver**
802 Great Sparrow*
803 Cape Sparrow*
804 Greyheaded Sparrow
806 Scalyfeathered Finch*
812 Chestnut Weaver
814 Masked Weaver
815 Lesser Masked Weaver
834 Melba Finch
845 Violeteared Waxbill*
846 **Common Waxbill**
847 Blackcheeked Waxbill
856 Redheaded Finch*
860 Pintailed Whydah
861 Shafttailed Whydah*
870 Blackthroated Canary
876 Blackheaded Canary
878 Yellow Canary*
879 Whitethroated Canary*
885 Cape Bunting
886 Rock Bunting
887 Larklike Bunting*

HARDAP

approximately 300 species recorded to date

The Hardap Dam and Recreational Resort (25 000 ha) is situated 24 km north-west of Mariental and 245 km south of Windhoek, in the dwarf shrub savanna vegetation type. Rainfall is variable but averages about 190 mm per year. The dam is on the upper Fish River, and is surrounded by rolling hills and rocky slopes. A number of islands and dead trees in the dam provide safe nesting and roosting sites for the rich variety of waterbirds attracted to the area.

SPECIAL AND INTERESTING SPECIES

The Hardap Recreational Resort contains a rich diversity of birdlife in an otherwise harsh, dry environment. A number of species reach the northern limit of their range in this area, having followed the Fish River northwards. These include **African Black Duck**, **Sclater's Lark**, **Olive Thrush**, **Cape Robin**, **Karoo Robin**, **Cinnamonbreasted Warbler**, **Fairy Flycatcher** and **Pintailed Whydah**. Hardap is best known for its waterbirds. These include **White Pelican**, which sometimes numbers up to 800 birds; over 100 pairs breed regularly on one of the islands, making this the only man-made wetland in southern Africa where pelicans breed. **Whitebreasted** and **Reed Cormorants**, **Darters** and 15 species of herons (including **Goliath**, **Purple**, **Squacco** and **Rufousbellied Herons**) and **Little** and **Dwarf Bitterns** are all recorded, most breeding regularly on the dam. At least four pairs of **African Fish Eagles** are resident, one pair nesting on a cliff overlooking the water. **Ospreys** are present

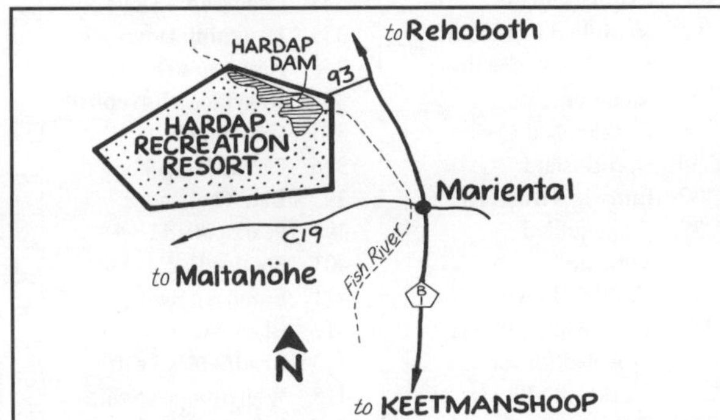

ALSO RECORDED

Lesser Blackbacked Gulls are seen at Hardap most years, as is Blacknecked Grebe which has been recorded breeding there. Pinkbacked Pelicans and Pygmy Geese are reliably reported from time to time. In years of particularly good rain, Steppe Eagles may occur as far south and west as Hardap and a Gymnogene was recently found breeding in the park.

Chris Brown

Turn west of the B1 highway 11 km north of Mariental onto district road 93. Proceed 12 km to the park entrance gate and a further 9 km to the reception centre. A variety of bungalows and camping facilities (overnight and day), a restaurant and other amenities are available. Visitors may travel around the park by car, on foot (a self-guided hiking trail has been established) or by boat.

at the dam every year, with a bird or two overwintering from time to time. Other waterbirds include 14 species of duck, both **Lesser** and **Greater Flamingos**, 23 species of waders, **Kelp** and **Greyheaded Gulls**, **Caspian**, **Whiskered** and **Whitewinged Terns**, **Pied** and **Giant Kingfishers** and a number of warblers and weavers in the reedbeds. Species typical of the arid terrestrial habitat include **Ostrich**, **Black Eagle**, **Pale Chanting Goshawk**, **Pygmy Falcon**, **Redbilled Francolin**, **Ludwig's Bustard**, **Namaqua Sandgrouse**, **Rock Pigeon**, **Laughing** and **Namaqua Doves**, **Rosyfaced Lovebird** (which breeds under the roofs of the buildings at Hardap), a number of swifts, including **Bradfield's**, plus **Shorttoed Rock Thrush** and **Dusky Sunbird**.

56% OF SPECIES

001 **Ostrich**
008 Dabchick
049 **White Pelican**
055 **Whitebreasted Cormorant**
058 **Reed Cormorant**
060 **Darter**
062 Grey Heron
063 Blackheaded Heron
064 **Goliath Heron**
065 **Purple Heron**
066 Great White Egret
067 Little Egret
071 Cattle Egret
072 **Squacco Heron**
075 **Rufousbellied Heron**
076 Blackcrowned Night Heron
078 **Little Bittern**
079 **Dwarf Bittern**
081 Hamerkop
084 Black Stork
089 Marabou Stork
090 Yellowbilled Stork
091 Sacred Ibis
095 African Spoonbill
096 **Greater Flamingo**
097 **Lesser Flamingo**
102 Egyptian Goose
103 South African Shelduck**
105 **African Black Duck**
106 Cape Teal
108 Redbilled Teal
116 Spurwinged Goose
123 Whitebacked Vulture
127 Blackshouldered Kite
131 **Black Eagle**
137 African Hawk Eagle
140 Martial Eagle
143 Blackbreasted Snake Eagle
148 **African Fish Eagle**
161 Gabar Goshawk
162 **Pale Chanting Goshawk***
170 **Osprey**
181 Rock Kestrel
186 **Pygmy Falcon**
194 **Redbilled Francolin***
203 Helmeted Guineafowl
226 Moorhen
228 Redknobbed Coot
230 Kori Bustard
232 **Ludwig's Bustard***
239a Whitequilled Korhaan**
248 Kittlitz's Plover
249 Threebanded Plover
255 Crowned Plover
258 Blacksmith Plover
264 Common Sandpiper
266 Wood Sandpiper
270 Greenshank
272 Curlew Sandpiper
274 Little Stint
284 Ruff
294 Avocet
295 Blackwinged Stilt
301 Doublebanded Courser
312 **Kelp Gull**
315 **Greyheaded Gull**
322 **Caspian Tern**
338 **Whiskered Tern**
339 **Whitewinged Tern**
344 **Namaqua Sandgrouse***
349 **Rock Pigeon**
354 Cape Turtle Dove
355 **Laughing Dove**
356 **Namaqua Dove**
367 **Rosyfaced Lovebird***
373 Grey Lourie
386 Diederik Cuckoo
392 Barn Owl
398 Pearlspotted Owl
401 Spotted Eagle Owl
411 European Swift
412 Black Swift
413 **Bradfield's Swift***
415 Whiterumped Swift
417 Little Swift

421 Palm Swift
425 **Whitebacked Mousebird****
426 Redfaced Mousebird
428 **Pied Kingfisher**
429 **Giant Kingfisher**
438 European Bee-eater
445 Swallowtailed Bee-eater
447 Lilacbreasted Roller
449 Purple Roller
451 Hoopoe
454 Scimitarbilled Woodhoopoe
457 Grey Hornbill
459 Southern Yellowbilled Hornbill*
465 Pied Barbet*
483 Goldentailed Woodpecker
486 Cardinal Woodpecker
497 Fawncoloured Lark
498 Sabota Lark*
500 Longbilled Lark*
506 Spikeheeled Lark*
510 **Sclater's Lark****
516 Greybacked Finchlark*
518 European Swallow
520 Whitethroated Swallow
526 Greater Striped Swallow*
529 Rock Martin
533 Brownthroated Martin
541 Forktailed Drongo
552 Ashy Tit*
557 Cape Penduline Tit*
567 Redeyed Bulbul*
577 **Olive Thrush**
580 Groundscraper Thrush
583 **Shorttoed Rock Thrush***
586 Mountain Chat*
587 Capped Wheatear
589 Familiar Chat
595 Anteating Chat**
601 **Cape Robin**
614 **Karoo Robin****
615 Kalahari Robin*
621 Titbabbler*
631 African Marsh Warbler
643 Willow Warbler
651 Longbilled Crombec
653 Yellowbellied Eremomela
656 Burntnecked Eremomela
658 Barred Warbler*
660 **Cinnamonbreasted Warbler****
665 Desert Cisticola
669 Greybacked Cisticola*
685 Blackchested Prinia*
689 Spotted Flycatcher
695 Marico Flycatcher*
697 Chat Flycatcher*
703 Pririt Batis*
706 **Fairy Flycatcher****
713 Cape Wagtail
717 Longbilled Pipit
731 Lesser Grey Shrike
732 Fiscal Shrike
733 Redbacked Shrike
739 Crimsonbreasted Boubou*
741 Brubru
743 Threestreaked Tchagra
746 Bokmakierie*
760 Wattled Starling
764 Glossy Starling*
770 Palewinged Starling*
779 Marico Sunbird
788 **Dusky Sunbird***
791 Scarletchested Sunbird
799 Whitebrowed Sparrowweaver
800 Sociable Weaver**
801 House Sparrow
802 Great Sparrow*
803 Cape Sparrow*
804 Greyheaded Sparrow
806 Scalyfeathered Finch*
814 Masked Weaver
821 Redbilled Quelea
824 Red Bishop
834 Melba Finch
845 Violeteared Waxbill*
846 Common Waxbill
847 Blackcheeked Waxbill
856 Redheaded Finch*
860 **Pintailed Whydah**
861 Shafttailed Whydah*
870 Blackthroated Canary
878 Yellow Canary*
879 Whitethroated Canary*
887 Larklike Bunting*

OTHER BIRDING SPOTS WORTH VISITING

Avis Dam
Within the eastern limits of the city of Windhoek, this dam is a favourite spot for local birders. Lots of waterbirds can be seen here, as well as interesting arid-zone birds on the surrounding hills. A pleasant place for a casual stroll.

Bushmanland
(Tsumkwe area) Drive north and then east from Grootfontein to get to Bushmanland; alternatively drive south from the Kaudom Game Reserve. Four-wheel drive vehicles are necessary, especially in the wet season when widespread flooding attracts very large numbers of waterbirds, especially ducks, grebes, rails and crakes, terns, waders, herons and cranes. This is one of the richest wetlands in southern Africa.

Fish River Canyon
Ai-Ais Hot Springs is 82 km on the D316 from the main Keetmanshoop-Upington road. It offers luxury flat accommodation, a restaurant and camping facilities. Birdlife is rich, especially around waterholes.

Kaudom Game Reserve
The region is reached from Grootfontein via Tsumkwe. From here four-wheel drive vehicles are necessary to negotiate the soft, sandy tracks. There are two camps with hutted accommodation and camping facilities. Advance booking is necessary.

USEFUL TELEPHONE NUMBERS

Directorate of Nature Conservation and Recreation Resorts
P/Bag X1327, Windhoek 9000
(Booking office)
(061) 3-6975

Department of Nature and Environmental Conservation
(in Walvis Bay)
PO Box 94, Walvis Bay 9190
(0642) 5972

State Museum of Namibia
PO Box 1203, Windhoek 9000
(061) 29-3300

3 Botswana

Co-ordinator Dave Bishop

1 Chobe River/Kasane
2 Shakawe Fishing Camp
3 Okavango Delta, Xaxaba Region
4 Nxai Pan National Park
5 Phakalane Sewage Ponds
6 Kgale Hill and Siding
7 Otse

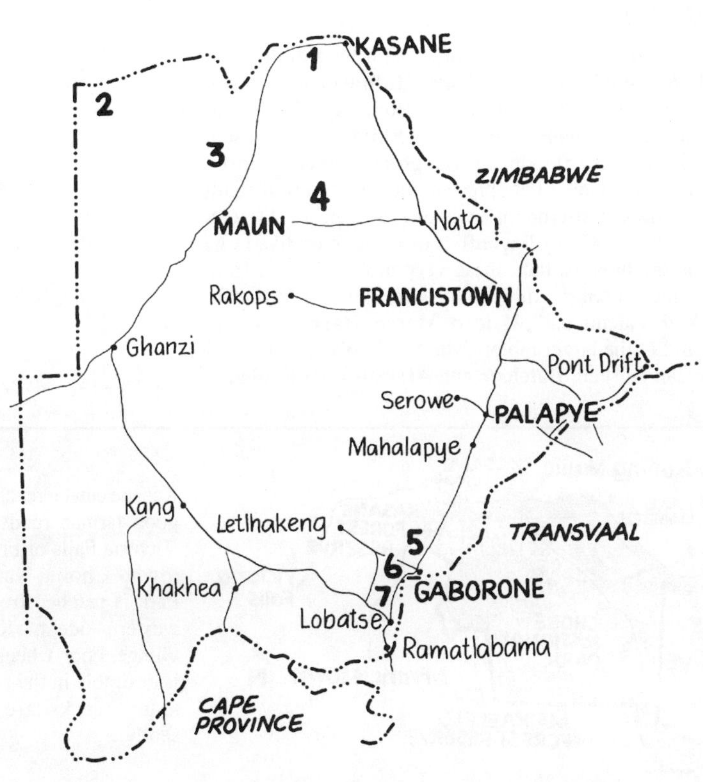

CHOBE RIVER/KASANE

approximately 300 species recorded to date

Because of its location on the northern boundary of southern Africa and its rich variety of habitats, this is an extremely interesting and rewarding birding area. Of particular note are the floodplains of the Chobe River, the riverside vegetation at Kasane and the woodland in Chobe National Park. This account deals with the area surrounding Kasane and the nearby Chobe floodplain. An entry fee is charged to Chobe National Park. Hotel accommodation is available at Kasane in addition to the luxury Chobe Game Lodge inside the national park. Camping is also available. Four-wheel drive vehicles can be hired at Kubu Lodge.

ALSO RECORDED

Rock Pratincole (summer) and Halfcollared Kingfisher can be seen at the rapids near Kasane. A large number of rarities and uncommon species have been recorded, including Angola Pitta, Emerald Cuckoo, Olive Bee-eater, Trumpeter Hornbill and Sousa's Shrike.

David Bishop

SPECIAL AND INTERESTING SPECIES

Waterside birds are well represented, with **Openbilled** and **Saddlebilled Storks**, **Wattled Crane**, **Rufousbellied Heron** and **Slaty Egret** not difficult to find. Both **Redwinged** and **Blackwinged Pratincoles** and **African Skimmer** are present in summer along the floodplain. **Longtoed Plover**, **Painted Snipe** and **Black Coucal** are present but sometimes difficult to find. In the late afternoon, keep an eye open for **African Hobby Falcon** hawking dragonflies over the river: like large bee-eaters the hobbies hunt these very mobile insects from riverside trees, often returning to the same perch. **Bat Hawk**, **Rednecked Falcon** and **African Marsh Harrier** are recorded, and of the larger raptors **Martial Eagle** and **Hooded Vulture** can be seen. **Bateleur** and **African Fish Eagle** are

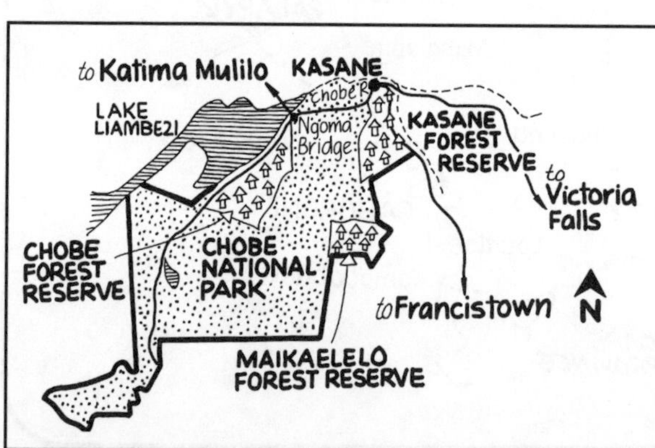

Kasane can be reached by good tarmac roads from Victoria Falls or Francistown. Chobe National Park is reached from the western side of Kasane village. Four-wheel drive is desirable in the park as many tracks are very sandy.

common. In summer **Broadbilled Rollers** are evident by their noisy calls; **Carmine Bee-eaters**, which rate among the most beautiful birds in southern Africa, breed in riverside banks. The reedbeds and riverside vegetation yield a long list of interesting and endemic species, including **Thrush Nightingale** (summer), **Brown Firefinch**, **Bearded** and **Heuglin's Robins**, **Crimsonbreasted Boubou**, **Redbilled Helmetshrike**, **Golden** and **Thickbilled Weavers**, **Redfaced** and **Blackbacked Cisticolas**, and the beautiful **Pinkthroated Longclaw**. The quality of birding more than compensates for the difficulties caused by the poor and sandy roads in the region.

55% OF SPECIES

058 Reed Cormorant ☐
060 Darter ☐
066 Great White Egret ☐
070 **Slaty Egret*** ☐
071 Cattle Egret ☐
072 Squacco Heron ☐
074 Greenbacked Heron ☐
075 **Rufousbellied Heron** ☐
081 Hamerkop ☐
087 **Openbilled Stork** ☐
088 **Saddlebilled Stork** ☐
090 Yellowbilled Stork ☐
102 Egyptian Goose ☐
115 Knobbilled Duck ☐
116 Spurwinged Goose ☐
118 Secretarybird ☐
121 **Hooded Vulture** ☐
123 Whitebacked Vulture ☐
126a Yellowbilled Kite ☐
127 Blackshouldered Kite ☐
129 **Bat Hawk** ☐
132 Tawny Eagle ☐
135 Wahlberg's Eagle ☐
140 **Martial Eagle** ☐
146 **Bateleur** ☐
148 **African Fish Eagle** ☐
157 Little Sparrowhawk ☐
159 Little Banded Goshawk ☐
165 African Marsh Harrier ☐
173 **Hobby Falcon** ☐
189 Crested Francolin ☐
194 Redbilled Francolin* ☐
199 Swainson's Francolin* ☐
203 Helmeted Guineafowl ☐
207 **Wattled Crane** ☐
240 African Jacana ☐
242 **Painted Snipe** ☐
258 Blacksmith Plover ☐
261 **Longtoed Plover** ☐
264 Common Sandpiper ☐
266 Wood Sandpiper ☐
270 Greenshank ☐
295 Blackwinged Stilt ☐
300 Temminck's Courser ☐
304 **Redwinged Pratincole** ☐
305 **Blackwinged Pratincole** ☐
339 Whitewinged Tern ☐
343 **African Skimmer** ☐
352 Redeyed Dove ☐
353 Mourning Dove ☐
354 Cape Turtle Dove ☐
355 Laughing Dove ☐
356 Namaqua Dove ☐
358 Greenspotted Dove ☐
373 Grey Lourie ☐
377 Redchested Cuckoo ☐
382 Jacobin Cuckoo ☐
386 Diederik Cuckoo ☐
388 **Black Coucal** ☐
391a Whitebrowed Coucal ☐
396 Scops Owl ☐
411 European Swift ☐
415 Whiterumped Swift ☐
426 Redfaced Mousebird ☐
428 Pied Kingfisher ☐
429 Giant Kingfisher ☐
430 Halfcollared Kingfisher ☐
433 Woodland Kingfisher ☐
435 Brownhooded Kingfisher ☐
436 Greyhooded Kingfisher ☐
438 European Bee-eater ☐
440 Bluecheeked Bee-eater ☐
441 **Carmine Bee-eater** ☐
443 Whitefronted Bee-eater ☐
444 Little Bee-eater ☐
447 Lilacbreasted Roller ☐
449 Purple Roller ☐
450 **Broadbilled Roller** ☐
452 Redbilled Woodhoopoe ☐
457 Grey Hornbill ☐
458 Redbilled Hornbill ☐
464 Blackcollared Barbet ☐
470 Yellowfronted Tinker Barbet ☐
473 Crested Barbet ☐
476 Lesser Honeyguide ☐
486 Cardinal Woodpecker ☐

487 Bearded Woodpecker ☐
518 European Swallow ☐
520 Whitethroated Swallow ☐
524 Redbreasted Swallow ☐
527 Lesser Striped Swallow ☐
534 Banded Martin ☐
541 Forktailed Drongo ☐
544 African Golden Oriole ☐
545 Blackheaded Oriole ☐
547 Black Crow ☐
560 Arrowmarked Babbler ☐
562 Whiterumped Babbler ☐
567 Redeyed Bulbul* ☐
568 Blackeyed Bulbul ☐
569 Terrestrial Bulbul ☐
574 Yellowbellied Bulbul ☐
587 Capped Wheatear ☐
599 **Heuglin's Robin** ☐
609 **Thrush Nightingale** ☐
617 **Bearded Robin** ☐
625 Icterine Warbler ☐
628 Great Reed Warbler ☐
634 European Sedge Warbler ☐
643 Willow Warbler ☐
648 Yellowbreasted Apalis ☐
657a Greybacked Bleating Warbler ☐
664 Fantailed Cisticola ☐
674 **Redfaced Cisticola** ☐
675 **Blackbacked Cisticola** ☐
683 Tawnyflanked Prinia ☐
689 Spotted Flycatcher ☐
694 Black Flycatcher ☐
701 Chinspot Batis ☐
710 Paradise Flycatcher ☐
711 African Pied Wagtail ☐
714 Yellow Wagtail ☐
716 Grassveld Pipit ☐
730 **Pinkthroated Longclaw** ☐
731 Lesser Grey Shrike ☐
733 Redbacked Shrike ☐
735 Longtailed Shrike ☐
739 **Crimsonbreasted Boubou*** ☐
740 Puffback ☐
743 Threestreaked Tchagra ☐
748 Orangebreasted Bush Shrike ☐
753 White Helmetshrike ☐
754 **Redbilled Helmetshrike** ☐
760 Wattled Starling ☐
761 Plumcoloured Starling ☐
762 Burchell's Starling* ☐
764 Glossy Starling* ☐
765 Greater Blue-eared Starling ☐
772 Redbilled Oxpecker ☐
792 Black Sunbird ☐
797 Yellow White-eye ☐
804 Greyheaded Sparrow ☐
807 **Thickbilled Weaver** ☐
811 Spottedbacked Weaver ☐
815 Lesser Masked Weaver ☐
816 **Golden Weaver** ☐
821 Redbilled Quelea ☐
834 Melba Finch ☐
842 Redbilled Firefinch ☐
843 **Brown Firefinch** ☐
844 Blue Waxbill ☐
860 Pintailed Whydah ☐
861 Shafttailed Whydah* ☐
862 Paradise Whydah ☐
867 Steelblue Widowfinch ☐
870 Blackthroated Canary ☐
884 Goldenbreasted Bunting ☐
☐
☐

Woodland Kingfisher

SHAKAWE FISHING CAMP

approximately 350 species recorded to date

Shakawe Fishing Camp, established in 1969, is a privately run licensed bush hotel and campsite. It is situated on the banks of the Okavango River near the north-western Botswana border, at the start of the Panhandle. The species listed are those recorded in riverine forest, floodplain, grassland, riverbanks, woodland and thorn scrub. These habitats are accessible within a 10 km radius of the hotel. A wide variety of bird species can be seen on the 16 ha premises comprising riverine forest, thorn scrub and approximately 1 km of open vertical riverbank frontage. This popular birding spot rates among the best in Botswana.

SPECIAL AND INTERESTING SPECIES

Pel's Fishing Owl can be seen on day forest walks or from a boat at night on forest edges. Best views are possible during the breeding season between February and June when it calls more frequently. The **African Skimmer**, which normally arrives in July and nests on exposed sandbanks until December, is best seen during boat trips on the river. **Western Banded Snake Eagles** are not uncommon and have very distinctive calls. Active nests have been found in the area in late summer. **Whitebacked Night Herons** frequent the vertical riverbank, papyrus or low overhanging branches in front of the camp and are best seen or heard at night. **Brown Firefinches** are quite

ALSO RECORDED

Osprey, African Hobby Falcon, Halfcollared Kingfisher and Cuckoo Hawk have been recorded.

Elaine Pryce

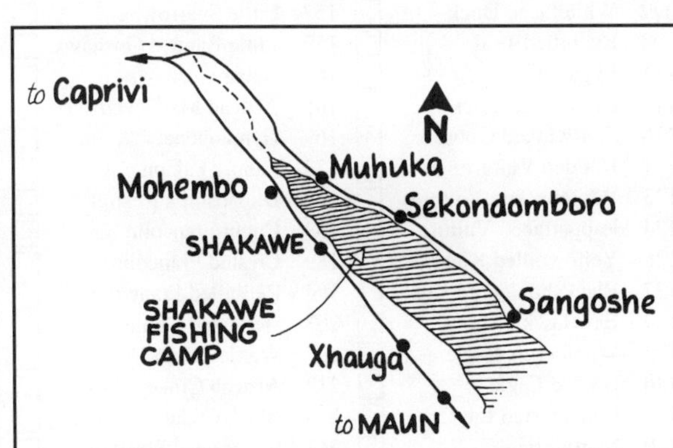

The signposted turnoff is on the main Maun/Shakawe road, 13 km south of Shakawe village. From the north one can enter Botswana via the Caprivi or Rundu, pass through Shakawe and take the Maun road past the airfield. There are other new camps in the area.

tame with groups of 20-30 foraging on the ground in open areas near thorn thickets, often in the company of **Blue Waxbills**. The large **Copperytailed Coucal** exposes itself by sitting on the papyrus in the early mornings and can sometimes be seen feeding in open floodplain areas. **Swamp Boubou** has a pretty duet call and is easily seen all year round in riverine habitat. **Carmine** and **Whitefronted Bee-eaters** nest in riverbanks in both large and small colonies. **Longtoed Plover** can be seen on open river edges, floodplains or backwaters and is common during the summer months. **Bradfield's Hornbill** can easily be overlooked in its preferred dry habitat where species such as **Bearded Woodpecker**, **Yellowbellied Eremomela**, **White** and **Redbilled Helmetshrikes** and **Violeteared Waxbill** may also be found. **Barred Owl** is resident and nests close to buildings. The **Bat Hawk**, which hunts in the early evening and on moonlit nights, is often around but not easily seen. **Broadbilled Rollers**, which arrive in October and nest in tall trees overlooking the campsites, give themselves away by their raucous calls and behaviour. **Pygmy Geese** and the friendly **African Jacanas** move quietly among the water lilies.

67% OF SPECIES

No.	Species	☐
049	White Pelican	☐
050	Pinkbacked Pelican	☐
058	Reed Cormorant	☐
060	Darter	☐
062	Grey Heron	☐
064	Goliath Heron	☐
065	Purple Heron	☐
066	Great White Egret	☐
067	Little Egret	☐
068	Yellowbilled Egret	☐
069	Black Egret	☐
070	Slaty Egret	☐
071	Cattle Egret	☐
072	Squacco Heron	☐
074	Greenbacked Heron	☐
075	Rufousbellied Heron	☐
076	Blackcrowned Night Heron	☐
077	**Whitebacked Night Heron**	☐
078	Little Bittern	☐
081	Hamerkop	☐
084	Black Stork	☐
085	Abdim's Stork	☐
087	Openbilled Stork	☐
089	Marabou Stork	☐
090	Yellowbilled Stork	☐
091	Sacred Ibis	☐
093	Glossy Ibis	☐
094	Hadeda Ibis	☐
095	African Spoonbill	☐
099	Whitefaced Duck	☐
108	Redbilled Teal	☐
114	Pygmy Goose	☐
115	Knobbilled Duck	☐
116	Spurwinged Goose	☐
121	Hooded Vulture	☐
123	Whitebacked Vulture	☐
124	Lappetfaced Vulture	☐
126a	Yellowbilled Kite	☐
127	Blackshouldered Kite	☐
129	Bat Hawk	☐
135	Wahlberg's Eagle	☐
136	Booted Eagle	☐
139	Longcrested Eagle	☐
140	Martial Eagle	☐
143	Blackbreasted Snake Eagle	☐
145	**Western Banded Snake Eagle**	☐
146	Bateleur	☐
148	African Fish Eagle	☐
154	Lizard Buzzard	☐
156	Ovambo Sparrowhawk	☐
157	Little Sparrowhawk	☐
159	Little Banded Goshawk	☐
161	Gabar Goshawk	☐
165	African Marsh Harrier	☐
169	Gymnogene	☐
172	Lanner Falcon	☐
185	Dickinson's Kestrel	☐
188	Coqui Francolin	☐
189	Crested Francolin	☐
194	Redbilled Francolin	☐
203	Helmeted Guineafowl	☐
207	Wattled Crane	☐
212	African Crake	☐
213	Black Crake	☐
217	Redchested Flufftail	☐

223 Purple Gallinule ☐
224 **Lesser Gallinule** ☐
226 Moorhen ☐
227 **Lesser Moorhen** ☐
237 Redcrested Korhaan* ☐
240 African Jacana ☐
241 **Lesser Jacana** ☐
242 Painted Snipe ☐
249 Threebanded Plover ☐
255 Crowned Plover ☐
258 Blacksmith Plover ☐
259 Whitecrowned Plover ☐
260 Wattled Plover ☐
261 Longtoed Plover ☐
264 Common Sandpiper ☐
266 Wood Sandpiper ☐
270 Greenshank ☐
284 Ruff ☐
286 Ethiopian Snipe ☐
295 Blackwinged Stilt ☐
298 Water Dikkop ☐
304 Redwinged Pratincole ☐
338 Whiskered Tern ☐
339 Whitewinged Tern ☐
343 **African Skimmer** ☐
344 Namaqua Sandgrouse* ☐
347 Doublebanded Sandgrouse* ☐
352 Redeyed Dove ☐
353 Mourning Dove ☐
354 Cape Turtle Dove ☐
355 Laughing Dove ☐
356 Namaqua Dove ☐
358 Greenspotted Dove ☐
361 Green Pigeon ☐
364 Meyer's Parrot ☐
373 Grey Lourie ☐
375 African Cuckoo ☐
378 Black Cuckoo ☐
381 Striped Cuckoo ☐
382 Jacobin Cuckoo ☐
386 Diederik Cuckoo ☐
389 **Copperytailed Coucal** ☐
390 Senegal Coucal ☐
392 Barn Owl ☐
394 Wood Owl ☐
396 Scops Owl ☐
397 Whitefaced Owl ☐
398 Pearlspotted Owl ☐
399 **Barred Owl** ☐
402 Giant Eagle Owl ☐
403 **Pel's Fishing Owl** ☐
405 Fierynecked Nightjar ☐
410 Pennantwinged Nightjar ☐
421 Palm Swift ☐
426 Redfaced Mousebird ☐
427 Narina Trogon ☐
428 Pied Kingfisher ☐
429 Giant Kingfisher ☐
431 Malachite Kingfisher ☐
433 Woodland Kingfisher ☐
436 Greyhooded Kingfisher ☐
440 Bluecheeked Bee-eater ☐
441 **Carmine Bee-eater** ☐
443 **Whitefronted Bee-eater** ☐
444 Little Bee-eater ☐
445 Swallowtailed Bee-eater ☐
447 Lilacbreasted Roller ☐
449 Purple Roller ☐
450 **Broadbilled Roller** ☐
451 Hoopoe ☐
452 Redbilled Woodhoopoe ☐
454 Scimitarbilled Woodhoopoe ☐
457 Grey Hornbill ☐
459 Southern Yellowbilled Hornbill* ☐
461 **Bradfield's Hornbill*** ☐
463 Ground Hornbill ☐
464 Blackcollared Barbet ☐
470 Yellowfronted Tinker Barbet ☐
473 Crested Barbet ☐
476 Lesser Honeyguide ☐
483 Goldentailed Woodpecker ☐
486 Cardinal Woodpecker ☐
487 **Bearded Woodpecker** ☐
522 Wiretailed Swallow ☐
523 Pearlbreasted Swallow ☐
527 Lesser Striped Swallow ☐
531 Greyrumped Swallow ☐
533 Brownthroated Martin ☐
534 Banded Martin ☐
539 Whitebreasted Cuckooshrike ☐
541 Forktailed Drongo ☐
544 African Golden Oriole ☐
545 Blackheaded Oriole ☐
554 Southern Black Tit* ☐
560 Arrowmarked Babbler ☐
562 Whiterumped Babbler ☐
563 Pied Babbler** ☐
567 Redeyed Bulbul* ☐
568 Blackeyed Bulbul ☐
569 Terrestrial Bulbul ☐
574 Yellowbellied Bulbul ☐
576 Kurrichane Thrush ☐
596 Stonechat ☐
599 Heuglin's Robin ☐
613 Whitebrowed Robin ☐
617 Bearded Robin ☐
621 Titbabbler* ☐
628 Great Reed Warbler ☐
638 African Sedge Warbler ☐
648 Yellowbreasted Apalis ☐
651 Longbilled Crombec ☐
653 **Yellowbellied Eremomela** ☐
657a Greybacked Bleating Warbler ☐
675 Blackbacked Cisticola ☐
676 **Chirping Cisticola** ☐
683 Tawnyflanked Prinia ☐

691 Bluegrey Flycatcher ☐
694 Black Flycatcher ☐
695 Marico Flycatcher* ☐
701 Chinspot Batis ☐
710 Paradise Flycatcher ☐
711 African Pied Wagtail ☐
713 Cape Wagtail ☐
714 YellowWagtail ☐
733 Redbacked Shrike ☐
735 Longtailed Shrike ☐
738 **Swamp Boubou** ☐
739 Crimsonbreasted Boubou* ☐
740 Puffback ☐
741 Brubru ☐
743 Threestreaked Tchagra ☐
748 Orangebreasted Bush Shrike ☐
753 **White Helmetshrike** ☐
754 **Redbilled Helmetshrike** ☐
760 Wattled Starling ☐
761 Plumcoloured Starling ☐
762 Burchell's Starling* ☐
763 Longtailed Starling* ☐
764 Glossy Starling ☐
765 Greater Blue-eared Starling ☐
771 Yellowbilled Oxpecker ☐
772 Redbilled Oxpecker ☐
779 Marico Sunbird ☐
787 Whitebellied Sunbird ☐
791 Scarletchested Sunbird ☐
793 Collared Sunbird ☐
797 Yellow White-eye ☐
798 Redbilled Buffalo Weaver ☐
799 Whitebrowed Sparrowweaver ☐
804 Greyheaded Sparrow ☐
807 Thickbilled Weaver ☐
811 Spottedbacked Weaver ☐
815 Lesser Masked Weaver ☐
816 Golden Weaver ☐
818 Brownthroated Weaver ☐
821 Redbilled Quelea ☐
824 Red Bishop ☐
828 Redshouldered Widow ☐
834 Melba Finch ☐
841 Jameson's Firefinch ☐
842 Redbilled Firefinch ☐
843 Brown Firefinch ☐
844 Blue Waxbill ☐
845 Violeteared Waxbill ☐
860 Pintailed Whydah ☐
861 Shafttailed Whydah ☐
862 Paradise Whydah ☐
884 Goldenbreasted Bunting ☐

Pygmy Geese

OKAVANGO DELTA, XAXABA REGION

over 400 species recorded to date

The area around Xaxaba in the central Okavango Delta is used here as an example of the avifauna that may be found in this rich and beautiful birding paradise. Most areas in the delta would produce exciting birding even during the dry season in late summer. Species diversity is evident to some extent from the north of the region to the south, but it is the fluctuation of water levels that creates the seasonal variation to a great extent. Xaxaba, at the edge of the Moremi Wildlife Reserve, encompasses the following habitats: perennial, clear flowing channels (seasonally flooded), vegetated floodplains and wooded islands. The high flood season is from May to August, after which the floodwaters recede until the arrival of the next annual flooding, usually in April. The altitude averages 900 m. There are many islands, variable in size and fringed with large trees and palms. One may walk freely in the delta part of Moremi, a great advantage to birders.

ALSO RECORDED

Over 400 species have been recorded from the Okavango Delta and recent additions include Striped Crake and Whinchat.

Richard Randall

SPECIAL AND INTERESTING SPECIES

Slaty Egrets always provide an attraction and are generally found in the shallow floodplains where there is short vegetation. The delta boasts southern Africa's finest habitat for herons and egrets and in this central region, all species except two (Whitebacked Night Heron and Madagascar Squacco

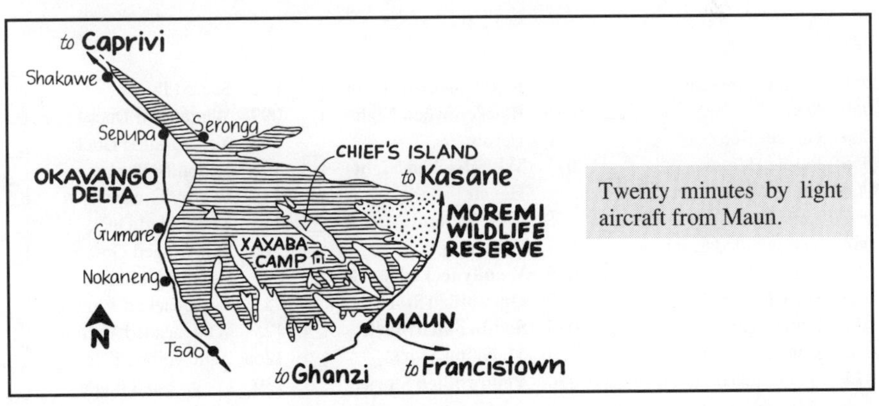

Twenty minutes by light aircraft from Maun.

Heron) occur. The best time to see them is from October to December, during the time of rapidly diminishing floodwater. **Saddlebilled, Marabou, Woollynecked, Openbilled** and **Yellowbilled Storks** can also be seen, sometimes in large numbers. Southern Africa's largest flocks of **Wattled Cranes** occur here. The floodplain edges are a good place to see **Black Coucal**, **Natal Nightjar** and **Pinkthroated Longclaw**. The large trees along the watercourses provide daytime refuge for the spectacular **Pel's Fishing Owl**. This is perhaps the best place in Africa to see this bird. **Swamp Boubous** with their pure white underparts are common close to the water. Specials to look for away from the waterside vegetation include **Mourning Dove, Brown Firefinch, Greencapped Eremomela, Whiterumped Babbler, Heuglin's Robin** and **Western Banded Snake Eagle**. In the reeds and along the channel edges are found **Rufousbellied Heron**, **Longtoed Plover**, **Copperytailed Coucal** and **Greater Swamp Warbler**. The **Chirping Cisticola** can be distinguished from the **Blackbacked Cisticola** by call. On the quieter waters where there are lilies, both **Lesser Jacana** and **Pygmy Geese** can be found. **African Fish Eagles**, **Green Pigeons** and **Meyer's Parrots** are common. A walk throuh the woodland could produce endemics such as **Burchell's**, **Longtailed** and **Glossy Starlings**. The three small owls, **Scops**, **Pearlspotted** and **Barred**, are normally not difficult to see especially if their calls are known. Colourful insectivores include **Carmine Bee-eaters**, **Lilacbreasted**, **Purple** and **Broadbilled Rollers**. Look at the bulbuls carefully as both **Redeyed** and **Blackeyed** occur. The drier woodland can produce species such as **Yellowbellied** and **Burntnecked Eremomelas**, **Arrowmarked Babbler**, **Yellow** and **Redbilled Oxpeckers**, **Redheaded Weaver** and **Jameson's** and **Redbilled Firefinches**

52% 0F SPECIES

058	Reed Cormorant	☐	075	**Rufousbellied Heron**	☐	091	Sacred Ibis	☐
060	Darter	☐	076	Blackcrowned Night Heron	☐	099	Whitefaced Duck	☐
064	Goliath Heron	☐				104	Yellowbilled Duck	☐
065	Purple Heron	☐	077	**Whitebacked Night Heron**	☐	108	Redbilled Teal	☐
066	Great White Egret	☐				114	**Pygmy Goose**	☐
067	Little Egret	☐	078	Little Bittern	☐	115	Knobbilled Duck	☐
068	Yellowbilled Egret	☐	081	Hamerkop	☐	116	Spurwinged Goose	☐
069	Black Egret	☐	086	**Woollynecked Stork**	☐	121	Hooded Vulture	☐
070	**Slaty Egret***	☐	087	**Openbilled Stork**	☐	123	Whitebacked Vulture	☐
071	Cattle Egret	☐	088	**Saddlebilled Stork**	☐	125	Whiteheaded Vulture	☐
072	Squacco Heron	☐	089	**Marabou Stork**	☐	126a	Yellowbilled Kite	☐
074	Greenbacked Heron	☐	090	**Yellowbilled Stork**	☐	139	Longcrested Eagle	☐

142 Brown Snake Eagle
145 **Western Banded Snake Eagle**
146 Bateleur
148 **African Fish Eagle**
158 Black Sparrowhawk
161 Gabar Goshawk
165 African Marsh Harrier
169 Gymnogene
189 Crested Francolin
194 Redbilled Francolin*
199 Swainson's Francolin*
207 **Wattled Crane**
213 Black Crake
223 Purple Gallinule
226 Moorhen
240 African Jacana
241 **Lesser Jacana**
255 Crowned Plover
258 Blacksmith Plover
260 Wattled Plover
261 **Longtoed Plover**
264 Common Sandpiper
266 Wood Sandpiper
270 Greenshank
284 Ruff
298 Water Dikkop
338 Whiskered Tern
347 Doublebanded Sandgrouse*
352 Redeyed Dove
353 **Mourning Dove**
354 Cape Turtle Dove
355 Laughing Dove
356 Namaqua Dove
358 Greenspotted Dove
361 **Green Pigeon**
364 **Meyer's Parrot**
373 Grey Lourie
377 Redchested Cuckoo
378 Black Cuckoo
381 Striped Cuckoo
382 Jacobin Cuckoo
386 Diederik Cuckoo
388 **Black Coucal**
389 **Copperytailed Coucal**
390 Senegal Coucal
394 Wood Owl
396 **Scops Owl**
397 Whitefaced Owl
398 **Pearlspotted Owl**
399 **Barred Owl**
402 Giant Eagle Owl
403 **Pel's Fishing Owl**
405 Fierynecked Nightjar
407 **Natal Nightjar**
421 Palm Swift
426 Redfaced Mousebird
428 Pied Kingfisher
431 Malachite Kingfisher
433 Woodland Kingfisher
435 Brownhooded Kingfisher
437 Striped Kingfisher
438 European Bee-eater
440 Bluecheeked Bee-eater
441 **Carmine Bee-eater**
444 Little Bee-eater
445 **Swallowtailed Bee-eater**
447 **Lilacbreasted Roller**
449 **Purple Roller**
450 **Broadbilled Roller**
451 Hoopoe
452 Redbilled Woodhoopoe
457 Grey Hornbill
458 Redbilled Hornbill
459 Southern Yellowbilled Hornbill*
463 Ground Hornbill
464 Blackcollared Barbet
470 Yellowfronted Tinker Barbet
473 Crested Barbet
474 Greater Honeyguide
476 Lesser Honeyguide
481 Bennett's Woodpecker
483 Goldentailed Woodpecker
486 Cardinal Woodpecker
487 Bearded Woodpecker
494 Rufousnaped Lark
496 Flappet Lark
498 Sabota Lark*
518 European Swallow
522 Wiretailed Swallow
524 Redbreasted Swallow
526 Greater Striped Swallow*
527 Lesser Striped Swallow
531 Greyrumped Swallow
534 Banded Martin
538 Black Cuckooshrike
541 Forktailed Drongo
544 African Golden Oriole
545 Blackheaded Oriole
554 Southern Black Tit*
560 **Arrowmarked Babbler**
562 **Whiterumped Babbler**
567 **Redeyed Bulbul***
568 **Blackeyed Bulbul**
569 Terrestrial Bulbul
576 Kurrichane Thrush
596 Stonechat
599 **Heuglin's Robin**
613 Whitebrowed Robin
635 Cape Reed Warbler
636 **Greater Swamp Warbler**
638 African Sedge Warbler
648 Yellowbreasted Apalis
651 Longbilled Crombec
653 **Yellowbellied Eremomela**
655 **Greencapped Eremomela**
656 **Burntnecked Eremomela**
657a Greybacked Bleating Warbler
664 Fantailed Cisticola
672 Rattling Cisticola
675 **Blackbacked Cisticola**
676 **Chirping Cisticola**

683 Tawnyflanked Prinia ☐
689 Spotted Flycatcher ☐
691 Bluegrey Flycatcher ☐
695 Marico Flycatcher* ☐
701 Chinspot Batis ☐
710 Paradise Flycatcher ☐
713 Cape Wagtail ☐
714 Yellow Wagtail ☐
716 Grassveld Pipit ☐
719 Buffy Pipit ☐
730 **Pinkthroated Longclaw** ☐
733 Redbacked Shrike ☐
735 Longtailed Shrike ☐
738 **Swamp Boubou** ☐
740 Puffback ☐
741 Brubru ☐
743 Threestreaked Tchagra ☐
744 Blackcrowned Tchagra ☐
748 Orangebreasted Bush Shrike ☐
754 Redbilled Helmetshrike ☐
760 Wattled Starling ☐
762 **Burchell's Starling*** ☐
763 **Longtailed Starling*** ☐
764 **Glossy Starling*** ☐
765 Greater Blue-eared Starling ☐
771 **Yellowbilled Oxpecker** ☐
772 **Redbilled Oxpecker** ☐
779 Marico Sunbird ☐
787 Whitebellied Sunbird ☐
791 Scarletchested Sunbird ☐
792 Black Sunbird ☐
793 Collared Sunbird ☐
797 Yellow White-eye ☐
798 Redbilled Buffalo Weaver ☐
799 Whitebrowed Sparrowweaver ☐
804 Greyheaded Sparrow ☐
805 Yellowthroated Sparrow ☐
814 Masked Weaver ☐
816 Golden Weaver ☐
818 Brownthroated Weaver ☐
819 **Redheaded Weaver** ☐
824 Red Bishop ☐
828 Redshouldered Widow ☐
834 Melba Finch ☐
841 **Jameson's Firefinch** ☐
842 **Redbilled Firefinch** ☐
843 **Brown Firefinch** ☐
844 Blue Waxbill ☐
846 Common Waxbill ☐
847 Blackcheeked Waxbill ☐
860 Pintailed Whydah ☐
861 Shafttailed Whydah* ☐
862 Paradise Whydah ☐
867 Steelblue Widowfinch ☐
870 Blackthroated Canary ☐
☐
☐
☐
☐
☐

African Skimmers

NXAI PAN NATIONAL PARK

approximately 217 species recorded to date

Nxai Pan National Park, situated north of the Nata-Maun road and the Makgadikgadi Game Reserve, is all too often missed by travellers on their way to the great birding areas of the Okavango Delta. The park is managed by a warden and game scouts who also maintain the two campsites, which have flush toilets and cold showers. The park consists of a large grass pan with tree "islands", surrounded by bushveld-covered sand dunes.

SPECIAL AND INTERESTING SPECIES

Greybacked Bleating and **Barred Warblers**, **Chinspot Batis** and **Whitebrowed Robin** can easily be located by call in the bush around the campsite, as well as a wide variety of woodland species. The short grass on the pan affords good opportunities to observe the many species of larks that occur, such as **Clapper**, **Fawncoloured**, **Sabota**, **Dusky** and **Redcapped**. After good rains (usually between December and March) fantastic sightings of raptors can be had when hundreds of **Steppe Buzzards**, **Western Redfooted Kestrels** and **Yellowbilled Kites** descend on emerging termites. The occasional **Lesser Spotted Eagle** or **Hobby Falcon** can also be found. Raptors are generally well represented in this area. **Carmine** and **Bluecheeked Bee-eaters** hawk insects on the fringe of the pan, often following the huge herds of springbok

ALSO RECORDED

Wattled Cranes have been recorded in small numbers, feeding in shallow pools after exceptional rains. Montagu's Harrier has been seen during the summer months.

Gill McGowan

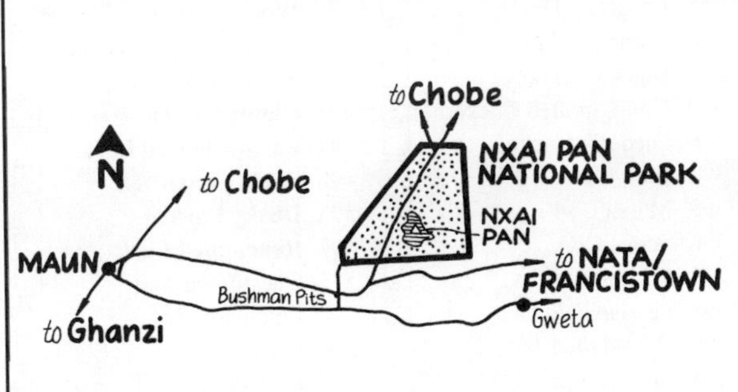

From the main Nata-Maun road, approximately 170 km from Nata or 135 km from Maun, take the well-used track northwards; after 35 km the entrance gate is reached. This track is very sandy and a four-wheel drive vehicle is recommended.

and zebra. On the open pan **Kori Bustards** and **Secretarybirds** mingle with the visiting **White Storks**. Look out for both **Redbilled** and **Yellowbilled Oxpeckers** on their zebra and giraffe hosts. The thorny acacias on the sand dunes are ideal habitat for **Violeteared**, **Blackcheeked** and **Blue Waxbills** as well as **Scalyfeathered** and **Melba Finches**, which are present all year.

72% OF SPECIES

001 Ostrich ☐
083 **White Stork** ☐
085 Abdim's Stork ☐
089 Marabou Stork ☐
118 **Secretarybird** ☐
123 Whitebacked Vulture ☐
124 Lappetfaced Vulture ☐
125 Whiteheaded Vulture ☐
126a **Yellowbilled Kite** ☐
127 Blackshouldered Kite ☐
132 Tawny Eagle ☐
134 **Lesser Spotted Eagle** ☐
135 Wahlberg's Eagle ☐
137 African Hawk Eagle ☐
140 Martial Eagle ☐
142 Brown Snake Eagle ☐
143 Blackbreasted Snake Eagle ☐
146 Bateleur ☐
149 **Steppe Buzzard** ☐
157 Little Sparrowhawk ☐
159 Little Banded Goshawk ☐
161 Gabar Goshawk ☐
162 Pale Chanting Goshawk* ☐
166 Montagu's Harrier ☐
169 Gymnogene ☐
172 Lanner Falcon ☐
173 **Hobby Falcon** ☐
179 **Western Redfooted Kestrel** ☐
182 Greater Kestrel ☐
189 Crested Francolin ☐
193 Orange River Francolin* ☐
194 Redbilled Francolin* ☐
199 Swainson's Francolin* ☐
201 Harlequin Quail ☐
203 Helmeted Guineafowl ☐
230 **Kori Bustard** ☐
237 Redcrested Korhaan* ☐
239a Whitequilled Korhaan** ☐
252 Caspian Plover ☐
255 Crowned Plover ☐
258 Blacksmith Plover ☐
297 Spotted Dikkop ☐
300 Temminck's Courser ☐
301 Doublebanded Courser ☐
303 Bronzewinged Courser ☐
305 Blackwinged Pratincole ☐
345 Burchell's Sandgrouse* ☐
347 Doublebanded Sandgrouse* ☐
354 Cape Turtle Dove ☐
355 Laughing Dove ☐
356 Namaqua Dove ☐
378 Black Cuckoo ☐
380 Great Spotted Cuckoo ☐
386 Diederik Cuckoo ☐
392 Barn Owl ☐
395 Marsh Owl ☐
396 Scops Owl ☐
397 Whitefaced Owl ☐
398 Pearlspotted Owl ☐
399 Barred Owl ☐
401 Spotted Eagle Owl ☐
405 Fierynecked Nightjar ☐
406 Rufouscheeked Nightjar ☐
411 European Swift ☐
421 Palm Swift ☐
426 Redfaced Mousebird ☐
438 European Bee-eater ☐
440 **Bluecheeked Bee-eater** ☐
441 **Carmine Bee-eater** ☐
444 Little Bee-eater ☐
445 Swallowtailed Bee-eater ☐
446 European Roller ☐
447 Lilacbreasted Roller ☐
449 Purple Roller ☐
451 Hoopoe ☐
454 Scimitarbilled Woodhoopoe ☐
457 Grey Hornbill ☐
458 Redbilled Hornbill ☐
459 Southern Yellowbilled Hornbill* ☐
465 Pied Barbet* ☐
483 Goldentailed Woodpecker ☐
486 Cardinal Woodpecker ☐
494 Rufousnaped Lark ☐
495 **Clapper Lark**** ☐
497 **Fawncoloured Lark** ☐
498 **Sabota Lark*** ☐
505 **Dusky Lark** ☐
507 **Redcapped Lark** ☐
515 Chestnutbacked Finchlark ☐
516 Greybacked Finchlark* ☐
518 European Swallow ☐

541 Forktailed Drongo ☐
543 European Golden Oriole ☐
547 Black Crow ☐
548 Pied Crow ☐
552 Ashy Tit* ☐
554 Southern Black Tit* ☐
557 Cape Penduline Tit* ☐
560 Arrowmarked Babbler ☐
563 Pied Babbler** ☐
567 Redeyed Bulbul* ☐
580 Groundscraper Thrush ☐
587 Capped Wheatear ☐
595 Anteating Chat** ☐
613 **Whitebrowed Robin** ☐
615 Kalahari Robin* ☐
621 Titbabbler* ☐
643 Willow Warbler ☐
651 Longbilled Crombec ☐
653 Yellowbellied Eremomela ☐
657a **Greybacked Bleating Warbler** ☐
658 **Barred Warbler*** ☐
664 Fantailed Cisticola ☐
665 Desert Cisticola ☐
671 Tinkling Cisticola ☐
672 Rattling Cisticola ☐
685 Blackchested Prinia* ☐
689 Spotted Flycatcher ☐
695 Marico Flycatcher* ☐
697 Chat Flycatcher* ☐
701 **Chinspot Batis** ☐
716 Grassveld Pipit ☐
718 Plainbacked Pipit ☐
719 Buffy Pipit ☐
731 Lesser Grey Shrike ☐
733 Redbacked Shrike ☐
735 Longtailed Shrike ☐
739 Crimsonbreasted Boubou* ☐
741 Brubru ☐
743 Threestreaked Tchagra ☐
744 Blackcrowned Tchagra ☐
753 White Helmetshrike ☐
760 Wattled Starling ☐
761 Plumcoloured Starling ☐
764 Glossy Starling* ☐
771 **Yellowbilled Oxpecker** ☐
772 **Redbilled Oxpecker** ☐
779 Marico Sunbird ☐
787 Whitebellied Sunbird ☐
798 Redbilled Buffalo Weaver ☐
799 Whitebrowed Sparrowweaver ☐
802 Great Sparrow* ☐
804 Greyheaded Sparrow ☐
806 **Scalyfeathered Finch*** ☐
814 Masked Weaver ☐
815 Lesser Masked Weaver ☐
819 Redheaded Weaver ☐
821 Redbilled Quelea ☐
834 **Melba Finch** ☐
844 **Blue Waxbill** ☐
845 **Violeteared Waxbill*** ☐
847 **Blackcheeked Waxbill** ☐
855 Cutthroat Finch ☐
856 Redheaded Finch* ☐
861 Shafttailed Whydah* ☐
862 Paradise Whydah ☐
878 Yellow Canary* ☐
884 Goldenbreasted Bunting ☐
886 Rock Bunting ☐
☐
☐

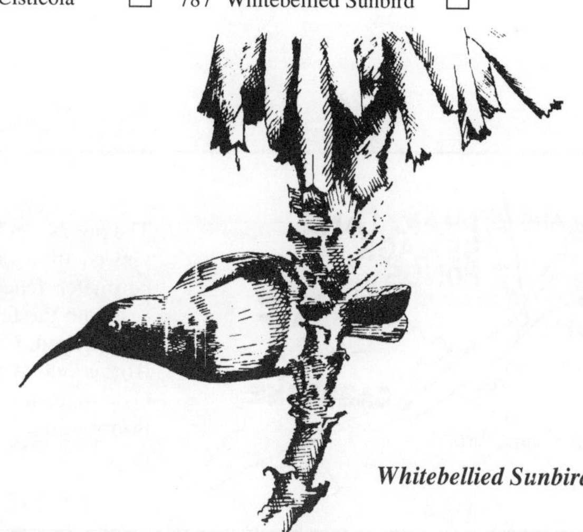

Whitebellied Sunbird

PHAKALANE SEWAGE PONDS

approximately 110 species recorded to date

The newly constructed Phakalane sewage ponds are situated 8 km north of Gaborone. Earth banks and dead trees in the ponds have increased the number of birds attracted to the area.

SPECIAL AND INTERESTING SPECIES

Waterbirds are the main attraction with several thousand birds present during the summer. Ducks are very well represented, **South African Shelduck**, **Hottentot Teal**, **Fulvous**, **Whitebacked** and **Maccoa Ducks** all having been recorded. Waders are also present in large numbers, most noticeable being **Marsh**, **Curlew** and **Wood Sandpipers**, **Little Stint**, **Ruff**, **Greenshank** and **Blackwinged Stilt**. **Avocet** and **Whitefronted Plover** have been seen occasionally. Other species normally present are **African Fish Eagle** and **Blacknecked Grebe**. In the surrounding bush check for **Swallowtailed Bee-eater** and **Buffy Pipit**. The size of the ponds makes a telescope beneficial, although not essential.

ALSO RECORDED

In the first six months since the construction of the new ponds, Blacktailed Godwit, Blackwinged Pratincole and Eastern Redfooted Kestrel have been seen. Additional rare species can be expected now that disturbance here is minimal.

David Bishop

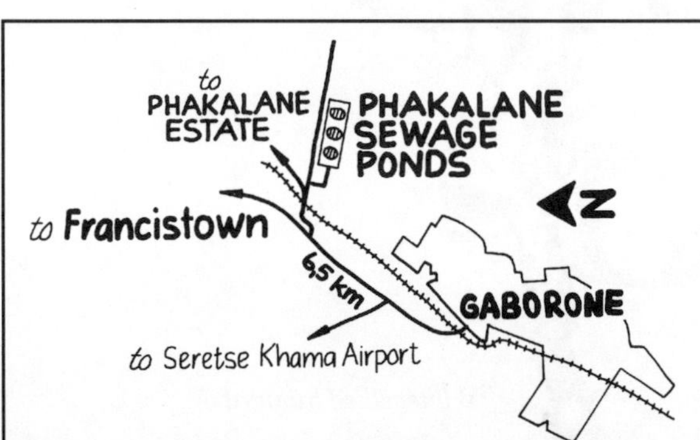

The ponds can be readily viewed from outside the perimeter fence but access into the fenced area is restricted. Contact the Botswana Bird Club, Gaborone, for the latest information.

100% OF SPECIES

007 **Blacknecked Grebe** ☐
008 Dabchick ☐
055 Whitebreasted Cormorant ☐
058 Reed Cormorant ☐
060 Darter ☐
062 Grey Heron ☐
063 Blackheaded Heron ☐
071 Cattle Egret ☐
072 Squacco Heron ☐
074 Greenbacked Heron ☐
085 Abdim's Stork ☐
091 Sacred Ibis ☐
094 Hadeda Ibis ☐
095 African Spoonbill ☐
096 Greater Flamingo ☐
097 Lesser Flamingo ☐
099 Whitefaced Duck ☐
100 **Fulvous Duck** ☐
101 **Whitebacked Duck** ☐
102 Egyptian Goose ☐
103 **South African Shelduck**** ☐
104 Yellowbilled Duck ☐
106 Cape Teal ☐
107 **Hottentot Teal** ☐
108 Redbilled Teal ☐
112 Cape Shoveller* ☐
113 Southern Pochard ☐
115 Knobbilled Duck ☐
116 Spurwinged Goose ☐
117 **Maccoa Duck** ☐
126a Yellowbilled Kite ☐
135 Wahlberg's Eagle ☐
148 **African Fish Eagle** ☐
172 Lanner Falcon ☐
199 Swainson's Francolin* ☐
226 Moorhen ☐
228 Redknobbed Coot ☐
246 **Whitefronted Plover** ☐
248 Kittlitz's Plover ☐
249 Threebanded Plover ☐
255 Crowned Plover ☐
258 Blacksmith Plover ☐
264 Common Sandpiper ☐
266 **Wood Sandpiper** ☐
269 **Marsh Sandpiper** ☐
270 **Greenshank** ☐
272 **Curlew Sandpiper** ☐
274 **Little Stint** ☐
284 **Ruff** ☐
287 Blacktailed Godwit ☐
294 **Avocet** ☐
295 **Blackwinged Stilt** ☐
339 Whitewinged Tern ☐
349 Rock Pigeon ☐
354 Cape Turtle Dove ☐
355 Laughing Dove ☐
356 Namaqua Dove ☐
373 Grey Lourie ☐
386 Diederik Cuckoo ☐
406 Rufouscheeked Nightjar ☐
415 Whiterumped Swift ☐
425 Whitebacked Mousebird** ☐
426 Redfaced Mousebird ☐
435 Brownhooded Kingfisher ☐
440 Bluecheeked Bee-eater ☐
444 Little Bee-eater ☐
445 **Swallowtailed Bee-eater** ☐
451 Hoopoe ☐
459 Southern Yellow-billed Hornbill* ☐
465 Pied Barbet* ☐
498 Sabota Lark* ☐
518 European Swallow ☐
524 Redbreasted Swallow ☐
526 Greater Striped Swallow* ☐
527 Lesser Striped Swallow ☐
530 House Martin ☐
533 Brownthroated Martin ☐
541 Forktailed Drongo ☐
548 Pied Crow ☐
567 Redeyed Bulbul* ☐
613 Whitebrowed Robin ☐
615 Kalahari Robin* ☐
621 Titbabbler* ☐
643 Willow Warbler ☐
651 Longbilled Crombec ☐
664 Fantailed Cisticola ☐
672 Rattling Cisticola ☐
685 Blackchested Prinia* ☐
695 Marico Flycatcher* ☐
701 Chinspot Batis ☐
713 Cape Wagtail ☐
719 **Buffy Pipit** ☐
731 Lesser Grey Shrike ☐
733 Redbacked Shrike ☐
739 Crimsonbreasted Boubou* ☐
743 Threestreaked Tchagra ☐
764 Glossy Starling* ☐
779 Marico Sunbird ☐
787 Whitebellied Sunbird ☐
798 Redbilled Buffalo Weaver ☐
799 Whitebrowed Sparrowweaver ☐
804 Greyheaded Sparrow ☐
806 Scalyfeathered Finch* ☐
814 Masked Weaver ☐
821 Redbilled Quelea ☐
826 Golden Bishop ☐
829 Whitewinged Widow ☐
834 Melba Finch ☐
844 Blue Waxbill ☐
862 Paradise Whydah ☐
☐
☐
☐
☐
☐
☐

KGALE HILL AND SIDING

approximately 250 species recorded to date

Kgale Hill, just south of Gaborone, is a bush-covered koppie with steep sides. Kgale Siding nearby gives access to the Gaborone Dam where a variety of waterbirds can be seen.

SPECIAL AND INTERESTING SPECIES

Typical koppie species can be seen at Kgale Hill, such as **Black Eagle**, **Mocking Chat**, **Natal Francolin** and **Shorttoed Rock Thrush**. **Lazy Cisticola** and **Striped Pipit** have been recorded. Other species to see include **Grey Hornbill**, **Pied Barbet**, **Familiar Chat**, **Kalahari Robin**, **Lesser Grey Shrike**, **Crimsonbreasted Boubou**, **Jameson's Firefinch**, **Shafttailed Whydah** and **Blackthroated Canary**. **Whitebreasted Cormorants** nest at Kgale Siding. **Reed Cormorant**, **Darter**, **Greenbacked Heron**, **Black Egret** and **Burchell's Coucal** are regularly recorded here.

ALSO RECORDED

Ospreys have been seen in recent summers at Kgale Siding.
David Bishop

Little Egrets

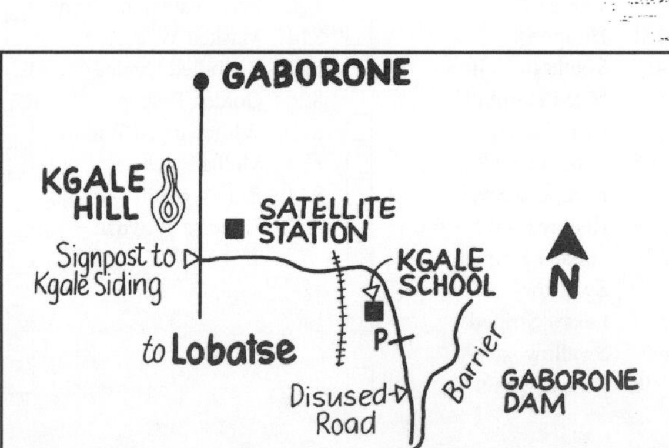

Kgale Hill is adjacent to the Gaborone/Lobatse road and is accessed via a stile. The energetic may want to climb the hill; most birds can, however, be seen by walking around its base. Kgale Siding can be reached by vehicle, from where it is possible to walk the final kilometre on a disused road to the dam.

50% OF SPECIES

055 **Whitebreasted Cormorant** ☐
058 **Reed Cormorant** ☐
060 **Darter** ☐
062 Grey Heron ☐
063 Blackheaded Heron ☐
066 Great White Egret ☐
067 Little Egret ☐
069 **Black Egret** ☐
071 Cattle Egret ☐
074 **Greenbacked Heron** ☐
099 Whitefaced Duck ☐
104 Yellowbilled Duck ☐
106 Cape Teal ☐
108 Redbilled Teal ☐
126a Yellowbilled Kite ☐
131 **Black Eagle** ☐
148 African Fish Eagle ☐
149 Steppe Buzzard ☐
196 **Natal Francolin*** ☐
199 Swainson's Francolin* ☐
213 Black Crake ☐
249 Threebanded Plover ☐
255 Crowned Plover ☐
258 Blacksmith Plover ☐
264 Common Sandpiper ☐
266 Wood Sandpiper ☐
269 Marsh Sandpiper ☐
270 Greenshank ☐
272 Curlew Sandpiper ☐
274 Little Stint ☐
284 Ruff ☐
295 Blackwinged Stilt ☐
339 Whitewinged Tern ☐
349 Rock Pigeon ☐
352 Redeyed Dove ☐
354 Cape Turtle Dove ☐
355 Laughing Dove ☐
356 Namaqua Dove ☐
358 Greenspotted Dove ☐
373 Grey Lourie ☐
382 Jacobin Cuckoo ☐
386 Diederik Cuckoo ☐
391 **Burchell's Coucal** ☐
415 Whiterumped Swift ☐
417 Little Swift ☐
425 Whitebacked Mousebird** ☐
426 Redfaced Mousebird ☐
428 Pied Kingfisher ☐
431 Malachite Kingfisher ☐
435 Brownhooded Kingfisher ☐
440 Bluecheeked Bee-eater ☐
444 Little Bee-eater ☐
457 **Grey Hornbill** ☐
459 Southern Yellowbilled Hornbill* ☐
464 Blackcollared Barbet ☐
465 **Pied Barbet*** ☐
473 Crested Barbet ☐
494 Rufousnaped Lark ☐
498 Sabota Lark* ☐
518 European Swallow ☐
520 Whitethroated Swallow ☐
524 Redbreasted Swallow ☐
526 Greater Striped Swallow* ☐
527 Lesser Striped Swallow ☐
530 House Martin ☐
533 Brownthroated Martin ☐
541 Forktailed Drongo ☐
545 Blackheaded Oriole ☐
548 Pied Crow ☐
560 Arrowmarked Babbler ☐
567 Redeyed Bulbul* ☐
576 Kurrichane Thrush ☐
583 **Shorttoed Rock Thrush*** ☐
589 **Familiar Chat** ☐
593 **Mocking Chat** ☐
602 Whitethroated Robin** ☐
613 Whitebrowed Robin ☐
615 **Kalahari Robin*** ☐
621 Titbabbler* ☐
628 Great Reed Warbler ☐
631 African Marsh Warbler ☐
634 European Sedge Warbler ☐
635 Cape Reed Warbler ☐
643 Willow Warbler ☐
651 Longbilled Crombec ☐
657a Greybacked Bleating Warbler ☐
664 Fantailed Cisticola ☐
672 Rattling Cisticola ☐
679 **Lazy Cisticola** ☐
681 Neddicky ☐
683 Tawnyflanked Prinia ☐
685 Blackchested Prinia* ☐
695 Marico Flycatcher* ☐
701 Chinspot Batis ☐
713 Cape Wagtail ☐
720 **Striped Pipit** ☐
731 **Lesser Grey Shrike** ☐
733 Redbacked Shrike ☐
739 **Crimsonbreasted Boubou*** ☐
740 Puffback ☐
743 Threestreaked Tchagra ☐
761 Plumcoloured Starling ☐
764 Glossy Starling* ☐
769 Redwinged Starling ☐
779 Marico Sunbird ☐
787 Whitebellied Sunbird ☐
796 Cape White-eye** ☐
806 Scalyfeathered Finch* ☐
814 Masked Weaver ☐
821 Redbilled Quelea ☐
824 Red Bishop ☐
829 Whitewinged Widow ☐
834 Melba Finch ☐
841 **Jameson's Firefinch** ☐
842 Redbilled Firefinch ☐
844 Blue Waxbill ☐
846 Common Waxbill ☐
847 Blackcheeked Waxbill ☐
860 Pintailed Whydah ☐
861 **Shafttailed Whydah*** ☐
862 Paradise Whydah ☐
867 Steelblue Widowfinch ☐
869 Yelloweyed Canary ☐
870 **Blackthroated Canary** ☐
884 Goldenbreasted Bunting ☐
886 Rock Bunting ☐

OTSE

approximately 320 species recorded to date

The Otse area has a number of ancient red sandstone hills, patches of tall woodland, two large dams and pockets of Kalahari sandveld. A cliff on the south-west face of Mannyelenong Hill supports the largest Cape Vulture nesting site in Botswana. There are no restrictions on camping in the area, although birders camping within sight of worked farmlands or villages should explain themselves to the nearby occupants. No accommodation is available in the immediate area. Four localities are included (three on the map) but the area is sparsely populated, and any of the tracks shown will provide a good starting point for birders.

SPECIAL AND INTERESTING SPECIES

Mannyelonong Hill. About 30 pairs of **Cape Vultures** breed on the hill in winter. On the large boulders at the base of the cliff look for **Shorttoed Rock Thrush** and in the kloofs for **Barthroated Apalis**. Other Botswana specials here include

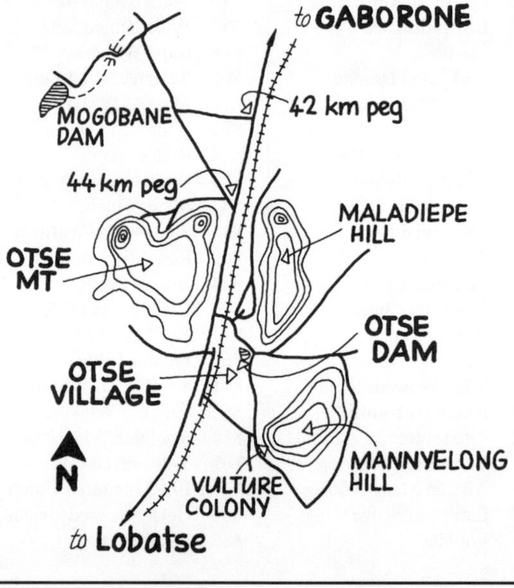

Otse village is 50 km south of Gaborone on the Gaborone-Lobatse road. Kilometre pegs referred to are distances south of Gabarone.

1. ***Mannyelenong Hill/ Game Reserve.*** There are two access roads: either take the northern entrance into Otse (signposted both "Otse" and "Moeding College"), take the right fork after crossing the railway line, continue through the village, passing the dam on your right. Turn right immediately after the dam, crossing a causeway below the dam wall, then turn left as soon as you come off the causeway. The track skirts the village; take the left fork which goes south-east across the plain towards the hill. At the fork is a Department of Wildlife camp. A small entrance fee is charged. For the second approach, take the southern entrance into Otse (signposted "Otse"), turn right at the T-junction, follow the road beside the railway line for 1 km, then turn left and cross the line at the first crossing, take the right fork and follow the main track through the village and across the plain to the hill. The vultures nest on the south-west cliff face. There is a network of tracks in the area, nearly all passable in a saloon

Mocking Chat, **Whitethroated Robin**, **Ovambo Sparrowhawk**, **Booted Eagle** and **White Helmetshrike**.

Otse Mountain. Birds of prey include **Black** and **Booted Eagles**, **Gymnogene** and **Little Sparrowhawk**. Cuckoos that may be seen are **Klaas's**, **Redchested** and **Black**. Look for **Barthroated Apalis**, **Greyheaded Bush Shrike**, **Pearlspotted Owl** and **Spotted Eagle Owl**. This is a good place to see all four species of barbet that occur in Botswana: **Pied**, **Crested**, **Blackcollared** and **Yellowfronted Tinker Barbet**. **Lanner Falcon** and **Black Stork** breed at the manganese pit in winter, where **Rock Martin** and **Mocking Chat** may also be found. The track leading up to the kloof can yield good sightings of all six Botswana francolins, and **Coqui**, **Crested**, **Natal** and **Swainson's** are not difficult to find.

Mogobane reedbeds can produce **Little Bittern** and **Blackcrowned Night Heron**, **Black Crake** and **Great Reed Warbler**. In the surrounding grasslands **Blackcheeked Waxbills** and **Whitewinged Widows** can be found. Around *Mogobane Dam* **Marsh Owl**, **Goliath** and **Blackheaded Herons**, **Lesser** and **Greater Flamingos**, **Hottentot Teal**, **Maccoa Duck**, **Great Crested Grebe** and **Kittlitz's Plover** can be seen. **Blackwinged Pratincoles** sometimes frequent the sandpits. Rare waders that have been recorded include **Knot** and **Sanderling**. Both **Whitequilled** and **Redcrested Korhaans** occur on the grassland to the west. In Botswana this is one of the best places to see **Orangebreasted Waxbill**. The cattle coming in to drink are sometimes accompanied by **Redbilled Oxpeckers**. **Shortclawed Larks** can be found in the grassland to the west of the dam. The extensive mud flats and shallow water attract waders, ducks and geese in large numbers, some of which breed on the islands.

Nnywane Dam. The woodland below the dam wall is good for **Pearlspotted** and **Barn Owls**. **Bat Hawk**, **Giant Kingfisher** and **African Black Duck** can be found along the secluded river below the dam wall, while **African Hawk Eagles** are recorded in the surrounding hills. **South African Shelduck** is found on the dam. The surrouding woodland has **Black Cuckooshrike**, **Cape Penduline Tit**, **Burntnecked** and **Yellowbellied Eremomelas**, **Fairy Flycatcher** (mainly in winter), **Barred Warbler** and **Yellow Canary**.

Stephen Spawls

car. If you go anticlockwise around the hill and keep turning left, you will get back to Otse village. Tracks leading southwest from the hill pass some small pans.

2. ***Otse Mountain.*** Take the track leading northwest off the tar road, at the 44 km peg. This track is only suitable for fourwheel drive or high-clearance vehicles. Approximately 250 m along this track take the small track on the left; it leads up into a magnificent kloof. The track forks after approximately 2,2 km from the turnoff; turn left and drive a further 200 m up into the kloof. This is an excellent camping spot, with big, shady trees along a watercourse. The right fork is impassable to vehicles, but crosses the watercourse and continues along the shoulder of the mountain to an abandoned manganese pit.

3. ***Mogobane Dam and reedbeds.*** Take the Mogobane/Ranaka road (signposted 42 km south of Gaborone). The road drops down the escarpment and crosses the plain, enters a settlement and swings left. Take the right fork past a dairy, then proceed right across a causeway. The reedbeds are on the right at the causeway and a small track goes off to the right, following the river. The

65% OF SPECIES

006 **Great Crested Grebe** ☐
008 Dabchick ☐
055 Whitebreasted Cormorant ☐
058 Reed Cormorant ☐
062 Grey Heron ☐
063 **Blackheaded Heron** ☐
064 **Goliath Heron** ☐
066 Great White Egret ☐
071 Cattle Egret ☐
076 **Blackcrowned Night Heron** ☐
078 **Little Bittern** ☐
081 Hamerkop ☐
083 White Stork ☐
084 **Black Stork** ☐
094 Hadeda Ibis ☐
095 African Spoonbill ☐
096 **Greater Flamingo** ☐
097 **Lesser Flamingo** ☐
099 Whitefaced Duck ☐
102 Egyptian Goose ☐
103 **South African Shelduck**** ☐
104 Yellowbilled Duck ☐
105 **African Black Duck** ☐
107 **Hottentot Teal** ☐
108 Redbilled Teal ☐
115 Knobbilled Duck ☐
116 Spurwinged Goose ☐
117 **Maccoa Duck** ☐
122 **Cape Vulture**** ☐
123 Whitebacked Vulture ☐
126a Yellowbilled Kite ☐
129 **Bat Hawk** ☐
131 **Black Eagle** ☐
136 **Booted Eagle** ☐
137 **African Hawk Eagle** ☐
143 Blackbreasted Snake Eagle ☐
149 Steppe Buzzard ☐
156 **Ovambo Sparrowhawk** ☐
157 **Little Sparrowhawk** ☐
159 Little Banded Goshawk ☐
161 Gabar Goshawk ☐
169 **Gymnogene** ☐
172 **Lanner Falcon** ☐
181 Rock Kestrel ☐
188 **Coqui Francolin** ☐
189 **Crested Francolin** ☐
196 **Natal Francolin*** ☐
199 **Swainson's Francolin*** ☐
205 Kurrichane Buttonquail ☐
213 **Black Crake** ☐
228 Redknobbed Coot ☐
237 **Redcrested Korhaan*** ☐
239a **Whitequilled Korhaan**** ☐
245 Ringed Plover ☐
248 **Kittlitz's Plover** ☐
249 Threebanded Plover ☐
255 Crowned Plover ☐
258 Blacksmith Plover ☐
264 Common Sandpiper ☐
266 Wood Sandpiper ☐
270 Greenshank ☐
271 **Knot** ☐
274 Little Stint ☐
281 **Sanderling** ☐
284 Ruff ☐
294 Avocet ☐
295 Blackwinged Stilt ☐
297 Spotted Dikkop ☐
305 **Blackwinged Pratincole** ☐
339 Whitewinged Tern ☐
349 Rock Pigeon ☐
352 Redeyed Dove ☐
354 Cape Turtle Dove ☐
355 Laughing Dove ☐
356 Namaqua Dove ☐
358 Greenspotted Dove ☐
361 Green Pigeon ☐

main road continues up slope and forks right; Mogobane Dam is on the left. Just past the dam, a small track goes off to the left along the north-west shore of the dam, an excellent birding spot.

*4. **Nnywane Dam.*** Take the turning signposted "Water Utilities Corporation: Lobatse Water Supply. Nnywane Dam and Purification Works", just before the 57 km peg. The track leads past the purification plant. Immediately beyond the plant take the left fork. The road follows the side of the narrow valley up to the dam.

364 Meyer's Parrot ☐
373 Grey Lourie ☐
377 **Redchested Cuckoo** ☐
378 **Black Cuckoo** ☐
381 Striped Cuckoo ☐
382 Jacobin Cuckoo ☐
385 **Klaas's Cuckoo** ☐
386 Diederik Cuckoo ☐
392 **Barn Owl** ☐
395 **Marsh Owl** ☐
398 **Pearlspotted Owl** ☐
401 **Spotted Eagle Owl** ☐
408 Freckled Nightjar ☐
411 European Swift ☐
415 Whiterumped Swift ☐
417 Little Swift ☐
426 Redfaced Mousebird ☐
429 **Giant Kingfisher** ☐
433 Woodland Kingfisher ☐
435 Brownhooded Kingfisher ☐

437 Striped Kingfisher ☐
438 European Bee-eater ☐
440 Bluecheeked Bee-eater ☐
444 Little Bee-eater ☐
447 Lilacbreasted Roller ☐
449 Purple Roller ☐
451 Hoopoe ☐
452 Redbilled Woodhoopoe ☐
457 Grey Hornbill ☐
458 Redbilled Hornbill ☐
459 Southern Yellowbilled Hornbill* ☐
464 **Blackcollared Barbet** ☐
465 **Pied Barbet*** ☐
470 **Yellowfronted Tinker Barbet** ☐
473 **Crested Barbet** ☐
474 Greater Honeyguide ☐
486 Cardinal Woodpecker ☐
494 Rufousnaped Lark ☐
497 Fawncoloured Lark ☐
498 Sabota Lark* ☐
501 **Shortclawed Lark**** ☐
515 Chestnutbacked Finchlark ☐
518 European Swallow ☐
524 Redbreasted Swallow ☐
526 Greater Striped Swallow* ☐
527 Lesser Striped Swallow ☐
529 **Rock Martin** ☐
534 Banded Martin ☐
538 **Black Cuckooshrike** ☐
541 Forktailed Drongo ☐
545 Blackheaded Oriole ☐
548 Pied Crow ☐
554 Southern Black Tit* ☐
557 **Cape Penduline Tit*** ☐
560 Arrowmarked Babbler ☐
567 Redeyed Bulbul* ☐
576 Kurrichane Thrush ☐
577 Olive Thrush ☐
580 Groundscraper Thrush ☐
583 **Shorttoed Rock Thrush*** ☐
589 Familiar Chat ☐
593 **Mocking Chat** ☐
596 Stonechat ☐
602 **Whitethroated Robin**** ☐
613 Whitebrowed Robin ☐
615 Kalahari Robin* ☐
621 Titbabbler* ☐
628 **Great Reed Warbler** ☐
635 Cape Reed Warbler ☐
643 Willow Warbler ☐
645 **Barthroated Apalis** ☐
651 Longbilled Crombec ☐
653 **Yellowbellied Eremomela** ☐
656 **Burntnecked Eremomela** ☐
657a Greybacked Bleating Warbler ☐
658 **Barred Warbler*** ☐
664 Fantailed Cisticola ☐
672 Rattling Cisticola ☐
685 Blackchested Prinia* ☐
689 Spotted Flycatcher ☐
695 Marico Flycatcher* ☐
701 Chinspot Batis ☐
706 **Fairy Flycatcher**** ☐
710 Paradise Flycatcher ☐
713 Cape Wagtail ☐
719 Buffy Pipit ☐
731 Lesser Grey Shrike ☐
732 Fiscal Shrike ☐
735 Longtailed Shrike ☐
739 Crimsonbreasted Boubou* ☐
740 Puffback ☐
741 Brubru ☐
743 Threestreaked Tchagra ☐
751 **Greyheaded Bush Shrike** ☐
753 **White Helmetshrike** ☐
756 Whitecrowned Shrike* ☐
761 Plumcoloured Starling ☐
764 Glossy Starling* ☐
769 Redwinged Starling ☐
772 **Redbilled Oxpecker** ☐
779 Marico Sunbird ☐
787 Whitebellied Sunbird ☐
792 Black Sunbird ☐
794 Bluethroated Sunbird ☐
801 House Sparrow ☐
803 Cape Sparrow* ☐
806 Scalyfeathered Finch* ☐
814 Masked Weaver ☐
819 Redheaded Weaver ☐
821 Redbilled Quelea ☐
824 Red Bishop ☐
826 Golden Bishop ☐
829 **Whitewinged Widow** ☐
834 Melba Finch ☐
841 Jameson's Firefinch ☐
844 Blue Waxbill ☐
845 Violeteared Waxbill* ☐
847 **Blackcheeked Waxbill** ☐
854 **Orangebreasted Waxbill** ☐
855 Cutthroat Finch ☐
856 Redheaded Finch* ☐
860 Pintailed Whydah ☐
862 Paradise Whydah ☐
867 Steelblue Widowfinch ☐
869 Yelloweyed Canary ☐
870 Blackthroated Canary ☐
878 **Yellow Canary*** ☐
884 Goldenbreasted Bunting ☐
886 Rock Bunting ☐
☐
☐

OTHER BIRDING SPOTS WORTH VISITING

Ramatlabama/Pitsane/Good Hope
This area in south-eastern Botswana, primarily open grassland, is likely to produce typical grassland species such as Lesser Kestrel, Whitequilled Korhaan and the speciality of the area, Shortclawed Lark. To explore the area west of the Lobatse/Mafikeng road either take the road to Good Hope from Pitsane or the road through Ramatlabama village, which is signposted immediately north of the Bophuthatswana/Botswana border post.

Tsholofelo Sewage Ponds, Gaborone
Arriving from Francistown turn left at the junction marked Tsholofelo shortly after crossing the railway line. Passing the Broadhurst Shopping Mall on your right go straight on to the two circles and turn left at the electrical substation immediately after a sharp right-hand bend. Proceed on the gravel road for about 1 km to the sewage ponds. Drive around the ponds for views of the reedbed in the adjacent Gaborone Game Reserve. Likely species include South African Shelduck, Maccoa Duck, Purple Gallinule, Painted Snipe and Marsh Owl.

Stevensford
The camp is located on the Limpopo River approximately 100 km east of Pelapye close to the South African border post at Martin's Drift. This is a good area for riverine forest species. Contact Stevensford Safaris, PO Box 26, Sherwood Ranch, Botswana.

Nata Lodge
The lodge is situated approximately 190 km north of Francistown on the road to Kasane. Enquire at the lodge for good birding areas nearby. Four-wheel drive guided tours may be possible to the Makgadikgadi Pans. Camping is available. Nata Lodge, Private Bag 10, Francistown.

Gweta Rest Camp
This camp is situated approximately 100 km west of Nata just off the rather rough road to Maun (currently being upgraded). Access is possible to the Makgadikgadi Pans where flamingos, pelicans and grassland species may be seen. Four-wheel drive is recommended. Gweta Rest Camp, PO Box 124, Gweta.

USEFUL TELEPHONE NUMBERS

Botswana Bird Club
PO Box 71, Gaborone

Botswana Society
PO Box 71, Gaborone
(09267) 35-1500

Tourism Division (Ministry of Commerce and Industry)
Private Bag 004, Gaborone
(09267) 35-3024

Department of Wildlife and National Parks
1 Gaborone, PO Box 131
(09267) 37-1405
2 Maun, PO Box 11
(09267) 66-0230
3 Kasane, PO Box 17
(09267) 65-0235

Kalahari Conservation Society
PO Box 859, Gaborone
(09267) 31-4259

4 Transvaal

Co-ordinator John McAllister

1 Messina Nature Reserve
2 Kruger National Park
3 Langjan Nature Reserve
4 Hans Merensky Nature Reserve
5 Woodbush Reserve, Magoebaskloof and Surrounding Area
6 Hans Strijdom Dam Nature Reserve
7 Lapalala Wilderness
8 Eastern Transvaal Escarpment
9 Nyl Floodplain and Surrounding Bushveld
10 Rust de Winter Nature Reserve
11 Dullstroom District
12 Vaalkop Dam Nature Reserve
13 Nelspruit Nature Reserve and Adjoining Trim Park
14 Loskop Dam
15 Pilanesberg National Park
16 Saddleback Pass and Peddlars Bush, Barberton
17 Diepsloot Nature Reserve and Associated Area
18 Carlos Rolfes Bird Sanctuary
19 Leeupan
20 Rondebult Bird Sanctuary
21 Blesbokspruit (Marievale Bird Sanctuary)
22 Suikerbosrand Nature Reserve
23 Barberspan Nature Reserve
24 Potchefstroom
25 Wakkerstroom
26 Far Western Transvaal

MESSINA NATURE RESERVE

approximately 192 species recorded to date

The prime purpose of this 3 700 ha nature reserve, the northernmost reserve under the control of the Chief Directorate: Nature and Environmental Conservation, is to provide protection for the large number of baobab trees *Adansonia digitata* within the confines of the reserve. Although the bird diversity here is not as large as for most other Transvaal localities it does afford birders the opportunity to see some species that are not always easy to find in the rest of the province. The reserve mainly consists of hilly, rocky country dominated by the baobabs, with a variety of corkwood trees *Commiphera spp.,* lowveld cluster-leaf *Sesamothamnus lugardii* and stands of mopane *Colophospermum mopane* also occurring. The riparian vegetation along the Sand River (at 3 852 million years the exposed gneiss in the riverbed is one of the oldest dated rocks in the world) is dominated by tall umbrella thorns *Acacia tortilis* and apple-leaf *Lonchocarpus capassa.* There is a circular drive through the reserve and a picnic area for visitors. Birders wishing to walk in the reserve should make prior arrangements to do so with the officer in charge. An overnight hiking trail is in the planning stages, but there are no facilities for visitors to overnight in the reserve at present. There is, however, a hotel and a municipal caravan park in the town of Messina, a mere 4 km away, and there is an Overvaal Resort at Tshipise, 40 km away.

The reserve entrance is 4 km south of the town of Messina on the N1 from Pretoria.

SPECIAL AND INTERESTING SPECIES

The reserve is one of the easiest places in the Transvaal to see **Meyer's Parrots** which are often heard before they are seen in the taller trees, particularly near the Sand River. **Whitebreasted Cuckooshrike**, **African Golden Oriole**, **Brubru**, **Crested Guineafowl** and **Scimitarbilled Woodhoopoe** are found in this habitat, although the cuckooshrike may be found where there are large mopane trees as well. **Crested Francolin** occur throughout the reserve, but **Natal Francolin** should be looked for in areas where there is a dense woody cover with little or no grass. **Kori Bustard**, **Spotted Dikkop**, **Bronzewinged Courser** (late summer and winter) and **Redcrested Korhaan** generally occur in the more open or scrubby areas. **Doublebanded Sandgrouse** may be flushed by the lucky birder from the stony hillsides or mopane stands, but are easier to find by patiently waiting at dusk (please get permission from the officer in charge to be in the reserve this late) beside one of the small earth dams. **Southern Black Tit**, **White** and **Redbilled Helmetshrikes**, **Whitecrowned Shrike**, **Redbilled Buffalo Weaver**, **Redheaded Weaver** and **European** (summer), **Lilacbreasted** and **Purple Rollers** can all be found in the deciduous woodland. The skies should be scanned for **Black Eagle**, **Wahlberg's Eagle** (from late August to March), **Brown** and **Blackbreasted Snake Eagles**, **Gymnogene** and **Bateleur**.

John McAllister

42% OF SPECIES

071 Cattle Egret ☐
126a Yellowbilled Kite ☐
127 Blackshouldered Kite ☐
131 **Black Eagle** ☐
135 **Wahlberg's Eagle** ☐
142 **Brown Snake Eagle** ☐
143 **Blackbreasted Snake Eagle** ☐
146 **Bateleur** ☐
163 Dark Chanting Goshawk ☐
169 **Gymnogene** ☐
189 **Crested Francolin** ☐
196 **Natal Francolin*** ☐
203 Helmeted Guineafowl ☐
204 **Crested Guineafowl** ☐
230 **Kori Bustard** ☐
237 **Redcrested Korhaan*** ☐
297 **Spotted Dikkop** ☐
303 **Bronzewinged Courser** ☐
347 **Doublebanded Sandgrouse*** ☐
354 Cape Turtle Dove ☐
355 Laughing Dove ☐
356 Namaqua Dove ☐
358 Greenspotted Dove ☐
364 **Meyer's Parrot** ☐
373 Grey Lourie ☐
375 African Cuckoo ☐
381 Striped Cuckoo ☐
382 Jacobin Cuckoo ☐
385 Klaas's Cuckoo ☐
398 Pearlspotted Owl ☐
401 Spotted Eagle Owl ☐
405 Fierynecked Nightjar ☐
417 Little Swift ☐
421 Palm Swift ☐
424 Speckled Mousebird ☐
426 Redfaced Mousebird ☐
433 Woodland Kingfisher ☐
435 Brownhooded Kingfisher ☐
438 European Bee-eater ☐
441 Carmine Bee-eater ☐
444 Little Bee-eater ☐
445 Swallowtailed Bee-eater ☐
446 **European Roller** ☐
447 **Lilacbreasted Roller** ☐

449 **Purple Roller** ☐
451 Hoopoe ☐
452 Redbilled Woodhoopoe ☐
454 **Scimitarbilled Woodhoopoe** ☐
457 Grey Hornbill ☐
458 Redbilled Hornbill ☐
459 Southern Yellowbilled Hornbill* ☐
498 Sabota Lark* ☐
518 European Swallow ☐
527 Lesser Striped Swallow ☐
539 **Whitebreasted Cuckooshrike** ☐
541 Forktailed Drongo ☐
544 **African Golden Oriole** ☐
548 Pied Crow ☐
554 **Southern Black Tit*** ☐
560 Arrowmarked Babbler ☐
568 Blackeyed Bulbul ☐
580 Groundscraper Thrush ☐
589 Familiar Chat ☐
672 Rattling Cisticola ☐
689 Spotted Flycatcher ☐
695 Marico Flycatcher* ☐
701 Chinspot Batis ☐
710 Paradise Flycatcher ☐
733 Redbacked Shrike ☐
739 Crimsonbreasted Boubou* ☐
740 Puffback ☐
741 **Brubru** ☐
743 Threestreaked Tchagra ☐
744 Blackcrowned Tchagra ☐
753 **White Helmetshrike** ☐
754 **Redbilled Helmetshrike** ☐
756 **Whitecrowned Shrike*** ☐
761 Plumcoloured Starling ☐
787 Whitebellied Sunbird ☐
798 **Redbilled Buffalo Weaver** ☐
814 Masked Weaver ☐
819 **Redheaded Weaver** ☐
844 Blue Waxbill ☐
845 Violeteared Waxbill* ☐
862 Paradise Whydah ☐
869 Yelloweyed Canary ☐
884 Goldenbreasted Bunting ☐
886 Rock Bunting ☐

Blackcollared Barbets

KRUGER NATIONAL PARK

approximately 495 species recorded to date

The original proclamation of the Kruger National Park (KNP) occurred in 1903, but not until 1926 was it declared a national park. Since then it has been administered by the National Parks Board. Located in the eastern Transvaal, it covers an area of 1 948 528 ha (19 485 sq km) and consists of a variety of habitats. The eastern half is mainly grassland savanna, while the west is predominantly woodland savanna. North of the Olifants River mopane is the dominant tree species; to the south marula and knob thorn dominate. The major rivers of the KNP traverse it from west to east and they provide varying degrees of development in their riparian vegetation – some are almost gallery forests (e.g. the Sabie and Luvuvhu) while others are more open (e.g. the Olifants and Letaba). Eighty dams have been built on both the permanent and perennial rivers: these attract a variety of waterbird species that has gradually increased with time. A network of tourist roads gives access to most habitats, and six wilderness trails for visitors can be booked through the National Parks Board. These trails offer the enthusiast the best way to see the birds of the KNP. It is suggested that the excellent road map on sale at all gates and rest camps be acquired, as all the roads have serial numbers which of necessity are quoted in this text. It is worth remembering that in December and January the rest camp gates are opened well before dawn and this gives birders the opportunity of seeing some of the night birds which may be impossible to record during the day.

NORTHERN KRUGER NATIONAL PARK

Four main habitats comprise the area accessible from the three northern camps, Punda Maria, Shingwedzi and Mopani, and this region encompasses the area as far south as the Mopani rest camp. Most of the western half of this area is dominated by the mopane or red bushwillow vegetation type on granitic soils. At present the absence of roads into this area restricts access, but as it is not a very good habitat for birds, the bird enthusiast will not miss much. The eastern grassland (on basaltic soils) with mopane shrubveld is worth visiting for its own sake: it has a unique character and this is where most of the game can be seen. To the east and south-east of Punda Maria is an area of mopane forest. The fourth habitat type is the sandveld to the north of Punda Maria, access to which can be gained by the Mahogany Loop or by booking the Nyalaland Trail, which operates in this area. The best birding spot is Pafuri and every attempt should be made to experience this tropical riverine forest. Many birds reach the southern limit of their range here, and can be seen nowhere else south of the Limpopo River. Most of the roads follow the drainage lines and always provide something for the birder.

SPECIAL AND INTERESTING SPECIES

Pafuri offers both **Mottled and Böhm's Spinetails:** they can be recorded fairly easily here. In summer check all baobabs that have attendant "swifts"; at other times scan the skies from the bridge over the Luvuvhu River – this usually reveals spinetails. The Mottled breeds in a baobab in the Nyalaland Trail Camp. Baobabs are also favoured for nesting by **Mosque Swallows**, which are not uncommon in this area. **Whitecrowned Plovers** are common in the riverbed, as are **Goliath Herons** and other members of the heron family, as well as **Great White Egrets**. In the riverine forest (along roads S63 and S64) a host of interesting species are to be found. **Tropical Boubous** are common – difficult to see but often heard. **Crested Guineafowl,** also common, can usually be seen without difficulty. **Cape (Swahili) Parrot** can be located by call (this species occurs to the north and is thought to be different from the parrot of the Cape). **Narina Trogon,**

ALSO RECORDED

The building of dams to provide drinking water for game has resulted in a wide variety of waterbirds turning up occasionally. Pygmy Goose, Hottentot Teal, Glossy Ibis, African Rail, Black Egret, both flamingo and both pelican species could turn up at any of these waters. Peregrine Falcons breed in the Luvuvhu River's gorges and may (with much luck) be seen on the S64. Green Sandpipers appear occasionally: they should be looked for in summer at the quieter pans and pools. In years of good rainfall, African Crake occurs. Caspian Plover has been recorded at Nshawu Dam. At Pafuri Yellowbellied Sunbird has been recorded, as has Thickbilled Cuckoo. Lesser Blue-eared Starling (with characteristic juveniles) has been seen at

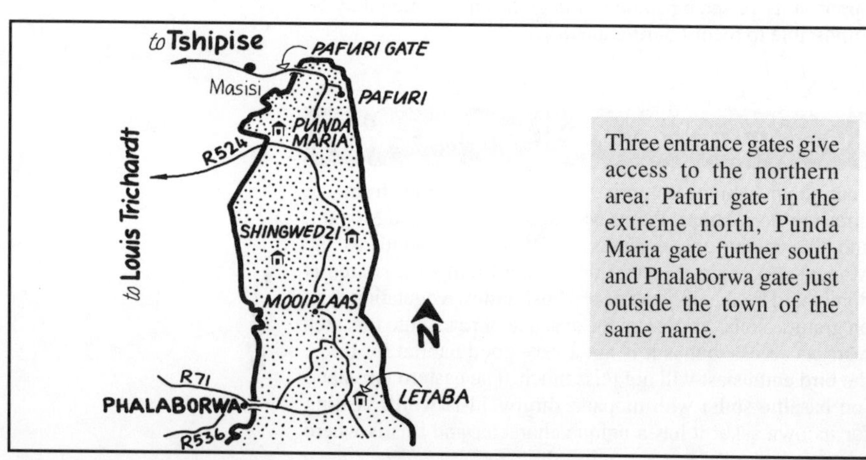

Three entrance gates give access to the northern area: Pafuri gate in the extreme north, Punda Maria gate further south and Phalaborwa gate just outside the town of the same name.

Yellow White-eye and **Wattle-eyed Flycatcher** can often be located at the picnic spot. **Broadbilled Rollers**, quite common in summer, are easily located by their raucous calls. **Longtailed Starling** is common. West of the picnic spot, where the road (S63) bears south away from the river towards the WNLA station, **Lemonbreasted Canaries** breed in summer in the lala palms. All canaries in this area should be carefully examined if you are trying to find this species. **Black** and **Crowned Eagles** occur here, the former mostly to the west along the Nyala Drive (S64), which is fairly mountainous, and the latter in the riverine forest. En route between Pafuri and Punda Maria, check the dead trees in the Klopperfontein area for **Dickinson's Kestrel**. All buffalo (particularly the larger herds) should be carefully scanned for **Yellowbilled Oxpecker**. In Punda Maria **Bearded Robin** and **Paradise Flycatcher** (in summer) can be seen. **Barred Owls** are often heard in the camp at night and with judicious use of a torch a view of one may be obtained. To the east and south-east of Punda Maria on roads S59, S60 and H13-1 **Arnot's Chats** are quite common in the mopane forest. A very early drive round the Mahogany Loop (S99) in summer could produce **Pennantwinged Nightjar**. A new tourist road to the east of Klopperfontein gives access to the grassland where **Ostrich**, **Kori Bustard**, **Dickinson's Kestrel** and **Montagu's** and **Pallid Harriers** may be recorded. In the Shingwedzi area, the Kanniedood Dam is an excellent birding locality. It has many viewing points and a host of waterbirds can always be found, particularly when receding waterlines expose the mud flats. All the large herons occur here, particularly **Goliath** and **Grey**. **Great White Egrets**, **Squacco Herons** and many storks – **Openbilled** and **Yellowbilled** in particular – are found here. Inland waders can be abundant in summer. **Saddlebilled Storks** can usually be found in the riverbeds around Shingwedzi. The low-water bridge at Shingwedzi is always worth a stop and in summer both **Broadbilled Rollers** and **Mosque Swallows** breed here. Shingwedzi rest camp specials are **Bennett's Woodpecker**, **Redheaded Weaver** and plentiful **Greater Blue-eared** and **Glossy Starlings**. Check the **Redheaded Weavers'** nests in the camp as **Cutthroat Finches** breed in them in late summer and early winter, and they roost in these nests at other times. Further south in the Mopani rest camp area is the Pioneer Dam, which promises to be good for waterbirds once the camp has been completed. **Redwinged Pratincoles** breed at the Nshawu Dam and can easily be seen. **Quail Finches** are common in the vicinity of this dam, and this is the only place in the park where **Kittlitz's Plover** regularly occurs.

the police post and WNLA station. The Nyalaland Trail offers the best opportunity to see Pel's Fishing Owl. Rackettailed Rollers are infrequently recorded. At the H13-1 and the H1-7 T-junction, there is a long vlei where Black Coucal and Black-backed Cisticola have been recorded.

Ian Whyte

CENTRAL KRUGER NATIONAL PARK

This includes the areas accessible from the three central rest camps, Letaba, Olifants and Satara, and encompasses the area south of the Mopani rest camp to the Kumana Dam (south of Satara). In the Letaba/Olifants area the habitat types are the same as those further north, but to the south in the western half, the habitat is mainly undulating and dominated by mixed combretum veld, while in the eastern half marula or knob thorn on grassveld dominates. These two vegetation types are separated by a narrow belt of very thick *Acacia welwitschii* on sandy soils – a good habitat for the small leaf-gleaners. The three rest camps each support their own interesting bird communities, and a few hours spent wandering around are usually well rewarded. Two wilderness trails operate in this central area, the Olifants Trail on the Olifants River and the Sweni Trail in the big-game area on the Sweni Spruit between Satara and Nwanedsi.

SPECIAL AND INTERESTING SPECIES

To the north of Letaba, the Mopani rest camp area and the Nshawu Dam are worth visiting (see previous section). On the way north is the Letaba high-water bridge which houses large colonies of **Little Swifts** and bats. At sunrise and sunset the bats attract a wide variety of raptors including **Bat Hawk**, **Gabar Goshawk**, **Hobby Falcon** and even **Wahlberg's Eagle** (summer). Further north is the Kondlanjovo Plain where **Kori Bustard** and **Sabota**, **Redcapped** and **Rufousnaped Larks** are easily seen. The Letaba/Olifants area is very good for water

Easy access is gained to all these camps through the Phalaborwa and Orpen entrance gates.

and river-associated birds. **African Fish Eagles** have become very tame at Letaba and sometimes perch virtually inside the camp. **Brownthroated Martins** nest in the sandbanks in front of the restaurant and elsewhere along both the Letaba and Olifants rivers. **Natal Robins** occur in Letaba camp. **Redbilled Oxpeckers** have colonised the lala palms at the entrance to the restaurant and arrive in scores to roost here at night. **Greyrumped Swallows** have been recorded nesting at Engelhard Dam in holes in the ground and **Horus Swifts** nest in the sandbanks there. **Redwinged Pratincoles** have bred next to the road on the southern side of the dam and in summer can usually be found there with ease. On the exposed sandbars in the dam, **Whitefronted Plover** has become quite common. Check these sandbars with care as they usually have something of interest to offer. On the Olifants River to the south **White-crowned Plovers** are common but they are paradoxically absent from the Letaba, which appears to offer an identical habitat. The lookout point at Olifants is a good spot to spend a few hours. **Saddlebilled Storks** nest below the camp. **Black Storks** nest on the cliffs to the east where the two rivers cut through the Lebombo Mountains and they can often be recorded moving up and down stream. Beware of the **Yellowbilled Kites** around your braaivleis fires as they have become accomplished meat thieves. **Yellowbellied Bulbuls** can be seen in Olifants camp. Satara is the big-game area of the park and as such offers the best opportunities for recording the five vulture species. Any kill will usually have **Hooded** and **Whitebacked Vultures** in attendance while a buffalo or giraffe kill will attract **Whiteheaded**, **Lappetfaced** and **Cape Vultures** over a few days. Specials in Satara camp are **Burchell's Starling** and **Redbilled Buffalo Weaver** while **Black Crakes** occupy and now breed in the water feature near the camp's gate, and can be viewed and photographed at leisure. Over large tracts of the grassland on the eastern side of Satara, dwarf knob thorn occurs and this is the favoured nesting habitat of both **Redbilled Quelea** and **Wattled Starling**. These species nest in large colonies – the starlings sometimes in thousands and the queleas in millions! Both species nest in summer, and if such a colony can be located it will be of absorbing interest. This is particularly so at a quelea colony, as eagles such as the **Tawny**, **Steppe** and **Lesser Spotted** are usually present, as are **Marabou Storks**. Many of the mammal predators are also in attendance and even hyenas take quelea nestlings. The grassland also supports large numbers of **Swainson's Francolin**, **Harlequin Quail** and **Kurrichane Buttonquail**, particularly in very wet summers. Between 10 km and 20 km north of Satara on the tarred road is an extensive

ALSO RECORDED

An Angola Pitta was recently seen at the Letaba bridge on the Phalaborwa/Shingwedzi road (H14). Osprey has been seen on a few occasions on the Letaba and Olifants rivers. Whitebacked and Fulvous Ducks have been recorded at the Nsemane Dam near Satara. At the Sweni Drift near Nwanedsi (S37), Bluecheeked Bee-eaters have been seen. A European Marsh Harrier was seen at the confluence of the Olifants and Timbavati rivers. Yellowbilled Oxpeckers have been reported at a few scattered localities throughout this area, and buffalo herds should be carefully examined. There is a record of a Collared Palm Thrush in the rest camp at Letaba. At the Engelhard Dam, where White and Pinkbacked Pelicans and Greater and Lesser Flamingos regularly turn up but seldom remain for long, Crowned Crane has been recorded. At Nsemane Dam to the west of Satara, Hottentot Teal and Pygmy Geese have been recorded. Both Pel's Fishing Owl and White-backed Night Heron can be seen on the Olifants Trail which operates from Letaba camp.

Ian Whyte

area of grassland where both **Montagu's** and **Pallid Harriers** can be seen. South of Satara is the Kumana Dam, a good locality for storks: both the **Woollynecked** and **Black** are often recorded there.

SOUTHERN KRUGER NATIONAL PARK

This section includes the whole area south of the Kumana Dam, which is accessible from Skukuza, Pretoriuskop, Berg-en-dal, Crocodile Bridge and Lower Sabie rest camps. It includes a few additional habitats to those found further north, but as is the case further north the Lebombo Mountains form the eastern boundary and to the west of these is grassland on basaltic soils. West of this again are the sandy soils that support a very dense shrubveld known as Gomondwane bush. Further west, in the same sequence as further north, are the undulating granitic soils supporting mixed combretum veld, but along the Sabie and Crocodile rivers are broad belts of thorn thickets. The south-western corner of the park is a mountainous area comprised mainly of rocky, grass-covered slopes intersected by heavily wooded kloofs. These mountains are the highest in the park, and together with the high-lying areas to the north of this (around Pretoriuskop), they support the only habitats where "middle-

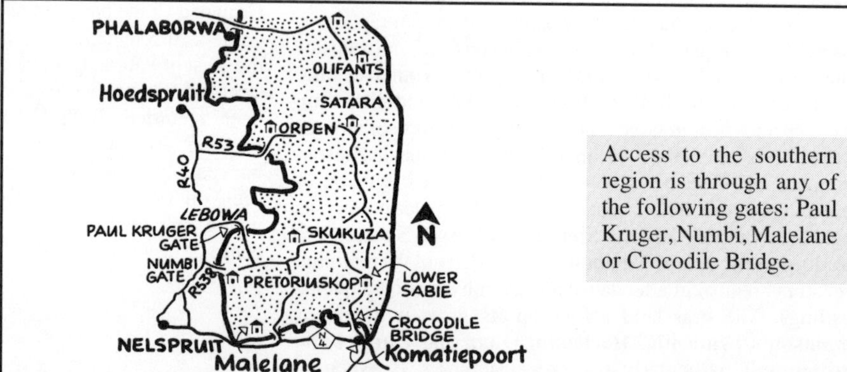

Access to the southern region is through any of the following gates: Paul Kruger, Numbi, Malelane or Crocodile Bridge.

veld" bird species occur in the park. Three wilderness trails operate in this area: the Metsi-metsi Trail is in the Tshokwane area and the Wolhuter and Bushman trails in the mountainous south-west between Pretoriuskop and Malelane. Wilderness trails are probably the best way to go birding in the park.

SPECIAL AND INTERESTING SPECIES

The low-water bridge near Skukuza has proved very good for **African Finfoot**. As these birds seem to be active in the evening, this is a good spot to spend the last few minutes before closing time. **Halfcollared Kingfisher** may also be seen here. Skukuza supports a large population of bats and **Bat Hawks** have quite often been recorded. Skywatching at dusk may prove fruitful. In summer **Hobby Falcons** also hunt bats here and up to six have been seen doing so at one time (care should be taken not to confuse them with Bat Hawks). **Marabou Storks** roost in the trees just outside the camp gates. The camp itself is a good locality for **Scarletchested** and **Marico Sunbirds**, **Purplecrested Lourie**, **Groundscraper** and **Kurrichane Thrushes**, and **Spottedbacked** and **Lesser Masked Weavers**, which nest in large numbers in the fig tree in front of the restaurant. This tree also attracts **Green Pigeons**. **Crowned Hornbills** visit the camp. On the loop to the nursery at Skukuza there is a dam where **Thickbilled Weavers** nest in summer. Check all the river views on the Lower Sabie road (H4-1) for African Finfoot. **African Black Duck** and **Goliath Heron** are quite common. **Violeteared Waxbills** occur in the thorn thickets along this road. **Whitecrowned Plover** may be found in small numbers on the Sabie River between the Nkuhlu picnic spot and the Nwatimhiri causeway on the S79. Lower Sabie has two dams within very close proximity. Just west of the camp is a dam right on the road's edge which attracts a wide variety of waterbirds. **Openbilled Storks** are nearly always present and **Woollynecked** and **Black Storks** can be seen there. Many of the birds visiting this dam have become very tame and it is a good spot for photographers. The camp at Lower Sabie has produced some interesting species.The open plains to the north and south of Lower Sabie are good for grassland species such as **Ostrich**, **Secretarybird**, **Swainson's Francolin**, **Harlequin Quail** and **Kurrichane Buttonquail**. **Shelley's Francolin** can be seen around Nkumbe Mountain on the H10. The tarred road between Lower Sabie and Crocodile Bridge cuts through the thick Gomondwane bush, which is good for small leaf-gleaners such as **Stierling's**

ALSO RECORDED

Black Sawwing Swallow and Purplebanded Sunbird have been recorded along the Crocodile River near Malelane. Grassbird was recorded on high ground in the mountainous south-western corner and Redthroated Wrynecks have been seen at Numbi gate. Crowned Crane and Rufousbellied Heron have turned up at some of the dams in this southern area. Blackcrowned Night Herons breed at Orpen Dam near Tshokwane (the Metsi-metsi Trail has access to these) and Whitebacked Night Herons have been recorded at a number of quiet backwaters throughout the area. Broadtailed Warblers have been recorded in the long-grass area near Pretoriuskop. Pygmy Geese have been recorded at Leeupan (near Tshokwane on the H1-2) and also at Vutome Dam (west of Tshokwane on the S33). The camp at Lower Sabie has produced some interesting species. Both Wattle-eyed Flycatcher and Bluethroated Sunbird (three records) have been seen here, the latter having been photographed as well. To the south of Lower Sabie on the S28 gravel road near Crocodile Bridge, there is an open vlei on the western side of the road where Black Coucal has been recorded.

Ian Whyte

Barred Warbler, **Burntnecked Eremomela** and **Yellowbreasted Apalis. Goldenrumped Tinker Barbet** occurs on the Crocodile River in the Crocodile Bridge area and can be seen in the camp itself. In the mountainous area around Berg-en-dal, **Gorgeous Bush Shrike** and occasionally **Narina Trogon** occur in the well-wooded kloofs, while **Redwinged Starling** and **Mocking Chat** can be seen higher up among the boulders. Pretoriuskop offers some of the middleveld species such as **Yellowfronted Tinker Barbet** and **Black Sunbird**. Gorgeous Bush Shrike can nearly always be heard on the loop road around Shabeni Kop and a pre-dawn drive there in summer may produce **Pennantwinged** and **Freckled Nightjars. Greyhooded Kingfishers** nest at Numbi gate in summer.

57% OF SPECIES

001 **Ostrich** ☐
008 Dabchick ☐
058 Reed Cormorant ☐
060 Darter ☐
062 **Grey Heron** ☐
064 **Goliath Heron** ☐
066 **Great White Egret** ☐
067 Little Egret ☐
072 **Squacco Heron** ☐
074 Greenbacked Heron ☐
076 Blackcrowned Night Heron ☐
081 Hamerkop ☐
084 **Black Stork** ☐
086 **Woollynecked Stork** ☐
087 **Openbilled Stork** ☐
088 **Saddlebilled Stork** ☐
089 **Marabou Stork** ☐
090 **Yellowbilled Stork** ☐
094 Hadeda Ibis ☐
099 Whitefaced Duck ☐
102 Egyptian Goose ☐
105 **African Black Duck** ☐
107 **Hottentot Teal** ☐
115 Knobbilled Duck ☐
118 **Secretarybird** ☐
121 **Hooded Vulture** ☐
122 **Cape Vulture**** ☐
123 **Whitebacked Vulture** ☐
124 **Lappetfaced Vulture** ☐
125 **Whiteheaded Vulture** ☐
126a **Yellowbilled Kite** ☐
129 **Bat Hawk** ☐
131 **Black Eagle** ☐
132 **Tawny Eagle** ☐
133 **Steppe Eagle** ☐
134 **Lesser Spotted Eagle** ☐
135 **Wahlberg's Eagle** ☐
137 African Hawk Eagle ☐
140 Martial Eagle ☐
141 **Crowned Eagle** ☐
142 Brown Snake Eagle ☐
143 Blackbreasted Snake Eagle ☐
146 Bateleur ☐
148 **African Fish Eagle** ☐
154 Lizard Buzzard ☐
157 Little Sparrowhawk ☐
159 Little Banded Goshawk ☐
161 **Gabar Goshawk** ☐
163 Dark Chanting Goshawk ☐
166 **Montagu's Harrier** ☐
167 **Pallid Harrier** ☐
169 Gymnogene ☐
173 **Hobby Falcon** ☐
180 Eastern Redfooted Kestrel ☐
185 **Dickinson's Kestrel** ☐
189 Crested Francolin ☐
191 **Shelley's Francolin** ☐
196 Natal Francolin* ☐
199 **Swainson's Francolin*** ☐
201 **Harlequin Quail** ☐
203 Helmeted Guineafowl ☐
204 **Crested Guineafowl** ☐
205 **Kurrichane Buttonquail** ☐
213 **Black Crake** ☐
229 **African Finfoot** ☐
230 **Kori Bustard** ☐
237 Redcrested Korhaan* ☐
238 Blackbellied Korhaan ☐
240 African Jacana ☐
246 **Whitefronted Plover** ☐
248 **Kittlitz's Plover** ☐
249 Threebanded Plover ☐
255 Crowned Plover ☐
256 **Lesser Blackwinged Plover** ☐

258 Blacksmith Plover
259 **Whitecrowned Plover**
264 Common Sandpiper
266 Wood Sandpiper
270 Greenshank
274 Little Stint
284 Ruff
295 Blackwinged Stilt
297 Spotted Dikkop
298 Water Dikkop
300 Temminck's Courser
304 **Redwinged Pratincole**
339 Whitewinged Tern
347 Doublebanded Sandgrouse*
352 Redeyed Dove
353 **Mourning Dove**
354 Cape Turtle Dove
355 Laughing Dove
356 Namaqua Dove
358 Greenspotted Dove
361 **Green Pigeon**
362 **Cape Parrot**
363 Brownheaded Parrot
371 **Purplecrested Lourie**
373 Grey Lourie
375 African Cuckoo
377 Redchested Cuckoo
380 Great Spotted Cuckoo
381 Striped Cuckoo
382 Jacobin Cuckoo
385 Klaas's Cuckoo
386 Diederik Cuckoo
391 Burchell's Coucal*
396 Scops Owl
398 Pearlspotted Owl
399 **Barred Owl**
402 Giant Eagle Owl
405 Fierynecked Nightjar
408 **Freckled Nightjar**
409 Mozambique Nightjar
410 **Pennantwinged Nightjar**
415 Whiterumped Swift
416 **Horus Swift**
417 **Little Swift**
421 Palm Swift
422 **Mottled Spinetail**
423 **Böhm's Spinetail**
424 Speckled Mousebird
426 Redfaced Mousebird
427 **Narina Trogon**
428 Pied Kingfisher
429 Giant Kingfisher
430 **Halfcollared Kingfisher**
431 Malachite Kingfisher
433 Woodland Kingfisher
435 Brownhooded Kingfisher
436 **Greyhooded Kingfisher**
437 Striped Kingfisher
438 European Bee-eater
441 Carmine Bee-eater
443 Whitefronted Bee-eater
444 Little Bee-eater
446 European Roller
447 Lilacbreasted Roller
449 Purple Roller
450 **Broadbilled Roller**
451 Hoopoe
452 Redbilled Woodhoopoe
454 Scimitarbilled Woodhoopoe*
455 Trumpeter Hornbill
457 Grey Hornbill
458 Redbilled Hornbill
459 Southern Yellowbilled Hornbill*
460 **Crowned Hornbill**
463 Ground Hornbill
464 Blackcollared Barbet
470 **Yellowfronted Tinker Barbet**
471 **Goldenrumped Tinker Barbet**
473 Crested Barbet
474 Greater Honeyguide
481 **Bennett's Woodpecker**
483 Goldentailed Woodpecker
486 Cardinal Woodpecker
487 Bearded Woodpecker
493 Monotonous Lark*
494 **Rufousnaped Lark**
496 Flappet Lark
498 **Sabota Lark***
507 **Redcapped Lark**
515 Chestnutbacked Finchlark
518 European Swallow
522 Wiretailed Swallow
524 **Redbreasted Swallow**
525 **Mosque Swallow**
527 Lesser Striped Swallow
531 **Greyrumped Swallow**
533 **Brownthroated Martin**
538 Black Cuckooshrike
541 Forktailed Drongo
545 Blackheaded Oriole
554 Southern Black Tit*
560 Arrowmarked Babbler
568 Blackeyed Bulbul
569 Terrestrial Bulbul
572 Sombre Bulbul
574 **Yellowbellied Bulbul**
575 **Yellowspotted Nicator**
576 **Kurrichane Thrush**
580 **Groundscraper Thrush**
593 **Mocking Chat**

594 **Arnot's Chat** ☐
599 Heuglin's Robin ☐
600 **Natal Robin** ☐
602 Whitethroated Robin** ☐
613 Whitebrowed Robin ☐
617 **Bearded Robin** ☐
635 Cape Reed Warbler ☐
638 African Sedge Warbler ☐
643 Willow Warbler ☐
648 **Yellowbreasted Apalis** ☐
651 Longbilled Crombec ☐
655 Greencapped Eremomela ☐
656 **Burntnecked Eremomela** ☐
657 Bleating Warbler ☐
657a Greybacked Bleating Warbler ☐
659 **Stierling's Barred Warbler** ☐
664 Fantailed Cisticola ☐
665 Desert Cisticola ☐
672 Rattling Cisticola ☐
674 Redfaced Cisticola ☐
683 Tawnyflanked Prinia ☐
689 Spotted Flycatcher ☐
690 Dusky Flycatcher ☐
691 Bluegrey Flycatcher ☐
693 Fantailed Flycatcher ☐
694 Black Flycatcher ☐
696 Mousecoloured Flycatcher ☐
701 Chinspot Batis ☐
705 **Wattle-eyed Flycatcher** ☐
710 **Paradise Flycatcher** ☐
711 African Pied Wagtail ☐
713 Cape Wagtail ☐
716 Grassveld Pipit ☐
728 Yellowthroated Longclaw ☐
731 Lesser Grey Shrike ☐
733 Redbacked Shrike ☐
735 Longtailed Shrike ☐
736 Southern Boubou** ☐
737 **Tropical Boubou** ☐
740 Puffback ☐
741 Brubru ☐
743 Threestreaked Tchagra ☐
744 Blackcrowned Tchagra ☐
747 **Gorgeous Bush Shrike** ☐
748 Orangebreasted Bush Shrike ☐
751 Greyheaded Bush Shrike ☐
753 White Helmetshrike ☐
754 Redbilled Helmetshrike ☐
756 Whitecrowned Shrike* ☐
760 **Wattled Starling** ☐
761 Plumcoloured Starling ☐
762 **Burchell's Starling*** ☐
763 **Longtailed Starling*** ☐
764 **Glossy Starling*** ☐
765 **Greater Blue-eared Starling** ☐
769 **Redwinged Starling** ☐
771 **Yellowbilled Oxpecker** ☐
772 **Redbilled Oxpecker** ☐
779 **Marico Sunbird** ☐
787 Whitebellied Sunbird ☐
791 **Scarletchested Sunbird** ☐
792 **Black Sunbird** ☐
793 **Collared Sunbird** ☐
796 Cape White-eye** ☐
797 **Yellow White-eye** ☐
798 **Redbilled Buffalo Weaver** ☐
801 House Sparrow ☐
804 Greyheaded Sparrow ☐
805 Yellowthroated Sparrow ☐
807 **Thickbilled Weaver** ☐
810 Spectacled Weaver ☐
811 **Spottedbacked Weaver** ☐
814 Masked Weaver ☐
815 **Lesser Masked Weaver** ☐
819 **Redheaded Weaver** ☐
821 **Redbilled Quelea** ☐
824 Red Bishop ☐
829 Whitewinged Widow ☐
834 Melba Finch ☐
840 Bluebilled Firefinch ☐
841 Jameson's Firefinch ☐
842 Redbilled Firefinch ☐
844 Blue Waxbill ☐
845 **Violeteared Waxbill*** ☐
846 Common Waxbill ☐
852 **Quail Finch** ☐
855 **Cutthroat Finch** ☐
857 Bronze Mannikin ☐
860 Pintailed Whydah ☐
861 Shafttailed Whydah* ☐
862 Paradise Whydah ☐
867 Steelblue Widowfinch ☐
869 Yelloweyed Canary ☐
871 **Lemonbreasted Canary*** ☐
881 Streakyheaded Canary ☐
884 Goldenbreasted Bunting ☐
886 Rock Bunting ☐

LANGJAN NATURE RESERVE

approximately 263 species recorded to date

Langjan Nature Reserve is under the control of the Chief Directorate: Nature and Environmental Conservation, and is situated in the arid, sweet bushveld north-west of the Soutpansberg range approximately 120 km north of Pietersburg. To the west of the Brak River the vegetation consists of scrub bushveld on shallow, hard calcerous soil dominated by wild raisin bush *Grewia spp.*, shepherd's tree *Boscia albitrunca*, lowveld cluster-leaf *Terminalia prunioides* and sickle bush *Dichrostachys cinerea*, with scattered marula *Sclerocarya birrea* and patches of corkwood trees *Commiphera spp.* here and there. East of the river (normally dry) the vegetation is dominated by large trees such as knob thorn *Acacia nigrescens*, camel thorn *A. erioloba*, silver cluster-leaf *Terminalia sericea* and tamboti *Spirostachys africana* on deep Kalahari sand. Along the Brak River the riparian bush is dominated by sweet thorn *Acacia karoo* and wild date palm *Phoenix reclinata*. The looming bulk of the Blouberg massif to the south-west and the Soutpansberg range to the south-east overlook the scenery. A network of roads and tracks criss-crosses the reserve (a detailed map is available at the office), but visitors should enquire which of these are negotiable by two-wheel drive vehicle at the time of their visit. Accommodation is available on the reserve in prefabricated huts and there is a hotel in Alldays, about 20 km away.

ALSO RECORDED

The Egyptian Vulture (thought to be extinct in South Africa) that turned up here in January 1989 served, like the Golden Pipit at Rust der Winter, to make Langjan a household name among twitchers in the country. Olivetree Warbler has been recorded in the Acacia scrub and Tropical Boubou has been found (and may be an overlooked resident) in the riparian woodland along the banks of the Brak River.

John McAllister

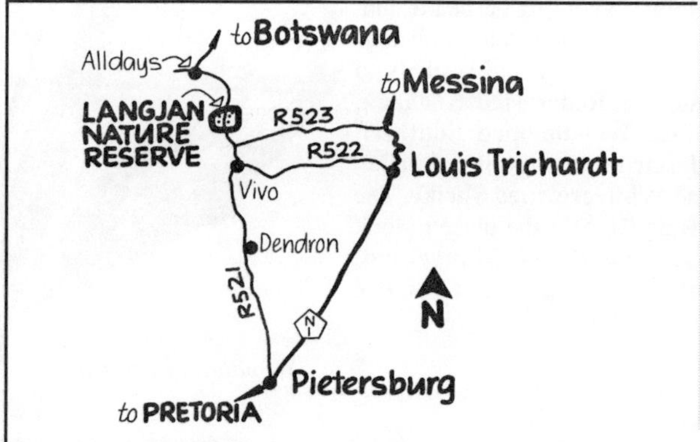

The reserve is not generally open to the public but, provided visits are arranged in advance, birders and other interested parties are welcome. Leave Pietersburg on the R521 to Alldays and the Botswana border. The reserve entrance (signposted) is on the left about 20 km beyond the grain silos and the junction with the R522 from Louis Trichardt at Vivo (103 km from Pietersburg). Please report to the reserve office on arrival.

SPECIAL AND INTERESTING SPECIES

On arrival at the office one of the first species that can be seen is **Pied Barbet**, and **Whitefaced Owl** often roosts in the trees here. Specials in the scrub bushveld include **Pale Chanting Goshawk** (examine the birds' rumps carefully as Dark Chanting Goshawk also occurs here from time to time), **Kori Bustard** (as many as 20 of these birds are sometimes seen in loose groups), **Namaqua Dove**, **Sabota Lark**, **Carmine Bee-eater** (summer), **Swallowtailed Bee-eater** (summer), **Blackchested Prinia**, **Marico Flycatcher**, **Scalyfeathered Finch**, **Melba Finch**, **Blue Waxbill**, **Violeteared Waxbill**, **Blackcheeked Waxbill**, **Shafttailed Whydah**, **Wattled Starling**, **Great Sparrow** and **Kalahari Robin**. **Lesser Grey Shrike** is also best looked for here during summer, especially if there had been good rains. The bare patches of ground provide ideal habitat for the nomadic **Temminck's Courser**, while **Bronzewinged Courser** visits these areas between July and December, and **Dusky Lark** is a regular summer visitor. Wherever there are large trees **Whitebrowed Sparrowweavers** and **Redbilled Buffalo Weavers** are likely to be found. The skies should always be scanned for **Wahlberg's Eagle** (summer), **Cape Vulture** (there is a large breeding colony on the cliffs of the nearby Blouberg), **Brown** and **Blackbreasted Snake Eagles** and **Bateleur**. Heavy downpours occasionally occur during summer. After these storms there are massive hatchings of termite alates and then the skies are often filled with hawking **Yellowbilled Kites**, **Steppe Eagles**, **European** and **Lilacbreasted Rollers**, **Forktailed Drongos** and **European Bee-eaters**. Hundreds of **White Storks** can be seen riding the thermals. A patient (and quiet) dusk wait at one of the many waterholes is likely to yield **Doublebanded Sandgrouse**. **Pearlspotted Owl** and **Fierynecked Nightjar** are almost bound to be heard and, with the aid of a spotlight, seen on the way back to camp after such a wait. The tall woodland in the sandveld is likely to reward birders with species such as **Redcrested Korhaan**, **Jacobin Cuckoo**, **Scimitarbilled Woodhoopoe**, **Southern Yellowbilled Hornbill**, **Pied Barbet**, **Longtailed Shrike**, **Crimsonbreasted Boubou** and **Whitecrowned Shrike**. The riparian woodland along the Brak River is the place to look for **Greenspotted Dove** and **Speckled Mousebird**. **Whitebrowed Robin**, **Titbabbler**, **Longbilled Crombec** and **Barred Warbler** can turn up almost anywhere.

Woodland Kingfisher

43% OF SPECIES

001 Ostrich ☐
062 Grey Heron ☐
071 Cattle Egret ☐
081 Hamerkop ☐
083 White Stork ☐
085 Abdim's Stork ☐
089 Marabou Stork ☐
094 Hadeda Ibis ☐
118 Secretarybird ☐
122 **Cape Vulture**** ☐
126a **Yellowbilled Kite** ☐
127 Blackshouldered Kite ☐
132 Tawny Eagle ☐
133 **Steppe Eagle** ☐
135 **Wahlberg's Eagle** ☐
142 **Brown Snake Eagle** ☐
143 **Blackbreasted Snake Eagle** ☐
146 **Bateleur** ☐
149 Steppe Buzzard ☐
159 Little Banded Goshawk ☐
161 Gabar Goshawk ☐
162 **Pale Chanting Goshawk*** ☐
169 Gymnogene ☐
189 Crested Francolin ☐
196 Natal Francolin* ☐
199 Swainson's Francolin* ☐
203 Helmeted Guineafowl ☐
230 **Kori Bustard** ☐
237 **Redcrested Korhaan*** ☐
255 Crowned Plover ☐
264 Common Sandpiper ☐
270 Greenshank ☐
297 Spotted Dikkop ☐
300 **Temminck's Courser** ☐
303 **Bronzewinged Courser** ☐
347 **Doublebanded Sandgrouse*** ☐
354 Cape Turtle Dove ☐
355 Laughing Dove ☐
356 **Namaqua Dove** ☐
358 **Greenspotted Dove** ☐
373 Grey Lourie ☐
378 Black Cuckoo ☐
382 **Jacobin Cuckoo** ☐
385 Klaas's Cuckoo ☐
386 Diederik Cuckoo ☐
391 **Burchell's Coucal*** ☐
392 Barn Owl ☐
397 **Whitefaced Owl** ☐
398 **Pearlspotted Owl** ☐
405 **Fierynecked Nightjar** ☐
418 Alpine Swift ☐
424 **Speckled Mousebird** ☐
438 **European Bee-eater** ☐
441 **Carmine Bee-eater** ☐
444 **Little Bee-eater** ☐
445 **Swallowtailed Bee-eater** ☐
446 **European Roller** ☐
447 **Lilacbreasted Roller** ☐
449 Purple Roller ☐
451 Hoopoe ☐
454 **Scimitarbilled Woodhoopoe** ☐
457 Grey Hornbill ☐
458 Redbilled Hornbill ☐
459 **Southern Yellow-billed Hornbill*** ☐
465 **Pied Barbet*** ☐
473 Crested Barbet ☐
498 **Sabota Lark*** ☐
505 **Dusky Lark** ☐
518 European Swallow ☐
527 Lesser Striped Swallow ☐
541 **Forktailed Drongo** ☐
554 Southern Black Tit* ☐
563 **Pied Babbler**** ☐
568 Blackeyed Bulbul ☐
580 Groundscraper Thrush ☐
613 **Whitebrowed Robin** ☐
615 **Kalahari Robin*** ☐
621 **Titbabbler*** ☐
643 Willow Warbler ☐
651 **Longbilled Crombec** ☐
658 **Barred Warbler*** ☐
672 Rattling Cisticola ☐
685 **Blackchested Prinia*** ☐
689 Spotted Flycatcher ☐
695 **Marico Flycatcher*** ☐
701 Chinspot Batis ☐
731 **Lesser Grey Shrike** ☐
733 Redbacked Shrike ☐
735 **Longtailed Shrike** ☐
739 **Crimsonbreasted Boubou*** ☐
740 Puffback ☐
741 Brubru ☐
743 Threestreaked Tchagra ☐
753 White Helmetshrike ☐
756 **Whitecrowned Shrike*** ☐
760 **Wattled Starling** ☐
761 Plumcoloured Starling ☐
764 Glossy Starling* ☐
779 Marico Sunbird ☐
787 Whitebellied Sunbird ☐
798 **Redbilled Buffalo Weaver** ☐
799 **Whitebrowed Sparrowweaver** ☐
802 **Great Sparrow*** ☐
804 Greyheaded Sparrow ☐
806 **Scalyfeathered Finch*** ☐
814 Masked Weaver ☐
821 Redbilled Quelea ☐
834 **Melba Finch** ☐
844 **Blue Waxbill** ☐
845 **Violeteared Waxbill*** ☐
847 **Blackcheeked Waxbill** ☐
861 **Shafttailed Whydah*** ☐
862 Paradise Whydah ☐
884 Goldenbreasted Bunting ☐
☐
☐

HANS MERENSKY NATURE RESERVE

approximately 280 species recorded to date

This 5 300 ha reserve, controlled by the Chief Directorate: Nature and Environmental Conservation, lies 66 km north-east of Tzaneen in the northern Transvaal lowveld. The major habitat in the reserve comprises arid, open woodland dominated by *Colophospermum mopane* (mopane) and *Combretum apiculatum* (red bushwillow) trees and scrub. There are rocky hills along the eastern boundary, and the Letaba River, with its gallery forest, forms the northern boundary. There are four day walks, a three-day hiking trail and a circular drive. Crocodiles and hippos are present in the Letaba and in some of the dams, so visitors should exercise caution at all times. Accommodation is available at the Overvaal Eiland Resort where camping is allowed.

SPECIAL AND INTERESTING SPECIES

The undisputed special of the mopane woodland is **Arnot's Chat**. Look for it in mopane forest, not scrub. Other birds to look for here include **Brownhooded**, **Striped**, **Pygmy** and **Woodland Kingfishers** (the last two in summer only). **Redbilled** and **Scimitarbilled Woodhoopoes** are plentiful, while **Redcrested Korhaan**, **Whitebrowed Robin**, **Longbilled Crombec**, **Cardinal**, **Goldentailed, Bennett's** and **Bearded Woodpeckers** are usually heard before they are seen. Make sure to scan the skies now and again for

ALSO RECORDED

Woollynecked, Openbilled and Saddlebilled Storks are occasionally seen at the dams. Steppe and Lesser Spotted Eagles are rare summer visitors. African Finfoot has been seen on the Letaba River. Barred Owl, both African and European Golden Orioles and Whitebreasted Cuckooshrike all occasionally visit the mopane woodland, especially in the large trees along the drainage systems.

John McAllister

Take the Gravelotte (R71) road from Tzaneen and turn left, shortly after crossing the Letsitele River, onto the R529 towards the reserve.

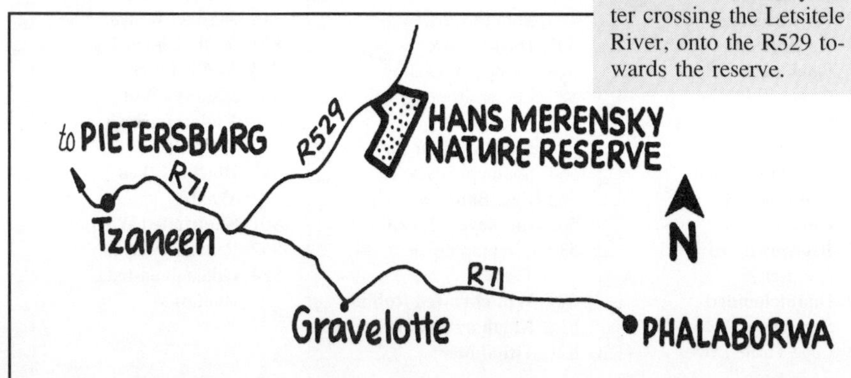

Bateleur, **Brown Snake Eagle**, **Wahlberg's** (summer) and **Martial Eagles**. **Marabou Storks** often gather in small numbers at the many dams and these are the best places to find **African Jacana**. During early summer the resounding call of **Redchested Cuckoos** and the mournful cry of **Black Cuckoos** can be heard throughout the day and often throughout the night. You should also be on the lookout for **African** and **Klaas's Cuckoos**. On the walk to the Letaba River look for **White** and **Redbilled Helmetshrikes**, which often accompany mixed bird parties, as do **Orangebreasted Bush Shrikes**. **Blackbellied Korhaan** may be found in open areas along the way. In the gallery forest you should find **Heuglin's** and **Whitethroated Robins**, **Tambourine Dove**, **Green Pigeon**, **Purplecrested Lourie**, **Yellowbreasted Apalis** and **Collared Sunbird**. Search the undergrowth carefully for **Terrestrial Bulbul**, which often gives itself away with its growling call. **Little Sparrowhawk** breeds here, but you'll need lots of patience to see it. **Malachite** and **Pied Kingfishers**, **African Pied Wagtail** and **African Black Duck** can be expected along the river. **Stierling's Barred Warbler** frequents the indigenous garden near the reserve offices. **Greater Blue-eared** and **Glossy Starlings**, best separated by their calls, are found in the resort grounds, as is **Scarletchested Sunbird**. **Fierynecked Nightjar** can be heard on moonlit nights and **Dark Chanting Goshawks** often sit on the power lines alongside the tarred road between the reserve entrance and the resort.

52% OF SPECIES

008 Dabchick ☐
058 Reed Cormorant ☐
060 Darter ☐
062 Grey Heron ☐
066 Great White Egret ☐
074 Greenbacked Heron ☐
081 Hamerkop ☐
089 **Marabou Stork** ☐
090 Yellowbilled Stork ☐
094 Hadeda Ibis ☐
095 African Spoonbill ☐
099 Whitefaced Duck ☐
102 Egyptian Goose ☐
105 **African Black Duck** ☐
115 Knobbilled Duck ☐
123 Whitebacked Vulture ☐
126a Yellowbilled Kite ☐
135 **Wahlberg's Eagle** ☐
140 **Martial Eagle** ☐
142 **Brown Snake Eagle** ☐
146 **Bateleur** ☐
148 African Fish Eagle ☐
157 **Little Sparrowhawk** ☐
163 **Dark Chanting Goshawk** ☐
189 Crested Francolin ☐
196 Natal Francolin* ☐
203 Helmeted Guineafowl ☐
205 Kurrichane Buttonquail ☐
237 **Redcrested Korhaan*** ☐
238 **Blackbellied Korhaan** ☐
240 **African Jacana** ☐
249 Threebanded Plover ☐
258 Blacksmith Plover ☐
264 Common Sandpiper ☐
266 Wood Sandpiper ☐
269 Marsh Sandpiper ☐
270 Greenshank ☐
347 Doublebanded Sandgrouse* ☐
352 Redeyed Dove ☐
354 Cape Turtle Dove ☐
355 Laughing Dove ☐
356 Namaqua Dove ☐
358 Greenspotted Dove ☐

359 **Tambourine Dove**
361 **Green Pigeon**
371 **Purplecrested Lourie**
373 Grey Lourie
375 **African Cuckoo**
377 **Redchested Cuckoo**
378 **Black Cuckoo**
385 **Klaas's Cuckoo**
386 Diederik Cuckoo
391 Burchell's Coucal*
392 Barn Owl
396 Scops Owl
398 Pearlspotted Owl
401 Spotted Eagle Owl
405 **Fierynecked Nightjar**
415 Whiterumped Swift
417 Little Swift
424 Speckled Mousebird
426 Redfaced Mousebird
428 **Pied Kingfisher**
431 **Malachite Kingfisher**
432 **Pygmy Kingfisher**
433 **Woodland Kingfisher**
435 **Brownhooded Kingfisher**
437 **Striped Kingfisher**
438 European Bee-eater
441 Carmine Bee-eater
446 European Roller
447 Lilacbreasted Roller
449 Purple Roller
451 Hoopoe
452 **Redbilled Woodhoopoe**
454 **Scimitarbilled Woodhoopoe**
457 Grey Hornbill
458 Redbilled Hornbill
459 Southern Yellowbilled Hornbill*
464 Blackcollared Barbet
473 Crested Barbet
474 Greater Honeyguide
476 Lesser Honeyguide
481 **Bennett's Woodpecker**
483 **Goldentailed Woodpecker**
486 **Cardinal Woodpecker**
487 **Bearded Woodpecker**
496 Flappet Lark
498 Sabota Lark*
518 European Swallow
524 Redbreasted Swallow
527 Lesser Striped Swallow
538 Black Cuckooshrike
541 Forktailed Drongo
545 Blackheaded Oriole
548 Pied Crow
554 Southern Black Tit*
558 Grey Penduline Tit
560 Arrowmarked Babbler
568 Blackeyed Bulbul
569 **Terrestrial Bulbul**
576 Kurrichane Thrush
580 Groundscraper Thrush
594 **Arnot's Chat**
599 **Heuglin's Robin**
602 **Whitethroated Robin****
613 **Whitebrowed Robin**
643 Willow Warbler
648 **Yellowbreasted Apalis**
651 **Longbilled Crombec**
657 Bleating Warbler
657a Greybacked Bleating Warbler
659 **Stierling's Barred Warbler**
672 Rattling Cisticola
677 Levaillant's Cisticola
681 Neddicky
683 Tawnyflanked Prinia
689 Spotted Flycatcher
694 Black Flycatcher
701 Chinspot Batis
710 Paradise Flycatcher
711 **African Pied Wagtail**
733 Redbacked Shrike
740 Puffback
741 Brubru
743 Threestreaked Tchagra
744 Blackcrowned Tchagra
748 **Orangebreasted Bush Shrike**
751 Greyheaded Bush Shrike
753 **White Helmetshrike**
754 **Redbilled Helmetshrike**
761 Plumcoloured Starling
764 **Glossy Starling***
765 **Greater Blue-eared Starling**
787 Whitebellied Sunbird
791 **Scarletchested Sunbird**
793 **Collared Sunbird**
796 Cape White-eye**
804 Greyheaded Sparrow
810 Spectacled Weaver
811 Spottedbacked Weaver
814 Masked Weaver
815 Lesser Masked Weaver
819 Redheaded Weaver
821 Redbilled Quelea
841 Jameson's Firefinch
844 Blue Waxbill
846 Common Waxbill
857 Bronze Mannikin
860 Pintailed Whydah
869 Yelloweyed Canary
884 Goldenbreasted Bunting

WOODBUSH RESERVE, MAGOEBASKLOOF AND SURROUNDING AREA

approximately 309 species recorded to date

Woodbush, on the escarpment between Pietersburg and Tzaneen on the R71, consists of extensive indigenous evergreen forest covering steep slopes and is well watered by fast flowing streams. The reserve is interspersed with patches of exotic pine and gum plantations. The forest lies on an alternative route down the escarpment and there is a 15 km detour from the main road through the forest which is best traversed downhill from west to east because of steep gradients. The detour is a gravel road and birding can be conducted by walking up and down the main road, after stopping at the various parking areas and view sites. Accommodation is available at the local hotels.

SPECIAL AND INTERESTING SPECIES

Many forest specials of southern Africa are found in the Woodbush forest and it is recommended that birders acquaint themselves with their calls, as forest birds are more often heard than seen. The use of a tape recorder could be very rewarding. Species such as **Chorister** and **Starred Robins**, **Olive Bush Shrike**, **Yellowstreaked Bulbul**, **Olive Woodpecker**, **Grey Cuckooshrike**, **Squaretailed Drongo**, **Bluemantled Flycatcher**, **Knysna Lourie**, **Black Sawwing Swallow**, **Sombre Bulbul**, **Olive Thrush**, **Yellowthroated Warbler**,

ALSO RECORDED

A bird more often heard than seen is the Buffspotted Flufftail. Both Redchested and Striped Flufftails (in montane grassland) have been recorded. Grey Wagtail has been recorded twice at Debenjeni Falls and Green Twinspot can be seen or heard in the forest.

Rodd Kippen

Take the turnoff to Woodbush from the R71 and thereafter follow the signs for Forest Drive. The turnoff to the Debenjeni Falls is near the bottom of the detour and there is adequate parking. Continue on the R71 towards Tzaneen to the Fanie Botha Dam on the northern side of the route; it is clearly signposted.

Barthroated Apalis, **Cape Batis** and **Forest Canary** may be found. Other unusual species such as **Emerald Cuckoo**, the elusive **Narina Trogon**, **Scalythroated Honeyguide** and **Bush Blackcap** may be encountered, and **Orange Thrush** and **Blackfronted Bush Shrike** are worth pursuing. A visit to Debenjeni Falls usually results in good sightings of **Longtailed Wagtail** and **Redbacked Mannikin**. Along the verges of the forest **Longcrested** and **Crowned Eagles**, **Forest Buzzard** and **African Goshawk** may be seen. **Wood Owl** and **Yellow Warbler** are present. **Swee Waxbills** can also be found in parties with **Common Waxbills**.

100% OF SPECIES (IN RESERVE)

008 Dabchick
055 Whitebreasted Cormorant
058 Reed Cormorant
062 Grey Heron
063 Blackheaded Heron
071 Cattle Egret
094 Hadeda Ibis
099 Whitefaced Duck
105 African Black Duck
126 Black Kite
126 Yellowbilled Kite
127 Blackshouldered Kite
129 Bat Hawk
131 Black Eagle
135 Wahlberg's Eagle
139 **Longcrested Eagle**
140 Martial Eagle
141 **Crowned Eagle**
149 Steppe Buzzard
150 **Forest Buzzard****
152 Jackal Buzzard**
155 Redbreasted Sparrowhawk
160 **African Goshawk**
169 Gymnogene
181 Rock Kestrel
196 Natal Francolin*
203 Helmeted Guineafowl
213 Black Crake
217 Redchested Flufftail
218 Buffspotted Flufftail
349 Rock Pigeon
350 Rameron Pigeon
352 Redeyed Dove
354 Cape Turtle Dove
359 Tambourine Dove
360 Cinnamon Dove
363 Brownheaded Parrot
370 **Knysna Lourie****
377 Redchested Cuckoo
378 Black Cuckoo
384 **Emerald Cuckoo**
394 **Wood Owl**
412 Black Swift
417 Little Swift
418 Alpine Swift
424 Speckled Mousebird
426 Redfaced Mousebird
427 **Narina Trogon**
428 Pied Kingfisher
429 Giant Kingfisher
435 Brownhooded Kingfisher
438 European Bee-eater
451 Hoopoe
452 Redbilled Woodhoopoe
475 **Scalythroated Honeyguide**
488 **Olive Woodpecker**
518 European Swallow
520 Whitethroated Swallow
529 Rock Martin
530 House Martin
537 **Black Sawwing Swallow**
540 **Grey Cuckooshrike**
542 **Squaretailed Drongo**
550 Whitenecked Raven
565 **Bush Blackcap****
568 Blackeyed Bulbul
569 Terrestrial Bulbul
570 **Yellowstreaked Bulbul**
572 **Sombre Bulbul**
576 Kurrichane Thrush
577 **Olive Thrush**
579 **Orange Thrush**
596 Stonechat
598 **Chorister Robin****
599 Heuglin's Robin
601 Cape Robin
606 **Starred Robin**
616 Brown Robin**
635 Cape Reed Warbler
637 **Yellow Warbler**
639 Barratt's Warbler**
644 **Yellowthroated Warbler**

645 **Barthroated Apalis** ☐
648 Yellowbreasted Apalis ☐
657 Bleating Warbler ☐
661 Grassbird** ☐
664 Fantailed Cisticola ☐
679 Lazy Cisticola ☐
683 Tawnyflanked Prinia ☐
690 Dusky Flycatcher ☐
700 **Cape Batis**** ☐
708 **Bluemantled Flycatcher** ☐
710 Paradise Flycatcher ☐
712 **Longtailed Wagtail** ☐
713 Cape Wagtail ☐
740 Puffback ☐
749 **Blackfronted Bush Shrike** ☐
750 **Olive Bush Shrike*** ☐
785 Greater Double-collared Sunbird** ☐
787 Whitebellied Sunbird ☐
792 Black Sunbird ☐
793 Collared Sunbird ☐
796 Cape White-eye** ☐
804 Greyheaded Sparrow ☐
807 Thickbilled Weaver ☐
813 Cape Weaver** ☐
816 Golden Weaver ☐
824 Red Bishop ☐
826 Golden Bishop ☐
827 Yellowrumped Widow ☐
831 Redcollared Widow ☐
835 Green Twinspot ☐
840 Bluebilled Firefinch ☐
846 **Common Waxbill** ☐
850 **Swee Waxbill*** ☐
858 **Redbacked Mannikin** ☐
872 Cape Canary ☐
873 **Forest Canary**** ☐

HANS STRIJDOM DAM NATURE RESERVE

approximately 257 species recorded to date

Hans Strijdom Dam Nature Reserve lies on the Mogol (or Mokolo) River in the heart of the Waterberg Mountains in the north-western Transvaal, 55 km south of Ellisras and 130 km north-west of Nylstroom. The reserve, including 914 ha of dam, is 4 600 ha in size and is under the control of the Chief Directorate: Nature and Environmental Conservation. Camp-

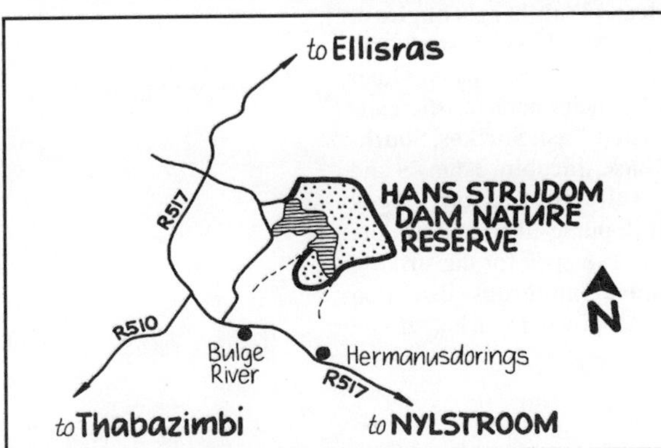

Turn off the N1 north of Pretoria at the Kranskop toll gate towards Nylstroom (R33). Proceed through the town and follow the R517 towards Ellisras. Follow this road through Vaalwater (60 km) to the Bulge River Post Office and trading store (a further 60 km). Turn right here onto the gravel road signposted to the dam. The camping area is on your right after 13 km. Directions to reach the office can be obtained here.

ing is allowed; the nearest hotels are at Ellisras or Vaalwater. The terrain is mountainous and the greater part of the reserve lies on Waterberg sandstone and comprises *Combretum-Burkea* or *Grewia-Pterocarpus* veld. The Mogol Hiking Trail traverses this part of the reserve. The campsite vegetation is dominated by *Acacia erioloba* (camel thorn) and *Terminalia sericea* (silver cluster-leaf). There are dense thickets of *Syzygium guineense* (water pear) along the Mogol River. A boat is essential if you wish to explore the dam and its shoreline, but landing other than at the campsite is not permitted.

SPECIAL AND INTERESTING SPECIES

The *Acacias* at the campsite should be scanned carefully for **Cape Penduline Tit**. **Longtailed Shrikes** and **Crimson-breasted Boubous** are other *Acacia* specialities while **Brubru**, **Puffback**, **Marico Sunbird** and **Chinspot Batis** may be found in any of the trees here. Scan the rocky shoreline opposite for **Water Dikkop** and **African Pied Wagtail**. Keep an eye open for hunting **Gymnogene** (over the hillsides) and in summer **Osprey** (over the water). If you have a boat and can get out onto the dam watch the cliff faces for **Black Eagles**, as well as **Black** and **Alpine Swifts**. On the flooded trees you also have a good chance of seeing **African Fish Eagle**. On the steep, rocky slopes, where there is good grass and tree cover, the prinia-like birds hopping around on the rocks will probably be **Lazy Cisticolas**. In the area around the office **Halfcollared Kingfisher** can often be seen in the waterside vegetation along the Mogol River and, if you are very lucky, you may see the elusive **African Finfoot** or the even shier **Whitebacked Night Heron**. In the broadleafed woodland (special permission required), or along the hiking trail, one often sees **African Hawk** and **Wahlberg's Eagles** or **Jackal Buzzard**. **Coqui**, **Crested**, **Natal**, **Swainson's** and **Shelley's Francolins** are best located by their calls. Other birds that give themselves away by their characteristic calls are **Greyheaded** and **Orangebreasted Bush Shrikes**, **Southern Boubou** and **Redchested**, **Black**, **Jacobin**, **Klaas's** and **Diederik Cuckoos**. Look carefully for the tiny **Grey Penduline Tit** and its beautiful purse-like nest in the broadleafed woodland and keep an eye open for the striking **Redheaded Weaver**. **Doublebanded Sandgrouse** can often be seen at dusk when they come down to drink at the waterholes on the reserve.

ALSO RECORDED

Meyer's Parrot, Yellowbilled Storks, Caspian Terns, Whitefronted Plover, Yellowbellied Bulbuls, Swee Waxbills and Bronzewinged Coursers have been seen in the reserve at various times in the past. Greyhooded Kingfisher is an erratic summer visitor.

Donovan Sykes

52% OF SPECIES

- 008 Dabchick ☐
- 055 Whitebreasted Cormorant ☐
- 058 Reed Cormorant ☐
- 060 Darter ☐
- 062 Grey Heron ☐
- 063 Blackheaded Heron ☐
- 071 Cattle Egret ☐
- 074 Greenbacked Heron ☐
- 077 **Whitebacked Night Heron** ☐
- 081 Hamerkop ☐
- 094 Hadeda Ibis ☐
- 102 Egyptian Goose ☐
- 105 African Black Duck ☐
- 131 **Black Eagle** ☐
- 135 **Wahlberg's Eagle** ☐
- 137 **African Hawk Eagle** ☐
- 148 **African Fish Eagle** ☐
- 152 **Jackal Buzzard**** ☐
- 169 **Gymnogene** ☐
- 170 **Osprey** ☐
- 181 Rock Kestrel ☐
- 188 **Coqui Francolin** ☐
- 189 **Crested Francolin** ☐
- 191 **Shelley's Francolin** ☐
- 196 **Natal Francolin*** ☐
- 199 **Swainson's Francolin*** ☐
- 205 Kurrichane Buttonquail ☐
- 213 Black Crake ☐
- 229 **African Finfoot** ☐
- 249 Threebanded Plover ☐
- 255 Crowned Plover ☐
- 258 Blacksmith Plover ☐
- 260 Wattled Plover ☐
- 298 **Water Dikkop** ☐
- 347 **Doublebanded Sandgrouse*** ☐
- 349 Rock Pigeon ☐
- 352 Redeyed Dove ☐
- 354 Cape Turtle Dove ☐
- 355 Laughing Dove ☐
- 356 Namaqua Dove ☐
- 358 Greenspotted Dove ☐
- 361 Green Pigeon ☐
- 364 Meyer's Parrot ☐
- 373 Grey Lourie ☐
- 377 **Redchested Cuckoo** ☐
- 378 **Black Cuckoo** ☐
- 382 **Jacobin Cuckoo** ☐
- 385 **Klaas's Cuckoo** ☐
- 386 **Diederik Cuckoo** ☐
- 391 Burchell's Coucal* ☐
- 412 **Black Swift** ☐
- 415 Whiterumped Swift ☐
- 418 **Alpine Swift** ☐
- 426 Redfaced Mousebird ☐
- 428 Pied Kingfisher ☐
- 429 Giant Kingfisher ☐
- 430 **Halfcollared Kingfisher** ☐
- 431 Malachite Kingfisher ☐
- 433 Woodland Kingfisher ☐
- 435 Brownhooded Kingfisher ☐
- 436 Greyhooded Kingfisher ☐
- 438 European Bee-eater ☐
- 441 Carmine Bee-eater ☐
- 444 Little Bee-eater ☐
- 447 Lilacbreasted Roller ☐
- 451 Hoopoe ☐
- 452 Redbilled Woodhoopoe ☐
- 457 Grey Hornbill ☐
- 458 Redbilled Hornbill ☐
- 459 Southern Yellow-billed Hornbill* ☐
- 464 Blackcollared Barbet ☐
- 470 Yellowfronted Tinker Barbet ☐
- 473 Crested Barbet ☐
- 474 Greater Honeyguide ☐
- 483 Goldentailed Woodpecker ☐
- 486 Cardinal Woodpecker ☐
- 487 Bearded Woodpecker ☐
- 518 European Swallow ☐
- 520 Whitethroated Swallow ☐
- 524 Redbreasted Swallow ☐
- 527 Lesser Striped Swallow ☐
- 541 Forktailed Drongo ☐
- 545 Blackheaded Oriole ☐
- 554 Southern Black Tit* ☐
- 557 **Cape Penduline Tit*** ☐
- 558 **Grey Penduline Tit** ☐
- 560 Arrowmarked Babbler ☐
- 568 Blackeyed Bulbul ☐
- 576 Kurrichane Thrush ☐
- 580 Groundscraper Thrush ☐
- 589 Familiar Chat ☐
- 593 Mocking Chat ☐
- 602 Whitethroated Robin** ☐
- 651 Longbilled Crombec ☐
- 653 Yellowbellied Eremomela ☐
- 679 **Lazy Cisticola** ☐
- 681 Neddicky ☐
- 683 Tawnyflanked Prinia ☐
- 694 Black Flycatcher ☐
- 695 Marico Flycatcher* ☐
- 701 **Chinspot Batis** ☐
- 710 Paradise Flycatcher ☐
- 711 **African Pied Wagtail** ☐
- 733 Redbacked Shrike ☐
- 735 **Longtailed Shrike** ☐
- 736 **Southern Boubou**** ☐
- 739 **Crimsonbreasted Boubou*** ☐
- 740 **Puffback** ☐
- 741 **Brubru** ☐
- 743 Threestreaked Tchagra ☐
- 744 Blackcrowned Tchagra ☐

748 **Orangebreasted Bush Shrike** ☐
751 **Greyheaded Bush Shrike** ☐
753 White Helmetshrike ☐
761 Plumcoloured Starling ☐
764 Glossy Starling* ☐
769 Redwinged Starling ☐
779 **Marico Sunbird** ☐
787 Whitebellied Sunbird ☐
792 Black Sunbird ☐
796 Cape White-eye** ☐
801 House Sparrow ☐
804 Greyheaded Sparrow ☐
814 Masked Weaver ☐
819 **Redheaded Weaver** ☐
834 Melba Finch ☐
841 Jameson's Firefinch ☐
842 Redbilled Firefinch ☐
844 Blue Waxbill ☐
846 Common Waxbill ☐
860 Pintailed Whydah ☐
869 Yelloweyed Canary ☐
884 Goldenbreasted Bunting ☐
886 Rock Bunting ☐
☐
☐
☐
☐

LAPALALA WILDERNESS

approximately 270 species recorded to date

Lapalala Wilderness is a privately owned 24 000 ha nature reserve in the Waterberg Mountains of the north-western Transvaal. There are several bush camps and a lodge, giving visitors access to the wilderness area. The reserve can be visualised as a large plateau, with a mean altitude of 1 100 m, dissected by many drainage valleys. There are two main drainage rivers within the reserve, namely the Lephalala (the Barrier), which flows for 50 km in a northerly direction, and the Blocklands River which flows in a north-easterly direction. Accommodation in bush camps of various sizes is available. No day visitors are allowed.

ALSO RECORDED

Unusual bushveld species include Saddlebilled Stork, Cape Vulture, Jackal Buzzard, Hobby Falcon, Anteating Chat, Sentinel Rock Thrush and Longtailed Wagtail.

C.B. Ravenhill and I. Davidson

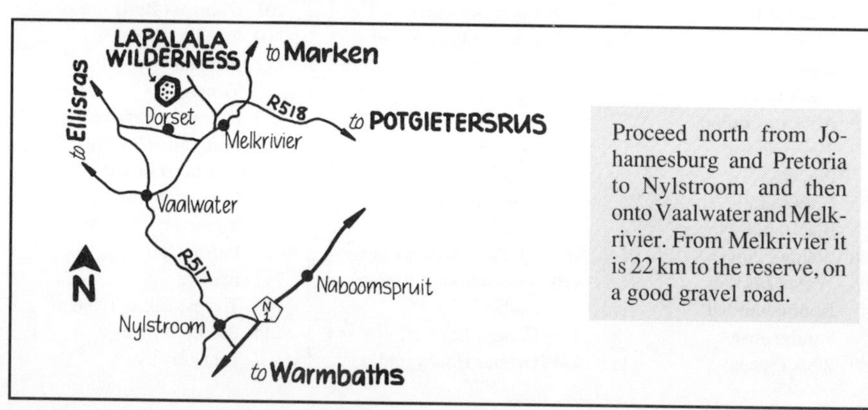

Proceed north from Johannesburg and Pretoria to Nylstroom and then onto Vaalwater and Melkrivier. From Melkrivier it is 22 km to the reserve, on a good gravel road.

SPECIAL AND INTERESTING SPECIES

Along the Lephalala River a number of uncommon species occur. **African Finfoot** are found in large pools and flowing water where reeds are dense. **Whitebacked Night Heron** and **Water Dikkop** can be seen along both rivers in the reserve. Look for **Black Stork** in shallow pools along the rivers; this bird breeds on cliffs. **Black Sparrowhawks** are found in open bushveld and have bred along the smaller streams. During summer **Greyhooded Kingfisher** is present, but is very shy. Both **Kori** and **Stanley's Bustards** can be found in open areas, especially after fires. **Shelley's Francolin** is seen or heard throughout the year. This is an excellent locality for a number of large raptors. **Martial**, **African Fish** and **African Hawk Eagles**, **Gymnogene**, **Blackbreasted** and **Brown Snake Eagles** all breed in the reserve. Small raptors include **Lizard Buzzard**, **Little Sparrowhawk** and **Little Banded Goshawk**. **African Jacana** can be seen among lilies. Kingfishers are well represented and include **Halfcollared**, **Pygmy** (summer) and **Woodland** (summer) **Kingfishers**. **Meyer's Parrot** occupies this woodland and some of the smaller, colourful species to look for are **Violeteared** and **Blackcheeked Waxbills**. Dry woodland endemics include **Southern Yellowbilled Hornbill**, **Pied Barbet**, **Southern Black Tit**, **Whitethroated Robin**, **Southern** and **Crimsonbreasted Boubous**.

55% OF SPECIES

- 008 Dabchick ☐
- 055 Whitebreasted Cormorant ☐
- 058 Reed Cormorant ☐
- 060 Darter ☐
- 071 Cattle Egret ☐
- 074 Greenbacked Heron ☐
- 077 **Whitebacked Night Heron** ☐
- 081 Hamerkop ☐
- 084 **Black Stork** ☐
- 094 Hadeda Ibis ☐
- 105 African Black Duck ☐
- 118 Secretarybird ☐
- 126a Yellowbilled Kite ☐
- 127 Blackshouldered Kite ☐
- 131 Black Eagle ☐
- 135 Wahlberg's Eagle ☐
- 137 **African Hawk Eagle** ☐
- 140 **Martial Eagle** ☐
- 142 **Brown Snake Eagle** ☐
- 143 **Blackbreasted Snake Eagle** ☐
- 148 **African Fish Eagle** ☐
- 149 Steppe Buzzard ☐
- 154 **Lizard Buzzard** ☐
- 157 **Little Sparrowhawk** ☐
- 158 **Black Sparrowhawk** ☐
- 159 **Little Banded Goshawk** ☐
- 169 **Gymnogene** ☐
- 181 Rock Kestrel ☐
- 188 Coqui Francolin ☐
- 189 Crested Francolin ☐
- 191 **Shelley's Francolin** ☐
- 196 Natal Francolin* ☐
- 213 Black Crake ☐
- 229 **African Finfoot** ☐
- 230 **Kori Bustard** ☐
- 231 **Stanley's Bustard** ☐
- 237 Redcrested Korhaan* ☐
- 240 **African Jacana** ☐
- 255 Crowned Plover ☐
- 260 Wattled Plover ☐
- 297 Spotted Dikkop ☐
- 298 **Water Dikkop** ☐
- 352 Redeyed Dove ☐
- 354 Cape Turtle Dove ☐
- 355 Laughing Dove ☐
- 356 Namaqua Dove ☐

358 Greenspotted Dove
361 Green Pigeon
364 **Meyer's Parrot**
373 Grey Lourie
375 African Cuckoo
377 Redchested Cuckoo
382 Jacobin Cuckoo
386 Diederik Cuckoo
391 Burchell's Coucal*
396 Scops Owl
401 Spotted Eagle Owl
405 Fierynecked Nightjar
406 Rufouscheeked Nightjar
412 Black Swift
415 Whiterumped Swift
424 Speckled Mousebird
426 Redfaced Mousebird
428 Pied Kingfisher
429 Giant Kingfisher
430 **Halfcollared Kingfisher**
432 **Pygmy Kingfisher**
433 **Woodland Kingfisher**
435 Brownhooded Kingfisher
436 **Greyhooded Kingfisher**
437 Striped Kingfisher
438 European Bee-eater
444 Little Bee-eater
447 Lilacbreasted Roller
449 Purple Roller
451 Hoopoe
452 Redbilled Woodhoopoe
454 Scimitarbilled Woodhoopoe
457 Grey Hornbill
459 **Southern Yellowbilled Hornbill***
464 Blackcollared Barbet
465 **Pied Barbet***
470 Yellowfronted Tinker Barbet
473 Crested Barbet
474 Greater Honeyguide
476 Lesser Honeyguide
481 Bennett's Woodpecker
486 Cardinal Woodpecker
494 Rufousnaped Lark
498 Sabota Lark*
518 European Swallow
526 Greater Striped Swallow*
527 Lesser Striped Swallow
529 Rock Martin
541 Forktailed Drongo
545 Blackheaded Oriole
554 **Southern Black Tit***
560 Arrowmarked Babbler
568 Blackeyed Bulbul
569 Terrestrial Bulbul
574 Yellowbellied Bulbul
576 Kurrichane Thrush
580 Groundscraper Thrush
589 Familiar Chat
593 Mocking Chat
602 **Whitethroated Robin****
613 Whitebrowed Robin
645 Barthroated Apalis
664 Fantailed Cisticola
672 Rattling Cisticola
689 Spotted Flycatcher
694 Black Flycatcher
701 Chinspot Batis
710 Paradise Flycatcher
720 Striped Pipit
723 Bushveld Pipit
733 Redbacked Shrike
736 **Southern Boubou****
739 **Crimsonbreasted Boubou***
740 Puffback
741 Brubru
743 Threestreaked Tchagra
744 Blackcrowned Tchagra
748 Orangebreasted Bush Shrike
751 Greyheaded Bush Shrike
753 White Helmetshrike
761 Plumcoloured Starling
764 Glossy Starling*
769 Redwinged Starling
779 Marico Sunbird
787 Whitebellied Sunbird
792 Black Sunbird
796 Cape White-eye**
804 Greyheaded Sparrow
811 Spottedbacked Weaver
819 Redheaded Weaver
821 Redbilled Quelea
841 Jameson's Firefinch
842 Redbilled Firefinch
844 Blue Waxbill
845 **Violeteared Waxbill***
846 Common Waxbill
847 **Blackcheeked Waxbill**
857 Bronze Mannikin
860 Pintailed Whydah
869 Yelloweyed Canary
884 Goldenbreasted Bunting
886 Rock Bunting

EASTERN TRANSVAAL ESCARPMENT

approximately 362 species recorded to date

The area included in this locality stretches from Long Tom Pass in the south to the Blydepoort Dam in the north. Birders should ensure that they have the permission of the various landowners before they enter areas away from the main roads and the various public view sites. Detailed maps of the area and permits to walk along the various trails can be obtained from the Department of Forestry (National Hiking Way) in Sabie or the Chief Directorate: Nature and Environmental Conservation offices at Bourke's Luck. Most of the hiking trails include overnight stops, but day walks can also be arranged. Accommodation of all grades is available in Sabie, Pilgrim's Rest, Graskop and at Paradise Camp and the F. H. Odendaal and Sybrand van Niekerk public resorts. Advance booking of both accommodation and trails is essential and peak holiday periods should be avoided if at all possible. Much of the area has been planted with alien trees and these plantations are virtually devoid of any animal life, but there are fairly extensive tracts of montane grassland, cliffs, indigenous forest, riverine vegetation and, in the north, lowveld bush.

ALSO RECORDED

Southern Tchagra along the Blyde River near Pilgrim's Rest, Blackfronted Bush Shrike in the indigenous bush below the escarpment cliffs and Bat Hawk in the higher lying areas.

Ken Gamble

The town of Sabie is approximately 60 km north-west of Nelspruit or 50 km east of Lydenburg on the R37. Tarred roads connect the town with the historic village of Pilgrim's Rest (42 km), Graskop (30 km) and the Blyde River Canyon Nature Reserve (64 km to Bourke's Luck) in the north. To reach the Sybrand van Niekerk Public Resort one should descend the spectacular Abel Erasmus Pass on the R36 and then travel along the R531 towards Klaserie. The turnoff to the resort (signposted) is on the right after 30 km.

SPECIAL AND INTERESTING SPECIES

The cliff faces at places like God's Window and along the Blyde River Canyon are good spots to find **Black Eagle**, **Black Stork**, **Whitenecked Raven**, **Jackal Buzzard**, **Lanner Falcon** and the rare **Peregrine Falcon**, while the cliffs at Manoutsa, best viewed from the R531 on the way to the Sybrand van Niekerk resort, host the third largest **Cape Vulture** breeding colony. The patches of indigenous forest found along the various trails provide a habitat for shy forest species such as **Narina Trogon**, **Orange Thrush**, **Knysna Lourie**, **Yellowstreaked** and **Sombre Bulbuls**, **Chorister Robin**, **Wood Owl** (particularly if you spend a night in one of the trail huts), **Cinnamon Dove**, **Olive Woodpecker**, **Barratt's** and **Yellowthroated Warblers**, **Bluemantled Flycatcher**, **Olive Bush Shrike**, **Barthroated Apalis**, **Cape Batis**, **Forest Canary** and, along the streams, **Buffspotted Flufftail**, which are often best located by their calls. **Lesser Doublecollared Sunbird**, **Swee Waxbill**, **Rednecked Francolin** and **Purplecrested Lourie** occur at the forest edge. The open tracts of rocky, montane grassland should be searched for **Wailing Cisticola**, **Buffstreaked Chat**, **Cape Rock Thrush**, **Yellowrumped Widow** and **Striped Flufftail** (in the moister areas). At some of the overnight huts in this habitat you may also hear **Cape Eagle Owl** and **Freckled Nightjar**. One should look for **Longtailed Wagtails** on the fast flowing, rocky streams of the area. On the last portion of the Blyde River Trail one should be on the lookout for **Crowned Eagle** and **Bald Ibis**. On the upper reaches of the dam there is also the possibility of catching a glimpse of **African Finfoot** and perhaps **Whitebacked Night Heron**. The bush around the dam should be searched for **Brownheaded Parrot**. A walk along the Blyde River downstream from Pilgrim's Rest should produce **Broadtailed** and **Yellow Warblers**, **Greater Doublecollared Sunbird**, **Spotted Prinia**, **Grassbird**, **Southern Boubou**, **Redbacked Mannikin**, **Halfcollared Kingfisher** and **African Black Duck**. The cliffs between the second and third bridges on the gravel road to Bourke's Luck provide a breeding site for thousands of **Black** and **Alpine Swifts** during the summer. **Longcrested Eagles** and **Black Sawwing Swallows** are also commonly seen in this area.

41% OF SPECIES

055 Whitebreasted Cormorant ☐
060 Darter ☐
062 Grey Heron ☐
063 Blackheaded Heron ☐
071 Cattle Egret ☐
077 **Whitebacked Night Heron** ☐
081 Hamerkop ☐
083 White Stork ☐
084 **Black Stork** ☐
092 **Bald Ibis**** ☐
094 Hadeda Ibis ☐
105 **African Black Duck** ☐
118 Secretarybird ☐
122 **Cape Vulture**** ☐
127 Blackshouldered Kite ☐
131 **Black Eagle** ☐
135 Wahlberg's Eagle ☐
139 **Longcrested Eagle** ☐
140 Martial Eagle ☐
141 **Crowned Eagle** ☐
148 African Fish Eagle ☐
149 Steppe Buzzard ☐
152 **Jackal Buzzard**** ☐
160 African Goshawk ☐
169 Gymnogene ☐
170 Osprey ☐
171 **Peregrine Falcon** ☐
172 **Lanner Falcon** ☐
181 Rock Kestrel ☐
189 Crested Francolin ☐
192 Redwing Francolin ☐
196 Natal Francolin* ☐
198 **Rednecked Francolin** ☐
199 Swainson's Francolin* ☐
218 **Buffspotted Flufftail** ☐
221 **Striped Flufftail** ☐
229 **African Finfoot** ☐
255 Crowned Plover ☐
260 Wattled Plover ☐
297 Spotted Dikkop ☐
349 Rock Pigeon ☐
350 Rameron Pigeon ☐
352 Redeyed Dove ☐
354 Cape Turtle Dove ☐
355 Laughing Dove ☐
356 Namaqua Dove ☐
358 Greenspotted Dove ☐
359 Tambourine Dove ☐
360 **Cinnamon Dove** ☐
361 Green Pigeon ☐
363 **Brownheaded Parrot** ☐
370 **Knysna Lourie**** ☐
371 **Purplecrested Lourie** ☐
373 Grey Lourie ☐
377 Redchested Cuckoo ☐
386 Diederik Cuckoo ☐
391 Burchell's Coucal* ☐
394 **Wood Owl** ☐
400 **Cape Eagle Owl** ☐
405 Fierynecked Nightjar ☐
408 **Freckled Nightjar** ☐
412 **Black Swift** ☐
415 Whiterumped Swift ☐
418 **Alpine Swift** ☐
424 Speckled Mousebird ☐
427 **Narina Trogon** ☐
428 Pied Kingfisher ☐
429 Giant Kingfisher ☐
430 **Halfcollared Kingfisher** ☐
431 Malachite Kingfisher ☐
435 Brownhooded Kingfisher ☐
438 European Bee-eater ☐
443 Whitefronted Bee-eater ☐
447 Lilacbreasted Roller ☐
455 Trumpeter Hornbill ☐
457 Grey Hornbill ☐
458 Redbilled Hornbill ☐
459 Southern Yellowbilled Hornbill* ☐
464 Blackcollared Barbet ☐
473 Crested Barbet ☐
483 Goldentailed Woodpecker ☐
486 Cardinal Woodpecker ☐
487 Bearded Woodpecker ☐
488 **Olive Woodpecker** ☐
518 European Swallow ☐
520 Whitethroated Swallow ☐
521 Blue Swallow ☐
529 Rock Martin ☐
536 **Black Sawwing Swallow** ☐
541 Forktailed Drongo ☐
550 **Whitenecked Raven** ☐
570 **Yellowstreaked Bulbul** ☐
572 **Sombre Bulbul** ☐
579 **Orange Thrush** ☐
580 Groundscraper Thrush ☐
581 **Cape Rock Thrush**** ☐
586 Mountain Chat* ☐
588 **Buffstreaked Chat**** ☐
589 Familiar Chat ☐
593 Mocking Chat ☐
596 Stonechat ☐
598 **Chorister Robin**** ☐
601 Cape Robin ☐
635 Cape Reed Warbler ☐
637 **Yellow Warbler** ☐
639 **Barratt's Warbler**** ☐
642 **Broadtailed Warbler** ☐
644 **Yellowthroated Warbler** ☐
645 **Barthroated Apalis** ☐
651 Longbilled Crombec ☐
657 Bleating Warbler ☐
661 **Grassbird**** ☐
667 Ayres' Cisticola ☐
670 **Wailing Cisticola** ☐
672 Rattling Cisticola ☐
681 Neddicky ☐
686 **Spotted Prinia**** ☐
690 Dusky Flycatcher ☐
698 Fiscal Flycatcher** ☐
700 **Cape Batis**** ☐
701 Chinspot Batis ☐
708 **Bluemantled Flycatcher** ☐
710 Paradise Flycatcher ☐

711 African Pied Wagtail ☐
712 **Longtailed Wagtail** ☐
713 Cape Wagtail ☐
732 Fiscal Shrike ☐
736 **Southern Boubou**** ☐
740 Puffback ☐
744 Blackcrowned Tchagra ☐
746 Bokmakierie* ☐
750 **Olive Bush Shrike*** ☐
769 Redwinged Starling ☐
775 Malachite Sunbird ☐
783 **Lesser Double-collared Sunbird**** ☐
785 **Greater Double-collared Sunbird**** ☐
792 Black Sunbird ☐
807 Thickbilled Weaver ☐
810 Spectacled Weaver ☐
813 Cape Weaver** ☐
814 Masked Weaver ☐
816 Golden Weaver ☐
827 **Yellowrumped Widow** ☐
831 Redcollared Widow ☐
840 Bluebilled Firefinch ☐
850 **Swee Waxbill*** ☐
857 Bronze Mannikin ☐
858 **Redbacked Mannikin** ☐
872 Cape Canary ☐
873 **Forest Canary**** ☐
886 Rock Bunting ☐

NYL FLOODPLAIN AND SURROUNDING BUSHVELD

approximately 389 species recorded to date

The Nyl floodplain, a mere two-hour drive from Johannesburg, is one of the prime birding areas in southern Africa. It is situated on the interface between the Waterberg Mountains and the Springbok Flats in the central Transvaal bushveld. The floodplain itself covers an area of 16 000 ha from the farm Middelfontein, just north of Nylstroom, to the farm Vaalkop just south of Potgietersrus, but the area that we will concentrate on here includes only Nylsvley Provincial Nature Reserve, Mosdene Private Nature Reserve and the

Nylsvley and Vogelfontein: Turn off the N1 from Pretoria to Pietersburg onto the gravel road signposted to Boekenhout Station (approximately 11 km south of Naboomspruit). The Nylsvley entrance is on the left after 8 km. To get to Vogelfontein turn left onto the road signposted "Rutland" and then take the first turn right. Carry on for about 2 km and the road crosses the floodplain. Stop near a large gate. You can walk across the dykes here to a hide, but PLEASE remember that you are on private property.

Mosdene: Continue along the N1 to the town of Naboomspruit. From here take the R519 towards Roedtan. Take the first turn to your left after having left town (signposted "Boekenhout"). The entrance to the farm is on the left about 3 km along this road. A detailed map of the reserve can be obtained here.

farm Vogelfontein. Camping is permitted on Nylsvley (basic facilities such as cold showers) and Mosdene (no facilities) and there are hotels in Naboomspruit and Nylstroom. One can also hire cottages on some of the nearby farms. Unless there has been a flood (this happened nine times in the last 27 years) the floodplain looks like a large tract of grassland with pools of water here and there. When it floods, however, it is transformed into a huge waterbird paradise and much of the *Acacia* savanna on the alluvial plains bordering the grassland is also flooded. On either side of the floodplain are broadleafed woodland and savanna ecosystems – a *Combretum apiculatum* (red bushwillow) dominated savanna on the felsite ridges and a woodland with tree species such as *Ochna pulchra* (lekkerbreek or peeling plane), *Terminalia sericea* (silver cluster-leaf) and *Burkea africana* (wild seringa) on sandier soils.

SPECIAL AND INTERESTING SPECIES

The floodplain: When flooded this area is truly a bird paradise offering birders a spectacle that can hardly be equalled anywhere else. Of the 102 waterbird species recorded here 58 have bred – this compares to 47 for St Lucia and 42 for Barberspan. Under these conditions 70-100 pairs of **Purple Heron**, 200-250 pairs of **Great White Egret**, 100-150 pairs of **Little Egret**, 100 pairs of **Yellowbilled Egret**, 40 pairs of **Black Egret**, 300-550 pairs of **Squacco Heron**, 500-700 pairs of **Blackcrowned Night Heron**, 20-30 pairs of **Little Bittern**, 100 pairs of **Dwarf Bittern** (in the flooded *Acacia* savanna), 10-20 pairs of **Bittern** (best located by the booming call of breeding males), 5 000+ pairs of **Purple Gallinule**, 1 000+ pairs of **Lesser Gallinule**, 6 000+ pairs of **Moorhen** and 8 000+ pairs of **Lesser Moorhen** breed in this area. **African Spoonbills** (up to 600 birds) are also present and breed during wet years, as do **Whitefaced Ducks** (up to 3 000 birds), **Fulvous** and **Whitebacked Ducks**, **African Rail**, **African Crake**, **African Jacana** (up to 800 birds), **Ethiopian Snipe** and **Blackwinged Stil**t. This is also one of the few localities where **European Marsh Harrier** can regularly be seen during wet summers.

The surrounding bushveld: Of the 389 species recorded in the area 291 are not dependent on the Nyl River being in flood, so the area is well worth a visit even if the floodplain is dry. The *Acacia* savanna on the flat alluvial soils bordering the floodplain proper is the most productive birding area here. **Crested Francolin**, **Whitefaced Owl** (best located

ALSO RECORDED

The floodplain: A Lesser Jacana turned up in the grasses of the floodplain in 1987. In January 1988 the only Streakybreasted Flufftail to be recorded in South Africa visited one of the few places where its call would have been recognised: Mr Warwick Tarboton's farm, Sericea. Later during the same year a Striped Crake pitched up at Vogelfontein. 1989 brought a Spotted Crake; a lone Slaty Egret (the first South African record since 1895) was present at Vogelfontein from May to October. A Grey Phalarope (fourth Transvaal record) and a River Warbler visited the area during the first quarter of 1991. Up to 20 Rufousbellied Herons and up to 30 Pygmy Geese have been recorded with both species having bred here. Whiskered Terns occur from time to time and have bred at Vogelfontein. Black Storks, which breed in the nearby Waterberg, are sometimes seen overhead and an occasional Saddlebilled Stork comes up from the lowveld. Other species that turn up at fairly regular intervals include Greyheaded Gull, Corncrake, Baillon's Crake, African Skimmer, Green Sandpiper and Bluecheeked Bee-eater.

The surrounding bushveld: A lone Bat Hawk and a single Osprey were recorded on a neighbouring farm in 1985. During 1987 an African Goshawk turned up on the same farm and a Rackettailed Roller was present for

from its call after dark and picked out by torchlight), **Lesser Honeyguide**, **Sabota Lark**, **Ashy Tit**, **Kalahari Robin**, **Burntnecked Eremomela** (which doesn't always have a "burnt" neck), **Greybacked Bleating Warbler**, **Barred Warbler** (best located by its call: somewhat similar to, but more shrill than, a Brubru's), **Longtailed Shrike**, **Crimsonbreasted Boubou**, **Orangebreasted Bush Shrike** (also found in the broadleafed woodland), **Marico Sunbird**, **Melba Finch**, **Jameson's** and **Redbilled Firefinches** and **Violeteared Waxbill** are all specials to be found in this habitat. Birds most often encountered in the broadleafed woodland include **Fierynecked** and **Rufouscheeked Nightjars** (best located by their calls at night), **Woodland Kingfisher** (mid- to late summer), **Grey Hornbill**, **Sharpbilled Honeyguide**, **Bennett's Woodpecker**, **Pearlbreasted Swallow**, **Black Cuckooshrike** and **Southern Black Tit**. **Fawncoloured Lark** and **Tinkling Cisticola** also occur in this habitat, but should be looked for specifically on *sandy soils*. **Pearlspotted Owl**, best located by its call, occurs in any woodland or savanna and can most easily be found during winter or on overcast days when it hunts during the day as well as at night. **Pygmy Kingfisher** (in summer), **Redbilled** and **Southern Yellowbilled Hornbills**, **Yellowfronted Tinker Barbet**, **Whitethroated** and **Whitebrowed Robins** and **Longbilled Crombec** occur almost anywhere in the bushveld areas.

51% OF SPECIES

001	Ostrich	☐
008	Dabchick	☐
058	Reed Cormorant	☐
060	Darter	☐
063	Blackheaded Heron	☐
065	**Purple Heron**	☐
066	**Great White Egret**	☐
067	**Little Egret**	☐
068	**Yellowbilled Egret**	☐
069	**Black Egret**	☐
071	Cattle Egret	☐
072	**Squacco Heron**	☐
076	**Blackcrowned Night Heron**	☐
078	**Little Bittern**	☐
079	**Dwarf Bittern**	☐
080	**Bittern**	☐
081	Hamerkop	☐
091	Sacred Ibis	☐
093	Glossy Ibis	☐
094	Hadeda Ibis	☐
095	**African Spoonbill**	☐
099	**Whitefaced Duck**	☐
100	**Fulvous Duck**	☐
101	**Whitebacked Duck**	☐
102	Egyptian Goose	☐
104	Yellowbilled Duck	☐
107	Hottentot Teal	☐
108	Redbilled Teal	☐
113	Southern Pochard	☐
116	Spurwinged Goose	☐
118	Secretarybird	☐
123	Whitebacked Vulture	☐
127	Blackshouldered Kite	☐

a few months on a nearby hill of the Waterberg. 1989 saw an African Golden Oriole arrive at Torino Ranch and in 1990 a Longtailed Wagtail pair was found breeding in a densely wooded Waterberg kloof. Hooded and Lappetfaced Vultures are seen on the odd occasion and single Longcrested Eagles wander over from the escarpment from time to time. Other birds that are seen now and again include Cuckoo Hawk, Montagu's and Pallid Harriers, Mozambique and Pennantwinged Nightjars, Carmine and Swallowtailed Bee-eaters and Dusky Lark. Striped Pipits, Cape and Grey Penduline Tits are seldom-seen breeding residents, as are Yellowbellied and Greencapped Eremomelas. European Wheatear and Collared Flycatcher are two rare Palaearctic migrants that found their way to Nylsvley prior to 1985. Kori Bustard and Doublebanded Sandgrouse are two species that were once plentiful but have not been recorded in the area during the past 20 years.

John McAllister

135 Wahlberg's Eagle
137 African Hawk Eagle
142 Brown Snake Eagle
143 Blackbreasted Snake Eagle
148 African Fish Eagle
157 Little Sparrowhawk
158 Black Sparrowhawk
159 Little Banded Goshawk
161 Gabar Goshawk
164 **European Marsh Harrier**
169 Gymnogene
188 Coqui Francolin
189 **Crested Francolin**
199 Swainson's Francolin*
203 Helmeted Guineafowl
210 **African Rail**
212 **African Crake**
213 Black Crake
223 **Purple Gallinule**
224 **Lesser Gallinule**
226 **Moorhen**
227 **Lesser Moorhen**
228 Redknobbed Coot
237 Redcrested Korhaan*
239a Whitequilled Korhaan**
240 **African Jacana**
249 Threebanded Plover
255 Crowned Plover
258 Blacksmith Plover
260 Wattled Plover
266 Wood Sandpiper
286 **Ethiopian Snipe**
295 **Blackwinged Stilt**
297 Spotted Dikkop
339 Whitewinged Tern
349 Rock Pigeon
352 Redeyed Dove
354 Cape Turtle Dove
355 Laughing Dove
356 Namaqua Dove
358 Greenspotted Dove
361 Green Pigeon
373 Grey Lourie
375 African Cuckoo
377 Redchested Cuckoo
378 Black Cuckoo
381 Striped Cuckoo
382 Jacobin Cuckoo
386 Diederik Cuckoo
391 Burchell's Coucal*
392 Barn Owl
397 **Whitefaced Owl**
398 **Pearlspotted Owl**
401 Spotted Eagle Owl
405 **Fierynecked Nightjar**
406 **Rufouscheeked Nightjar**
415 Whiterumped Swift
417 Little Swift
418 Alpine Swift
424 Speckled Mousebird
426 Redfaced Mousebird
428 Pied Kingfisher
431 Malachite Kingfisher
432 **Pygmy Kingfisher**
433 **Woodland Kingfisher**
435 Brownhooded Kingfisher
438 European Bee-eater
443 Whitefronted Bee-eater
447 Lilacbreasted Roller
452 Redbilled Woodhoopoe
457 **Grey Hornbill**
458 **Redbilled Hornbill**
459 **Southern Yellow-billed Hornbill***
464 Blackcollared Barbet
470 **Yellowfronted Tinker Barbet**
473 Crested Barbet
474 Greater Honeyguide
476 **Lesser Honeyguide**
478 **Sharpbilled Honeyguide**
481 **Bennett's Woodpecker**
483 Goldentailed Woodpecker
486 Cardinal Woodpecker
494 Rufousnaped Lark
497 **Fawncoloured Lark**
498 **Sabota Lark***
518 European Swallow
520 Whitethroated Swallow
523 **Pearlbreasted Swallow**
524 Redbreasted Swallow
526 Greater Striped Swallow*
527 Lesser Striped Swallow
529 Rock Martin
533 Brownthroated Martin
538 **Black Cuckooshrike**
541 Forktailed Drongo
545 Blackheaded Oriole
552 **Ashy Tit***
554 **Southern Black Tit***
560 Arrowmarked Babbler
568 Blackeyed Bulbul
576 Kurrichane Thrush
580 Groundscraper Thrush
596 Stonechat
602 **Whitethroated Robin****
613 **Whitebrowed Robin**
615 **Kalahari Robin***
621 Titbabbler*
635 Cape Reed Warbler
638 African Sedge Warbler
643 Willow Warbler
651 **Longbilled Crombec**
656 **Burntnecked Eremomela**
657a **Greybacked Bleating Warbler**
658 **Barred Warbler***
664 Fantailed Cisticola
665 Desert Cisticola
671 **Tinkling Cisticola**
672 Rattling Cisticola
677 Levaillant's Cisticola

681 Neddicky ☐
683 Tawnyflanked Prinia ☐
685 Blackchested Prinia* ☐
689 Spotted Flycatcher ☐
694 Black Flycatcher ☐
695 Marico Flycatcher* ☐
701 Chinspot Batis ☐
710 Paradise Flycatcher ☐
716 Grassveld Pipit ☐
723 Bushveld Pipit ☐
727 Orangethroated Longclaw** ☐
732 Fiscal Shrike ☐
733 Redbacked Shrike ☐
735 **Longtailed Shrike** ☐
736 Southern Boubou** ☐
739 **Crimsonbreasted Boubou*** ☐
740 Puffback ☐
741 Brubru ☐
743 Threestreaked Tchagra ☐
744 Blackcrowned Tchagra ☐
748 **Orangebreasted Bush Shrike** ☐
753 White Helmetshrike ☐
761 Plumcoloured Starling ☐
762 Burchell's Starling* ☐
764 Glossy Starling* ☐
769 Redwinged Starling ☐
779 **Marico Sunbird** ☐
787 Whitebellied Sunbird ☐
796 Cape White-eye** ☐
799 Whitebrowed Sparrowweaver ☐
804 Greyheaded Sparrow ☐
805 Yellowthroated Sparrow ☐
806 Scalyfeathered Finch* ☐
811 Spottedbacked Weaver ☐
814 Masked Weaver ☐
821 Redbilled Quelea ☐
824 Red Bishop ☐
829 Whitewinged Widow ☐
832 Longtailed Widow ☐
834 **Melba Finch** ☐
841 **Jameson's Firefinch** ☐
842 **Redbilled Firefinch** ☐
844 Blue Waxbill ☐
845 **Violeteared Waxbill*** ☐
846 Common Waxbill ☐
860 Pintailed Whydah ☐
869 Yelloweyed Canary ☐
884 Goldenbreasted Bunting ☐

RUST DE WINTER NATURE RESERVE

approximately 348 species recorded to date

The reserve is approximately 80 km north of Pretoria. Camping is allowed, but facilities are limited to field toilets and braai sites (no wood). Birders should make prior ar-

Turn off the Pretoria/Pietersburg freeway (N1) towards Boekenhoutkloof 45 km north of Pretoria. Turn left shortly afterwards to Rust de Winter. After 27 km turn right at a T-junction. The turnoff to the dam is signposted on the right 6 km further on. Follow this gravel road for 3 km to the reserve entrance gate. The reserve office is located on the right shortly before reaching the gate.

rangements with the officer in charge if they wish to walk in any part of the reserve other than the area open for angling. The riverine bush below the dam wall lies in a Water Affairs Department security area and special permission should be obtained before visiting here. Petrol is not available at the nearby settlement of Rust de Winter. The terrain is hilly and rocky with a flat area of alluvial soils in the west. The hills are covered with *Combretum apiculatum* (red bushwillow), *Faurea saligna* (Transvaal beech), *Euphorbia cooperi* (Transvaal candelabra tree) savanna which grades into woodland dominated by species such as *Syzygium guineense* (water pear), *Heteropyxis natalensis* (lavender tree) and *Bridelia mollis* (velvet sweetberry) along the seasonal watercourses. *Acacia* savanna occurs on the alluvial soils and, when the dam has been at a consistently low level for a number of years, fairly extensive grasslands also develop.

SPECIAL AND INTERESTING SPECIES

When the water level is rising the reedbeds and other emergent vegetation around the edges of the dam provide habitat for **Purple** and **Greenbacked Herons**, **Blackcrowned Night Heron**, **African Spoonbill**, **Whitefaced Duck**, **Black Crake**, **Burchell's Coucal** and **African Jacana**. **Great Crested Grebe** breed here under these conditions. **Gabar Goshawk**, **Redcrested Korhaan**, **Namaqua Dove**, **Cardinal Woodpecker**, **Sabota Lark**, **Whitebrowed** and **Kalahari Robins**, **Titbabbler**, **Barred Warbler**, **Rattling Cisticola**, **Marico Flycatcher**, **Longtailed Shrike**, **Crimsonbreasted Boubou**, **Jameson's Firefinch** and **Violeteared Waxbill** are all best looked for in the *Acacia* savanna. The rocky hills with their *Combretum*-dominated woodland are favoured areas for **Coqui Francolin**, **Grey**, **Redbilled** and **Southern Yellowbilled Hornbills**, **Flappet Lark**, **Southern Black Tit**, **Black Cuckooshrike**, **Longbilled Crombec**, **Mousecoloured Flycatcher**, **Redheaded Weaver**, **Rock Bunting** and, in summer, **Cape Bunting**. **Pied Barbet** (in the *Acacia* savanna), **Yellowfronted Tinker Barbet** and **Quail Finch** (particularly in short grass near the water's edge) are more often than not located by their calls. Among the raptors **Secretarybird**, **African Hawk Eagle**, **Blackbreasted Snake Eagle** and **African Fish Eagle** breed here. **Wahlberg's Eagles** breed nearby.

ALSO RECORDED

Whitethroat and the rare Olivetree Warbler are two of the more interesting migrants that are sometimes found in the *Acacia* savanna during summer. The Golden Pipit that was present in this area from January to March 1986 ensured that the reserve became a household name among South African twitchers. Ringed and Grey Plovers and Curlew are three rare waders (inland) that have been seen here recently. Temminck's Courser has been recorded in the grassland after long dry spells and Bronzewinged Courser should be looked for in savanna areas that have recently been burnt. African Finfoot is occasionally seen in the upper reaches of the dam. Bateleur and Ayres', Booted and Longcrested Eagles have also been recorded.

John McAllister

43% OF SPECIES

- 006 **Great Crested Grebe** ☐
- 008 Dabchick ☐
- 055 Whitebreasted Cormorant ☐
- 058 Reed Cormorant ☐
- 060 Darter ☐
- 062 Grey Heron ☐
- 063 Blackheaded Heron ☐
- 065 **Purple Heron** ☐
- 066 Great White Egret ☐
- 071 Cattle Egret ☐
- 074 **Greenbacked Heron** ☐
- 076 **Blackcrowned Night Heron** ☐
- 081 Hamerkop ☐
- 083 White Stork ☐
- 091 Sacred Ibis ☐
- 094 Hadeda Ibis ☐
- 095 **African Spoonbill** ☐
- 099 **Whitefaced Duck** ☐
- 102 Egyptian Goose ☐
- 104 Yellowbilled Duck ☐
- 108 Redbilled Teal ☐
- 116 Spurwinged Goose ☐
- 118 **Secretarybird** ☐
- 126 Black Kite ☐
- 126a Yellowbilled Kite ☐
- 127 Blackshouldered Kite ☐
- 135 **Wahlberg's Eagle** ☐
- 137 **African Hawk Eagle** ☐
- 143 **Blackbreasted Snake Eagle** ☐
- 148 **African Fish Eagle** ☐
- 149 Steppe Buzzard ☐
- 161 **Gabar Goshawk** ☐
- 180 Eastern Redfooted Kestrel ☐
- 182 Greater Kestrel ☐
- 183 Lesser Kestrel ☐
- 188 **Coqui Francolin** ☐
- 189 Crested Francolin ☐
- 196 Natal Francolin* ☐
- 199 Swainson's Francolin* ☐
- 203 Helmeted Guineafowl ☐
- 213 **Black Crake** ☐
- 237 **Redcrested Korhaan*** ☐
- 240 **African Jacana** ☐
- 249 Threebanded Plover ☐
- 255 Crowned Plover ☐
- 258 Blacksmith Plover ☐
- 260 Wattled Plover ☐
- 297 Spotted Dikkop ☐
- 349 Rock Pigeon ☐
- 352 Redeyed Dove ☐
- 354 Cape Turtle Dove ☐
- 355 Laughing Dove ☐
- 356 **Namaqua Dove** ☐
- 358 Greenspotted Dove ☐
- 373 Grey Lourie ☐
- 377 Redchested Cuckoo ☐
- 382 Jacobin Cuckoo ☐
- 386 Diederik Cuckoo ☐
- 391 **Burchell's Coucal*** ☐
- 415 Whiterumped Swift ☐
- 417 Little Swift ☐
- 426 Redfaced Mousebird ☐
- 428 Pied Kingfisher ☐
- 431 Malachite Kingfisher ☐
- 433 Woodland Kingfisher ☐
- 438 European Bee-eater ☐
- 443 Whitefronted Bee-eater ☐
- 444 Little Bee-eater ☐
- 446 European Roller ☐
- 447 Lilacbreasted Roller ☐
- 452 Redbilled Woodhoopoe ☐
- 457 **Grey Hornbill** ☐
- 458 **Redbilled Hornbill** ☐
- 459 **Southern Yellow-billed Hornbill*** ☐
- 464 Blackcollared Barbet ☐
- 465 **Pied Barbet*** ☐
- 470 **Yellowfronted Tinker Barbet** ☐
- 473 Crested Barbet ☐
- 486 **Cardinal Woodpecker** ☐
- 494 Rufousnaped Lark ☐
- 496 **Flappet Lark** ☐
- 498 **Sabota Lark*** ☐
- 518 European Swallow ☐
- 520 Whitethroated Swallow ☐
- 524 Redbreasted Swallow ☐
- 527 Lesser Striped Swallow ☐
- 538 **Black Cuckooshrike** ☐
- 541 Forktailed Drongo ☐
- 545 Blackheaded Oriole ☐
- 548 Pied Crow ☐
- 554 **Southern Black Tit*** ☐
- 560 Arrowmarked Babbler ☐
- 568 Blackeyed Bulbul ☐
- 576 Kurrichane Thrush ☐
- 580 Groundscraper Thrush ☐
- 581 Cape Rock Thrush** ☐
- 613 **Whitebrowed Robin** ☐
- 615 **Kalahari Robin*** ☐
- 621 **Titbabbler*** ☐
- 643 Willow Warbler ☐
- 651 **Longbilled Crombec** ☐
- 658 **Barred Warbler*** ☐
- 664 Fantailed Cisticola ☐
- 672 **Rattling Cisticola** ☐
- 681 Neddicky ☐
- 683 Tawnyflanked Prinia ☐
- 685 Blackchested Prinia* ☐
- 689 Spotted Flycatcher ☐
- 695 **Marico Flycatcher*** ☐
- 696 **Mousecoloured Flycatcher** ☐
- 701 Chinspot Batis ☐
- 710 Paradise Flycatcher ☐
- 716 Grassveld Pipit ☐
- 732 Fiscal Shrike ☐
- 733 Redbacked Shrike ☐
- 735 **Longtailed Shrike** ☐
- 736 Southern Boubou** ☐
- 739 **Crimsonbreasted Boubou*** ☐
- 740 Puffback ☐
- 741 Brubru ☐

743 Threestreaked Tchagra ☐
744 Blackcrowned Tchagra ☐
761 Plumcoloured Starling ☐
764 Glossy Starling* ☐
769 Redwinged Starling ☐
779 Marico Sunbird ☐
787 Whitebellied Sunbird ☐
792 Black Sunbird ☐
796 Cape White-eye** ☐
803 Cape Sparrow* ☐
804 Greyheaded Sparrow ☐
806 Scalyfeathered Finch* ☐
811 Spottedbacked Weaver ☐
814 Masked Weaver ☐
819 **Redheaded Weaver** ☐
821 Redbilled Quelea ☐
824 Red Bishop ☐
826 Golden Bishop ☐
829 Whitewinged Widow ☐
841 **Jameson's Firefinch** ☐
844 Blue Waxbill ☐
845 **Violeteared Waxbill*** ☐
852 **Quail Finch** ☐
857 Bronze Mannikin ☐
860 Pintailed Whydah ☐
862 Paradise Whydah ☐
869 Yelloweyed Canary ☐
884 Goldenbreasted Bunting ☐
885 **Cape Bunting** ☐
886 **Rock Bunting** ☐

DULLSTROOM DISTRICT

approximately 219 species recorded to date

The Dullstroom area is mostly above 2 000 m above sea level and consists of rolling grasslands and many large sponges or marshes. The climate is classified as sub-alpine with cold winters and mild summers. Most of the land is privately owned, much of it by trout syndicates, but very good birding can be had from the roads criss-crossing the area. There is a hotel in the village as well as a caravan park and campsite run by the town council at the Dullstroom Dam, where some good birding can be done.

Turn off the N4 from Pretoria to Nelspruit at Belfast. Take the R540 from here to Dullstroom. Two circular drives that will take you through some excellent birding country are detailed below. Roads on both of these drives can become slippery when wet.

1. Eight kilometres from Dullstroom on the Belfast road turn left onto a gravel road signposted "Machadodorp". After 4,5 km turn left towards Valleyspruit and then, 7 km later, turn right towards Kruisfontein. After 14 km turn left towards Morgenzon (dry weather only). This road eventually rejoins the Dullstroom/Lydenburg (13 km) road about 3 km north of Dullstroom.

2. Leave Dullstroom via Slachtersnek Street, turn-

ing right at the T-junction after the railway crossing towards Tonteldoos. Pass through Tonteldoos village after 22 km and continue on for another 14 km to Draaikraal where the road joins the tarred Roossenekal/ Lydenburg road. Turn right here and proceed up to the top of the Steenkampsberg Pass (13 km) and turn right again onto the gravel road to Nederhorst (14 km), which is 8 km from Dullstroom.

SPECIAL AND INTERESTING SPECIES

Scan the many sponges for **Wattled** and **Crowned Cranes** and look for **Blue Crane** in the drier grassland. **Jackal Buzzard**, **Stanley's Bustard**, **Ground Woodpecker**, **Longbilled Lark**, **Sentinel Rock Thrush** and **Buffstreaked Chat** are best looked for in the high-lying rocky areas while **Greywing Francolin** and **Yellowbreasted Pipit** prefer areas with short grass. **Redwing Francolin** and **Whitebellied Korhaan** prefer long grass and can often be found at lower altitudes. Recently burnt areas are the favoured haunts of **Bald Ibis** and **Blackwinged Plover** (rocky summits in summer).The thin, piping call of **Ayres' Cisticola** is perhaps the most characteristic sound heard here. **Palecrowned Cisticola**, **Malachite Sunbird**, **Yellowrumped Widow** and **Golden Bishop** may be found in wet lowlands where there is rank grass and weeds. The *Protea* dotted rocky slopes of the mountain pass to the east of the Nederhorst turn-off on the Roossenekal/Lydenburg road are the best places to find **Wailing Cisticola** and **Gurney's Sugarbird**. **Horus Swift**, **Banded Martin** and **Cape Eagle Owl** can also be found along this road. The many plantations are the best places to look for **Redbreasted** and **Black Sparrowhawk** while **African Marsh Harrier** is often seen quartering the sponges. **Cape Vulture** and **Black Crow** can turn up almost anywhere.

57% OF SPECIES

No.	Species		No.	Species	
008	Dabchick	☐	118	Secretarybird	☐
055	Whitebreasted Cormorant	☐	122	**Cape Vulture****	☐
058	Reed Cormorant	☐	127	Blackshouldered Kite	☐
062	Grey Heron	☐	149	Steppe Buzzard	☐
063	Blackheaded Heron	☐	152	**Jackal Buzzard****	☐
065	Purple Heron	☐	155	**Redbreasted Sparrowhawk**	☐
066	Great White Egret	☐	158	**Black Sparrowhawk**	☐
068	Yellowbilled Egret	☐	165	**African Marsh Harrier**	☐
071	Cattle Egret	☐	172	Lanner Falcon	☐
081	Hamerkop	☐	180	Eastern Redfooted Kestrel	☐
083	White Stork	☐	181	Rock Kestrel	☐
084	Black Stork	☐	183	Lesser Kestrel	☐
091	Sacred Ibis	☐	190	**Greywing Francolin****	☐
092	**Bald Ibis****	☐	192	**Redwing Francolin**	☐
094	Hadeda Ibis	☐	199	Swainson's Francolin*	☐
099	Whitefaced Duck	☐			
102	Egyptian Goose	☐			
104	Yellowbilled Duck	☐			
116	Spurwinged Goose	☐			

ALSO RECORDED

The elusive Grass Owl, which breeds here, may be flushed near a marsh by the lucky birder. Redchested Flufftail may be heard in the marshes and the rare Whitewinged Flufftail also occurs here. Striped Flufftail may be heard in the montane grassland. Blue Korhaan has been recorded in short grassland.

John McAllister

200 Common Quail ☐
203 Helmeted Guineafowl ☐
207 **Wattled Crane** ☐
208 **Blue Crane**** ☐
209 **Crowned Crane** ☐
210 African Rail ☐
212 African Crake ☐
223 Purple Gallinule ☐
226 Moorhen ☐
228 Redknobbed Coot ☐
231 **Stanley's Bustard** ☐
233 **Whitebellied Korhaan** ☐
255 Crowned Plover ☐
257 **Blackwinged Plover** ☐
258 Blacksmith Plover ☐
260 Wattled Plover ☐
266 Wood Sandpiper ☐
286 Ethiopian Snipe ☐
295 Blackwinged Stilt ☐
297 Spotted Dikkop ☐
339 Whitewinged Tern ☐
349 Rock Pigeon ☐
350 Rameron Pigeon ☐
352 Redeyed Dove ☐
354 Cape Turtle Dove ☐
355 Laughing Dove ☐
377 Redchested Cuckoo ☐
386 Diederik Cuckoo ☐
395 Marsh Owl ☐
400 **Cape Eagle Owl** ☐
401 Spotted Eagle Owl ☐
412 Black Swift ☐
415 Whiterumped Swift ☐
416 **Horus Swift** ☐
417 Little Swift ☐
418 Alpine Swift ☐
424 Speckled Mousebird ☐
426 Redfaced Mousebird ☐
428 Pied Kingfisher ☐
430 Halfcollared Kingfisher ☐
431 Malachite Kingfisher ☐
438 European Bee-eater ☐
444 Little Bee-eater ☐
464 Blackcollared Barbet ☐
473 Crested Barbet ☐
480 **Ground Woodpecker**** ☐
500 **Longbilled Lark*** ☐
507 Redcapped Lark ☐
518 European Swallow ☐
520 Whitethroated Swallow ☐
524 Redbreasted Swallow ☐
526 Greater Striped Swallow* ☐
529 Rock Martin ☐
530 House Martin ☐
533 Brownthroated Martin ☐
534 **Banded Martin** ☐
547 **Black Crow** ☐
568 Blackeyed Bulbul ☐
577 Olive Thrush ☐
580 Groundscraper Thrush ☐
581 Cape Rock Thrush** ☐
582 **Sentinel Rock Thrush**** ☐
586 Mountain Chat* ☐
588 **Buffstreaked Chat**** ☐
593 Mocking Chat ☐
595 Anteating Chat** ☐
596 Stonechat ☐
601 Cape Robin ☐
631 African Marsh Warbler ☐
635 Cape Reed Warbler ☐
638 African Sedge Warbler ☐
643 Willow Warbler ☐
645 Barthroated Apalis ☐
667 **Ayres' Cisticola** ☐
668 **Palecrowned Cisticola** ☐
670 **Wailing Cisticola** ☐
677 Levaillant's Cisticola ☐
686 Spotted Prinia** ☐
713 Cape Wagtail ☐
716 Grassveld Pipit ☐
725 **Yellowbreasted Pipit**** ☐
727 Orangethroated Longclaw** ☐
732 Fiscal Shrike ☐
736 Southern Boubou** ☐
746 Bokmakierie* ☐
759 Pied Starling** ☐
769 Redwinged Starling ☐
774 **Gurney's Sugarbird**** ☐
775 **Malachite Sunbird** ☐
801 House Sparrow ☐
803 Cape Sparrow* ☐
804 Greyheaded Sparrow ☐
813 Cape Weaver** ☐
814 Masked Weaver ☐
824 Red Bishop ☐
826 **Golden Bishop** ☐
827 **Yellowrumped Widow** ☐
828 Redshouldered Widow ☐
831 Redcollared Widow ☐
832 Longtailed Widow ☐
846 Common Waxbill ☐
852 Quail Finch ☐
854 Orangebreasted Waxbill ☐
860 Pintailed Whydah ☐
872 Cape Canary ☐
881 Streakyheaded Canary ☐
885 Cape Bunting ☐

☐

☐

☐

☐

☐

☐

VAALKOP DAM NATURE RESERVE

approximately 339 species recorded to date

This reserve, at present controlled by the Chief Directorate: Nature and Environmental Conservation, is a mere 135 km from Johannesburg and Pretoria and about 60 km north-west of Brits. It is one of the prime bushveld and waterbird reserves in the Transvaal. The 1 873 ha reserve is comprised mainly of the dam (1 045 ha) surrounded by a narrow strip of land below the 100-year floodline, which is made up of a heterogeneous mixture of *Acacia* thornveld (mostly umbrella thorn *Acacia tortilis*, scented thorn *Acacia nilotica* and sweet thorn *Acacia karoo*), open broadleafed savanna dominated by weeping wattle *Peltophorum africanum*, buffalo thorn or wag-'n-bietjie *Ziziphus mucronata* and mountain karee *Rhus leptodictya*. Below the dam wall is a strip of riverine vegetation. This wide variety of habitats results in a rich diversity of birds being recorded in this relatively small area.

SPECIAL AND INTERESTING SPECIES

Immediately after passing through the entrance gate there is a fork in the road. The *Acacia* scrub in the vicinity of the entrance gate and along the left hand fork is a good place to look for **Great Sparrow** and **Scalyfeathered Finch**. Other *Acacia* specials in the reserve are **Blue** and **Violeteared Waxbills**, **Crimsonbreasted Boubou**, **Marico Sunbird**,

Take the R511 from Brits towards Thabazimbi. Turn left at Beestekraal siding (38 km). Shortly after crossing the Crocodile River a T-junction is reached. To reach the northern and eastern shores of the dam (the most popular birding area) turn right and continue along the tarred road for about 12 km and turn left (signposted) to the dam. The reserve entrance is on the right, a short way along this gravel road. To reach the southern shore and the reserve office turn left at the T-junction and right shortly afterwards. Travel along this tarred road for approximately 19 km and turn right onto a road signposted "Moorddrif". Turn right again at a T-junction about 10 km further on. The entrance to the reserve is on your right after another 10 km or so, shortly before crossing the Elands River and the upper reaches of the dam. Camping and caravanning are allowed on the reserve, but facilities are fairly primitive: a few cold water taps and toilets.

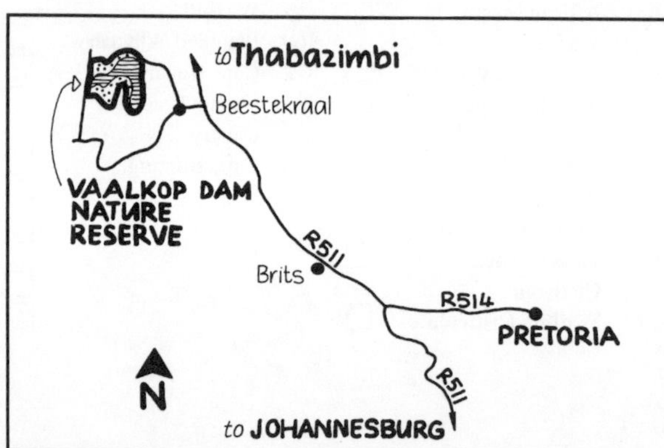

Marico Flycatcher, **Blackchested Prinia**, **Titbabbler**, **Kalahari Robin**, **Pied Barbet** and **Sabota Lark**. **Whitebacked Mousebird**, a bird of dense scrub and bush thickets, should also be looked for here. The righ-hand fork crosses the Elands River below the dam wall where **Whitethroated Robin** and **Southern Boubou** frequent the riverine bush. Other species that are best found in this dense bush are **Tawnyflanked Prinia**, **Puffback**, **Brubru** and **Black Sunbird**. The reedbeds on the riverbanks are the favoured haunt of **Black Crake**, **Malachite Kingfisher**, **Orangebreasted Waxbill** and **Burchell's Coucal**. After crossing the river the road climbs up to the dam and good views can be had over the water. Scan the rocky shoreline carefully for **Water Dikkop** – this is the closest locality to the Witwatersrand where this lowveld species, which has colonised the area via the Limpopo and Crocodile rivers, can be regularly seen. Also look for **Wattled Plover**. Further on the road passes through more *Acacia* woodland (keep a sharp eye open for **Pale Chanting Goshawk** and **Redcrested Korhaan** here and, if you camp overnight, listen for **Rufouscheeked Nightjar**) before coming to some open savanna with scattered broadleafed trees. Here one should look for **Whitequilled Korhaan**, **Spotted Dikkop**, **Grey**, **Redbilled** and **Southern Yellowbilled Hornbills**, **Pearlbreasted Swallow**, **Whitebrowed Robin**, **Three-streaked Tchagra** and **Longtailed Shrike**. The very attractive **Whitefronted** and **Little Bee-eaters** can also be found in this habitat. Good views of the upper reaches of the dam can be had from here and the flooded trees are often used by **Whitebreasted** and **Reed Cormorants**, **Darters** and **Grey Herons** as breeding sites, and by **Bluecheeked Bee-eaters** (late summer), **Pied Kingfishers** and **African Fish Eagles** as hunting perches. Most of the ducks, especially **Whitefaced** and **Knobbilled Ducks** also prefer these shallower and quieter waters. On the southern shore (please get permission from the officer in charge of the reserve first) **Pearlspotted Owls** call almost continually on cloudy days and during winter.

ALSO RECORDED

A single Ringed Teal (probably an escapee), a Sanderling, a Whiterumped Sandpiper and an African Skimmer (1984) are probably the most surprising birds to be recorded here recently. Redbilled Oxpeckers have been seen with increasing frequency of late.

John McAllister

44% OF SPECIES

006	Great Crested Grebe	☐	063	Blackheaded Heron	☐	081	Hamerkop	☐
008	Dabchick	☐	066	Great White Egret	☐	085	Abdim's Stork	☐
055	**Whitebreasted Cormorant**	☐	067	Little Egret	☐	091	Sacred Ibis	☐
			068	Yellowbilled Egret	☐	094	Hadeda Ibis	☐
058	**Reed Cormorant**	☐	071	Cattle Egret	☐	095	African Spoonbill	☐
060	**Darter**	☐	076	Blackcrowned Night Heron	☐	099	**Whitefaced Duck**	☐
062	**Grey Heron**	☐				102	Egyptian Goose	☐

104 Yellowbilled Duck ☐
108 Redbilled Teal ☐
115 **Knobbilled Duck** ☐
116 Spurwinged Goose ☐
126a Yellowbilled Kite ☐
127 Blackshouldered Kite ☐
135 Wahlberg's Eagle ☐
143 Blackbreasted Snake Eagle ☐
148 **African Fish Eagle** ☐
149 Steppe Buzzard ☐
161 Gabar Goshawk ☐
162 **Pale Chanting Goshawk*** ☐
189 Crested Francolin ☐
196 Natal Francolin* ☐
199 Swainson's Francolin* ☐
203 Helmeted Guineafowl ☐
213 **Black Crake** ☐
228 Redknobbed Coot ☐
237 **Redcrested Korhaan*** ☐
239a **Whitequilled Korhaan**** ☐
249 Threebanded Plover ☐
255 Crowned Plover ☐
258 Blacksmith Plover ☐
260 **Wattled Plover** ☐
264 Common Sandpiper ☐
274 Little Stint ☐
297 **Spotted Dikkop** ☐
298 **Water Dikkop** ☐
339 Whitewinged Tern ☐
349 Rock Pigeon ☐
352 Redeyed Dove ☐
354 Cape Turtle Dove ☐
355 Laughing Dove ☐
356 Namaqua Dove ☐
373 Grey Lourie ☐
382 Jacobin Cuckoo ☐
386 Diederik Cuckoo ☐
391 **Burchell's Coucal*** ☐
398 **Pearlspotted Owl** ☐
401 Spotted Eagle Owl ☐
406 **Rufouscheeked Nightjar** ☐
415 Whiterumped Swift ☐
417 Little Swift ☐
424 Speckled Mousebird ☐
425 **Whitebacked Mousebird**** ☐
426 Redfaced Mousebird ☐
428 **Pied Kingfisher** ☐
431 **Malachite Kingfisher** ☐
435 Brownhooded Kingfisher ☐
438 European Bee-eater ☐
440 **Bluecheeked Bee-eater** ☐
443 **Whitefronted Bee-eater** ☐
444 **Little Bee-eater** ☐
446 European Roller ☐
447 Lilacbreasted Roller ☐
451 Hoopoe ☐
452 Redbilled Woodhoopoe ☐
457 **Grey Hornbill** ☐
458 **Redbilled Hornbill** ☐
459 **Southern Yellow-billed Hornbill*** ☐
464 Blackcollared Barbet ☐
465 **Pied Barbet*** ☐
473 Crested Barbet ☐
494 Rufousnaped Lark ☐
498 **Sabota Lark*** ☐
518 European Swallow ☐
520 Whitethroated Swallow ☐
523 **Pearlbreasted Swallow** ☐
524 Redbreasted Swallow ☐
526 Greater Striped Swallow* ☐
527 Lesser Striped Swallow ☐
533 Brownthroated Martin ☐
541 Forktailed Drongo ☐
548 Pied Crow ☐
560 Arrowmarked Babbler ☐
568 Blackeyed Bulbul ☐
576 Kurrichane Thrush ☐
596 Stonechat ☐
602 **Whitethroated Robin**** ☐
613 **Whitebrowed Robin** ☐
615 **Kalahari Robin*** ☐
621 **Titbabbler*** ☐
631 African Marsh Warbler ☐
633 European Marsh Warbler ☐
634 European Sedge Warbler ☐
643 Willow Warbler ☐
651 Longbilled Crombec ☐
664 Fantailed Cisticola ☐
665 Desert Cisticola ☐
672 Rattling Cisticola ☐
677 Levaillant's Cisticola ☐
681 Neddicky ☐
683 **Tawnyflanked Prinia** ☐
685 **Blackchested Prinia** ☐
689 Spotted Flycatcher ☐
695 **Marico Flycatcher*** ☐
701 Chinspot Batis ☐
710 Paradise Flycatcher ☐
713 Cape Wagtail ☐
732 Fiscal Shrike ☐
733 Redbacked Shrike ☐
735 **Longtailed Shrike** ☐
736 **Southern Boubou**** ☐
739 **Crimsonbreasted Boubou*** ☐
740 **Puffback** ☐
741 **Brubru** ☐
743 **Threestreaked Tchagra** ☐
764 Glossy Starling* ☐
779 **Marico Sunbird** ☐
787 Whitebellied Sunbird ☐
792 **Black Sunbird** ☐
796 Cape White-eye** ☐
799 Whitebrowed Sparrowweaver ☐
801 House Sparrow ☐
802 **Great Sparrow*** ☐
803 Cape Sparrow* ☐

804 Greyheaded Sparrow ☐
806 **Scalyfeathered Finch*** ☐
814 Masked Weaver ☐
821 Redbilled Quelea ☐
824 Red Bishop ☐
826 Golden Bishop ☐
844 **Blue Waxbill** ☐
845 **Violeteared Waxbill*** ☐
846 Common Waxbill ☐
852 Quail Finch ☐
854 **Orangebreasted Waxbill** ☐
860 Pintailed Whydah ☐
869 Yelloweyed Canary ☐
870 Blackthroated Canary ☐
886 Rock Bunting ☐
☐
☐
☐
☐

NELSPRUIT NATURE RESERVE AND ADJOINING TRIM PARK

approximately 152 species recorded to date

The Nelspruit Nature Reserve, a small protected area under the control of the Nelspruit Town Council, is situated in a residential area of Nelspruit. The reserve lies in a valley with steep slopes and bare granitic domes on the one side. Densely vegetated with broadleaf woodland and riverine vegetation, it is characterised by tall trees. The western boundary adjoins the trim park, which levels out and has a sizeable vlei area forming an important habitat for wetland species. Vehicles are not permitted within the reserve but there are well laid out footpaths to follow. The reserve is open all hours.

SPECIAL AND INTERESTING SPECIES

African Goshawk can often be seen flying overhead in the early morning and giving its characteristic "krit" call at two-

ALSO RECORDED

Towards the end of winter and in early spring Narina Trogon sometimes visits the reserve from forest areas nearby. Cinnamon Dove has been recorded on a couple of occasions. Broadtailed Warbler has been seen on the plateau and on the granite slopes Mocking Chat is occasionally seen although it is rare in the reserve. Occasionally Shelley's Francolin has been recorded calling from the northern slopes. Raptors

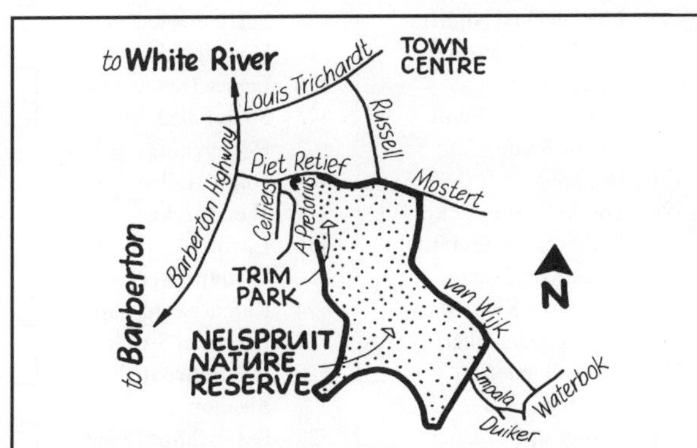

Follow van Wijk Street south of the business centre and at the top of the hill turn right into Waterbok Street, and right again into Impala Street. At the cul-de-sac you will find a parking area and the entrance gate. There is no entrance fee. An alternate entrance is from the car park at the trim park in Andries Pretorius Street. Follow the footpath under the road culvert and keep to the right to reach the nature reserve or to the left to circuit the vlei area.

second intervals. **Purplecrested Lourie** and **Green Pigeon** will be found in the tall riverine trees. In the early mornings the valley echoes with birdsong. **Black Cuckoos** call from the tall trees, as do **Yellowbreasted Apalises**, while **Heuglin's** and **Natal Robins** frequent the dense scrub. **Whitethroated Robin** may also be seen. At night and on rainy days the eerie call of **Buffspotted Flufftail** can sometimes be heard. Other night birds often heard are **Fierynecked Nightjar** on the wooded slopes and **Freckled Nightjar** on the granite domes. **Wood Owl** can be heard calling from the riverine trees. The dense vegetation attracts forest birds such as **Olive Bush Shrike**, **Green Twinspot** and **Redbacked Mannikin**. The loud call of the **Goldentailed Woodpecker** makes this species easy to distinguish from the smaller **Cardinal Woodpecker**. The vlei area in the trim park is well worth a visit in late summer. **Redchested Flufftail** can be heard calling from within the marsh vegetation, and there is much activity from breeding **Redshouldered** and **Redcollared Widows** and from **Golden** and **Thickbilled Weavers**. A pair of **Whitethroated Swallows** nest under a road bridge at the edge of the vlei each year.

such as Wahlberg's and Martial Eagles and Brown Snake Eagle are not resident in the reserve but may be seen flying overhead. Goldenrumped Tinker Barbet appears to move up the larger rivers from the coast, and is sometimes recorded in the reserve.

Peter Lawson

94% OF SPECIES

No.	Species		No.	Species		No.	Species	
058	Reed Cormorant	☐	361	**Green Pigeon**	☐	444	Little Bee-eater	☐
071	Cattle Egret	☐	371	**Purplecrested Lourie**	☐	451	Hoopoe	☐
074	Greenbacked Heron	☐	377	Redchested Cuckoo	☐	454	Scimitarbilled Woodhoopoe	☐
081	Hamerkop	☐	378	**Black Cuckoo**	☐	464	Blackcollared Barbet	☐
085	Abdim's Stork	☐	385	Klaas's Cuckoo	☐	470	Yellowfronted Tinker Barbet	☐
094	Hadeda Ibis	☐	386	Diederik Cuckoo	☐	473	Crested Barbet	☐
126a	Yellowbilled Kite	☐	391	Burchell's Coucal*	☐	474	Greater Honeyguide	☐
154	Lizard Buzzard	☐	394	**Wood Owl**	☐	475	Scalythroated Honeyguide	☐
157	Little Sparrowhawk	☐	401	Spotted Eagle Owl	☐	476	Lesser Honeyguide	☐
160	**African Goshawk**	☐	405	**Fierynecked Nightjar**	☐	478	Sharpbilled Honeyguide	☐
173	Hobby Falcon	☐	408	**Freckled Nightjar**	☐	483	**Goldentailed Woodpecker**	☐
196	Natal Francolin*	☐	412	Black Swift	☐	486	**Cardinal Woodpecker**	☐
203	Helmeted Guineafowl	☐	415	Whiterumped Swift	☐	494	Rufousnaped Lark	☐
213	Black Crake	☐	418	Alpine Swift	☐	518	European Swallow	☐
217	**Redchested Flufftail**	☐	421	Palm Swift	☐	520	**Whitethroated Swallow**	☐
218	**Buffspotted Flufftail**	☐	424	Speckled Mousebird	☐	527	Lesser Striped Swallow	☐
264	Common Sandpiper	☐	426	Redfaced Mousebird	☐			
350	Rameron Pigeon	☐	429	Giant Kingfisher	☐			
352	Redeyed Dove	☐	431	Malachite Kingfisher	☐			
354	Cape Turtle Dove	☐	432	Pygmy Kingfisher	☐			
355	Laughing Dove	☐	435	Brownhooded Kingfisher	☐			
358	Greenspotted Dove	☐	438	European Bee-eater	☐			
359	Tambourine Dove	☐						

533 Brownthroated Martin ☐
536 Black Sawwing Swallow ☐
538 Black Cuckooshrike ☐
541 Forktailed Drongo ☐
545 Blackheaded Oriole ☐
548 Pied Crow ☐
554 Southern Black Tit* ☐
558 Grey Penduline Tit ☐
560 Arrowmarked Babbler ☐
568 Blackeyed Bulbul ☐
569 Terrestrial Bulbul ☐
572 Sombre Bulbul ☐
576 Kurrichane Thrush ☐
599 **Heuglin's Robin** ☐
600 **Natal Robin** ☐
601 Cape Robin ☐
602 **Whitethroated Robin**** ☐
613 Whitebrowed Robin ☐
619 Garden Warbler ☐
631 African Marsh Warbler ☐
633 European Marsh Warbler ☐
638 African Sedge Warbler ☐
643 Willow Warbler ☐
645 Barthroated Apalis ☐
648 **Yellowbreasted Apalis** ☐
651 Longbilled Crombec ☐
657 Bleating Warbler ☐
674 Redfaced Cisticola ☐
677 Levaillant's Cisticola ☐
679 Lazy Cisticola ☐
681 Neddicky ☐
683 Tawnyflanked Prinia ☐
689 Spotted Flycatcher ☐
690 Dusky Flycatcher ☐
691 Bluegrey Flycatcher ☐
693 Fantailed Flycatcher ☐
694 Black Flycatcher ☐
701 Chinspot Batis ☐
710 Paradise Flycatcher ☐
720 Striped Pipit ☐
728 Yellowthroated Longclaw ☐
732 Fiscal Shrike ☐
736 Southern Boubou** ☐
740 Puffback ☐
743 Threestreaked Tchagra ☐
744 Blackcrowned Tchagra ☐
747 Gorgeous Bush Shrike ☐
748 Orangebreasted Bush Shrike ☐
750 **Olive Bush Shrike*** ☐
751 Greyheaded Bush Shrike ☐
761 Plumcoloured Starling ☐
769 Redwinged Starling ☐
787 Whitebellied Sunbird ☐
791 Scarletchested Sunbird ☐
792 Black Sunbird ☐
793 Collared Sunbird ☐
796 Cape White-eye** ☐
801 House Sparrow ☐
805 Yellowthroated Sparrow ☐
807 **Thickbilled Weaver** ☐
810 Spectacled Weaver ☐
811 Spottedbacked Weaver ☐
815 Lesser Masked Weaver ☐
816 **Golden Weaver** ☐
819 Redheaded Weaver ☐
824 Red Bishop ☐
828 **Redshouldered Widow** ☐
829 Whitewinged Widow ☐
831 **Redcollared Widow** ☐
835 **Green Twinspot** ☐
840 Bluebilled Firefinch ☐
842 Redbilled Firefinch ☐
846 Common Waxbill ☐
854 Orangebreasted Waxbill ☐
857 Bronze Mannikin ☐
858 **Redbacked Mannikin** ☐
860 Pintailed Whydah ☐
864 Black Widowfinch ☐
869 Yelloweyed Canary ☐
877 Bully Canary ☐
881 Streakyheaded Canary ☐
886 Rock Bunting ☐
☐
☐
☐
☐
☐

Tambourine Doves

LOSKOP DAM

approximately 297 species recorded to date

The area covered here lies at the interface of the Transvaal highveld and bushveld biomes and includes Overvaal Loskopdam, controlled by the Overvaal Resorts Board, Loskop Dam Nature Reserve (14 800 ha) and the dam itself (2 332 ha), both controlled by the Chief Directorate: Nature and Environmental Conservation. The area is mountainous and mostly covered with a *Combretum* or bushwillow dominated broadleafed woodland with species such as Transvaal beech *Faurea saligna*, wild seringa *Burkea africana* and lavender fever-berry *Croton gratissimus* also occurring. On the higher lying ground this woodland gives way to a *Protea* dominated savanna and finally to open grassland. *Acacia* woodland and scrub occurs on the alluvial soils west of the Olifants River and along the Dennilton road. Riparian vegetation fringes the Olifants River. Accommodation ranging from chalets to camping sites is available at the Overvaal resort. Visitors may drive through the reserve on the demarcated roads, but because of the presence of buffalo and white rhinoceros, they may not leave their vehicles.

SPECIAL AND INTERESTING SPECIES

The reserve was the site of one of the first successful re-introduction attempts of **Redbilled Oxpeckers** in the Transvaal in September 1985 and the birds are now well-established breeding residents. They are often seen on the backs of their hosts – mainly giraffe, buffalo and impala. The well-

ALSO RECORDED

Black Stork, Black and Crowned Eagles and Bald Ibis have been recorded breeding in the area and may be seen by the lucky birder. Stanley's Bustard may sometimes be seen along the road to Verena. Crowned Crane, Dwarf Bittern and Racket-tailed Roller are out of range rarities that have been recorded recently.

John McAllister

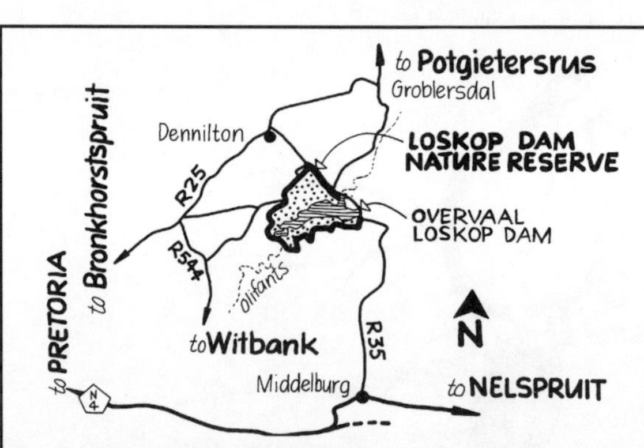

The easiest way to reach the dam is to leave the N4 from Pretoria to the lowveld at Middelburg and take the R35 towards Groblersdal. The resort, on the left after about 50 km, is open 24 hours a day, but the reserve is only open between 07h00 and 17h00 (entry allowed only until 15h00) daily.

wooded grounds of the resort provide good birding and between late August and mid-April this is a good place to study the differences between **Greater** and **Lesser Striped Swallows. Green Pigeon**, **Palm Swift**, **Whitefronted** and **Little Bee-eaters**, **Longbilled Crombec**, **Neddicky** and **Paradise Flycatcher** (summer) are among the species commonly found here. The dam is best viewed from the resort. Scan the water for **Egyptian Goose**, **Yellowbilled Duck**, **Whitebreasted** and **Reed Cormorants** and **Darter** and the skies for **African Fish Eagle** and **Osprey** (summer). The quieter parts of the shoreline, best seen from a boat, should produce **Grey Heron**, **Yellowbilled Egret**, **Water Dikkop** and **Hamerkop**. The narrow bridge crossing the Olifants River on the way to the reserve is a good place to stop for a while. Both **Little** and **Whiterumped Swifts** breed under the bridge, **African Black Duck** can often be seen in the river and the reeds should be scanned for **Burchell's Coucal**, **Cape Reed Warbler**, **African Sedge Warbler** and **Cape** and **Thickbilled Weavers**. The long grass and tangled vegetation on the riverbanks may produce **Redfaced Cisticola**, **Redcollared Widow** and **Grassbird** while the riverine bush is a good place to look for **Southern Boubou** and **Puffback**. After crossing the Olifants the road to the reserve entrance passes through a small patch of *Acacia* savanna (the road to Dennilton also passes through some *Acacia* scrub) and a walk in this area is often rewarded by good views of **Swainson's Francolin**, **Scimitarbilled Woodhoopoe**, **Titbabbler**, **Crimsonbreasted Boubou**, **Threestreaked Tchagra**, **Blue** and **Violeteared Waxbills** and **Redheaded Finch**. The drive through the reserve traverses mountainous broadleafed woodland. Stops along this road (please remember not to get out of your vehicle) may reward birders with species such as **Redchested Cuckoo** (more often heard than seen), **Jacobin Cuckoo** and **Woodland Kingfisher** in summer. **Flappet Lark** can often be seen displaying overhead during summer, but it is inconspicuous at other times. Mixed bird parties here often include **Southern Black Tit**, **Yellowfronted Tinker Barbet**, **Chinspot Batis** (particularly in winter), **Brubru** and **White Helmetshrike**. Search the surrounding bush for **Lazy Cisticola**, **Striped Pipit**, **Mocking Chat** and **Shelley's Francolin** where the road passes through well-wooded, rocky gorges. **Greencapped Eremomela** and **Greybacked Bleating Warbler** are often heard before they are seen and should be looked for in the upper canopy of tall trees. Scan the skies for **African Hawk** and **Martial Eagles**. The gravel road to Verena winds up through the hills into the *Protea* savanna. The open rocky slopes are home to **Cape Rock Thrush**, **Wailing Cisticola** and **Rock Bunting**.

Transvaal

51% OF SPECIES

001 Ostrich
008 Dabchick
055 **Whitebreasted Cormorant**
058 **Reed Cormorant**
060 **Darter**
062 **Grey Heron**
068 **Yellowbilled Egret**
071 Cattle Egret
081 Hamerkop
094 Hadeda Ibis
102 **Egyptian Goose**
104 **Yellowbilled Duck**
105 **African Black Duck**
126a Yellowbilled Kite
137 **African Hawk Eagle**
140 **Martial Eagle**
148 **African Fish Eagle**
170 **Osprey**
181 Rock Kestrel
188 Coqui Francolin
189 Crested Francolin
191 **Shelley's Francolin**
196 Natal Francolin*
199 **Swainson's Francolin***
203 Helmeted Guineafowl
249 Threebanded Plover
258 Blacksmith Plover
260 Wattled Plover
297 Spotted Dikkop
298 **Water Dikkop**
349 Rock Pigeon
352 Redeyed Dove
354 Cape Turtle Dove
355 Laughing Dove
358 Greenspotted Dove
361 **Green Pigeon**
373 Grey Lourie
377 **Redchested Cuckoo**
382 **Jacobin Cuckoo**
386 Diederik Cuckoo
391 **Burchell's Coucal***
392 Barn Owl
396 Scops Owl
398 Pearlspotted Owl
405 Fierynecked Nightjar
412 Black Swift
415 **Whiterumped Swift**
416 Horus Swift
417 **Little Swift**
421 **Palm Swift**
424 Speckled Mousebird
426 Redfaced Mousebird
428 **Pied Kingfisher**
431 Malachite Kingfisher
433 **Woodland Kingfisher**
435 Brownhooded Kingfisher
437 Striped Kingfisher
443 **Whitefronted Bee-eater**
444 **Little Bee-eater**
451 Hoopoe
452 Redbilled Woodhoopoe
454 **Scimitarbilled Woodhoopoe**
457 Grey Hornbill
458 Redbilled Hornbill
459 Southern Yellow-billed Hornbill*
464 Blackcollared Barbet
465 Pied Barbet*
470 **Yellowfronted Tinker Barbet**
473 Crested Barbet
483 Goldentailed Woodpecker
486 Cardinal Woodpecker
494 Rufousnaped Lark
496 **Flappet Lark**
518 European Swallow
524 Redbreasted Swallow
526 **Greater Striped Swallow***
527 **Lesser Striped Swallow**
529 Rock Martin
541 Forktailed Drongo
545 Blackheaded Oriole
554 **Southern Black Tit***
560 Arrowmarked Babbler
568 Blackeyed Bulbul
576 Kurrichane Thrush
580 Groundscraper Thrush
581 **Cape Rock Thrush****
589 Familiar Chat
593 **Mocking Chat**
601 Cape Robin
602 Whitethroated Robin**
613 Whitebrowed Robin
621 **Titbabbler***
635 **Cape Reed Warbler**
638 **African Sedge Warbler**
643 Willow Warbler
645 Barthroated Apalis
651 **Longbilled Crombec**
655 **Greencapped Eremomela**
657a **Greybacked Bleating Warbler**
661 **Grassbird****
664 Fantailed Cisticola
665 Desert Cisticola
670 **Wailing Cisticola**
672 Rattling Cisticola
674 **Redfaced Cisticola**
677 Levaillant's Cisticola
679 **Lazy Cisticola**
681 **Neddicky**
683 Tawnyflanked Prinia
689 Spotted Flycatcher
694 Black Flycatcher
701 **Chinspot Batis**
710 **Paradise Flycatcher**
716 Grassveld Pipit
720 **Striped Pipit**
732 Fiscal Shrike
736 **Southern Boubou****
739 **Crimsonbreasted Boubou***

- 740 **Puffback** ☐
- 741 **Brubru** ☐
- 743 **Threestreaked Tchagra** ☐
- 744 Blackcrowned Tchagra ☐
- 751 Greyheaded Bush Shrike ☐
- 753 **White Helmetshrike** ☐
- 761 Plumcoloured Starling ☐
- 764 Glossy Starling* ☐
- 769 Redwinged Starling ☐
- 772 **Redbilled Oxpecker** ☐
- 787 Whitebellied Sunbird ☐
- 792 Black Sunbird ☐
- 796 Cape White-eye** ☐
- 804 Greyheaded Sparrow ☐
- 805 Yellowthroated Sparrow ☐
- 806 Scalyfeathered Finch* ☐
- 807 **Thickbilled Weaver** ☐
- 813 **Cape Weaver**** ☐
- 814 Masked Weaver ☐
- 819 Redheaded Weaver ☐
- 824 Red Bishop ☐
- 829 Whitewinged Widow ☐
- 831 **Redcollared Widow** ☐
- 844 **Blue Waxbill** ☐
- 845 **Violeteared Waxbill*** ☐
- 846 Common Waxbill ☐
- 856 **Redheaded Finch*** ☐
- 857 Bronze Mannikin ☐
- 860 Pintailed Whydah ☐
- 869 Yelloweyed Canary ☐
- 884 Goldenbreasted Bunting ☐
- 886 **Rock Bunting** ☐

PILANESBERG NATIONAL PARK

approximately 346 species recorded to date

The Pilanesberg National Park, under the control of the National Parks and Wildlife Management Board of Bophuthatswana, is the fourth largest in southern Africa, with an area of 500 square km. It covers habitats such as the large Mankwe Dam, savanna grassland, ravines and dense woodland. There are over 100 km of good roads and accommodation at various camps ranges from safari tents, chalets and a caravan park to a luxury hotel.

ALSO RECORDED

Uncommon water-associated species that may be seen are Osprey, Blackcrowned Night Heron and Greenbacked Heron. Booted Eagle, Honey Buzzard and Tree Pipit are unusual summer visitors. Green Sandpiper has been trapped at Mankwe Dam.

Clive Hopcroft

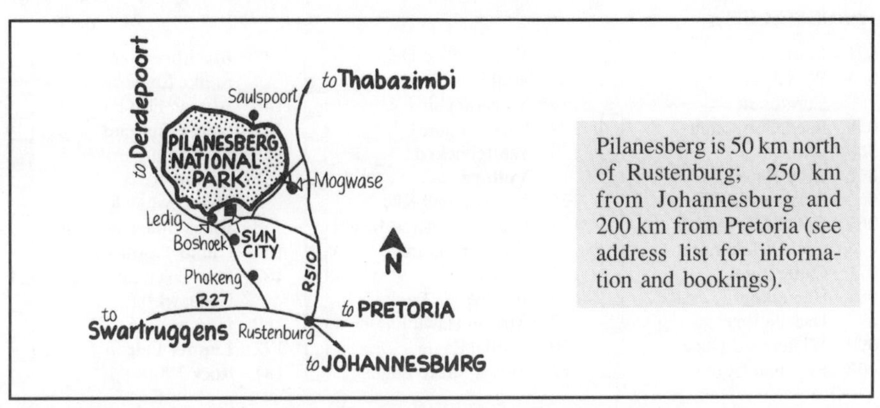

Pilanesberg is 50 km north of Rustenburg; 250 km from Johannesburg and 200 km from Pretoria (see address list for information and bookings).

SPECIAL AND INTERESTING SPECIES

Secretarybird is a regular breeding resident in Pilanesberg. The carcass hide attracts many vultures and **Whitebacked Vulture** is regularly seen there or on nearby pylons. One of the four nightjars recorded is the **Freckled Nightjar**, which calls during the breeding season around the koppies and from the roof of the hotel. **Flappet Lark** can be seen and heard overhead while one drives through the grassland and **Pied Babblers** and **Great Sparrows** nest in *Acacias* in the caravan park at the Manyane camp. Visitors may enter the bushveld on accompanied and self-guided trails where **Fantailed Flycatchers** can be seen and heard as they move through the canopy. Sitting on the upper branches will be **Longtailed Shrikes** and the occasional **Bushveld Pipit**. **Plumcoloured Starling** is common. Fifteen shrike species occur in the area; listen for the calls of **Brubru**, **Puffback**, **Crimsonbreasted Boubou**, **Greyheaded Bush Shrike**, **Threestreaked** and **Blackcrowned Tchagras**. The most attractive of the waxbills, the **Violeteared**, as well as the **Blackcheeked Waxbill** may be seen foraging low down. **Monotonous Lark** (after rains) and **Great Spotted Cuckoo** (summer) are frequent visitors. **Icterine Warbler** (summer) is not uncommon in the scattered *Acacia* trees. Scan the sky for **Blackbreasted Snake Eagle** and **Lanner Falcon**. Other raptors that occur regularly are **Black** and **Ovambo Sparrowhawks** and **Gabar Goshawk**. The **Gymnogene** breeds at Pilanesberg and is often mobbed by **Black** and **Alpine Swifts**. Endemics to look out for include **Shorttoed Rock Thrush**, **Swainson's Francolin**, **Whitebacked Mousebird**, **Southern Yellowbilled Hornbill**, **Southern Black Tit**, **Whitethroated Robin** and **Barred Warbler**.

47% OF SPECIES

No.	Species	
001	Ostrich	☐
055	Whitebreasted Cormorant	☐
058	Reed Cormorant	☐
060	Darter	☐
062	Grey Heron	☐
063	Blackheaded Heron	☐
064	Goliath Heron	☐
066	Great White Egret	☐
071	Cattle Egret	☐
081	Hamerkop	☐
094	Hadeda Ibis	☐
099	Whitefaced Duck	☐
102	Egyptian Goose	☐
104	Yellowbilled Duck	☐
108	Redbilled Teal	☐
118	**Secretarybird**	☐
122	Cape Vulture**	☐
123	**Whitebacked Vulture**	☐
126a	Yellowbilled Kite	☐
127	Blackshouldered Kite	☐
130	Honey Buzzard	☐
131	Black Eagle	☐
135	Wahlberg's Eagle	☐
137	African Hawk Eagle	☐
140	Martial Eagle	☐
142	Brown Snake Eagle	☐
143	**Blackbreasted Snake Eagle**	☐
148	African Fish Eagle	☐
149	Steppe Buzzard	☐
152	Jackal Buzzard**	☐
156	**Ovambo Sparrowhawk**	☐
158	**Black Sparrowhawk**	☐
161	**Gabar Goshawk**	☐
162	Pale Chanting Goshawk*	☐
169	**Gymnogene**	☐
172	**Lanner Falcon**	☐
181	Rock Kestrel	☐

188 Coqui Francolin ☐
189 Crested Francolin ☐
196 Natal Francolin* ☐
199 **Swainson's Francolin*** ☐
203 Helmeted Guineafowl ☐
228 Redknobbed Coot ☐
255 Crowned Plover ☐
258 Blacksmith Plover ☐
339 Whitewinged Tern ☐
352 Redeyed Dove ☐
354 Cape Turtle Dove ☐
355 Laughing Dove ☐
358 Greenspotted Dove ☐
373 Grey Lourie ☐
377 Redchested Cuckoo ☐
378 Black Cuckoo ☐
380 **Great Spotted Cuckoo** ☐
381 Striped Cuckoo ☐
382 Jacobin Cuckoo ☐
385 Klaas's Cuckoo ☐
386 Diederik Cuckoo ☐
398 Pearlspotted Owl ☐
406 Rufouscheeked Nightjar ☐
408 **Freckled Nightjar** ☐
412 **Black Swift** ☐
415 Whiterumped Swift ☐
417 Little Swift ☐
418 **Alpine Swift** ☐
424 Speckled Mousebird ☐
425 **Whitebacked Mousebird**** ☐
426 Redfaced Mousebird ☐
435 Brownhooded Kingfisher ☐
438 European Bee-eater ☐
447 Lilacbreasted Roller ☐
457 Grey Hornbill ☐
458 Redbilled Hornbill ☐
459 **Southern Yellow-billed Hornbill*** ☐
464 Blackcollared Barbet ☐
470 Yellowfronted Tinker Barbet ☐
473 Crested Barbet ☐
483 Goldentailed Woodpecker ☐
493 **Monotonous Lark*** ☐
494 Rufousnaped Lark ☐
496 **Flappet Lark** ☐
498 Sabota Lark* ☐
518 European Swallow ☐
520 Whitethroated Swallow ☐
524 Redbreasted Swallow ☐
526 Greater Striped Swallow* ☐
527 Lesser Striped Swallow ☐
541 Forktailed Drongo ☐
545 Blackheaded Oriole ☐
548 Pied Crow ☐
554 **Southern Black Tit*** ☐
560 Arrowmarked Babbler ☐
563 **Pied Babbler**** ☐
568 Blackeyed Bulbul ☐
580 Groundscraper Thrush ☐
583 **Shorttoed Rock Thrush*** ☐
589 Familiar Chat ☐
602 **Whitethroated Robin**** ☐
613 Whitebrowed Robin ☐
615 Kalahari Robin* ☐
621 Titbabbler* ☐
625 **Icterine Warbler** ☐
643 Willow Warbler ☐
645 Barthroated Apalis ☐
651 Longbilled Crombec ☐
657a Greybacked Bleating Warbler ☐
658 **Barred Warbler*** ☐
666 Cloud Cisticola ☐
672 Rattling Cisticola ☐
681 Neddicky ☐
683 Tawnyflanked Prinia ☐
685 Blackchested Prinia* ☐
689 Spotted Flycatcher ☐
693 **Fantailed Flycatcher** ☐
694 Black Flycatcher ☐
695 Marico Flycatcher* ☐
701 Chinspot Batis ☐
710 Paradise Flycatcher ☐
713 Cape Wagtail ☐
716 Grassveld Pipit ☐
723 **Bushveld Pipit** ☐
727 Orangethroated Longclaw** ☐
731 Lesser Grey Shrike ☐
732 Fiscal Shrike ☐
733 Redbacked Shrike ☐
735 **Longtailed Shrike** ☐
736 Southern Boubou ☐
739 **Crimsonbreasted Boubou*** ☐
740 **Puffback** ☐
741 **Brubru** ☐
743 **Threestreaked Tchagra** ☐
744 **Blackcrowned Tchagra** ☐
751 **Greyheaded Bush Shrike** ☐
756 Whitecrowned Shrike* ☐
761 **Plumcoloured Starling** ☐
764 Glossy Starling* ☐
769 Redwinged Starling ☐
787 Whitebellied Sunbird ☐
792 Black Sunbird ☐
796 Cape White-eye** ☐
799 Whitebrowed Sparrowweaver ☐
802 **Great Sparrow*** ☐
803 Cape Sparrow* ☐
804 Greyheaded Sparrow ☐
805 Yellowthroated Sparrow ☐
806 Scalyfeathered Finch* ☐
814 Masked Weaver ☐
815 Lesser Masked Weaver ☐
821 Redbilled Quelea ☐
826 Golden Bishop ☐
832 Longtailed Widow ☐
834 Melba Finch ☐
840 Bluebilled Firefinch ☐
841 Jameson's Firefinch ☐
842 Redbilled Firefinch ☐
844 Blue Waxbill ☐
845 **Violeteared Waxbill*** ☐
846 Common Waxbill ☐
847 **Blackcheeked Waxbill** ☐
869 Yelloweyed Canary ☐
881 Streakyheaded Canary ☐
884 Goldenbreasted Bunting ☐

SADDLEBACK PASS AND PEDDLARS BUSH, BARBERTON

approximately 125 species recorded to date

This locality includes state-owned and private land owned by Twello Bosbou. It includes the Barberton Mountain area which has steep montane grassland and *Protea* veld on Saddleback Pass, as well as evergreen forest at Peddlars Bush, with exotic pine plantations. The species listed are those occurring along the steep road up the pass, as well as in the forest. The forest is 1 250 m above sea level in the mist belt, and averages 1 118 mm of rainfall annually.

SPECIAL AND INTERESTING SPECIES

Many interesting birds can be seen on the drive up the mountain before one reaches the forest. **Redbreasted Sparrowhawk** should be looked for halfway up the pass where there is a small patch of old wattle scrub and some indigenous bush. **Redwing Francolin** occurs nearby and can sometimes be heard calling in the early morning. **Malachite Sunbird** and **Gurney's Sugarbird** occur in the *Protea* scrub on the right of the road. The best time to see these birds is when the *Proteas* are flowering in November/December; a good viewing spot is on the right where there is an eroded excavation caused by road building. **Buffstreaked Chat** is often seen among rocks on the same slope. After turning onto the gravel road at the top of the pass look out for **Forest Buzzard** in the pine plantations on your right. Care must be

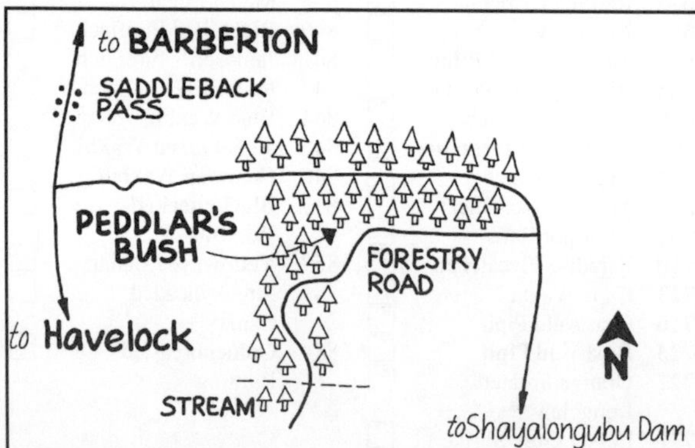

ALSO RECORDED

Southern Tchagra has been recorded near the top of Saddleback Pass. Both Rednecked Francolin and Cape Eagle Owl have been recorded. Goldenrumped Tinker Barbet has been heard although it usually occurs at much lower altitudes.

Peter Lawson

From Barberton take the Kaapmuiden road and on the outskirts of Barberton turn right on a road signposted "Havelock". The road is tarred and winds steeply up a mountain pass. There are various rewarding stopping places before you reach the top of the pass, where you turn left onto a gravel road signposted "Shayalongubu Dam". Follow this road through an exotic plantation for approximately 10 km until you reach indigenous evergreen forest. Birdwatching is good along this stretch of road. Take the first forestry road to the right as soon as you leave the indigenous forest and keep to the right until you reach the forest once more. At this point you should leave your car and walk until you reach a small stream that crosses the road. Prior permission should be obtained from the local forester.

taken however as **Steppe Buzzard** also occurs. Winter is the best time to make sure of your identification. **Swee Waxbill** and **Redbacked Mannikin** can be seen on the verge of the road in the plantation area when the grass is long in late summer. On reaching the indigenous forest, stop and listen. If your visit is in the summer, you will probably hear **Emerald Cuckoo**, **Chorister Robin** and **Narina Trogon**. Look for movement in the dense canopy and you may pick out **Knysna Lourie**, **Olive Woodpecker** and **Yellowstreaked Bulbul** with its characteristic flicking of one wing at a time. **Squaretailed Drongo** is easily located as it is a noisy bird. **Grey Cuckooshrike** is quite tame, and sometimes you can see it at close quarters. **Olive Bush Shrike** can also be located by its call and very often responds to "spishing". Travel for some distance through the forest to where the pines start again at the far end. **Buffspotted Flufftail** may be heard here, particularly on overcast days. This is also a good spot to locate **Barratt's Warbler** in rank growth of bracken and brambles. If you are very quiet and still you can call it up, but you will probably only get a glimpse. This is also the spot to play your tape for **Bush Blackcap**, which comes to the forest verge. Turn sharply to the right at this point and drive on a forestry road until you once more reach the indigenous forest. Stop your car and walk slowly along the road where **Cinnamon Dove** is sometimes located at the edge of the road, and **Green Twinspots** have been seen feeding. You will probably hear the rolling froglike call of **Scalythroated Honeyguide**. For many years it has had a callsite where the road turns sharply to the left. Other species to look for are **Orange Thrush** and **Crowned Eagle**. Follow the small stream that crosses the road. This is a good spot to call up both **Brown** and **Starred Robins**. **Bluemantled Flycatcher**, **Olive Sunbird** and **Forest Canary** also occur near the stream.

97% OF SPECIES

094 Hadeda Ibis ☐
126a Yellowbilled Kite ☐
141 **Crowned Eagle** ☐
149 Steppe Buzzard ☐
150 Forest Buzzard** ☐
152 **Jackal Buzzard**** ☐
155 **Redbreasted Sparrowhawk** ☐
158 Black Sparrowhawk ☐
160 African Goshawk ☐
173 Hobby Falcon ☐
181 Rock Kestrel ☐
192 **Redwing Francolin** ☐
196 Natal Francolin* ☐
218 **Buffspotted Flufftail** ☐
350 Rameron Pigeon ☐
352 Redeyed Dove ☐
354 Cape Turtle Dove ☐
355 Laughing Dove ☐
358 Greenspotted Dove ☐
359 Tambourine Dove ☐
360 **Cinnamon Dove** ☐
361 Green Pigeon ☐
370 **Knysna Lourie**** ☐
377 Redchested Cuckoo ☐
378 Black Cuckoo ☐
384 **Emerald Cuckoo** ☐
385 Klaas's Cuckoo ☐
386 Diederik Cuckoo ☐
391 Burchell's Coucal* ☐
394 Wood Owl ☐
405 Fierynecked Nightjar ☐
412 Black Swift ☐

417 Little Swift ☐
418 Alpine Swift ☐
424 Speckled Mousebird ☐
427 **Narina Trogon** ☐
438 European Bee-eater ☐
444 Little Bee-eater ☐
455 Trumpeter Hornbill ☐
464 Blackcollared Barbet ☐
470 Yellowfronted Tinker Barbet ☐
475 **Scalythroated Honeyguide** ☐
476 Lesser Honeyguide ☐
483 Goldentailed Woodpecker ☐
488 **Olive Woodpecker** ☐
494 Rufousnaped Lark ☐
518 European Swallow ☐
526 Greater Striped Swallow* ☐
529 Rock Martin ☐
536 Black Sawwing Swallow ☐
540 **Grey Cuckooshrike** ☐
541 Forktailed Drongo ☐
542 **Squaretailed Drongo** ☐
545 Blackheaded Oriole ☐
550 Whitenecked Raven ☐
554 Southern Black Tit* ☐
565 **Bush Blackcap**** ☐
568 Blackeyed Bulbul ☐
569 Terrestrial Bulbul ☐
570 **Yellowstreaked Bulbul** ☐
572 Sombre Bulbul ☐
577 Olive Thrush ☐
579 **Orange Thrush** ☐
581 Cape Rock Thrush** ☐
588 **Buffstreaked Chat**** ☐
589 Familiar Chat ☐
596 Stonechat ☐
598 **Chorister Robin**** ☐
600 Natal Robin ☐
601 Cape Robin ☐
606 **Starred Robin** ☐
616 **Brown Robin**** ☐
639 **Barratt's Warbler**** ☐
643 Willow Warbler ☐
644 Yellowthroated Warbler ☐
645 Barthroated Apalis ☐
657 Bleating Warbler ☐
670 Wailing Cisticola ☐
679 Lazy Cisticola ☐
681 Neddicky ☐
683 Tawnyflanked Prinia ☐
686 Spotted Prinia** ☐
690 Dusky Flycatcher ☐
700 Cape Batis** ☐
708 **Bluemantled Flycatcher** ☐
710 Paradise Flycatcher ☐
712 Longtailed Wagtail ☐
717 Longbilled Pipit ☐
720 Striped Pipit ☐
727 Orangethroated Longclaw** ☐
732 Fiscal Shrike ☐
736 Southern Boubou** ☐
740 Puffback ☐
744 Blackcrowned Tchagra ☐
747 Gorgeous Bush Shrike ☐
748 Orangebreasted Bush Shrike ☐
750 **Olive Bush Shrike*** ☐
751 Greyheaded Bush Shrike ☐
768 Blackbellied Starling ☐
769 Redwinged Starling ☐
774 **Gurney's Sugarbird**** ☐
775 **Malachite Sunbird** ☐
783 Lesser Double-collared Sunbird** ☐
787 Whitebellied Sunbird ☐
790 **Olive Sunbird** ☐
792 Black Sunbird ☐
793 Collared Sunbird ☐
796 Cape White-eye** ☐
807 Thickbilled Weaver ☐
810 Spectacled Weaver ☐
831 Redcollared Widow ☐
835 **Green Twinspot** ☐
840 Bluebilled Firefinch ☐
846 Common Waxbill ☐
850 **Swee Waxbill*** ☐
858 **Redbacked Mannikin** ☐
860 Pintailed Whydah ☐
872 Cape Canary ☐
873 **Forest Canary**** ☐
881 Streakyheaded Canary ☐
886 Rock Bunting ☐

DIEPSLOOT NATURE RESERVE AND ASSOCIATED AREA

approximately 310 species recorded to date

Diepsloot Nature Reserve and the northern sewage works are located on the R28 approximately 8 km north of the Lion Park. Interspersed in the area are nine large dams, which feed into the Jukskei River. The route from Johannesburg to the Hartebeespoort Dam is via the Lion Park and along the R512. This road follows the banks of the Crocodile River for approximately 25 km through beautiful passes and kloofs before reaching the Hartebeespoort Dam. The area comprises an extensive variety of habitats varying from open water, rivers and grasslands to kloofs and mountains. Accommodation is available at various places in the vicinity and there are camping facilities at Kommandonek and Oberon in the Hartebeespoort Dam Nature Reserve. Entrance to Diepsloot Nature Reserve and the northern sewage works is by permit only and private visits are not allowed. Birders wishing to visit this site should contact the Witwatersrand Bird Club to find out when the next outing to the site will take place.

SPECIAL AND INTERESTING SPECIES

The main special to be found at Diepsloot is the **Yellow Wagtail**, which will be located in the cattle camps during the summer months. Up to 30 birds may be seen in different groups. The wetland areas are full of grassland and water associated species including **Glossy**, **Sacred** and **Hadeda**

ALSO RECORDED

Fantailed Flycatcher has been recorded breeding along the Crocodile River. Longcrested Eagle and Peregrine Falcon have been recorded at Diepsloot, as well as Rufousbellied Heron. Pygmy Goose has been recorded at Hartebeespoort Dam.

Rodd Kippen

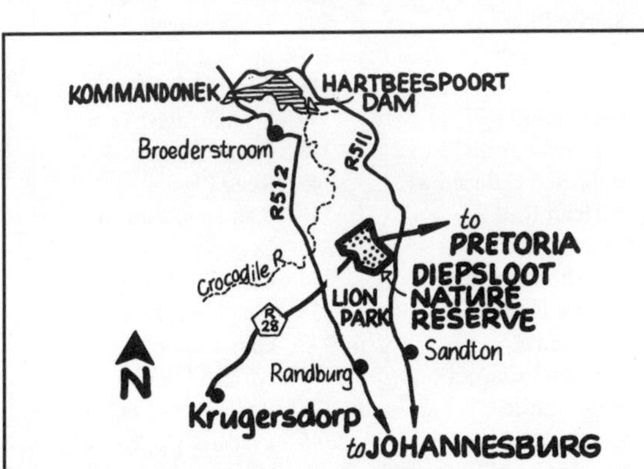

Take the R512 from Randburg or Sandton and turn right at Lion Park corner onto the R28. The Diepsloot Nature Reserve entrance is approximately 8 km from Lion Park corner. The route to Hartebeespoort Dam is along the R511.

Ibises, Ethiopian Snipe, Swainson's Francolin, Whitequilled Korhaan and **Wattled Plover** (common). The exposed waters are full of **Yellowbilled**, **African Black** and **Whitefaced Ducks** and occasionally **Knobbilled** and **Whitebacked Ducks** are encountered. Reedbeds will produce good sightings of **Purple Gallinule** and **Black Crake**, while **African Rail** and **Redchested Flufftail** are more often heard than seen. **Redcapped Lark** may be found on the roadways. Along the Crocodile River in the mountainous areas **Rameron Pigeon**, **Mocking Chat** and many different raptors will be recorded, with up to seven species of cuckoo being found in the summer months. Hartebeespoort Dam supports a high population of kingfishers and **Malachite**, **Halfcollared**, **Giant** and **Pied** are often encountered. **Blacknecked** and **Great Crested Grebes** will be found on the open water. The mountain area to the north of Hartebeespoort Dam has one of the last large breeding colonies of **Cape Vulture**. **Black Eagles** also breed in these mountains.

45% OF SPECIES

No.	Species	
006	**Great Crested Grebe**	☐
007	**Blacknecked Grebe**	☐
008	Dabchick	☐
055	Whitebreasted Cormorant	☐
058	Reed Cormorant	☐
060	Darter	☐
062	Grey Heron	☐
063	Blackheaded Heron	☐
071	Cattle Egret	☐
072	Squacco Heron	☐
075	**Rufousbellied Heron**	☐
081	Hamerkop	☐
091	**Sacred Ibis**	☐
093	**Glossy Ibis**	☐
094	**Hadeda Ibis**	☐
099	**Whitefaced Duck**	☐
101	**Whitebacked Duck**	☐
102	Egyptian Goose	☐
104	**Yellowbilled Duck**	☐
105	**African Black Duck**	☐
108	Redbilled Teal	☐
112	Cape Shoveller*	☐
113	Southern Pochard	☐
115	**Knobbilled Duck**	☐
116	Spurwinged Goose	☐
122	**Cape Vulture**	☐
126	Black Kite	☐
126a	Yellowbilled Kite	☐
127	Blackshouldered Kite	☐
131	**Black Eagle**	☐
148	African Fish Eagle	☐
149	Steppe Buzzard	☐
182	Greater Kestrel	☐
199	**Swainson's Francolin***	☐
200	Common Quail	☐
203	Helmeted Guineafowl	☐
210	**African Rail**	☐
213	**Black Crake**	☐
217	**Redchested Flufftail**	☐
223	**Purple Gallinule**	☐
226	Moorhen	☐
228	Redknobbed Coot	☐
239a	**Whitequilled Korhaan****	☐
255	Crowned Plover	☐
258	Blacksmith Plover	☐
260	**Wattled Plover**	☐
264	Common Sandpiper	☐
266	Wood Sandpiper	☐
269	Marsh Sandpiper	☐
270	Greenshank	☐
284	Ruff	☐
286	**Ethiopian Snipe**	☐
295	Blackwinged Stilt	☐
297	Spotted Dikkop	☐
315	Greyheaded Gull	☐
339	Whitewinged Tern	☐
348	Feral Pigeon	☐
349	Rock Pigeon	☐
350	**Rameron Pigeon**	☐
352	Redeyed Dove	☐
354	Cape Turtle Dove	☐
355	Laughing Dove	☐
373	Grey Lourie	☐
375	African Cuckoo	☐
377	Redchested Cuckoo	☐
386	Diederik Cuckoo	☐

391 Burchell's Coucal* ☐
393 Grass Owl ☐
395 Marsh Owl ☐
401 Spotted Eagle Owl ☐
412 Black Swift ☐
415 Whiterumped Swift ☐
416 Horus Swift ☐
417 Little Swift ☐
418 Alpine Swift ☐
422 Mottled Spinetail ☐
424 Speckled Mousebird ☐
426 Redfaced Mousebird ☐
428 **Pied Kingfisher** ☐
429 **Giant Kingfisher** ☐
430 **Halfcollared Kingfisher** ☐
431 **Malachite Kingfisher** ☐
438 European Bee-eater ☐
443 Whitefronted Bee-eater ☐
451 Hoopoe ☐
452 Redbilled Woodhoopoe ☐
464 Blackcollared Barbet ☐
473 Crested Barbet ☐
476 Lesser Honeyguide ☐
486 Cardinal Woodpecker ☐
489 Redthroated Wryneck ☐
494 Rufousnaped Lark ☐
507 **Redcapped Lark** ☐

515 Chestnutbacked Finchlark ☐
518 European Swallow ☐
520 Whitethroated Swallow ☐
523 Pearlbreasted Swallow ☐
526 Greater Striped Swallow* ☐
527 Lesser Striped Swallow** ☐
528 South African Cliff Swallow** ☐
530 House Martin ☐
533 Brownthroated Martin ☐
541 Forktailed Drongo ☐
548 Pied Crow ☐
560 Arrowmarked Babbler ☐
568 Blackeyed Bulbul ☐
577 Olive Thrush ☐
593 **Mocking Chat** ☐
596 Stonechat ☐
601 Cape Robin ☐
631 African Marsh Warbler ☐
635 Cape Reed Warbler ☐
643 Willow Warbler ☐
661 Grassbird** ☐
664 Fantailed Cisticola ☐
665 Desert Cisticola ☐
666 Cloud Cisticola ☐
667 Ayres' Cisticola ☐

677 Levaillant's Cisticola ☐
681 Neddicky ☐
683 Tawnyflanked Prinia ☐
685 Blackchested Prinia* ☐
698 Fiscal Flycatcher** ☐
713 Cape Wagtail ☐
714 **Yellow Wagtail** ☐
716 Grassveld Pipit ☐
727 Orangethroated Longclaw** ☐
732 Fiscal Shrike ☐
740 Puffback ☐
746 Bokmakierie* ☐
758 Indian Myna ☐
764 Glossy Starling* ☐
779 Marico Sunbird ☐
787 Whitebellied Sunbird ☐
792 Black Sunbird ☐
796 Cape White-eye** ☐
801 House Sparrow ☐
803 Cape Sparrow* ☐
804 Greyheaded Sparrow ☐
814 Masked Weaver ☐
824 Red Bishop ☐
826 Golden Bishop ☐
831 Redcollared Widow ☐
832 Longtailed Widow ☐
846 Common Waxbill ☐
860 Pintailed Whydah ☐
☐
☐

Black Egret

CARLOS ROLFES BIRD SANCTUARY

approximately 170 species recorded to date

This large, circular pan was donated by Carlos Rolfes (an industrialist on whose land it is situated) to the Chief Directorate: Nature and Environmental Conservation. It has been declared a bird sanctuary, is fully fenced and administered by the Witwatersrand Bird Club, which is now (1992) developing it. One hide has already being constructed and others will follow. It lies within a heavily industrialised region some 3 km south of Jan Smuts Airport. The water input is controlled and the pan is never empty. The shoreline is mostly grass and sedges with some reedbeds. On the western side there is a stand of old *Eucalyptus* trees and there are areas of dry shoreline on the eastern side. Rolfes Pan is a haven for waterbirds, the dominant species varying according to prevailing water levels.

SPECIAL AND INTERESTING SPECIES

With low water levels both species of flamingo may occur in large numbers, although the **Greater** normally outnumbers the **Lesser Flamingo**. Also, with low water levels, stands of emergent watergrass grow in the pan and these attract nesting **Whiskered Terns**, **Great Crested** and **Blacknecked Grebes** as well as **Dabchicks**. The sanctuary's close proximity to Johannesburg and Jan Smuts Airport makes it an ideal locality for overseas birders to see the following endemics,

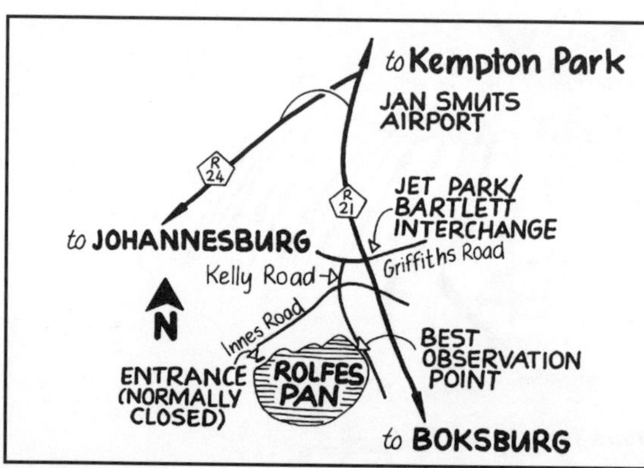

ALSO RECORDED

All indigenous duck species could be expected to appear at any time of the year although species such as South African Shelduck are far less frequent. Blackheaded and Franklin's Gulls, Grey Phalarope, Blacktailed Godwit and Redthroated Wryneck have all been recorded in recent years, the phalarope, gulls and godwits enjoying a prolonged stay. The Franklin's Gull actually returned the following season and attempted mating with the Greyheaded Gulls.

Ken Newman

To reach the sanctuary from Johannesburg take the R24 towards Jan Smuts Airport. On reaching the airport interchange take the East Rand offramp onto the R21; after about 2 km exit at the Jet Park/Bartlett offramp and turn right over the R21 into Griffiths Road and almost immediately left into Kelly Road. The pan will be seen about 500 m further. At present access to the sanctuary area is not possible and birding must be done through the fence: a telescope and tripod are useful. The Witwatersrand Bird Club, however, plans to arrange for access to the pan. Contact the club for details.

all of which breed at this site: **Cape Shoveller**, **Swainson's Francolin**, **Greater Striped Swallow**, **Orangethroated Longclaw** and **Cape Sparrow**. Other breeding birds that are normally common include **Squacco Heron**, **Fulvous** and **Whitebacked Ducks**, **Hottentot** and **Redbilled Teal**, **Spurwinged Goose**, **Purple Gallinule**, **Moorhen**, **Redknobbed Coot**, **Blacksmith Plover**, **Stonechat**, **Fantailed** and **Levaillant's Cisticolas** and **Red** and **Golden Bishops**. **Goliath**, **Grey**, **Blackheaded** and **Purple Herons** are usually present as is **Blackcrowned Night Heron** and all species of egrets. **African Spoonbill** and **African Jacana** are regulars as are **Glossy**, **Sacred** and **Hadeda Ibises**. In recent years (late 1980s) **Greyheaded Gulls** have moved into Rolfes Pan in very large numbers and now breed regularly during winter and early spring months.

69% OF SPECIES

006 **Great Crested Grebe** ☐
007 **Blacknecked Grebe** ☐
008 **Dabchick** ☐
055 Whitebreasted Cormorant ☐
058 Reed Cormorant ☐
060 Darter ☐
062 **Grey Heron** ☐
063 **Blackheaded Heron** ☐
064 **Goliath Heron** ☐
065 **Purple Heron** ☐
066 Great White Egret ☐
067 Little Egret ☐
068 Yellowbilled Egret ☐
069 **Black Egret** ☐
071 Cattle Egret ☐
072 Squacco Heron ☐
074 Greenbacked Heron ☐
076 Blackcrowned Night Heron ☐
078 Little Bittern ☐
081 Hamerkop ☐
091 **Sacred Ibis** ☐
093 **Glossy Ibis** ☐
094 **Hadeda Ibis** ☐
095 **African Spoonbill** ☐
096 **Greater Flamingo** ☐
097 **Lesser Flamingo** ☐
099 Whitefaced Duck ☐
100 Fulvous Duck ☐
101 **Whitebacked Duck** ☐
102 Egyptian Goose ☐
103 South African Shelduck** ☐
104 Yellowbilled Duck ☐
105 African Black Duck ☐
106 Cape Teal ☐
107 Hottentot Teal ☐
108 Redbilled Teal ☐
112 Cape Shoveller* ☐
113 Southern Pochard ☐
115 **Knobbilled Duck** ☐
116 Spurwinged Goose ☐
117 Maccoa Duck ☐
126a Yellowbilled Kite ☐
127 Blackshouldered Kite ☐
199 Swainson's Francolin* ☐
203 Helmeted Guineafowl ☐
213 Black Crake ☐
223 Purple Gallinule ☐
226 Moorhen ☐
228 Redknobbed Coot ☐
240 **African Jacana** ☐
249 Threebanded Plover ☐
255 Crowned Plover ☐
258 Blacksmith Plover ☐
260 Wattled Plover ☐
264 Common Sandpiper ☐
266 Wood Sandpiper ☐
269 Marsh Sandpiper ☐
270 Greenshank ☐
272 Curlew Sandpiper ☐
274 Little Stint ☐
284 Ruff ☐
286 Ethiopian Snipe ☐
294 Avocet ☐
295 Blackwinged Stilt ☐
297 Spotted Dikkop ☐
315 **Greyheaded Gull** ☐
322 **Caspian Tern** ☐
338 **Whiskered Tern** ☐
339 **Whitewinged Tern** ☐
348 Feral Pigeon ☐
349 Rock Pigeon ☐
352 Redeyed Dove ☐
354 Cape Turtle Dove ☐
355 Laughing Dove ☐
386 Diederik Cuckoo ☐
391 Burchell's Coucal* ☐
392 Barn Owl ☐
395 Marsh Owl ☐
415 Whiterumped Swift ☐
417 Little Swift ☐

426 Redfaced Mousebird ☐	638 African Sedge Warbler ☐	803 Cape Sparrow* ☐
428 Pied Kingfisher ☐	643 Willow Warbler ☐	814 Masked Weaver ☐
431 Malachite Kingfisher ☐	661 Grassbird** ☐	821 Redbilled Quelea ☐
494 Rufousnaped Lark ☐	664 Fantailed Cisticola ☐	824 Red Bishop ☐
518 European Swallow ☐	677 Levaillant's Cisticola ☐	826 Golden Bishop ☐
520 Whitethroated Swallow ☐	683 Tawnyflanked Prinia ☐	832 Longtailed Widow ☐
526 Greater Striped Swallow* ☐	713 Cape Wagtail ☐	846 Common Waxbill ☐
530 House Martin ☐	716 Grassveld Pipit ☐	852 Quail Finch ☐
533 Brownthroated Martin ☐	727 Orangethroated Longclaw** ☐	854 Orangebreasted Waxbill ☐
568 Blackeyed Bulbul ☐	732 Fiscal Shrike ☐	860 Pintailed Whydah ☐
596 Stonechat ☐	758 Indian Myna ☐	870 Blackthroated Canary ☐
631 African Marsh Warbler ☐	760 Wattled Starling ☐	☐
635 Cape Reed Warbler ☐	796 Cape White-eye** ☐	☐
	801 House Sparrow ☐	☐

LEEUPAN

approximately 160 species recorded to date

Leeupan is situated on municipal grounds on the outskirts of Benoni and consists of a single, large, roughly circular pan within grassland. On the southern side there is a small group of poplar trees and a fisherman's hut. At the northern end a small stream seeps into the pan through a marshy area. There are a few reedbeds and the shoreline is mostly bare and stony. The best way of birding at Leeupan, which is not a declared bird sanctuary, is from a motor car. There are no hides and for satisfactory spotting of the more distant birds a telescope is recommended.

From Johannesburg take the R22 eastwards and exit at the Benoni/Bonaero Park offramp; turn right onto Atlas Road and continue until the traffic lights at Dunswart Steel are reached. At this point turn left onto Main Reef Road which becomes Princess Avenue. Turn right into Tom Jones Street which, in turn, becomes Rangeview Road, and follow this road about 5 km south out of Benoni, where the pan will be found on the right. Entrance is via a simple farm gate in the wire fence. The tracks around the pan are in poor condition.

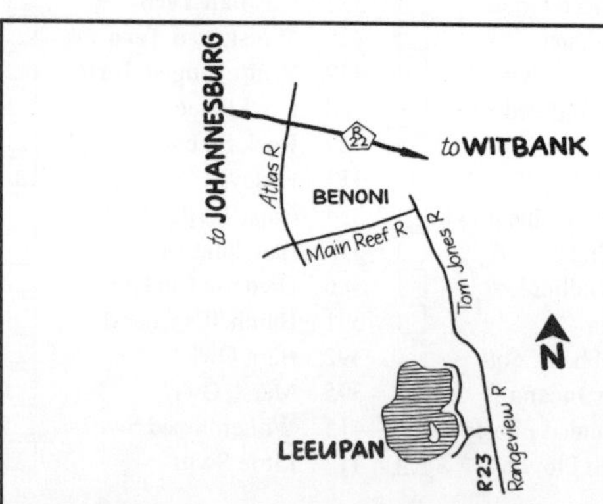

SPECIAL AND INTERESTING SPECIES

The main attractions at Leeupan are the often large flocks of flamingos, the **Greater** being the most common with influxes of **Lesser Flamingo** from time to time. Most of our duck species can be expected in addition to **Great Crested Grebe**, **Avocet**, **Blackwinged Stilt**, **African Spoonbill**, **Great White** and **Little Egrets**. The marshy region is good for both **Glossy** and **Sacred Ibises**, **Ethiopian Snipe** and, in summer, migrant waders. The stony shoreline is excellent for many small wading birds, especially **Kittlitz's**, **Ringed** and **Threebanded Plovers**, while **Turnstone** is a tantalisingly irregular summer passage migrant. In spring, following veld burning, Kittlitz's Plover and **Capped Wheatear** breed along with **Redcapped Lark** and **Crowned Plover**. Once the grass has grown again **Orangethroated Longclaw**, **Grassveld Pipit** and **Rufousnaped Lark** become common.

ALSO RECORDED

The first Longtoed Stint for southern Africa was recorded in the late 1960s at Leeupan. A vagrant African Skimmer has been sighted in recent years and from time to time Whiskered Tern occurs.

Ken Newman

63% OF SPECIES

006 **Great Crested Grebe** ☐
007 Blacknecked Grebe ☐
008 Dabchick ☐
055 Whitebreasted Cormorant ☐
058 Reed Cormorant ☐
060 Darter ☐
062 Grey Heron ☐
063 Blackheaded Heron ☐
064 Goliath Heron ☐
065 Purple Heron ☐
066 **Great White Egret** ☐
067 **Little Egret** ☐
071 Cattle Egret ☐
076 Blackcrowned Night Heron ☐
090 Yellowbilled Stork ☐
091 **Sacred Ibis** ☐
093 **Glossy Ibis** ☐
094 Hadeda Ibis ☐
095 **African Spoonbill** ☐
096 **Greater Flamingo** ☐
097 **Lesser Flamingo** ☐
099 Whitefaced Duck ☐
100 Fulvous Duck ☐
101 Whitebacked Duck ☐
102 Egyptian Goose ☐
104 Yellowbilled Duck ☐
106 Cape Teal ☐
107 Hottentot Teal ☐
108 Redbilled Teal ☐
112 Cape Shoveller* ☐
113 Southern Pochard ☐
116 Spurwinged Goose ☐
117 Maccoa Duck ☐
127 Blackshouldered Kite ☐
165 African Marsh Harrier ☐
180 Eastern Redfooted Kestrel ☐
182 Greater Kestrel ☐
199 Swainson's Francolin* ☐
203 Helmeted Guineafowl ☐
213 Black Crake ☐
223 Purple Gallinule ☐
226 Moorhen ☐
228 Redknobbed Coot ☐
245 **Ringed Plover** ☐
248 **Kittlitz's Plover** ☐
249 **Threebanded Plover** ☐
255 **Crowned Plover** ☐
258 Blacksmith Plover ☐
262 **Turnstone** ☐
264 Common Sandpiper ☐
266 Wood Sandpiper ☐
269 Marsh Sandpiper ☐
270 Greenshank ☐
272 Curlew Sandpiper ☐
274 Little Stint ☐
284 Ruff ☐
286 **Ethiopian Snipe** ☐
294 **Avocet** ☐
295 **Blackwinged Stilt** ☐
297 Spotted Dikkop ☐
315 Greyheaded Gull ☐
339 Whitewinged Tern ☐
349 Rock Pigeon ☐
354 Cape Turtle Dove ☐
355 Laughing Dove ☐
395 Marsh Owl ☐
415 Whiterumped Swift ☐
417 Little Swift ☐
428 Pied Kingfisher ☐
431 Malachite Kingfisher ☐
494 **Rufousnaped Lark** ☐
506 Spikeheeled Lark* ☐
507 **Redcapped Lark** ☐
518 European Swallow ☐
526 Greater Striped Swallow* ☐
547 Black Crow ☐
548 Pied Crow ☐
568 Blackeyed Bulbul ☐
587 **Capped Wheatear** ☐

595 Anteating Chat** ☐	716 **Grassveld Pipit** ☐	832 Longtailed Widow ☐
596 Stonechat ☐	717 Longbilled Pipit ☐	846 Common Waxbill ☐
635 Cape Reed Warbler ☐	727 **Orangethroated Longclaw**** ☐	852 Quail Finch ☐
664 Fantailed Cisticola ☐	732 Fiscal Shrike ☐	854 Orangebreasted Waxbill ☐
665 Desert Cisticola ☐	758 Indian Myna ☐	860 Pintailed Whydah ☐
666 Cloud Cisticola ☐	803 Cape Sparrow* ☐	☐
677 Levaillant's Cisticola ☐	814 Masked Weaver ☐	☐
713 Cape Wagtail ☐	824 Red Bishop ☐	☐
714 Yellow Wagtail ☐		☐

RONDEBULT BIRD SANCTUARY

approximately 170 species recorded to date

Rondebult (95 ha) belongs to the Germiston City Council and consists of a number of large ponds originally created as settlement pans for a nearby sewage treatment plant. The sewage plant no longer functions but the waters are nevertheless rich in organic content and their levels are controlled. Extensive marshlands, reedbeds and islands provide refuge for numerous birds. This is regarded as one of the finest places to see waterbirds in the Transvaal. The warm summer months of the highveld bring thousands of migrant waders while in the harshness of winter, when a heavy layer of frost often whitens the region, the duck populations build up, and much breeding occurs. Herons, ibises, spoonbills and many other water associated birds are present all year. Eight well situated viewing hides are available.

From Johannesburg take the N3 motorway towards Heidelberg and Durban. After passing Alberton leave the N3 at the Alrode/Wadeville offramp which is signposted "Rondebult". At the traffic lights at the end of the long offramp filter left and travel on the R554 towards Brakpan, passing through industrial sites on the left and Leondale township on the right. After passing over a railway bridge, Rondebult will be seen on the right. The entrance, which is signposted, is 1 km further on beyond a line of tall gum trees.

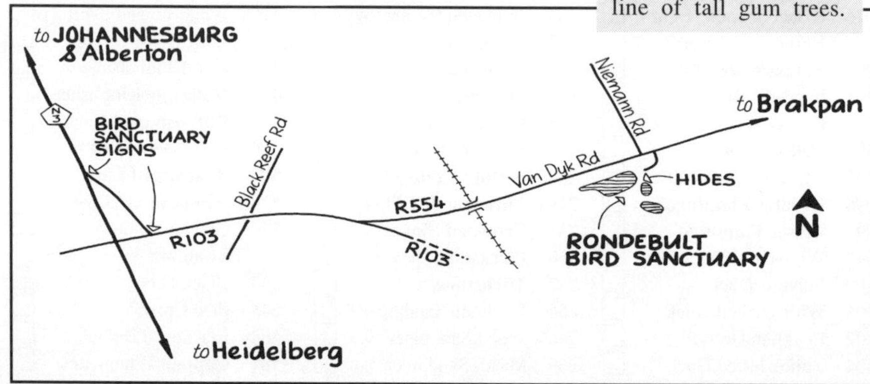

SPECIAL AND INTERESTING SPECIES

The pan at hides number 1 and 2 usually supports a number of **Avocets** and **Blackwinged Stilts** which can be seen at close range. In early summer **Ruff**, **Greenshank**, **Marsh Sandpiper**, **Little Stint**, **Curlew Sandpiper**, **Glossy Ibis** and **Whitewinged Tern** are usually in evidence while, at any time, **Ethiopian Snipe** and **Purple Gallinule** are virtual certainties. These two hides and hide number 8 are the best places from which to watch for **African Rail**, **Black** and **Baillon's Crakes**. Hides 3-7 are best for viewing ducks and herons, and good views of **Maccoa Duck**, **Southern Pochard**, **Whitefaced** and **Fulvous Ducks** plus **Hottentot Teal** can usually be assured in addition to **Greater Flamingo**. **Goliath Heron** is frequently present as are **Spurwinged Geese**, while **Blackcrowned Night Heron** and the occasional **Little Bittern** roost by day in the reeds. From hides 4 and 5, which are elevated, it is possible to look across the pans and reeds to the marshlands beyond where **African Marsh Harrier**, **Jackal Buzzard** and **Marsh Owl** can often be seen flying or perched. When **Sacred Ibis**, **Cattle Egret**, **Blackheaded** and **Grey Herons** choose to breed (usually in summer) it is possible to look down from these hides into the colonies. On the shoreline below the hides watch for **Yellow Wagtail** during summer. The eastern side of the sanctuary is fringed by a row of mature willow trees. Search these in summer for **Barn Owl** and **African** and **European Cuckoos**. Away from the hides watch for **Orangebreasted Waxbill** (especially in late summer when the bishops and weavers are vacating their nests), **Quail Finch**, **Pied Starling**, **Stonechat** and **Levaillant's Cisticola**. Check the sky for the many flocks of waterbirds that are continually arriving.

From the centre of Johannesburg the journey to Rondebult takes about 35 minutes. The sanctuary is open to the public 12 hours a day, a caretaker is on duty and toilets are available. There is no accommodation and camping is not permitted. Please sign the visitors' book before leaving.

ALSO RECORDED

Rarities that have been recorded at Rondebult include European Shoveller, Garganey, Redshank, Pectoral Sandpiper, Ringed Plover, Blacknecked Grebe and European Wheatear.

Ken Newman

75% OF SPECIES

008	Dabchick	☐
058	Reed Cormorant	☐
062	**Grey Heron**	☐
063	**Blackheaded Heron**	☐
064	**Goliath Heron**	☐
065	Purple Heron	☐
067	Little Egret	☐
071	**Cattle Egret**	☐
076	**Blackcrowned Night Heron**	☐
078	**Little Bittern**	☐
091	**Sacred Ibis**	☐
093	**Glossy Ibis**	☐
094	Hadeda Ibis	☐
095	African Spoonbill	☐
096	**Greater Flamingo**	☐
097	Lesser Flamingo	☐
099	**Whitefaced Duck**	☐
100	**Fulvous Duck**	☐
102	Egyptian Goose	☐
104	Yellowbilled Duck	☐
106	Cape Teal	☐
107	**Hottentot Teal**	☐
108	Redbilled Teal	☐
112	Cape Shoveller*	☐
113	**Southern Pochard**	☐
116	**Spurwinged Goose**	☐
117	**Maccoa Duck**	☐
127	Blackshouldered Kite	☐
149	Steppe Buzzard	☐
152	**Jackal Buzzard****	☐
165	**African Marsh Harrier**	☐
180	Eastern Redfooted Kestrel	☐
199	Swainson's Francolin*	☐
203	Helmeted Guineafowl	☐
210	**African Rail**	☐
213	**Black Crake**	☐

215 **Baillon's Crake**
223 **Purple Gallinule**
226 Moorhen
228 Redknobbed Coot
245 Ringed Plover
249 Threebanded Plover
255 Crowned Plover
258 Blacksmith Plover
260 Wattled Plover
264 Common Sandpiper
266 Wood Sandpiper
269 **Marsh Sandpiper**
270 **Greenshank**
272 **Curlew Sandpiper**
274 **Little Stint**
284 **Ruff**
286 **Ethiopian Snipe**
294 **Avocet**
295 **Blackwinged Stilt**
297 Spotted Dikkop
315 Greyheaded Gull
339 **Whitewinged Tern**
348 Feral Pigeon
349 Rock Pigeon
352 Redeyed Dove
354 Cape Turtle Dove
355 Laughing Dove
356 Namaqua Dove
374 **European Cuckoo**
375 **African Cuckoo**
377 Redchested Cuckoo
386 Diederik Cuckoo
391 Burchell's Coucal*
392 **Barn Owl**
395 **Marsh Owl**
415 Whiterumped Swift
416 Horus Swift
417 Little Swift
424 Speckled Mousebird
426 Redfaced Mousebird
428 Pied Kingfisher
431 Malachite Kingfisher
451 Hoopoe
473 Crested Barbet
494 Rufousnaped Lark
507 Redcapped Lark
518 European Swallow
520 Whitethroated Swallow
526 Greater Striped Swallow*
528 South African Cliff Swallow**
530 House Martin
533 Brownthroated Martin
534 Banded Martin
548 Pied Crow
568 Blackeyed Bulbul
577 Olive Thrush
587 Capped Wheatear
596 **Stonechat**
601 Cape Robin
628 Great Reed Warbler
631 African Marsh Warbler
635 Cape Reed Warbler
638 African Sedge Warbler
643 Willow Warbler
664 Fantailed Cisticola
665 Desert Cisticola
667 Ayres' Cisticola
677 **Levaillant's Cisticola**
683 Tawnyflanked Prinia
713 Cape Wagtail
714 **Yellow Wagtail**
716 Grassveld Pipit
727 Orangethroated Longclaw**
732 Fiscal Shrike
746 Bokmakierie*
758 Indian Myna
759 **Pied Starling****
796 Cape White-eye**
801 House Sparrow
803 Cape Sparrow*
813 Cape Weaver**
814 Masked Weaver
821 Redbilled Quelea
824 Red Bishop
826 Golden Bishop
832 Longtailed Widow
846 Common Waxbill
852 **Quail Finch**
854 **Orangebreasted Waxbill**
860 Pintailed Whydah
870 Blackthroated Canary
881 Streakyheaded Canary

BLESBOKSPRUIT (MARIEVALE BIRD SANCTUARY)

approximately 252 species recorded to date

The Blesbokspruit area, almost 2 000 ha in extent, is situated on the far east rand, some 10 km east of the town of Springs and extending to 10 km north-east of Nigel. It consists of shallow open water with extensive *Phragmites* and *Typha* reedbeds surrounded by grassland, mining and agricultural activity. This area, a Ramsar Convention Wetland site, is jointly controlled by the Chief Directorate: Nature and Environmental Conservation, Anglo American Corporation and Springs Town Council. Only two areas are open daily to the public: Marievale Bird Sanctuary and Springs Bird Sanctuary. No camping is allowed, but Marievale has a pleasant picnic site and excellent hides. There are toilets.

SPECIAL AND INTERESTING SPECIES

Hottentot Teal are seen on most of the pans; they prefer the pan fringes. During winter up to 2 500 **Spurwinged Geese** are present, the birds using the area to moult. Rails and crakes are heard occasionally, and if one is lucky **African Rail** and **Black Crake** may be seen. During winter **Redcapped Lark** and **Capped Wheatear** occur, especially on the northern section (look for them on overgrazed or burnt areas). During summer this area also supports **Yellow Wagtail**. (A telescope is however necessary.) Both **African** and **European** (summer) **Marsh Harriers** occur, with the European bird recorded more often than its African counterpart during the last few seasons. The

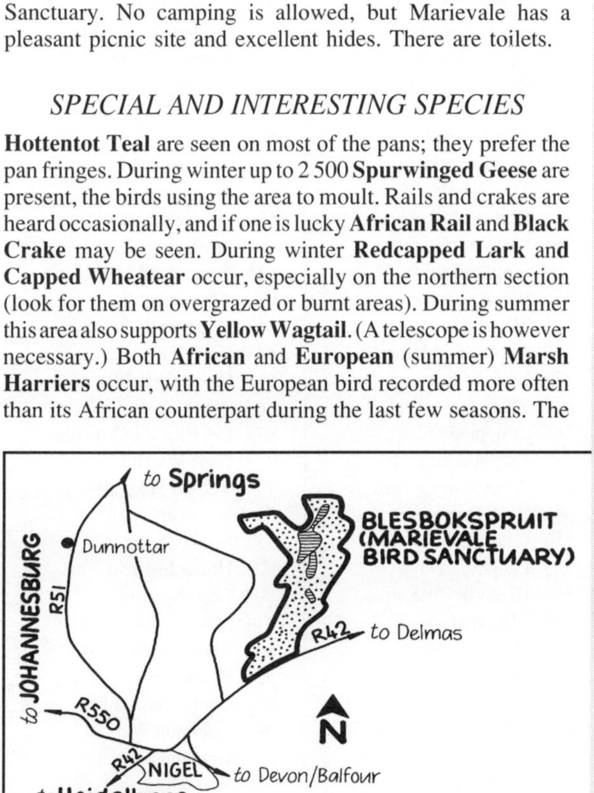

Marievale can be reached from Johannesburg via either Nigel or Springs. The route via Nigel is as follows: take the N3 towards Heidelberg as far as the Nigel/Kliprivier exit (R550). Follow the road into Nigel and then take the Delmas Road (R42) until the signposts to the sanctuary on the left side are reached. The route via Springs: take the N12 freeway from Johannesburg as far as the Springs/Daveyton (R51) exit. Follow the R51 (towards Springs) for about 20 km until on the southern outskirts of Springs an unnumbered route on the left-hand side marked "Nigel" is reached. Take this road for about 3 km. Here you will find a turnoff on the left side marked "Marievale Voëlpark". Take this road for a further 3 km until a gravel road turning off to the right and signposted "Marievale Consolidated Mines Ltd" is reached. Follow this for about 2 km and at the T-junction turn left and follow the signs to "Marievale Bird Sanctuary". The Springs Bird Sanctuary can be reached by taking the Welgedacht/Delmas road (R550) from Springs. After about 10 km the Blesbokspruit is crossed and on the left-hand side is the sign to the sanctuary.

adjacent grasslands support up to 20 **Marsh Owls**, seen at their best during the winter. **European Swallows** use the reedbeds to roost and during summer up to 500 000 birds can be seen swarming and diving into the reeds. Warblers are well represented, with **Cape Reed** and **African Sedge Warblers** being the most common. The area is also rich in herons and other colonial nesting birds – **Blackheaded**, **Goliath** and **Squacco Herons**, **Whitebreasted** and **Reed Cormorants**, **Darter**, **Sacred** and **Glossy Ibises** and **Cattle Egret** all breed here. **Great White**, **Little**, **Black** and **Yellowbilled Egrets** are all commonly seen.

ALSO RECORDED

Blacktailed Godwits occur from time to time at Springs Bird Sanctuary. Migrant waders include Common and Marsh Sandpipers, Greenshank and Grey Plover.

Mike Crowther

38% OF SPECIES

006 Great Crested Grebe ☐
008 Dabchick ☐
055 **Whitebreasted Cormorant** ☐
058 **Reed Cormorant** ☐
060 **Darter** ☐
063 **Blackheaded Heron** ☐
064 **Goliath Heron** ☐
066 **Great White Egret** ☐
067 **Little Egret** ☐
068 **Yellowbilled Egret** ☐
069 **Black Egret** ☐
071 **Cattle Egret** ☐
072 **Squacco Heron** ☐
078 Little Bittern ☐
091 **Sacred Ibis** ☐
093 **Glossy Ibis** ☐
094 Hadeda Ibis ☐
095 African Spoonbill ☐
096 Greater Flamingo ☐
099 Whitefaced Duck ☐
100 Fulvous Duck ☐
102 Egyptian Goose ☐
103 South African Shelduck** ☐
104 Yellowbilled Duck ☐
107 **Hottentot Teal** ☐
108 Redbilled Teal ☐
112 Cape Shoveller* ☐
113 Southern Pochard ☐
116 **Spurwinged Goose** ☐
127 Blackshouldered Kite ☐
152 Jackal Buzzard** ☐
164 **European Marsh Harrier** ☐
165 **African Marsh Harrier** ☐
199 Swainson's Francolin* ☐
203 Helmeted Guineafowl ☐
210 **African Rail** ☐
213 **Black Crake** ☐
223 Purple Gallinule ☐
226 Moorhen ☐
228 Redknobbed Coot ☐
248 Kittlitz's Plover ☐
249 Threebanded Plover ☐
255 Crowned Plover ☐
258 Blacksmith Plover ☐
260 Wattled Plover ☐
266 Wood Sandpiper ☐
269 Marsh Sandpiper ☐
272 Curlew Sandpiper ☐
274 Little Stint ☐
284 Ruff ☐
286 Ethiopian Snipe ☐
315 Greyheaded Gull ☐
339 Whitewinged Tern ☐
349 Rock Pigeon ☐
354 Cape Turtle Dove ☐
355 Laughing Dove ☐
386 Diederik Cuckoo ☐
395 **Marsh Owl** ☐
415 Whiterumped Swift ☐
416 Horus Swift ☐
417 Little Swift ☐
426 Redfaced Mousebird ☐
428 Pied Kingfisher ☐
473 Crested Barbet ☐
489 Redthroated Wryneck ☐
507 **Redcapped Lark** ☐
518 **European Swallow** ☐
520 Whitethroated Swallow ☐
526 Greater Striped Swallow* ☐
533 Brownthroated Martin ☐
586 Mountain Chat* ☐
587 **Capped Wheatear** ☐
596 Stonechat ☐
633 European Marsh Warbler ☐
634 European Sedge Warbler ☐
635 **Cape Reed Warbler** ☐
638 **African Sedge Warbler** ☐
664 Fantailed Cisticola ☐
666 Cloud Cisticola ☐
667 Ayres' Cisticola ☐
677 Levaillant's Cisticola ☐
713 Cape Wagtail ☐
714 **Yellow Wagtail** ☐
716 Grassveld Pipit ☐
732 Fiscal Shrike ☐
801 House Sparrow ☐
803 Cape Sparrow* ☐
814 Masked Weaver ☐
821 Redbilled Quelea ☐
824 Red Bishop ☐
832 Longtailed Widow ☐
846 Common Waxbill ☐
854 Orangebreasted Waxbill ☐
869 Yelloweyed Canary ☐
870 Blackthroated Canary ☐

SUIKERBOSRAND NATURE RESERVE

approximately 250 species recorded to date

This 13 337 ha reserve, controlled by the Chief Directorate: Nature and Environmental Conservation, lies about 50 km south of Johannesburg and 25 km west of Heidelberg. The major habitat is grassland, which can be divided into montane (above 1 800 m) and "non-montane". Broadleafed woodland occurs in the valleys, *Acacia* savanna has developed in the south-west and *Protea* veld covers the eastern section. There is an extensive network of overnight trails, two day-walks, two picnic sites and a 60 km circular drive. Camping is not allowed. Gates are open between 06h00 (07h00 in winter) and 17h30.

SPECIAL AND INTERESTING SPECIES

Cape Weavers breed at Kareekloof; **Familiar Chat** and **Rock Bunting** (summer) are abundant at the Diepkloof picnic site. This is the closest place to Johannesburg where **Redeyed Bulbul** is common. **Redthroated Wryneck** and **Malachite Sunbird** should also be looked for here. **Black Eagles** breed on the south facing cliffs and **Jackal Buzzards** are common. **Titbabbler**, **Cape White-eye** and **Ashy Tit** occur in the *Acacia* savanna. If you enjoy the challenge of sorting out look-alikes this is your place. The montane grassland is home to **Mountain** and **Anteating Chats**, and **Pied Starlings** are everywhere. **Sentinel Rock Thrush** visits the summit in

ALSO RECORDED

Spotted Eagle Owl can often be heard from some of the trail huts at night and Cape Eagle Owl has also been recorded recently.

John McAllister

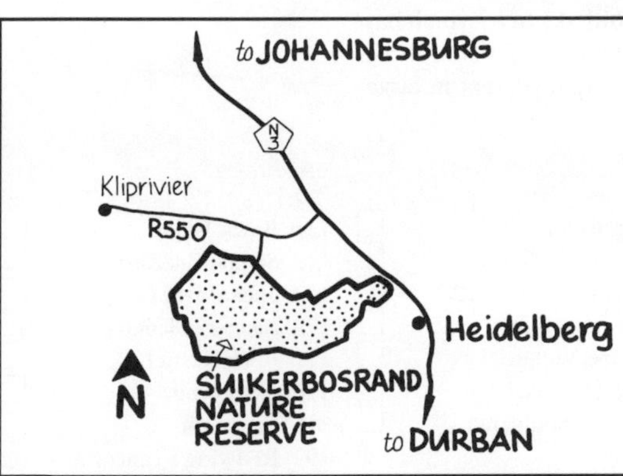

Turn off the N3 from Johannesburg to Durban onto the R550 towards Kliprivier. Turn left to the reserve (signposted) 6 km further on.

winter and **Cape Rock Thrush** is common throughout the year. An isolated population of **Greywing Francolin** occurs at high altitude while **Redwing Francolins** are found lower down in the wetter north. **Orange River Francolin** should be looked for in the drier grasslands to the south. **Fiscal Flycatcher** and **Fiscal Shrike** are common. During summer **Fantailed Cisticolas** "zitt" about above the rank grassland near the Diepkloof entrance gate. **Ayres' Cisticola** can be heard over the sparsely grassed highlands where the rainfall is the highest. **Wailing Cisticola** can be seen on the more open rocky, grass-covered hillsides dotted with *Protea caffra*. **Lazy Cisticola** occurs where hillsides are more densely wooded. **Levaillant's Cisticola** should be looked for in the marshy areas; **Cloud Cisticola** prefers the drier grasslands in the south; **Rattling Cisticola** is best found in the *Acacia* savanna and **Neddicky** occurs wherever there are trees. Both **Yelloweyed** and **Yellow Canaries** occur, with the latter showing a preference for the *Acacia* savanna. **Cape Canary** prefers the montane grassland, **Bully Canary** the *Protea* dotted hillsides and **Streakyheaded Canary** the well-wooded areas; **Blackthroated Canary** can be found almost anywhere. **Golden Bishop** and **Yellowrumped Widow** enjoy a similar habitat – rank grass and weeds. **Grassveld Pipit** is found in short open grassland as are **Plainbacked** and **Buffy Pipits**, but the latter two also occur in open woodland and savanna. **Longbilled Pipit** favours short *rocky* grassland or open woodland and **Striped Pipit** prefers wooded, rocky hillsides. To add to your woes Rock Pipit has also been recorded recently, but its status is uncertain. **Rufousnaped Lark** calls from a conspicuous perch in grassland and open savanna in summer. **Redcapped Lark** can be found in short, sparsely grassed areas and **Spikeheeled Lark** likes shortly grazed or burnt grassland. **Clapper Lark** displays conspicuously over long grass during summer while **Longbilled Lark**, which has a similar display flight without the clapping, favours more rocky areas and **Pinkbilled Larks** are often present in large numbers.

54% OF SPECIES

058 Reed Cormorant ☐
060 Darter ☐
062 Grey Heron ☐
063 Blackheaded Heron ☐
065 Purple Heron ☐
071 Cattle Egret ☐
081 Hamerkop ☐
091 Sacred Ibis ☐
094 Hadeda Ibis ☐
102 Egyptian Goose ☐
104 Yellowbilled Duck ☐
118 Secretarybird ☐
122 Cape Vulture** ☐
126a Yellowbilled Kite ☐
127 Blackshouldered Kite ☐
131 **Black Eagle** ☐
149 Steppe Buzzard ☐
152 **Jackal Buzzard**** ☐
172 Lanner Falcon ☐
181 Rock Kestrel ☐
190 **Greywing Francolin**** ☐
192 **Redwing Francolin** ☐

193 **Orange River Francolin***
199 Swainson's Francolin*
203 Helmeted Guineafowl
226 Moorhen
228 Redknobbed Coot
249 Threebanded Plover
255 Crowned Plover
258 Blacksmith Plover
260 Wattled Plover
264 Common Sandpiper
266 Wood Sandpiper
286 Ethiopian Snipe
297 Spotted Dikkop
349 Rock Pigeon
352 Redeyed Dove
354 Cape Turtle Dove
355 Laughing Dove
356 Namaqua Dove
377 Redchested Cuckoo
386 Diederik Cuckoo
392 Barn Owl
415 Whiterumped Swift
417 Little Swift
424 Speckled Mousebird
426 Redfaced Mousebird
428 Pied Kingfisher
451 Hoopoe
464 Blackcollared Barbet
465 Pied Barbet*
473 Crested Barbet
489 **Redthroated Wryneck**
494 **Rufousnaped Lark**
495 **Clapper Lark****
500 **Longbilled Lark***
506 **Spikeheeled Lark***
507 **Redcapped Lark**
508 **Pinkbilled Lark***
518 European Swallow
520 Whitethroated Swallow
526 Greater Striped Swallow*
530 House Martin
548 Pied Crow
552 **Ashy Tit***
567 **Redeyed Bulbul***
577 Olive Thrush
581 **Cape Rock Thrush****
582 **Sentinel Rock Thrush****
586 **Mountain Chat***
589 **Familiar Chat**
593 **Mocking Chat**
595 **Anteating Chat****
596 Stonechat
601 Cape Robin
615 Kalahari Robin*
621 **Titbabbler***
643 Willow Warbler
645 Barthroated Apalis
664 **Fantailed Cisticola**
665 Desert Cisticola
666 **Cloud Cisticola**
667 **Ayres' Cisticola**
670 **Wailing Cisticola**
672 **Rattling Cisticola**
677 **Levaillant's Cisticola**
679 **Lazy Cisticola**
681 **Neddicky**
683 Tawnyflanked Prinia
685 Blackchested Prinia*
689 Spotted Flycatcher
698 **Fiscal Flycatcher****
706 Fairy Flycatcher**
710 Paradise Flycatcher
713 Cape Wagtail
716 **Grassveld Pipit**
717 **Longbilled Pipit**
718 **Plainbacked Pipit**
719 **Buffy Pipit**
720 **Striped Pipit**
727 Orangethroated Longclaw**
732 **Fiscal Shrike**
743 Threestreaked Tchagra
746 Bokmakierie*
759 **Pied Starling****
760 Wattled Starling
764 Glossy Starling*
769 Redwinged Starling
775 **Malachite Sunbird**
796 **Cape White-eye****
799 Whitebrowed Sparrowweaver
801 House Sparrow
803 Cape Sparrow*
804 Greyheaded Sparrow
813 **Cape Weaver****
815 Lesser Masked Weaver
821 Redbilled Quelea
824 Red Bishop
826 **Golden Bishop**
827 **Yellowrumped Widow**
831 Redcollared Widow
832 Longtailed Widow
834 Melba Finch
846 Common Waxbill
852 Quail Finch
854 Orangebreasted Waxbill
856 Redheaded Finch*
860 Pintailed Whydah
869 **Yelloweyed Canary**
870 **Blackthroated Canary**
872 **Cape Canary**
877 **Bully Canary**
878 **Yellow Canary***
881 **Streakyheaded Canary**
885 Cape Bunting
886 **Rock Bunting**

BARBERSPAN NATURE RESERVE

approximately 287 species recorded to date

The reserve, which covers 3 060 ha and is controlled by the Chief Directorate: Nature and Environmental Conservation, is situated in the south-western Transvaal approximately 80 km south-west of Lichtenburg. When full the pan (a declared wetland of international importance) covers an area of 2 000 ha. The other major habitat in the reserve is arid *Themeda-Cymbopogon* grassland. There is a camping site with limited facilities including pit toilets, running water and outdoor fireplaces. Accommodation is available at the Barberspan Hotel.

SPECIAL AND INTERESTING SPECIES

When full the pan provides a waterbird spectacle that would be difficult to match anywhere. During September/October numbers can build up to 27 000 **Redknobbed Coot**, 5 000 **Yellowbilled Duck**, 5 000 **Redbilled Teal**, 3 000 **Spurwinged Geese**, 2 000 **Egyptian Geese**, 1 000 **South African Shelduck**, 900 **Whitebreasted Cormorant**, 500 **Southern Pochard** and 250 **Cape Shoveller**. With the onset of the summer rains these birds tend to disperse to breed on the numerous small ephemeral pans in the area. When the water levels are high, rafts of up to 200 **Blacknecked Grebe** can be seen fishing in the deep water and **Great Crested Grebe** breed in large numbers in the emergent vegetation at the edge of the pan.

Leave the Pretoria-Johannesburg area on the R47 via Tarlton and Ventersdorp to Coligny. Turn left onto the R375 to Biesiesvlei, then left again onto the R47 towards Sannieshof. About 20 km past Sannieshof turn right onto a gravel road signposted "Deelpan". Continue along this road for about 5 km to the reserve office. Permission to enter the nature area should be obtained here.

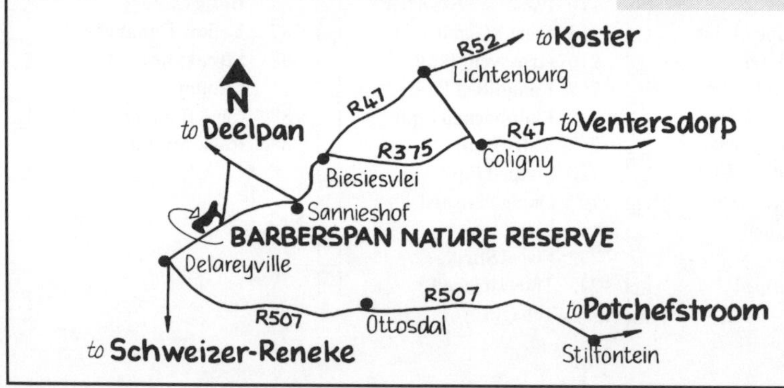

This is also one of the best inland sites for **Caspian Tern** (up to 70 birds). **Goliath Heron**, **Avocet** and **Blackwinged Stilt** are usually present in fair numbers. During drought periods when Barberspan shrinks dramatically in size and the surrounding pans dry up, the water becomes extremely saline. At times like this up to 15 000 **Lesser** and 5 000 **Greater Flamingo** have been seen on neighbouring Leeupan. **Maccoa Duck** also like these saline conditions and up to 200 birds have been recorded here. The threatened **Chestnutbanded Plover** (up to 50 birds) may be seen feeding along the shoreline, particularly where there are large salt patches. In between these two extemes the bare shores of the pan become a wader paradise during summer. It is undoubtedly the best inland site for coastal species such as **Turnstone**, **Ringed** and **Grey Plovers**. **Curlew Sandpiper**, **Little Stint** and **Ruff** are found in large numbers with **Greenshank**, **Common**, **Wood** and **Marsh Sandpipers** also present. **Marsh Owls** can often be seen hunting during the late afternoon, or on overcast days, over the rank vegetation on the eastern boundary of the reserve. **Rufouseared Warbler** is a special of the karroid vegetation in the north-eastern corner of the reserve. In the grassland one should look for **Swainson's Francolin**, **Whitequilled Korhaan**, **Blackchested Prinia**, **Anteating Chat**, **Grassveld Pipit**, **Orangethroated Longclaw**, **Spikeheeled** and **Pinkbilled Larks**. The short grass near the pan is the best place to find **Redcapped Lark**, **Quail Finch**, **Chestnutbacked** and **Greybacked Finchlarks**. **Swallowtailed Bee-eater**, **Namaqua Sandgrouse** and **Fairy Flycatcher** are regular winter visitors to the reserve. The gardens at the reserve buildings (old research station) should produce **Yellow Canary**, **Redheaded Finch**, **Fiscal Flycatcher** and **Redeyed Bulbul**.

ALSO RECORDED

Unexpected vagrants are an exciting feature of Barberspan and Rednecked Falcon, Baillon's Crake, Painted Snipe, Whitefronted Plover, Green Sandpiper, Sanderling, Buffbreasted Sandpiper, Blacktailed and Bartailed Godwits, Burchell's and Temminck's Coursers, Lesser Blackbacked Gull, Tinkling Cisticola and Chat Flycatcher have all been recorded here recently.

John McAllister

52% OF SPECIES

001 Ostrich ☐
006 **Great Crested Grebe** ☐
007 **Blacknecked Grebe** ☐
008 Dabchick ☐
050 Pinkbacked Pelican ☐
055 **Whitebreasted Cormorant** ☐
058 Reed Cormorant ☐
060 Darter ☐
062 Grey Heron ☐
063 Blackheaded Heron ☐
064 **Goliath Heron** ☐
066 Great White Egret ☐
067 Little Egret ☐
068 Yellowbilled Egret ☐
069 Black Egret ☐
071 Cattle Egret ☐
076 Blackcrowned Night Heron ☐
081 Hamerkop ☐
085 Abdim's Stork ☐
091 Sacred Ibis ☐
093 Glossy Ibis ☐
094 Hadeda Ibis ☐
095 African Spoonbill ☐
096 **Greater Flamingo** ☐
097 **Lesser Flamingo** ☐
102 **Egyptian Goose** ☐
103 **South African Shelduck**** ☐
104 **Yellowbilled Duck** ☐
106 Cape Teal ☐
108 **Redbilled Teal** ☐
112 **Cape Shoveller*** ☐
113 **Southern Pochard** ☐
116 **Spurwinged Goose** ☐

117 **Maccoa Duck**
118 Secretarybird
127 Blackshouldered Kite
148 African Fish Eagle
149 Steppe Buzzard
170 Osprey
172 Lanner Falcon
181 Rock Kestrel
182 Greater Kestrel
183 Lesser Kestrel
199 **Swainson's Francolin***
203 Helmeted Guineafowl
223 Purple Gallinule
226 Moorhen
228 **Redknobbed Coot**
239a **Whitequilled Korhaan****
245 **Ringed Plover**
247 **Chestnutbanded Plover**
248 Kittlitz's Plover
249 Threebanded Plover
254 **Grey Plover**
255 Crowned Plover
258 Blacksmith Plover
262 **Turnstone**
264 **Common Sandpiper**
266 **Wood Sandpiper**
269 **Marsh Sandpiper**
270 **Greenshank**
272 **Curlew Sandpiper**
274 **Little Stint**
284 **Ruff**
294 **Avocet**
295 **Blackwinged Stilt**
297 Spotted Dikkop
315 Greyheaded Gull
322 **Caspian Tern**
338 Whiskered Tern
339 Whitewinged Tern
344 **Namaqua Sandgrouse***
349 Rock Pigeon
352 Redeyed Dove
354 Cape Turtle Dove
355 Laughing Dove
356 Namaqua Dove
386 Diederik Cuckoo
395 **Marsh Owl**
401 Spotted Eagle Owl
415 Whiterumped Swift
417 Little Swift
421 Palm Swift
425 Whitebacked Mousebird**
426 Redfaced Mousebird
428 Pied Kingfisher
438 European Bee-eater
445 **Swallowtailed Bee-eater**
451 Hoopoe
465 Pied Barbet*
473 Crested Barbet
494 Rufousnaped Lark
506 **Spikeheeled Lark***
507 **Redcapped Lark**
508 **Pinkbilled Lark***
515 **Chestnutbacked Finchlark**
516 **Greybacked Finchlark***
518 European Swallow
520 Whitethroated Swallow
526 Greater Striped Swallow*
528 South African Cliff Swallow**
547 Black Crow
548 Pied Crow
567 **Redeyed Bulbul***
595 **Anteating Chat****
596 Stonechat
601 Cape Robin
615 Kalahari Robin*
621 Titbabbler*
635 Cape Reed Warbler
643 Willow Warbler
664 Fantailed Cisticola
665 Desert Cisticola
666 Cloud Cisticola
672 Rattling Cisticola
677 Levaillant's Cisticola
681 Neddicky
685 **Blackchested Prinia***
688 **Rufouseared Warbler****
689 Spotted Flycatcher
698 **Fiscal Flycatcher****
706 **Fairy Flycatcher****
713 Cape Wagtail
716 **Grassveld Pipit**
727 **Orangethroated Longclaw****
732 Fiscal Shrike
733 Redbacked Shrike
743 Threestreaked Tchagra
746 Bokmakierie*
764 Glossy Starling*
796 Cape White-eye**
799 Whitebrowed Sparrowweaver
801 House Sparrow
803 Cape Sparrow*
804 Greyheaded Sparrow
814 Masked Weaver
821 Redbilled Quelea
824 Red Bishop
826 Golden Bishop
832 Longtailed Widow
842 Redbilled Firefinch
846 Common Waxbill
852 **Quail Finch**
856 **Redheaded Finch***
860 Pintailed Whydah
867 Steelblue Widowfinch
870 Blackthroated Canary
878 **Yellow Canary***
887 Larklike Bunting*

POTCHEFSTROOM

approximately 300 species recorded to date

Potchefstroom is situated on the Mooi River in the southern Transvaal. To many people it seems unthinkable that a big variety of birds can occur in an area as flat and barren as that of Potchefstroom. However, the presence of water habitats, i.e. the Mooi and Vaal rivers, Potchefstroom and Boskop dams, the hills of the Vredefort Dome and the open grassveld leads the birdwatcher to a magnificent variety of species. Boskop Dam is in a provincial nature reserve, which also includes a couple of thousand hectares of short grassveld. At the O.P.M. Prozesky Bird Sanctuary a hundred species can be seen in as many minutes. Situated on the floodplain of the Mooi River and around disused sewage pans, this sanctuary gives one a good idea of what the whole area must have looked like a century ago when Thomas Ayres collected species such as Angola Pitta, Rufousbellied Heron and Great Snipe here. Because of extensive geological activity the Vredefort Dome's hills and kloofs have a very mild climate and birds expected in more temperate areas occur here.

SPECIAL AND INTERESTING SPECIES

Osprey can be found in the old trees in the little bay on the western side of Boskop Dam Nature Reserve. **Great Crested Grebes** breed on the dam and **Black Sparrowhawk** can be seen in the gum plantation. In the grasslands one should look for **Doublebanded Courser**, **Whitequilled Korhaan**, **Orangethroated Longclaw**, **Orange River Francolin**,

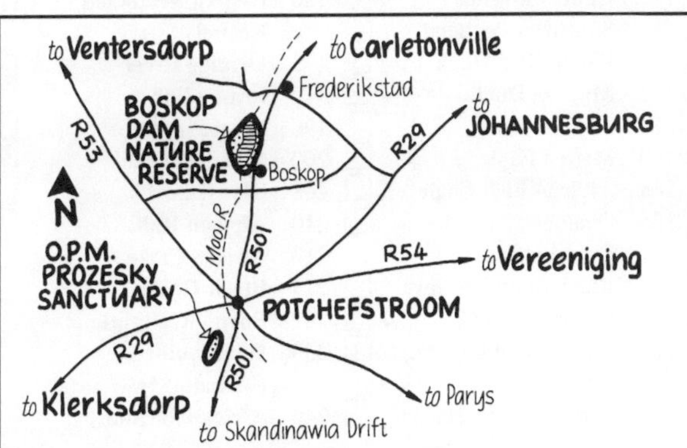

Boskop Dam: From the town of Potchefstroom drive north on the R501 towards Carletonville. After 14 km turn left into the Boskop Dam Nature Reserve, or after 18 km turn left on the Muiskraal road. After 2 km turn left after the bridge over the Mooi River and follow the gravel road to the reserve.

O.P.M. Prozesky Bird Sanctuary: From the town of Potchefstroom proceed southwards on Mooi River Drive (R501) towards Skandinawia Drift. Beyond the golf course is the northern, undeveloped part of the sanctuary between the road and the river. Turn right after 3,7 km into Viljoen Street, then turn left after 250 m into the O.P.M. Prozesky Sanctuary. A Y4 key will give you access to both hides and the toilets. If you continue on Mooi River Drive (R501) towards Schoemansdrif for 23,5 km and turn right towards Nooitgedacht, you'll soon be driving on a road between the hills and the Vaal River, towards Skandinawia Drift. Follow this road for 16 km and turn right to get back to Potchefstroom. Excellent birding can be had along this road.

Clapper, **Spikeheeled** and **Pinkbilled Larks**. **Orange-breasted Waxbill** can usually be found in the reedbeds and **Yellow Canary** should be looked for wherever there are trees. The O.P.M. Prozesky Sanctuary gives you access to a great variety of waterbirds. **Knobbilled**, **Fulvous** and **Maccoa Ducks**, **South African Shelduck**, **Southern Pochard**, **Hottentot Teal** and **Cape Shoveller** are easily seen from the hides as are **African Rail**, **Black Crake** and **Purple Gallinule**. **Little Bittern**, **Blackcrowned Night Heron**, **Squacco**, **Purple** and **Goliath Herons** are all frequently seen. **Longtailed**, **Redcollared** and **Whitewinged Widows**, **Golden** and **Red Bishops** are always buzzing around over the reeds. A wide variety of sedge and reed warblers including **Cape Reed** and **African Sedge Warblers** are found in the reeds. The road alongside the Vaal River is the ideal place from which to see **Goliath Heron** and **African Black Duck** on the river. **Chinspot** and **Pririt Batis** can be found in the trees on the hillside. **Ashy Tit**, **Scimitarbilled Woodhoopoe** and **Goldentailed Woodpecker** can easily be called up. **Blue**, **Violeteared**, **Blackcheeked** and **Common Waxbills** are often seen, as are **African Fish Eagle** and **African Jacana**. The haunting call of **Redthroated Wrynecks** often leads you to a hole in a tree where they breed. **Rufouscheeked** and **Fierynecked Nightjars** can be heard at night, with the puppylike yelp of the **Freckled Nightjar** heard in the vicinity of the granitic outcrops near Parys.

ALSO RECORDED

Yellow Wagtail has been seen walking among fishermen at Boskop Dam and Honey Buzzard has been seen raiding wasps' nests in a poplar tree. With patience Baillon's Crake can be seen feeding at the O.P.M. Prozesky Sanctuary on the edge of one of the marshes at dawn and dusk. Peregrine Falcon has taken a pigeon above one of the hides and Pectoral Sandpiper was recorded on the mudflats near the Mooi River. Black Eagle and Plumcoloured Starling are sometimes seen in the hills around the Vaal River and the rare Whitebacked Night Heron and Greenbacked Heron can be found on the river.

Sam de Beer

49% OF SPECIES

006	**Great Crested Grebe**	☐
064	**Goliath Heron**	☐
065	**Purple Heron**	☐
066	Great White Egret	☐
068	Yellowbilled Egret	☐
069	Black Egret	☐
072	**Squacco Heron**	☐
076	**Blackcrowned Night Heron**	☐
078	**Little Bittern**	☐
090	Yellowbilled Stork	☐
093	Glossy Ibis	☐
095	African Spoonbill	☐
099	Whitefaced Duck	☐
100	**Fulvous Duck**	☐
103	**South African Shelduck****	☐
105	**African Black Duck**	☐
106	Cape Teal	☐
107	**Hottentot Teal**	☐
112	**Cape Shoveller***	☐
113	**Southern Pochard**	☐
115	**Knobbilled Duck**	☐
117	**Maccoa Duck**	☐
118	Secretarybird	☐
140	Martial Eagle	☐
148	**African Fish Eagle**	☐
156	Ovambo Sparrowhawk	☐
158	**Black Sparrowhawk**	☐
161	Gabar Goshawk	☐
162	Pale Chanting Goshawk*	☐
165	African Marsh Harrier	☐
169	Gymnogene	☐
170	**Osprey**	☐
172	Lanner Falcon	☐
180	Eastern Redfooted Kestrel	☐
193	**Orange River Francolin***	☐
196	Natal Francolin*	☐
200	Common Quail	☐
208	Blue Crane**	☐
210	**African Rail**	☐
212	African Crake	☐
213	**Black Crake**	☐
223	**Purple Gallinule**	☐
239a	**Whitequilled Korhaan****	☐
240	**African Jacana**	☐

260 Wattled Plover ☐
270 Greenshank ☐
286 Ethiopian Snipe ☐
294 Avocet ☐
300 Temminck's Courser ☐
301 **Doublebanded Courser** ☐
305 Blackwinged Pratincole ☐
322 Caspian Tern ☐
338 Whiskered Tern ☐
356 Namaqua Dove ☐
382 Jacobin Cuckoo ☐
385 Klaas's Cuckoo ☐
393 Grass Owl ☐
401 Spotted Eagle Owl ☐
405 **Fierynecked Nightjar** ☐
406 **Rufouscheeked Nightjar** ☐
408 **Freckled Nightjar** ☐
416 Horus Swift ☐
421 Palm Swift ☐
430 Halfcollared Kingfisher ☐
440 Bluecheeked Bee-eater ☐
445 Swallowtailed Bee-eater ☐
452 Redbilled Woodhoopoe ☐
454 **Scimitarbilled Woodhoopoe** ☐
474 Greater Honeyguide ☐
478 Sharpbilled Honeyguide ☐
483 **Goldentailed Woodpecker** ☐
486 Cardinal Woodpecker ☐
489 **Redthroated Wryneck** ☐
494 Rufousnaped Lark ☐
495 **Clapper Lark**** ☐
498 Sabota Lark* ☐
506 **Spikeheeled Lark*** ☐
507 Redcapped Lark ☐
508 **Pinkbilled Lark*** ☐
515 Chestnutbacked Finchlark ☐
516 Greybacked Finchlark* ☐
524 Redbreasted Swallow ☐
530 House Martin ☐
532 Sand Martin ☐
534 Banded Martin ☐
547 Black Crow ☐
548 Pied Crow ☐
552 **Ashy Tit*** ☐
580 Groundscraper Thrush ☐
586 Mountain Chat* ☐
587 Capped Wheatear ☐
593 Mocking Chat ☐
602 Whitethroated Robin** ☐
615 Kalahari Robin* ☐
621 Titbabbler* ☐
628 Great Reed Warbler ☐
631 African Marsh Warbler ☐
633 European Marsh Warbler ☐
634 European Sedge Warbler ☐
635 **Cape Reed Warbler** ☐
638 **African Sedge Warbler** ☐
651 Longbilled Crombec ☐
653 Yellowbellied Eremomela ☐
665 Desert Cisticola ☐
666 Cloud Cisticola ☐
672 Rattling Cisticola ☐
701 **Chinspot Batis** ☐
703 **Pririt Batis*** ☐
706 Fairy Flycatcher** ☐
711 African Pied Wagtail ☐
714 Yellow Wagtail ☐
718 Plainbacked Pipit ☐
719 Buffy Pipit ☐
727 **Orangethroated Longclaw**** ☐
731 Lesser Grey Shrike ☐
733 Redbacked Shrike ☐
741 Brubru ☐
743 Threestreaked Tchagra ☐
746 Bokmakierie* ☐
769 Redwinged Starling ☐
775 Malachite Sunbird ☐
792 Black Sunbird ☐
805 Yellowthroated Sparrow ☐
806 Scalyfeathered Finch* ☐
824 **Red Bishop** ☐
826 **Golden Bishop** ☐
829 **Whitewinged Widow** ☐
831 **Redcollared Widow** ☐
832 **Longtailed Widow** ☐
834 Melba Finch ☐
841 Jameson's Firefinch ☐
842 Redbilled Firefinch ☐
844 **Blue Waxbill** ☐
845 **Violeteared Waxbill*** ☐
846 **Common Waxbill** ☐
847 **Blackcheeked Waxbill** ☐
852 Quail Finch ☐
854 **Orangebreasted Waxbill** ☐
857 Bronze Mannikin ☐
861 Shafttailed Whydah* ☐
864 Black Widowfinch ☐
867 Steelblue Widowfinch ☐
878 **Yellow Canary*** ☐
881 Streakyheaded Canary ☐
884 Goldenbreasted Bunting ☐
885 Cape Bunting ☐
886 Rock Bunting ☐
☐
☐
☐
☐

WAKKERSTROOM

approximately 250 species recorded to date

Bush Blackcap

Wakkerstroom, situated on the escarpment of the south-eastern Transvaal, has a varied range of habitats and greatly varying altitudes. It is one of the best localities in southern Africa to find the rarer highveld species, and the abundance of vleis in the area offers ideal wetland birding. A 500 ha wetland (vlei) lying within the municipal boundaries of Wakkerstroom is being developed as a nature reserve. Hills, valleys, ravines, patches of indigenous forest, montane grassland and rocky outcrops surround the town. There are many pans, marshes and dams in the district, this being one of the south-eastern Transvaal's major catchment areas. A municipal caravan park adjoins the Martins Dam. Accommodation is also available at the Weaver's Nest Guest House, which is run by birders for birders. Birding information is available here.

Wakkerstroom is 27 km from Volksrust on the Piet Retief road and is an ideal halfway stopover from the Reef to the northern Natal parks, which also makes it a feasible weekend destination from both directions. There are many circular drives in the area, all covering at least four varying habitats and offering excellent birding.

SPECIAL AND INTERESTING SPECIES

Bush Blackcap, **Barthroated Apalis** and **Olive Bush Shrike** can be found in *Leucosidea* and *Buddleja* thickets in valleys and ravines. On the rocky mountain slopes look out for **Rock Pipit** (which stands upright on a rock and points its bill upwards while singing), **Ground Woodpecker**, **Sentinel Rock Thrush**, **Buffstreaked Chat**, **Cape Bunting** and **Longbilled Lark**. A walk in the short open grassland areas could produce **Yellowbreasted Pipit** – which may be difficult to flush – and **Pinkbilled Lark**, which usually occurs in small

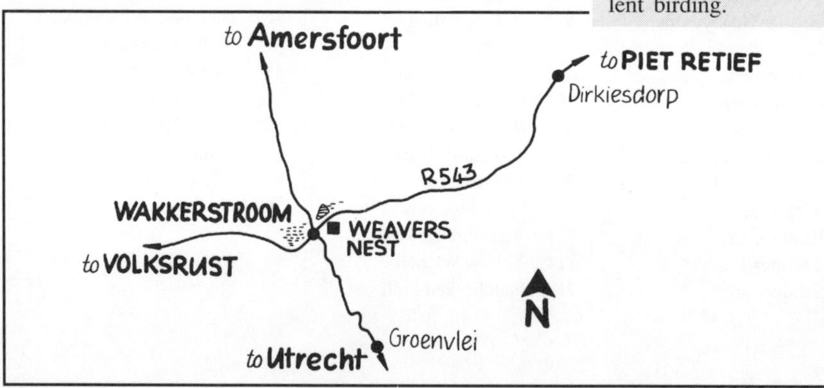

parties. **Spikeheeled Lark** favours short grazed or burnt open grassland. **Botha's Lark** is similar to Pinkbilled Lark, but the bill is more slender, breast and flanks are more heavily streaked. This species may be found in short grassland on the upper slopes of hillsides. **Rudd's Lark** occurs in short, dense *Themeda-Heteropogon* grassland on the edges of pans and vleis. The very short tail and thin, white stripe from forehead to crown is diagnostic. **Blue** and **Whitebellied Korhaans** are both regulars, but favour different habitats. The first prefers short grazed grassland and the latter longer, dense grassland. A visit to the bridge on the Wakkerstroom/Amersfoort road provides magnificent views of the extensive wetland, which has large stands of *Phragmites* reeds. **African Rail**, **Ethiopian Snipe**, **Little Bittern**, **Wood Sandpiper** (summer), **Ruff** (summer), **Purple Gallinule**, **African Marsh**, **African Sedge** and **Yellow Warblers**, **Great White**, **Little** and **Yellowbilled Egrets**, **Purple** and **Squacco Herons** and **African Marsh Harrier** are but a few of the many species that you could see and hear. **Blackcrowned Night Heron** may be seen in the willow trees along the wetland edge. Other pans and dams produce **Blacknecked** and **Great Crested Grebes**, **Whiskered** and **Whitewinged Terns**, **Yellowbilled Duck**, **Southern Pochard**, **Maccoa Duck**, **Hottentot** and **Cape Teals**. A walk around the adjoining grassland should turn up **Palecrowned Cisticola**, **Orangethroated Longclaw** and **Wattled Plover**. **Redbreasted Sparrowhawk** likes plantations surrounded by grassland and has been sighted quite frequently. **Greywing** and **Redwing Francolins** are often heard. Look for Greywing (barred breast) in high montane grassland and Redwing (speckled upper breast) in lower grassland areas. Hundreds of birds roost at the dam at the caravan park for the night. Flocks of 120 **Bald Ibis**, 150 **Crowned Cranes**, numerous egrets and cormorants, **Sacred Ibis** and **African Spoonbills** are a regular feature of this dam at sunset.

ALSO RECORDED

Cape Eagle Owl may be found where extensive rock outcrops occur, and Blackwinged Plover and Shorttailed Pipit in short open grassland. While the call of Redchested Flufftail can often be heard in the large wetland after dark, the bird remains an elusive sight. Wattled Cranes are known to breed in the area. Montagu's Harrier has been recorded over the large vlei near Groenvlei.

Elna Kotze

65% OF SPECIES

006 **Great Crested Grebe** ☐
007 **Blacknecked Grebe** ☐
008 Dabchick ☐
055 Whitebreasted Cormorant ☐
058 Reed Cormorant ☐
060 Darter ☐
062 Grey Heron ☐
063 Blackheaded Heron ☐
065 **Purple Heron** ☐
066 **Great White Egret** ☐
067 **Little Egret** ☐
068 **Yellowbilled Egret** ☐
071 Cattle Egret ☐
072 **Squacco Heron** ☐
076 **Blackcrowned Night Heron** ☐
078 **Little Bittern** ☐
081 Hamerkop ☐
083 White Stork ☐
091 **Sacred Ibis** ☐
092 **Bald Ibis**** ☐
093 Glossy Ibis ☐
094 Hadeda Ibis ☐
095 **African Spoonbill** ☐
102 Egyptian Goose ☐
104 **Yellowbilled Duck** ☐
105 African Black Duck ☐
106 **Cape Teal** ☐
107 **Hottentot Teal** ☐

112 Cape Shoveller* ☐
113 **Southern Pochard** ☐
116 Spurwinged Goose ☐
117 **Maccoa Duck** ☐
118 Secretarybird ☐
127 Blackshouldered Kite ☐
131 Black Eagle ☐
140 Martial Eagle ☐
149 Steppe Buzzard ☐
152 Jackal Buzzard** ☐
155 **Redbreasted Sparrowhawk** ☐
158 Black Sparrowhawk ☐
165 **African Marsh Harrier** ☐
180 Eastern Redfooted Kestrel ☐
181 Rock Kestrel ☐
183 Lesser Kestrel ☐
190 **Greywing Francolin**** ☐
192 **Redwing Francolin** ☐
199 Swainson's Francolin* ☐
207 Wattled Crane ☐
208 Blue Crane** ☐
209 **Crowned Crane** ☐
210 **African Rail** ☐
217 Redchested Flufftail ☐
223 **Purple Gallinule** ☐
226 Moorhen ☐
228 Redknobbed Coot ☐
231 Stanley's Bustard ☐
233 **Whitebellied Korhaan** ☐
234 **Blue Korhaan**** ☐
248 Kittlitz's Plover ☐
249 Threebanded Plover ☐
255 Crowned Plover ☐
257 Blackwinged Plover ☐
258 Blacksmith Plover ☐
260 **Wattled Plover** ☐
264 Common Sandpiper ☐
266 **Wood Sandpiper** ☐
269 Marsh Sandpiper ☐
270 Greenshank ☐
274 Little Stint ☐
284 **Ruff** ☐
286 **Ethiopian Snipe** ☐
294 Avocet ☐
295 Blackwinged Stilt ☐
297 Spotted Dikkop ☐
338 **Whiskered Tern** ☐
339 **Whitewinged Tern** ☐
377 Redchested Cuckoo ☐
378 Black Cuckoo ☐
385 Klaas's Cuckoo ☐
386 Diederik Cuckoo ☐
395 Marsh Owl ☐
400 Cape Eagle Owl ☐
401 Spotted Eagle Owl ☐
412 Black Swift ☐
416 Horus Swift ☐
418 Alpine Swift ☐
428 Pied Kingfisher ☐
431 Malachite Kingfisher ☐
451 Hoopoe ☐
452 Redbilled Woodhoopoe ☐
464 Blackcollared Barbet ☐
480 **Ground Woodpecker**** ☐
489 Redthroated Wryneck ☐
494 Rufousnaped Lark ☐
499 **Rudd's Lark**** ☐
500 **Longbilled Lark*** ☐
506 **Spikeheeled Lark*** ☐
507 Redcapped Lark ☐
508 **Pinkbilled Lark*** ☐
509 **Botha's Lark**** ☐
518 European Swallow ☐
520 Whitethroated Swallow ☐
526 Greater Striped Swallow* ☐
527 Lesser Striped Swallow ☐
528 South African Cliff Swallow** ☐
533 Brownthroated Martin ☐
534 Banded Martin ☐
545 Blackheaded Oriole ☐
565 **Bush Blackcap**** ☐
568 Blackeyed Bulbul ☐
572 Sombre Bulbul ☐
577 Olive Thrush ☐
581 Cape Rock Thrush** ☐
582 **Sentinel Rock Thrush**** ☐
586 Mountain Chat* ☐
587 Capped Wheatear ☐
588 **Buffstreaked Chat**** ☐
589 Familiar Chat ☐
593 Mocking Chat ☐
595 Anteating Chat** ☐
596 Stonechat ☐
601 Cape Robin ☐
631 **African Marsh Warbler** ☐
637 **Yellow Warbler** ☐
638 **African Sedge Warbler** ☐
645 **Barthroated Apalis** ☐
661 Grassbird** ☐
664 Fantailed Cisticola ☐
668 **Palecrowned Cisticola** ☐
670 Wailing Cisticola ☐
716 Grassveld Pipit ☐
717 Longbilled Pipit ☐
721 **Rock Pipit**** ☐
725 **Yellowbreasted Pipit**** ☐
727 **Orangethroated Longclaw**** ☐
732 Fiscal Shrike ☐
746 Bokmakierie* ☐
750 **Olive Bush Shrike** ☐
753 White Helmetshrike ☐
759 Pied Starling** ☐
764 Glossy Starling* ☐
769 Redwinged Starling ☐
775 Malachite Sunbird ☐
785 Greater Double-collared Sunbird** ☐
792 Black Sunbird ☐
804 Greyheaded Sparrow ☐
813 Cape Weaver** ☐
814 Masked Weaver ☐
824 Red Bishop ☐
826 Golden Bishop ☐

827 Yellowrumped Widow	☐	829 Whitewinged Widow	☐	884 Goldenbreasted Bunting	☐
828 Redshouldered Widow	☐	831 Redcollared Widow	☐	**885 Cape Bunting**	☐
		860 Pintailed Whydah	☐	886 Rock Bunting	☐
		872 Cape Canary	☐		

FAR WESTERN TRANSVAAL

approximately 225 species recorded to date

The damming of the Vaal River near the town of Bloemhof in the far western Transvaal resulted in the formation of an immense body of water, nearly 85 km long and at places more than 5 km wide. This body of water attracts thousands of waterbirds, and the Bloemhof Dam and Wolwespruit Nature Reserves on the Transvaal side and the Sandveld Nature Reserve on the Free State side attract a great multitude of grassland, *Acacia* thornveld and Kalahari sandveld species, because of the destruction of their habitats outside these reserves. The SA Lombard Nature Reserve is situated approximately 10 km from Bloemhof in dry grassveld. These reserves are controlled by the Provincial Nature Conservation bodies.

The town of Bloemhof can be used as a base. The turnoff to the SA Lombard Nature Reserve is 5 km from the town on the Schweizer-Reneke road (R34). The Bloemhof Dam Nature Reserve and the Sandveld Nature Reserve are on the road to Hoopstad (R34). The turnoff to the Wolwespruit Nature Reserve is on the Transvaal side of the Vaal on the R504 between Leeudoringstad and Bothaville. Turn south at the bridge and follow the gravel road for 15 km to the entrance of the reserve.

SPECIAL AND INTERESTING SPECIES

This is one of the best localities in southern Africa to study larks and pipits; **Melodious**, **Spikeheeled**, **Rufousnaped**, **Clapper**, **Longbilled**, **Pinkbilled** and **Fawncoloured Larks** and **Chestnutbanded** and **Greybacked Finchlarks** occur in this area. **Grassveld**, **Plainbacked** and **Buffy Pipits** can be

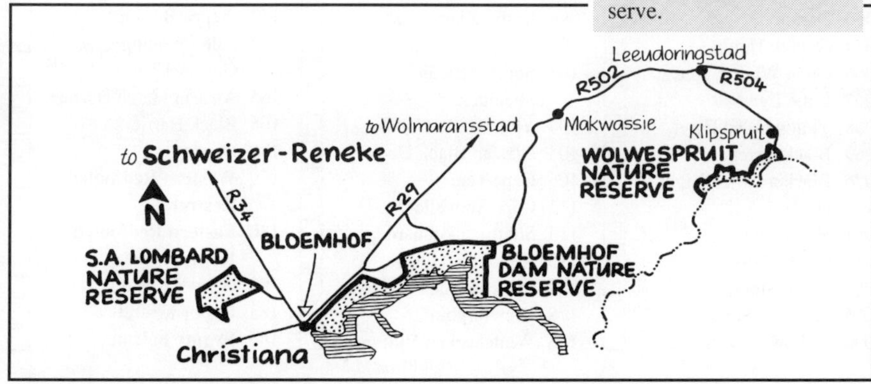

identified by studying their habits, tail feathers and calls. Away from human settlement among the *Acacia erioloba* (camel thorn) and *Acacia karoo* (sweet thorn) is the ideal place to look for **Orange River Francolin**, **Sabota Lark**, **Pied Barbet**, **Kalahari Robin**, **Yellow Canary**, **Redbilled Firefinch**, **Steelblue Widowfinch**, **Great Sparrow** and **Sociable Weaver**, with **Pygmy Falcon** in attendance. The wing pattern of **Redfooted Kestrels** will distinguish the **Western** from the **Eastern** species. **Whitequilled Korhaan**, **Kori Bustard**, **Doublebanded** and **Burchell's Coursers** are found on open, bare land with a few scattered trees. A big drawcard is the great variey of birds on the dams, pans and river. Several species of waterfowl such as **Whitefaced** and **Yellowbilled Ducks**, **South African Shelduck**, **Cape Shoveller** and **Redknobbed Coot** occur in their thousands. A trip along the banks of the Bloemhof Dam should reveal **Chestnutbanded Plover**, **Osprey** (in summer), **Caspian Tern**, **African Fish Eagle** and **Grass Owl**. There are so many **Goliath Herons** along the length of the dam shore that the area was largely responsible for this species being removed from the SA Red Data List. **Pririt Batis**, **Titbabbler**, **Ashy Tit**, **Marico Flycatcher**, **Whitebacked Mousebird**, **Sharpbilled Honeyguide** and **Whitebrowed Robin** may be heard and seen in the dense riverine bush, while **Shorttoed Rock Thrush** and **Blackwinged Pratincole** occur virtually anywhere. Both **Swallowtailed** (winter) and **Bluecheeked Bee-eaters** (summer) are recorded from this region.

ALSO RECORDED

Wahlberg's Eagle and Brown Snake Eagle may be found in the Bloemhof area. Montagu's, Pallid, Black and African Marsh Harriers have been recorded. Pinkbacked and White Pelicans have visited Bloemhof Dam, as have Arctic Tern and African Skimmer. Since a big body of water usually attracts a great variety of migrant waders, the likes of Curlew and Whitefronted Plover may be seen. An interesting breeding record from the last century is that of a Wattled Crane nest (the eggs were collected) near where the present bridge crosses the dam on the Bloemhof/Hoopstad road.

Sam de Beer

67% OF SPECIES

006 Great Crested Grebe ☐
007 Blacknecked Grebe ☐
055 Whitebreasted Cormorant ☐
060 Darter ☐
064 Goliath Heron ☐
066 Great White Egret ☐
067 Little Egret ☐
068 Yellowbilled Egret ☐
069 Black Egret ☐
076 Blackcrowned Night Heron ☐
081 Hamerkop ☐
083 White Stork ☐
084 Black Stork ☐
085 Abdim's Stork ☐
090 Yellowbilled Stork ☐
091 Sacred Ibis ☐
093 Glossy Ibis ☐
095 African Spoonbill ☐
096 Greater Flamingo ☐
097 Lesser Flamingo ☐
099 Whitefaced Duck ☐
103 South African Shelduck** ☐
104 Yellowbilled Duck ☐
105 African Black Duck ☐
106 Cape Teal ☐
112 Cape Shoveller* ☐
113 Southern Pochard ☐
115 Knobbilled Duck ☐
117 Maccoa Duck ☐
118 Secretarybird ☐
123 Whitebacked Vulture ☐
132 Tawny Eagle ☐
140 Martial Eagle ☐
142 Brown Snake Eagle ☐
148 African Fish Eagle ☐
149 Steppe Buzzard ☐
162 Pale Chanting Goshawk* ☐
165 African Marsh Harrier ☐
168 Black Harrier** ☐
170 **Osprey** ☐
179 **Western Redfooted Kestrel** ☐
180 **Eastern Redfooted Kestrel** ☐
182 Greater Kestrel ☐
183 Lesser Kestrel ☐
186 **Pygmy Falcon** ☐

193 Orange River Francolin* ☐
199 Swainson's Francolin* ☐
200 Common Quail ☐
208 Blue Crane ☐
230 **Kori Bustard** ☐
237 **Redcrested Korhaan*** ☐
245 Ringed Plover ☐
247 **Chestnutbanded Plover** ☐
248 Kittlitz's Plover ☐
269 Marsh Sandpiper ☐
270 Greenshank ☐
272 Curlew Sandpiper ☐
294 Avocet ☐
295 Blackwinged Stilt ☐
297 Spotted Dikkop ☐
299 **Burchell's Courser*** ☐
301 **Doublebanded Courser** ☐
305 **Blackwinged Pratincole** ☐
315 Greyheaded Gull ☐
322 **Caspian Tern** ☐
338 Whiskered Tern ☐
339 Whitewinged Tern ☐
344 Namaqua Sandgrouse* ☐
352 Redeyed Dove ☐
356 Namaqua Dove ☐
373 Grey Lourie ☐
382 Jacobin Cuckoo ☐
386 Diederik Cuckoo ☐
391 Burchell's Coucal* ☐
393 **Grass Owl** ☐
395 Marsh Owl ☐
415 Whiterumped Swift ☐
421 Palm Swift ☐
425 Whitebacked Mousebird** ☐
426 Redfaced Mousebird ☐
429 Giant Kingfisher ☐
431 Malachite Kingfisher ☐
435 Brownhooded Kingfisher ☐
440 Bluecheeked Bee-eater ☐
443 Whitefronted Bee-eater ☐
445 Swallowtailed Bee-eater ☐
447 Lilacbreasted Roller ☐
449 Purple Roller ☐
454 Scimitarbilled Woodhoopoe ☐
457 Grey Hornbill ☐
459 Southern Yellow-billed Hornbill* ☐
465 Pied Barbet* ☐
473 Crested Barbet ☐
478 Sharpbilled Honeyguide ☐
483 Goldentailed Woodpecker ☐
486 Cardinal Woodpecker ☐
492 **Melodious Lark**** ☐
494 Rufousnaped Lark ☐
495 Clapper Lark** ☐
497 **Fawncoloured Lark** ☐
498 Sabota Lark* ☐
500 **Longbilled Lark*** ☐
506 Spikeheeled Lark* ☐
507 Redcapped Lark ☐
508 **Pinkbilled Lark*** ☐
515 **Chestnutbacked Finchlark** ☐
516 **Greybacked Finchlark*** ☐
524 Redbreasted Swallow ☐
541 Forktailed Drongo ☐
552 Ashy Tit* ☐
583 **Shorttoed Rock Thrush*** ☐
587 Capped Wheatear ☐
589 Familiar Chat ☐
595 Anteating Chat** ☐
613 **Whitebrowed Robin** ☐
615 Kalahari Robin* ☐
620 Whitethroat ☐
621 Titbabbler* ☐
651 Longbilled Crombec ☐
664 Fantailed Cisticola ☐
665 Desert Cisticola ☐
666 Cloud Cisticola ☐
672 Rattling Cisticola ☐
677 Levaillant's Cisticola ☐
695 Marico Flycatcher* ☐
703 **Pririt Batis*** ☐
706 Fairy Flycatcher** ☐
711 African Pied Wagtail ☐
716 Grassveld Pipit ☐
718 **Plainbacked Pipit** ☐
719 **Buffy Pipit** ☐
727 Orangethroated Longclaw** ☐
731 Lesser Grey Shrike ☐
733 Redbacked Shrike ☐
739 Crimsonbreasted Boubou* ☐
743 Threestreaked Tchagra ☐
799 Whitebrowed Sparrowweaver ☐
800 **Sociable Weaver**** ☐
802 **Great Sparrow*** ☐
804 Greyheaded Sparrow ☐
806 Scalyfeathered Finch* ☐
826 Golden Bishop ☐
832 Longtailed Widow ☐
834 Melba Finch ☐
842 Redbilled Firefinch ☐
845 Violeteared Waxbill* ☐
852 Quail Finch ☐
861 Shafttailed Whydah* ☐
867 Steelblue Widowfinch ☐
878 Yellow Canary ☐
887 Larklike Bunting* ☐

OTHER BIRDING SPOTS WORTH VISITING

THE WITWATERSRAND METROPOLITAN AREA

Con Joubert Bird Sanctuary

This bird sanctuary, open daily from 08h00 to 17h00, consists primarily of a permanent pan in residential Randfontein. There is an excellent viewing hide. Enquiries to the Randfontein Centre of the SA Wildlife Society.

Florence Bloom Bird Sanctuary

A Johannesburg urban bird sanctuary near the Delta Park headquarters of the Southern African Ornithological Society and the SA Wildlife Society. Open 24 hours per day. Two viewing hides.

Kloofendal Nature Reserve

Mountain birding in an urban area.The reserve lies on the "Ridge of white waters" and is open daily from 1 September to 30 April, but may be closed at times. Enquiries to the Parks and Recreation Department, Roodepoort Municipality.

Korsman Bird Sanctuary

An East Rand bird sanctuary consisting primarily of a natural pan with some surrounding veld. Access is restricted to the perimeter fence so a telescope is desirable. Enquiries to the Parks and Recreation Department, Benoni Municipality.

Melrose Bird Sanctuary

This sanctuary consists of a dam, a reedswamp and surrounding veld. Offers a good opportunity to see Thickbilled Weavers. Open 24 hours per day.

Witwatersrand National Botanical Gardens

Offers good bush and mountain birding, including Black Eagle and Greater Doublecollared Sunbird, close to the centre of Roodepoort. Pleasant walks, cafeteria etc. Enquiries to the National Botanic Gardens.

THE PRETORIA AREA

L.C. de Villiers Sports Grounds

There are some interesting dams in the grounds, which belong to the University of Pretoria, where there is usually a large and very active heronry. Enquiries to the University of Pretoria.

Pretoria National Botanic Gardens

Interesting bushveld birding close to the city centre. Around 140 species recorded. Open 06h00 to 18h00 daily. Enquiries to Botanical Research Institute – Mr Dry or Mrs Fourie.

Roodeplaat Dam Nature Reserve
A provincial nature reserve with excellent bushveld and waterfowl birding almost in the city. Enquiries to the officer in charge or the Regional Head: West, Chief Directorate: Nature and Environmental Conservation.

Soutpan
A 2 000 ha Department of Agriculture experimental farm. Excellent bushveld birding in the volcanic crater, including African Hawk Eagle. Only 40 km from Pretoria, but access is restricted. Enquiries to Department of Agriculture or Northern Transvaal Ornithological Society.

SOUTHERN TRANSVAAL HIGHVELD

Abe Bailey Nature Reserve
This 5 000 ha provincial nature reserve, situated near Carletonville 100 km west of Johannesburg, offers fine wetland (hides) and grassland birding. Camping is not allowed, but the Carletonville Municipal Resort is nearby.

Christiana and the Rob Ferreira Resort and Nature Reserve
Overvaal resort and nature reserve on the outskirts of Christiana in the far western Transvaal, on the banks of the Vaal River. Good arid grassland and riverine birding. Ten kilometre trail along Vaal.

NORTHERN TRANSVAAL BUSHVELD

Atherstone Nature Reserve
A newly acquired (1990) provincial nature reserve (13 000 ha) in the arid bushveld west of Thabazimbi which offers excellent birding in the turf thornveld habitat. Contact the officer in charge prior to a visit.

Ben Lavin Nature Reserve
An SA Wildlife Society reserve near Louis Trichardt, with viewing hides, walks, drives, huts, camping. Gorgeous Bush Shrikes, Heuglin's and Bearded Robins are among the specials here. Enquiries to the warden.

Borakalalo National Park
This 14 000 ha park is run by the National Parks and Wildlife Management Board of Bophuthatswana. Tented accommodation, camping and caravanning are available. Excellent birding including African Finfoot. Enquiries to the warden.

Doorndraai Dam Nature Reserve
A 7 229 ha provincial nature reserve south of Potgietersrus with fine bushveld birding including Greencapped Eremomela and Fantailed Flycatcher. Camping and caravanning; walks. Enquiries to the officer in charge.

Pietersburg Game Reserve
This municipal reserve (3 200 ha) outside Pietersburg has about 200 species. The undisputed special is Shortclawed Lark. There are picnic sites, drives and a hiking trail. Accommodation, caravanning and camping facilities just outside the reserve. Enquiries to the Parks Department, Pietersburg Municipality.

Pietersburg Bird Sanctuary
This 60 ha sanctuary situated on the northern boundary of Pietersburg has three dams, four shallow pans and bird viewing hides. European Marsh Harrier can be seen in the summer.

Rustenburg Nature Reserve
A 4 257 ha provincial nature reserve in the Magaliesberg Mountains south of Rustenburg. Good bushveld and montane birding. Camping, caravanning, circular drives, walks and hikes. Enquiries to the officer in charge.

Tshipise and Honnet Nature Reserve
An Overvaal resort, nature reserve and mineral bath pleasantly situated in the far northern Transvaal between the Soutpansberg Mountains and Messina. On the way to either Zimbabwe or the Kruger National Park's Pafuri Gate. Good arid bushveld birding.

EASTERN TRANSVAAL ESCARPMENT, INCLUDING THE SOUTPANSBERG

Buzzard Mountain Retreat
A private farm in the Soutpansberg Mountains west of Louis Trichardt: the 220 species recorded include Knysna Lourie, Black Eagle, Narina Trogon and Gurney's Sugarbird. Trails in magnificent scenery, stone cottages and wooden cabins. Advance booking essential.

Hangklip State Forest
An indigenous montane forest reserve controlled by the Department of Forestry. Specials include Olive Bush Shrike and Grey Cuckooshrike. Picnic site and forest walks; no camping. Enquiries to the Hangklip Forestry Station.

Wolkberg Wilderness Area
A 22 000 ha mountain wilderness area administered by the Chief Directorate: Nature and Environmental Conservation. For the very energetic only. Walk anywhere you wish and camp anywhere you wish, but no vehicles. Specials include Peregrine Falcon and Striped Flufftail. Enquiries to the officer in charge.

USEFUL TELEPHONE NUMBERS

THE WITWATERSRAND METROPOLITAN AREA

Blesbokspruit
Officer-in-Charge,
Marievale Bird Sanctuary (Heidelberg)
(0151) 2181

Parks Division,
Springs Town Council
(for Springs Bird Sanctuary)
(011) 812-1244

Carlos Rolfes Bird Sanctuary
Witwatersrand Bird Club (mornings only)
(011) 782-7134

Con Joubert Bird Sanctuary
SA Wildlife Society (Randfontein)
(evenings)
(011) 693-3826

Diepsloot Nature Reserve and associated area
City Engineer's Department,
Johannesburg Municipality
(011) 407-6111

Witwatersrand Bird Club (mornings only)
(011) 782-7134

Officer-in-Charge,
Hartbeespoort Dam Nature Reserve
(Broederstroom)
(01205) 5-1353

Florence Bloom Bird Sanctuary
The SA Ornithological Society
(mornings only)
(011) 782-1547

The SA Wildlife Society
(011) 782-1934

Kloofendal Nature Reserve
Roodepoort Municipality,
Parks and Recreation Department
(011) 672-6641

Leeupan and Korsman Bird Sanctuary
Benoni Municipality,
Parks and Recreation Department
(011) 845-1650

Rondebult Bird Sanctuary
Germiston City Council, Parks Department
(011) 51-0911

Witwatersrand National Botanic Gardens
The Curator
(011) 662-1741

THE PRETORIA AREA

L.C. de Villiers Sports Grounds
University of Pretoria
(012) 43-7711

Pretoria National Botanical Gardens
Botanical Research Institute (Pretoria)
(012) 86-1164

Roodeplaat Dam Nature Reserve
Officer-in-Charge (Pretoria)
(012) 808-1164

Soutpan
Department of Agriculture (Pretoria)
(012) 326-8111

Northern Transvaal Ornithological Society
(evenings)
(012) 43-2168

THE SOUTHERN TRANSVAAL HIGHVELD

Abe Bailey Nature Reserve
Officer-in-Charge (Potchefstroom)
(0148) 6828

Barberspan Nature Reserve
Officer-in-Charge (Barberspan)
(0144322) 1202

Ornithological Research Station
(Barberspan)
(0144322) 1323

Barberspan Hotel (Barberspan)
(0144322) 28

Christiana and Rob Ferreira Resort and Nature Reserve
Overvaal Rob Ferreira (Christiana)
(0534) 2244

The Dullstroom District
The Dullstroom Inn (Dullstroom)
(01325) 4-0071

The Far Western Transvaal
Bloemhof Dam Nature Reserve
(Bloemhof)
(01802) 3-1706

Wesvaal Bird Club (evenings)
(Potchefstroom)
(0148) 6828

Vaal Reefs Bird Club (evenings)
(Klerksdorp)
(018) 78-2059

Potchefstroom Town Council
(Prozesky Sanctuary)
(0148) 99-5111

Suikerbosrand Nature Reserve
Officer-in-Charge (Heidelberg)
(0151) 2181

Overvaal Kareekloof (Meyerton)
(016) 6-5334

Overvaal Heidelberg Kloof (Heidelberg)
(0151) 2412

Wakkerstroom
Weaver's Nest Guest House
(Wakkerstroom)
(013339) 223

Wakkerstroom Municipality
(Wakkerstroom)
(013339) 331

THE NORTHERN TRANSVAAL BUSHVELD

Atherstone Nature Reserve
Officer-in-Charge (Dwaalboom)
(015378) 802

Ben Alberts Nature Reserve
The Warden (Thabazimbi)
(01537) 2-1509

Ben Lavin Nature Reserve
The Warden (Louis Trichardt)
(01551) 3834

Borakalalo National Park
The Warden (Jericho)
Jericho 1441

Doorndraai Dam Nature Reserve
Officer-in-Charge (Sterkrivier)
(015423) 629

Rietbokspruit Guest Farm (Naboomspruit)
(01534) 3-2525

Hans Strijdom Dam Nature Reserve
Officer-in-Charge (Ellisras)
(01536) 3-5148

Langjan Nature Reserve
Officer-in-Charge (Vivo)
(015562) 1211

Lapalala Wilderness
Central Booking Office (Johannesburg)
(011) 453-7645

Loskop Dam Nature Reserve
Overvaal Loskopdam (Groblersdal)
(01202) 3075

Messina Nature Reserve
Officer-in-Charge (Messina)
(01553) 3235

Impala Lily Motel (Messina)
(01553) 2197

The Nyl Floodplain and Surrounding Bushveld
Nylsvley Nature Reserve (Naboomspruit)
(01534) 3-1074

Mosdene Private Nature Reserve (Naboomspruit)
(01534) 3-1933

Owl Cottage (Johannesburg)
(011) 788-8916

Pietersburg Game Reserve
Parks Department,
Pietersburg Municipality
(01521) 93-1114

North-eastern Bird Club (evenings) (Pietersburg)
(01521) 82-1260

Pietersburg Bird Sanctuary
(01521) 82-1260

Pilanesberg National Park
(014652) 2405

Rust der Winter Nature Reserve
Officer-in-Charge (Rust der Winter)
(0121712) 2422

Rustenburg Nature Reserve
Officer-in-Charge (Rustenburg)
(0142) 3-1050

Tshipise Mineral Baths and Honnet Nature Reserve
Overvaal Tshipise
(015539) 624

Vaalkop Dam Nature Reserve
Officer-in-Charge (Beestekraal)
(012117) 676

THE EASTERN TRANSVAAL ESCARPMENT AND THE SOUTPANSBERG

Buzzard Mountain Retreat
John Greaves (Louis Trichardt)
(01551) 4196

The Eastern Transvaal Escarpment
Blyde River Canyon Nature Reserve:
Bourke's Luck
(01315) 8-1215

Swadini
(0131732) 4904

Paradise Camp (Graskop)
(01315) 7-1118

Overvaal F.H. Odendaal Resort (Ohrigstad)
(01323) 8-0158

Overvaal Sybrand van Niekerk (Hoedspruit)
(015282) 3-2300

Overvaal Pilgrim's Rest (Royal Hotel)
(01315) 4222

Department of Forestry (for trails) Sabie
(01315) 4-1031

Hangklip State Forest
Hangklip Forestry Station
(Louis Trichardt)
(01551) 2525

Saddleback Pass and Peddlars Bush, Barberton
Department of Forestry (Barberton)
(01314) 2-2704

Wolkberg Wilderness Area
Officer-in-Charge (Haenertsburg)
(0152222) 1303

Woodbush Reserve and Surrounding Area
Woodbush Forestry Station (Tzaneen)
(01523) 5-3152

THE EASTERN TRANSVAAL LOWVELD

Hans Merensky Nature Reserve
Officer-in-Charge (Lapariza)
(015238) 632

Overvaal Eiland (Lapariza)
(015238) 759

Kruger National Park
National Parks Board (Pretoria)
(012) 343-1991

Lawson's Bird Tours
(01311) 4-2257a/h
(01311) 55-2147

Nelspruit Nature Reserve and Adjoining Trim Park
Lowveld Bird Club (evenings) (Nelspruit)
(01311) 2-4308

5 Northern Cape

Co-ordinator Corné Anderson

1 Kalahari Gemsbok National Park
2 Ganspan Waterfowl Sanctuary
3 Witsand Tourist Resort
4 Upington
5 Augrabies Falls National Park
6 "Die Bos" Nature Reserve, Prieska
7 Goegap Provincial Nature Reserve
8 Bushmanland

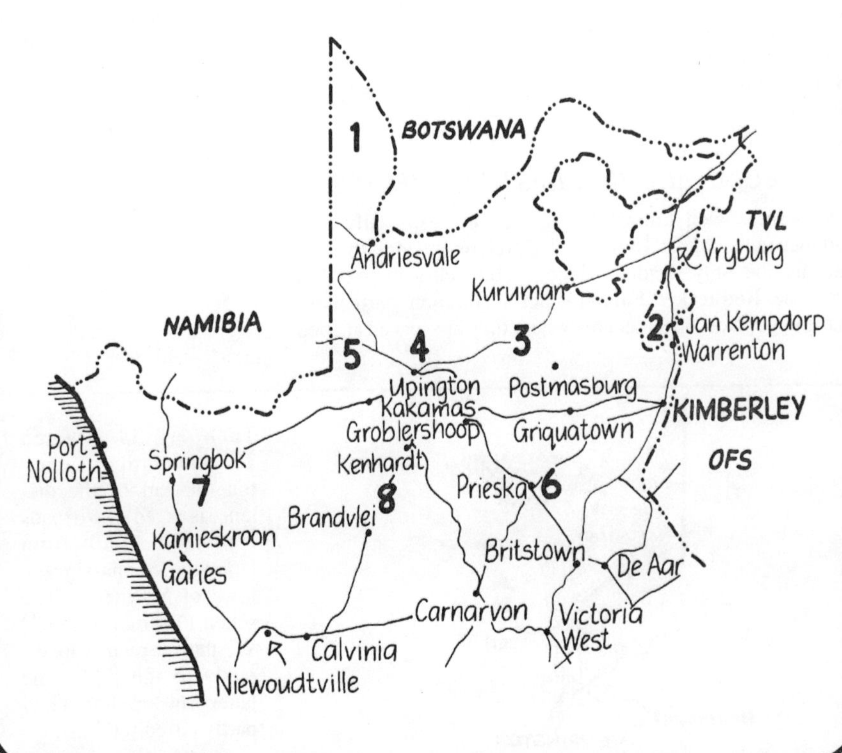

KALAHARI GEMSBOK NATIONAL PARK

approximately 278 species recorded to date

The Kalahari Gemsbok National Park, an area of 959 103 ha controlled by the National Parks Board, is situated in the extreme north-western corner of South Africa. It is an area of predominantly red sand dunes; the vegetation is semi-arid savanna. The northern parts of the park are more wooded than the southern. Temperatures are extreme; rainfall is low and occurs mostly between January and March. Although approximately 278 species have been recorded in the park, only about 82 are resident. The rest are either nomadic or seasonal visitors. In summer strong north-easterly or north-westerly winds are responsible for unusual records such as Purple Gallinule and Arctic Skua! During the wet summer months spectacular numbers of raptors gather around waterholes in the dry riverbeds. The 467 km of roads in the park follow the two dry riverbeds (Nossob and Auob), with a linking road over the dunes. No hiking is allowed but there are four picnic sites along the roads.

SPECIAL AND INTERESTING SPECIES

The park is well known for its raptors, especially after summer rains. About 15 pairs of **Bateleur** breed in the park and are the only resident breeding Bateleurs in the Cape Province. **Rednecked Falcon** is not uncommon, particularly in the upper Nossob River area where they are spaced at about

ALSO RECORDED

Unusual species such as Fulvous and Knobbilled Ducks, Turnstone, African Jacana, African Crake, Rufousbellied Heron, Lesser Flamingo and Little Bittern are blown in by strong winds during the rainy season. Other uncommon species include Black Stork, Redbilled Buffalo Weaver, Yellow Wagtail, African Hobby Falcon, Pallid Harrier, African Hawk Eagle and Gymnogene. Pipits are scarce but Grassveld Pipit may be seen. A Whitethroated Bee-eater, a new record for southern Africa, was recorded in the park.

Kotie Herholdt

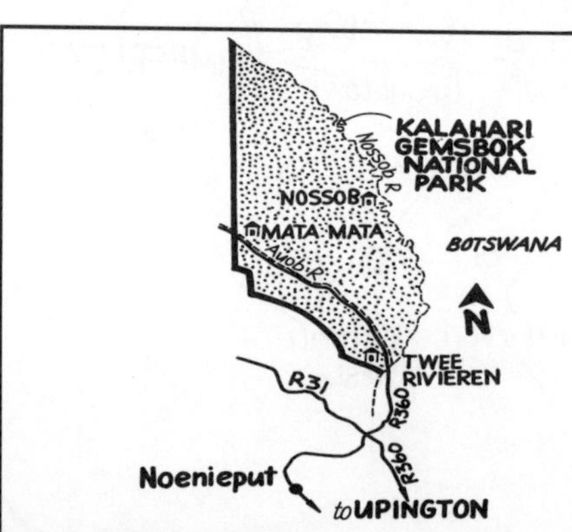

The park is situated 280 km north of Upington (80 km of the distance is tarred). Two roads lead to the park from Upington, one passing the town of Noenieput. The other (Theuns van der Westhuizen road) leads directly to the park. The latter is 60 km shorter and partly tarred (80 km).

one pair per 6 km. At least 34 pairs are resident in the park. This is one of the only places within South Africa to see this species. Sometimes one can see up to 30 **Lanner Falcons** and large numbers of **Steppe Eagles** flying around a single termite emergence. About 12 pairs of **Martial Eagle** live along the Nossob River and about six pairs along the Auob River. About 15 pairs of **Tawny Eagle** occupy the Nossob River. In winter large numbers of **Rock Kestrels** move into the park, as do Bateleurs (mostly immatures). Around midday vultures gather around the waterholes to bathe, especially at Kannagaus, Grootkolk and Rooiputs. The northern part of the park is the south-western distribution limit for **Whiteheaded Vulture**. Other less common birds of prey include **Wahlberg's**, **Booted** and **Lesser Spotted Eagles**. The smaller birds of prey include **Little Banded**, **Gabar** and **Pale Chanting Goshawks**. **Pygmy Falcon**, which breeds in the large **Sociable Weaver** nests, is common on the southern parts of the Nossob River from Twee Rivieren to Kijkij and in the Kaspersdraai/Kwang area. Pairs are spaced up to every 2,5-4 km where Sociable Weaver nests are available. At least 29 pairs of **Giant Eagle Owl** occur in the park; they are most common on the Auob River. Resident pairs of **Scops**, **Whitefaced** and **Pearlspotted Owl** breed in Nossob camp and can be found throughout most of the woodland areas. A total of 47 diurnal and seven nocturnal raptors have been recorded in the park. After summer rains **Marabou Stork** might be found in limited numbers, while **White** and **Abdim's Storks** can be quite common. **Common** and **Harlequin Quails** and **Kurrichane Buttonquail** also increase greatly in number at this time of the year. For those interested in tackling the larks, look for **Monotonous** and **Pinkbilled Larks** after summer rains. **Fawncoloured** and **Spikeheeled** (around pans) are present, while **Clapper** may be found in the areas with taller grass. The most common finchlark is the **Greybacked** but **Blackeared** and **Chestnutbacked Finchlarks** also occur. **Stark's Lark** is uncommon and best seen in years of good rainfall. **Redbilled Woodhoopoe**, **Striped Kingfisher**, **Grey Hornbill**, **Swallowtailed Bee-eater**, **Pied Babbler** and **Kalahari Robin** can be found in the woodland areas and along watercourses. **Great Spotted Cuckoo** is common in summer, parasitising crows and starlings. **European Golden Oriole** occurs every summer at Nossob. Other summer visitors include **Bradfield's Swift**, which can be seen together with large flocks of **European Swift**. **Ludwig's Bustards** are common on the Auob and southern Nossob rivers after the rains, while **Kori Bustard** is abundant all year round. **Rufouseared Warbler** is common, but the rufous ear coverts are not as dark or rich in colour as those of the birds to the south, in the Karoo. During winter large flocks of seedeaters such as **Redheaded Finch**, **Greyheaded Sparrow** and **Shafttailed Whydah** gather at the waterholes. This is also a good time to see **Namaqua** and **Burchell's Sandgrouse**, which gather in large numbers to drink.

52% OF SPECIES

- 001 Ostrich ☐
- 008 Dabchick ☐
- 063 Blackheaded Heron ☐
- 066 Great White Egret ☐
- 067 Little Egret ☐
- 068 Yellowbilled Egret ☐
- 071 Cattle Egret ☐
- 081 Hamerkop ☐
- 083 **White Stork** ☐
- 085 **Abdim's Stork** ☐
- 089 **Marabou Stork** ☐
- 102 Egyptian Goose ☐
- 108 Redbilled Teal ☐
- 116 Spurwinged Goose ☐
- 118 Secretarybird ☐
- 122 Cape Vulture** ☐
- 123 Whitebacked Vulture ☐
- 124 Lappetfaced Vulture ☐
- 125 **Whiteheaded Vulture** ☐
- 126 Black Kite ☐
- 126a Yellowbilled Kite ☐
- 127 Blackshouldered Kite ☐
- 132 **Tawny Eagle** ☐
- 133 **Steppe Eagle** ☐
- 134 **Lesser Spotted Eagle** ☐
- 135 **Wahlberg's Eagle** ☐
- 136 **Booted Eagle** ☐
- 140 **Martial Eagle** ☐
- 142 Brown Snake Eagle ☐
- 143 Blackbreasted Snake Eagle ☐
- 146 **Bateleur** ☐
- 149 Steppe Buzzard ☐
- 152 Jackal Buzzard** ☐
- 159 **Little Banded Goshawk** ☐
- 161 **Gabar Goshawk** ☐
- 162 **Pale Chanting Goshawk*** ☐
- 172 **Lanner Falcon** ☐
- 173 Hobby Falcon ☐
- 178 **Rednecked Falcon** ☐
- 179 Western Redfooted Kestrel ☐
- 181 **Rock Kestrel** ☐
- 182 Greater Kestrel ☐
- 183 Lesser Kestrel ☐
- 186 **Pygmy Falcon** ☐
- 200 **Common Quail** ☐
- 201 **Harlequin Quail** ☐
- 205 **Kurrichane Buttonquail** ☐
- 230 **Kori Bustard** ☐
- 232 **Ludwig's Bustard*** ☐
- 237 Redcrested Korhaan* ☐
- 239a Whitequilled Korhaan** ☐
- 249 Threebanded Plover ☐
- 255 Crowned Plover ☐
- 258 Blacksmith Plover ☐
- 297 Spotted Dikkop ☐
- 299 Burchell's Courser* ☐
- 300 Temminck's Courser ☐
- 301 Doublebanded Courser ☐
- 303 Bronzewinged Courser ☐
- 339 Whitewinged Tern ☐
- 344 Namaqua Sandgrouse* ☐
- 345 Burchell's Sandgrouse* ☐
- 354 Cape Turtle Dove ☐
- 355 Laughing Dove ☐
- 356 Namaqua Dove ☐
- 380 **Great Spotted Cuckoo** ☐
- 392 Barn Owl ☐
- 396 **Scops Owl** ☐
- 397 **Whitefaced Owl** ☐
- 398 **Pearlspotted Owl** ☐
- 401 Spotted Eagle Owl ☐
- 402 **Giant Eagle Owl** ☐
- 406 Rufouscheeked Nightjar ☐
- 411 **European Swift** ☐
- 413 **Bradfield's Swift*** ☐
- 426 Redfaced Mousebird ☐
- 437 **Striped Kingfisher** ☐
- 438 European Bee-eater ☐
- 445 **Swallowtailed Bee-eater** ☐
- 446 European Roller ☐
- 447 Lilacbreasted Roller ☐
- 449 Purple Roller ☐
- 451 Hoopoe ☐
- 452 **Redbilled Woodhoopoe** ☐
- 454 Scimitarbilled Woodhoopoe ☐
- 457 **Grey Hornbill** ☐
- 459 Southern Yellow-billed Hornbill* ☐
- 465 Pied Barbet* ☐
- 486 Cardinal Woodpecker ☐
- 493 **Monotonous Lark*** ☐
- 495 **Clapper Lark**** ☐

497 **Fawncoloured Lark** ☐
498 Sabota Lark* ☐
506 **Spikeheeled Lark*** ☐
508 **Pinkbilled Lark*** ☐
511 **Stark's Lark*** ☐
515 **Chestnutbacked Finchlark** ☐
516 **Greybacked Finchlark*** ☐
517 **Blackeared Finchlark**** ☐
518 European Swallow ☐
526 Greater Striped Swallow* ☐
529 Rock Martin ☐
531 Forktailed Drongo ☐
543 **European Golden Oriole** ☐
547 Black Crow ☐
552 Ashy Tit* ☐
557 Cape Penduline Tit* ☐
563 **Pied Babbler**** ☐
589 Familiar Chat ☐
590 Tractrac Chat* ☐
595 Anteating Chat** ☐
615 **Kalahari Robin*** ☐
621 Titbabbler* ☐
651 Longbilled Crombec ☐
664 Fantailed Cisticola ☐
665 Desert Cisticola ☐
685 Blackchested Prinia* ☐
688 **Rufouseared Warbler**** ☐
695 Marico Flycatcher* ☐
697 Chat Flycatcher* ☐
703 Pririt Batis* ☐
731 Lesser Grey Shrike ☐
732 Fiscal Shrike ☐
733 Redbacked Shrike ☐
739 Crimsonbreasted Boubou* ☐
741 Brubru ☐
746 Bokmakierie* ☐
760 Wattled Starling ☐
762 Burchell's Starling* ☐
764 Glossy Starling* ☐
788 Dusky Sunbird* ☐
799 Whitebrowed Sparrowweaver ☐
800 **Sociable Weaver**** ☐
801 House Sparrow ☐
802 Great Sparrow* ☐
803 Cape Sparrow* ☐
804 **Greyheaded Sparrow** ☐
806 Scalyfeathered Finch* ☐
814 Masked Weaver ☐
821 Redbilled Quelea ☐
834 Melba Finch ☐
845 Violeteared Waxbill* ☐
847 **Blackcheeked Waxbill** ☐
856 **Redheaded Finch*** ☐
861 **Shafttailed Whydah*** ☐
870 **Blackthroated Canary** ☐
878 Yellow Canary* ☐
887 Larklike Bunting* ☐
☐

Melba Finches

GANSPAN WATERFOWL SANCTUARY

approximately 205 species recorded to date

The Ganspan Waterfowl Sanctuary has at its centre a 100 ha shallow pan. The 180 ha sanctuary, situated in Kimberley thornveld, is controlled by the Jan Kempdorp Municipality and is open to the public from 06h00 to 18h00 daily. A small admission fee is charged. Picnic and overnight camping sites with limited toilet and braai facilities are available. Shade devices should be brought as the trees are still relatively small. A hiking trail leads off the 3,2 km road around the pan.

SPECIAL AND INTERESTING SPECIES

Ganspan is the ideal spot to see **Great Crested Grebes** perform their elaborate courtship behaviour. These birds are easiest to find early in the morning on the open water near the entrance gate. The best place to see **African Rail** is on the left side of the road approximately 1,4 km from the entrance where the road enters the thick reedbed. They usually respond quickly to a tape recorder in the early morning. The shy **Little Bittern** may also be seen skulking in the reeds at this spot, or flying off reluctantly, showing its diagnostic cream-coloured upperwing markings. The marshy area to the right of this spot is the place to find **Squacco Heron**, **Painted Snipe** and **Baillon's Crake**. Herons usually roost in the dead trees near the marsh, or they can be seen foraging in the shallows. **Painted Snipe** are easily overlooked where they forage in the marginal vegetation

ALSO RECORDED

Blacknecked Grebe may be found on the pan after heavy rains. Marsh Owl may be flushed along the trail, or can be seen perched on fence posts in the very early morning or late afternoon. Black Egret (a rare bird in the Cape) is sometimes seen on the muddy edges of the pan. Both Chestnutbanded Plover and Caspian Tern (the latter an uncommon inland visitor) have also been recorded.

Corné and Elmarie Anderson

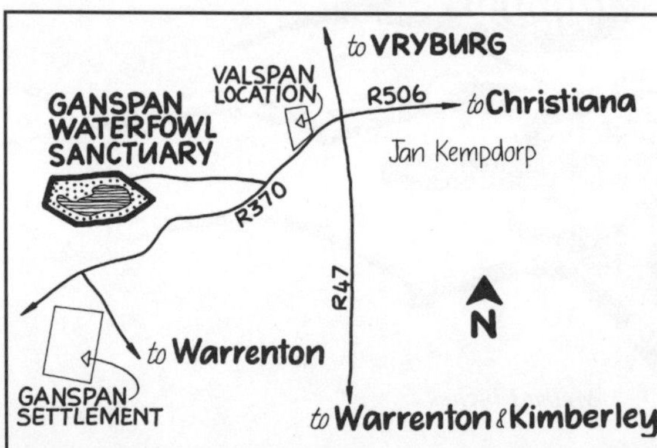

The Ganspan turnoff (R370) is 22 km from Warrenton on the Warrenton-Vryburg road (R47). From Warrenton, turn left and follow the tarmac road through the Jan Kempdorp industrial area for 2,5 km. Turn right at the Ganspan turnoff (signposted) and follow the gravel road for 4,5 km.

around the water. With enough patience **Baillon's Crake**, with its characteristic humpback posture, bluish chest and barred belly, can be seen skulking in habitat very similar to that of the Painted Snipe. **Hottentot Teal**, **Whitebacked** and **Fulvous Ducks** are normally present. While on the hiking trail, scan the summer sky for **Horus Swift**, which is an uncommon breeding intra-Africa migrant in the northern Cape. The surrounding woodland can yield both **Karoo** and **Kalahari Robins**, **Pied Barbet**, **Rufouseared Warbler**, **Pririt Batis**, **Crimson-breasted Boubou**, **Scalyfeathered Finch**, **Violeteared** and **Blackcheeked Waxbills** and **Blackthroated Canary**.

66% OF SPECIES

- 006 **Great Crested Grebe** ☐
- 008 Dabchick ☐
- 055 Whitebreasted Cormorant ☐
- 058 Reed Cormorant ☐
- 060 Darter ☐
- 062 Grey Heron ☐
- 063 Blackheaded Heron ☐
- 064 Goliath Heron ☐
- 065 Purple Heron ☐
- 066 Great White Egret ☐
- 067 Little Egret ☐
- 068 Yellowbilled Egret ☐
- 071 Cattle Egret ☐
- 072 **Squacco Heron** ☐
- 078 **Little Bittern** ☐
- 081 Hamerkop ☐
- 091 Sacred Ibis ☐
- 093 Glossy Ibis ☐
- 095 African Spoonbill ☐
- 096 Greater Flamingo ☐
- 097 Lesser Flamingo ☐
- 099 Whitefaced Duck ☐
- 100 **Fulvous Duck** ☐
- 101 **Whitebacked Duck** ☐
- 102 Egyptian Goose ☐
- 103 South African Shelduck** ☐
- 104 Yellowbilled Duck ☐
- 106 Cape Teal ☐
- 107 **Hottentot Teal** ☐
- 108 Redbilled Teal ☐
- 112 Cape Shoveller* ☐
- 113 Southern Pochard ☐
- 116 Spurwinged Goose ☐
- 127 Blackshouldered Kite ☐
- 149 Steppe Buzzard ☐
- 161 Gabar Goshawk ☐
- 162 Pale Chanting Goshawk* ☐
- 165 African Marsh Harrier ☐
- 210 **African Rail** ☐
- 213 Black Crake ☐
- 215 **Baillon's Crake** ☐
- 223 Purple Gallinule ☐
- 226 Moorhen ☐
- 228 Redknobbed Coot ☐
- 237 Redcrested Korhaan* ☐
- 239a Whitequilled Korhaan** ☐
- 242 **Painted Snipe** ☐
- 247 Chestnutbanded Plover ☐
- 248 Kittlitz's Plover ☐
- 249 Threebanded Plover ☐
- 255 Crowned Plover ☐
- 258 Blacksmith Plover ☐
- 264 Common Sandpiper ☐
- 266 Wood Sandpiper ☐
- 269 Marsh Sandpiper ☐
- 270 Greenshank ☐
- 274 Little Stint ☐
- 284 Ruff ☐
- 286 Ethiopian Snipe ☐
- 295 Blackwinged Stilt ☐
- 315 Greyheaded Gull ☐
- 338 Whiskered Tern ☐
- 339 Whitewinged Tern ☐
- 354 Cape Turtle Dove ☐
- 355 Laughing Dove ☐
- 356 Namaqua Dove ☐
- 386 Diederik Cuckoo ☐
- 391 Burchell's Coucal* ☐
- 415 Whiterumped Swift ☐
- 416 **Horus Swift** ☐
- 417 Little Swift ☐
- 428 Pied Kingfisher ☐
- 431 Malachite Kingfisher ☐
- 438 European Bee-eater ☐
- 454 Scimitarbilled Woodhoopoe ☐
- 465 **Pied Barbet*** ☐
- 486 Cardinal Woodpecker ☐
- 495 Clapper Lark** ☐
- 497 Fawncoloured Lark ☐
- 498 Sabota Lark* ☐
- 506 Spikeheeled Lark* ☐
- 507 Redcapped Lark ☐
- 518 European Swallow ☐
- 520 Whitethroated Swallow ☐
- 526 Greater Striped Swallow* ☐
- 528 South African Cliff Swallow** ☐
- 529 Rock Martin ☐

533 Brownthroated Martin ☐
541 Forktailed Drongo ☐
548 Pied Crow ☐
552 Ashy Tit* ☐
567 Redeyed Bulbul* ☐
577 Olive Thrush ☐
589 Familiar Chat ☐
595 Anteating Chat** ☐
601 Cape Robin ☐
614 **Karoo Robin**** ☐
615 **Kalahari Robin*** ☐
621 Titbabbler* ☐
628 Great Reed Warbler ☐
635 Cape Reed Warbler ☐
643 Willow Warbler ☐
653 Yellowbellied Eremomela ☐
664 Fantailed Cisticola ☐
665 Desert Cisticola ☐
677 Levaillant's Cisticola ☐
685 Blackchested Prinia* ☐
688 **Rufouseared Warbler**** ☐
689 Spotted Flycatcher ☐
697 Chat Flycatcher* ☐
698 Fiscal Flycatcher** ☐
703 **Pririt Batis*** ☐
711 African Pied Wagtail ☐
713 Cape Wagtail ☐
716 Grassveld Pipit ☐
731 Lesser Grey Shrike ☐
732 Fiscal Shrike ☐
733 Redbacked Shrike ☐
739 **Crimsonbreasted Boubou*** ☐
743 Threestreaked Tchagra ☐
760 Wattled Starling ☐
764 Glossy Starling* ☐
796 Cape White-eye** ☐
799 Whitebrowed Sparrowweaver ☐
801 House Sparrow ☐
803 Cape Sparrow* ☐
804 Greyheaded Sparrow ☐
806 **Scalyfeathered Finch*** ☐
814 Masked Weaver ☐
824 Red Bishop ☐
845 **Violeteared Waxbill*** ☐
846 Common Waxbill ☐
847 **Blackcheeked Waxbill** ☐
860 Pintailed Whydah ☐
870 **Blackthroated Canary** ☐
878 Yellow Canary* ☐
☐
☐
☐

WITSAND TOURIST RESORT

approximately 132 species recorded to date

The Witsand Tourist Resort is situated on the western side of the Langeberg mountain range with mountain passes on two of the access roads, which can be hazardous on the few occasions when the roads are wet. The privately owned resort

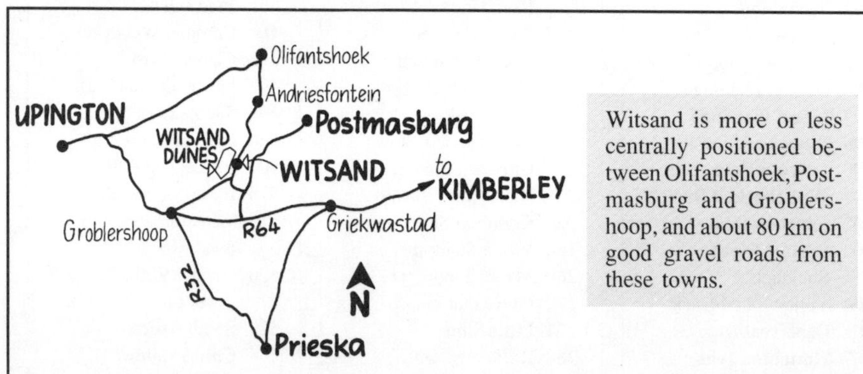

Witsand is more or less centrally positioned between Olifantshoek, Postmasburg and Groblershoop, and about 80 km on good gravel roads from these towns.

provides accommodation in the form of bungalows with an ablution block, open-air cooking facilities, firewood and running water. A new camping site with more facilities is being planned. Habitats include white sand dunes with little or no vegetation, open low mixed shrub-grass flats, stone outcrops, low ridges, open water (called "Gorras") and woodland. A walking trail about 10 km long, with shorter detours and covering all the above-mentioned habitats, is worth taking. An internal map of the area is available on arrival.

SPECIAL AND INTERESTING SPECIES

Early morning or late afternoon birding is advisable in this relatively hot area, when drinking places are most frequented. Species such as **Namaqua** and **Burchell's Sandgrouse** have restricted drinking periods (normally from 09h00 to 10h00). The fountain area, 200 m from the campsite, is a good place to see **Pied Barbet**, **Wattled Starling**, **Whitebacked** and **Redfaced Mousebirds**, and **Violeteared, Common** and **Blackcheeked Waxbills**. On the open stretch of water and its surroundings one can find **South African Shelduck**. The stony outcrops, ridges and surroundings are worth visiting for **Familiar** and **Mountain Chats** and **Fawncoloured** and **Spikeheeled Larks**. The adjacent low scrub and grassy plains with trees studded here and there accommodate the large communal **Sociable Weaver** nests. **Pygmy Falcon**, **Pearlspotted Owl** and Pied Barbet all use the chambers in these huge "haystacks" to breed in. Birds of prey such as **Spotted Eagle Owl**, **Greater Kestrel**, **Pale Chanting Goshawk** and even **Black Eagle** breed on top of these structures. A stroll through the woodlands may produce **Swallowtailed Bee-eater**, **Scimitarbilled Woodhoopoe**, **Grey Hornbill**, **Ashy Tit**, **Yellowbellied Eremomela**, **Rufouseared Warbler**, **Pririt Batis** and **Crimsonbreasted Boubou**.

ALSO RECORDED

Vagrants to the open water areas include African Fish Eagle, Giant and Malachite Kingfishers. Both Fairy Flycatcher and Namaqua Prinia have been recorded during the winter months. On the left of the road from Olifantshoek is a cliff face that used to be a breeding site for Cape Vultures in former times. According to early settlers these cliffs were once washed white with the birds' droppings.

Abrie Maritz

92% OF SPECIES

- 071 Cattle Egret ☐
- 103 **South African Shelduck**** ☐
- 118 Secretarybird ☐
- 123 Whitebacked Vulture ☐
- 124 Lappetfaced Vulture ☐
- 127 Blackshouldered Kite ☐
- 131 **Black Eagle** ☐
- 132 Tawny Eagle ☐
- 140 Martial Eagle ☐
- 149 Steppe Buzzard ☐
- 152 Jackal Buzzard ☐
- 161 Gabar Goshawk ☐
- 162 **Pale Chanting Goshawk*** ☐
- 181 Rock Kestrel ☐
- 182 **Greater Kestrel** ☐
- 186 **Pygmy Falcon** ☐
- 193 Orange River Francolin* ☐
- 200 Common Quail ☐
- 203 Helmeted Guineafowl ☐
- 205 Kurrichane Buttonquail ☐
- 230 Kori Bustard ☐
- 232 Ludwig's Bustard* ☐
- 237 Redcrested Korhaan* ☐

239a Whitequilled Korhaan** ☐
255 Crowned Plover ☐
258 Blacksmith Plover ☐
297 Spotted Dikkop ☐
301 Doublebanded Courser ☐
344 **Namaqua Sandgrouse*** ☐
345 **Burchell's Sandgrouse*** ☐
349 Rock Pigeon ☐
352 Redeyed Dove ☐
354 Cape Turtle Dove ☐
355 Laughing Dove ☐
356 Namaqua Dove ☐
382 Jacobin Cuckoo ☐
386 Diederik Cuckoo ☐
392 Barn Owl ☐
398 **Pearlspotted Owl** ☐
401 **Spotted Eagle Owl** ☐
406 Rufouscheeked Nightjar ☐
411 European Swift ☐
413 Bradfield's Swift* ☐
417 Little Swift ☐
425 **Whitebacked Mousebird**** ☐
426 **Redfaced Mousebird** ☐
445 **Swallowtailed Bee-eater** ☐
447 Lilacbreasted Roller ☐
451 Hoopoe ☐
454 **Scimitarbilled Woodhoopoe** ☐
457 **Grey Hornbill** ☐
459 Southern Yellow-billed Hornbill* ☐
465 **Pied Barbet*** ☐
483 Goldentailed Woodpecker ☐
486 Cardinal Woodpecker ☐
495 Clapper Lark** ☐
497 **Fawncoloured Lark** ☐
498 Sabota Lark* ☐
506 **Spikeheeled Lark*** ☐
516 Greybacked Finchlark* ☐
518 European Swallow ☐
520 Whitethroated Swallow ☐
526 Greater Striped Swallow* ☐
529 Rock Martin ☐
533 Brownthroated Martin ☐
541 Forktailed Drongo ☐
547 Black Crow ☐
552 **Ashy Tit*** ☐
557 Cape Penduline Tit* ☐
567 Redeyed Bulbul* ☐
577 Olive Thrush ☐
580 Groundscraper Thrush ☐
583 Shorttoed Rock Thrush* ☐
586 **Mountain Chat*** ☐
587 Capped Wheatear ☐
589 **Familiar Chat** ☐
595 Anteating Chat** ☐
615 Kalahari Robin* ☐
621 Titbabbler* ☐
651 Longbilled Crombec ☐
653 **Yellowbellied Eremomela** ☐
665 Desert Cisticola ☐
669 Greybacked Cisticola* ☐
685 Blackchested Prinia* ☐
688 **Rufouseared Warbler**** ☐
689 Spotted Flycatcher ☐
697 Chat Flycatcher* ☐
698 Fiscal Flycatcher** ☐
703 **Pririt Batis*** ☐
713 Cape Wagtail ☐
716 Grassveld Pipit ☐
731 Lesser Grey Shrike ☐
732 Fiscal Shrike ☐
733 Redbacked Shrike ☐
739 **Crimsonbreasted Boubou*** ☐
741 Brubru ☐
743 Threestreaked Tchagra ☐
746 Bokmakierie* ☐
760 **Wattled Starling** ☐
764 Glossy Starling* ☐
770 Palewinged Starling* ☐
788 Dusky Sunbird* ☐
796 Cape White-eye** ☐
799 Whitebrowed Sparrowweaver ☐
800 **Sociable Weaver**** ☐
801 House Sparrow ☐
803 Cape Sparrow* ☐
804 Greyheaded Sparrow ☐
806 Scalyfeathered Finch* ☐
814 Masked Weaver ☐
821 Redbilled Quelea ☐
845 **Violeteared Waxbill*** ☐
846 **Common Waxbill** ☐
847 **Blackcheeked Waxbill** ☐
856 Redheaded Finch* ☐
870 Blackthroated Canary ☐
878 Yellow Canary* ☐
879 Whitethroated Canary ☐
884 Goldenbreasted Bunting ☐
885 Cape Bunting ☐
886 Rock Bunting ☐
887 Larklike Bunting* ☐

UPINGTON

approximately 160 species recorded to date

The Eiland Holiday Resort in Upington lies on the banks of the Orange River and is managed by the town municipality. Driving to the entrance gate one passes through the longest avenue of palm trees in the southern hemisphere. In 1974 and 1988 the resort was completely flooded and extensive restoration has had to be done. The vegetation is lush and green, in sharp contrast to the surrounding countryside. The Tortelduif Nature Trail follows the banks of the Orange River for about 4 km. The resort has fully equipped cottages, chalets and caravan and camping grounds. Bookings can be made through the Upington Municipality. Other facilities include a swimming pool and a hall, ideal for conferences.

The Spitskop Nature Reserve, 15 km north of Upington, was proclaimed by the Upington City Coucil in 1967 as a nature reserve for the protection of game and indigenous plants. It has been privately managed since 1990. The reserve covers an area of 2 700 ha and has walking trails and 37 km of roads for game viewing and birding. No accommodation is available, but there is a picnic site. It is open from 08h00 to 17h00 during April to September and from 08h00 to 19h00 October to March.

SPECIAL AND INTERESTING SPECIES

When walking along the Tortelduif Nature Trail, be on the lookout for **Rosyfaced Lovebird**, **Lesser Honeyguide** and **Swallowtailed Bee-eater**. **Namaqua Prinia** is usually heard

ALSO RECORDED

Whitebacked Night Heron is an unconfirmed sighting along the river. Black-crowned Night Heron is recorded in the vicinity. Occasional summer migrants include European Golden Oriole and Redbacked Shrike. Tractrac Chat has been recorded at Spitskop Nature Reserve.

Riann de Klerk

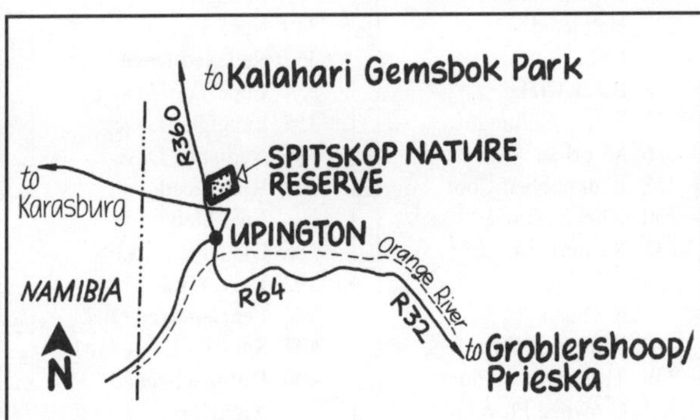

The Eiland Holiday Resort is adjacent to the bridge crossing the Orange River at Upington. The Spitskop Nature Reserve is north of the town on the R360 road and is signposted.

before being seen in the reeds along the river. **Scimitarbilled Woodhoopoe**, **Ashy Tit** and **Blackheaded Canary** can be found in the camel thorn trees at the campsite and along the river. In the evening or early morning one can hear **Pearlspotted** and **Barn Owls** and **Spotted Eagle Owl**. They are sometimes found in the lit palm tree lane, where **Rufouscheeked Nightjars** have also been recorded. Between December and March large flocks of **Abdim's Stork** can be seen soaring in the sky or foraging in cultivated lands. **African Fish Eagle**, with its pleasant call, can be seen flying above the river or perched in large trees. When driving to Spitskop Nature Reserve look for **Pygmy Falcon** on the telephone poles, especially in the vicinity of **Sociable Weaver** nests. **Kori Bustard**, **Doublebanded Courser**, **Capped Wheatear**, **Chat Flycatcher**, **Fawncoloured** and **Karoo Larks**, and **Karoo** and **Kalahari Robins** are present and normally not difficult to find. The display flight of the **Clapper Lark** is most evident in the early morning and late afternoon. After a good rainy season **Blackeared Finchlark** can, with luck, be seen among flocks of **Greybacked Finchlark.**

91% OF SPECIES

- 001 Ostrich ☐
- 008 Dabchick ☐
- 055 Whitebreasted Cormorant ☐
- 058 Reed Cormorant ☐
- 060 Darter ☐
- 062 Grey Heron ☐
- 063 Blackheaded Heron ☐
- 067 Little Egret ☐
- 068 Yellowbilled Egret ☐
- 071 Cattle Egret ☐
- 081 Hamerkop ☐
- 084 Black Stork ☐
- 085 **Abdim's Stork** ☐
- 091 Sacred Ibis ☐
- 094 Hadeda Ibis ☐
- 102 Egyptian Goose ☐
- 103 South African Shelduck** ☐
- 104 Yellowbilled Duck ☐
- 105 African Black Duck ☐
- 106 Cape Teal ☐
- 108 Redbilled Teal ☐
- 116 Spurwinged Goose ☐
- 126a Yellowbilled Kite ☐
- 127 Blackshouldered Kite ☐
- 148 **African Fish Eagle** ☐
- 162 Pale Chanting Goshawk* ☐
- 172 Lanner Falcon ☐
- 181 Rock Kestrel ☐
- 182 Greater Kestrel ☐
- 186 **Pygmy Falcon** ☐
- 203 Helmeted Guineafowl ☐
- 213 Black Crake ☐
- 223 Purple Gallinule ☐
- 226 Moorhen ☐
- 228 Redknobbed Coot ☐
- 230 **Kori Bustard** ☐
- 235 Karoo Korhaan** ☐
- 239a Whitequilled Korhaan** ☐
- 248 Kittlitz's Plover ☐
- 249 Threebanded Plover ☐
- 255 Crowned Plover ☐
- 258 Blacksmith Plover ☐
- 264 Common Sandpiper ☐
- 266 Wood Sandpiper ☐
- 270 Greenshank ☐
- 274 Little Stint ☐
- 295 Blackwinged Stilt ☐
- 297 Spotted Dikkop ☐
- 301 **Doublebanded Courser** ☐
- 344 Namaqua Sandgrouse* ☐
- 349 Rock Pigeon ☐
- 352 Redeyed Dove ☐
- 354 Cape Turtle Dove ☐
- 355 Laughing Dove ☐
- 356 Namaqua Dove ☐
- 367 **Rosyfaced Lovebird*** ☐
- 386 Diederik Cuckoo ☐
- 392 **Barn Owl** ☐
- 398 **Pearlspotted Owl** ☐
- 401 **Spotted Eagle Owl** ☐
- 406 **Rufouscheeked Nightjar** ☐
- 415 Whiterumped Swift ☐

417 Little Swift
421 Palm Swift
425 Whitebacked Mousebird**
426 Redfaced Mousebird
428 Pied Kingfisher
429 Giant Kingfisher
431 Malachite Kingfisher
438 European Bee-eater
445 **Swallowtailed Bee-eater**
451 Hoopoe
454 **Scimitarbilled Woodhoopoe**
465 Pied Barbet*
476 **Lesser Honeyguide**
486 Cardinal Woodpecker
495 **Clapper Lark****
497 **Fawncoloured Lark**
500 Longbilled Lark*
502 **Karoo Lark****
506 Spikeheeled Lark*
507 Redcapped Lark
512 Thickbilled Lark**
516 **Greybacked Finchlark***
517 **Blackeared Finchlark****
518 European Swallow
520 Whitethroated Swallow
526 Greater Striped Swallow*
529 Rock Martin
533 Brownthroated Martin
541 Forktailed Drongo
552 **Ashy Tit***
567 Redeyed Bulbul*
577 Olive Thrush
580 Groundscraper Thrush
583 Shorttoed Rock Thrush*
586 Mountain Chat*
587 **Capped Wheatear**
589 Familiar Chat
592 Karoo Chat*
595 Anteating Chat**
601 Cape Robin
614 **Karoo Robin****
615 **Kalahari Robin***
621 Titbabbler*
631 African Marsh Warbler
635 Cape Reed Warbler
651 Longbilled Crombec
653 Yellowbellied Eremomela
664 Fantailed Cisticola
677 Levaillant's Cisticola
685 Blackchested Prinia*
687 **Namaqua Prinia****
688 Rufouseared Warbler**
689 Spotted Flycatcher
697 **Chat Flycatcher***
698 Fiscal Flycatcher**
703 Pririt Batis*
711 African Pied Wagtail
713 Cape Wagtail
716 Grassveld Pipit
732 Fiscal Shrike
741 Brubru
746 Bokmakierie*
760 Wattled Starling
764 Glossy Starling*
788 Dusky Sunbird*
796 Cape White-eye**
799 Whitebrowed Sparrowweaver
800 **Sociable Weaver****
801 House Sparrow
802 Great Sparrow*
803 Cape Sparrow*
804 Greyheaded Sparrow
806 Scalyfeathered Finch*
814 Masked Weaver
821 Redbilled Quelea
824 Red Bishop
846 Common Waxbill
856 Redheaded Finch*
860 Pintailed Whydah
870 Blackthroated Canary
876 **Blackheaded Canary**
878 Yellow Canary*
879 Whitethroated Canary*

Namaqua Sandgrouse

AUGRABIES FALLS NATIONAL PARK

approximately 195 species recorded to date

Augrabies means "place of great noise". This national park (9 415 ha), situated 39 km north-west of Kakamas, was proclaimed in 1966. The falls are one of the natural wonders of South Africa and one of the six greatest falls in the world. Most striking is the contrasting scenery, lush vegetation on either side of the river with virtual desert and moon landscape stretching to beyond the horizon. The climate is arid, with hot summer days and cold winter nights. The Klipspringer Hiking Trail offers three days of hiking with two overnight huts. There are also three nature trails of approximately one hour each. An access road leads to vantage points such as Echo Corner and Oranjekom along the ravine downstream of the falls. There are fully equipped huts and cottages as well as a caravan park and camping ground. Advance bookings should be made through the National Parks Board.

SPECIAL AND INTERESTING SPECIES

As in other hot, arid parts of the world, the best time for birdwatching is early morning and late afternoon when one might be fortunate enough to see species such as **Ludwig's** and **Kori Bustards** searching for food over the broken veld. During good rainy seasons one can find **Blackeared Finchlark**. **White** and **Abdim's Storks** frequent the riverside

ALSO RECORDED

A number of raptors have been recorded at Augrabies, including Steppe Buzzard, Gymnogene, Peregrine and Rednecked Falcons. Barn, Spotted and Giant Eagle Owls, Rufouseared, Freckled and Pennantwinged Nightjars have all been seen or heard in the camp. Bluecheeked Bee-eater and Redbacked Shrike have also been recorded in the park.

Riann de Klerk

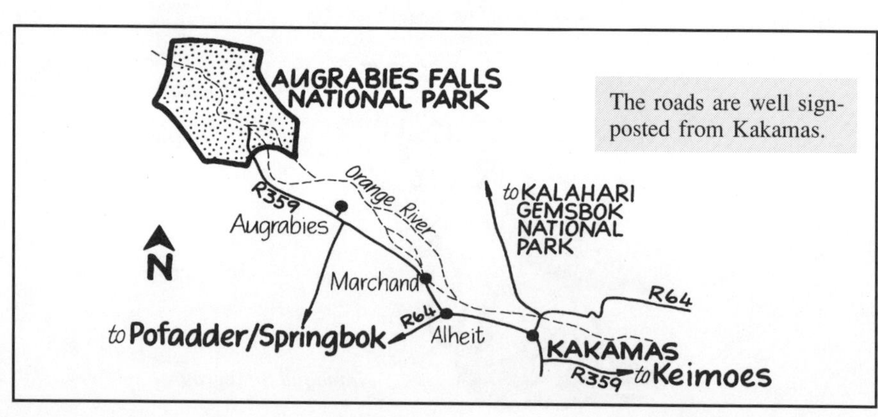

The roads are well signposted from Kakamas.

while **Black Storks** breed in the gorges. A pair of **Black Eagles** nest at Echo Corner, best seen during the late afternoon when they glide above the canyon. Other birds of prey include **African Fish Eagle** and **Pale Chanting Goshawk** (common). **Booted Eagle** can be seen in the veld west of the campsite. Be on the lookout for **Pygmy Falcon** near the large **Sociable Weaver** nests. Stop near the rocky outcrops and look for **Cinnamonbreasted** and **Rufouseared Warblers**. Larks are not abundant but species such as **Longbilled**, **Karoo** and **Spikeheeled** can be found. A stroll in the campsite is always worthwhile. Look and listen for **Rosyfaced Lovebird** and **Ashy Tit**, especially in the large camel thorn trees. **Blackchested Prinias** are common and **Namaqua Prinia** can be found in the vicinity of streams. Also look for **Pied Barbet**, **Titbabbler**, **Pririt Batis** and **Brubru**. Swifts are abundant, especially **Alpine** which occurs in large flocks.

73% OF SPECIES

008 Dabchick ☐
055 Whitebreasted Cormorant ☐
058 Reed Cormorant ☐
060 Darter ☐
062 Grey Heron ☐
063 Blackheaded Heron ☐
067 Little Egret ☐
078 Little Bittern ☐
081 Hamerkop ☐
083 **White Stork** ☐
084 **Black Stork** ☐
085 **Abdim's Stork** ☐
102 Egyptian Goose ☐
103 South African Shelduck** ☐
104 Yellowbilled Duck ☐
105 African Black Duck ☐
106 Cape Teal ☐
108 Redbilled Teal ☐
116 Spurwinged Goose ☐
126a Yellowbilled Kite ☐
127 Blackshouldered Kite ☐
131 **Black Eagle** ☐
136 **Booted Eagle** ☐
140 Martial Eagle ☐
148 **African Fish Eagle** ☐
162 **Pale Chanting Goshawk*** ☐
172 Lanner Falcon ☐
181 Rock Kestrel ☐
182 Greater Kestrel ☐
186 **Pygmy Falcon** ☐
203 Helmeted Guineafowl ☐
226 Moorhen ☐
228 Redknobbed Coot ☐
230 **Kori Bustard** ☐
232 **Ludwig's Bustard*** ☐
235 Karoo Korhaan** ☐
249 Threebanded Plover ☐
258 Blacksmith Plover ☐
264 Common Sandpiper ☐
266 Wood Sandpiper ☐
270 Greenshank ☐
297 Spotted Dikkop ☐
344 Namaqua Sandgrouse* ☐
349 Rock Pigeon ☐
352 Redeyed Dove ☐
354 Cape Turtle Dove ☐
355 Laughing Dove ☐
356 Namaqua Dove ☐
367 **Rosyfaced Lovebird*** ☐
386 Diederik Cuckoo ☐
412 Black Swift ☐
413 Bradfield's Swift* ☐
415 Whiterumped Swift ☐
417 Little Swift ☐
418 **Alpine Swift** ☐
425 Whitebacked Mousebird** ☐
426 Redfaced Mousebird ☐
428 Pied Kingfisher ☐
429 Giant Kingfisher ☐
431 Malachite Kingfisher ☐
438 European Bee-eater ☐
445 Swallowtailed Bee-eater ☐
451 Hoopoe ☐
454 Scimitarbilled Woodhoopoe ☐
465 **Pied Barbet*** ☐
474 Greater Honeyguide ☐
476 Lesser Honeyguide ☐
486 Cardinal Woodpecker ☐
498 Sabota Lark* ☐
500 **Longbilled Lark*** ☐
502 **Karoo Lark**** ☐
506 **Spikeheeled Lark*** ☐
516 Greybacked Finchlark* ☐

517 **Blackeared Finchlark**** ☐
518 European Swallow ☐
520 Whitethroated Swallow ☐
523 Pearlbreasted Swallow ☐
526 Greater Striped Swallow* ☐
528 South African Cliff Swallow** ☐
529 Rock Martin ☐
530 House Martin ☐
533 Brownthroated Martin ☐
534 Banded Martin ☐
541 Forktailed Drongo ☐
551 Southern Grey Tit** ☐
552 **Ashy Tit*** ☐
567 Redeyed Bulbul* ☐
577 Olive Thrush ☐
580 Groundscraper Thrush ☐
583 Shorttoed Rock Thrush* ☐
586 Mountain Chat* ☐
587 Capped Wheatear ☐
589 Familiar Chat ☐
592 Karoo Chat* ☐
595 Anteating Chat** ☐
601 Cape Robin ☐
614 Karoo Robin** ☐
615 Kalahari Robin* ☐
621 **Titbabbler*** ☐
631 African Marsh Warbler ☐
635 Cape Reed Warbler ☐
651 Longbilled Crombec ☐
653 Yellowbellied Eremomela ☐
660 **Cinnamonbreasted Warbler**** ☐
664 Fantailed Cisticola ☐
669 Greybacked Cisticola* ☐
677 Levaillant's Cisticola ☐
685 **Blackchested Prinia*** ☐
687 **Namaqua Prinia**** ☐
688 **Rufouseared Warbler**** ☐
689 Spotted Flycatcher ☐
695 Marico Flycatcher* ☐
697 Chat Flycatcher* ☐
698 Fiscal Flycatcher** ☐
703 **Pririt Batis*** ☐
711 African Pied Wagtail ☐
713 Cape Wagtail ☐
716 Grassveld Pipit ☐
732 Fiscal Shrike ☐
741 **Brubru** ☐
746 Bokmakierie* ☐
760 Wattled Starling ☐
764 Glossy Starling* ☐
770 Palewinged Starling* ☐
788 Dusky Sunbird* ☐
796 Cape White-eye** ☐
799 Whitebrowed Sparrowweaver ☐
800 **Sociable Weaver**** ☐
801 House Sparrow ☐
802 Great Sparrow* ☐
803 Cape Sparrow* ☐
804 Greyheaded Sparrow ☐
806 Scalyfeathered Finch* ☐
814 Masked Weaver ☐
821 Redbilled Quelea ☐
824 Red Bishop ☐
842 Redbilled Firefinch ☐
846 Common Waxbill ☐
860 Pintailed Whydah ☐
870 Blackthroated Canary ☐
876 Blackheaded Canary ☐
878 Yellow Canary* ☐
879 Whitethroated Canary* ☐
885 Cape Bunting ☐

Whitequilled Korhaan

"DIE BOS" NATURE RESERVE, PRIESKA

approximately 157 species recorded to date (in Prieska area)

"Die Bos" Nature Reserve, a small oasis of about 60 ha on the banks of the Orange River, is situated within the municipal boundaries of the small Karoo town of Prieska. The fenced-off campsite, surrounded by lush riverine woodland, has eight rondawels (self-contained except for bedding). Picnic and ablution facilities are available, and the municipal swimming pool also lies within the boundaries of the reserve. For birdwatchers the nearby sludge dams promise a wealth in waders. There is a launching place for boats suitably equipped to tackle the fast-flowing Orange River. The best time for birdwatching at "Die Bos" is during the week as the resort tends to become quite crowded during weekends.

SPECIAL AND INTERESTING SPECIES

The striking **Goliath Heron** can be seen throughout the day, hunting in the shallows and on the small islands. **White Storks** are present in large numbers during summer on the nearby lucerne fields. The best place to view the shy and elusive **African Black Duck** is on the quiet waters behind the reed islands in the river, where they usually shelter under the overhanging branches of willows. A bird more often heard than seen in the thick riverine bush is the **Cape Francolin**. Its presence is quite interesting as "Die Bos" is out of its normal

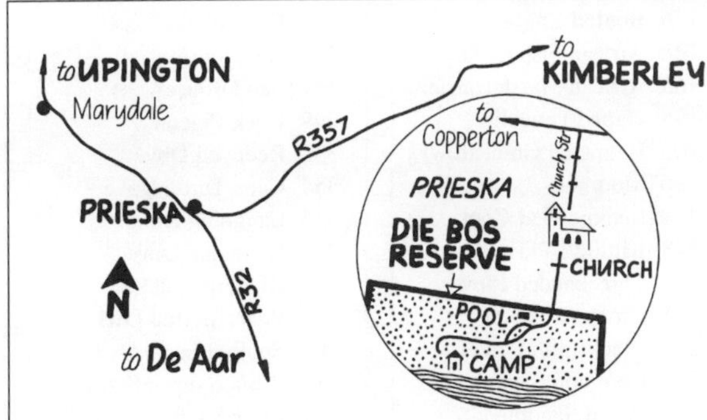

ALSO RECORDED

Black Eagle and Black-headed Canary are present in the hills surrounding Prieska, and Karoo Lark, Karoo Chat, Karoo Korhaan, Greybacked and Blackeared Finchlarks, as well as Ludwig's Bustard can be found among the local karroid shrubs.

Corné and Elmarie Anderson

If you travel via Douglas (R357), Prieska is approximately 250 km west of Kimberley. On entering Prieska from Douglas, follow the main road for approximately 800 m to a four-way stop, turn right into Church Street and continue past the church to the entrance of the reserve. To reach the campsite, follow the well-maintained gravel road for approximately 1 400 m (see map). Prieska can also be reached from de Aar (175 km) via Britstown (R32).

distribution range. It is a thrilling experience to look up and see a **Booted Eagle** soaring high over the reserve. These intra-Africa migrants are mainly seen in early and late summer and can be recognised by their cream-coloured underwing coverts contrasting with dark secondary and primary feathers. The white patches on the leading edges of the wings near the body, the so-called "landing lights", are also characteristic. Both **Southern Grey** and **Ashy Tits** are present. A bird usually overlooked in the campsite is the **Lesser Honeyguide**, which tends to use the same perch, where it sits motionless for long periods. The relatively thick bill, dark moustache and white outer tail feathers are diagnostic. The picnic area is the best place to look for one of our smaller owl species, the **Pearlspotted Owl**, which usually perches low down in thick bush. It responds readily at dusk to a tape recording of its drawn-out "peeuw peeuw" call. The **Namaqua Prinia** with its swift-like "triip triip" call can be encountered in the thick reeds near the river or in the undergrowth flanking the reserve roads. The large **European Golden Oriole**, a non-breeding Palaearctic migrant, has also been recorded. The males are quite spectacular with their golden plumage and contrasting black wings and tail. Endemics to look for include **Whitebacked Mousebird**, **Karoo Robin**, **Fiscal Flycatcher**, **Pririt Batis** and **Whitethroated Canary**.

70% OF SPECIES

- 008 Dabchick ☐
- 055 Whitebreasted Cormorant ☐
- 058 Reed Cormorant ☐
- 060 Darter ☐
- 062 Grey Heron ☐
- 063 Blackheaded Heron ☐
- 064 **Goliath Heron** ☐
- 067 Little Egret ☐
- 076 Blackcrowned Night Heron ☐
- 081 Hamerkop ☐
- 083 **White Stork** ☐
- 091 Sacred Ibis ☐
- 094 Hadeda Ibis ☐
- 099 Whitefaced Duck ☐
- 102 Egyptian Goose ☐
- 103 South African Shelduck** ☐
- 104 Yellowbilled Duck ☐
- 105 **African Black Duck** ☐
- 106 Cape Teal ☐
- 108 Redbilled Teal ☐
- 127 Blackshouldered Kite ☐
- 136 **Booted Eagle** ☐
- 148 African Fish Eagle ☐
- 165 African Marsh Harrier ☐
- 195 **Cape Francolin** ☐
- 203 Helmeted Guineafowl ☐
- 226 Moorhen ☐
- 228 Redknobbed Coot ☐
- 248 Kittlitz's Plover ☐
- 249 Threebanded Plover ☐
- 255 Crowned Plover ☐
- 258 Blacksmith Plover ☐
- 264 Common Sandpiper ☐
- 266 Wood Sandpiper ☐
- 272 Curlew Sandpiper ☐
- 274 Little Stint ☐
- 284 Ruff ☐
- 295 Blackwinged Stilt ☐
- 297 Spotted Dikkop ☐
- 301 Doublebanded Courser ☐
- 344 Namaqua Sandgrouse* ☐
- 349 Rock Pigeon ☐
- 352 Redeyed Dove ☐
- 354 Cape Turtle Dove ☐
- 355 Laughing Dove ☐
- 356 Namaqua Dove ☐
- 386 Diederik Cuckoo ☐
- 398 **Pearlspotted Owl** ☐
- 401 Spotted Eagle Owl ☐
- 415 Whiterumped Swift ☐
- 417 Little Swift ☐
- 418 Alpine Swift ☐

425 **Whitebacked Mousebird**** ☐
426 Redfaced Mousebird ☐
428 Pied Kingfisher ☐
429 Giant Kingfisher ☐
431 Malachite Kingfisher ☐
438 European Bee-eater ☐
443 Whitefronted Bee-eater ☐
451 Hoopoe ☐
454 Scimitarbilled Woodhoopoe ☐
465 Pied Barbet* ☐
473 Crested Barbet ☐
476 **Lesser Honeyguide** ☐
483 Goldentailed Woodpecker ☐
486 Cardinal Woodpecker ☐
498 Sabota Lark* ☐
518 European Swallow ☐
520 Whitethroated Swallow ☐
526 Greater Striped Swallow* ☐
529 Rock Martin ☐
533 Brownthroated Martin ☐
543 **European Golden Oriole** ☐
548 Pied Crow ☐
551 **Southern Grey Tit**** ☐
552 **Ashy Tit*** ☐
577 Olive Thrush ☐
580 Groundscraper Thrush ☐
595 Anteating Chat** ☐
601 Cape Robin ☐
614 **Karoo Robin**** ☐
621 Titbabbler* ☐
628 Great Reed Warbler ☐
635 Cape Reed Warbler ☐
643 Willow Warbler ☐
653 Yellowbellied Eremomela ☐
685 Blackchested Prinia* ☐
687 **Namaqua Prinia**** ☐
689 Spotted Flycatcher ☐
698 **Fiscal Flycatcher**** ☐
703 **Pririt Batis*** ☐
711 African Pied Wagtail ☐
713 Cape Wagtail ☐
716 Grassveld Pipit ☐
732 Fiscal Shrike ☐
741 Brubru ☐
746 Bokmakierie* ☐
764 Glossy Starling* ☐
788 Dusky Sunbird* ☐
796 Cape White-eye** ☐
801 House Sparrow ☐
803 Cape Sparrow* ☐
804 Greyheaded Sparrow ☐
814 Masked Weaver ☐
824 Red Bishop ☐
846 Common Waxbill ☐
856 Redheaded Finch* ☐
870 Blackthroated Canary ☐
878 Yellow Canary* ☐
879 **Whitethroated Canary*** ☐

☐
☐
☐
☐
☐

Namaqua Sandgrouse

GOEGAP PROVINCIAL NATURE RESERVE

approximately 93 species recorded to date

Goegap, previously known as the Hester Malan Nature Reserve, is a reserve of the Chief Directorate of Nature and Environmental Conservation in the Cape. The reserve is now 14 864 ha in size, having recently been extended. The largest part of the reserve represents Namaqualand broken veld. There is also a small area of transition between the former and false succulent karoo, while the south-eastern section of the reserve is false desert grassland. The reserve consists of dome-shaped granite hills with sandy flats in between. The rainfall is very low and erratic (162 mm average annual rainfall) and normally occurs in winter; summer rainfall is, however, experienced in the south-eastern section. The temperature varies between a maximum of 45 °C in summer to a minimum of 2 °C in winter. Recreation facilities include a picnic area, hiking trails, tourist roads and an exhibition of succulents.

SPECIAL AND INTERESTING SPECIES

Because the rainfall is erratic and the vegetation ephemeral, permanently resident species are few, and their numbers are low. One such species is the **Cape Eagle Owl**, which breeds in the reserve, and can often be heard and seen in the vicinity of the information centre at dusk. Another breeding resident, the **Black Eagle**, can regularly be seen soaring above granite

ALSO RECORDED

Blackbreasted Snake Eagle is occasionally seen, and there are several unconfirmed sightings of Peregrine Falcon from the more rugged areas. Greywing Francolins occur here on the north-western limit of their distribution, their early morning calls carrying clearly from the koppies on the crisp dry air. The eerie screech of the Barn Owl can be heard, particularly at times of rodent irruptions when the owl numbers appear to increase. More potential species have yet to be recorded for the reserve, mainly because a large portion of the reserve has been recently acquired, and also because of the transient use of the reserve by many species. Any confirmed additions to the species list and breeding records should be given to the reserve manager.

Guy Palmer

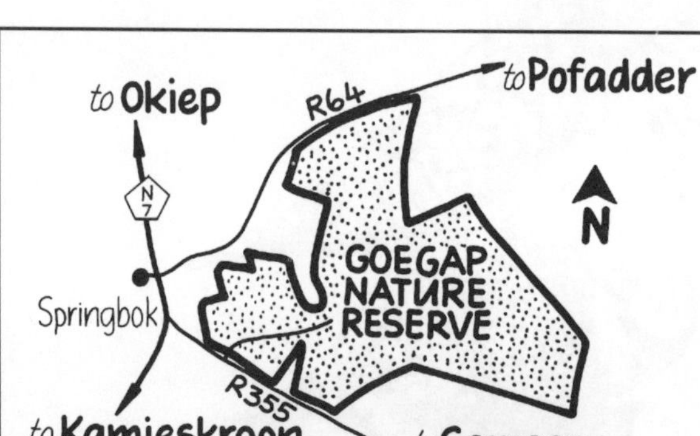

The entrance to the reserve is approximately 12 km east of Springbok, just past the airfield. Permits are required and can be obtained at the information centre.

koppies in search of dassies and red rock rabbits, its two main prey species in this area. Other raptors to be seen are **Martial** and **Booted Eagles** and **Lanner Falcon**. **Doublebanded Courser** can be found on the flats in the eastern section but is easily overlooked, as is **Karoo Korhaan**, which frequents the same area. The eroded gulleys in the koppies contain the handsome **Ground Woodpecker**, its presence often being revealed by its strident call. This reserve is probably one of the better places for getting to know the larks of the arid north-west. Of the dozen species that can be expected to occur here, several have already been recorded including the distributionally restricted **Red Lark** and **Stark's**, **Thickbilled**, **Karoo** and **Clapper Larks**. The best viewing time is in spring after good rains, as many species in this arid area are nomadic, moving to whichever areas offer the best foraging and nesting opportunities. This coincides with the best flowering period for the famous Namaqualand flowers, the reserve being one of the better places to view this spectacle. **Ludwig's Bustard** can also be seen in groups of up to six birds at this time, unfortunately flushing at some distance. Many species breed at this time of plenty: **Karoo Eremomela**, **Cinnamonbreasted Warbler** and **Dusky Sunbird** are among the opportunists. At times spishing can be particularly rewarding, often removing the frustration of stalking elusive species in this area virtually devoid of cover.

100% OF SPECIES

001 Ostrich ☐
063 Blackheaded Heron ☐
102 Egyptian Goose ☐
103 South African Shelduck** ☐
106 Cape Teal ☐
118 Secretarybird ☐
126a Yellowbilled Kite ☐
127 Blackshouldered Kite ☐
131 **Black Eagle** ☐
136 **Booted Eagle** ☐
140 **Martial Eagle** ☐
143 Blackbreasted Snake Eagle ☐
152 Jackal Buzzard** ☐
162 Pale Chanting Goshawk* ☐
168 Black Harrier** ☐
172 **Lanner Falcon** ☐
181 Rock Kestrel ☐
182 Greater Kestrel ☐
190 Greywing Francolin** ☐
232 **Ludwig's Bustard*** ☐
235 **Karoo Korhaan**** ☐
294 Avocet ☐
295 Blackwinged Stilt ☐
297 Spotted Dikkop ☐
301 **Doublebanded Courser** ☐
344 Namaqua Sandgrouse* ☐
349 Rock Pigeon ☐
354 Cape Turtle Dove ☐
355 Laughing Dove ☐
356 Namaqua Dove ☐
392 Barn Owl ☐
400 **Cape Eagle Owl** ☐
401 Spotted Eagle Owl ☐
405 Fierynecked Nightjar ☐
418 Alpine Swift ☐
425 Whitebacked Mousebird ☐
426 Redfaced Mousebird ☐
451 Hoopoe ☐
465 Pied Barbet* ☐
480 **Ground Woodpecker**** ☐
495 **Clapper Lark**** ☐
502 **Karoo Lark**** ☐
504 **Red Lark**** ☐
507 Redcapped Lark ☐
511 **Stark's Lark*** ☐
512 **Thickbilled Lark**** ☐
516 Greybacked Finchlark* ☐
529 Rock Martin ☐
547 Black Crow ☐

548 Pied Crow ☐
550 Whitenecked Raven ☐
551 Southern Grey Tit** ☐
566 Cape Bulbul** ☐
567 Redeyed Bulbul* ☐
577 Olive Thrush ☐
581 Cape Rock Thrush** ☐
586 Mountain Chat* ☐
587 Capped Wheatear ☐
589 Familiar Chat ☐
590 Tractrac Chat* ☐
592 Karoo Chat* ☐
595 Anteating Chat** ☐
614 Karoo Robin** ☐
622 Layard's Titbabbler** ☐
651 Longbilled Crombec ☐
654 **Karoo Eremomela**** ☐
660 **Cinnamonbreasted Warbler**** ☐
669 Greybacked Cisticola* ☐
686 Karoo Prinia** ☐
687 Namaqua Prinia** ☐
688 Rufouseared Warbler** ☐
697 Chat Flycatcher* ☐
698 Fiscal Flycatcher** ☐
706 Fairy Flycatcher** ☐
713 Cape Wagtail ☐
716 Grassveld Pipit ☐
717 Longbilled Pipit ☐
732 Fiscal Shrike ☐
746 Bokmakierie* ☐
759 Pied Starling** ☐
764 Glossy Starling* ☐
770 Palewinged Starling* ☐
775 Malachite Sunbird ☐
783 Lesser Doublecollared Sunbird** ☐
788 **Dusky Sunbird*** ☐
801 House Sparrow ☐
803 Cape Sparrow* ☐
813 Cape Weaver** ☐
814 Masked Weaver ☐
876 Blackheaded Canary ☐
879 Whitethroated Canary* ☐
885 Cape Bunting ☐
887 Larklike Bunting* ☐
☐
☐

BUSHMANLAND

approximately 192 species recorded to date

Surprisingly for most people, Bushmanland is one of the prize birding habitats in southern Africa, especially from September to December when the hot, arid region comes alive with vast numbers of larks and other semi-desert species. The region covers an area of approximately 40 000 square km and stretches from Calvinia in the south to Kenhardt in the north, from Springbok in the west to Van

ALSO RECORDED

Vagrant Grey Plovers have been recorded after good rains. Goliath Heron has been seen more regularly in recent years when the pans have been full.

Nico Myburgh

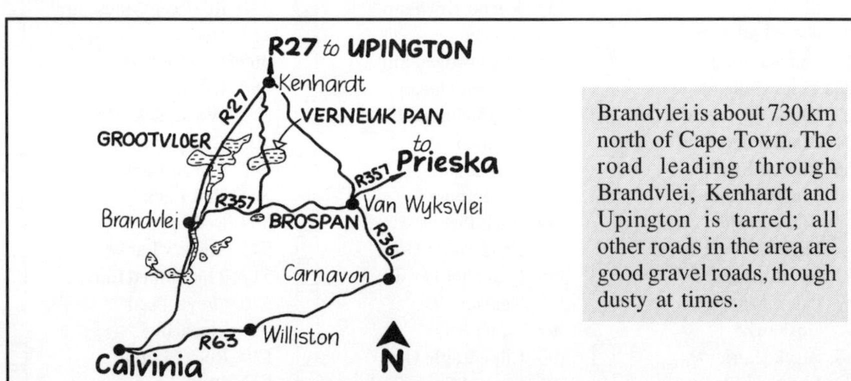

Brandvlei is about 730 km north of Cape Town. The road leading through Brandvlei, Kenhardt and Upington is tarred; all other roads in the area are good gravel roads, though dusty at times.

Wyksvlei in the east. It is a vast flat area with low scrub, dry riverbeds and a few rocky ridges. Rainfall ranges from 75 mm to 200 mm annually. The main road from Cape Town to Upington passes through Bushmanland with the town of Brandvlei almost in the centre. Hotel accommodation is available at Brandvlei and at most other small Bushmanland towns. One can rent cottages on farms in the Calvinia district, which can be arranged through the Calvinia municipality.

SPECIAL AND INTERESTING SPECIES

Birding can be done from the roadside as most species will be found in the road reserve where there is normally plenty of grass seed and cover. Farmers do not like strangers wandering through their farms but allow birders who have asked permission. Larks are of course abundant in this region and attract most birders to the area. The highlight for most will undoubtedly be **Red** and **Sclater's Larks**. Both are uncommon and the former can be found from 30 km south of Brandvlei through to the Orange River and mostly on the red sand dunes. The latter, with its diagnostic teardrop mark below the eye and conical, almost upturned bill, must be looked for in the driest areas, free of vegetation, where it breeds from October to November before moving on. It seldom seems to breed in the same area for more than one season and always nests completely in the open, often on shaly outcrops. Other larks worth looking out for are **Blackeared Finchlark**, **Thickbilled**, **Longbilled**, **Clapper** and **Karoo Larks**. Trees, which are few and far between, are in much demand by birds of prey as nest sites. **Pale Chanting Goshawk**, **Secretarybird**, **Blackbreasted Snake Eagle**, **Greater Kestrel**, **Jackal Buzzard** and **Martial Eagle** use whatever trees may be found. **Black** and **Booted Eagles** and **Gymnogene** nest on suitable cliff faces. Most of the road bridges host colonies of **South African Cliff Swallow**. Look for **Karoo Korhaan, Ludwig's Bustard** and **Doublebanded Courser**. **Namaqua Sandgrouse** are common nesters in the road reserve. The scrub country could yield **Cape Penduline Tit**, **Rufouseared Warbler**, **Namaqua** and **Karoo Prinias**, **Karoo** and **Yellowbellied Eremomelas** and **Chat Flycatcher**. When the pans, such as Brospan, Verneuk Pan and Flamink Pan fill after years of being dry, thousands of **Lesser** and **Greater Flamingos**, **African Spoonbill**, **South African Shelduck**, **Avocet**, and many other waders and herons appear overnight, feeding on the abundant supply of triops, shrimps, molluscs, frogs and even fish. One of the best pans to witness this spectacle is on the road 54 km north of Calvinia to Brandvlei. North of Van Rynsdorp, look out for **European Bee-eaters** perched on telephone wires: they breed in river or roadside banks during November and December.

65% OF SPECIES

- 001 Ostrich
- 062 Grey Heron
- 068 Yellowbilled Egret
- 083 White Stork
- 084 Black Stork
- 095 **African Spoonbill**
- 096 **Greater Flamingo**
- 097 **Lesser Flamingo**
- 103 South African Shelduck**
- 107 Hottentot Teal
- 118 **Secretarybird**
- 131 **Black Eagle**
- 136 **Booted Eagle**
- 140 **Martial Eagle**
- 143 **Blackbreasted Snake Eagle**
- 152 **Jackal Buzzard****
- 162 **Pale Chanting Goshawk***
- 168 Black Harrier**
- 169 **Gymnogene**
- 171 Peregrine Falcon
- 172 Lanner Falcon
- 181 Rock Kestrel
- 182 **Greater Kestrel**
- 183 Lesser Kestrel
- 208 Blue Crane**
- 230 Kori Bustard
- 232 **Ludwig's Bustard***
- 235 **Karoo Korhaan****
- 239a Whitequilled Korhaan**
- 248 Kittlitz's Plover
- 249 Threebanded Plover
- 254 Grey Plover
- 255 Crowned Plover
- 294 **Avocet**
- 297 Spotted Dikkop
- 299 Burchell's Courser*
- 301 **Doublebanded Courser**
- 344 **Namaqua Sandgrouse***
- 349 Rock Pigeon
- 354 Cape Turtle Dove
- 356 Namaqua Dove
- 386 Diederik Cuckoo
- 400 Cape Eagle Owl
- 401 Spotted Eagle Owl
- 405 Fierynecked Nightjar
- 406 Rufouscheeked Nightjar
- 417 Little Swift
- 425 Whitebacked Mousebird**
- 431 Malachite Kingfisher
- 438 **European Bee-eater**
- 451 Hoopoe
- 465 Pied Barbet*
- 474 Greater Honeyguide
- 480 Ground Woodpecker**
- 495 **Clapper Lark****
- 498 Sabota Lark*
- 500 **Longbilled Lark***
- 502 **Karoo Lark****
- 504 **Red Lark****
- 506 Spikeheeled Lark*
- 507 Redcapped Lark
- 510 **Sclater's Lark****
- 511 Stark's Lark*
- 512 **Thickbilled Lark****
- 516 Greybacked Finchlark*
- 517 **Blackeared Finchlark****
- 518 European Swallow
- 520 Whitethroated Swallow
- 526 Greater Striped Swallow*
- 528 **South African Cliff Swallow****
- 529 Rock Martin
- 534 Banded Martin
- 548 Pied Crow
- 550 Whitenecked Raven
- 551 Southern Grey Tit**
- 557 **Cape Penduline Tit***
- 567 Redeyed Bulbul*
- 577 Olive Thrush
- 586 Mountain Chat*
- 587 Capped Wheatear
- 589 Familiar Chat
- 590 Tractrac Chat*
- 591 Sicklewinged Chat**
- 592 Karoo Chat*
- 595 Anteating Chat**
- 596 Stonechat
- 601 Cape Robin
- 614 Karoo Robin**
- 621 Titbabbler*
- 622 Layard's Titbabbler**
- 651 Longbilled Crombec
- 653 **Yellowbellied Eremomela**
- 654 **Karoo Eremomela****
- 660 Cinnamonbreasted Warbler**
- 669 Greybacked Cisticola*
- 685 Blackchested Prinia*
- 686 **Karoo Prinia****
- 687 **Namaqua Prinia****
- 688 **Rufouseared Warbler****
- 697 **Chat Flycatcher***
- 706 Fairy Flycatcher**
- 710 Paradise Flycatcher
- 713 Cape Wagtail
- 717 Longbilled Pipit
- 732 Fiscal Shrike
- 746 Bokmakierie*
- 759 Pied Starling**
- 770 Palewinged Starling*
- 775 Malachite Sunbird
- 788 Dusky Sunbird*
- 796 Cape White-eye**
- 799 Whitebrowed Sparrowweaver
- 800 Sociable Weaver**
- 801 House Sparrow
- 803 Cape Sparrow*
- 814 Masked Weaver
- 824 Red Bishop
- 856 Redheaded Finch*
- 872 Cape Canary
- 876 Blackheaded Canary
- 877 Bully Canary
- 878 Yellow Canary*
- 879 Whitethroated Canary*
- 885 Cape Bunting

OTHER BIRDING SPOTS WORTH VISITING

Molopo Reserve, Vorstershoop
A 24 000 ha reserve administered by the Chief Directorate: Nature and Environmental Conservation (Cape Province) bordered by the Molopo River on the north-western boundary. Excellent for woodland birding. No accommodation is available.

Rolfontein Nature Reserve
A 47 000 ha reserve also controlled by the CDNEC (Cape Province), situated next to the P.K. le Roux Dam. Good for Karoo birding. Tented camp and trails with overnight facilities to be booked in advance.

Kamfersdam Flamingo Sanctuary
Approximately 5 km north of Kimberley on the Johannesburg road; rich in waders (summer) and waterfowl. Contact the northern Cape branch of the S.A. Wildlife Society (see telephone list) beforehand.

USEFUL TELEPHONE NUMBERS

Augrabies Falls National Park
(05442) 4

Jan Kempdorp Municipality (Ganspan)
(0533) 6-1775

Molopo Reserve
Ventersdorp (0020) 1311/22

National Parks Board
(012) 343-1991

Northern Cape Branch
(S.A. Wildlife Society)
(0531) 3-2645/6

Prieska – "Die Bos" Reserve
(0594) 3-1375

Rolfontein Nature Reserve
(05782) 160

Spitskop Nature Reserve
(054) 2-2336

Upington Municipality
(054) 2-6911

Witsand Tourist Resort
(0591) 7-2373

6 Swaziland

Co-ordinator Vincent Parker

1 Phophonyane Nature Reserve
2 Malolotja Nature Reserve
3 Mlawula Nature Reserve

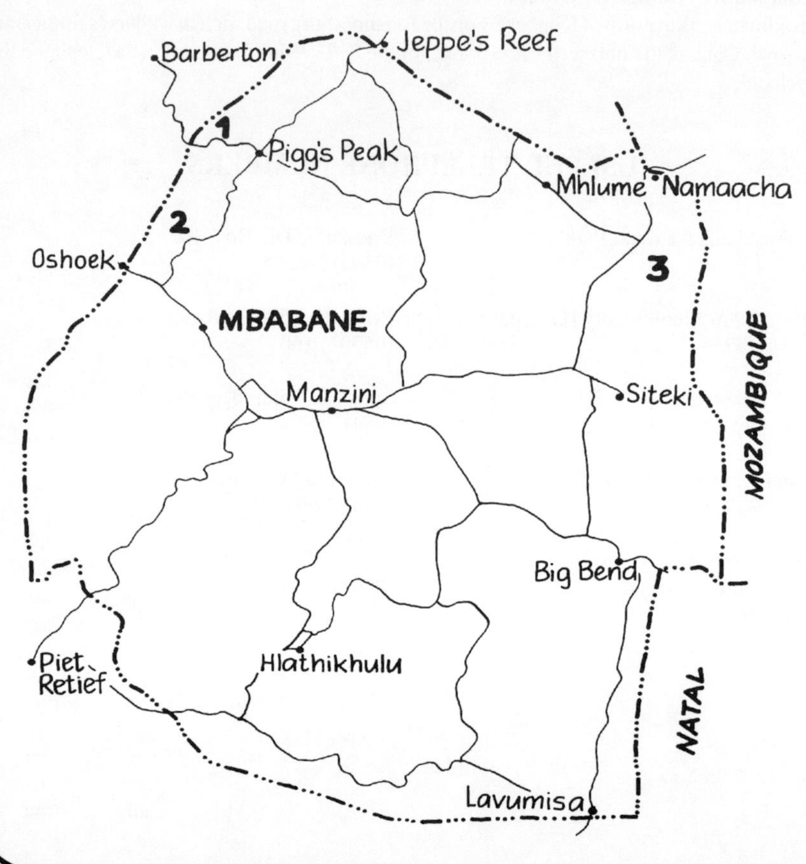

PHOPHONYANE NATURE RESERVE

approximately 185 species recorded to date

Phophonyane Nature Reserve is situated near the northern tip of Swaziland in a narrow middleveld belt between the Drakensberg escarpment to the south and west and the lowveld to the north and east. This reserve and the nearby Mlumati Valley Nature Reserve are privately owned and were established in 1985. The combined conservation area is about 2 000 ha. The vegetation consists largely of dense woodland and a rare middleveld forest type which is probably unique to this area. The tallest and most extensive of these forests occur in the Mlumati valley. The Phophonyane reserve includes a spectacular series of waterfalls and rock pools on the Phophonyane River. The habitat on Kobolondo Mountain is montane grassland and mistbelt forest patches. The altitude ranges from 600 m in the Mlumati valley to 1 277 m on the peak of Kobolondo.

SPECIAL AND INTERESTING SPECIES

During the summer months **Yellowspotted Nicator** and **Gorgeous Bush Shrike** can be heard calling from almost every thicket in the area. Unfortunately, they remain hidden in the foliage most of the time and it is a challenge to the birder's patience and perseverance to actually spot them. The brilliant **Narina Trogon** is a less vocal species which may be seen in the vicinity of the lodge. Two species that are more

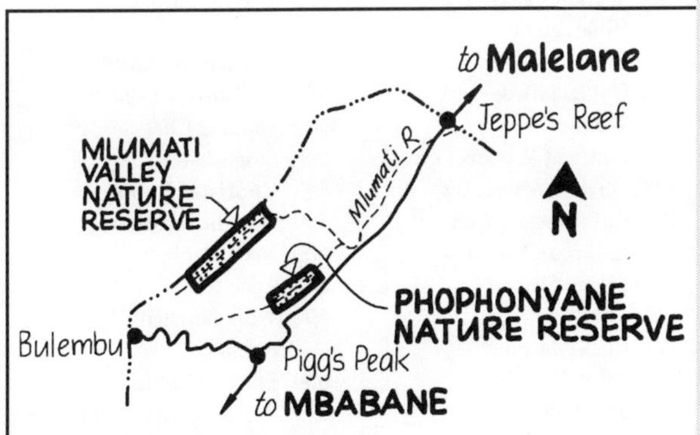

ALSO RECORDED

There has been one sighting of African Finfoot in a pool below the Phophonyane falls. Another species recorded only once to date in the Mlumati valley is Brown Robin.

Vincent Parker

The Phophonyane Lodge and Nature Reserve is 3 km off the main tar road from Piggs Peak to the Jeppes Reef border post, and 10 km north of Piggs Peak. From Phophonyane, an all-weather road leads to the peak of Kobolondo Mountain. Access to the Mlumati valley is by a four-wheel drive track from Phophonyane Lodge. Visitors can make arrangements to be driven to the Mlumati valley in a four-wheel drive vehicle.

conspicuous and also common throughout the area are the **Purplecrested Lourie** and **Olive Sunbird**. Perhaps the two most vocal species are the **Squaretailed Drongo** and **Heuglin's Robin**, which can be heard throughout the year. The mistbelt forest on Kobolondo Mountain has **Chorister** and **Starred Robins**, **Yellowthroated Warbler** and **Knysna Lourie**, which may also be seen in other parts of the Mlumati valley. On the main footpath through the Mlumati valley one may find **Yellowstreaked Bulbuls**. This is the only site in Swaziland where this species has been recorded. In the gardens around the lodge look out for **Redbacked Mannikin**, **Green Twinspot** and **Goldenrumped Tinker Barbet**. **Longtailed Wagtails** are to be found along the Phophonyane River between the waterfalls. **Crowned Eagles** are sometimes seen and heard from the lodge while displaying high overhead. **Longcrested Eagles** have also been seen in the vicinity of the lodge.

69% OF SPECIES

- 081 Hamerkop ☐
- 094 Hadeda Ibis ☐
- 105 African Black Duck ☐
- 139 **Longcrested Eagle** ☐
- 141 **Crowned Eagle** ☐
- 149 Steppe Buzzard ☐
- 160 African Goshawk ☐
- 196 Natal Francolin* ☐
- 218 Buffspotted Flufftail ☐
- 350 Rameron Pigeon ☐
- 352 Redeyed Dove ☐
- 354 Cape Turtle Dove ☐
- 358 Greenspotted Dove ☐
- 359 Tambourine Dove ☐
- 361 Green Pigeon ☐
- 370 **Knysna Lourie**** ☐
- 371 **Purplecrested Lourie** ☐
- 377 Redchested Cuckoo ☐
- 378 Black Cuckoo ☐
- 384 Emerald Cuckoo ☐
- 385 Klaas's Cuckoo ☐
- 386 Diederik Cuckoo ☐
- 391 Burchell's Coucal* ☐
- 424 Speckled Mousebird ☐
- 427 **Narina Trogon** ☐
- 432 Pygmy Kingfisher ☐
- 435 Brownhooded Kingfisher ☐
- 438 European Bee-eater ☐
- 444 Little Bee-eater ☐
- 455 Trumpeter Hornbill ☐
- 460 Crowned Hornbill ☐
- 464 Blackcollared Barbet ☐
- 471 **Goldenrumped Tinker Barbet** ☐
- 474 Greater Honeyguide ☐
- 475 Scalythroated Honeyguide ☐
- 476 Lesser Honeyguide ☐
- 483 Goldentailed Woodpecker ☐
- 486 Cardinal Woodpecker ☐
- 488 Olive Woodpecker ☐
- 494 Rufousnaped Lark ☐
- 518 European Swallow ☐
- 527 Lesser Striped Swallow ☐
- 529 Rock Martin ☐
- 536 Black Sawwing Swallow ☐
- 538 Black Cuckooshrike ☐
- 541 Forktailed Drongo ☐
- 542 **Squaretailed Drongo** ☐
- 545 Blackheaded Oriole ☐
- 548 Pied Crow ☐
- 550 Whitenecked Raven ☐
- 554 Southern Black Tit* ☐
- 568 Blackeyed Bulbul ☐
- 569 Terrestrial Bulbul ☐
- 570 **Yellowstreaked Bulbul** ☐
- 572 Sombre Bulbul ☐
- 575 **Yellowspotted Nicator** ☐
- 576 Kurrichane Thrush ☐
- 588 Buffstreaked Chat** ☐
- 589 Familiar Chat ☐
- 596 Stonechat ☐
- 598 **Chorister Robin**** ☐
- 599 **Heuglin's Robin** ☐
- 600 Natal Robin ☐
- 601 Cape Robin ☐
- 602 Whitethroated Robin** ☐
- 606 **Starred Robin** ☐
- 613 Whitebrowed Robin ☐
- 643 Willow Warbler ☐

644 **Yellowthroated Warbler** ☐
645 Barthroated Apalis ☐
648 Yellowbreasted Apalis ☐
657 Bleating Warbler ☐
661 Grassbird** ☐
664 Fantailed Cisticola ☐
670 Wailing Cisticola ☐
674 Redfaced Cisticola ☐
678 Croaking Cisticola ☐
679 Lazy Cisticola ☐
681 Neddicky ☐
683 Tawnyflanked Prinia ☐
690 Dusky Flycatcher ☐
691 Bluegrey Flycatcher ☐
694 Black Flycatcher ☐
700 Cape Batis** ☐
710 Paradise Flycatcher ☐
711 African Pied Wagtail ☐
712 **Longtailed Wagtail** ☐
718 Plainbacked Pipit ☐
720 Striped Pipit ☐
728 Yellowthroated Longclaw ☐
732 Fiscal Shrike ☐
736 Southern Boubou** ☐
740 Puffback ☐
744 Blackcrowned Tchagra ☐
747 **Gorgeous Bush Shrike** ☐
748 Orangebreasted Bush Shrike ☐
750 Olive Bush Shrike* ☐
751 Greyheaded Bush Shrike ☐
753 White Helmetshrike ☐
761 Plumcoloured Starling ☐
769 Redwinged Starling ☐
785 Greater Double-collared Sunbird** ☐
787 Whitebellied Sunbird ☐
790 **Olive Sunbird** ☐
791 Scarletchested Sunbird ☐
792 Black Sunbird ☐
793 Collared Sunbird ☐
796 Cape White-eye** ☐
804 Greyheaded Sparrow ☐
805 Yellowthroated Sparrow ☐
807 Thickbilled Weaver ☐
810 Spectacled Weaver ☐
811 Spottedbacked Weaver ☐
816 Golden Weaver ☐
828 Redshouldered Widow ☐
829 Whitewinged Widow ☐
831 Redcollared Widow ☐
835 **Green Twinspot** ☐
840 Bluebilled Firefinch ☐
846 Common Waxbill ☐
850 Swee Waxbill* ☐
857 Bronze Mannikin ☐
858 **Redbacked Mannikin** ☐
860 Pintailed Whydah ☐
869 Yelloweyed Canary ☐
872 Cape Canary ☐
881 Streakyheaded Canary ☐
884 Goldenbreasted Bunting ☐
☐
☐
☐

Knysna Lourie

MALOLOTJA NATURE RESERVE

approximately 290 species recorded to date

Malolotja is situated on the edge of the Drakensberg escarpment in the north-west of Swaziland, along the South African border. The nature reserve was established in 1979 and is administered by the Swaziland National Trust Commission. Its 18 000 ha include montane grassland, vleis, mistbelt forests and riverine woodland. The nearby Hawane Dam with a large expanse of open water and extensive reedbeds also falls under the jurisdiction of the reserve. The altitude within the reserve ranges from 760 m in the narrow Komati River valley to 1 837 m at the summit of Ngwenya Mountain. Within the reserve, the high-lying grassland areas are easily accessible via the main tourist road. However, in order to explore the forests and river valleys, it is necessary to take to the footpaths. The reserve has an extensive network of well marked hiking trails and offers hikes ranging in duration from a couple of hours to five or six days.

SPECIAL AND INTERESTING SPECIES

Blue Swallows are most likely to be seen in the vicinity of the main campsite during the summer months. Sometimes up to eight or nine birds can be seen together, skimming low over the open grassland. **Bald Ibis** are usually present between May and January and can be seen roosting on cliffs around the spectacular Malolotja Falls or feeding on recently burnt

ALSO RECORDED

Crowned Cranes have occasionally been seen in a vlei adjoining Hawane Dam. In the grasslands there have been a number of recent sightings of Anteating Chats. Prior to 1990, this species had been recorded only once in Swaziland. Grey Cuckooshrike has seldom been seen in Malolotja but is probably resident in several of the forests. Bush Blackcap has been seen in nearby forests, but has not yet been spotted within the reserve. A nesting site of Cape Vultures on Ngwenya Mountain was abandoned some 30 years ago, but there has been one recent sighting of Cape Vultures in the reserve.

Vincent Parker

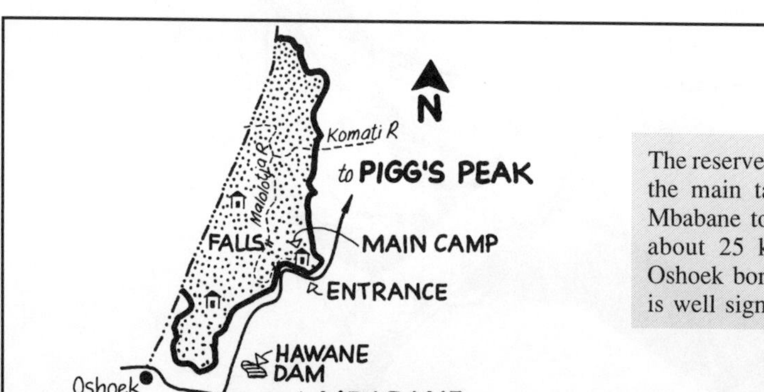

The reserve is situated on the main tar road from Mbabane to Piggs Peak, about 25 km from the Oshoek border post, and is well signposted.

grassland areas. More than 60 birds have been seen at the roosting site in the evening. Other notable species to be found in the montane grassland include **Blue Crane**, **Blackwinged Plover**, **Stanley's Bustard** and **Redwing Francolin**. **Broadtailed Warblers** can be found in rank vegetation associated with vleis in montane grasslands as well as on riverbanks in low-lying valleys. At night the eerie booming call of **Striped Flufftail** is to be heard from the vleis, especially near the main campsite. Those energetic enough to hike into the dense forest may be rewarded with sightings of spectacular forest birds such as **Knysna Lourie**, **Narina Trogon**, **Starred Robin** and **Green Twinspot**. The long, arduous hike up Ngwenya Mountain may be rewarded by views of **Gurney's Sugarbird** in a particularly impressive protea woodland near the summit. The handsome **Jackal Buzzard** is both common and conspicuous. **African Marsh Harrier** is easily spotted around the vleis, and **Redbreasted Sparrowhawk** is occasionally seen hunting over the grasslands. **Crowned Eagles** inhabit the large forests and are most likely to be seen when calling and circling high overhead. **Black Eagles** can be seen around Silotwane Mountain.

51% OF SPECIES

008 Dabchick ☐
058 Reed Cormorant ☐
063 Blackheaded Heron ☐
071 Cattle Egret ☐
081 Hamerkop ☐
083 White Stork ☐
092 **Bald Ibis****** ☐
094 Hadeda Ibis ☐
104 Yellowbilled Duck ☐
105 African Black Duck ☐
116 Spurwinged Goose ☐
118 Secretarybird ☐
126a Yellowbilled Kite ☐
131 **Black Eagle** ☐
141 **Crowned Eagle** ☐
149 Steppe Buzzard ☐
152 **Jackal Buzzard****** ☐
155 **Redbreasted Sparrowhawk** ☐
165 **African Marsh Harrier** ☐
192 **Redwing Francolin** ☐
200 Common Quail ☐
208 **Blue Crane****** ☐
221 **Striped Flufftail** ☐
228 Redknobbed Coot ☐
231 **Stanley's Bustard** ☐
257 **Blackwinged Plover** ☐
260 Wattled Plover ☐
352 Redeyed Dove ☐
354 Cape Turtle Dove ☐
358 Greenspotted Dove ☐
359 Tambourine Dove ☐
361 Green Pigeon ☐
370 **Knysna Lourie****** ☐
377 Redchested Cuckoo ☐
378 Black Cuckoo ☐
385 Klaas's Cuckoo ☐
391 Burchell's Coucal* ☐
416 Horus Swift ☐
417 Little Swift ☐
424 Speckled Mousebird ☐
427 **Narina Trogon** ☐
430 Halfcollared Kingfisher ☐
431 Malachite Kingfisher ☐
435 Brownhooded Kingfisher ☐
444 Little Bee-eater ☐
451 Hoopoe ☐
455 Trumpeter Hornbill ☐
464 Blackcollared Barbet ☐
474 Greater Honeyguide ☐
480 Ground Woodpecker** ☐
483 Goldentailed Woodpecker ☐
486 Cardinal Woodpecker ☐
488 Olive Woodpecker ☐
494 Rufousnaped Lark ☐
518 European Swallow ☐
520 Whitethroated Swallow ☐
521 **Blue Swallow** ☐
526 Greater Striped Swallow* ☐
527 Lesser Striped Swallow ☐
529 Rock Martin ☐

531 Greyrumped Swallow ☐
534 Banded Martin ☐
536 Black Sawwing Swallow ☐
538 Black Cuckooshrike ☐
541 Forktailed Drongo ☐
545 Blackheaded Oriole ☐
547 Black Crow ☐
550 Whitenecked Raven ☐
554 Southern Black Tit* ☐
568 Blackeyed Bulbul ☐
569 Terrestrial Bulbul ☐
572 Sombre Bulbul ☐
576 Kurrichane Thrush ☐
581 Cape Rock Thrush** ☐
588 Buffstreaked Chat** ☐
589 Familiar Chat ☐
593 Mocking Chat ☐
596 Stonechat ☐
598 Chorister Robin** ☐
601 Cape Robin ☐
606 **Starred Robin** ☐
613 Whitebrowed Robin ☐
637 Yellow Warbler ☐
642 **Broadtailed Warbler** ☐
643 Willow Warbler ☐
644 Yellowthroated Warbler ☐
645 Barthroated Apalis ☐
648 Yellowbreasted Apalis ☐
657 Bleating Warbler ☐
661 Grassbird** ☐
667 Ayres' Cisticola ☐
670 Wailing Cisticola ☐
677 Levaillant's Cisticola ☐
678 Croaking Cisticola ☐
679 Lazy Cisticola ☐
681 Neddicky ☐
683 Tawnyflanked Prinia ☐
686a Spotted Prinia** ☐
690 Dusky Flycatcher ☐
691 Bluegrey Flycatcher ☐
694 Black Flycatcher ☐
700 Cape Batis** ☐
708 Bluemantled Flycatcher ☐
710 Paradise Flycatcher ☐
711 African Pied Wagtail ☐
712 Longtailed Wagtail ☐
713 Cape Wagtail ☐
717 Longbilled Pipit ☐
718 Plainbacked Pipit ☐
720 Striped Pipit ☐
727 Orangethroated Longclaw** ☐
728 Yellowthroated Longclaw ☐
732 Fiscal Shrike ☐
736 Southern Boubou** ☐
740 Puffback ☐
744 Blackcrowned Tchagra ☐
746 Bokmakierie* ☐
761 Plumcoloured Starling ☐
769 Redwinged Starling ☐
774 **Gurney's Sugarbird**** ☐
775 Malachite Sunbird ☐
783 Lesser Doublecollared Sunbird** ☐
785 Greater Double-colared Sunbird** ☐
787 Whitebellied Sunbird ☐
792 Black Sunbird ☐
793 Collared Sunbird ☐
796 Cape White-eye** ☐
807 Thickbilled Weaver ☐
810 Spectacled Weaver ☐
813 Cape Weaver** ☐
827 Yellowrumped Widow ☐
828 Redshouldered Widow ☐
831 Redcollared Widow ☐
832 Longtailed Widow ☐
835 **Green Twinspot** ☐
840 Bluebilled Firefinch ☐
846 Common Waxbill ☐
850 Swee Waxbill* ☐
852 Quail Finch ☐
854 Orangebreasted Waxbill ☐
857 Bronze Mannikin ☐
860 Pintailed Whydah ☐
869 Yelloweyed Canary ☐
872 Cape Canary ☐
873 Forest Canary** ☐
881 Streakyheaded Canary ☐
884 Goldenbreasted Bunting ☐
885 Cape Bunting ☐
886 Rock Bunting ☐
☐
☐
☐

MLAWULA NATURE RESERVE

approximately 353 species recorded to date

Mlawula is owned and run by the Swaziland National Trust Commission. Situated in the north-eastern Swaziland lowveld, its 160 square kilometres cover a very diverse area, including part of the Lebombo Mountains. Habitats include thorn and broadleaved savanna, moist and dry forest thickets, extensive riverine zones and a limited amount of grassveld. The wide variety of habitats supports a wealth of bird life. There are two camping sites and a hiking trail system. The checklist includes species recorded at the Simunye settling ponds. Other areas worth visiting include the Simunye Nature Reserve and settling ponds, the Mbuluzi Nature Reserve (on the way to Mlawula Nature Reserve) and the Hlone Game Sanctuary, which has basic hutted accommodation.

SPECIAL AND INTERESTING SPECIES

The dry Lebombo ironwood forests and surrounding thickets are home to a number of local specials, including **African Broadbill**, which are most easily located by call, especially in the early morning and late afternoon; **Blackbellied Starling** is most common in the summer months, and **Pinkthroated Twinspot** is secretive, best located by its tinkling call; **Grey Sunbird** is to be seen at flowering *Schotia* trees and aloes. The large Siphiso valley is a good area to see **Redbilled Helmetshrike,** here near the southern limit of its distribution – again, most easily located by its loud, distinctive call. The dry

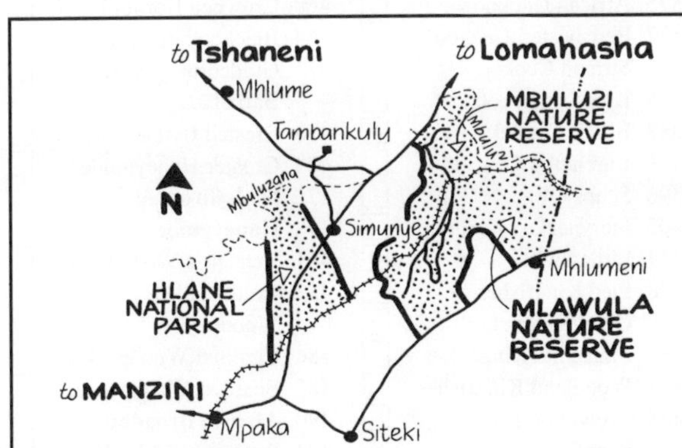

ALSO RECORDED

The several crossings over the Mlawula River are the best places to see White-backed Night Heron at night, and Green Sandpiper by day in summer. A pair of Broad-billed Rollers bred for some years just below the junction of the Mlawula and Mbuluzi rivers. There have been early summer sightings of Grey-hooded Kingfisher in the Siphiso valley. Greencapped Eremomela and Grey Waxbill are occasionally recorded.

James Culverwell

Mlawula Nature Reserve: Ten kilometres north-east of Simunye (Lusoti village) on the Lomahasha road, turn right to Mlawula Nature Reserve and Mlawula Station. The current entrance to the Mbuluzi area is about 1 km from this turnoff along this road.

Simunye Nature Reserve and settling ponds: It is necessary to obtain permission from the Royal Swazi Sugar Corporation first, from whom directions can be obtained. If staying on Mlawula proper, ask the senior warden to arrange permission.

thickets along the Mlawula River are the best places to find **Yellowspotted Nicator** and **Bearded Robin**, more easily found during summer. **Scalythroated Honeyguide** is easily located by its purring call: a number of call sites occur in the southern Siphiso and Mlawula valleys. **Longtailed Wagtail** frequents scattered localities throughout the reserve, particularly the junction of the Mluwula and Mbuluzi rivers and isolated pools in the upper Siphiso valley. Spring burns between the Mbuluzi gate and campground attract numbers of breeding **Lesser Blackwinged Plover**, and in midsummer this is also the preferred habitat of **Black Coucal**, whose "pop-pop" call should be listened for. Seedeaters such as **Swee Waxbill** and **Redbacked Mannikin** may be found feeding in the swards of *Panicum* grass. The wet summer months are a good time to find the elusive **African Crake** along the track from the Mbuluzi gate to the Mbuluzi campsite. The Mlawula and Mbuluzi rivers support a number of **African Finfoot**, which are fairly often seen.

38% OF SPECIES

058 Reed Cormorant ☐
062 Grey Heron ☐
074 Greenbacked Heron ☐
081 Hamerkop ☐
084 Black Stork ☐
089 Marabou Stork ☐
094 Hadeda Ibis ☐
099 Whitefaced Duck ☐
102 Egyptian Goose ☐
105 African Black Duck ☐
123 Whitebacked Vulture ☐
135 Wahlberg's Eagle ☐
141 Crowned Eagle ☐
148 African Fish Eagle ☐
154 Lizard Buzzard ☐
169 Gymnogene ☐
189 Crested Francolin ☐
196 Natal Francolin* ☐
203 Helmeted Guineafowl ☐
204 Crested Guineafowl ☐
212 **African Crake** ☐
213 Black Crake ☐
229 **African Finfoot** ☐
238 Blackbellied Korhaan ☐
240 African Jacana ☐
249 Threebanded Plover ☐
256 **Lesser Blackwinged Plover** ☐
264 Common Sandpiper ☐
266 Wood Sandpiper ☐
284 Ruff ☐
352 Redeyed Dove ☐
354 Cape Turtle Dove ☐
358 Greenspotted Dove ☐
359 Tambourine Dove ☐
361 Green Pigeon ☐
371 Purplecrested Lourie ☐
375 African Cuckoo ☐
377 Redchested Cuckoo ☐
381 Striped Cuckoo ☐
385 Klaas's Cuckoo ☐
388 **Black Coucal** ☐
391 Burchell's Coucal* ☐
396 Scops Owl ☐
405 Fierynecked Nightjar ☐
417 Little Swift ☐
428 Pied Kingfisher ☐
429 Giant Kingfisher ☐
431 Malachite Kingfisher ☐
433 Woodland Kingfisher ☐
435 Brownhooded Kingfisher ☐
437 Striped Kingfisher ☐
438 European Bee-eater ☐
446 European Roller ☐
451 Hoopoe ☐
452 Redbilled Woodhoopoe ☐
454 Scimitarbilled Woodhoopoe ☐
455 Trumpeter Hornbill ☐
457 Grey Hornbill ☐
459 Southern Yellowbilled Hornbill* ☐
460 Crowned Hornbill ☐
464 Blackcollared Barbet ☐
471 Goldenrumped Tinker Barbet ☐
473 Crested Barbet ☐
474 Greater Honeyguide ☐
475 **Scalythroated Honeyguide** ☐
481 Bennett's Woodpecker ☐
483 Goldentailed Woodpecker ☐
486 Cardinal Woodpecker ☐
487 Bearded Woodpecker ☐
490 **African Broadbill** ☐
494 Rufousnaped Lark ☐

496 Flappet Lark ☐
518 European Swallow ☐
527 Lesser Striped Swallow ☐
529 Rock Martin ☐
531 Forktailed Drongo ☐
542 Squaretailed Drongo ☐
545 Blackheaded Oriole ☐
548 Pied Crow ☐
550 Whitenecked Raven ☐
554 Southern Black Tit* ☐
560 Arrowmarked Babbler ☐
568 Blackeyed Bulbul ☐
569 Terrestrial Bulbul ☐
572 Sombre Bulbul ☐
575 **Yellowspotted Nicator** ☐
576 Kurrichane Thrush ☐
599 Heuglin's Robin ☐
613 Whitebrowed Robin ☐
617 **Bearded Robin** ☐
648 Yellowbreasted Apalis ☐
651 Longbilled Crombec ☐
657 Bleating Warbler ☐
672 Rattling Cisticola ☐
674 Redfaced Cisticola ☐
678 Croaking Cisticola ☐
683 Tawnyflanked Prinia ☐
694 Black Flycatcher ☐
701 Chinspot Batis ☐
710 Paradise Flycatcher ☐
711 African Pied Wagtail ☐
712 **Longtailed Wagtail** ☐
723 Bushveld Pipit ☐
728 Yellowthroated Longclaw ☐
733 Redbacked Shrike ☐
736 Southern Boubou** ☐
740 Puffback ☐
741 Brubru ☐
743 Threestreaked Tchagra ☐
744 Blackcrowned Tchagra ☐
748 Orangebreasted Bush Shrike ☐
751 Greyheaded Bush Shrike ☐
753 White Helmetshrike ☐
754 **Redbilled Helmetshrike** ☐
761 Plumcoloured Starling ☐
764 Glossy Starling* ☐
768 **Blackbellied Starling** ☐
769 Redwinged Starling ☐
772 Redbilled Oxpecker ☐
787 Whitebellied Sunbird ☐
789 **Grey Sunbird** ☐
791 Scarletchested Sunbird ☐
793 Collared Sunbird ☐
796 Cape White-eye** ☐
805 Yellowthroated Sparrow ☐
810 Spectacled Weaver ☐
811 Spottedbacked Weaver ☐
814 Masked Weaver ☐
829 Whitewinged Widow ☐
831 Redcollared Widow ☐
838 **Pinkthroated Twinspot**** ☐
841 Jameson's Firefinch ☐
844 Blue Waxbill ☐
846 Common Waxbill ☐
850 **Swee Waxbill*** ☐
857 Bronze Mannikin ☐
858 **Redbacked Mannikin** ☐
860 Pintailed Whydah ☐
869 Yelloweyed Canary ☐
884 Goldenbreasted Bunting ☐
☐

OTHER BIRDING SPOTS WORTH VISITING

Muti-Muti Nature Reserve
This reserve lies immediately south of Siteki on the road to Mbabane. The entrance is at the radio tower. The reserve contains forests and thornveld on a mountainside.

Sifunga Dam
Situated about 15 km north of Big Bend on the road past the sugar mill. This is an excellent site for waterbirds.

USEFUL TELEPHONE NUMBERS

Malolotja Nature Reserve
(09268) 4-3060

Mlawula
(09268) 3-8239

Phophonyane Nature Reserve
(09268) 7-1319

Swaziland National Trust Commission
(reservations) (09268) 6-1179

7 Orange Free State

Co-ordinator Deon du Plessis

1 Sandveld Nature Reserve (Bloemhof Dam)
2 O.F.S. Goldfields
3 Willem Pretorius Game Reserve and Resort
4 Golden Gate Highlands National Park
5 Tussen-die-Riviere Game Farm

SANDVELD NATURE RESERVE (BLOEMHOF DAM)

approximately 247 species recorded to date

Sandveld Nature Reserve, on the shores of the Bloemhof Dam, is administered by the Orange Free State Nature Conservation. This reserve was established to create a buffer zone along the Bloemhof Dam and to conserve the seriously depleted Kalahari thornveld protruding into the north-western Orange Free State. Here, at the confluence of the Vaal and Vet rivers, Kalahari thornveld with its magnificent *Acacia erioloba* (camel thorn) trees meets the Orange Free State grasslands, creating probably the richest diversity of avifauna found anywhere in this province. Camping facilities with electricity are available at Reserve Headquarters.

SPECIAL AND INTERESTING SPECIES

The Kalahari thornveld supports some very unlikely Orange Free State species. The huge camel thorn trees are used by **Sociable Weavers** in which to build their bulky nests and some of these chambers may be occupied by **Pygmy Falcon**. These trees are also utilised by a small colony of **Whitebacked Vultures** as nesting platforms, and both **Southern Yellowbilled Hornbill** and **Longtailed Shrike** are present. The Acacia woodland north and south of the campsite supports a wide variety of species including the brillantly coloured **Crimsonbreasted Boubou**. **Kalahari Robin**, **Titbabbler** and **Marico Flycatcher** are common. **Ashy Tit**,

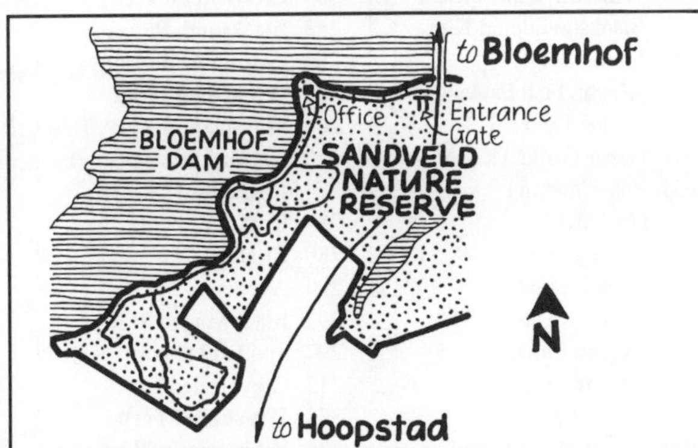

ALSO RECORDED

Some of the few records in the Orange Free State of Chestnutbanded Plover, Palm Swift and Goldentailed Woodpecker come from this area and this reserve is one of the best places where Gabar Goshawk still occurs. On large dead trees near the dam wall African Fish Eagle can be seen and Osprey has been recorded. Black Eagle, Squacco and Goliath Herons and African Jacana can be seen along the banks on the upper reaches of the dam.

Deon du Plessis

West of Welkom, take the Hoopstad-Bloemhof tarred road. The controlled entrance is on the Hoopstad side of the bridge across the Bloemhof Dam (Vaal River). From the gate follow the dirt road to Reserve Headquarters about 3 km away. The best Kalahari thornveld can be found in the game area, where additional entrance fees must be paid. Excellent birding can be had along the riverine bush around Reserve Headquarters and near the angling areas further upstream.

Willow Warbler, **Longbilled Crombec**, **Pririt Batis**, **Rattling Cisticola**, **Redbacked Shrike**, **Brubru** and **Threestreaked Tchagra** are among the thornveld species not difficult to find. Colourful seedeaters such as **Blue**, **Violeteared** and **Blackcheeked Waxbills** and **Redbilled Firefinch** frequent the thickets, while **Scalyfeathered Finch**, **Pintailed**, **Shafttailed** and **Paradise Whydahs** are found in more open bush. In the camp area and its surroundings, **Groundscraper Thrush**, **Glossy Starling**, **Whitebrowed Sparrowweaver** and **Yellow Canary** can be seen. The grasslands, created by the removal of thornbush, are home to **Whitequilled Korhaan**, **Redcapped Lark** and **Anteating Chat**. For waterbirds one should walk from the bridge to the fence in the east. Other than the normal quota of grebe, cormorant and duck, flocks of **Greater** and **Lesser Flamingos** can be seen flying past, while **Whitewinged** and, to a lesser extent, **Whiskered Terns** fish and hawk insects over the water and grassland. **Kittlitz's** and **Threebanded Plovers** are regular breeding species, while Palaearctic waders such as **Little Stint**, **Ruff**, **Greenshank**, **Curlew**, and **Common**, **Marsh** and **Wood Sandpipers** visit the dam in large numbers.

60% OF SPECIES

- 006 Great Crested Grebe ☐
- 008 Dabchick ☐
- 055 Whitebreasted Cormorant ☐
- 058 Reed Cormorant ☐
- 060 Darter ☐
- 062 Grey Heron ☐
- 063 Blackheaded Heron ☐
- 064 Goliath Heron ☐
- 066 Great White Egret ☐
- 067 Little Egret ☐
- 071 Cattle Egret ☐
- 072 Squacco Heron ☐
- 076 Blackcrowned Night Heron ☐
- 090 Yellowbilled Stork ☐
- 091 Sacred Ibis ☐
- 094 Hadeda Ibis ☐
- 095 African Spoonbill ☐
- 096 **Greater Flamingo** ☐
- 097 **Lesser Flamingo** ☐
- 099 Whitefaced Duck ☐
- 102 Egyptian Goose ☐
- 103 South African Shelduck** ☐
- 104 Yellowbilled Duck ☐
- 106 Cape Teal ☐
- 108 Redbilled Teal ☐
- 112 Cape Shoveller* ☐
- 116 Spurwinged Goose ☐
- 118 Secretarybird ☐
- 123 **Whitebacked Vulture** ☐
- 127 Blackshouldered Kite ☐
- 140 Martial Eagle ☐
- 148 African Fish Eagle ☐
- 149 Steppe Buzzard ☐
- 161 Gabar Goshawk ☐
- 162 Pale Chanting Goshawk* ☐
- 170 Osprey ☐
- 181 Rock Kestrel ☐
- 183 Lesser Kestrel ☐
- 186 **Pygmy Falcon** ☐
- 193 Orange River Francolin* ☐
- 199 Swainson's Francolin* ☐
- 203 Helmeted Guineafowl ☐
- 228 Redknobbed Coot ☐
- 230 Kori Bustard ☐
- 237 Redcrested Korhaan* ☐
- 239a **Whitequilled Korhaan**** ☐
- 248 **Kittlitz's Plover** ☐
- 249 **Threebanded Plover** ☐
- 255 Crowned Plover ☐
- 258 Blacksmith Plover ☐
- 264 **Common Sandpiper** ☐
- 266 **Wood Sandpiper** ☐
- 269 **Marsh Sandpiper** ☐
- 270 **Greenshank** ☐
- 274 **Little Stint** ☐
- 284 **Ruff** ☐
- 289 **Curlew** ☐
- 294 Avocet ☐
- 295 Blackwinged Stilt ☐
- 297 Spotted Dikkop ☐
- 315 Greyheaded Gull ☐
- 338 **Whiskered Tern** ☐
- 339 **Whitewinged Tern** ☐

349 Rock Pigeon
352 Redeyed Dove
354 Cape Turtle Dove
355 Laughing Dove
356 Namaqua Dove
382 Jacobin Cuckoo
386 Diederik Cuckoo
415 Whiterumped Swift
417 Little Swift
425 Whitebacked Mousebird**
426 Redfaced Mousebird
428 Pied Kingfisher
429 Giant Kingfisher
431 Malachite Kingfisher
435 Brownhooded Kingfisher
438 European Bee-eater
443 Whitefronted Bee-eater
447 Lilacbreasted Roller
451 Hoopoe
454 Scimitarbilled Woodhoopoe
457 Grey Hornbill
459 **Southern Yellow-billed Hornbill***
465 Pied Barbet*
473 Crested Barbet
486 Cardinal Woodpecker
494 Rufousnaped Lark
495 Clapper Lark**
498 Sabota Lark*
506 Spikeheeled Lark*
507 **Redcapped Lark**
518 European Swallow
520 Whitethroated Swallow
524 Redbreasted Swallow
526 Greater Striped Swallow*
528 South African Cliff Swallow**
533 Brownthroated Martin
541 Forktailed Drongo
552 **Ashy Tit***
567 Redeyed Bulbul*
577 Olive Thrush
580 **Groundscraper Thrush**
595 **Anteating Chat****
596 Stonechat
601 Cape Robin
615 **Kalahari Robin***
621 **Titbabbler***
643 **Willow Warbler**
651 **Longbilled Crombec**
664 Fantailed Cisticola
672 **Rattling Cisticola**
677 Levaillant's Cisticola
681 Neddicky
685 Blackchested Prinia*
695 **Marico Flycatcher***
698 Fiscal Flycatcher**
703 **Pririt Batis***
706 Fairy Flycatcher**
713 Cape Wagtail
716 Grassveld Pipit
727 Orangethroated Longclaw**
731 Lesser Grey Shrike
732 Fiscal Shrike
733 **Redbacked Shrike**
735 **Longtailed Shrike**
739 **Crimsonbreasted Boubou***
741 **Brubru**
743 **Threestreaked Tchagra**
746 Bokmakierie*
760 Wattled Starling
764 **Glossy Starling***
796 Cape White-eye**
799 **Whitebrowed Sparrowweaver**
800 **Sociable Weaver****
801 House Sparrow
803 Cape Sparrow*
804 Greyheaded Sparrow
806 **Scalyfeathered Finch***
814 Masked Weaver
824 Red Bishop
832 Longtailed Widow
834 Melba Finch
842 **Redbilled Firefinch**
844 **Blue Waxbill**
845 **Violeteared Waxbill***
847 **Blackcheeked Waxbill**
852 Quail Finch
856 Redheaded Finch*
860 **Pintailed Whydah**
861 **Shafttailed Whydah***
862 **Paradise Whydah**
870 Blackthroated Canary
878 **Yellow Canary***

O.F.S. GOLDFIELDS

approximately 263 species recorded to date

The Goldfields are situated in the central Orange Free State, approximately 270 km from Johannesburg on the main Cape route, 570 km from Durban and 150 km from Bloemfontein. Two major towns around which the wetlands occur are Welkom and Virginia. This area is rich in bird life because of its diversity of habitats: large open pans, smaller pans, reed-filled pans, vleis, grasslands, Acacia thornveld and riverine bush. Accommodation is available at a number of local hotels and for caravanners and campers there are caravan parks in Virginia (on river banks) and in Welkom.

SPECIAL AND INTERESTING SPECIES

Interesting species occurring in the bush areas and along the river are **Crimsonbreasted Boubou** (listen for its call), **Whitefronted Bee-eater** (large colonies in the banks), **Threestreaked Tchagra**, **Paradise Flycatcher**, **Karoo** and **Kalahari Robins**, **African Black Duck**, **Greater** and **Lesser Honeyguides**. **Gabar Goshawk**, **Violeteared** and **Blackcheeked Waxbills**, **Paradise** and **Shafttailed Whydahs**, **Steelblue Widowfinch**, **Melba** and **Scalyfeathered Finches**. **Goliath** and **Purple Herons** are quite common. **Little Bittern** and **Squacco Heron** are to be seen in the bullrushes. **Blackcrowned Night Herons** are common in the willow trees along the riverbanks. **Lanner Falcon** may be seen flying overhead. Four species of kingfishers commonly

All areas are accessible to the general public except for the Virginia Nature Reserve where visits can be arranged by contacting the Parks and Recreation Department. For larger groups birdwatching trips on the river can be undertaken on a motorised raft at minimal cost. For bookings contact the Parks and Recreation Department, Virginia Municipality. The Goldfields Bird Club sanctuary is entered through a gate adjacent to the Theronia sewage works main gate. The sanctuary consists of a number of water areas. Walk past the first large pan, follow the path to the smaller reed-filled pan, where large numbers of birds congregate. For other walks, see map. Two official nature trails exist, one in Virginia and the other in Welkom. Pans worth visiting are Rietpan, Witpan and St Hele-

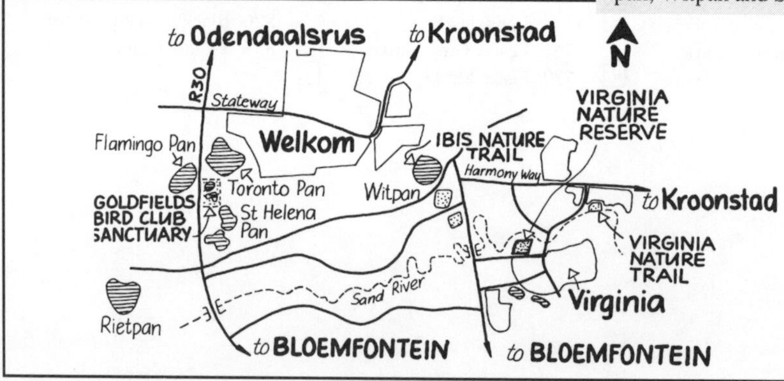

seen are **Giant**, **Malachite**, **Brownhooded** and **Pied**. Duck species of interest around the pans are **Fulvous Duck**, **Hottentot Teal** and **Maccoa Duck**. Large numbers of migrant waders occur during the summer, including **Wood**, **Marsh** and **Curlew Sandpipers**, **Ruff**, **Greenshank**, **Ringed** and **Chestnutbanded Plovers**. **Blackwinged Stilt** and **Avocet** are common. **Glossy Ibis** is a common breeding resident. Small groups of **Lesser Flamingo** as well as small numbers of **Greater Flamingo** can be seen at St Helena and Rietpan. Numbers fluctuate because of water depth and availability of food. **Ethiopian Snipe** occur on the reed perimeters as do large numbers of **Purple Gallinule**. **African Jacana** are now resident in some areas.

62% OF SPECIES

- 001 Ostrich ☐
- 006 Great Crested Grebe ☐
- 007 Blacknecked Grebe ☐
- 008 Dabchick ☐
- 055 Whitebreasted Cormorant ☐
- 058 Reed Cormorant ☐
- 060 Darter ☐
- 062 Grey Heron ☐
- 063 Blackheaded Heron ☐
- 064 **Goliath Heron** ☐
- 065 **Purple Heron** ☐
- 066 Great White Egret ☐
- 067 Little Egret ☐
- 071 Cattle Egret ☐
- 072 **Squacco Heron** ☐
- 076 **Blackcrowned Night Heron** ☐
- 078 **Little Bittern** ☐
- 081 Hamerkop ☐
- 093 **Glossy Ibis** ☐
- 094 Hadeda Ibis ☐
- 095 African Spoonbill ☐
- 096 **Greater Flamingo** ☐
- 097 **Lesser Flamingo** ☐
- 099 Whitefaced Duck ☐
- 100 **Fulvous Duck** ☐
- 101 Whitebacked Duck ☐
- 102 Egyptian Goose ☐
- 103 South African Shelduck** ☐
- 104 Yellowbilled Duck ☐
- 105 **African Black Duck** ☐
- 106 Cape Teal ☐
- 107 **Hottentot Teal** ☐
- 108 Redbilled Teal ☐
- 112 Cape Shoveller* ☐
- 113 Southern Pochard ☐
- 116 Spurwinged Goose ☐
- 117 **Maccoa Duck** ☐
- 127 Blackshouldered Kite ☐
- 161 **Gabar Goshawk** ☐
- 172 **Lanner Falcon** ☐
- 183 Lesser Kestrel ☐
- 199 Swainson's Francolin* ☐
- 203 Helmeted Guineafowl ☐
- 223 **Purple Gallinule** ☐
- 226 Moorhen ☐
- 228 Redknobbed Coot ☐
- 239a Whitequilled Korhaan** ☐
- 240 **African Jacana** ☐
- 245 **Ringed Plover** ☐
- 247 **Chestnutbanded Plover** ☐
- 248 Kittlitz's Plover ☐
- 249 Threebanded Plover ☐
- 255 Crowned Plover ☐
- 258 Blacksmith Plover ☐
- 264 Common Sandpiper ☐
- 266 **Wood Sandpiper** ☐
- 269 **Marsh Sandpiper** ☐

na pan plus the vlei areas between the pans. The reed-filled pans in Virginia are worth a visit, as well as the vlei area in the Virginia Nature Reserve.

ALSO RECORDED

On the river Greenbacked and Rufousbellied Herons have been sighted. Redthroated Wryneck have established themselves at Virginia Park. Redbilled Woodhoopoe and Redbreasted Swallows are occasional visitors. In the grasslands Kurrichane Buttonquail have been found. On the pans regular sightings of European Marsh Harrier have recently been made. Booted Eagle has been seen from the Goldfields Bird Club sanctuary. Turnstone and Great Crested Grebe have also been recorded.

John and Debbie Wesson

Orange Free State

- 270 **Greenshank** ☐
- 272 **Curlew Sandpiper** ☐
- 274 Little Stint ☐
- 284 **Ruff** ☐
- 286 **Ethiopian Snipe** ☐
- 294 **Avocet** ☐
- 295 **Blackwinged Stilt** ☐
- 297 Spotted Dikkop ☐
- 301 Doublebanded Courser ☐
- 315 Greyheaded Gull ☐
- 338 Whiskered Tern ☐
- 339 Whitewinged Tern ☐
- 349 Rock Pigeon ☐
- 352 Redeyed Dove ☐
- 354 Cape Turtle Dove ☐
- 355 Laughing Dove ☐
- 356 Namaqua Dove ☐
- 377 Redchested Cuckoo ☐
- 380 Great Spotted Cuckoo ☐
- 382 Jacobin Cuckoo ☐
- 386 Diederik Cuckoo ☐
- 415 Whiterumped Swift ☐
- 417 Little Swift ☐
- 425 Whitebacked Mousebird** ☐
- 426 Redfaced Mousebird ☐
- 428 **Pied Kingfisher** ☐
- 429 **Giant Kingfisher** ☐
- 431 **Malachite Kingfisher** ☐
- 435 **Brownhooded Kingfisher** ☐
- 438 European Bee-eater ☐
- 443 **Whitefronted Bee-eater** ☐
- 454 Scimitarbilled Woodhoopoe ☐
- 465 Pied Barbet* ☐
- 473 Crested Barbet ☐
- 474 **Greater Honeyguide** ☐
- 476 **Lesser Honeyguide** ☐
- 486 Cardinal Woodpecker ☐
- 489 Redthroated Wryneck ☐
- 494 Rufousnaped Lark ☐
- 506 Spikeheeled Lark* ☐
- 507 Redcapped Lark ☐
- 516 Greybacked Finchlark* ☐
- 518 European Swallow ☐
- 520 Whitethroated Swallow ☐
- 526 Greater Striped Swallow* ☐
- 528 South African Cliff Swallow** ☐
- 529 Rock Martin ☐
- 532 Sand Martin ☐
- 533 Brownthroated Martin ☐
- 548 Pied Crow ☐
- 552 Ashy Tit* ☐
- 567 Redeyed Bulbul* ☐
- 577 Olive Thrush ☐
- 580 Groundscraper Thrush ☐
- 586 Mountain Chat* ☐
- 589 Familiar Chat ☐
- 595 Anteating Chat** ☐
- 596 Stonechat ☐
- 601 Cape Robin ☐
- 614 **Karoo Robin**** ☐
- 615 **Kalahari Robin*** ☐
- 621 Titbabbler* ☐
- 631 African Marsh Warbler ☐
- 651 Longbilled Crombec ☐
- 677 Levaillant's Cisticola ☐
- 681 Neddicky ☐
- 685 Blackchested Prinia* ☐
- 698 Fiscal Flycatcher** ☐
- 710 **Paradise Flycatcher** ☐
- 713 Cape Wagtail ☐
- 716 Grassveld Pipit ☐
- 727 Orangethroated Longclaw** ☐
- 732 Fiscal Shrike ☐
- 733 Redbacked Shrike ☐
- 739 **Crimsonbreasted Boubou*** ☐
- 743 **Threestreaked Tchagra** ☐
- 746 Bokmakierie* ☐
- 759 Pied Starling** ☐
- 760 Wattled Starling ☐
- 764 Glossy Starling* ☐
- 769 Redwinged Starling ☐
- 775 Malachite Sunbird ☐
- 787 Whitebellied Sunbird ☐
- 796 Cape White-eye** ☐
- 801 House Sparrow ☐
- 803 Cape Sparrow* ☐
- 804 Greyheaded Sparrow ☐
- 806 **Scalyfeathered Finch*** ☐
- 814 Masked Weaver ☐
- 821 Redbilled Quelea ☐
- 824 Red Bishop ☐
- 826 Golden Bishop ☐
- 832 Longtailed Widow ☐
- 834 **Melba Finch** ☐
- 842 Redbilled Firefinch ☐
- 844 Blue Waxbill ☐
- 845 **Violeteared Waxbill*** ☐
- 846 Common Waxbill ☐
- 847 **Blackcheeked Waxbill** ☐
- 852 Quail Finch ☐
- 854 Orangebreasted Waxbill ☐
- 856 Redheaded Finch* ☐
- 860 Pintailed Whydah ☐
- 861 **Shafttailed Whydah*** ☐
- 862 **Paradise Whydah** ☐
- 867 **Steelblue Widowfinch** ☐
- 870 Blackthroated Canary ☐
- 878 Yellow Canary* ☐
- 885 Cape Bunting ☐
- 886 Rock Bunting ☐

WILLEM PRETORIUS GAME RESERVE AND RESORT

approximately 198 species recorded to date

The Allemanskraal Dam is surrounded by the 9 311 ha Willem Pretorius Game Reserve. The area consists of four distinct habitats:

- The area around the rondawels, situated on a hill overlooking the dam, with extensive plantings of aloes on some of the slopes below the rondawels.
- The dam, islands and shoreline.
- Hills with well-wooded gorges, consisting mainly of *Celtis africana, Rhus lancea, Ziziphus mucronata* and *Olea africana.*
- Mixed Acacia thornveld, grassland.

Accommodation is available in the resort. Facilities include rondawels, bungalows and a large caravan park. The game reserve gates open at 07h00 and close at 18h00 (enquire at office). Care must be taken when driving up the gravel roads into the hills after rain.

ALSO RECORDED

Uncommon species occurring from time to time are Black Harrier, Tawny Eagle, Lilacbreasted Roller, Bronzewinged Courser and Lesser Grey Shrike. Temminck's and Burchell's Coursers have been recorded from the dry open areas, and Namaqua Sandgrouse have been seen and heard in flight.

John and Debbie Wesson

SPECIAL AND INTERESTING SPECIES

- *In and around the camp and rondawels*: **Mocking** and **Mountain Chats** are often found in the rock garden or around the restaurant. **Malachite** and **Whitebellied Sunbirds** can be seen when the aloes are in flower (winter). Among the rocks one will find **Cape** and **Rock Buntings** with **Yellow Canaries** frequenting the weeds and grass fringes. **Redwinged**

The dam and the game reserve are situated 10 km off the N1 highway between Kroonstad and Bloemfontein, about 30 km north of Winburg. The reserve is approximately 280 km from Johannesburg and 30 km from Virginia and the Goldfields.

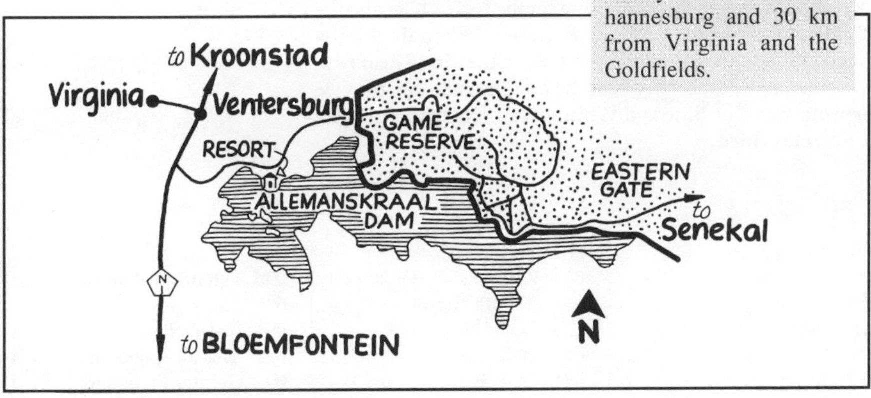

Starlings are usually active around the camp while **Alpine Swifts** can be seen flying overhead.

• *The dam* can be approached from the resort side but it is busy over weekends and holidays. The best time is early morning and late afternoon when a drive along the edge will provide views of **African Spoonbill**, **Darter**, **Goliath Heron**, **Yellowbilled Stork** (summer) and **African Fish Eagle**. In patches of seeding grass one can see small flocks of **Common Waxbill**; **Whitebrowed Sparrowweaver** is abundant in this area. The islands, with species such as **South African Shelduck**, are best seen from the restaurant. Drive up from the dam past the caravan park and take the gravel road to the reserve. On the way look out for **Spikeheeled** and **Rufousnaped Larks**, as well as **Swainson's Francolin**.

• Once in the game reserve, drive up into *the hills* by turning right at the T-junction. Magnificent views can be obtained of the plains and dam below, as well as of the wooded gorges. There is a lookout point on top of one of these hills. Here and in the wooded areas are **Cape Canary**, **Jacobin**, **Redchested** and **Great Spotted Cuckoos**. **Sabota Lark** can be found on the Acacia fringe. **Black** and **Martial Eagles** are also seen in this area.

• *Open plains, Acacia thornveld and grassland*: While driving through this area **Redcapped Lark** and **Quail Finch** are quite common in the grassy plains. In areas where the grass is short, look out for **Doublebanded Courser**. On the edge of the shoreline look for **Kittlitz's** and **Threebanded Plovers**, as well as migrant waders such as **Curlew** and **Wood Sandpipers**. **Greater Flamingo** and **Goliath Heron** (normally solitary) may be found. During summer there is an influx of **Redbacked Shrikes** to these areas, as well as a few **European Rollers**. The **Bokmakierie** is the most striking of the shrike species occurring in the area (listen for the call). Other species of interest occurring here are **Paradise Whydah**, **Melba Finch**, **Violeteared Waxbill** and **Pale Chanting Goshawk**. The grasslands, especially near the eastern gate, can provide one with views of **Blue** and **Whitequiled Korhaans** as well as **Secretarybird**.

73% OF SPECIES

001 Ostrich ☐
008 Dabchick ☐
055 Whitebreasted Cormorant ☐
058 Reed Cormorant ☐
060 **Darter** ☐
062 Grey Heron ☐
063 Blackheaded Heron ☐
064 **Goliath Heron** ☐
066 Great White Egret ☐
067 Little Egret ☐
071 Cattle Egret ☐
081 Hamerkop ☐
090 **Yellowbilled Stork** ☐
091 Sacred Ibis ☐
094 Hadeda Ibis ☐
095 **African Spoonbill** ☐
096 **Greater Flamingo** ☐

099 Whitefaced Duck
102 Egyptian Goose
103 **South African Shelduck****
104 Yellowbilled Duck
116 Spurwinged Goose
118 **Secretarybird**
126a Yellowbilled Kite
131 **Black Eagle**
140 **Martial Eagle**
148 **African Fish Eagle**
161 Gabar Goshawk
162 **Pale Chanting Goshawk***
181 Rock Kestrel
182 Greater Kestrel
183 Lesser Kestrel
196 Natal Francolin*
199 **Swainson's Francolin***
203 Helmeted Guineafowl
226 Moorhen
228 Redknobbed Coot
234 **Blue Korhaan****
239a **Whitequilled Korhaan****
248 **Kittlitz's Plover**
249 **Threebanded Plover**
255 Crowned Plover
258 Blacksmith Plover
264 Common Sandpiper
266 **Wood Sandpiper**
270 Greenshank
272 **Curlew Sandpiper**
274 Little Stint
284 Ruff
295 Blackwinged Stilt
297 Spotted Dikkop
301 **Doublebanded Courser**
315 Greyheaded Gull
338 Whiskered Tern
339 Whitewinged Tern
349 Rock Pigeon
352 Redeyed Dove
354 Cape Turtle Dove
355 Laughing Dove
356 Namaqua Dove
377 **Redchested Cuckoo**
380 **Great Spotted Cuckoo**
382 **Jacobin Cuckoo**
386 Diederik Cuckoo
415 Whiterumped Swift
417 Little Swift
418 **Alpine Swift**
425 Whitebacked Mousebird**
426 Redfaced Mousebird
428 Pied Kingfisher
438 European Bee-eater
443 Whitefronted Bee-eater
446 **European Roller**
454 Scimitarbilled Woodhoopoe
465 Pied Barbet*
473 Crested Barbet
476 Lesser Honeyguide
486 Cardinal Woodpecker
489 Redthroated Wryneck
494 **Rufousnaped Lark**
498 **Sabota Lark***
506 **Spikeheeled Lark***
507 **Redcapped Lark**
516 Greybacked Finchlark*
518 European Swallow
520 Whitethroated Swallow
526 Greater Striped Swallow*
528 South African Cliff Swallow**
532 Sand Martin
533 Brownthroated Martin
552 Ashy Tit*
567 Redeyed Bulbul*
577 Olive Thrush
586 **Mountain Chat***
589 Familiar Chat
593 **Mocking Chat**
595 Anteating Chat**
596 Stonechat
601 Cape Robin
615 Kalahari Robin*
621 Titbabbler*
651 Longbilled Crombec
677 Levaillant's Cisticola
681 Neddicky
685 Blackchested Prinia*
698 Fiscal Flycatcher**
713 Cape Wagtail
716 Grassveld Pipit
727 Orangethroated Longclaw**
732 Fiscal Shrike
733 **Redbacked Shrike**
743 Threestreaked Tchagra
746 **Bokmakierie***
759 Pied Starling**
760 Wattled Starling
764 Glossy Starling*
769 **Redwinged Starling**
775 **Malachite Sunbird**
787 **Whitebellied Sunbird**
796 Cape White-eye**
799 **Whitebrowed Sparrowweaver**
801 House Sparrow
803 Cape Sparrow*
804 Greyheaded Sparrow
806 Scalyfeathered Finch*
814 Masked Weaver
821 Redbilled Quelea
824 Red Bishop
826 Golden Bishop
832 Longtailed Widow
834 **Melba Finch**
842 Redbilled Firefinch
844 Blue Waxbill
845 **Violeteared Waxbill***
846 **Common Waxbill**
852 **Quail Finch**
856 Redheaded Finch*
860 Pintailed Whydah
861 Shafttailed Whydah*
862 **Paradise Whydah**
867 Steelblue Widowfinch
870 Blackthroated Canary
872 **Cape Canary**
878 **Yellow Canary***
885 **Cape Bunting**
886 **Rock Bunting**

GOLDEN GATE HIGHLANDS NATIONAL PARK

approximately 150 species recorded to date

The Golden Gate Highlands National Park in the eastern Orange Free State is the only national park in this province. It has recently been expanded to 11 630 ha and now borders on Qwa-Qwa in the east and Lesotho in the south. The camp at Glen Reenen consists of a campsite, caravan park and rondawels, while the Brandwag section provides more luxurious accommodation in the form of fully equipped chalets and hotel rooms. Hiking trails crisscross the park and the two-day Ribbok Hiking Trail offers overnight facilities. The predominant vegetation can be described as montane grassland; the altitude ranges from 1 800 m to 2 837 m above sea level. Not many species can survive the harsh climate in winter, but magnificent sandstone cliffs, patches of montane forest and numerous streams add a welcome variety to the grass-covered hills.

SPECIAL AND INTERESTING SPECIES

Bald Ibis breed at two sites and a guided tour to the Cathedral Cave breeding cliffs can be arranged. Always keep an eye on the sky for **Cape Vulture**, **Bearded Vulture**, **Black Eagle** and **Jackal Buzzard** – the first, unfortunately, no longer breeds here. **Black Crow** and **Whitenecked Raven** are often seen performing aerial acrobatics. Golden Gate is a very good locality to get to know the swifts. The crevices in the rock

ALSO RECORDED

Barratt's Warbler was first recorded in the O.F.S. in 1987 in the scrub just below Echo Cave. The most likely owl to be heard at night is the Cape Eagle Owl: at least four pairs are resident in the park. Black Harriers often visit the park in summer and autumn. The recently acquired eastern section of the park contains good patches of montane forest and unlikely forest species (for the O.F.S.) such as Rameron Pigeon, Bush Blackcap and Cape Batis can be found there.

Deon du Plessis

The park can be approached on a tarred road from Clarens, which lies on the Bethlehem-Fouriesburg road. Gravel roads (not always recommended for caravans) also link the park to Kestell and Witsieshoek. Entrance to the park is free.

faces of the cliffs are used by **Alpine**, **Black** and **Whiterumped Swifts** for roosting and breeding. **Horus Swifts** breed in the roadside banks along the game viewing drive. **Greywing Francolin** are not uncommon along this drive. Typical montane species such as **Buffstreaked Chat**, **Wailing Cisticola** and **Rock Pipit** may be found on the rocky slopes, while **Sentinel Rock Thrush** and **Orangebreasted Rockjumper** frequent the highest mountain tops. Small groups of **Ground Woodpeckers** can be found in boulder-strewn areas. Keep a lookout for **Redbreasted Sparrowhawk** in the clumps of poplar trees at the Glen Reenen caravan park. The vlei along the main road between Glen Reenen and the information centre is the favourite habitat of many bishops, widows and weavers. Take care not to confuse the **Golden Bishop** with the **Yellowrumped Widow**. **Cape Rock Thrush** perch on the Glen Reenen rondawel roofs while **Rock Pigeon** and **Redwinged Starling** frequent both cliffs and buildings, and noisy groups of **Pied Starlings** can be seen everywhere. In spring and early summer the **Redchested Cuckoo** is more often heard than seen, while a flash of orange along the wooded streams gives the **Paradise Flycatcher** away. There are two fair-sized dams in the park where **Yellowbilled Duck**, **Redknobbed Coot** and **Moorhen** occur. **Levaillant's Cisticola** are most common along the lower damp vleis and **Malachite Kingfisher** frequent the reed edges.

80% OF SPECIES

- 008 Dabchick ☐
- 055 Whitebreasted Cormorant ☐
- 058 Reed Cormorant ☐
- 060 Darter ☐
- 062 Grey Heron ☐
- 063 Blackheaded Heron ☐
- 065 Purple Heron ☐
- 071 Cattle Egret ☐
- 081 Hamerkop ☐
- 083 White Stork ☐
- 084 Black Stork ☐
- 091 Sacred Ibis ☐
- 092 **Bald Ibis**** ☐
- 094 Hadeda Ibis ☐
- 102 Egyptian Goose ☐
- 104 **Yellowbilled Duck** ☐
- 105 African Black Duck ☐
- 113 Southern Pochard ☐
- 116 Spurwinged Goose ☐
- 118 Secretarybird ☐
- 119 **Bearded Vulture** ☐
- 122 **Cape Vulture**** ☐
- 127 Blackshouldered Kite ☐
- 131 **Black Eagle** ☐
- 152 **Jackal Buzzard**** ☐
- 155 **Redbreasted Sparrowhawk** ☐
- 168 Black Harrier** ☐
- 169 Gymnogene ☐
- 172 Lanner Falcon ☐
- 180 Eastern Redfooted Kestrel ☐
- 181 Rock Kestrel ☐
- 183 Lesser Kestrel ☐
- 190 **Greywing Francolin**** ☐
- 199 Swainson's Francolin* ☐
- 203 Helmeted Guineafowl ☐
- 208 Blue Crane** ☐
- 226 **Moorhen** ☐
- 228 **Redknobbed Coot** ☐
- 249 Threebanded Plover ☐
- 286 Ethiopian Snipe ☐
- 349 **Rock Pigeon** ☐
- 350 Rameron Pigeon ☐
- 352 Redeyed Dove ☐
- 354 Cape Turtle Dove ☐
- 355 Laughing Dove ☐
- 377 **Redchested Cucko** ☐
- 386 Diederik Cuckoo ☐

392 Barn Owl
400 Cape Eagle Owl
401 Spotted Eagle Owl
412 **Black Swift**
415 **Whiterumped Swift**
416 **Horus Swift**
417 Little Swift
418 **Alpine Swift**
424 Speckled Mousebird
428 Pied Kingfisher
429 Giant Kingfisher
431 **Malachite Kingfisher**
451 Hoopoe
473 Crested Barbet
480 **Ground Woodpecker****
489 Redthroated Wryneck
518 European Swallow
520 Whitethroated Swallow
526 Greater Striped Swallow*
529 Rock Martin
547 **Black Crow**
550 **Whitenecked Raven**
567 Redeyed Bulbul*
568 Blackeyed Bulbul
577 Olive Thrush
581 **Cape Rock Thrush****
582 **Sentinel Rock Thrush****
586 Mountain Chat*
588 **Buffstreaked Chat****
589 Familiar Chat
595 Anteating Chat**
596 Stonechat
601 Cape Robin
612 **Orangebreasted Rockjumper****
635 Cape Reed Warbler
661 Grassbird**
664 Fantailed Cisticola
670 **Wailing Cisticola**
677 **Levaillant's Cisticola**
681 Neddicky
686 Spotted Prinia**
700 Cape Batis**
706 Fairy Flycatcher**
710 **Paradise Flycatcher**
713 Cape Wagtail
716 Grassveld Pipit
717 Longbilled Pipit
721 **Rock Pipit****
727 Orangethroated Longclaw**
732 Fiscal Shrike
736 Southern Boubou**
746 Bokmakierie*
759 **Pied Starling****
769 **Redwinged Starling**
775 Malachite Sunbird
796 Cape White-eye**
801 House Sparrow
803 Cape Sparrow*
804 Greyheaded Sparrow
813 Cape Weaver**
814 Masked Weaver
824 Red Bishop
826 **Golden Bishop**
827 **Yellowrumped Widow**
831 Redcollared Widow
832 Longtailed Widow
846 Common Waxbill
860 Pintailed Whydah
870 Blackthroated Canary
872 Cape Canary
881 Streakyheaded Canary
885 Cape Bunting
886 Rock Bunting

Buffstreaked Chats

TUSSEN-DIE-RIVIERE GAME FARM

approximately 225 species recorded to date

This provincial nature reserve of 22 000 ha is situated between the confluence of the Orange and the Caledon rivers and caters for both tourists and game hunters. The reserve is closed to the public during the hunting season, from May to August (check exact dates beforehand). Excellent accommodation is available in chalets overlooking the Orange River (for weekends, book well in advance), while various camping facilities are also available. The wide variety of habitats, including typical Karoo scrub, themeda grassland, rocky koppies and wooded kloofs, and its position on the upper reaches of the Hendrik Verwoed Dam, is reflected in a diverse avifauna. Roads in the reserve are well laid out with long sections following the riverine bush of the Caledon River, and others crossing over hills and plains. The old homestead at the De Wet picnic site, together with the old farm dam, is as rewarding a birding site as you will get anywhere in the southern Orange Free State.

SPECIAL AND INTERESTING SPECIES

The hill behind the entrance gate (Aasvoëlkop) is home to a pair of **Black Eagles**, while **Martial Eagles** can be found around the De Wet picnic site. **Tawny Eagles** are also resident in the reserve and **African Fish Eagle** can often be heard calling along the Orange and Caledon rivers. Keep a lookout for **Redbreasted Sparrowhawk** in the poplars near

ALSO RECORDED

Dusky Sunbirds have been recorded, which could indicate an eastward expansion of range. Check all pigeons in thick stands of olive trees on the rocky hillsides in the centre of the reserve for the occasional Rameron Pigeon. Blue Cranes used to occur

Following the 1988 floods, the only remaining entrance is on the north-eastern boundary of the reserve. From Bloemfontein proceed to Smithfield. Then take the Bethulie tarred road and turn off on to the Goedemoed gravel road. The entrance is on the road just south of the Caledon River. The reserve is also accessible from Aliwal North via Goedemoed, a distance of 45 km, partly tarred.

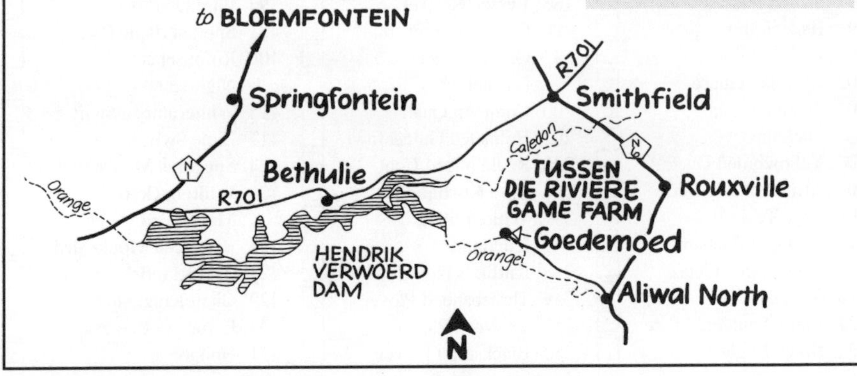

the old homesteads. In summer the reserve is used as a hunting ground by some of the thousands of **Lesser Kestrels** which roost at night in Bethulie, Rouxville and Aliwal North. Larks really abound here with the **Clapper Lark** everywhere. **Thickbilled Larks** are found on the plains, **Redcapped Larks** like trampled and open ground, and **Spikeheeled Larks** are found on stony level areas. Chats are also common and **Mountain**, **Familiar**, **Sicklewing**, **Karoo**, **Anteating** and **Stonechat** may be found in quick succession. **Rock Bunting** is often heard calling in rocky areas. The indigenous garden in front of the information centre is a real oasis in the dry season. **Malachite Sunbird** visits the flowers, while the berries are a favourite of all three species of mousebirds: **Speckled**, **Whitebacked** and **Redfaced**. **Karoo Robin**, **Titbabbler** and **Rufouseared Warbler** frequent any thicket, while **Namaqua Prinia** keeps to the riverine bush. Both **Blue** and **Whitequilled Korhaans** are found on the grass-covered plains.

in large numbers, but like other large species such as Ludwig's Bustard, they are less common today. The Cape Vulture roosting colony at Aasvoëlkop is sadly no longer active. Goliath Heron has found the man-made lake created by the Hendrik Verwoed Dam to its liking and even breeds there.

Deon du Plessis

67% OF SPECIES

001 Ostrich ☐
008 Dabchick ☐
055 Whitebreasted Cormorant ☐
058 Reed Cormorant ☐
060 Darter ☐
062 Grey Heron ☐
063 Blackheaded Heron ☐
071 Cattle Egret ☐
081 Hamerkop ☐
083 White Stork ☐
084 Black Stork ☐
091 Sacred Ibis ☐
094 Hadeda Ibis ☐
095 African Spoonbill ☐
102 Egyptian Goose ☐
103 South African Shelduck** ☐
104 Yellowbilled Duck ☐
105 African Black Duck ☐
106 Cape Teal ☐
113 Southern Pochard ☐
116 Spurwinged Goose ☐
118 Secretarybird ☐
127 Blackshouldered Kite ☐
131 **Black Eagle** ☐
132 **Tawny Eagle** ☐
140 **Martial Eagle** ☐
148 **African Fish Eagle** ☐
149 Steppe Buzzard ☐
152 Jackal Buzzard** ☐
155 **Redbreasted Sparrowhawk** ☐
162 Pale Chanting Goshawk* ☐
168 Black Harrier** ☐
181 Rock Kestrel ☐
182 Greater Kestrel ☐
183 **Lesser Kestrel** ☐
190 Greywing Francolin** ☐
193 Orange River Francolin* ☐
200 Common Quail ☐
203 Helmeted Guineafowl ☐
228 Redknobbed Coot ☐
234 **Blue Korhaan**** ☐
239a **Whitequilled Korhaan**** ☐
248 Kittlitz's Plover ☐
249 Threebanded Plover ☐
255 Crowned Plover ☐
258 Blacksmith Plover ☐
264 Common Sandpiper ☐
270 Greenshank ☐
294 Avocet ☐
295 Blackwinged Stilt ☐
297 Spotted Dikkop ☐
301 Doublebanded Courser ☐
349 Rock Pigeon ☐
352 Redeyed Dove ☐
354 Cape Turtle Dove ☐
355 Laughing Dove ☐
356 Namaqua Dove ☐
386 Diederik Cuckoo ☐
392 Barn Owl ☐
401 Spotted Eagle Owl ☐
406 Rufouscheeked Nightjar ☐
415 Whiterumped Swift ☐
417 Little Swift ☐
424 **Speckled Mousebird** ☐
425 **Whitebacked Mousebird**** ☐
426 **Redfaced Mousebird** ☐
428 Pied Kingfisher ☐
429 Giant Kingfisher ☐
438 European Bee-eater ☐
451 Hoopoe ☐

465 Pied Barbet* ☐
495 **Clapper Lark**** ☐
500 Longbilled Lark* ☐
506 **Spikeheeled Lark*** ☐
507 **Redcapped Lark** ☐
512 **Thickbilled Lark**** ☐
518 European Swallow ☐
520 Whitethroated Swallow ☐
526 Greater Striped Swallow* ☐
529 Rock Martin ☐
533 Brownthroated Martin ☐
547 Black Crow ☐
548 Pied Crow ☐
550 Whitenecked Raven ☐
551 Southern Grey Tit** ☐
567 Redeyed Bulbul* ☐
577 Olive Thrush ☐
581 Cape Rock Thrush** ☐
586 **Mountain Chat*** ☐
589 **Familiar Chat** ☐
590 Tractrac Chat* ☐
591 **Sicklewinged Chat**** ☐
592 **Karoo Chat*** ☐
595 **Anteating Chat**** ☐
596 **Stonechat** ☐
601 Cape Robin ☐
614 **Karoo Robin**** ☐
621 **Titbabbler*** ☐
622 Layard's Titbabbler** ☐
635 Cape Reed Warbler ☐
651 Longbilled Crombec ☐
653 Yellowbellied Eremomela ☐
664 Fantailed Cisticola ☐
665 Desert Cisticola ☐
666 Cloud Cisticola ☐
669 Greybacked Cisticola* ☐
677 Levaillant's Cisticola ☐
681 Neddicky ☐
685 Blackchested Prinia* ☐
686 Karoo Prinia** ☐
687 **Namaqua Prinia**** ☐
688 **Rufouseared Warbler**** ☐
689 Spotted Flycatcher ☐
698 Fiscal Flycatcher** ☐
706 Fairy Flycatcher** ☐
711 African Pied Wagtail ☐
713 Cape Wagtail ☐
716 Grassveld Pipit ☐
717 Longbilled Pipit ☐
719 Buffy Pipit ☐
721 Rock Pipit** ☐
727 Orangethroated Longclaw** ☐
732 Fiscal Shrike ☐
733 Redbacked Shrike ☐
746 Bokmakierie* ☐
759 Pied Starling** ☐
760 Wattled Starling ☐
764 Glossy Starling* ☐
769 Redwinged Starling ☐
770 Palewinged Starling* ☐
775 **Malachite Sunbird** ☐
796 Cape White-eye** ☐
799 Whitebrowed Sparrowweaver ☐
801 House Sparrow ☐
803 Cape Sparrow* ☐
804 Greyheaded Sparrow ☐
813 Cape Weaver** ☐
814 Masked Weaver ☐
824 Red Bishop ☐
832 Longtailed Widow ☐
846 Common Waxbill ☐
852 Quail Finch ☐
860 Pintailed Whydah ☐
870 Blackthroated Canary ☐
872 Cape Canary ☐
878 Yellow Canary* ☐
879 Whitethroated Canary* ☐
885 Cape Bunting ☐
886 **Rock Bunting** ☐
☐
☐

OTHER BIRDING SPOTS WORTH VISITING

Soetdoring Nature Reserve
Situated north-west of Bloemfontein on the Bultfontein road. Excellent birding spots are the picnic sites along the Modder River, while drives through the prime grasslands and to the upper reaches of the Kruger's Drift Dam will be rewarding.

The National Botanic Garden
Situated on the north-western outskirts of Bloemfontein; an abundance of bird species frequent the well-known indigenous tree and shrub gardens.

Kroonpark and the Kroonstad Bird Park
Forms a green belt (especially on the southern bank) along the False River in Kroonstad. Both camping and chalet accommodation is available at Kroonstad.

Korannaberg
Situated near Marquard on private land, but various hiking trails and farm lodges make this beautiful, mountainous area accessible to birders who want to get away from the noisy and busy city life.

USEFUL TELEPHONE NUMBERS

Willem Pretorius Game Reserve
(01734) 4229

Sandveld Nature Reserve
(018022) 1103

Tussen-die-Riviere
(05862) 2803

National Parks Board
(Golden Gate)
(012) 343-1991

Korannaberg
(Farm Lodge Bookings)
(012) 46-5365

Whitebacked Night Heron

8 Natal

Co-ordinators Hugh Chittenden (Coastal)
Nigel Robson (Inland)

1 Ndumu Game Reserve
2 Lake Sibaya
3 Itala Game Reserve
4 Mkuzi Game Reserve
5 Vryheid Nature Reserve and Surrounding Area
6 Cape Vidal
7 Lake St Lucia – Western Shores
8 Hluhluwe-Umfolozi Game Reserves
9 Weenen Nature Reserve
10 Richards Bay
11 Dlinza Forest, Ntumeni Nature Reserve and Umgoye Forest
12 Mlalazi Nature Reserve and Mtunzini Village
13 Giant's Castle Game Reserve
14 Umgeni Valley Nature Reserve
15 Sani Pass
16 Darvill Sewage Works
17 Umhlanga Sewage Works
18 Shongweni Dam
19 Beachwood Mangroves and Umgeni River Mouth
20 Natal Estuarine and Pelagic
21 Xumeni Forest, Donnybrook
22 Vernon Crookes Nature Reserve
23 Matatiele
24 Oribi Gorge Nature Reserve

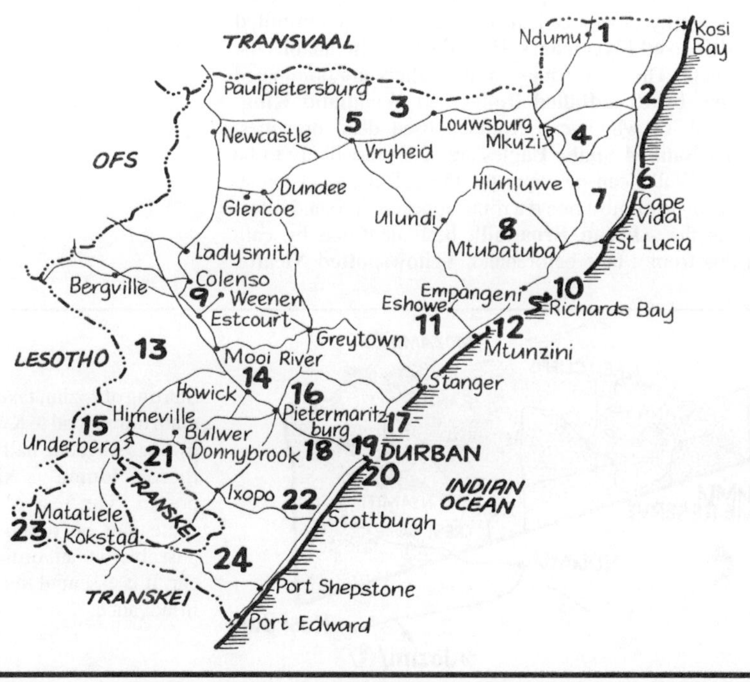

NDUMU GAME RESERVE

approximately 403 species recorded to date

Ndumu Game Reserve, controlled by the KwaZulu Bureau of Natural Resources, is located on the Usutu floodplain adjacent to Mozambique. The habitat is diverse, consisting of a variety of deciduous woodland types, sand forest, riverine gallery forest, grassland and permanent rivers and pans. Ndumu boasts more species of birds than any place of comparable size in the whole of South Africa, a function not only of habitat diversity, but of its northerly position on the coastal plain, where it is best positoned to pick up tropical stragglers.

SPECIAL AND INTERESTING SPECIES

A guided walk through the gallery forest will produce **Narina Trogon**, **Wood Owl**, **Green Coucal** and, with luck, **Pel's Fishing Owl**. **White-eared Barbets** nest in the dead branches of the fig trees. Ripe fig crops are attended not only by **Green Pigeons**, but by clouds of fruit-flies, the prey of **Fantailed** and **Wattle-eyed Flycatchers**. **Heuglin's Robin** inhabits the undergrowth. The open fringes of the gallery are dominated in summer by **Broadbilled Roller** and **Woodland Kingfisher**, both of which call from exposed dead branches. **Southern Banded Snake Eagles** are also most likely to be seen here. Walks can be requested through the sand forest, but get ready to climb a tree if a rhino appears. The sand forest special is the **African Broadbill**, best identified by call. Learn this from a tape beforehand. **Yellowspotted Nicator**

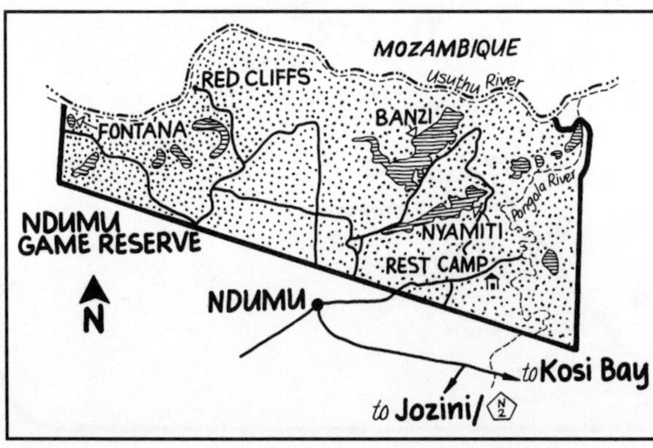

Starting at Jozini, take the main tarred road to Kwangwanase. About halfway there, Ndumu is signposted. The rest of the route can be rough but passable in an ordinary car. It is essential to book in advance.

and **Gorgeous Bush Shrike** are two other shy beauties whose calls dominate the sand forest chorus. **Neergaard's Sunbird** is fairly common in the sand forest, although not confined to it. This is a coastal plain endemic, rarely seen outside Ndumu and Mkuzi game reserves and False Bay Park. **Grey Waxbills** and **Pinkthroated Twinspots** are easily seen on sand forest fringes. In grassy places with sparse or low bush look out for **Jameson's Firefinch**, **Stierling's Barred Warbler** and **Paradise Whydah**. **Harlequin Quails** are common in some summers and are presumed to breed in Ndumu. **Lesser Blackwinged Plovers** nest in heavily grazed grassland. **Water Dikkops** are always to be found around the pan edges, and nest on the hippo lawns right out in the open. Waterbird displays are not as reliable as they were once reputed, and much depends upon the time since the last flood. At present (1991) Nyamithi Pan has little aquatic vegetation, so it cannot support the large numbers of birds seen a few years ago. **Openbilled Storks** are sometimes present and once bred just outside the reserve. **Pygmy Goose** and **Knobbilled Duck** are usually to be seen, sometimes in fair numbers. In general all the other typical waterbirds are present, but often only in ones or twos. Waterside thickets are the haunt of **Blackcrowned Night Heron**, and **Goliath Herons** nest in tall trees overhanging the Pongola. The most exciting of the pan birds is the **Sooty Falcon** (summer), which forages alongside the fringing fever trees.

ALSO RECORDED

Vanga Flycatcher has been seen several times in the gallery forest. Palmnut Vultures visit on occasion, and join other vultures at carcases. Longtoed Plovers are sometimes present, preferring open river fringes to the pans. Striped Cuckoos are uncommon summer visitors; also look out for Thickbilled Cuckoo and its host, the Redbilled Helmetshrike. Black Coucals occur in the wet grassland bordering the reserve's southern boundary, an area due to be incorporated into the reserve. A few northern species, virtually unknown elsewhere in Natal, just extend into Ndumu. Examples are Longtailed Shrike and Redbilled Buffalo Weaver. Finally there is always a chance of something really unusual like Eastern Sawwing Swallow, Greyhooded Kingfisher or Chestnutfronted Helmetshrike.

David Johnson

51% OF SPECIES

058 Reed Cormorant ☐
060 Darter ☐
062 Grey Heron ☐
064 **Goliath Heron** ☐
065 Purple Heron ☐
066 Great White Egret ☐
067 Little Egret ☐
068 Yellowbilled Egret ☐
071 Cattle Egret ☐
072 Squacco Heron ☐
074 Greenbacked Heron ☐
076 **Blackcrowned Night Heron** ☐
081 Hamerkop ☐
086 Woollynecked Stork ☐
087 **Openbilled Stork** ☐
090 Yellowbilled Stork ☐
091 Sacred Ibis ☐
093 Glossy Ibis ☐
094 Hadeda Ibis ☐
095 African Spoonbill ☐
099 Whitefaced Duck ☐
100 Fulvous Duck ☐
102 Egyptian Goose ☐
114 **Pygmy Goose** ☐
115 **Knobbilled Duck** ☐
116 Spurwinged Goose ☐
123 Whitebacked Vulture ☐
126a Yellowbilled Kite ☐
132 Tawny Eagle ☐
135 Wahlberg's Eagle ☐
140 Martial Eagle ☐
142 Brown Snake Eagle ☐

144 **Southern Banded Snake Eagle**
146 Bateleur
148 African Fish Eagle
154 Lizard Buzzard
160 African Goshawk
169 Gymnogene
170 Osprey
175 **Sooty Falcon**
189 Crested Francolin
196 Natal Francolin*
200 Common Quail
201 **Harlequin Quail**
203 Helmeted Guineafowl
204 Crested Guineafowl
213 Black Crake
223 Purple Gallinule
226 Moorhen
237 Redcrested Korhaan*
238 Blackbellied Korhaan
240 African Jacana
248 Kittlitz's Plover
249 Threebanded Plover
256 **Lesser Blackwinged Plover**
258 Blacksmith Plover
260 Wattled Plover
264 Common Sandpiper
266 Wood Sandpiper
270 Greenshank
274 Little Stint
284 Ruff
294 Avocet
295 Blackwinged Stilt
297 Spotted Dikkop
298 **Water Dikkop**
322 Caspian Tern
338 Whiskered Tern
339 Whitewinged Tern
352 Redeyed Dove
354 Cape Turtle Dove
355 Laughing Dove
358 Greenspotted Dove
359 Tambourine Dove
361 **Green Pigeon**
371 Purplecrested Lourie
373 Grey Lourie
377 Redchested Cuckoo
378 Black Cuckoo
382 Jacobin Cuckoo
385 Klaas's Cuckoo
386 Diederik Cuckoo
387 **Green Coucal**
391 Burchell's Coucal*
392 Barn Owl
394 **Wood Owl**
401 Spotted Eagle Owl
403 **Pel's Fishing Owl**
404 European Nightjar
405 Fierynecked Nightjar
409 Mozambique Nightjar
424 Speckled Mousebird
426 Redfaced Mousebird
427 **Narina Trogon**
428 Pied Kingfisher
429 Giant Kingfisher
431 Malachite Kingfisher
432 Pygmy Kingfisher
433 **Woodland Kingfisher**
435 Brownhooded Kingfisher
437 Striped Kingfisher
438 European Bee-eater
444 Little Bee-eater
447 Lilacbreasted Roller
450 **Broadbilled Roller**
452 Redbilled Woodhoopoe
454 Scimitarbilled Woodhoopoe
455 Trumpeter Hornbill
460 Crowned Hornbill
464 Blackcollared Barbet
466 **White-eared Barbet**
469 Redfronted Tinker Barbet
471 Goldenrumped Tinker Barbet
483 Goldentailed Woodpecker
486 Cardinal Woodpecker
487 Bearded Woodpecker
490 **African Broadbill**
494 Rufousnaped Lark
496 Flappet Lark
518 European Swallow
522 Wiretailed Swallow
527 Lesser Striped Swallow
538 Black Cuckooshrike
541 Forktailed Drongo
542 Squaretailed Drongo
545 Blackheaded Oriole
554 Southern Black Tit*
568 Blackeyed Bulbul
569 Terrestrial Bulbul
572 Sombre Bulbul
574 Yellowbellied Bulbul
575 **Yellowspotted Nicator**
576 Kurrichane Thrush
599 **Heuglin's Robin**
600 Natal Robin
602 Whitethroated Robin**
613 Whitebrowed Robin
617 Bearded Robin
635 Cape Reed Warbler
638 African Sedge Warbler
643 Willow Warbler
648 Yellowbreasted Apalis
649 Rudd's Apalis*
651 Longbilled Crombec
656 Burntnecked Eremomela
657 Bleating Warbler
659 **Stierling's Barred Warbler**
664 Fantailed Cisticola
672 Rattling Cisticola
681 Neddicky
683 Tawnyflanked Prinia
689 Spotted Flycatcher
690 Dusky Flycatcher
691 Bluegrey Flycatcher
693 **Fantailed Flycatcher**
694 Black Flycatcher
696 Mousecoloured Flycatcher
701 Chinspot Batis
705 **Wattle-eyed Flycatcher**
710 Paradise Flycatcher
711 African Pied Wagtail
716 Grassveld Pipit

728 Yellowthroated Longclaw ☐	780 Purplebanded Sunbird ☐	817 Yellow Weaver ☐
733 Redbacked Shrike ☐	782 **Neergaard's Sunbird**** ☐	824 Red Bishop ☐
736 Southern Boubou** ☐	787 Whitebellied Sunbird ☐	828 Redshouldered Widow ☐
740 Puffback ☐	790 Olive Sunbird ☐	829 Whitewinged Widow ☐
741 Brubru ☐	791 Scarletchested Sunbird ☐	834 Melba Finch ☐
743 Threestreaked Tchagra ☐	793 Collared Sunbird ☐	838 **Pinkthroated Twinspot**** ☐
744 Blackcrowned Tchagra ☐	796 Cape White-eye** ☐	840 Bluebilled Firefinch ☐
747 **Gorgeous Bush Shrike** ☐	797 Yellow White-eye ☐	841 **Jameson's Firefinch** ☐
748 Orangebreasted Bush Shrike ☐	805 Yellowthroated Sparrow ☐	844 Blue Waxbill ☐
751 Greyheaded Bush Shrike ☐	807 Thickbilled Weaver ☐	846 Common Waxbill ☐
753 White Helmetshrike ☐	808 Forest Weaver ☐	848 **Grey Waxbill** ☐
761 Plumcoloured Starling ☐	810 Spectacled Weaver ☐	857 Bronze Mannikin ☐
764 Glossy Starling* ☐	811 Spottedbacked Weaver ☐	860 Pintailed Whydah ☐
768 Blackbellied Starling ☐	815 Lesser Masked Weaver ☐	862 **Paradise Whydah** ☐
		869 Yelloweyed Canary ☐
		884 Goldenbreasted Bunting ☐

LAKE SIBAYA

approximately 296 species recorded to date

Lake Sibaya, the largest fresh-water lake in South Africa, is situated near the coast and separated from the sea by high forest-covered dunes. The low nutrient levels in the lake do not make it conducive to good fishing so the lake, which is administered by the Kwazulu Bureau of Natural Resources, is

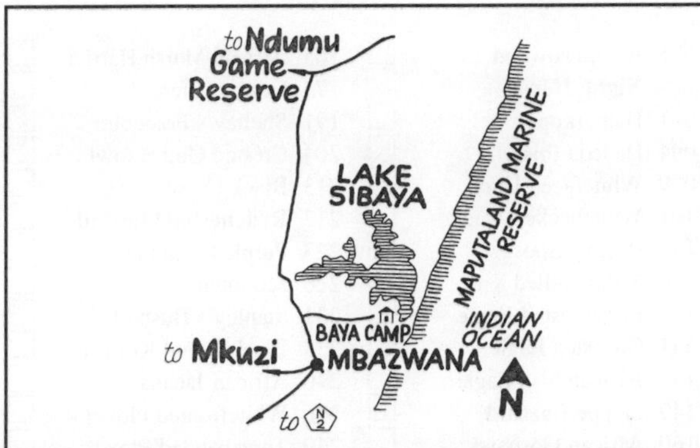

Take the road to Sordwana Bay from the N2, which leads through Mbazwana. Baya Camp is situated on the southern side of the lake and is 18 km north-east of Mbazwana. The road, which is sandy, is adequately signposted. From Baya Camp a track leads to the eastern dune forests. From here, four-wheel drive is necessary to reach Nine Mile Beach and Mabibi.

unspoilt and its surroundings are ideal for birding. Private boats are not permitted, but lake trips are available from Baya Camp, which offers hutted accommodation and walking trails in the adjacent woodland.

SPECIAL AND INTERESTING SPECIES

The moist grassland areas around parts of the lake are ideal habitat for **Pinkthroated Longclaw**. From Baya Camp drive 5,8 km towards Nine Mile Beach. On either side of the track are long stretches of wet grassland, where these beautiful birds can be flushed with ease. They can be separated from **Yellowthroated Longclaws** in flight by their darker upperparts and white wing bars. The rolling sandy grassland areas are home to **Natal Nightjar**. In the camp itself **Yellow White-eyes** are common. Look for **Purplebanded** and **Grey Sunbirds**. **Greyrumped Swallows** fly low over the grassland in front of the camp. While on the woodland trails look for **Brown Robin**, **Natal Robin**, **Terrestrial Bulbul**, **Yellowspotted Nicator** and **Gorgeous Bush Shrike**. **Redchested Flufftails** can be heard calling in most of the Papyrus beds in the vicinity. A trip to the coastal dune forest will yield **Woodwards' Batis**, which can easily be located by its characteristic "who" call. Other species to be found are **Narina Trogon**, **Green Twinspot**, **Grey Waxbill** (verges) and **Squaretailed Drongo**. Waterbirds one can see on a boat trip include **Whitewinged**, **Whiskered** and **Caspian Terns**, **Little Egret**, **Greenbacked** and **Squacco Herons**, **Blackcrowned Night Heron** and the largest in the world, **Goliath Heron**.

ALSO RECORDED

Both Hobby Falcon and Cuckoo Hawk may be found over the broken indigenous woodland and the exotic plantations. Bat Hawk has been recorded and the lake supports one of the few Great Crested Grebe populations in Natal. Rufousbellied Herons are recorded on the lake edge and the adjacent pans.

Hugh Chittenden

52% OF SPECIES

- 008 Dabchick ☐
- 055 Whitebreasted Cormorant ☐
- 058 Reed Cormorant ☐
- 060 Darter ☐
- 062 Grey Heron ☐
- 064 **Goliath Heron** ☐
- 065 Purple Heron ☐
- 067 **Little Egret** ☐
- 068 Yellowbilled Egret ☐
- 071 Cattle Egret ☐
- 072 **Squacco Heron** ☐
- 074 **Greenbacked Heron** ☐
- 076 **Blackcrowned Night Heron** ☐
- 081 Hamerkop ☐
- 094 Hadeda Ibis ☐
- 099 Whitefaced Duck ☐
- 101 Whitebacked Duck ☐
- 114 Pygmy Goose ☐
- 126a Yellowbilled Kite ☐
- 139 Longcrested Eagle ☐
- 141 Crowned Eagle ☐
- 148 African Fish Eagle ☐
- 149 Steppe Buzzard ☐
- 160 African Goshawk ☐
- 165 African Marsh Harrier ☐
- 173 Hobby Falcon ☐
- 191 Shelley's Francolin ☐
- 204 Crested Guineafowl ☐
- 213 Black Crake ☐
- 217 **Redchested Flufftail** ☐
- 223 Purple Gallinule ☐
- 226 Moorhen ☐
- 231 Stanley's Bustard ☐
- 238 Blackbellied Korhaan ☐
- 240 African Jacana ☐
- 246 Whitefronted Plover ☐
- 249 Threebanded Plover ☐

- 260 Wattled Plover ☐
- 264 Common Sandpiper ☐
- 266 Wood Sandpiper ☐
- 270 Greenshank ☐
- 286 Ethiopian Snipe ☐
- 295 Blackwinged Stilt ☐
- 315 Greyheaded Gull ☐
- 322 **Caspian Tern** ☐
- 327 Common Tern ☐
- 338 **Whiskered Tern** ☐
- 339 **Whitewinged Tern** ☐
- 352 Redeyed Dove ☐
- 354 Cape Turtle Dove ☐
- 358 Greenspotted Dove ☐
- 359 Tambourine Dove ☐
- 361 Green Pigeon ☐
- 370a **Livingstone's Lourie** ☐
- 371 Purplecrested Lourie ☐
- 377 Redchested Cuckoo ☐
- 385 Klaas's Cuckoo ☐
- 386 Diederik Cuckoo ☐
- 387 Green Coucal ☐
- 391 Burchell's Coucal* ☐
- 394 Wood Owl ☐
- 401 Spotted Eagle Owl ☐
- 405 Fierynecked Nightjar ☐
- 407 **Natal Nightjar** ☐
- 424 Speckled Mousebird ☐
- 427 **Narina Trogon** ☐
- 428 Pied Kingfisher ☐
- 429 Giant Kingfisher ☐
- 431 Malachite Kingfisher ☐
- 432 Pygmy Kingfisher ☐
- 435 Brownhooded Kingfisher ☐
- 444 Little Bee-eater ☐
- 452 Redbilled Woodhoopoe ☐
- 455 Trumpeter Hornbill ☐
- 460 Crowned Hornbill ☐
- 464 Blackcollared Barbet ☐
- 471 Goldenrumped Tinker Barbet ☐
- 475 Scalythroated Honeyguide ☐
- 483 Goldentailed Woodpecker ☐
- 486 Cardinal Woodpecker ☐
- 490 African Broadbill ☐
- 494 Rufousnaped Lark ☐
- 518 European Swallow ☐
- 527 Lesser Striped Swallow ☐
- 531 **Greyrumped Swallow** ☐
- 534 Banded Martin ☐
- 538 Black Cuckooshrike ☐
- 541 Forktailed Drongo ☐
- 542 **Squaretailed Drongo** ☐
- 545 Blackheaded Oriole ☐
- 548 Pied Crow ☐
- 554 Southern Black Tit* ☐
- 568 Blackeyed Bulbul ☐
- 569 **Terrestrial Bulbul** ☐
- 572 Sombre Bulbul ☐
- 574 Yellowbellied Bulbul ☐
- 575 **Yellowspotted Nicator** ☐
- 596 Stonechat ☐
- 600 **Natal Robin** ☐
- 616 **Brown Robin**** ☐
- 635 Cape Reed Warbler ☐
- 638 African Sedge Warbler ☐
- 643 Willow Warbler ☐
- 648 Yellowbreasted Apalis ☐
- 649 Rudd's Apalis* ☐
- 651 Longbilled Crombec ☐
- 657 Bleating Warbler ☐
- 664 Fantailed Cisticola ☐
- 675 Blackbacked Cisticola ☐
- 678 Croaking Cisticola ☐
- 681 Neddicky ☐
- 683 Tawnyflanked Prinia ☐
- 690 Dusky Flycatcher ☐
- 691 Bluegrey Flycatcher ☐
- 694 Black Flycatcher ☐
- 701 Chinspot Batis ☐
- 704 **Woodwards' Batis*** ☐
- 705 Wattle-eyed Flycatcher ☐
- 710 Paradise Flycatcher ☐
- 711 African Pied Wagtail ☐
- 713 Cape Wagtail ☐
- 716 Grassveld Pipit ☐
- 728 Yellowthroated Longclaw ☐
- 730 **Pinkthroated Longclaw** ☐
- 732 Fiscal Shrike ☐
- 733 Redbacked Shrike ☐
- 736 Southern Boubou** ☐
- 740 Puffback ☐
- 744 Blackcrowned Tchagra ☐
- 747 **Gorgeous Bush Shrike** ☐
- 748 Orangebreasted Bush Shrike ☐
- 751 Greyheaded Bush Shrike ☐
- 761 Plumcoloured Starling ☐
- 768 Blackbellied Starling ☐
- 780 **Purplebanded Sunbird** ☐
- 787 Whitebellied Sunbird ☐
- 789 **Grey Sunbird** ☐
- 790 Olive Sunbird ☐
- 791 Scarletchested Sunbird ☐
- 793 Collared Sunbird ☐
- 797 **Yellow White-eye** ☐
- 807 Thickbilled Weaver ☐
- 808 Forest Weaver ☐
- 810 Spectacled Weaver ☐
- 817 Yellow Weaver ☐
- 828 Redshouldered Widow ☐
- 831 Redcollared Widow ☐
- 835 **Green Twinspot** ☐
- 840 Bluebilled Firefinch ☐
- 846 Common Waxbill ☐
- 848 **Grey Waxbill** ☐
- 857 Bronze Mannikin ☐
- 860 Pintailed Whydah ☐
- 869 Yelloweyed Canary ☐
- 877 Bully Canary ☐
- 884 Goldenbreasted Bunting ☐
- ☐
- ☐
- ☐
- ☐

ITALA GAME RESERVE

approximately 314 species recorded to date

Itala, controlled by the Natal Parks Board, is located on the south bank of the Pongola River near Louwsburg. The habitat ranges from a warm floodplain close to sea level, to cool highveld. Much of the reserve consists of spectacular slopes of rock and woodland, and it is famous for its diversity of vegetation and bird species.

SPECIAL AND INTERESTING SPECIES

Itala is noted for its birds of prey. **Crowned Eagles** are conspicuous, and a nest can be seen a few kilometres down an old track north of the warden's office. Itala is one of the best places in Natal to see **African Hawk Eagle**, always patrolling the steep rocky bush below the escarpment edge. A nest has yet to be found in the reserve, something to look out for. **Lesser Spotted Eagles** are frequent summer visitors and are best seen attending termite emergences. The rocky jumbles are a haven for chats, notably **Mountain**, **Familiar** and **Mocking** and, in winter, **Buffstreaked Chat**. This habitat surrounds the main tourist camp and is alive with bird noises, the raucous **Natal Francolin** dominating. **Rudd's Apalis** is particularly noticeable in the surrounding thorn trees. Robins are common among this bush, and one koppie near Craigadam boasts five robins, **Heuglin's**, **Cape**, **Natal**, **Whitethroated** and **Whitebrowed**. In areas of sparser bush **Jameson's Firefinch** can be found, and where there is bare eroded ground, **Rock Bunting**. Itala is well served with

ALSO RECORDED

Via the Pongola connection all sorts of Zululand birds just extend into Itala. Typical examples are Brownheaded Parrot, Lilacbreasted Roller, Bearded Woodpecker, Grey Penduline Tit and Bearded Robin. Because of its far northern position in Natal, Itala also collects a few species more typical of the Transvaal: Longtailed Shrike, Temminck's Courser and Grey Lourie. Itala also finds itself on the extremity of another avifauna, that of the arid west, which extends a distributional tongue eastwards in this vicinity. This supplies Titbabbler, Cape Bunting and Arrowmarked Babbler. Redbilled Oxpeckers are occasionally seen, although never in sufficient numbers for a viable breeding population. Once numbers of host animals – rhino, buffalo, giraffe and eland – have built up, oxpeckers

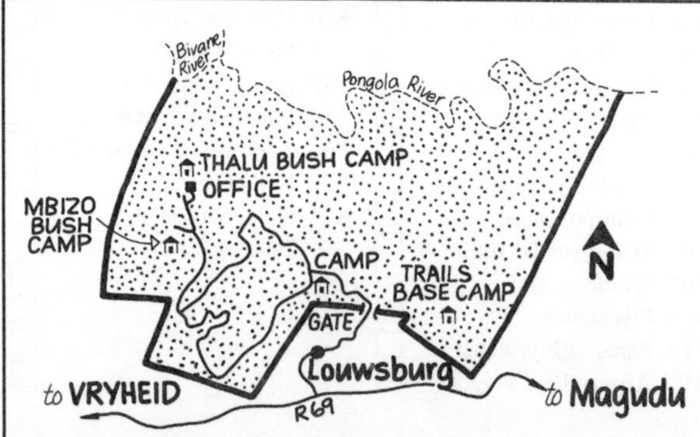

Louwsburg can be reached from Vryheid or from Pongola via Magudu. The reserve entrance is signposted from Louwsburg. There are tourist roads within the reserve and walks can be arranged. Accommodation ranges from luxury cabins and bush camps down to camping.

rivers for the Pongola has several permanent tributaries, all suitable for a swim after a hot day's birding. The faster stretches are home to **Longtailed Wagtail**, while **Whitebacked Night Heron** and **Halfcollared Kingfisher** inhabit still waters where there is dense overhanging vegetation. The best place to see these rare species is just below the warden's office on the Thalu River. In the south of the reserve the high grasslands are the place to see **Whitebellied Korhaan**. **Alpine** and **Black Swifts** are present for much of the year, especially where the grassland meets the escarpment edge. In summer they are joined by **Banded Martin**. **Longbilled Pipits** use small rocky outcrops in the grassland. **Bald Ibis** are frequently seen there too, and nest on the ledges just below the main escarpment.

should become established. Ostriches are being reintroduced, research having shown that the species once occurred in Itala.

David Johnson

52% OF SPECIES

- 077 **Whitebacked Night Heron** ☐
- 092 **Bald Ibis**** ☐
- 126a Yellowbilled Kite ☐
- 131 Black Eagle ☐
- 134 **Lesser Spotted Eagle** ☐
- 137 **African Hawk Eagle** ☐
- 141 **Crowned Eagle** ☐
- 149 Steppe Buzzard ☐
- 152 Jackal Buzzard** ☐
- 160 African Goshawk ☐
- 169 Gymnogene ☐
- 172 Lanner Falcon ☐
- 181 Rock Kestrel ☐
- 196 **Natal Francolin*** ☐
- 200 Common Quail ☐
- 203 Helmeted Guineafowl ☐
- 233 **Whitebellied Korhaan** ☐
- 300 Temminck's Courser ☐
- 349 Rock Pigeon ☐
- 352 Redeyed Dove ☐
- 354 Cape Turtle Dove ☐
- 355 Laughing Dove ☐
- 358 Greenspotted Dove ☐
- 359 Tambourine Dove ☐
- 361 Green Pigeon ☐
- 363 Brownheaded Parrot ☐
- 371 Purplecrested Lourie ☐
- 375 African Cuckoo ☐
- 377 Redchested Cuckoo ☐
- 382 Jacobin Cuckoo ☐
- 385 Klaas's Cuckoo ☐
- 386 Diederik Cuckoo ☐
- 391 Burchell's Coucal* ☐
- 401 Spotted Eagle Owl ☐
- 404 European Nightjar ☐
- 405 Fierynecked Nightjar ☐
- 412 **Black Swift** ☐
- 418 **Alpine Swift** ☐
- 424 Speckled Mousebird ☐
- 426 Redfaced Mousebird ☐
- 429 Giant Kingfisher ☐
- 430 **Halfcollared Kingfisher** ☐
- 432 Pygmy Kingfisher ☐
- 435 Brownhooded Kingfisher ☐
- 438 European Bee-eater ☐
- 444 Little Bee-eater ☐
- 446 European Roller ☐
- 447 Lilacbreasted Roller ☐
- 451 Hoopoe ☐
- 452 Redbilled Woodhoopoe ☐
- 454 Scimitarbilled Woodhoopoe ☐
- 455 Trumpeter Hornbill ☐
- 464 Blackcollared Barbet ☐
- 465 Pied Barbet* ☐
- 469 Redfronted Tinker Barbet ☐
- 473 Crested Barbet ☐
- 474 Greater Honeyguide ☐
- 475 Scalythroated Honeyguide ☐
- 483 Goldentailed Woodpecker ☐
- 486 Cardinal Woodpecker ☐
- 487 Bearded Woodpecker ☐
- 489 Redthroated Wryneck ☐
- 494 Rufousnaped Lark ☐
- 496 Flappet Lark ☐
- 498 Sabota Lark* ☐
- 518 European Swallow ☐
- 524 Redbreasted Swallow ☐
- 526 Greater Striped Swallow* ☐
- 529 Rock Martin ☐
- 534 **Banded Martin** ☐
- 536 Black Sawwing Swallow ☐
- 538 Black Cuckooshrike ☐
- 541 Forktailed Drongo ☐
- 545 Blackheaded Oriole ☐
- 548 Pied Crow ☐
- 550 Whitenecked Raven ☐
- 554 Southern Black Tit* ☐
- 558 Grey Penduline Tit ☐
- 560 Arrowmarked Babbler ☐

568 Blackeyed Bulbul ☐
572 Sombre Bulbul ☐
576 Kurrichane Thrush ☐
580 Groundscraper Thrush ☐
581 Cape Rock Thrush** ☐
586 **Mountain Chat*** ☐
588 **Buffstreaked Chat**** ☐
589 **Familiar Chat** ☐
593 **Mocking Chat** ☐
596 Stonechat ☐
599 **Heuglin's Robin** ☐
600 **Natal Robin** ☐
601 **Cape Robin** ☐
602 **Whitethroated Robin**** ☐
613 **Whitebrowed Robin** ☐
617 Bearded Robin ☐
621 Titbabbler* ☐
642 Broadtailed Warbler ☐
643 Willow Warbler ☐
648 Yellowbreasted Apalis ☐
649 **Rudd's Apalis*** ☐
651 Longbilled Crombec ☐
657 Bleating Warbler ☐
661 Grassbird** ☐
664 Fantailed Cisticola ☐
667 Ayres' Cisticola ☐
670 Wailing Cisticola ☐
672 Rattling Cisticola ☐
674 Redfaced Cisticola ☐
678 Croaking Cisticola ☐
679 Lazy Cisticola ☐
681 Neddicky ☐
683 Tawnyflanked Prinia ☐
689 Spotted Flycatcher ☐
690 Dusky Flycatcher ☐
691 Bluegrey Flycatcher ☐
694 Black Flycatcher ☐
696 Mousecoloured Flycatcher ☐
701 Chinspot Batis ☐
710 Paradise Flycatcher ☐
712 **Longtailed Wagtail** ☐
713 Cape Wagtail ☐
716 Grassveld Pipit ☐
717 **Longbilled Pipit** ☐
720 Striped Pipit ☐
727 Orangethroated Longclaw** ☐
728 Yellowthroated Longclaw ☐
732 Fiscal Shrike ☐
733 Redbacked Shrike ☐
735 Longtailed Shrike ☐
736 Southern Boubou** ☐
740 Puffback ☐
741 Brubru ☐
742 Southern Tchagra** ☐
744 Blackcrowned Tchagra ☐
747 Gorgeous Bush Shrike ☐
748 Orangebreasted Bush Shrike ☐
751 Greyheaded Bush Shrike ☐
761 Plumcoloured Starling ☐
764 Glossy Starling* ☐
769 Redwinged Starling ☐
785 Greater Double-collared Sunbird** ☐
787 Whitebellied Sunbird ☐
791 Scarletchested Sunbird ☐
792 Black Sunbird ☐
796 Cape White-eye** ☐
804 Greyheaded Sparrow ☐
805 Yellowthroated Sparrow ☐
810 Spectacled Weaver ☐
834 Melba Finch ☐
840 Bluebilled Firefinch ☐
841 **Jameson's Firefinch** ☐
842 Redbilled Firefinch ☐
844 Blue Waxbill ☐
846 Common Waxbill ☐
850 Swee Waxbill* ☐
852 Quail Finch ☐
857 Bronze Mannikin ☐
860 Pintailed Whydah ☐
864 Black Widowfinch ☐
869 Yelloweyed Canary ☐
884 Goldenbreasted Bunting ☐
886 **Rock Bunting** ☐

☐
☐
☐
☐
☐

Redbreasted Swallow

MKUZI GAME RESERVE

over 400 species recorded to date

This Natal Parks Board game reserve is one of the most popular among birdwatchers and, apart possibly from Ndumu Game Reserve, has the largest checklist in the province. Its major asset is its wide range of habitats which include pans, swamps, Acacia thornveld, woodland and riverine forest. There are even some cliff and mountainous habitats as well as open grassland.

SPECIAL AND INTERESTING SPECIES

A well-marked network of roads covers much of the reserve and a number of areas may be visited on foot with a game guard. The riverine forest below the hutted camp on the Mkuzi River and near Nsumo Pan have superb walks and are good places to see **Southern Banded Snake Eagle**, **Pel's Fishing Owl**, **Heuglin's Robin** and **Grey Waxbill**, while **Whitefronted Bee-eaters** breed in holes along the riverbank during the summer months. The sand forest areas between the hutted camp and the airstrip, and also around Kumasinga Hide, are the place to look for **Neergaard's Sunbird**, **Rudd's Apalis**, **Fantailed Flycatcher**, **Gorgeous Bush Shrike**, **Yellowspotted Nicator**, **Whitethroated** and **Bearded Robins** and **Pinkthroated Twinspot**. The grassland on and adjacent to the airstrip holds **Desert Cisticola** and from the nearby thornveld the grating call of the elusive **Olivetree Warbler**, as well as that of **Stierling's Barred Warbler**,

ALSO RECORDED

The Kubube and Kumasinga hides with their small pans set in the thicker woodland annually host Dwarf Bittern and Green Sandpiper, while one of the few occurrences of Grey Wagtail in the country was recorded here. Listen for African Broadbill near the Kubube Hide parking area. The reserve supports a wide range of raptors with Hooded Vulture (very rare in Natal), Bat Hawk, Honey Buzzard and Ayres' Eagle having been recorded. Apart from the Bat Hawk, which has mostly occurred in the riverine forest, the other three may be encountered anywhere in the reserve. Pennantwinged Nightjar has been recorded once, in the Lebombo foothills, while the most recent addition to the Mkuzi Game Reserve list has been Yellowbilled Oxpecker, which presumably

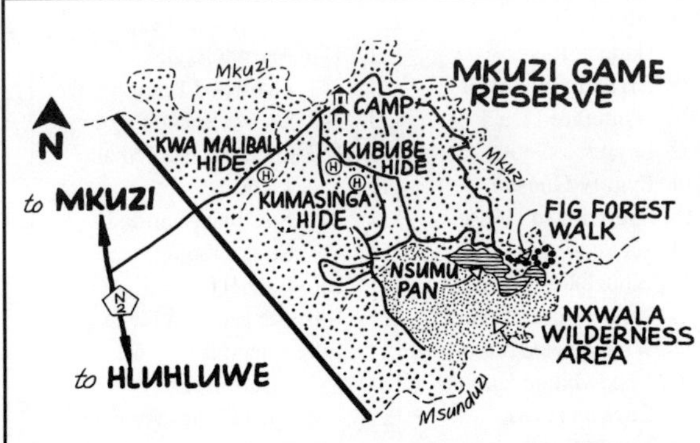

32 km north of Hluhluwe village on the N2, the reserve is signposted on the right, thereafter follow the signs for about 15 km to the park gate. Adjacent to the gate is the caravan park and campsite, while the hutted camp is some 10 km further inside the reserve.

may be heard. To have a reasonable chance of seeing these two species one really needs to have a tape recording of their calls; however, patience is often rewarded. Also look for **Burntnecked Eremomela** in the thorn trees. The tall open woodland on the loop road is good for **Steppe** and **Lesser Spotted Eagles** particularly after heavy rains, as these species gather like chickens around the nest holes from which termite alates emerge, attempting to snap them up with their beaks. In the same area **Brownheaded Parrot** and **Bushveld Pipit** occur. The presence of the former species is usually detected when its loud shrieking call is heard as it hurtles overhead. The latter species is most frequently flushed from the roadside. The fairly extensive Nsumo Pan can be excellent for waterbirds, but this is very much dependent on the water levels. The largest numbers occur when levels are fairly low and the mud flats are exposed. Species that breed in the fever trees along the shoreline include **Pinkbacked Pelican**, **Yellowbilled Stork**, **African Spoonbill** and **Goliath Heron**. These trees are also a good place to see **Woodland Kingfisher. Pygmy Goose** and **Lesser Jacana** can with determined scanning be located among the mass of water lilies which often cover large areas of the pan. The fig forest walk should produce **Broadbilled Roller**, **Green Coucal**, **White-eared Barbet**, **Scalythroated Honeyguide**, **Natal Robin**, **Bluegrey Flycatcher**, **Black Cuckooshrike** and **Crowned Eagle**. Keep an eye open for **Cuckoo Hawk** along the walk.

originated from those birds that were released, and have bred, in the Umfolozi/ Hluhluwe complex as part of a reintroduction programme of this species in Natal.

Digby Cyrus

56% OF SPECIES

008 Dabchick	☐	
049 White Pelican	☐	
050 **Pinkbacked Pelican**	☐	
055 Whitebreasted Cormorant	☐	
058 Reed Cormorant	☐	
060 Darter	☐	
062 Grey Heron	☐	
063 Blackheaded Heron	☐	
064 **Goliath Heron**	☐	
065 Purple Heron	☐	
066 Great White Egret	☐	
067 Little Egret	☐	
068 Yellowbilled Egret	☐	
071 Cattle Egret	☐	
072 Squacco Heron	☐	
074 Greenbacked Heron	☐	
081 Hamerkop	☐	
086 Woollynecked Stork	☐	
090 **Yellowbilled Stork**	☐	
093 Glossy Ibis	☐	
094 Hadeda Ibis	☐	
095 **African Spoonbill**	☐	
099 Whitefaced Duck	☐	
102 Egyptian Goose	☐	
114 **Pygmy Goose**	☐	
116 Spurwinged Goose	☐	
118 Secretarybird	☐	
123 Whitebacked Vulture	☐	
124 Lappetfaced Vulture	☐	
125 Whiteheaded Vulture	☐	
126a Yellowbilled Kite	☐	
128 **Cuckoo Hawk**	☐	
132 Tawny Eagle	☐	
133 **Steppe Eagle**	☐	
134 **Lesser Spotted Eagle**	☐	
135 Wahlberg's Eagle	☐	
139 Longcrested Eagle	☐	
140 Martial Eagle	☐	
141 **Crowned Eagle**	☐	
142 Brown Snake Eagle	☐	
143 Blackbreasted Snake Eagle	☐	
144 **Southern Banded Snake Eagle**	☐	
146 Bateleur	☐	
148 African Fish Eagle	☐	
149 Steppe Buzzard	☐	
154 Lizard Buzzard	☐	
160 African Goshawk	☐	
169 Gymnogene	☐	

189 Crested Francolin ☐
196 Natal Francolin* ☐
203 Helmeted Guineafowl ☐
204 Crested Guineafowl ☐
213 Black Crake ☐
223 Purple Gallinule ☐
226 Moorhen ☐
238 Blackbellied Korhaan ☐
240 African Jacana ☐
241 **Lesser Jacana** ☐
249 Threebanded Plover ☐
255 Crowned Plover ☐
258 Blacksmith Plover ☐
264 Common Sandpiper ☐
266 Wood Sandpiper ☐
269 Marsh Sandpiper ☐
270 Greenshank ☐
272 Curlew Sandpiper ☐
274 Little Stint ☐
284 Ruff ☐
295 Blackwinged Stilt ☐
298 Water Dikkop ☐
338 Whiskered Tern ☐
339 Whitewinged Tern ☐
352 Redeyed Dove ☐
354 Cape Turtle Dove ☐
358 Greenspotted Dove ☐
359 Tambourine Dove ☐
361 Green Pigeon ☐
363 **Brownheaded Parrot** ☐
371 Purplecrested Lourie ☐
377 Redchested Cuckoo ☐
378 Black Cuckoo ☐
382 Jacobin Cuckoo ☐
384 Emerald Cuckoo ☐
385 Klaas's Cuckoo ☐
386 Diederik Cuckoo ☐
387 **Green Coucal** ☐
391 Burchell's Coucal* ☐
394 Wood Owl ☐
401 Spotted Eagle Owl ☐
403 **Pel's Fishing Owl** ☐
405 Fierynecked Nightjar ☐
415 Whiterumped Swift ☐
424 Speckled Mousebird ☐
426 Redfaced Mousebird ☐
427 Narina Trogon ☐
428 Pied Kingfisher ☐
429 Giant Kingfisher ☐
431 Malachite Kingfisher ☐
432 Pygmy Kingfisher ☐
433 **Woodland Kingfisher** ☐
435 Brownhooded Kingfisher ☐
437 Striped Kingfisher ☐
438 European Bee-eater ☐
443 **Whitefronted Bee-eater** ☐
444 Little Bee-eater ☐
446 European Roller ☐
447 Lilacbreasted Roller ☐
450 **Broadbilled Roller** ☐
451 Hoopoe ☐
452 Redbilled Woodhoopoe ☐
454 Scimitarbilled Woodhoopoe ☐
455 Trumpeter Hornbill ☐
459 Southern Yellowbilled Hornbill* ☐
460 Crowned Hornbill ☐
463 Ground Hornbill ☐
464 Blackcollared Barbet ☐
466 **White-eared Barbet** ☐
469 Redfronted Tinker Barbet ☐
471 Goldenrumped Tinker Barbet ☐
473 Crested Barbet ☐
474 Greater Honeyguide ☐
475 **Scalythroated Honeyguide** ☐
476 Lesser Honeyguide ☐
483 Goldentailed Woodpecker ☐
486 Cardinal Woodpecker ☐
487 Bearded Woodpecker ☐
494 Rufousnaped Lark ☐
496 Flappet Lark ☐
498 Sabota Lark* ☐
518 European Swallow ☐
522 Wiretailed Swallow ☐
527 Lesser Striped Swallow ☐
533 Brownthroated Martin ☐
536 Black Sawwing Swallow ☐
538 **Black Cuckooshrike** ☐
540 Grey Cuckooshrike ☐
541 Forktailed Drongo ☐
542 Squaretailed Drongo ☐
545 Blackheaded Oriole ☐
548 Pied Crow ☐
554 Southern Black Tit* ☐
558 Grey Penduline Tit ☐
568 Blackeyed Bulbul ☐
569 Terrestrial Bulbul ☐
572 Sombre Bulbul ☐
574 Yellowbellied Bulbul ☐
575 **Yellowspotted Nicator** ☐
576 Kurrichane Thrush ☐
580 Groundscraper Thrush ☐
596 Stonechat ☐
599 Heuglin's Robin ☐
600 **Natal Robin** ☐
602 **Whitethroated Robin**** ☐
613 Whitebrowed Robin ☐
617 **Bearded Robin** ☐
626 **Olivetree Warbler** ☐
635 Cape Reed Warbler ☐
638 African Sedge Warbler ☐
643 Willow Warbler ☐
648 Yellowbreasted Apalis ☐
649 **Rudd's Apalis*** ☐
651 Longbilled Crombec ☐
656 **Burntnecked Eremomela** ☐
657 Bleating Warbler ☐
659 **Stierling's Barred Warbler** ☐
664 Fantailed Cisticola ☐
665 **Desert Cisticola** ☐
672 Rattling Cisticola ☐
674 Redfaced Cisticola ☐
675 Blackbacked Cisticola ☐

681 Neddicky ☐
683 Tawnyflanked Prinia ☐
689 Spotted Flycatcher ☐
690 Dusky Flycatcher ☐
691 **Bluegrey Flycatcher** ☐
693 **Fantailed Flycatcher** ☐
694 Black Flycatcher ☐
696 Mousecoloured Flycatcher ☐
701 Chinspot Batis ☐
710 Paradise Flycatcher ☐
711 African Pied Wagtail ☐
713 Cape Wagtail ☐
716 Grassveld Pipit ☐
723 **Bushveld Pipit** ☐
728 Yellowthroated Longclaw ☐
733 Redbacked Shrike ☐
736 Southern Boubou** ☐
740 Puffback ☐
741 Brubru ☐
743 Threestreaked Tchagra ☐
744 Blackcrowned Tchagra ☐
747 **Gorgeous Bush Shrike** ☐
748 Orangebreasted Bush Shrike ☐
751 Greyheaded Bush Shrike ☐
753 White Helmetshrike ☐
760 Wattled Starling ☐
761 Plumcoloured Starling ☐
764 Glossy Starling* ☐
768 Blackbellied Starling ☐
769 Redwinged Starling ☐
772 Redbilled Oxpecker ☐
780 Purplebanded Sunbird ☐
782 **Neergaard's Sunbird**** ☐
787 Whitebellied Sunbird ☐
789 Grey Sunbird ☐
790 Olive Sunbird ☐
791 Scarletchested Sunbird ☐
792 Black Sunbird ☐
793 Collared Sunbird ☐
796 Cape White-eye** ☐
801 House Sparrow ☐
804 Greyheaded Sparrow ☐
805 Yellowthroated Sparrow ☐
807 Thickbilled Weaver ☐
808 Forest Weaver ☐
810 Spectacled Weaver ☐
811 Spottedbacked Weaver ☐
814 Masked Weaver ☐
815 Lesser Masked Weaver ☐
817 Yellow Weaver ☐
824 Red Bishop ☐
828 Redshouldered Widow ☐
829 Whitewinged Widow ☐
831 Redcollared Widow ☐
834 Melba Finch ☐
838 **Pinkthroated Twinspot**** ☐
840 Bluebilled Firefinch ☐
844 Blue Waxbill ☐
846 Common Waxbill ☐
848 **Grey Waxbill** ☐
850 Swee Waxbill* ☐
860 Pintailed Whydah ☐
864 Black Widowfinch ☐
869 Yelloweyed Canary ☐
884 Goldenbreasted Bunting ☐

☐
☐
☐

VRYHEID NATURE RESERVE AND SURROUNDING AREA

approximately 249 species recorded to date

This reserve, controlled by the Natal Parks Board, is approximately 800 ha in size and is situated on the northern side of the town on Vryheid Hill. Patches of evergreen forest, grassland, wetland and protea veld provide habitats for the 174 species that have been recorded so far in this small reserve itself. The hiking trail in the reserve passes through all these major habitats. The Klipfontein Dam area on the southern side of the town is also controlled by the Natal Parks Board and 136 species have been recorded on the dam and in the adjacent grassland. Esikhuma is the name of a mountain further south just off the Melmoth-Vryheid road and is an excellent birding spot for thornveld, grassland and krans species.

SPECIAL AND INTERESTING SPECIES

Crowned Eagles breed in the evergreen forest that overlooks the town and **Tambourine** and **Cinnamon Doves**, **Olive Woodpecker**, **Bush Blackcap** and **Chorister Robin** are regularly recorded. On the top of the hill **Redwing Francolin**, **Alpine Swift**, **Longbilled Lark**, **Buffstreaked Chat**, **Cloud Cisticola** and **Plainbacked Pipit** are common. In the bush thickets **Black Sparrowhawk**, **African Goshawk**, **Purplecrested Lourie**, **Jacobin Cuckoo** and **Black Cuckooshrike** can be seen. Other grassland-associated spe-

ALSO RECORDED

Dabchick, Dwarf Bittern, Black Stork and Halfcollared Kingfisher have been seen at the dam next to the picnic site in Vryheid Nature Reserve. European and Lilac-breasted Rollers have been recorded on the top of Vryheid Hill. Great Crested Grebe has been recorded on the dam just north of Vryheid Nature Reserve.

Stoffel de Jager

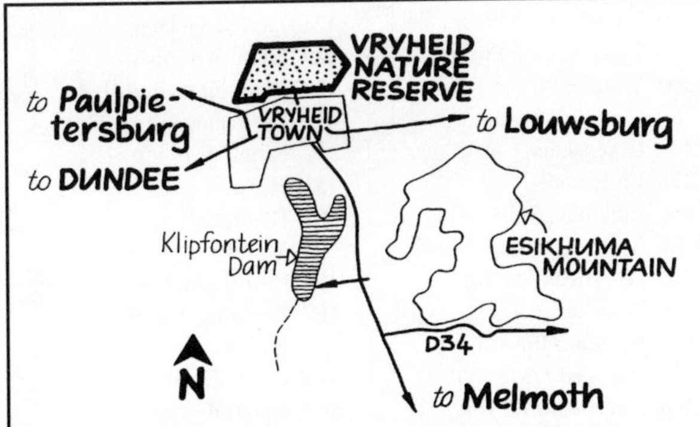

The entrance gate to Vryheid Nature Reserve is via East Street past the provincial hospital (a small entrance fee is charged). The Klipfontein Dam is 8 km from Vryheid to the right of the road to Melmoth. To reach the krans on Esikhuma Mountain, drive for 10 km towards Melmoth from Vryheid, then proceed left for 2 km on the D34.

cies include **Wailing Cisticola**, **Broadtailed Warbler** and **Grass Owl**. Along the Klipfontein Dam shore **Purple Heron**, **Little Egret**, **African Spoonbill**, **African Jacana** and **Giant Kingfisher** can be found. **African Fish Eagle** breed at the dam and **Greyheaded Gull** and **Whiskered Tern** may be found over the water. Various plover species including **Kittlitz's Plover** feed on the edge of the dam. The krans on Esikhuma Mountain is the breeding site for **Bald Ibis**, **Lanner Falcon**, **Rock Kestrel** and **Gymnogene**. Look out for **Black Eagles** flying overhead and for **Mountain Chat**, **Ground Woodpecker** and **Grassbird** on the adjacent slopes. The thornveld nearby has **Redbilled Woodhoopoe**, **Orangebreasted Bush Shrike**, **Black Cuckoo**, **Greenspotted Dove** and, closer to Vryheid, **Titbabbler** and **Yellow Warbler** in the adjoining vlei areas. Other species normally not difficult to find include **Jackal Buzzard**, **Mocking Chat** and **Shelley's** and **Coqui Francolins**.

61% OF SPECIES

008 Dabchick ☐
055 Whitebreasted Cormorant ☐
062 Grey Heron ☐
065 **Purple Heron** ☐
067 **Little Egret** ☐
081 Hamerkop ☐
083 White Stork ☐
091 Sacred Ibis ☐
092 **Bald Ibis**** ☐
095 **African Spoonbill** ☐
099 Whitefaced Duck ☐
102 Egyptian Goose ☐
104 Yellowbilled Duck ☐
105 African Black Duck ☐
108 Redbilled Teal ☐
113 Southern Pochard ☐
116 Spurwinged Goose ☐
118 Secretarybird ☐
126a Yellowbilled Kite ☐
131 **Black Eagle** ☐
141 **Crowned Eagle** ☐
148 **African Fish Eagle** ☐
152 **Jackal Buzzard**** ☐
157 Little Sparrowhawk ☐
158 **Black Sparrowhawk** ☐
160 **African Goshawk** ☐
165 African Marsh Harrier ☐
169 **Gymnogene** ☐
172 **Lanner Falcon** ☐
180 Eastern Redfooted Kestrel ☐
181 **Rock Kestrel** ☐
188 **Coqui Francolin** ☐
191 **Shelley's Francolin** ☐
192 **Redwing Francolin** ☐
200 Common Quail ☐
238 Blackbellied Korhaan ☐
240 **African Jacana** ☐
248 **Kittlitz's Plover** ☐
249 Threebanded Plover ☐
257 Blackwinged Plover ☐
260 Wattled Plover ☐
264 Common Sandpiper ☐
270 Greenshank ☐
274 Little Stint ☐
286 Ethiopian Snipe ☐
297 Spotted Dikkop ☐
315 **Greyheaded Gull** ☐
338 **Whiskered Tern** ☐
350 Rameron Pigeon ☐
352 Redeyed Dove ☐
358 **Greenspotted Dove** ☐
359 **Tambourine Dove** ☐
360 **Cinnamon Dove** ☐
361 Green Pigeon ☐
371 **Purplecrested Lourie** ☐
378 **Black Cuckoo** ☐
382 **Jacobin Cuckoo** ☐
385 Klaas's Cuckoo ☐
393 **Grass Owl** ☐
401 Spotted Eagle Owl ☐
412 Black Swift ☐
415 Whiterumped Swift ☐
418 **Alpine Swift** ☐
421 Palm Swift ☐
426 Redfaced Mousebird ☐
428 Pied Kingfisher ☐
429 **Giant Kingfisher** ☐
431 Malachite Kingfisher ☐
435 Brownhooded Kingfisher ☐
451 Hoopoe ☐
452 **Redbilled Woodhoopoe** ☐
465 Pied Barbet* ☐
469 Redfronted Tinker Barbet ☐
473 Crested Barbet ☐
480 **Ground Woodpecker**** ☐

483 Goldentailed Woodpecker ☐
488 **Olive Woodpecker** ☐
489 Redthroated Wryneck ☐
494 Rufousnaped Lark ☐
500 **Longbilled Lark*** ☐
507 Redcapped Lark ☐
520 Whitethroated Swallow ☐
526 Greater Striped Swallow* ☐
527 Lesser Striped Swallow ☐
529 Rock Martin ☐
534 Banded Martin ☐
536 Black Sawwing Swallow ☐
538 **Black Cuckooshrike** ☐
545 Blackheaded Oriole ☐
550 Whitenecked Raven ☐
554 Southern Black Tit* ☐
565 **Bush Blackcap**** ☐
572 Sombre Bulbul ☐
576 Kurrichane Thrush ☐
577 Olive Thrush ☐
586 **Mountain Chat*** ☐
588 **Buffstreaked Chat**** ☐
589 Familiar Chat ☐
593 **Mocking Chat** ☐
596 Stonechat ☐
598 **Chorister Robin**** ☐
601 Cape Robin ☐
613 Whitebrowed Robin ☐
621 **Titbabbler*** ☐
637 **Yellow Warbler** ☐
642 **Broadtailed Warbler** ☐
645 Barthroated Apalis ☐
657 Bleating Warbler ☐
661 **Grassbird**** ☐
664 Fantailed Cisticola ☐
666 **Cloud Cisticola** ☐
670 **Wailing Cisticola** ☐
677 Levaillant's Cisticola ☐
678 Croaking Cisticola ☐
679 Lazy Cisticola ☐
681 Neddicky ☐
683 Tawnyflanked Prinia ☐
690 Dusky Flycatcher ☐
694 Black Flycatcher ☐
698 Fiscal Flycatcher** ☐
701 Chinspot Batis ☐
710 Paradise Flycatcher ☐
716 Grassveld Pipit ☐
718 **Plainbacked Pipit** ☐
733 Redbacked Shrike ☐
736 Southern Boubou** ☐
741 Brubru ☐
744 Blackcrowned Tchagra ☐
746 Bokmakierie* ☐
748 **Orangebreasted Bush Shrike** ☐
750 Olive Bush Shrike* ☐
775 Malachite Sunbird ☐
785 Greater Double-collared Sunbird** ☐
787 Whitebellied Sunbird ☐
792 Black Sunbird ☐
804 Greyheaded Sparrow ☐
805 Yellowthroated Sparrow ☐
810 Spectacled Weaver ☐
821 Redbilled Quelea ☐
826 Golden Bishop ☐
827 Yellowrumped Widow ☐
829 Whitewinged Widow ☐
840 Bluebilled Firefinch ☐
844 Blue Waxbill ☐
850 Swee Waxbill* ☐
852 Quail Finch ☐
854 Orangebreasted Waxbill ☐
857 Bronze Mannikin ☐
872 Cape Canary ☐
884 Goldenbreasted Bunting ☐
886 Rock Bunting ☐
☐
☐
☐

CAPE VIDAL

approximately 254 species recorded to date

Cape Vidal, controlled by the Natal Parks Board, is situated in tall evergreen dune forest on the eastern shores of Lake St Lucia. The species described inhabit the grassland, floodplains and part of the excellent dune forest that has been threatened by mining activities. Hiking trails on the eastern shores may be booked through the Natal Parks Board, and the forest trail which leaves the campsite at Cape Vidal is one of the best along the Natal coast for dune forest species. Camping facilities within the dune forest and log-cabin chalets are available through the Natal Parks Board head office.

SPECIAL AND INTERESTING SPECIES

This is one of the best localities in southern Africa to find **Woodwards' Batis**, **Brown Robin** and **Rudd's Apalis**. The first two are very easy to locate within the campsite. Woodwards' Batis is best located in the early morning when it gives itself away by its monotonous "whoo" call. **Brown Robins** are generally very tame and often hop around the tents and deck chairs, even when these are occupied by campers! **Rudd's Apalis** is strictly an Acacia loving bird that seldom leaves these thickets which occur within the coastal woodland. Its loud and fast "tok tok tok" call is easy to separate from the call of the **Yellowbreasted Apalis** with which it mixes. **Livingstone's Lourie** is common and easy to locate in the campsite. Parties of **Green Twinspot** may be found anywhere

ALSO RECORDED

Redwinged Pratincole may be found in the grassland region during the summer months where there is short grass adjacent to small ponds. This too is the habitat of Pinkthroated Longclaw, so it is advisable to check out each longclaw that may flush from the grassland or road verge. All three longclaw species have been recorded in this region. After good rains, interesting waterbirds such a Rufousbellied Heron, Pygmy Goose, Whitebacked and Fulvous Ducks may be found, the latter together with Whitefaced Duck, sometimes in large numbers. The seldom recorded Natal Nightjar has been found in this locality. The most northern records for the southern African race of the Spotted Thrush are for this woodland during winter months. The Wattle-eyed

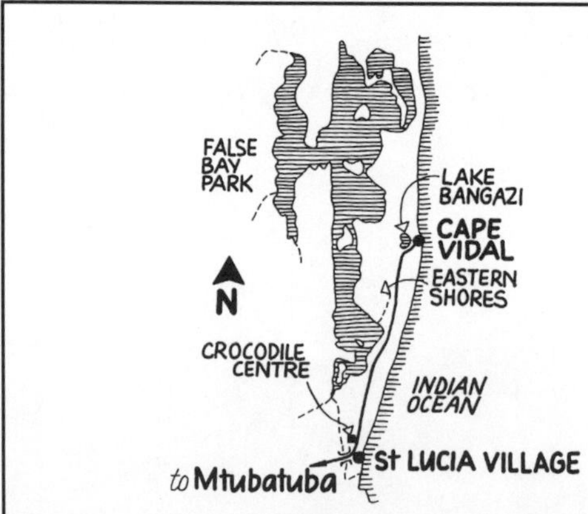

From St Lucia village proceed northwards through the Natal Parks Board gate on a gravel road for about 30 km into the eastern shores nature reserve.

in the forest, even on campsite verges. The best place to see **Grey Waxbills** is on road verges or on the edge of open forest patches where they feed on grass seeds. Both **Grey Sunbird** and **Green Coucal** give themselves away by their characteristic calls. This sunbird is a noisy species: its three-note call may be heard high in the tree tops throughout the coastal woodland. Another noisy resident of this evergreen woodland is the **Yellowspotted Nicator**. This is as far south as it occurs in southern Africa. On the forest trail during the summer months, look out for **Broadbilled Roller**, which perches high on dead branches. **Southern Banded Snake Eagle** can be seen along the road or on telephone poles between St Lucia and Cape Vidal. It is also not uncommon close to St Lucia on the road from Mtubatuba, where it often perches on power pylons. Cape Vidal boasts a high population of **Crested Guineafowl**. Look for **Bluecheeked Bee-eaters** on the telephone lines.

Flycatcher prefers swampy retreats and may be found in thickets close to water. Look out for seedeaters such as Redbacked Mannikin and Bully Canary.

Hugh Chittenden

45% OF SPECIES

058 Reed Cormorant ☐
060 Darter ☐
066 Great White Egret ☐
068 Yellowbilled Egret ☐
074 Greenbacked Heron ☐
081 Hamerkop ☐
086 Woollynecked Stork ☐
088 Saddlebilled Stork ☐
094 Hadeda Ibis ☐
095 African Spoonbill ☐
099 Whitefaced Duck ☐
102 Egyptian Goose ☐
104 Yellowbilled Duck ☐
116 Spurwinged Goose ☐
126a Yellowbilled Kite ☐
139 Longcrested Eagle ☐
141 Crowned Eagle ☐
142 Brown Snake Eagle ☐
143 Blackbreasted Snake Eagle ☐
144 **Southern Banded Snake Eagle** ☐
148 African Fish Eagle ☐
149 Steppe Buzzard ☐
160 African Goshawk ☐
165 African Marsh Harrier ☐
204 **Crested Guineafowl** ☐
218 Buffspotted Flufftail ☐
240 African Jacana ☐
246 Whitefronted Plover ☐
248 Kittlitz's Plover ☐
264 Common Sandpiper ☐
266 Wood Sandpiper ☐
269 Marsh Sandpiper ☐
270 Greenshank ☐
272 Curlew Sandpiper ☐
281 Sanderling ☐
295 Blackwinged Stilt ☐
312 Kelp Gull ☐
315 Greyheaded Gull ☐
324 Swift Tern ☐
326 Sandwich Tern ☐
327 Common Tern ☐
352 Redeyed Dove ☐
358 Greenspotted Dove ☐
359 Tambourine Dove ☐
370a **Livingstone's Lourie** ☐
371 Purplecrested Lourie ☐
377 Redchested Cuckoo ☐
386 Diederik Cuckoo ☐
387 **Green Coucal** ☐
391 Burchell's Coucal* ☐
394 Wood Owl ☐
424 Speckled Mousebird ☐
427 Narina Trogon ☐
428 Pied Kingfisher ☐
432 Pygmy Kingfisher ☐
435 Brownhooded Kingfisher ☐
440 **Bluecheeked Bee-eater** ☐
444 Little Bee-eater ☐
450 **Broadbilled Roller** ☐
455 Trumpeter Hornbill ☐
460 Crowned Hornbill ☐
464 Blackcollared Barbet ☐
466 White-eared Barbet ☐
471 Goldenrumped Tinker Barbet ☐
475 Scalythroated Honeyguide ☐
483 Goldentailed Woodpecker ☐
594 Rufousnaped Lark ☐
518 European Swallow ☐
536 Black Sawwing Swallow ☐
541 Forktailed Drongo ☐
542 Squaretailed Drongo ☐
568 Blackeyed Bulbul ☐
569 Terrestrial Bulbul ☐

572 Sombre Bulbul ☐
574 Yellowbellied Bulbul ☐
575 **Yellowspotted Nicator** ☐
600 Natal Robin ☐
616 **Brown Robin**** ☐
635 Cape Reed Warbler ☐
643 Willow Warbler ☐
648 **Yellowbreasted Apalis** ☐
649 **Rudd's Apalis*** ☐
657 Bleating Warbler ☐
664 Fantailed Cisticola ☐
675 Blackbacked Cisticola ☐
678 Croaking Cisticola ☐
683 Tawnyflanked Prinia ☐
690 Dusky Flycatcher ☐
691 Bluegrey Flycatcher ☐
704 **Woodwards' Batis*** ☐
710 Paradise Flycatcher ☐
713 Cape Wagtail ☐
716 Grassveld Pipit ☐
728 Yellowthroated Longclaw ☐
732 Fiscal Shrike ☐
736 Southern Boubou** ☐
740 Puffback ☐
744 Blackcrowned Tchagra ☐
747 Gorgeous Bush Shrike ☐
751 Greyheaded Bush Shrike ☐
768 Blackbellied Starling ☐
789 **Grey Sunbird** ☐
790 Olive Sunbird ☐
791 Scarletchested Sunbird ☐
793 Collared Sunbird ☐
796 Cape White-eye** ☐
808 Forest Weaver ☐
810 Spectacled Weaver ☐
811 Spottedbacked Weaver ☐
835 **Green Twinspot** ☐
840 Bluebilled Firefinch ☐
846 Common Waxbill ☐
848 **Grey Waxbill** ☐
857 Bronze Mannikin ☐
869 Yelloweyed Canary ☐

LAKE ST LUCIA – WESTERN SHORES

approximately 358 species recorded to date

Lake St Lucia is the largest estuarine system in Africa, covering an area of 325 square km, with a mean depth of 1,5 m and a maximum of 2,04 m. It supports large flocks of flamingos, pelicans and other waterbirds. The three accommodation sites, Charters Creek, Fanie's Island and False Bay, are administered by the Natal Parks Board. These sites are

ALSO RECORDED

Redheaded Queleas breed in the reedbeds around the lake and in isolated swamps within the adjacent exotic timber plantations. Mangrove Kingfishers are recorded from the southern end of the lake, particularly in the narrows near St Lucia

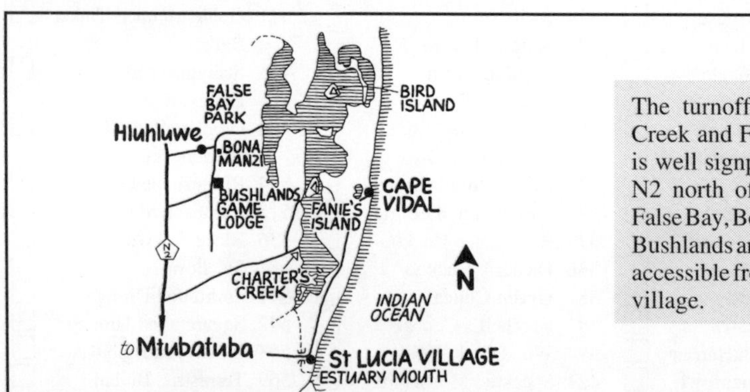

The turnoff to Charters Creek and Fanie's Island is well signposted on the N2 north of Mtubatuba. False Bay, Bonamanzi and Bushlands are close to and accessible from Hluhluwe village.

close to the lake edge and all have walking trails in the adjacent woodland. Two privately owned game reserves near Hluhluwe, Bonamanzi and Bushlands, offer excellent birding and tree-house accommodation.

SPECIAL AND INTERESTING SPECIES

The Hluhluwe River mouth at False Bay used to be the only breeding site for **Pinkbacked Pelicans** in South Africa. In recent years this colony has moved to Nsumu Pan in the Mkuzi Game Reserve; the reason for this is uncertain but could be human disturbance. Up to 1 000 pairs of **White Pelicans** breed on the lake islands. Most of the southern African breeding population of about 400 pairs of **Caspian Tern** also breed on these islands and about 290 pairs, the largest number recorded to date, bred in 1990. A boat trip is necessary to get good views of **Lesser** and **Greater Flamingos**, **Woollynecked**, **Yellowbilled** and **Saddlebilled Storks**. Waders include **Ruff**, **Turnstone** and **Ringed** and **Grey Plovers**. Look for **Lesser Crested**, **Swift** and **Sandwich Terns** on the boat jetties as well as **Whitewinged** and **Whiskered Terns** over the lake. The adjacent woodland habitats are home to many interesting species. The shy **African Broadbill** may be found deep in the wooded gulleys around False Bay, and **Whitethroated Robin** and **Neergaard's Sunbird** are not uncommon at this locality. One of the easiest spots to find the sunbird is around the offices at False Bay. **Pinkthroated Twinspots** are shy but not too difficult to find on any of the walks through woodland, particularly where there are small open clearings with clumps of grass. Other woodland specials include **Yellowspotted Nicator**, **Yellow White-eye** and **Brown** and **Bearded Robins**; the flocks of **Crested Guineafowl** are quite tame. It is possible in the evenings to find **Natal Nightjar** on the sandier sections of roads around the lake. The very localised **Southern Banded Snake Eagle** is more likely to be found in the moist woodland at the southern end of the lake than in the drier Acacia woodland further north. Keep an eye open for this species on the power pylons or telephone poles close to St Lucia village. during the winter months. Redchested Flufftails call from surrounding reedbeds and Sand Martin can be seen from the bridge crossing the narrows near St Lucia village. Shorttailed Pipits are recorded from the short grassland areas.

Hugh Chittenden

44% OF SPECIES

008 Dabchick
049 **White Pelican**
050 **Pinkbacked Pelican**
055 Whitebreasted Cormorant
058 Reed Cormorant
060 Darter
062 Grey Heron
064 Goliath Heron
065 Purple Heron
066 Great White Egret
067 Little Egret
068 Yellowbilled Egret
072 Squacco Heron
074 Greenbacked Heron
081 Hamerkop
086 **Woollynecked Stork**
088 **Saddlebilled Stork**
090 **Yellowbilled Stork**
094 Hadeda Ibis
095 African Spoonbill
096 **Greater Flamingo**
097 **Lesser Flamingo**
099 Whitefaced Duck
102 Egyptian Goose
104 Yellowbilled Duck
116 Spurwinged Goose
126a Yellowbilled Kite
139 Longcrested Eagle
144 **Southern Banded Snake Eagle**
148 African Fish Eagle
149 Steppe Buzzard
160 African Goshawk
165 African Marsh Harrier
189 Crested Francolin
196 Natal Francolin*
204 **Crested Guineafowl**
213 Black Crake
240 African Jacana
245 **Ringed Plover**
249 Threebanded Plover
254 **Grey Plover**
258 Blacksmith Plover
262 **Turnstone**
264 Common Sandpiper
266 Wood Sandpiper
269 Marsh Sandpiper
270 Greenshank
272 Curlew Sandpiper
274 Little Stint
284 **Ruff**
295 Blackwinged Stilt
315 Greyheaded Gull
322 **Caspian Tern**
324 **Swift Tern**
325 **Lesser Crested Tern**
326 **Sandwich Tern**
327 Common Tern
338 **Whiskered Tern**
339 **Whitewinged Tern**
352 Redeyed Dove
358 Greenspotted Dove
359 Tambourine Dove
370a Livingstone's Lourie
371 Purplecrested Lourie
377 Redchested Cuckoo
385 Klaas's Cuckoo
386 Diederik Cuckoo
387 Green Coucal
391 Burchell's Coucal*
405 Fierynecked Nightjar
407 **Natal Nightjar**
427 Narina Trogon
428 Pied Kingfisher
429 Giant Kingfisher
431 Malachite Kingfisher
434 Mangrove Kingfisher
435 Brownhooded Kingfisher
444 Little Bee-eater
446 European Roller
447 Lilacbreasted Roller
454 Scimitarbilled Woodhoopoe
455 Trumpeter Hornbill
460 Crowned Hornbill
464 Blackcollared Barbet
466 White-eared Barbet
471 Goldenrumped Tinker Barbet
476 Lesser Honeyguide
490 **African Broadbill**
494 Rufousnaped Lark
518 European Swallow
524 Redbreasted Swallow
527 Lesser Striped Swallow
532 Sand Martin
533 Brownthroated Martin
541 Forktailed Drongo
542 Squaretailed Drongo
545 Blackheaded Oriole
554 Southern Black Tit*
568 Blackeyed Bulbul
569 Terrestrial Bulbul
572 Sombre Bulbul
574 Yellowbellied Bulbul
575 **Yellowspotted Nicator**
600 Natal Robin
602 **Whitethroated Robin****
616 **Brown Robin****
617 **Bearded Robin**
631 African Marsh Warbler
633 European Marsh Warbler
635 Cape Reed Warbler
638 African Sedge Warbler
643 Willow Warbler
648 Yellowbreasted Apalis
649 Rudd's Apalis*
651 Longbilled Crombec
657 Bleating Warbler
664 Fantailed Cisticola
672 Rattling Cisticola
675 Blackbacked Cisticola
678 Croaking Cisticola
690 Dusky Flycatcher
691 Bluegrey Flycatcher
694 Black Flycatcher
696 Mousecoloured Flycatcher
701 Chinspot Batis
710 Paradise Flycatcher

711	African Pied Wagtail	☐	780	Purplebanded Sunbird	☐	810	Spectacled Weaver	☐
716	Grassveld Pipit	☐	782	**Neergaard's Sunbird****	☐	817	Yellow Weaver	☐
728	Yellowthroated Longclaw	☐	789	Grey Sunbird	☐	828	Redshouldered Widow	☐
732	Fiscal Shrike	☐	790	Olive Sunbird	☐	831	Redcollared Widow	☐
736	Southern Boubou**	☐	791	Scarletchested Sunbird	☐	838	**Pinkthroated Twinspot****	☐
740	Puffback	☐	793	Collared Sunbird	☐	840	Bluebilled Firefinch	☐
744	Blackcrowned Tchagra	☐	796	Cape White-eye**	☐	846	Common Waxbill	☐
747	Gorgeous Bush Shrike	☐	797	**Yellow White-eye**	☐	857	Bronze Mannikin	☐
748	Orangebreasted Bush Shrike	☐	805	Yellowthroated Sparrow	☐	860	Pintailed Whydah	☐
761	Plumcoloured Starling	☐	807	Thickbilled Weaver	☐	869	Yelloweyed Canary	☐
768	Blackbellied Starling	☐	808	Forest Weaver	☐	877	Bully Canary	☐
								☐

HLUHLUWE-UMFOLOZI GAME RESERVES

approximately 378 species recorded to date

The Hluhluwe and Umfolozi game reserves were proclaimed in 1897, making them the oldest reserves in Africa. This region ranging between 45 m and 579 m above sea level, the birthplace of conservation in Natal, is administered by the Natal Parks Board. The reserves, which are now linked by a central corridor section, comprise about 96 000 ha, making the complex the third largest conservation area in South Africa after the Kruger National Park and the Kalahari

ALSO RECORDED

Dwarf Bittern is recorded at small pans during the summer months. Although Bald Ibis have small, irregular nesting colonies within the reserve, there are insufficient feeding habitats, so these birds feed mainly outside the reserve. Little Banded and Gabar Goshawks are uncommon. Other species to look out for are Southern Banded

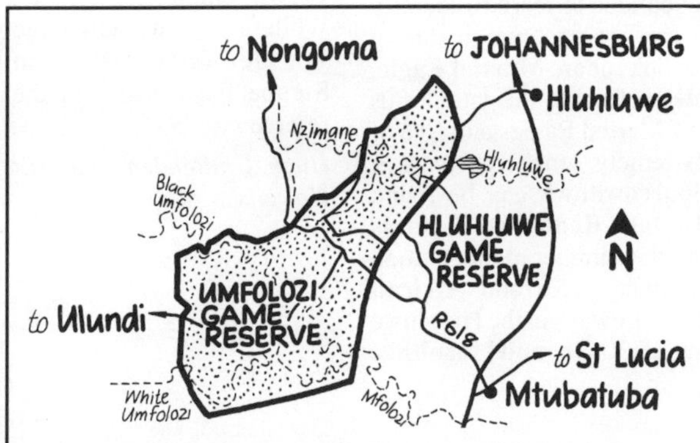

The reserve is 18 km west of Hluhluwe but access is also available from Mtubatuba: proceed westwards on the Nongoma road, which is well signposted. The access road eastwards from Ulundi is open all year but road conditions are variable.

Gemsbok National Park. Accommodation is available at three hutted camps as well as bush camps.

SPECIAL AND INTERESTING SPECIES

The reintroduction of the **Yellowbilled Oxpecker** is an interesting feature of the reserve.This species had last been recorded in Natal just after the turn of the century. Although population numbers are still low, this species, which favours big game, mixes freely with the **Redbilled Oxpecker**. Both **Black** and **Jacobin Cuckoos** are common and even the black morph of the latter species is regularly seen. **Redbreasted Swallows** breed under most culverts. **European Rollers** are uncommon migrants but **Lilacbreasted Roller** and **Southern Yellowbilled Hornbill** breed here and are most likely to be seen in the Umfolozi sector. The uncommon **Bearded Woodpecker** can be found in large trees with plenty of dead wood. Listen for **Flappet Lark**, an aptly named species performing aerial cruises above the broken grassland. **Rudd's Apalis** can be located by its characteristic fast "tok tok tok" call. Other uncommon bushveld species to look for are **Fantailed Flycatcher**, **Bearded Robin**, **Grey Penduline Tit**, **Melba Finch** and **Yellowbellied** and **Burntnecked Eremomelas**. **Bushveld Pipit** is regularly recorded but **Southern Tchagra** is the most uncommon tchagra and difficult to find. Both **Crested** and **Natal Francolins** are common and with luck **Shelley's Francolin** may be heard on the higher grassland slopes. Listen for **Heuglin's Robin** in the riverine bush, especially in the north-east of the complex. **Redthroated Wryneck** has been recorded at selected areas such as Mpila Camp in the Umfolozi region, and breeds at Cengeni Gate. Both **Lappetfaced** and **Whiteheaded Vultures** breed, with about 16 and nine pairs active in the region (late 1980s). The complex is a good area to learn to identify **Lesser Spotted Eagles**, which are not uncommon during rainy conditions. Other raptors to look for are **Martial Eagle**, **Brown Snake Eagle** and **Bateleur**. During the late 1980s there were seven breeding pairs of Martial Eagles and five of Bateleur, the latter being an extremely sensitive breeding species. The secretive **Black Sparrowhawk** can be found along the riverine thickets and **Eastern Redfooted Kestrels** can be seen in fair numbers during the summer months. Look for **Water Dikkops** along the river edges and **African Finfoot** on the still waters near the causeways in the Hluhluwe sector. The reserve supports about 25-30 **Ground Hornbills**. Snake Eagle, Coqui Francolin, Osprey, Namaqua Dove and Temminck's Courser: all have been recorded here in the past. Olive Woodpecker and Delegorgue's Pigeon occur in the forests in the north. The Purple Roller is an irregular visitor to Natal, especially this far south, but has been seen in the past. In spite of excellent Natal Parks Board management, especially in recent years, vlei degradation and river reedbed erosion have taken their toll on species such as African Marsh Harrier. Pallid Harrier appears in old lists but has not been recorded recently. Cyclone Demoina was responsible for the disappearance in 1984 of the Umfolozi riverine bush, together with its population of Brownheaded Parrots. The Longtailed Shrike has not been seen for approximately 40 years and the Grey Lourie, which was recorded regularly in the past, has seldom been seen since the early 1970s. Giant Eagle Owl, Whitefaced Owl, Olivetree Warbler (summer) and Steppe Eagle occur in the reserve.

Hugh Chittenden and Bill Howells

51% OF SPECIES

058 Reed Cormorant
060 Darter
062 Grey Heron
066 Great White Egret
067 Little Egret
081 Hamerkop
086 Woollynecked Stork
094 Hadeda Ibis
099 Whitefaced Duck
102 Egyptian Goose
105 African Black Duck
116 Spurwinged Goose
118 Secretarybird
123 Whitebacked Vulture
124 **Lappetfaced Vulture**
125 **Whiteheaded Vulture**
126a Yellowbilled Kite
127 Blackshouldered Kite
132 Tawny Eagle
134 **Lesser Spotted Eagle**
135 Wahlberg's Eagle
140 **Martial Eagle**
141 Crowned Eagle
142 **Brown Snake Eagle**
143 Blackbreasted Snake Eagle
146 **Bateleur**
148 African Fish Eagle
149 Steppe Buzzard
152 Jackal Buzzard**
158 **Black Sparrowhawk**
160 African Goshawk
169 Gymnogene
172 Lanner Falcon
180 **Eastern Redfooted Kestrel**
189 **Crested Francolin**
191 **Shelley's Francolin**
196 **Natal Francolin***
203 Helmeted Guineafowl
204 Crested Guineafowl
213 Black Crake
229 **African Finfoot**
238 Blackbellied Korhaan
249 Threebanded Plover
255 Crowned Plover
264 Common Sandpiper
270 Greenshank
297 Spotted Dikkop
298 **Water Dikkop**
352 Redeyed Dove
354 Cape Turtle Dove
358 Greenspotted Dove
359 Tambourine Dove
361 Green Pigeon
371 Purplecrested Lourie
377 Redchested Cuckoo
378 **Black Cuckoo**
382 **Jacobin Cuckoo**
384 Emerald Cuckoo
385 Klaas's Cuckoo
386 Diederik Cuckoo
391 Burchell's Coucal*
405 Fierynecked Nightjar
415 Whiterumped Swift
417 Little Swift
424 Speckled Mousebird
426 Redfaced Mousebird
427 Narina Trogon
428 Pied Kingfisher
429 Giant Kingfisher
432 Pygmy Kingfisher
435 Brownhooded Kingfisher
437 Striped Kingfisher
443 Whitefronted Bee-eater
444 Little Bee-eater
446 **European Roller**
447 **Lilacbreasted Roller**
451 Hoopoe
452 Redbilled Woodhoopoe
454 Scimitarbilled Woodhoopoe
455 Trumpeter Hornbill
459 **Southern Yellow-billed Hornbill***
460 Crowned Hornbill
463 **Ground Hornbill**
464 Blackcollared Barbet
469 Redfronted Tinker Barbet
471 Goldenrumped Tinker Barbet
473 Crested Barbet
474 Greater Honeyguide
475 Scalythroated Honeyguide
476 Lesser Honeyguide
483 Goldentailed Woodpecker
486 Cardinal Woodpecker
487 **Bearded Woodpecker**
489 **Redthroated Wryneck**
494 Rufousnaped Lark
496 **Flappet Lark**
498 Sabota Lark*
518 European Swallow
522 Wiretailed Swallow
524 **Redbreasted Swallow**
527 Lesser Striped Swallow
538 Black Cuckooshrike
541 Forktailed Drongo
542 Squaretailed Drongo
545 Blackheaded Oriole
548 Pied Crow
554 Southern Black Tit*
558 **Grey Penduline Tit**
568 Blackeyed Bulbul
569 Terrestrial Bulbul
572 Sombre Bulbul
575 Yellowspotted Nicator
576 Kurrichane Thrush
589 Familiar Chat
596 Stonechat
599 **Heuglin's Robin**
600 Natal Robin
602 Whitethroated Robin**
613 Whitebrowed Robin
617 **Bearded Robin**
628 Great Reed Warbler
635 Cape Reed Warbler

643 Willow Warbler ☐
648 Yellowbreasted Apalis ☐
649 **Rudd's Apalis*** ☐
651 Longbilled Crombec ☐
653 **Yellowbellied Eremomela** ☐
656 **Burntnecked Eremomela** ☐
657 Bleating Warbler ☐
664 **Fantailed Cisticola** ☐
672 Rattling Cisticola ☐
674 Redfaced Cisticola ☐
678 Croaking Cisticola ☐
681 Neddicky ☐
683 Tawnyflanked Prinia ☐
689 Spotted Flycatcher ☐
690 Dusky Flycatcher ☐
691 Bluegrey Flycatcher ☐
693 Fantailed Flycatcher ☐
694 Black Flycatcher ☐
696 Mousecoloured Flycatcher ☐
701 Chinspot Batis ☐
710 Paradise Flycatcher ☐
711 African Pied Wagtail ☐
716 Grassveld Pipit ☐
723 **Bushveld Pipit** ☐
728 Yellowthroated Longclaw ☐
732 Fiscal Shrike ☐
733 Redbacked Shrike ☐
736 Southern Boubou** ☐
740 Puffback ☐
741 Brubru ☐
742 **Southern Tchagra**** ☐
743 Threestreaked Tchagra ☐
744 Blackcrowned Tchagra ☐
747 Gorgeous Bush Shrike ☐
748 Orangebreasted Bush Shrike ☐
751 Greyheaded Bush Shrike ☐
753 White Helmetshrike ☐
761 Plumcoloured Starling ☐
764 Glossy Starling* ☐
769 Redwinged Starling ☐
771 **Yellowbilled Oxpecker** ☐
772 **Redbilled Oxpecker** ☐
780 Purplebanded Sunbird ☐
787 Whitebellied Sunbird ☐
789 Grey Sunbird ☐
791 Scarletchested Sunbird ☐
793 Collared Sunbird ☐
796 Cape White-eye** ☐
801 House Sparrow ☐
804 Greyheaded Sparrow ☐
805 Yellowthroated Sparrow ☐
810 Spectacled Weaver ☐
811 Spottedbacked Weaver ☐
814 Masked Weaver ☐
821 Redbilled Quelea ☐
824 Red Bishop ☐
828 Redshouldered Widow ☐
829 Whitewinged Widow ☐
831 Redcollared Widow ☐
834 **Melba Finch** ☐
840 Bluebilled Firefinch ☐
844 Blue Waxbill ☐
846 Common Waxbill ☐
858 Redbacked Mannikin ☐
860 Pintailed Whydah ☐
862 Paradise Whydah ☐
864 Black Widowfinch ☐
869 Yelloweyed Canary ☐
884 Goldenbreasted Bunting ☐
886 Rock Bunting ☐

Shelley's Francolin

WEENEN NATURE RESERVE

approximately 233 species recorded to date

Weenen Nature Reserve, controlled by the Natal Parks Board, is situated between Estcourt and Weenen in the heart of the Natal midlands. This land was farmed as far back as 1850. Sir Theophilus Shepstone and the son of Andries Pretorius were among its previous owners. During the years prior to 1948 the land was severely abused and became so badly eroded that in 1975 the area was handed over to the Natal Parks Board. This 4 909 ha reserve is dominated by Acacias with open areas of grassland. The Bushmans River flows through a steep valley in the south. There are three picnic sites with braai facilities and two self-guided trails. Visitors wishing to sleep in the reserve can make use of campsites served by an ablution block with hot and cold water.

SPECIAL AND INTERESTING SPECIES

During the summer months one may locate eight species of cuckoo. **African Cuckoo** is fairly common and can always be heard in the early part of the morning and late afternoon during early and mid-summer. **Great Spotted Cuckoo** is usually found in open woodland, noisily chattering as it hunts for caterpillars. **Striped Cuckoo** is easier to locate during October and into November, and again during late March and April, although it is present throughout the summer. The other cuckoos are all common and **Klaas's Cuckoo** may be

ALSO RECORDED

In some summers Blackbellied Korhaans visit alongside the resident Whitebellied Korhaans in the area near the entrance gate. Wahlberg's Eagle is a summer visitor and a white-morph individual has nested in the same tree for many years. If you camp in the reserve you will hear Fiery-necked Nightjar, Cape and Spotted Eagle Owls and Spotted Dikkop. The latest arrival is Purplecrested Lourie, no doubt via the Tugela and Bushmans rivers. This is the furthest inland that this species is found in Natal.

Les Nutting

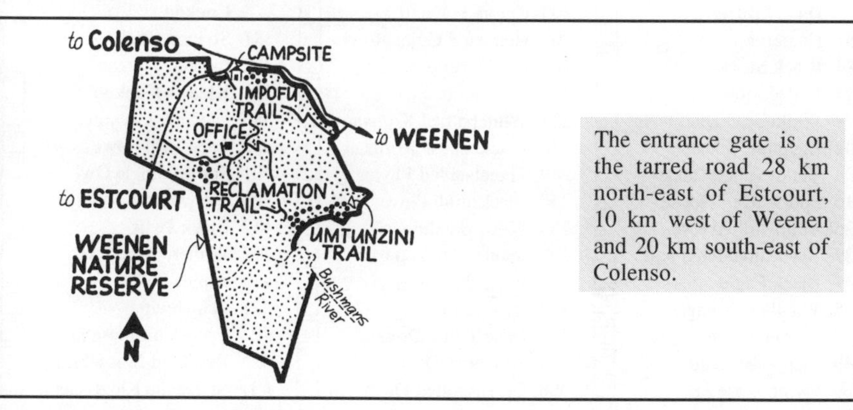

The entrance gate is on the tarred road 28 km north-east of Estcourt, 10 km west of Weenen and 20 km south-east of Colenso.

found all year. **Bearded Woodpecker** is almost at the southern tip of its range here, as is the fairly common **Whitethroated Robin**, which frequently sings in the undergrowth. Weenen is located at the south-eastern margin of the arid west avifauna, so it boasts some unlikely species, notably **Titbabbler**, **Blackthroated Canary** and **Redheaded Finch**. The former two are common and the Blackthroated Canary is easily recognised as the LBJ with the yellow rump, which gathers around roadside puddles. **Blue Cranes** forage in the reserve, although no nest has yet been found. **Black Storks** are present and probably do nest, suitable habitat being found on the less accessible kranses on the Bushmans River. The Impofu Trail will reveal grass and reed birds and waterfowl as you pass the dam. The Beacon View Trail starts from the Umtunzini picnic site and will take you to the highest point in the reserve. This walk should produce many swallows, martins, swifts and various birds of prey, gliding along the valley edge, with the Bushmans River 400 m below. A short stroll to the view site can be equally rewarding. There is a hide at the dam below the office where you can see bishops, weavers, widows and some waterfowl. **Little** and **Dwarf Bitterns** may skulk around in the reeds above the dam. **Icterine Warblers** are not uncommon and Weenen is one of the best places to see this furtive bird.

62% OF SPECIES

- 008 Dabchick ☐
- 062 Grey Heron ☐
- 063 Blackheaded Heron ☐
- 071 Cattle Egret ☐
- 078 **Little Bittern** ☐
- 079 **Dwarf Bittern** ☐
- 081 Hamerkop ☐
- 084 **Black Stork** ☐
- 094 Hadeda Ibis ☐
- 099 Whitefaced Duck ☐
- 102 Egyptian Goose ☐
- 104 Yellowbilled Duck ☐
- 116 Spurwinged Goose ☐
- 126a Yellowbilled Kite ☐
- 127 Blackshouldered Kite ☐
- 131 Black Eagle ☐
- 135 Wahlberg's Eagle ☐
- 140 Martial Eagle ☐
- 149 Steppe Buzzard ☐
- 169 Gymnogene ☐
- 172 Lanner Falcon ☐
- 180 Eastern Redfooted Kestrel ☐
- 181 Rock Kestrel ☐
- 196 Natal Francolin* ☐
- 200 Common Quail ☐
- 203 Helmeted Guineafowl ☐
- 208 **Blue Crane**** ☐
- 228 Redknobbed Coot ☐
- 233 Whitebellied Korhaan ☐
- 238 Blackbellied Korhaan ☐
- 249 Threebanded Plover ☐
- 258 Blacksmith Plover ☐
- 266 Wood Sandpiper ☐
- 297 Spotted Dikkop ☐
- 349 Rock Pigeon ☐
- 352 Redeyed Dove ☐
- 354 Cape Turtle Dove ☐
- 355 Laughing Dove ☐
- 358 Greenspotted Dove ☐
- 371 Purplecrested Lourie ☐
- 375 **African Cuckoo** ☐
- 377 Redchested Cuckoo ☐
- 378 Black Cuckoo ☐
- 380 **Great Spotted Cuckoo** ☐
- 381 **Striped Cuckoo** ☐
- 382 Jacobin Cuckoo ☐
- 385 **Klaas's Cuckoo** ☐
- 386 Diederik Cuckoo ☐
- 400 Cape Eagle Owl ☐
- 401 Spotted Eagle Owl ☐
- 405 Fierynecked Nightjar ☐
- 412 Black Swift ☐
- 415 Whiterumped Swift ☐
- 418 Alpine Swift ☐
- 421 Palm Swift ☐
- 424 Speckled Mousebird ☐
- 426 Redfaced Mousebird ☐
- 431 Malachite Kingfisher ☐

435 Brownhooded Kingfisher ☐
451 Hoopoe ☐
452 Redbilled Woodhoopoe ☐
454 Scimitarbilled Woodhoopoe ☐
463 Ground Hornbill ☐
464 Blackcollared Barbet ☐
465 Pied Barbet* ☐
483 Goldentailed Woodpecker ☐
486 Cardinal Woodpecker ☐
487 **Bearded Woodpecker** ☐
494 Rufousnaped Lark ☐
498 Sabota Lark* ☐
518 European Swallow ☐
526 Greater Striped Swallow* ☐
527 Lesser Striped Swallow ☐
529 Rock Martin ☐
538 Black Cuckooshrike ☐
541 Forktailed Drongo ☐
545 Blackheaded Oriole ☐
547 Black Crow ☐
548 Pied Crow ☐
554 Southern Black Tit* ☐
560 Arrowmarked Babbler ☐
568 Blackeyed Bulbul ☐
576 Kurrichane Thrush ☐
581 Cape Rock Thrush** ☐
589 Familiar Chat ☐
593 Mocking Chat ☐
601 Cape Robin ☐
602 **Whitethroated Robin**** ☐
613 Whitebrowed Robin ☐
621 **Titbabbler*** ☐
625 **Icterine Warbler** ☐
643 Willow Warbler ☐
651 Longbilled Crombec ☐
657 Bleating Warbler ☐
661 Grassbird** ☐
664 Fantailed Cisticola ☐
672 Rattling Cisticola ☐
678 Croaking Cisticola ☐
679 Lazy Cisticola ☐
681 Neddicky ☐
683 Tawnyflanked Prinia ☐
690 Dusky Flycatcher ☐
698 Fiscal Flycatcher** ☐
701 Chinspot Batis ☐
710 Paradise Flycatcher ☐
713 Cape Wagtail ☐
716 Grassveld Pipit ☐
727 Orangethroated Longclaw** ☐
732 Fiscal Shrike ☐
733 Redbacked Shrike ☐
736 Southern Boubou** ☐
740 Puffback ☐
741 Brubru ☐
744 Blackcrowned Tchagra ☐
748 Orangebreasted Bush Shrike ☐
751 Greyheaded Bush Shrike ☐
761 Plumcoloured Starling ☐
764 Glossy Starling* ☐
769 Redwinged Starling ☐
787 Whitebellied Sunbird ☐
792 Black Sunbird ☐
796 Cape White-eye** ☐
801 House Sparrow ☐
804 Greyheaded Sparrow ☐
805 Yellowthroated Sparrow ☐
810 Spectacled Weaver ☐
811 Spottedbacked Weaver ☐
814 Masked Weaver ☐
815 Lesser Masked Weaver ☐
824 Red Bishop ☐
829 Whitewinged Widow ☐
831 Redcollared Widow ☐
832 Longtailed Widow ☐
840 Bluebilled Firefinch ☐
844 Blue Waxbill ☐
846 Common Waxbill ☐
850 Swee Waxbill* ☐
856 **Redheaded Finch*** ☐
860 Pintailed Whydah ☐
864 Black Widowfinch ☐
869 Yelloweyed Canary ☐
870 **Blackthroated Canary** ☐
881 Streakyheaded Canary ☐
884 Goldenbreasted Bunting ☐
886 Rock Bunting ☐
☐
☐
☐
☐
☐

RICHARDS BAY

approximately 301 species recorded to date

Although vastly changed from the early days when the bay area was in pristine condition, areas within the town boundary still support an extremely wide range of bird species. The majority of these species are associated with either aquatic and associated habitats or swamp and dune forest areas.

SPECIAL AND INTERESTING SPECIES

The Berm Wall is excellent for waders: **Broadbilled Sandpiper**, **Sand Plover**, **Bartailed Godwit**, **Terek Sandpiper**, **Curlew** and **Knot** occur each summer, while **Osprey** is present all year (check poles sticking out above the water). A telescope is essential here, particularly when the waders and numerous tern species are sitting out on the mudbanks. In contrast Thulazihleka Pan boasts a wide range of freshwater-associated species and by sitting quietly in the hide one may be rewarded with views of **Baillon's Crake**, **Lesser Jacana**, **Pygmy Goose**, **Yellow Wagtail**, **Brownthroated Weaver** and **Redwinged Pratincole**. On the harbour fence en route to the hide numerous **Bluecheeked Bee-eaters** may be seen during summer. The swamp forest locality is good for **Wattle-eyed Flycatcher** and **Scalythroated Honeyguide** as well as a wide range of forest species. At the Bay Hall one has a second chance to see some of the wader species as well as **Little, Sandwich**, **Caspian, Lesser Crested, Swift** and **Common Terns**, which are present during the summer months.

Four localities are included (see map), with the approach being taken from the Empangeni-Richards Bay road.

• *Berm Wall* (harbour): take the *first* harbour turnoff at the traffic lights, follow the road to the customs post. Normally a permit, obtainable from the Port Manager, is required to enter the area. Proceed straight on until you reach the Berm Wall area. The best time to be there is three hours before high tide.

• *Thulazihleka Pan:* retrace your steps almost to the customs post, take a right turn as indicated on the map and follow the route to the exit via a second harbour entrance. Outside the gate turn left up the fence line until you see a hide in the reedbed on the right (approximately 1,5 km); follow the path through the reeds.

• *Mzingazi Swamp Forest:* back on the main road, turn left at the sign marked "Greenhill & SAP", then left at the fork to the Natal Sharks Board; continue until a no entry sign is reached. Park your vehicle: 50 m further a second road comes in at right angles. The swamp forest borders on the opposite side, where interesting

50% OF SPECIES

008 Dabchick ☐
049 White Pelican ☐
050 Pinkbacked Pelican ☐
055 Whitebreasted Cormorant ☐
058 Reed Cormorant ☐
060 Darter ☐
062 Grey Heron ☐
063 Blackheaded Heron ☐
064 Goliath Heron ☐
065 Purple Heron ☐
066 Great White Egret ☐
067 Little Egret ☐
068 Yellowbilled Egret ☐
069 Black Egret ☐
072 Squacco Heron ☐
081 Hamerkop ☐
086 Woollynecked Stork ☐
090 Yellowbilled Stork ☐
091 Sacred Ibis ☐
093 Glossy Ibis ☐
094 Hadeda Ibis ☐
095 African Spoonbill ☐
096 Greater Flamingo ☐
099 Whitefaced Duck ☐
101 Whitebacked Duck ☐
102 Egyptian Goose ☐
104 Yellowbilled Duck ☐
107 Hottentot Teal ☐
114 **Pygmy Goose** ☐
116 Spurwinged Goose ☐
126a Yellowbilled Kite ☐
148 African Fish Eagle ☐
165 African Marsh Harrier ☐
170 **Osprey** ☐
213 Black Crake ☐
215 **Baillon's Crake** ☐
223 Purple Gallinule ☐
226 Moorhen ☐
228 Redknobbed Coot ☐
240 African Jacana ☐
241 **Lesser Jacana** ☐
245 Ringed Plover ☐
246 Whitefronted Plover ☐
248 Kittlitz's Plover ☐
249 Threebanded Plover ☐
251 **Sand Plover** ☐
254 Grey Plover ☐
258 Blacksmith Plover ☐
262 Turnstone ☐
263 **Terek Sandpiper** ☐
264 Common Sandpiper ☐
266 Wood Sandpiper ☐
269 Marsh Sandpiper ☐
270 Greenshank ☐
271 **Knot** ☐
272 Curlew Sandpiper ☐
274 Little Stint ☐
281 Sanderling ☐
283 **Broadbilled Sandpiper** ☐
284 Ruff ☐
288 **Bartailed Godwit** ☐
289 **Curlew** ☐
290 Whimbrel ☐
295 Blackwinged Stilt ☐
304 **Redwinged Pratincole** ☐
315 Greyheaded Gull ☐
322 **Caspian Tern** ☐
324 **Swift Tern** ☐
325 **Lesser Crested Tern** ☐
326 **Sandwich Tern** ☐
327 **Common Tern** ☐
335 **Little Tern** ☐
338 Whiskered Tern ☐
339 Whitewinged Tern ☐
352 Redeyed Dove ☐
359 Tambourine Dove ☐
385 Klaas's Cuckoo ☐
386 Diederik Cuckoo ☐
387 Green Coucal ☐
391 Burchell's Coucal* ☐
415 Whiterumped Swift ☐
417 Little Swift ☐
424 Speckled Mousebird ☐
428 Pied Kingfisher ☐
429 Giant Kingfisher ☐
431 Malachite Kingfisher ☐
432 Pygmy Kingfisher ☐

swamp forest species can be found in either direction.

• *Bay Hall* : turn left off the main road at the "Bay Area" sign. Follow the route through a small patch of coastal forest to the parking area on the edge of the bay. The best time is mid-tide.

ALSO RECORDED

Richards Bay is well known for the number of rare species that have been recorded here. These include Redshank, Buffbreasted Sandpiper (first southern African record), Whitecheeked Tern (first southern African record), Crab Plover, Mongolian Plover and European Oystercatcher, all of which turned up along the Berm Wall area. Thulazihleka Pan has hosted Basra Reed Warbler and Temminck's Stint (both first southern African records) while Gullbilled Tern and Lesser Blackbacked Gull have occurred at Bay Hall. The construction of hides in recent years has facilitated good sightings of species such as Bittern.

Digby Cyrus

Natal

435 Brownhooded Kingfisher ☐
440 **Bluecheeked Bee-eater** ☐
455 Trumpeter Hornbill ☐
464 Blackcollared Barbet ☐
466 White-eared Barbet ☐
469 Redfronted Tinker Barbet ☐
471 Goldenrumped Tinker Barbet ☐
475 **Scalythroated Honeyguide** ☐
518 European Swallow ☐
522 Wiretailed Swallow ☐
524 Redbreasted Swallow ☐
527 Lesser Striped Swallow ☐
533 Brownthroated Martin ☐
536 Black Sawwing Swallow ☐
541 Forktailed Drongo ☐
548 Pied Crow ☐
568 Blackeyed Bulbul ☐
572 Sombre Bulbul ☐
574 Yellowbellied Bulbul ☐
600 Natal Robin ☐
628 Great Reed Warbler ☐
631 African Marsh Warbler ☐
633 European Marsh Warbler ☐
634 European Sedge Warbler ☐
635 Cape Reed Warbler ☐
638 African Sedge Warbler ☐
643 Willow Warbler ☐
648 Yellowbreasted Apalis ☐
657 Bleating Warbler ☐
675 Blackbacked Cisticola ☐
683 Tawnyflanked Prinia ☐
690 Dusky Flycatcher ☐
705 **Wattle-eyed Flycatcher** ☐
710 Paradise Flycatcher ☐
711 African Pied Wagtail ☐
713 Cape Wagtail ☐
714 **Yellow Wagtail** ☐
716 Grassveld Pipit ☐
728 Yellowthroated Longclaw ☐
732 Fiscal Shrike ☐
736 Southern Boubou** ☐
740 Puffback ☐
744 Blackcrowned Tchagra ☐
758 Indian Myna ☐
768 Blackbellied Starling ☐
780 Purplebanded Sunbird ☐
787 Whitebellied Sunbird ☐
789 Grey Sunbird ☐
790 Olive Sunbird ☐
793 Collared Sunbird ☐
796 Cape White-eye** ☐
807 Thickbilled Weaver ☐
810 Spectacled Weaver ☐
811 Spottedbacked Weaver ☐
817 Yellow Weaver ☐
818 **Brownthroated Weaver** ☐
824 Red Bishop ☐
828 Redshouldered Widow ☐
840 Bluebilled Firefinch ☐
846 Common Waxbill ☐
857 Bronze Mannikin ☐
860 Pintailed Whydah ☐
869 Yelloweyed Canary ☐
872 Cape Canary ☐
☐
☐
☐
☐

DLINZA FOREST, NTUMENI NATURE RESERVE AND UMGOYE FOREST

approximately 78 species recorded to date

Dlinza Forest is situated on the south-western side of Eshowe and has two roads leading through the forest. The one, Natural Arch Drive, is tarred and gives residents access from one end of town to the other. The second is a forked and winding gravel road enabling one to drive through the centre of the forest. There are also well maintained paths, and a picnic site off Kangella Street. Ntumeni Nature Reserve is reached by driving through Eshowe towards Nkandla and turning left after 9 km; the entrance is 3,5 km further on the right. Umgoye Forest can be reached in a two-wheel drive vehicle only in reasonable weather conditions. Turn left off the N2, 12 km north of Mtunzini village. From the north, turn right 5 km past the turnoff to the University of Zululand.

Dlinza Forest, which is about 205 ha in size and averages 500 m above sea level, falls within the town borough of Eshowe but is controlled by the Natal Parks Board. To the east, closer to the coast, lies the larger Umgoye Forest, which covers an area of about 2 000 ha and averages 450 m above sea level. Unfortunately access is difficult because of the poorly maintained road leading to the forest. Inland or west of Eshowe lies the Ntumeni Nature Reserve (also controlled by the Natal Parks Board) which is 650 m above sea level and over 560 ha in size.

SPECIAL AND INTERESTING SPECIES

Delegorgue's Pigeon occurs in all three forests but is most readily seen in Dlinza and Ntumeni. It is easy to locate in summer if you know its characteristic loud ascending then descending call, but to get a glimpse of this forest canopy bird is a different matter. In southern Africa the only place where **Green Barbet** occurs is Umgoye Forest. This species is normally not difficult to find if you locate its loud "choc-choc" call. The endangered **Spotted Thrush** breeds in all three forests but is extremely shy and elusive during the breeding season. At least 20 breeding pairs have been recorded in Dlinza Forest. Interestingly **Yellowstreaked Bulbuls** occur in Umgoye

and Ntumeni but not in the central forest, Dlinza. **Brown Robins** are only present in certain parts of the forest, and absent in others. They do not overlap in territory with the Spotted Thrushes during the breeding season. These robins give themselves away by their characteristic alarm note: their song is very similar to that of the thrush. At least two pairs of **Black Sparrowhawks** breed in Dlinza Forest and **Crowned Eagles** can be found in all three forests. **African Broadbill** has only recently been recorded in Ntumeni but other shy species such as **Olive Bush Shrike** and **Green Coucal** are not uncommon. Both **White-eared** and Green Barbets are parasitised by **Scalythroated Honeyguides**. **Lesser Honeyguide** also occasionally enters these forests to parasitise barbets. Parties of **Green Twinspot** occur throughout the forests and are easiest to find on windless days when their soft "tik" call is easier to hear. Other forest species to look for are **Olive Woodpecker**, **Grey Cuckooshrike** and **Redbacked Mannikin**. In the grass and scrub verge above Ntumeni Forest three additional species may be found: **Spotted Prinia**, **Southern Tchagra** and **Lazy Cisticola. Wood Owls** are not difficult to locate at night. **Yellowthroated Warbler** is found only in Ntumeni Forest.

After 4,6 km turn right, at the 9,4 km mark bear right and then left at 10,1 km. Entry permits from Kwa-Zulu are required and the book must be signed at the gate, 11 km from the N2.

ALSO RECORDED

Bush Blackcap has been recorded during winter in Dlinza. Although unusual as a forest species, two or three pairs of African Sedge Warbler occupy the thick sedge grass in a marshy patch at the centre of Dlinza Forest.

Hugh Chittenden

100% OF SPECIES

094 Hadeda Ibis ☐
141 **Crowned Eagle** ☐
157 Little Sparrowhawk ☐
158 **Black Sparrowhawk** ☐
160 African Goshawk ☐
169 Gymnogene ☐
218 Buffspotted Flufftail ☐
350 Rameron Pigeon ☐
351 **Delegorgue's Pigeon** ☐
352 Redeyed Dove ☐
359 Tambourine Dove ☐
360 Cinnamon Dove ☐
361 Green Pigeon ☐
371 Purplecrested Lourie ☐
377 Redchested Cuckoo ☐
378 Black Cuckoo ☐
384 Emerald Cuckoo ☐
385 Klaas's Cuckoo ☐
387 **Green Coucal** ☐
391 Burchell's Coucal* ☐
394 **Wood Owl** ☐
401 Spotted Eagle Owl ☐
424 Speckled Mousebird ☐
427 Narina Trogon ☐
432 Pygmy Kingfisher ☐
452 Redbilled Woodhoopoe ☐
455 Trumpeter Hornbill ☐
460 Crowned Hornbill ☐
466 **White-eared Barbet** ☐
468 **Green Barbet** ☐
469 Redfronted Tinker Barbet ☐
471 Goldenrumped Tinker Barbet ☐
475 **Scalythroated Honeyguide** ☐
476 **Lesser Honeyguide** ☐
478 Sharpbilled Honeyguide ☐
483 Goldentailed Woodpecker ☐
488 **Olive Woodpecker** ☐
490 **African Broadbill** ☐
536 Black Sawwing Swallow ☐
538 Black Cuckooshrike ☐
540 **Grey Cuckooshrike** ☐
541 Forktailed Drongo ☐
542 Squaretailed Drongo ☐
545 Blackheaded Oriole ☐
565 **Bush Blackcap**** ☐
568 Blackeyed Bulbul ☐
569 Terrestrial Bulbul ☐
570 **Yellowstreaked Bulbul** ☐
572 Sombre Bulbul ☐
574 Yellowbellied Bulbul ☐
577 Olive Thrush ☐
578 **Spotted Thrush** ☐
598 Chorister Robin** ☐
600 Natal Robin ☐
606 Starred Robin ☐

616 **Brown Robin**** ☐
638 African Sedge Warbler ☐
644 **Yellowthroated Warbler** ☐
645 Barthroated Apalis ☐
648 Yellowbreasted Apalis ☐
657 Bleating Warbler ☐
679 **Lazy Cisticola** ☐
686 **Spotted Prinia**** ☐
690 Dusky Flycatcher ☐
691 Bluegrey Flycatcher ☐
700 Cape Batis** ☐
708 Bluemantled Flycatcher ☐
710 Paradise Flycatcher ☐
712 Longtailed Wagtail ☐
736 Southern Boubou** ☐
740 Puffback ☐
742 **Southern Tchagra**** ☐
750 **Olive Bush Shrike*** ☐
751 Greyheaded Bush Shrike ☐
768 Blackbellied Starling ☐
783 Lesser Double-collared Sunbird** ☐
789 Grey Sunbird ☐
790 Olive Sunbird ☐
793 Collared Sunbird ☐
796 Cape White-eye** ☐
808 Forest Weaver ☐
835 **Green Twinspot** ☐
857 Bronze Mannikin ☐
858 **Redbacked Mannikin** ☐

MLALAZI NATURE RESERVE AND MTUNZINI VILLAGE

approximately 309 species recorded to date

The Natal Parks Board Mlalazi Nature Reserve stretches southwards from the Mlalazi estuary and includes one of the finest examples of dune plant succession known still to exist along the entire east coast. The reserve and the adjacent Mtunzini town area combine to provide a wide range of habitats, which accounts for the high species count in this rather small area. Several habitat types are readily accessible, and walks have been established which cover coastline, dune forest, swamps and reedbeds, mangrove forests, estuarine margins, some open grassland and the unique raffia palm (*Raphia australis*) swamp. Detailed information on the area

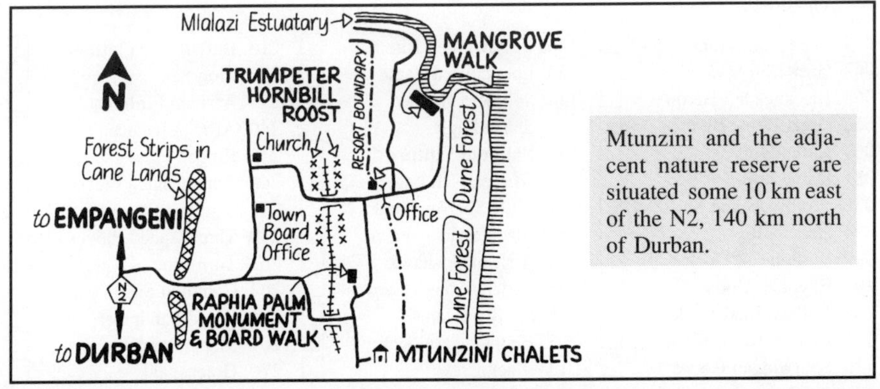

Mtunzini and the adjacent nature reserve are situated some 10 km east of the N2, 140 km north of Durban.

and bookings for accommodation in the form of log cabins are obtainable from the Natal Parks Board office in the reserve and the Mtunzini Town Board office.

SPECIAL AND INTERESTING SPECIES

Mtunzini is best known for its small breeding population of some three to five pairs of **Palmnut Vulture.** The best spot to see this species is the raffia palm boardwalk trail, along the beach or by scanning the strips of forest which remain along the drainage lines in the sugarcane lands around the town. A walk along the edge of the estuary, which also includes the mangrove forest, is good for **African Finfoot**, which often flushes out onto open water. During the winter this is the best place to try and track down the elusive **Mangrove Kingfisher**. If one is out early in the morning, or in the early evening, **Pel's Fishing Owl** may well be heard calling from the thickly wooded areas near the water's edge. However, only the lucky ones get to see this bird. The coastal dune forest walks can be very productive and it is here that the **Spotted Thrush** can be located during the winter months as it forages among the undergrowth, particularly buckweed, below the forest canopy. Other species regularly encountered are **Green Coucal**, **Bluemantled Flycatcher**, **Wattle-eyed Flycatcher**, **White-eared Barbet**, **Cinnamon Dove**, **Scalythroated Honeyguide**, **Olive Sunbird**, **Grey Sunbird**, **Gorgeous Bush Shrike**, **Narina Trogon**, **Forest Weaver**, **Grey Waxbill** and **Green Twinspot**.

ALSO RECORDED

Two raptors, the Sooty Falcon and Southern Banded Snake Eagle, have in recent years been observed in the area, as have Halfcollared Kingfishers. While Trumpeter Hornbills are a common species along coastal Natal, Mtunzini is known for the large flock, often exceeding 100 birds, that frequents the area in the nonbreeding season. They are a spectacular sight when coming in to roost in the stands of large exotic trees between the town and the Mlalazi Nature Reserve. The rare White-backed Night Heron has been recorded on one or two occasions along the Mlalazi estuary and the nearby Siyaya Lagoon, as has Redheaded Quelea. Six Swallowtailed Bee-eaters recorded during a dry spell in 1971 constitute one of only six occurrences ever of this species in Natal.

Digby Cyrus

47% OF SPECIES

058 Reed Cormorant ☐
062 Grey Heron ☐
063 Blackheaded Heron ☐
066 Great White Egret ☐
067 Little Egret ☐
081 Hamerkop ☐
086 Woollynecked Stork ☐
094 Hadeda Ibis ☐
099 Whitefaced Duck ☐
102 Egyptian Goose ☐
104 Yellowbilled Duck ☐
105 African Black Duck ☐
116 Spurwinged Goose ☐
126a Yellowbilled Kite ☐
139 Longcrested Eagle ☐
144 Southern Banded Snake Eagle ☐
147 **Palmnut Vulture** ☐
148 African Fish Eagle ☐
157 Little Sparrowhawk ☐
158 Black Sparrowhawk ☐
160 African Goshawk ☐
165 African Marsh Harrier ☐
175 Sooty Falcon ☐
203 Helmeted Guineafowl ☐
213 Black Crake ☐
218 Buffspotted Flufftail ☐
226 Moorhen ☐
229 **African Finfoot** ☐
240 African Jacana ☐
245 Ringed Plover ☐
246 Whitefronted Plover ☐
248 Kittlitz's Plover ☐
249 Threebanded Plover ☐
262 Turnstone ☐
264 Common Sandpiper ☐
266 Wood Sandpiper ☐
269 Marsh Sandpiper ☐
270 Greenshank ☐

272 Curlew Sandpiper ☐
274 Little Stint ☐
281 Sanderling ☐
284 Ruff ☐
297 Spotted Dikkop ☐
315 Greyheaded Gull ☐
327 Common Tern ☐
350 Rameron Pigeon ☐
352 Redeyed Dove ☐
359 Tambourine Dove ☐
360 **Cinnamon Dove** ☐
361 Green Pigeon ☐
371 Purplecrested Lourie ☐
385 Klaas's Cuckoo ☐
386 Diederik Cuckoo ☐
387 **Green Coucal** ☐
391 Burchell's Coucal* ☐
401 Spotted Eagle Owl ☐
403 **Pel's Fishing Owl** ☐
405 Fierynecked Nightjar ☐
415 Whiterumped Swift ☐
417 Little Swift ☐
421 Palm Swift ☐
424 Speckled Mousebird ☐
427 **Narina Trogon** ☐
428 Pied Kingfisher ☐
429 Giant Kingfisher ☐
431 Malachite Kingfisher ☐
432 Pygmy Kingfisher ☐
434 **Mangrove Kingfisher** ☐
435 Brownhooded Kingfisher ☐
444 Little Bee-eater ☐
455 Trumpeter Hornbill ☐
460 Crowned Hornbill ☐
464 Blackcollared Barbet ☐
466 **White-eared Barbet** ☐
471 Goldenrumped Tinker Barbet ☐
475 **Scalythroated Honeyguide** ☐
483 Goldentailed Woodpecker ☐
518 European Swallow ☐
522 Wiretailed Swallow ☐
527 Lesser Striped Swallow ☐
533 Brownthroated Martin ☐
536 Black Sawwing Swallow ☐
541 Forktailed Drongo ☐
542 Squaretailed Drongo ☐
545 Blackheaded Oriole ☐
548 Pied Crow ☐
568 Blackeyed Bulbul ☐
569 Terrestrial Bulbul ☐
572 Sombre Bulbul ☐
574 Yellowbellied Bulbul ☐
576 Kurrichane Thrush ☐
578 **Spotted Thrush** ☐
596 Stonechat ☐
600 Natal Robin ☐
613 Whitebrowed Robin ☐
631 African Marsh Warbler ☐
635 Cape Reed Warbler ☐
643 Willow Warbler ☐
648 Yellowbreasted Apalis ☐
657 Bleating Warbler ☐
664 Fantailed Cisticola ☐
672 Rattling Cisticola ☐
674 Redfaced Cisticola ☐
675 Blackbacked Cisticola ☐
681 Neddicky ☐
683 Tawnyflanked Prinia ☐
689 Spotted Flycatcher ☐
690 Dusky Flycatcher ☐
691 Bluegrey Flycatcher ☐
694 Black Flycatcher ☐
705 **Wattle-eyed Flycatcher** ☐
708 **Bluemantled Flycatcher** ☐
710 Paradise Flycatcher ☐
711 African Pied Wagtail ☐
713 Cape Wagtail ☐
716 Grassveld Pipit ☐
728 Yellowthroated Longclaw ☐
732 Fiscal Shrike ☐
736 Southern Boubou** ☐
740 Puffback ☐
744 Blackcrowned Tchagra ☐
747 **Gorgeous Bush Shrike** ☐
758 Indian Myna ☐
768 Blackbellied Starling ☐
789 **Grey Sunbird** ☐
790 **Olive Sunbird** ☐
791 Scarletchested Sunbird ☐
793 Collared Sunbird ☐
796 Cape White-eye** ☐
801 House Sparrow ☐
807 Thickbilled Weaver ☐
808 **Forest Weaver** ☐
810 Spectacled Weaver ☐
811 Spottedbacked Weaver ☐
817 Yellow Weaver ☐
824 Red Bishop ☐
828 Redshouldered Widow ☐
831 Redcollared Widow ☐
835 **Green Twinspot** ☐
840 Bluebilled Firefinch ☐
846 Common Waxbill ☐
848 **Grey Waxbill** ☐
857 Bronze Mannikin ☐
860 Pintailed Whydah ☐
864 Black Widowfinch ☐
869 Yelloweyed Canary ☐
☐
☐
☐
☐
☐
☐
☐

GIANT'S CASTLE GAME RESERVE

approximately 160 species recorded to date

This game reserve, proclaimed in 1903, is under the control of the Natal Parks Board and has accommodation for approximately 70 visitors in a popular hutted camp. Reservations and enquiries must be made well in advance through the Natal Parks Board. Camping facilities are also available. The Giant's Castle area is mountainous, varying in height from about 1 650 m at the main entrance gate to over 3 400 m on top of the Drakensberg escarpment. The deep valleys have small patches of relic canopy forest and in the higher regions Leucosidea scrub patches. Sandstone cliffs border the valleys and these constitute what is called the Little Berg. The top of the sandstone averages about 2 050 m. Above this is a basalt grassland plateau which runs up to the main escarpment.

SPECIAL AND INTERESTING SPECIES

Bearded Vultures are regularly seen, particularly in the winter months, and a visit to the Bearded Vulture Hide is a must. It operates from May to September. Bookings for this is through the warden at the game reserve (see telephone list). Other species that may be seen at the hide are **Black Eagle**, **Lanner Falcon**, **Cape Vulture**, **Jackal Buzzard** and **Cape Rock Thrush**. The rest camp has a delightful indigenous garden where species such as **Malachite** and **Greater**

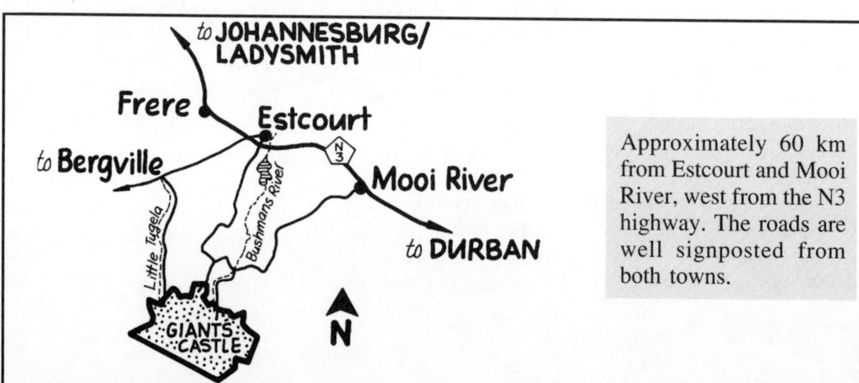

Approximately 60 km from Estcourt and Mooi River, west from the N3 highway. The roads are well signposted from both towns.

Doublecollared Sunbirds are common. **Cape Batis**, **Cape Robin**, **Bush Blackcap** and **Barratt's Warbler** are common in the summer months. Many birds prefer very distinct altitudinal habitats. If one takes a walk from the rest camp (altitude about 1 800 m) to the top of the escarpment via Langalibalele Pass (2 860 m) bird species change greatly as the altitude increases. The path starts along the Bushmans River where one can expect to see **Yellow Warbler**, **Grassbird**, **Yellowrumped Widow**, **African Black Duck**, **Giant Kingfisher**, **Spotted Prinia** and **Familiar Chat**. As one leaves the valley floor and ascends the ridge into the open grassland look carefully for **Yellowbreasted Pipit**, which prefers altitudes between 2 000 m and 2 300 m. **Grassveld Pipit**, **Orangethroated Longclaw** and **Ayres' Cisticola** are common up to about the 2 200 m level. In the pass itself the ringing call of the **Orangebreasted Rockjumper** may be heard. At the top of the pass into Lesotho, bird species are completely different from those of the rest camp and the lower altitudes. Look out for **Fairy Flycatcher**, **Thickbilled Lark**, **Yellow Canary**, **Drakensberg Siskin** and **Sicklewinged Chat**. The francolin found at this high altitude is the **Greywing. Redwing Francolin** may be encountered on the lower ridges long before one nears the contour path. The forest patches immediately beneath the sandstone cliffs harbour additional species such as **Barthroated Apalis**, **Yellowthroated Warbler**, **Olive Thrush**, **Paradise** and **Dusky Flycatchers**, **Cinnamon Dove** and **Chorister Robin**. In the Protea savanna around the camp and up the road from the main gate be sure to look for **Gurney's Sugarbird**, **Buffstreaked Chat** and **Ground Woodpecker**. Other species to look for are **Bald Ibis**, **Black Stork** and **Stanley's Bustard**.

Bill Barnes

Shelley's Francolin

71% OF SPECIES

- 063 Blackheaded Heron ☐
- 081 Hamerkop ☐
- 083 White Stork ☐
- 084 **Black Stork** ☐
- 092 **Bald Ibis****** ☐
- 094 Hadeda Ibis ☐
- 105 **African Black Duck** ☐
- 118 Secretarybird ☐
- 119 **Bearded Vulture** ☐
- 122 **Cape Vulture****** ☐
- 126a Yellowbilled Kite ☐
- 127 Blackshouldered Kite ☐
- 131 **Black Eagle** ☐
- 140 Martial Eagle ☐
- 149 Steppe Buzzard ☐
- 152 **Jackal Buzzard****** ☐
- 155 Redbreasted Sparrowhawk ☐
- 160 African Goshawk ☐
- 165 African Marsh Harrier ☐
- 168 Black Harrier** ☐
- 169 Gymnogene ☐
- 172 **Lanner Falcon** ☐
- 181 Rock Kestrel ☐
- 190 **Greywing Francolin****** ☐
- 192 **Redwing Francolin** ☐
- 198 Rednecked Francolin ☐
- 200 Common Quail ☐
- 203 Helmeted Guineafowl ☐
- 208 Blue Crane** ☐
- 231 **Stanley's Bustard** ☐
- 349 Rock Pigeon ☐

- 350 Rameron Pigeon ☐
- 352 Redeyed Dove ☐
- 354 Cape Turtle Dove ☐
- 360 **Cinnamon Dove** ☐
- 377 Redchested Cuckoo ☐
- 382 Jacobin Cuckoo ☐
- 385 Klaas's Cuckoo ☐
- 386 Diederik Cuckoo ☐
- 393 Grass Owl ☐
- 395 Marsh Owl ☐
- 401 Spotted Eagle Owl ☐
- 405 Fierynecked Nightjar ☐
- 412 Black Swift ☐
- 415 Whiterumped Swift ☐
- 418 Alpine Swift ☐
- 429 **Giant Kingfisher** ☐
- 431 Malachite Kingfisher ☐
- 480 **Ground Woodpecker**** ☐
- 488 Olive Woodpecker ☐
- 512 **Thickbilled Lark**** ☐
- 518 European Swallow ☐
- 520 Whitethroated Swallow ☐
- 526 Greater Striped Swallow* ☐
- 529 Rock Martin ☐
- 533 Brownthroated Martin ☐
- 536 Black Sawwing Swallow ☐
- 541 Forktailed Drongo ☐
- 547 Black Crow ☐
- 550 Whitenecked Raven ☐
- 554 Southern Black Tit* ☐
- 565 **Bush Blackcap**** ☐
- 568 Blackeyed Bulbul ☐
- 577 **Olive Thrush** ☐
- 581 **Cape Rock Thrush**** ☐
- 582 Sentinel Rock Thrush** ☐
- 588 **Buffstreaked Chat**** ☐
- 589 **Familiar Chat** ☐
- 591 **Sicklewinged Chat**** ☐
- 596 Stonechat ☐
- 598 **Chorister Robin**** ☐
- 601 **Cape Robin** ☐
- 612 **Orangebreasted Rockjumper**** ☐
- 637 **Yellow Warbler** ☐
- 639 **Barratt's Warbler**** ☐
- 644 **Yellowthroated Warbler** ☐
- 645 **Barthroated Apalis** ☐
- 661 **Grassbird**** ☐
- 667 **Ayres' Cisticola** ☐
- 670 Wailing Cisticola ☐
- 677 Levaillant's Cisticola ☐
- 681 Neddicky ☐
- 686a **Spotted Prinia**** ☐
- 690 **Dusky Flycatcher** ☐
- 700 **Cape Batis**** ☐
- 706 **Fairy Flycatcher**** ☐
- 710 **Paradise Flycatcher** ☐
- 713 Cape Wagtail ☐
- 716 **Grassveld Pipit** ☐
- 725 **Yellowbreasted Pipit**** ☐
- 727 **Orangethroated Longclaw**** ☐
- 740 Puffback ☐
- 746 Bokmakierie* ☐
- 759 Pied Starling** ☐
- 769 Redwinged Starling ☐
- 774 **Gurney's Sugarbird**** ☐
- 775 **Malachite Sunbird** ☐
- 783 Lesser Double-collared Sunbird** ☐
- 785 **Greater Double-collared Sunbird**** ☐
- 796 Cape White-eye** ☐
- 804 Greyheaded Sparrow ☐
- 813 Cape Weaver** ☐
- 827 **Yellowrumped Widow** ☐
- 831 Redcollared Widow ☐
- 832 Longtailed Widow ☐
- 846 Common Waxbill ☐
- 850 Swee Waxbill* ☐
- 852 Quail Finch ☐
- 860 Pintailed Whydah ☐
- 872 Cape Canary ☐
- 873 Forest Canary** ☐
- 875 **Drakensberg Siskin**** ☐
- 878 **Yellow Canary*** ☐
- 881 Streakyheaded Canary ☐
- 884 Goldenbreasted Bunting ☐
- 885 Cape Buntin ☐
- 886 Rock Bunting ☐
- ☐
- ☐
- ☐

UMGENI VALLEY NATURE RESERVE

approximately 213 species recorded to date

Umgeni Valley Nature Reserve is owned and managed by the Wildlife Society of Southern Africa through the Umgeni Valley Project. The reserve, established in 1976, is situated to the east of Howick and just downstream from Howick Falls on the Umgeni River. A wide variety of habitats are found in the reserve, including undulating and flat grassland above the sandstone cliff faces and steep rocky, bushy and aloe-strewn slopes extending to the Umgeni River in the valley floor, where there are patches of thicker vegetation and large trees. A large area of Acacia thornveld stocked with giraffe and wildebeest is found at the eastern end of the reserve. The nature reserve is open from dawn to dusk and an entry fee is payable at the office. Overnight accommodation is available in the form of a six-bed cottage.

SPECIAL AND INTERESTING SPECIES

Wailing Cisticolas are found in the upper grassland areas, often perched in the morning on tall grass stems and first noticed by their characteristic "wailing" call. **Mocking Chats** are found on the cliff faces and around the large boulders on the steep slopes below the cliffs. **Cape** and **Sentinel Rock Thrushes** (in winter) may be seen sitting on vantage points along the top of the cliff faces. Dassies, which live on the cliffs, provide an attraction for **Black Eagles** which are usually seen planing

ALSO RECORDED

Shorttailed Pipit has been recorded in the grassland areas. Raptors that may be seen include Martial, Wahlberg's, Tawny and Booted Eagles, Black Sparrowhawk and Hobby Falcon. The cliff top near the parking area at the eastern end of the road network is a good point for raptor and swallow/swift watching. Lesser Grey Shrike (summer) and Fairy Flycatcher (winter) have occurred in the Acacia thornveld area. Green Pigeons occasionally visit the larger fruiting trees in the reserve.

Roger Horner

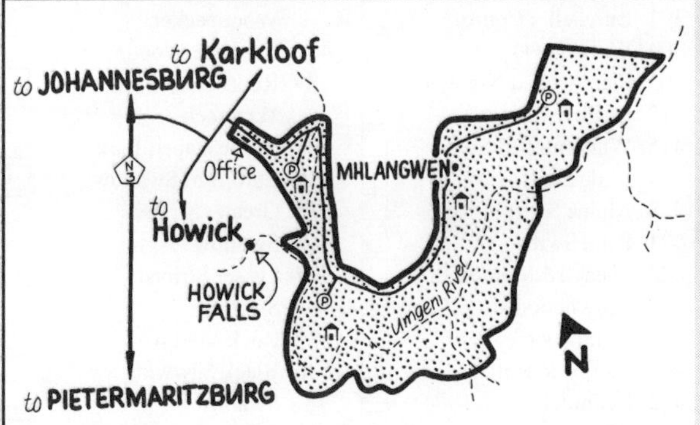

Howick lies on the eastern side of the N3 about 25 km north of Pietermaritzburg. From the main street of Howick take the tarred road to Karkloof and Rietvlei. Only 1,2 km from this junction the entrance to Umgeni Nature Reserve will be found on the right. A gravel road system allows vehicles access to the upper grassland areas and a network of trails gives access to most other areas.

back and forth on up-currents of air along the cliff top. Breeding has occurred just outside the reserve. There are two **Crowned Eagle** nests in the reserve and these large raptors may often be seen flying with the Black Eagles. The **Lanner Falcon** also uses up-currents from the cliff face or may be seen flying across the valley. The grassy slopes at the foot of the cliff provide suitable habitat for **Lazy Cisticola** and rock-strewn areas may turn up **Striped Pipit**. **Longtailed Wagtails** use the swift-flowing streams on the hillsides, and the stream below Mhlangwen Cottage, where it crosses the Grassland Trail, is an excellent spot for this species. **Trumpeter** and **Crowned Hornbills** and **Knysna Lourie** may be heard and seen as they feed in the larger trees along the Umgeni River and part of the Grassland Trail at the foot of the cliff. **Lesser** and **Greater Honeyguides** are usually picked up by call and **Sharpbilled Honeyguide** may be found in the Acacia thornveld areas, especially during the winter months. This same area will yield **Redthroated Wryneck**. Scan dead branches and trees.

62% OF SPECIES

- 055 Whitebreasted Cormorant ☐
- 063 Blackheaded Heron ☐
- 071 Cattle Egret ☐
- 081 Hamerkop ☐
- 083 White Stork ☐
- 094 Hadeda Ibis ☐
- 102 Egyptian Goose ☐
- 126a Yellowbilled Kite ☐
- 131 **Black Eagle** ☐
- 139 Longcrested Eagle ☐
- 141 **Crowned Eagle** ☐
- 149 Steppe Buzzard ☐
- 152 Jackal Buzzard** ☐
- 160 African Goshawk ☐
- 169 Gymnogene ☐
- 172 **Lanner Falcon** ☐
- 181 Rock Kestrel ☐
- 188 Coqui Francolin ☐
- 196 Natal Francolin* ☐
- 200 Common Quail ☐
- 203 Helmeted Guineafowl ☐
- 226 Moorhen ☐
- 349 Rock Pigeon ☐
- 350 Rameron Pigeon ☐
- 352 Redeyed Dove ☐
- 354 Cape Turtle Dove ☐
- 355 Laughing Dove ☐
- 358 Greenspotted Dove ☐
- 359 Tambourine Dove ☐
- 370 **Knysna Lourie**** ☐
- 377 Redchested Cuckoo ☐
- 378 Black Cuckoo ☐
- 385 Klaas's Cuckoo ☐
- 386 Diederik Cuckoo ☐
- 391 Burchell's Coucal* ☐
- 394 Wood Owl ☐
- 405 Fierynecked Nightjar ☐
- 412 Black Swift ☐
- 415 Whiterumped Swift ☐
- 417 Little Swift ☐
- 418 Alpine Swift ☐
- 421 Palm Swift ☐
- 424 Speckled Mousebird ☐
- 435 Brownhooded Kingfisher ☐
- 446 European Roller ☐
- 452 Redbilled Woodhoopoe ☐
- 454 Scimitarbilled Woodhoopoe ☐
- 455 **Trumpeter Hornbill** ☐
- 460 **Crowned Hornbill** ☐
- 464 Blackcollared Barbet ☐
- 473 Crested Barbet ☐
- 474 **Greater Honeyguide** ☐
- 476 **Lesser Honeyguide** ☐
- 478 **Sharpbilled Honeyguide** ☐
- 483 Goldentailed Woodpecker ☐
- 486 Cardinal Woodpecker ☐
- 489 **Redthroated Wryneck** ☐
- 494 Rufousnaped Lark ☐
- 518 European Swallow ☐
- 526 Greater Striped Swallow* ☐
- 527 Lesser Striped Swallow ☐
- 529 Rock Martin ☐
- 536 Black Sawwing Swallow ☐
- 538 Black Cuckooshrike ☐

541 Forktailed Drongo ☐
545 Blackheaded Oriole ☐
550 Whitenecked Raven ☐
554 Southern Black Tit* ☐
568 Blackeyed Bulbul ☐
572 Sombre Bulbul ☐
576 Kurrichane Thrush ☐
577 Olive Thrush ☐
581 **Cape Rock Thrush**** ☐
582 **Sentinel Rock Thrush**** ☐
589 Familiar Chat ☐
593 **Mocking Chat** ☐
596 Stonechat ☐
598 Chorister Robin** ☐
601 Cape Robin ☐
613 Whitebrowed Robin ☐
643 Willow Warbler ☐
645 Barthroated Apalis ☐
651 Longbilled Crombec ☐
657 Bleating Warbler ☐
664 Fantailed Cisticola ☐
667 Ayres' Cisticola ☐
670 **Wailing Cisticola** ☐
677 Levaillant's Cisticola ☐
678 Croaking Cisticola ☐
679 **Lazy Cisticola** ☐
681 Neddicky ☐
683 Tawnyflanked Prinia ☐
690 Dusky Flycatcher ☐
694 Black Flycatcher ☐
700 Cape Batis** ☐
701 Chinspot Batis ☐
710 Paradise Flycatcher ☐
712 **Longtailed Wagtail** ☐
713 Cape Wagtail ☐
716 Grassveld Pipit ☐
720 **Striped Pipit** ☐
727 Orangethroated Longclaw** ☐
732 Fiscal Shrike ☐
736 Southern Boubou** ☐
740 Puffback ☐
741 Brubru ☐
744 Blackcrowned Tchagra ☐
748 Orangebreasted Bush Shrike ☐
758 Indian Myna ☐
761 Plumcoloured Starling ☐
764 Glossy Starling* ☐
769 Redwinged Starling ☐
787 Whitebellied Sunbird ☐
792 Black Sunbird ☐
793 Collared Sunbird ☐
796 Cape White-eye** ☐
804 Greyheaded Sparrow ☐
805 Yellowthroated Sparrow ☐
807 Thickbilled Weaver ☐
810 Spectacled Weaver ☐
811 Spottedbacked Weaver ☐
813 Cape Weaver** ☐
824 Red Bishop ☐
828 Redshouldered Widow ☐
831 Redcollared Widow ☐
840 Bluebilled Firefinch ☐
846 Common Waxbill ☐
850 Swee Waxbill* ☐
857 Bronze Mannikin ☐
860 Pintailed Whydah ☐
869 Yelloweyed Canary ☐
872 Cape Canary ☐
881 Streakyheaded Canary ☐
884 Goldenbreasted Bunting ☐
☐
☐
☐

Knysna Lourie

SANI PASS

approximately 132 species recorded to date

This mountain pass over the high Drakensberg from Natal to Lesotho is 125 km by road west of Pietermaritzburg. This description covers the 90 square km catchment of the Umkomazana River within the Drakensberg park in Natal (administered by the Natal Parks Board), and 270 square km of the catchments of the Sani and Sekongkong rivers in Lesotho. The altitude ranges from 1 600 m to 3 482 m, where substantially sub-zero night temperatures prevail during the winter months and snow may lie for some weeks. Many of the bird species throughout the locality are altitudinal migrants and observations suggest that the Sani Pass is a migration route for certain Palaearctic species. Accommodation is available at Underberg, Himeville and at the Sani Pass Hotel. Hiking permits are available from the Natal Parks Board. Passports are essential for entry into Lesotho except for RSA citizens accompanying organised day tours who have identity books. Sani Top Chalet in Lesotho has self-catering accommodation.

SPECIAL AND INTERESTING SPECIES

The species mentioned follow the order in which they might be encountered on the way up the pass. Associated with the mixed Leucosidea scrub and thicket around Good Hope, **Bush Blackcap**, **Yellow Warbler**, **Barratt's Warbler** (by call) and **Sharpbilled Honeyguide**. A half-hour walk up the

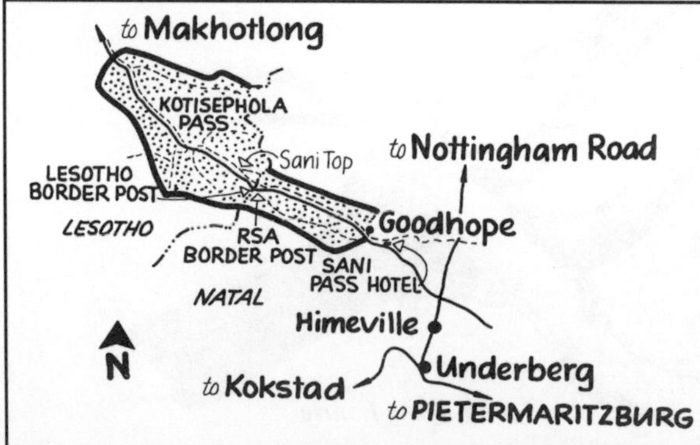

ALSO RECORDED

Peregrine Falcon, Cape Eagle Owl and Booted Eagle are recorded.

Robin Guy

From the Cape Province via Transkei the road is tarred to Underberg/Himeville. From the Transvaal take the tarred road signposted "Bulwer", turning off the N3 at Merrivale (110 km to Underberg). Turn left 9 km from Underberg via Himeville at the signposted crossroads near the Polela River bridge. The locality described here begins 14 km further at the Good Hope Store where the pass continues a further 11 km up to the RSA border control post (open 08h00 to 16h00 daily). Only four-wheel drive vehicles are permitted to continue the last 8 km to the Lesotho border post at Sani Top, and the 24 km along the Mokhotlong road to the Sekongkong River.

Gxalingenwa footpath (starts in gum plantation 50 m from bridge) into evergreen forest for **Chorister Robin**, **Yellowthroated Warbler**, **Olive Woodpecker** and **Buffspotted Flufftail**. Beyond Good Hope the road climbs to Protea grassland with sandstone scarps, tumbled boulders and rank growth in gulleys, the habitat of **Gurney's Sugarbird**, **Buffstreaked Chat**, **Ground Woodpecker**, **Cape Rock Trush** and **Grassbird**. In the roadside vlei listen for **Redchested Flufftail**. As the basalt lava cliffs of the main escarpment are approached beyond the RSA border post, there is a high-altitude grassland above the road: **Black Harrier** habitat. Below the road is dense thicket, which has resulted from a century of heavy grazing pressure by pack animals wandering from an old outspan, with subsequent colonisation by a wealth of heath plants: unique habitat. Look here for **Fairy Flycatcher**, **Layard's Titbabbler**, **Wailing Cisticola** and **Spotted Prinia**. On the final zig-zags through the head of the pass expect **Drakensberg Siskin**, **Orangebreasted Rockjumper**, **Cape Bunting** and, as you reach the top, **Sicklewinged Chat** and **Sentinal Rock Thrush**. Listen for the unmistakable call of **Rock Pipit** in the vicinity of the Sani Top Chalet, on the escarpment. In Lesotho, in subalpine heath, **Mountain Pipit** may first be seen in the vicinity of a ruin 2 km along the road to Mokhotlong from Sani Top. This species, which is only present from September to April, occurs in the same terrain as **Thickbilled Lark**, which has an unmistakable thin musical call. **Greywing Francolin** is resident and **Yellow Canary** can usually be seen. It is noteworthy that the Lesotho highlands support considerable populations of insectivorous birds, which may be related to the high nutrient content of the volcanic soil. Raptors are well represented, particularly **Jackal Buzzard**, which benefits from the abundance of ice rats (*Otomys sloggetti*). **Pale Chanting Goshawk** is regularly recorded in the autumn. Short-grass vleis are preferred by **Bald Ibis** and **Redcapped Lark**, and the streams by **Black Stork**. On the steep descent beyond Kotisephola Pass you can see a **Bearded Vulture** nest cave, often with wool straggling out. Listen here for Rock Pipit and expect Layard's Titbabbler and **Southern Grey Tit**. Allow two hours back to the RSA border post which closes at 16h00.

90% OF SPECIES

055 Whitebreasted Cormorant ☐
062 Grey Heron ☐
063 Blackheaded Heron ☐
071 Cattle Egret ☐
081 Hamerkop ☐
083 White Stork ☐
084 **Black Stork** ☐
091 Sacred Ibis ☐
092 **Bald Ibis**** ☐
094 Hadeda Ibis ☐
102 Egyptian Goose ☐

Natal

104 Yellowbilled Duck ☐
105 African Black Duck ☐
118 Secretarybird ☐
119 **Bearded Vulture** ☐
122 Cape Vulture** ☐
127 Blackshouldered Kite ☐
131 Black Eagle ☐
136 **Booted Eagle** ☐
149 Steppe Buzzard ☐
152 **Jackal Buzzard**** ☐
155 Redbreasted Sparrowhawk ☐
160 African Goshawk ☐
162 **Pale Chanting Goshawk*** ☐
168 **Black Harrier**** ☐
169 Gymnogene ☐
171 Peregrine Falcon ☐
172 Lanner Falcon ☐
181 Rock Kestrel ☐
190 **Greywing Francolin**** ☐
192 Redwing Francolin ☐
200 Common Quail ☐
205 Kurrichane Buttonquail ☐
208 Blue Crane** ☐
217 **Redchested Flufftail** ☐
218 **Buffspotted Flufftail** ☐
249 Threebanded Plover ☐
266 Wood Sandpiper ☐
349 Rock Pigeon ☐
350 Rameron Pigeon ☐
352 Redeyed Dove ☐
354 Cape Turtle Dove ☐
356 Namaqua Dove ☐
377 Redchested Cuckoo ☐
378 Black Cuckoo ☐
382 Jacobin Cuckoo ☐
386 Diederik Cuckoo ☐
400 Cape Eagle Owl ☐
411 European Swift ☐
412 Black Swift ☐
415 Whiterumped Swift ☐
416 Horus Swift ☐
418 Alpine Swift ☐
424 Speckled Mousebird ☐
428 Pied Kingfisher ☐
429 Giant Kingfisher ☐
451 Hoopoe ☐
478 **Sharpbilled Honeyguide** ☐
480 **Ground Woodpecker**** ☐
488 **Olive Woodpecker** ☐
507 **Redcapped Lark** ☐
512 **Thickbilled Lark**** ☐
518 European Swallow ☐
526 Greater Striped Swallow* ☐
529 Rock Martin ☐
530 House Martin ☐
533 Brownthroated Martin ☐
536 Black Sawwing Swallow ☐
541 Forktailed Drongo ☐
545 Blackheaded Oriole ☐
547 Black Crow ☐
550 Whitenecked Raven ☐
551 **Southern Grey Tit**** ☐
554 Southern Black Tit* ☐
565 **Bush Blackcap**** ☐
568 Blackeyed Bulbul ☐
572 Sombre Bulbul ☐
576 Kurrichane Thrush ☐
577 Olive Thrush ☐
581 **Cape Rock Thrush**** ☐
582 **Sentinel Rock Thrush**** ☐
588 **Buffstreaked Chat**** ☐
589 Familiar Chat ☐
591 **Sicklewinged Chat**** ☐
596 Stonechat ☐
598 **Chorister Robin**** ☐
601 Cape Robin ☐
612 **Orangebreasted Rockjumper**** ☐
622 **Layard's Titbabbler**** ☐
637 **Yellow Warbler** ☐
639 **Barratt's Warbler**** ☐
644 **Yellowthroated Warbler** ☐
645 Barthroated Apalis ☐
661 **Grassbird**** ☐
667 Ayres' Cisticola ☐
670 **Wailing Cisticola** ☐
677 Levaillant's Cisticola ☐
681 Neddicky ☐
686a **Spotted Prinia**** ☐
690 Dusky Flycatcher ☐
700 Cape Batis** ☐
706 **Fairy Flycatcher**** ☐
710 Paradise Flycatcher ☐
713 Cape Wagtail ☐
901 **Mountain Pipit*** ☐
717 Longbilled Pipit ☐
721 **Rock Pipit**** ☐
727 Orangethroated Longclaw** ☐
732 Fiscal Shrike ☐
736 Southern Boubou** ☐
746 Bokmakierie* ☐
769 Redwinged Starling ☐
774 **Gurney's Sugarbird**** ☐
775 Malachite Sunbird ☐
785 Greater Double-collared Sunbird** ☐
796 Cape White-eye** ☐
801 House Sparrow ☐
803 Cape Sparrow* ☐
804 Greyheaded Sparrow ☐
813 Cape Weaver** ☐
827 Yellowrumped Widow ☐
831 Redcollared Widow ☐
846 Common Waxbill ☐
850 Swee Waxbill* ☐
860 Pintailed Whydah ☐
864 Black Widowfinch ☐
872 Cape Canary ☐
875 **Drakensberg Siskin**** ☐
878 **Yellow Canary*** ☐
881 Streakyheaded Canary ☐
884 Goldenbreasted Bunting ☐
885 **Cape Bunting** ☐

DARVILL SEWAGE WORKS

approximately 247 species recorded to date

The Darvill sewage works are controlled by the City Engineer of Pietermaritzburg and are located near the Umsindusi River. The habitat is almost entirely exotic, consisting of man-made ponds surrounded by alien weeds, reedbeds and poplar plantations. Management is informal and the area is deliberately left "untidy" for the benefit of birds. The bird community is a mixture of wetland, scrub and forest species and in summer there is always a high population of Palaearctic migrants.

SPECIAL AND INTERESTING SPECIES

Darvill is famous for its ducks, **Hottentot Teal** being especially common and even **Fulvous Duck** can sometimes be seen. **Baillon's Crake** and **Little Bittern** both occur in thick weedy edges. Probably Darvill's most renowned breeding bird is the **Redheaded Quelea**, which first appeared in 1983 when the species was presumed rare. The same population arrives each October, sometimes in their thousands, departing before the end of March. The best place to see the queleas is beside the lower strip ponds. Huge numbers of swallows and swifts forage low over Darvill in overcast weather. In winter the dominant species are **Brownthroated** and **Rock Martin**, in spring **Lesser Striped Swallows** dominate and in summer **European Swallows** take over. Palaearctic warblers concentrate at Darvill, particularly in late summer. **Willow**

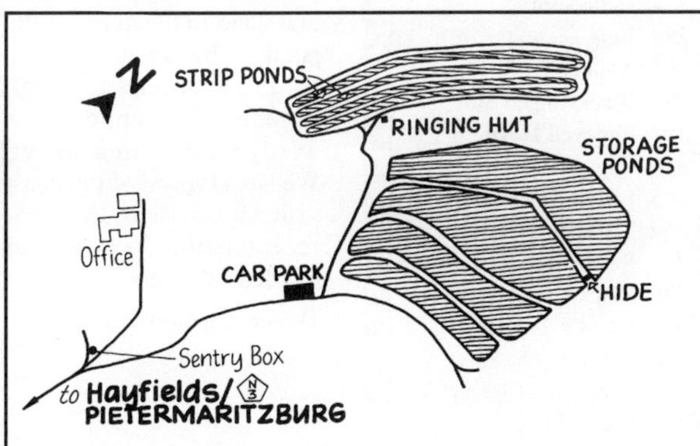

Take the Hayfields turn-off from the Pietermaritzburg bypass. After 200 m the road forks: take the left fork which leads straight on through the golf course. The Darvill entrance is clearly signposted on the left, about 2 km along this road. Follow the internal tarred road for 300 m and sign in at the sentry box. Entry permits are obtainable at the office near the sentry box during office hours. Take the gravel track to the car park.

Warblers are especially common, and diligence will reveal **European Sedge**, **European Marsh**, **Great Reed** and **Garden Warblers**. Darvill is also noted for its winter migrants. **Bully** and **Cape Canaries**, **Orangebreasted Waxbill**, **African Pied Wagtail** and **Rock Martin** appear only in winter, the latter being abundant if there is cold weather in the Drakensberg. Raptors are sparse but **Longcrested** and **African Fish Eagles** both breed in the poplars. At dusk a **Black Sparrowhawk**, which specialises in bat-catching, can be seen. One of the charms of Darvill is the constant changes in the larger water birds. **Squacco Herons** "invaded" for much of 1990, and then vanished. **Avocets** and **Glossy Ibis** appear frequently and **Yellow Wagtails** arrived for the first time in the spring of 1990.

61% OF SPECIES

- 008 **Dabchick** ☐
- 058 Reed Cormorant ☐
- 060 Darter ☐
- 062 Grey Heron ☐
- 063 Blackheaded Heron ☐
- 071 Cattle Egret ☐
- 072 **Squacco Heron** ☐
- 078 **Little Bittern** ☐
- 081 Hamerkop ☐
- 091 Sacred Ibis ☐
- 093 **Glossy Ibis** ☐
- 094 Hadeda Ibis ☐
- 099 Whitefaced Duck ☐
- 100 **Fulvous Duck** ☐
- 101 Whitebacked Duck ☐
- 102 Egyptian Goose ☐
- 104 Yellowbilled Duck ☐
- 106 Cape Teal ☐
- 107 **Hottentot Teal** ☐
- 108 Redbilled Teal ☐
- 112 Cape Shoveller* ☐
- 113 Southern Pochard ☐
- 116 Spurwinged Goose ☐
- 126a Yellowbilled Kite ☐
- 135 Wahlberg's Eagle ☐
- 139 **Longcrested Eagle** ☐
- 148 **African Fish Eagle** ☐
- 149 Steppe Buzzard ☐
- 158 **Black Sparrowhawk** ☐
- 160 African Goshawk ☐
- 169 Gymnogene ☐
- 196 Natal Francolin* ☐
- 203 Helmeted Guineafowl ☐
- 213 Black Crake ☐
- 215 **Baillon's Crake** ☐
- 217 Redchested Flufftail ☐
- 218 Buffspotted Flufftail ☐
- 226 Moorhen ☐
- 228 Redknobbed Coot ☐
- 240 African Jacana ☐
- 249 Threebanded Plover ☐
- 258 Blacksmith Plover ☐
- 264 Common Sandpiper ☐
- 266 Wood Sandpiper ☐
- 270 Greenshank ☐
- 274 Little Stint ☐
- 284 Ruff ☐
- 294 **Avocet** ☐
- 295 Blackwinged Stilt ☐
- 352 Redeyed Dove ☐
- 354 Cape Turtle Dove ☐
- 355 Laughing Dove ☐
- 359 Tambourine Dove ☐
- 377 Redchested Cuckoo ☐
- 378 Black Cuckoo ☐
- 385 Klaas's Cuckoo ☐
- 386 Diederik Cuckoo ☐
- 391 Burchell's Coucal* ☐
- 401 Spotted Eagle Owl ☐
- 405 Fierynecked Nightjar ☐

ALSO RECORDED

Because Darvill is well watched, all sorts of unlikely birds are recorded from time to time. Famous one-off records in the last five years are Natal Robin, Wattle-eyed Flycatcher, Marabou Stork, Black Tern, Purplecrested Lourie, Mozambique Nightjar, Pearlbreasted Swallow, Wattled Starling and Lesser Masked Weaver, all well out of range and habitat. Perhaps the most exciting rare bird to be seen more than once at Darvill is the Peregrine Falcon. One individual hunts swallows, and ringing has shown that it is the same bird which roosts on the Natalia building in the town centre. Crowned Cranes occasionally roost in the willows above the top ponds. In some summers Pygmy Kingfishers are common with a good proportion of black-beaked juveniles. Broadtailed Warblers occur in the small area of natural grassland to the north of the ponds. The Spotted Prinia, an upland species in Natal, occasionally appears in weedy scrub during winter. Weavers typical of the coast visit on occasion, the most recent being Yellow and Golden Weavers.

David Johnson

411 European Swift ☐
412 Black Swift ☐
415 Whiterumped Swift ☐
417 Little Swift ☐
421 Palm Swift ☐
424 Speckled Mousebird ☐
426 Redfaced Mousebird ☐
428 Pied Kingfisher ☐
429 Giant Kingfisher ☐
431 Malachite Kingfisher ☐
432 Pygmy Kingfisher ☐
435 Brownhooded Kingfisher ☐
464 Blackcollared Barbet ☐
473 Crested Barbet ☐
474 Greater Honeyguide ☐
478 Sharpbilled Honeyguide ☐
483 Goldentailed Woodpecker ☐
486 Cardinal Woodpecker ☐
518 **European Swallow** ☐
520 Whitethroated Swallow ☐
526 Greater Striped Swallow* ☐
527 **Lesser Striped Swallow** ☐
529 **Rock Martin** ☐
530 House Martin ☐
532 Sand Martin ☐
533 **Brownthroated Martin** ☐
536 Black Sawwing Swallow ☐
541 Forktailed Drongo ☐
545 Blackheaded Oriole ☐
548 Pied Crow ☐
554 Southern Black Tit* ☐
568 Blackeyed Bulbul ☐
572 Sombre Bulbul ☐
576 Kurrichane Thrush ☐
577 Olive Thrush ☐
601 Cape Robin ☐
619 **Garden Warbler** ☐
628 **Great Reed Warbler** ☐
631 African Marsh Warbler ☐
633 **European Marsh Warbler** ☐
634 **European Sedge Warbler** ☐
635 Cape Reed Warbler ☐
637 Yellow Warbler ☐
638 African Sedge Warbler ☐
643 **Willow Warbler** ☐
645 Barthroated Apalis ☐
657 Bleating Warbler ☐
664 Fantailed Cisticola ☐
677 Levaillant's Cisticola ☐
683 Tawnyflanked Prinia ☐
689 Spotted Flycatcher ☐
690 Dusky Flycatcher ☐
694 Black Flycatcher ☐
710 Paradise Flycatcher ☐
711 **African Pied Wagtail** ☐
713 Cape Wagtail ☐
714 **Yellow Wagtail** ☐
716 Grassveld Pipit ☐
728 Yellowthroated Longclaw ☐
732 Fiscal Shrike ☐
736 Southern Boubou** ☐
758 Indian Myna ☐
764 Glossy Starling* ☐
787 Whitebellied Sunbird ☐
790 Olive Sunbird ☐
792 Black Sunbird ☐
793 Collared Sunbird ☐
796 Cape White-eye** ☐
801 House Sparrow ☐
803 Cape Sparrow* ☐
804 Greyheaded Sparrow ☐
807 Thickbilled Weaver ☐
810 Spectacled Weaver ☐
811 Spottedbacked Weaver ☐
813 Cape Weaver** ☐
822 **Redheaded Quelea** ☐
824 Red Bishop ☐
828 Redshouldered Widow ☐
829 Whitewinged Widow ☐
831 Redcollared Widow ☐
840 Bluebilled Firefinch ☐
846 Common Waxbill ☐
852 Quail Finch ☐
854 **Orangebreasted Waxbill** ☐
857 Bronze Mannikin ☐
858 Redbacked Mannikin ☐
860 Pintailed Whydah ☐
864 Black Widowfinch ☐
869 Yelloweyed Canary ☐
872 **Cape Canary** ☐
873 Forest Canary** ☐
877 **Bully Canary** ☐
881 Streakyheaded Canary ☐
☐
☐

UMHLANGA SEWAGE WORKS

approximately 128 species recorded to date

The Umhlanga sewage works, controlled by the Umhlanga Municipality, are situated just north-west of Umhlanga Rocks on the banks of the Umhlanga River. The four settling ponds are completely separate from the sewage works and are well vegetated, with reeds, grass, sedges and lily pads. The walkways around the ponds are grassed and well maintained. A bird-ringing station has been established at the ponds with ringing usually taking place on the last Sunday of the month. Anyone is welcome to attend these sessions, which provide an ideal opportunity to see birds in the hand. None of the birds commonly seen are particularly special, but the concentration and opportunity to get close up make this a popular birding spot especially for waders, herons, warblers, weavers and other waterbirds. The best time of the year to visit the ponds is in summer, but a number of species use this sanctuary during winter. Expect to see between 40 and 50 species in an hour's birding.

SPECIAL AND INTERESTING SPECIES

The pond closest to the entrance provides the best birding as it is well vegetated. Scan the reeds and lily pads for interesting species such as **Black Crake**, **Purple Gallinule**, **Greenbacked** and **Purple Herons**, **Blackcrowned Night Heron** and **White Pelican**. Numerous weavers nest in the trees and reeds, including **Thickbilled** and **Yellow Weavers**. The two top ponds are less vegetated and a restricted walk-

ALSO RECORDED

A number of uncommon species have been recorded at the ponds including Little Bittern, Lesser Jacana, Wattle-eyed Flycatcher, Osprey, Lesser Moorhen, Greyhooded Kingfisher, Redbacked Mannikin and Brownthroated Weaver.

Gordon Holtshausen

Birders are welcome at the ponds and access is not restricted. The ponds are situated about 20 km north of Durban and 5 km from Umhlanga Rocks. From Durban, take the Leo Boyd highway (M4) to Umhlanga Rocks and take the Umhlanga/Lighthouse Road turnoff from the dual carriageway. Turn left into Umhlanga Rocks Drive. Proceed for 1,2 km and then turn right into Herwood Drive, which is 100 m from the Natal Sharks Board building. Proceed along Herwood Drive for 1,9 km on tar road, then 2,5 km on gravel to the ponds.

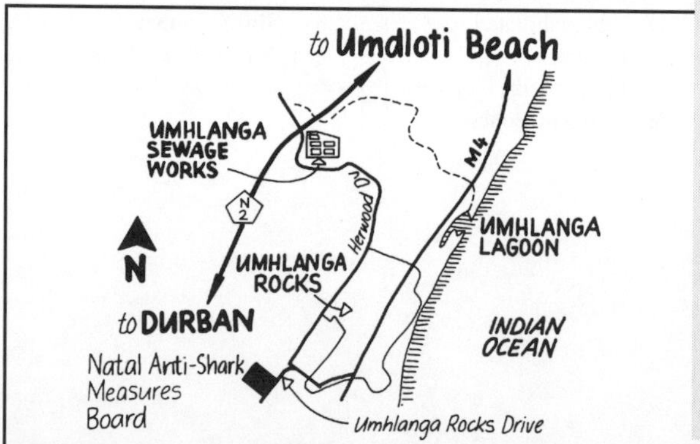

way provides a secure roost for **Whitebreasted Cormorant**, **Ruff**, **Wood Sandpiper**, **Whitefaced Duck** and **Water Dikkop**. The reeds and vegetation around the ponds provide habitat for warblers and cisticolas and one should look and listen for **Blackbacked** and **Redfaced Cisticolas**, and **Cape Reed**, **Great Reed**, **European Sedge**, **African Marsh** and **African Sedge Warblers**. In the evenings swallows, martins and swifts come in to roost in the reedbeds.

100% OF SPECIES

008 Dabchick ☐
049 **White Pelican** ☐
055 **Whitebreasted Cormorant** ☐
058 Reed Cormorant ☐
060 Darter ☐
062 Grey Heron ☐
063 Blackheaded Heron ☐
064 Goliath Heron ☐
065 **Purple Heron** ☐
066 Great White Egret ☐
067 Little Egret ☐
072 Squacco Heron ☐
074 **Greenbacked Heron** ☐
076 **Blackcrowned Night Heron** ☐
078 Little Bittern ☐
081 Hamerkop ☐
091 Sacred Ibis ☐
094 Hadeda Ibis ☐
099 **Whitefaced Duck** ☐
102 Egyptian Goose ☐
104 Yellowbilled Duck ☐
105 African Black Duck ☐
106 Cape Teal ☐
107 Hottentot Teal ☐
113 Southern Pochard ☐
116 Spurwinged Goose ☐
126a Yellowbilled Kite ☐
141 Crowned Eagle ☐
148 African Fish Eagle ☐
149 Steppe Buzzard ☐
170 Osprey ☐
191 Shelley's Francolin ☐
196 Natal Francolin* ☐
200 Common Quail ☐
204 Crested Guineafowl ☐
213 **Black Crake** ☐
223 **Purple Gallinule** ☐
226 Moorhen ☐
227 Lesser Moorhen ☐
228 Redknobbed Coot ☐
240 African Jacana ☐
241 Lesser Jacana ☐
249 Threebanded Plover ☐
258 Blacksmith Plover ☐
264 Common Sandpiper ☐
266 **Wood Sandpiper** ☐
269 Marsh Sandpiper ☐
270 Greenshank ☐
284 **Ruff** ☐
288 Bartailed Godwit ☐
295 Blackwinged Stilt ☐
298 **Water Dikkop** ☐
315 Greyheaded Gull ☐
327 Common Tern ☐
339 Whitewinged Tern ☐
348 Feral Pigeon ☐
352 Redeyed Dove ☐
354 Cape Turtle Dove ☐
355 Laughing Dove ☐
359 Tambourine Dove ☐
366 Roseringed Parakeet ☐
371 Purplecrested Lourie ☐
386 Diederik Cuckoo ☐
391 Burchell's Coucal* ☐
394 Wood Owl ☐
412 Black Swift ☐
415 Whiterumped Swift ☐
417 Little Swift ☐
421 Palm Swift ☐
424 Speckled Mousebird ☐
426 Redfaced Mousebird ☐
428 Pied Kingfisher ☐
429 Giant Kingfisher ☐
431 Malachite Kingfisher ☐
435 Brownhooded Kingfisher ☐
436 Greyhooded Kingfisher ☐
438 European Bee-eater ☐
444 Little Bee-eater ☐
451 Hoopoe ☐
464 Blackcollared Barbet ☐
473 Crested Barbet ☐
483 Goldentailed Woodpecker ☐
486 Cardinal Woodpecker ☐
494 Rufousnaped Lark ☐
518 European Swallow ☐
527 Lesser Striped Swallow ☐
533 Brownthroated Martin ☐
536 Black Sawwing Swallow ☐
541 Forktailed Drongo ☐
548 Pied Crow ☐
554 Southern Black Tit* ☐
568 Blackeyed Bulbul ☐
572 Sombre Bulbul ☐
596 Stonechat ☐
600 Natal Robin ☐
613 Whitebrowed Robin ☐
628 **Great Reed Warbler** ☐

631 **African Marsh Warbler** ☐
633 European Marsh Warbler ☐
634 **European Sedge Warbler** ☐
635 **Cape Reed Warbler** ☐
637 Yellow Warbler ☐
638 **African Sedge Warbler** ☐
643 Willow Warbler ☐
657 Bleating Warbler ☐
674 **Redfaced Cisticola** ☐
675 **Blackbacked Cisticola** ☐
681 Neddicky ☐
683 Tawnyflanked Prinia ☐
690 Dusky Flycatcher ☐
705 Wattle-eyed Flycatcher ☐
710 Paradise Flycatcher ☐
711 African Pied Wagtail ☐
713 Cape Wagtail ☐
716 Grassveld Pipit ☐
732 Fiscal Shrike ☐
736 Southern Boubou** ☐
742 Southern Tchagra** ☐
744 Blackcrowned Tchagra ☐
758 Indian Myna ☐
764 Glossy Starling* ☐
768 Blackbellied Starling ☐
780 Purplebanded Sunbird ☐
787 Whitebellied Sunbird ☐
789 Grey Sunbird ☐
791 Scarletchested Sunbird ☐
792 Black Sunbird ☐
793 Collared Sunbird ☐
796 Cape White-eye** ☐
801 House Sparrow ☐
807 **Thickbilled Weaver** ☐
810 Spectacled Weaver ☐
811 Spottedbacked Weaver ☐
817 **Yellow Weaver** ☐
824 Red Bishop ☐
828 Redshouldered Widow ☐
829 Whitewinged Widow ☐
831 Redcollared Widow ☐
840 Bluebilled Firefinch ☐
844 Blue Waxbill ☐
846 Common Waxbill ☐
857 Bronze Mannikin ☐
858 Redbacked Mannikin ☐
860 Pintailed Whydah ☐
869 Yelloweyed Canary ☐
877 Bully Canary ☐

SHONGWENI DAM

approximately 150 species recorded to date

This fairly isolated dam is situated in the Mlazi River valley about 30 km from Durban, off the N3 to Pietermaritzburg. The dam is controlled by the Umgeni Water Board, and the surrounding area is fenced and patrolled. Habitat varies from

The dam is easily located from either of the highways linking Durban and Pietermaritzburg. The offramp, marked Shongweni/Assagay, is the first after the tollgate on the N3 out of Durban, or the first after the Hillcrest offramp on the older R613. Whichever is used, turn left towards Shongweni and thereafter follow the signs to Shongweni Dam. The last 6 km are on a good gravel road which leads directly to the main gate, open from 06h00 to 18h00.

climax indigenous forest to woodland, grass, scrub and exotic plantations. The water attracts a good cross-section of birds while the forest areas are host to a number of specials. There is no accommodation available and no entry fee is charged.

SPECIAL AND INTERESTING SPECIES

The major feature of the area is immense sheer cliff faces which are utilised by a number of species for nesting. A pair of **Lanner Falcons** are always present, along with huge flocks of **Black Swifts** and **Redwinged Starlings**. **Black Storks** have nested for years in one particular site on the cliff. The road down to the picnic area is worth walking along. Just above the wall a pair of **Mocking Chats** regularly go through their mimicry routine. **Rock Martins** and **Whiterumped Swifts** forage around the wall, while **Cape Rock Thrush** and **Rock Pigeons** are also seen in this area. A little way up the road from the wall is a large, flat ledge that overlooks the dam and surrounding area. Look for **Striped Pipit** on the rock ledges above you, **African Black Duck** on the water and **African Fish**, **Black** and **Crowned Eagles** soaring overhead. **Crowned** and **Trumpeter Hornbills** are frequently present, along with visual stunners such as **Plumcoloured Starling, Narina Trogon**, **Pygmy Kingfisher** and **Collared Sunbird**. **Grey** and **Swee Waxbills** and **Redbacked Mannikins** are quite common in the bush fringe. **Black Cuckooshrike** may be located by its high-pitched trill. **Lesser Honeyguide** is often seen around the picnic site.

ALSO RECORDED

Grey Cuckooshrike can be seen in the bird parties that gather especially in winter. Redthroated Wryneck and Gorgeous Bush Shrike (with its loud and liquid "kong, kong, kowit" call) are more often heard than seen. Gabar Goshawk has been seen over the gorge below the dam wall. Follow the "pretty georgie" call of the Emerald Cuckoo and you may be lucky enough to get a glimpse of this brightly coloured bird.

Dave Bishop

100% OF SPECIES

- 055 Whitebreasted Cormorant ☐
- 058 Reed Cormorant ☐
- 060 Darter ☐
- 062 Grey Heron ☐
- 063 Blackheaded Heron ☐
- 067 Little Egret ☐
- 071 Cattle Egret ☐
- 074 Greenbacked Heron ☐
- 081 Hamerkop ☐
- 084 **Black Stork** ☐
- 094 Hadeda Ibis ☐
- 095 African Spoonbill ☐
- 099 Whitefaced Duck ☐
- 102 Egyptian Goose ☐
- 104 Yellowbilled Duck ☐
- 105 **African Black Duck** ☐
- 116 Spurwinged Goose ☐
- 126a Yellowbilled Kite ☐
- 127 Blackshouldered Kite ☐
- 131 **Black Eagle** ☐
- 141 **Crowned Eagle** ☐
- 148 **African Fish Eagle** ☐
- 149 Steppe Buzzard ☐
- 157 Little Sparrowhawk ☐
- 160 African Goshawk ☐
- 161 Gabar Goshawk ☐
- 169 Gymnogene ☐
- 172 **Lanner Falcon** ☐
- 191 Shelley's Francolin ☐
- 196 Natal Francolin* ☐
- 200 Common Quail ☐
- 249 Threebanded Plover ☐
- 258 Blacksmith Plover ☐
- 264 Common Sandpiper ☐
- 298 Water Dikkop ☐
- 349 **Rock Pigeon** ☐
- 352 Redeyed Dove ☐
- 354 Cape Turtle Dove ☐
- 355 Laughing Dove ☐
- 358 Greenspotted Dove ☐
- 359 Tambourine Dove ☐
- 371 Purplecrested Lourie ☐
- 377 Redchested Cuckoo ☐
- 378 Black Cuckoo ☐

384 Emerald Cuckoo ☐
385 Klaas's Cuckoo ☐
386 Diederik Cuckoo ☐
391 Burchell's Coucal* ☐
401 Spotted Eagle Owl ☐
412 **Black Swift** ☐
415 **Whiterumped Swift** ☐
424 Speckled Mousebird ☐
427 **Narina Trogon** ☐
428 Pied Kingfisher ☐
429 Giant Kingfisher ☐
432 **Pygmy Kingfisher** ☐
435 Brownhooded Kingfisher ☐
451 Hoopoe ☐
452 Redbilled Woodhoopoe ☐
455 **Trumpeter Hornbill** ☐
460 **Crowned Hornbill** ☐
464 Blackcollared Barbet ☐
469 Redfronted Tinker Barbet ☐
471 Goldenrumped Tinker Barbet ☐
473 Crested Barbet ☐
474 Greater Honeyguide ☐
476 **Lesser Honeyguide** ☐
483 Goldentailed Woodpecker ☐
486 Cardinal Woodpecker ☐
489 Redthroated Wryneck ☐
494 Rufousnaped Lark ☐
518 European Swallow ☐
526 Greater Striped Swallow ☐
527 Lesser Striped Swallow ☐
529 **Rock Martin** ☐
533 Brownthroated Martin ☐
536 Black Sawwing Swallow ☐
538 **Black Cuckooshrike** ☐
540 Grey Cuckooshrike ☐
541 Forktailed Drongo ☐
545 Blackheaded Oriole ☐
548 Pied Crow ☐
550 Whitenecked Raven ☐
554 Southern Black Tit* ☐
568 Blackeyed Bulbul ☐
569 Terrestrial Bulbul ☐
572 Sombre Bulbul ☐
577 Olive Thrush ☐
581 **Cape Rock Thrush**** ☐
589 Familiar Chat ☐
593 **Mocking Chat** ☐
596 Stonechat ☐
600 Natal Robin ☐
601 Cape Robin ☐
613 Whitebrowed Robin ☐
635 Cape Reed Warbler ☐
645 Barthroated Apalis ☐
657 Bleating Warbler ☐
672 Rattling Cisticola ☐
679 Lazy Cisticola ☐
681 Neddicky ☐
683 Tawnyflanked Prinia ☐
690 Dusky Flycatcher ☐
691 Bluegrey Flycatcher ☐
694 Black Flycatcher ☐
700 Cape Batis** ☐
701 Chinspot Batis ☐
710 Paradise Flycatcher ☐
711 African Pied Wagtail ☐
713 Cape Wagtail ☐
720 **Striped Pipit** ☐
728 Yellowthroated Longclaw ☐
732 Fiscal Shrike ☐
736 Southern Boubou** ☐
740 Puffback ☐
742 Southern Tchagra** ☐
747 Gorgeous Bush Shrike ☐
748 Orangebreasted Bush Shrike ☐
750 Olive Bush Shrike* ☐
751 Greyheaded Bush Shrike ☐
761 **Plumcoloured Starling** ☐
764 Glossy Starling* ☐
768 Blackbellied Starling ☐
769 **Redwinged Starling** ☐
787 Whitebellied Sunbird ☐
789 Grey Sunbird ☐
790 Olive Sunbird ☐
791 Scarletchested Sunbird ☐
792 Black Sunbird ☐
793 **Collared Sunbird** ☐
796 Cape White-eye** ☐
801 House Sparrow ☐
804 Greyheaded Sparrow ☐
805 Yellowthroated Sparrow ☐
807 Thickbilled Weaver ☐
808 Forest Weaver ☐
810 Spectacled Weaver ☐
811 Spottedbacked Weaver ☐
813 Cape Weaver** ☐
828 Redshouldered Widow ☐
831 Redcollared Widow ☐
840 Bluebilled Firefinch ☐
846 Common Waxbill ☐
848 **Grey Waxbill** ☐
850 **Swee Waxbill*** ☐
857 Bronze Mannikin ☐
858 **Redbacked Mannikin** ☐
860 Pintailed Whydah ☐
864 Black Widowfinch ☐
869 Yelloweyed Canary ☐
884 Goldenbreasted Bunting ☐
☐
☐

BEACHWOOD MANGROVES AND UMGENI RIVER MOUTH

approximately 201 species recorded to date

This tiny reserve situated on the north bank of the Umgeni River estuary is wedged in between the sea and the Leo Boyd highway. It is controlled by the Natal Parks Board and the southern entance gate (under the Ellis Brown viaduct) is kept locked. A hide has been erected by the Natal Bird Club and access to the area can be arranged by contacting the Natal Parks Board. The north gate is open during working hours but this requires a long walk on the beach. Habitats in the reserve consist of beach, mangrove forest, mud flats, grassland and reedbeds. A boardwalk has been laid out through the mangroves, and the extension of this walk leads to the hide. For the best birding start at the southern entrance and walk towards the sea. At the river, turn right and walk through the mangroves to a lookout point over the Umgeni River. Retrace your steps to the car park and follow the path north. Past the mud flats, turn right and cross the river via the wooden bridge and walk onto the beach. Now head south towards the sand spit at the mouth of the Umgeni. This walk will take you through all the reserve's habitats; the Umgeni River itself also provides excellent birding.

SPECIAL AND INTERESTING SPECIES

Purplebanded Sunbirds call from the tops of the mangroves and **Mozambique Nightjar** can be found on the dunes just

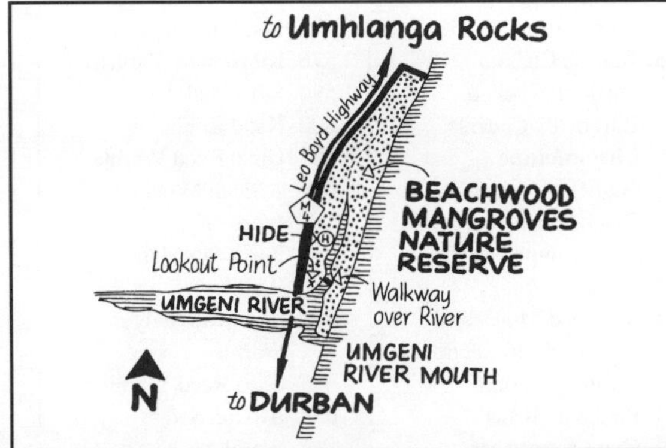

ALSO RECORDED

Over the years, some of the species that have been recorded here include Greater Frigatebird, Franklin's, Lesser Blackbacked and Sabine's Gulls, Lesser Golden and Crab Plovers, Sooty and Roseate Terns and Lesser Noddy.

Gordon Holtshausen

From Durban, head north on the Leo Boyd highway. The road crosses the Umgeni River and the first offramp is Prospect Hall Road/Riverside Drive. Take this offramp and approximately 300 m further turn left onto a gravel track which will lead you to the entrance gate situated under the bridge. The entrance is marked "Beachwood Mangroves Nature Reserve". In order to bird along the banks of the Umgeni, walk from the parking area under the bridge or drive along the north bank of the Umgeni River down Riverside Drive. You can also park at Blue Lagoon on the south bank and study the birds on the sand banks.

south of the north gate. The lagoon is one of the most southern localities where **Wiretailed Swallow** regularly occurs. Many waders and terns use this area: they include **Terek Sandpiper**, **Sand** and **Grey Plovers**, **Caspian**, **Swift**, **Lesser Crested**, **Sandwich**, **Common** and **Arctic Terns**. Beachwood is probably best known for the **Wattle-eyed Flycatchers** that breed near the information centre. **Mangrove Kingfishers** have been recorded in the mangroves during the winter. The river mouth has become the regular haunt of **White** and **Pinkbacked Pelicans** and **Woollynecked Storks** have taken to feeding here.

65% OF SPECIES

049 **White Pelican** ☐
050 **Pinkbacked Pelican** ☐
055 Whitebreasted Cormorant ☐
058 Reed Cormorant ☐
060 Darter ☐
062 Grey Heron ☐
064 Goliath Heron ☐
066 Great White Egret ☐
067 Little Egret ☐
072 Squacco Heron ☐
074 Greenbacked Heron ☐
081 Hamerkop ☐
086 **Woollynecked Stork** ☐
091 Sacred Ibis ☐
094 Hadeda Ibis ☐
095 African Spoonbill ☐
099 Whitefaced Duck ☐
102 Egyptian Goose ☐
104 Yellowbilled Duck ☐
126a Yellowbilled Kite ☐
148 African Fish Eagle ☐
172 Lanner Falcon ☐
223 Purple Gallinule ☐
226 Moorhen ☐
240 African Jacana ☐
245 Ringed Plover ☐
246 Whitefronted Plover ☐
247 Chestnutbanded Plover ☐
249 Threebanded Plover ☐
251 **Sand Plover** ☐
254 **Grey Plover** ☐
262 Turnstone ☐
263 **Terek Sandpiper** ☐
266 Wood Sandpiper ☐
270 Greenshank ☐
272 Curlew Sandpiper ☐
274 Little Stint ☐
281 Sanderling ☐
284 Ruff ☐
290 Whimbrel ☐
298 Water Dikkop ☐
312 Kelp Gull ☐
315 Greyheaded Gull ☐
322 **Caspian Tern** ☐
324 **Swift Tern** ☐
325 **Lesser Crested Tern** ☐
326 **Sandwich Tern** ☐
327 **Common Tern** ☐
328 **Arctic Tern** ☐
348 Feral Pigeon ☐
352 Redeyed Dove ☐
355 Laughing Dove ☐
371 Purplecrested Lourie ☐
385 Klaas's Cuckoo ☐
386 Diederik Cuckoo ☐
391 Burchell's Coucal* ☐
409 **Mozambique Nightjar** ☐
412 Black Swift ☐
415 Whiterumped Swift ☐
417 Little Swift ☐
424 Speckled Mousebird ☐
426 Redfaced Mousebird ☐
427 Narina Trogon ☐
428 Pied Kingfisher ☐
429 Giant Kingfisher ☐
434 **Mangrove Kingfisher** ☐
435 Brownhooded Kingfisher ☐
444 Little Bee-eater ☐
464 Blackcollared Barbet ☐
473 Crested Barbet ☐
518 European Swallow ☐
522 **Wiretailed Swallow** ☐
527 Lesser Striped Swallow ☐
529 Rock Martin ☐
533 Brownthroated Martin ☐
536 Black Sawwing Swallow ☐
541 Forktailed Drongo ☐
548 Pied Crow ☐
554 Southern Black Tit* ☐
568 Blackeyed Bulbul ☐
569 Terrestrial Bulbul ☐
572 Sombre Bulbul ☐
576 Kurrichane Thrush ☐
596 Stonechat ☐
600 Natal Robin ☐
628 Great Reed Warbler ☐
631 African Marsh Warbler ☐
633 European Marsh Warbler ☐
634 European Sedge Warbler ☐
635 Cape Reed Warbler ☐
638 African Sedge Warbler ☐

643 Willow Warbler
645 Barthroated Apalis
648 Yellowbreasted Apalis
651 Longbilled Crombec
657 Bleating Warbler
672 Rattling Cisticola
674 Redfaced Cisticola
675 Blackbacked Cisticola
681 Neddicky
683 Tawnyflanked Prinia
690 Dusky Flycatcher
701 Chinspot Batis
705 **Wattle-eyed Flycatcher**
710 Paradise Flycatcher
711 African Pied Wagtail
713 Cape Wagtail
728 Yellowthroated Longclaw
732 Fiscal Shrike
758 Indian Myna
768 Blackbellied Starling
769 Redwinged Starling
780 **Purplebanded Sunbird**
787 Whitebellied Sunbird
790 Olive Sunbird
791 Scarletchested Sunbird
792 Black Sunbird
793 Collared Sunbird
796 Cape White-eye**
801 House Sparrow
807 Thickbilled Weaver
811 Spottedbacked Weaver
817 Yellow Weaver
824 Red Bishop
828 Redshouldered Widow
831 Redcollared Widow
840 Bluebilled Firefinch
846 Common Waxbill
857 Bronze Mannikin
860 Pintailed Whydah
869 Yelloweyed Canary

NATAL ESTUARINE AND PELAGIC

approximately 222 species recorded to date

The Natal coast has a limited number of estuaries and lagoons which often provide the only opportunity to see certain marine estuarine species. Habitat consists largely of mud or sand flats (the former being much more productive), often with reedbed borders. There are usually brackish or even fresh water pans in association, particularly at St Lucia and Richards

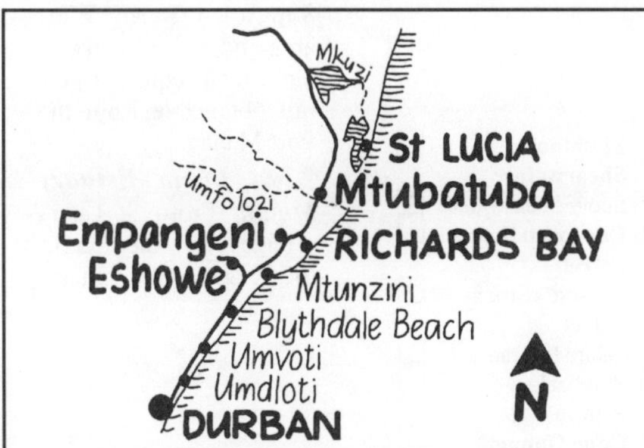

Six major localities are recommended:

- ***Durban Bayhead:*** Though a shadow of its former glory the area is still worth a visit. Travel along the southern freeway, turning left into Bayhead Road (just before the old Congella Power Station). Cross the Umhlatuzana River and as the road bears left turn sharp left into Langeberg Road. Proceed through the customs gate towards the container terminal. The best viewpoint is north of the mangroves overlooking the mud flats.
- ***Umgeni River Mouth:*** Drive north from Durban along the coast road. Turn left at Blue Lagoon and immediately right, passing back under the high-

Bay. These yield an even wider range of species. For purposes of this account, however, note will only be taken of species associated with a marine and estuarine environment. A telescope is recommended for birding in these areas. Although less renowned for pelagic seabirds than Cape waters the offshore waters of Natal are turning up an increasing number of specials and a long list of rarities. Unless you are in a position to convert a ski boating friend from sailfish to shearwaters you will probably be limited to an offshore trip on the *Isle of Capri*. Better still book a place on one of the Natal Bird Club sea trips or on a trawler with a private pelagic organiser.

SPECIAL AND INTERESTING SPECIES

Estuarine specials include **Sand**, **Mongolian** and **Grey Plovers**, **Turnstone**, **Bartailed Godwit**, **Curlew**, **Knot** and **Terek Sandpiper**. The rare **Broadbilled Sandpiper** turns up regularly at Richards Bay. **Lesser Crested Terns** are much in evidence in summer while **Mangrove Kingfisher** may be found in suitable habitat during winter. **Palmnut Vulture** can be seen at Mtunzini and occasionally at Richards Bay. Some pelagic sea-watching is available from the breakwaters at Richards Bay and Durban. After heavy weather **Cape Gannet** and **Whitechinned Petrel** will probably be seen and, if you are extremely lucky, **Greater Frigatebird**. Deep sea trips could yield **Greatwinged** and **Southern Giant Petrels**, **Wilson's Storm Petrel**, **Subantarctic Skua** (all year); **Blackbrowed** and **Shy Albatrosses**, **Softplumaged Petrel**, **Broadbilled Prion** and **Antarctic Tern** (winter), **European Storm Petrel**, **Cory's** and **Fleshfooted Shearwaters**, and **Arctic** and **Pomarine Skuas** (summer).

40% OF SPECIES

- 011 **Shy Albatross** ☐
- 012 **Blackbrowed Albatross** ☐
- 014 Yellownosed Albatross ☐
- 017 **Southern Giant Petrel** ☐
- 021 Pintado Petrel ☐
- 023 **Greatwinged Petrel** ☐
- 024 **Softplumaged Petrel** ☐
- 029 **Broadbilled Prion** ☐
- 032 **Whitechinned Petrel** ☐
- 034 **Cory's Shearwater** ☐
- 036 **Fleshfooted Shearwater** ☐
- 037 Sooty Shearwater ☐
- 042 **European Storm Petrel** ☐
- 044 **Wilson's Storm Petrel** ☐
- 049 White Pelican ☐
- 050 Pinkbacked Pelican ☐
- 053 **Cape Gannet*** ☐

way. Parking is available.

- ***Umdloti River Mouth:*** Drive north on the coast road. Turn right to Umdloti village. Park at the northern end of the village and walk along the beach to Umdloti Lagoon.
- ***Umvoti River Mouth:*** Travel north from Durban on the N2 and take the Groutville turnoff (approximately 60 km). Cross back over the N2 and proceed eastwards on a gravel road through sugar cane to the house of Mr and Mrs Jex. Ask permission before going down to the lagoon. Alternatively drive to the southern end of Blythdale Beach and walk to the lagoon.
- ***Richards Bay Harbour:*** Directions are given in the Richards Bay section. Prime areas are the Bay Hall mud flats, the small craft harbour pan (accessible without permit), and the Clean Berth sandspit, Sanctuary/Berm Wall area and south breakwater, which require a permit obtainable from the Port Manager.
- ***St Lucia Estuary Mouth***: From St Lucia village follow the signs to the St Lucia lake estuary.

055 Whitebreasted Cormorant
056 Cape Cormorant*
060 Darter
061 **Greater Frigatebird**
062 Grey Heron
064 Goliath Heron
066 Great White Egret
067 Little Egret
078 Little Bittern
081 Hamerkop
086 Woollynecked Stork
090 Yellowbilled Stork
091 Sacred Ibis
095 African Spoonbill
096 Greater Flamingo
097 Lesser Flamingo
099 Whitefaced Duck
102 Egyptian Goose
104 Yellowbilled Duck
106 Cape Teal
108 Redbilled Teal
116 Spurwinged Goose
147 **Palmnut Vulture**
148 African Fish Eagle
170 Osprey
245 Ringed Plover
246 Whitefronted Plover
248 Kittlitz's Plover
249 Threebanded Plover
250 **Mongolian Plover**
251 **Sand Plover**
254 **Grey Plover**
258 Blacksmith Plover
262 **Turnstone**
263 **Terek Sandpiper**
264 Common Sandpiper
266 Wood Sandpiper
269 Marsh Sandpiper
270 Greenshank
271 **Knot**
272 Curlew Sandpiper
274 Little Stint
281 Sanderling
283 **Broadbilled Sandpiper**
284 Ruff
288 **Bartailed Godwit**
289 **Curlew**
290 Whimbrel
294 Avocet
295 Blackwinged Stilt
298 Water Dikkop
304 Redwinged Pratincole
307 **Arctic Skua**
309 **Pomarine Skua**
310 **Subantarctic Skua**
312 Kelp Gull
315 Greyheaded Gull
322 Caspian Tern
324 Swift Tern
325 **Lesser Crested Tern**
326 Sandwich Tern
327 Common Tern
328 Arctic Tern
329 **Antarctic Tern**
335 Little Tern
338 Whiskered Tern
339 Whitewinged Tern
428 Pied Kingfisher
429 Giant Kingfisher
431 Malachite Kingfisher
434 **Mangrove Kingfisher**
440 Bluecheeked Bee-eater
711 African Pied Wagtail
713 Cape Wagtail

ALSO RECORDED

It is in the area of rarities and vagrants that estuarine and pelagic birds make their mark in the southern African bird list. Over 50 species seen along the Natal coast fit into this category. Notable among them are:

Estuarine: European Oystercatcher, Lesser Golden Plover, Redshank, Whiterumped Sandpiper, Buffbreasted Sandpiper, Blacktailed Godwit, Crab Plover, Gullbilled, Whitecheeked, Sooty, Roseate and Bridled Terns, Lesser Blackbacked Gull and Lesser Noddy.

Pelagic: Wandering and Greyheaded Albatrosses, Northern Giant Petrel, Antarctic Fulmar, Kerguelen Petrel, Audubon's Shearwater, Leach's, Whitebellied and Blackbellied Storm Petrels, South Polar and Longtailed Skuas and Sabine's Gull.

Pete Outhwaite

XUMENI FOREST, DONNYBROOK

approximately 82 species recorded to date

This mistbelt evergreen forest, controlled by the Department of Water Affairs and Forestry as part of Sarnia State Forest, lies on the southern slope of the hill above Donnybrook. The indigenous forest covers 380 ha bounded by plantations and open grassland. Huge yellowwoods and white stinkwoods dominate a typical variety of forest trees and undergrowth. Birding is easy when walking along the vehicle track that follows a contour from the entrance to the forester's staff accommodation. Smaller tracks lead into other parts of the forest, including up the slope to the grassland above.

SPECIAL AND INTERESTING SPECIES

The **Orange Thrush** is resident in small numbers. It is a skulker, singing mainly at dusk and best looked for along the quieter paths below the main track. Flocks of **Cape Parrot** come to roost in the forest, and small groups may remain to feed in the canopy throughout the day. Listen for the call of flying birds to establish their presence. **Barratt's Warbler** is common in the dense undergrowth beside the main track. It is very retiring, but if not singing, its soft contact call invariably gives its presence away. **Forest Buzzard** occurs occasionally as it is resident in the area, but care must be taken to separate individuals from the common migratory Steppe Buzzard. Typical forest birds that may easily be

ALSO RECORDED

Birds found in adjacent habitats are not included in the checklist, but those found above the forest in the upland grassland include Cape Vulture, Black and Martial Eagles, Rock Kestrel, Blue Crane, Blackwinged Plover, Banded Martin, Mountain and Buffstreaked Chats and Malachite Sunbird.

Nigel Robson

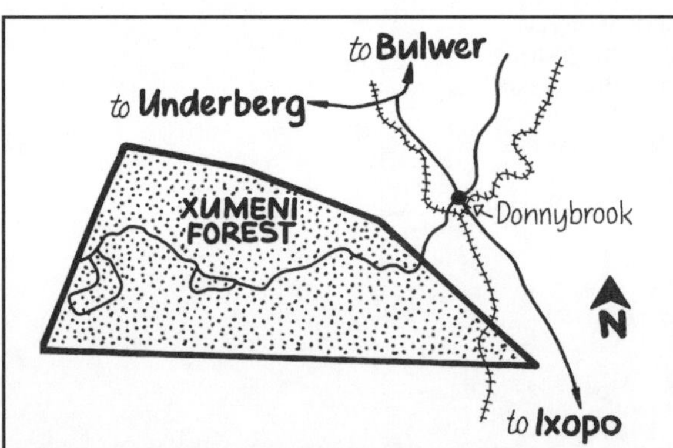

Donnybrook is 40 km north-west of Ixopo (from Durban) and 22 km north-east of Bulwer (from Pietermaritzburg). From Donnybrook travel just over a kilometre on the tar road towards Bulwer. Immediately after passing under the railway bridge, turn left onto gravel and cross the railway lines. Take the narrow track on the right which leads into the forest.

recognised by call include **Buffspotted Flufftail**, **Crowned Eagle**, **Knysna Lourie**, **Narina Trogon**, **Emerald Cuckoo**, **Olive Woodpecker**, **Chorister Robin**, **Bluemantled Flycatcher** and **Olive Bush Shrike**. Less vociferous are **Cinnamon Dove** and **Starred Robin**. **Crowned Hornbill**, **Forest Weaver** and **Green Twinspot** are not always to be found, being at the edge of their distribution range, and **Bush Blackcap** appears to be scarce. There are always parties of **Forest Canaries**.

100% OF SPECIES

094 Hadeda Ibis
126a Yellowbilled Kite
139 Longcrested Eagle
141 **Crowned Eagle**
149 Steppe Buzzard
150 **Forest Buzzard****
157 Little Sparrowhawk
158 Black Sparrowhawk
160 African Goshawk
169 Gymnogene
198 Rednecked Francolin
203 Helmeted Guineafowl
218 **Buffspotted Flufftail**
350 Rameron Pigeon
352 Redeyed Dove
354 Cape Turtle Dove
360 **Cinnamon Dove**
362 **Cape Parrot**
370 **Knysna Lourie****
377 Redchested Cuckoo
378 Black Cuckoo
384 **Emerald Cuckoo**
394 Wood Owl
424 Speckled Mousebird
427 **Narina Trogon**
451 Hoopoe
460 **Crowned Hornbill**
469 Redfronted Tinker Barbet
488 **Olive Woodpecker**
536 Black Sawwing Swallow
540 Grey Cuckooshrike
531 Forktailed Drongo
545 Blackheaded Oriole
554 Southern Black Tit*
565 **Bush Blackcap****
568 Blackeyed Bulbul
569 Terrestrial Bulbul
572 Sombre Bulbul
577 Olive Thrush
579 **Orange Thrush**
598 **Chorister Robin****
601 Cape Robin
606 **Starred Robin**
639 **Barratt's Warbler****
643 Willow Warbler
644 Yellowthroated Warbler
645 Barthroated Apalis
648 Yellowbreasted Apalis
657 Bleating Warbler
679 Lazy Cisticola
681 Neddicky
683 Tawnyflanked Prinia
686a Spotted Prinia**
689 Spotted Flycatcher
690 Dusky Flycatcher
700 Cape Batis**
708 **Bluemantled Flycatcher**
710 Paradise Flycatcher
732 Fiscal Shrike
736 Southern Boubou**
740 Puffback
746 Bokmakierie*
750 **Olive Bush Shrike***
751 Greyheaded Bush Shrike
769 Redwinged Starling
783 Lesser Double-collared Sunbird**
792 Black Sunbird
793 Collared Sunbird
796 Cape White-eye**
808 **Forest Weaver**
828 Redshouldered Widow
831 Redcollared Widow
835 **Green Twinspot**
840 Bluebilled Firefinch
846 Common Waxbill
850 Swee Waxbill*
857 Bronze Mannikin
860 Pintailed Whydah
869 Yelloweyed Canary
872 Cape Canary
873 **Forest Canary****
884 Goldenbreasted Bunting

VERNON CROOKES NATURE RESERVE

approximately 290 species recorded to date

Vernon Crookes Nature Reserve is a Natal Parks Board reserve proclaimed in January 1973. Situated south of Durban on the southern side of the Mpambinyoni Valley which reaches the sea at Scottburgh, it lies on the first escarpment, on the road from the coast to Ixopo and the Drakensberg. The highest point of the reserve is 900 m above sea level. The reserve's proximity to Durban and its popularity among birders have resulted in many vagrants being recorded. The new tented camp and roads will further facilitate birding in the future.

SPECIAL AND INTERESTING SPECIES

African Broadbill, first recorded here in 1979, is not uncommon and while seldom seen may be heard calling from the thickest bush throughout the year by early risers. Many people have recorded **Broadtailed Warbler** perform its display flight in the early morning. **Crowned Cranes** breed annually, as do **Black Sparrowhawk**, **African Goshawk** and **Lanner Falcon**. **Martial**, **Crowned** and **Longcrested Eagles** all breed in the reserve and are seen fairly frequently. **Gymnogene** has also been recorded breeding. **Redchested** and **Buffspotted Flufftails** can be heard during the summer months, as well as **Black** and **Emerald Cuckoos**. **Green Coucal** is common in summer. **Cape Rock Thrush**, **Famil-**

ALSO RECORDED

Shorttailed Pipit was first recorded in 1988 and breeds annually. A Cuckoo Hawk was found feeding a fledgling in April 1988 and it is probable that this bird bred in the reserve. Striped Flufftails are recorded and Cuckoo Finch has been seen twice in the little marsh near the picnic site. Two seasonal rarities in the reserve are Sentinel Rock Thrush (winter) and European Golden Oriole (summer).

Hamish Campbell

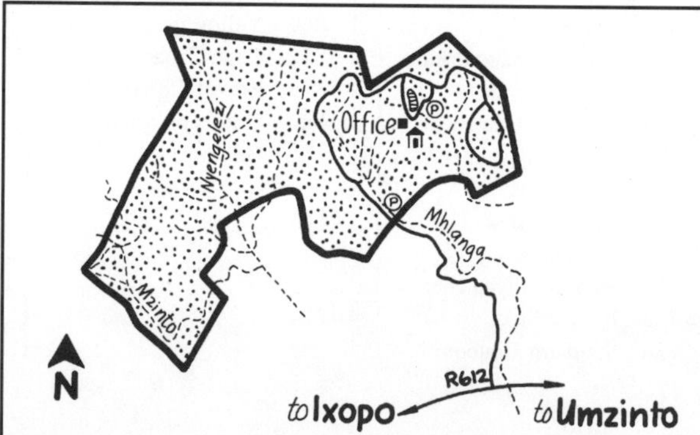

From the Westville interchange (where the N2 crosses the N3) proceed 60 km down the N2 South, bypassing Umkomaas and Scottburgh. Three km past Scottburgh turn off onto the R612, turn inland over the N2 (bypassing Umzinto); 12 km from the N2 turn right (north) onto a well signposted gravel road and proceed 4 km to the reserve gate.

iar and **Mocking Chats** can be seen on the rocks above the north-western krans down to the Mpambinyoni River. **Starred Robin** is a winter migrant from high altitudes. The Vernon Crookes Nature Reserve is an excellent place for learning cisticolas. **Fantailed**, **Ayres'** and **Palecrowned** are all audible and visible on the plains in spring and summer. **Croaking** and **Lazy Cisticolas** and **Neddicky** are common in grassland, while **Levaillant's Cisticola** may occasionally be heard near the dams. **Plainbacked Pipits** are frequently seen, but **Striped** and **Longbilled** are uncommon. **Green Twinspots** and **Quail Finch** are frequently heard but seldom seen. **Grey** and **Swee Waxbills** and **Redbacked Mannikins** occur on forest edges while **Orangebreasted Waxbill** has also been recorded.

56% OF SPECIES

008 Dabchick ☐
063 Blackheaded Heron ☐
081 Hamerkop ☐
094 Hadeda Ibis ☐
101 Whitebacked Duck ☐
104 Yellowbilled Duck ☐
116 Spurwinged Goose ☐
126a Yellowbilled Kite ☐
128 Cuckoo Hawk ☐
139 **Longcrested Eagle** ☐
140 **Martial Eagle** ☐
141 **Crowned Eagle** ☐
149 Steppe Buzzard ☐
158 **Black Sparrowhawk** ☐
160 **African Goshawk** ☐
169 **Gymnogene** ☐
172 **Lanner Falcon** ☐
173 Hobby Falcon ☐
196 Natal Francolin* ☐
200 Common Quail ☐
209 **Crowned Crane** ☐
217 **Redchested Flufftail** ☐
218 **Buffspotted Flufftail** ☐
221 Striped Flufftail ☐
226 Moorhen ☐
228 Redknobbed Coot ☐
240 African Jacana ☐
350 Rameron Pigeon ☐
352 Redeyed Dove ☐
358 Greenspotted Dove ☐
359 Tambourine Dove ☐
360 Cinnamon Dove ☐
370 Knysna Lourie** ☐
371 Purplecrested Lourie ☐
377 Redchested Cuckoo ☐
378 **Black Cuckoo** ☐
384 **Emerald Cuckoo** ☐
385 Klaas's Cuckoo ☐
387 **Green Coucal** ☐
391 Burchell's Coucal* ☐
394 Wood Owl ☐
405 Fierynecked Nightjar ☐
412 Black Swift ☐
415 Whiterumped Swift ☐
417 Little Swift ☐
424 Speckled Mousebird ☐
427 Narina Trogon ☐
432 Pygmy Kingfisher ☐
435 Brownhooded Kingfisher ☐
444 Little Bee-eater ☐
452 Redbilled Woodhoopoe ☐
455 Trumpeter Hornbill ☐
464 Blackcollared Barbet ☐
469 Redfronted Tinker Barbet ☐
471 Goldenrumped Tinker Barbet ☐
474 Greater Honeyguide ☐
475 Scalythroated Honeyguide ☐
476 Lesser Honeyguide ☐
478 Sharpbilled Honeyguide ☐
483 Goldentailed Woodpecker ☐
486 Cardinal Woodpecker ☐
488 Olive Woodpecker ☐
489 Redthroated Wryneck ☐
490 **African Broadbill** ☐
494 Rufousnaped Lark ☐
518 European Swallow ☐
527 Lesser Striped Swallow ☐
529 Rock Martin ☐
536 Black Sawwing Swallow ☐
538 Black Cuckooshrike ☐
540 Grey Cuckooshrike ☐
541 Forktailed Drongo ☐
542 Squaretailed Drongo ☐
545 Blackheaded Oriole ☐
550 Whitenecked Raven ☐
554 Southern Black Tit* ☐
568 Blackeyed Bulbul ☐
569 Terrestrial Bulbul ☐
572 Sombre Bulbul ☐
574 Yellowbellied Bulbul ☐
577 Olive Thrush ☐

581 **Cape Rock Thrush****
589 **Familiar Chat**
593 **Mocking Chat**
596 Stonechat
598 Chorister Robin**
600 Natal Robin
601 Cape Robin
606 **Starred Robin**
613 Whitebrowed Robin
616 Brown Robin**
639 Barratt's Warbler**
642 **Broadtailed Warbler**
644 Yellowthroated Warbler
645 Barthroated Apalis
648 Yellowbreasted Apalis
657 Bleating Warbler
661 Grassbird**
664 **Fantailed Cisticola**
667 **Ayres' Cisticola**
668 **Palecrowned Cisticola**
677 **Levaillant's Cisticola**
678 **Croaking Cisticola**
679 **Lazy Cisticola**
681 **Neddicky**
683 Tawnyflanked Prinia
690 Dusky Flycatcher
691 Bluegrey Flycatcher
694 Black Flycatcher
700 Cape Batis**
701 Chinspot Batis
708 Bluemantled Flycatcher
710 Paradise Flycatcher
712 Longtailed Wagtail
713 Cape Wagtail
717 **Longbilled Pipit**
718 **Plainbacked Pipit**
720 **Striped Pipit**
724 Shorttailed Pipit
727 Orangethroated Longclaw**
728 Yellowthroated Longclaw
732 Fiscal Shrike
736 Southern Boubou**
740 Puffback
742 Southern Tchagra**
747 Gorgeous Bush Shrike
748 Orangebreasted Bush Shrike
751 Greyheaded Bush Shrike
764 Glossy Starling*
768 Blackbellied Starling
769 Redwinged Starling
785 Greater Double-collared Sunbird**
787 Whitebellied Sunbird
789 Grey Sunbird
790 Olive Sunbird
792 Black Sunbird
793 Collared Sunbird
796 Cape White-eye**
801 House Sparrow
805 Yellowthroated Sparrow
807 Thickbilled Weaver
808 Forest Weaver
810 Spectacled Weaver
811 Spottedbacked Weaver
828 Redshouldered Widow
831 Redcollared Widow
835 **Green Twinspot**
840 Bluebilled Firefinch
846 Common Waxbill
848 **Grey Waxbill**
850 **Swee Waxbill***
852 Quail Finch
854 **Orangebreasted Waxbill**
857 Bronze Mannikin
858 **Redbacked Mannikin**
860 Pintailed Whydah
869 Yelloweyed Canary
872 Cape Canary
877 Bully Canary
881 Streakyheaded Canary

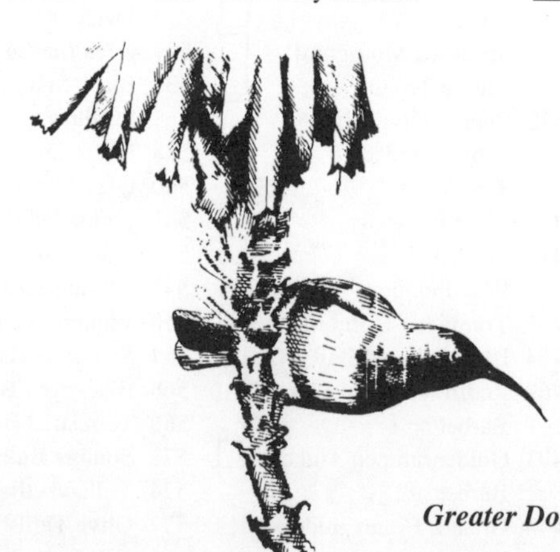

Greater Doublecollared Sunbird

MATATIELE

approximately 144 species recorded to date

Matatiele is situated in the most westerly part of southern Natal and is bordered in the north, west and south by Transkei. A notable feature of the landscape is the wide valley running east-west, known as the Cedarville Flats, flanked to the north by the foothills of the Drakensberg and to the south by high ground rising to over 2 000 m above sea level. The Cedarville Flats was mainly a wetland up to the early part of this century and was well known for vast numbers of waterfowl. As a result of drainage the area of wetland has been greatly reduced but this has been partly compensated for by numerous dams. The famous artist and ornithologist, C. Finch-Davies, did much of his work in this district around the turn of the century. A good locality for birding on the flats is the farm Golden Fleece (ask permission to visit first). There are several large dams and pans on Golden Fleece. From Matatiele proceed for 19 km along the Swartberg road, turn right at the fork on the farm Meadowbrook and watch for the farm signboard 3 km further at the dam. For the mountain areas follow the road to the radio tower south of the town for approximately 7 km and turn right at the gate marked "High Street". From here to the border of the commonage is good LBJ territory. Beyond the border the farm Avenham is well worth visiting. Another interesting area is the Mvenyane Valley between the Matatiele and Jumbla ranges running roughly west to east. The road branches off the Matatiele-Cedarville road to the south at the farm

ALSO RECORDED

Martial Eagle and Bearded Vulture are occasionally seen, as are Black Stork, Little Bittern, Dwarf Bittern, Squacco Heron and African Rail. Other unusual sightings have been Rameron Pigeon, Namaqua Dove, European Bee-eater, European Golden Oriole, Rock Pipit and Redbacked Shrike.

Sam Kirk

The town may be reached from Pietermaritzburg via Bulwer, Underberg and Swartberg or alternatively via Umzimkulu and Kokstad. Passports or identification books have to be produced at Umzimkulu. From Durban a convenient route is via Port Shepstone and Kokstad on the N2.

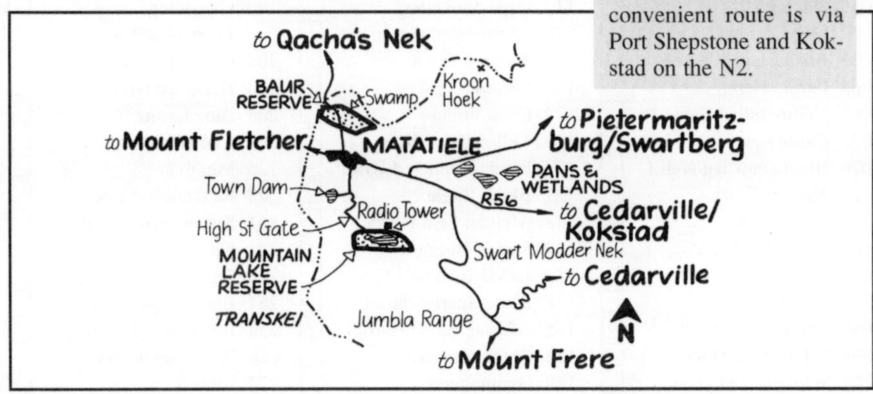

Compensation, 8 km from Matatiele, and gradually ascends to Swartmodder Nek, then down into the valley. This route eventually leads back to the Matatiele-Cedarville tarred road.

SPECIAL AND INTERESTING SPECIES

At Golden Fleece the following may be seen: **African Fish Eagle**, **Darter**, **Blackcrowned Night Heron**, **Ethiopian Snipe**, **Yellowbilled Egret**, **Avocet**, **Blackwinged Stilt**, **Blue Crane**, **South African Shelduck** and **Stanley's Bustard**. Interesting birds on Matatiele Mountain include **Gurney's Sugarbird**, **Yellowbreasted Pipit**, **Rudd's** and **Longbilled Larks**, **Orangebreasted Rockjumper**, **Cape** and **Sentinel Rock Thrushes**, **Cape Bunting** and **Ground Woodpecker**. **Greywing Francolin** and **Black Harrier** may be found in the higher rolling grasslands while **Wailing Cisticola** and **Marsh Owl** can be seen in the grassland lower down. **Crowned Crane** is not uncommon on the Cedarville Flats while the presence of **Maccoa Duck** is often unpredictable. **Redthroated Wryneck** are best found in exotic plantations especially near homesteads. There are five breeding pairs of **Black Eagle** in the Matatiele area. One nest is in plain view from the west end of town.

100% OF SPECIES

- 008 Dabchick ☐
- 055 Whitebreasted Cormorant ☐
- 058 Reed Cormorant ☐
- 060 **Darter** ☐
- 062 Grey Heron ☐
- 063 Blackheaded Heron ☐
- 065 Purple Heron ☐
- 068 **Yellowbilled Egret** ☐
- 071 Cattle Egret ☐
- 076 **Blackcrowned Night Heron** ☐
- 081 Hamerkop ☐
- 083 White Stork ☐
- 091 Sacred Ibis ☐
- 094 Hadeda Ibis ☐
- 095 African Spoonbill ☐
- 099 Whitefaced Duck ☐
- 101 Whitebacked Duck ☐
- 103 **South African Shelduck**** ☐
- 104 Yellowbilled Duck ☐
- 108 Redbilled Teal ☐
- 112 Cape Shoveller* ☐
- 116 Spurwinged Goose ☐
- 117 **Maccoa Duck** ☐
- 118 Secretarybird ☐
- 122 Cape Vulture** ☐
- 126a Yellowbilled Kite ☐
- 127 Blackshouldered Kite ☐
- 131 **Black Eagle** ☐
- 148 **African Fish Eagle** ☐
- 149 Steppe Buzzard ☐
- 152 Jackal Buzzard** ☐
- 158 Black Sparrowhawk ☐
- 165 African Marsh Harrier ☐
- 168 **Black Harrier**** ☐
- 169 Gymnogene ☐
- 172 Lanner Falcon ☐
- 180 Eastern Redfooted Kestrel ☐
- 181 Rock Kestrel ☐
- 190 **Greywing Francolin**** ☐
- 200 Common Quail ☐
- 203 Helmeted Guineafowl ☐
- 208 **Blue Crane**** ☐
- 209 **Crowned Crane** ☐
- 226 Moorhen ☐
- 228 Redknobbed Coot ☐
- 231 **Stanley's Bustard** ☐
- 248 Kittlitz's Plover ☐
- 249 Threebanded Plover ☐
- 257 Blackwinged Plover ☐
- 258 Blacksmith Plover ☐
- 266 Wood Sandpiper ☐
- 274 Little Stint ☐

284 Ruff ☐
286 **Ethiopian Snipe** ☐
294 **Avocet** ☐
295 **Blackwinged Stilt** ☐
297 Spotted Dikkop ☐
338 Whiskered Tern ☐
348 Feral Pigeon ☐
349 Rock Pigeon ☐
352 Redeyed Dove ☐
354 Cape Turtle Dove ☐
355 Laughing Dove ☐
356 Namaqua Dove ☐
377 Redchested Cuckoo ☐
378 Black Cuckoo ☐
386 Diederik Cuckoo ☐
395 **Marsh Owl** ☐
412 Black Swift ☐
415 Whiterumped Swift ☐
418 Alpine Swift ☐
421 Palm Swift ☐
424 Speckled Mousebird ☐
428 Pied Kingfisher ☐
429 Giant Kingfisher ☐
431 Malachite Kingfisher ☐
451 Hoopoe ☐
474 Greater Honeyguide ☐
480 **Ground Woodpecker**** ☐
486 Cardinal Woodpecker ☐
489 **Redthroated Wryneck** ☐
499 **Rudd's Lark**** ☐
500 **Longbilled Lark*** ☐
507 Redcapped Lark ☐
526 Greater Striped Swallow* ☐
529 Rock Martin ☐
534 Banded Martin ☐
541 Forktailed Drongo ☐
547 Black Crow ☐
548 Pied Crow ☐
550 Whitenecked Raven ☐
568 Blackeyed Bulbul ☐
572 Sombre Bulbul ☐
581 **Cape Rock Thrush**** ☐
582 **Sentinel Rock Thrush**** ☐
586 Mountain Chat* ☐
588 Buffstreaked Chat** ☐
595 Anteating Chat** ☐
596 Stonechat ☐
601 Cape Robin ☐
612 **Orangebreasted Rockjumper**** ☐
635 Cape Reed Warbler ☐
638 African Sedge Warbler ☐
667 Ayres' Cisticola ☐
670 **Wailing Cisticola** ☐
677 Levaillant's Cisticola ☐
681 Neddicky ☐
686a Spotted Prinia** ☐
700 Cape Batis** ☐
710 Paradise Flycatcher ☐
713 Cape Wagtail ☐
716 Grassveld Pipit ☐
717 Longbilled Pipit ☐
725 **Yellowbreasted Pipit**** ☐
727 Orangethroated Longclaw** ☐
732 Fiscal Shrike ☐
736 Southern Boubou** ☐
746 Bokmakierie* ☐
757 European Starling ☐
759 Pied Starling** ☐
764 Glossy Starling* ☐
769 Redwinged Starling ☐
774 **Gurney's Sugarbird**** ☐
775 Malachite Sunbird ☐
792 Black Sunbird ☐
796 Cape White-eye** ☐
801 House Sparrow ☐
803 Cape Sparrow* ☐
804 Greyheaded Sparrow ☐
813 Cape Weaver** ☐
814 Masked Weaver ☐
821 Redbilled Quelea ☐
824 Red Bishop ☐
826 Golden Bishop ☐
827 Yellowrumped Widow ☐
832 Longtailed Widow ☐
846 Common Waxbill ☐
852 Quail Finch ☐
854 Orangebreasted Waxbill ☐
860 Pintailed Whydah ☐
872 Cape Canary ☐
881 Streakyheaded Canary ☐
884 Goldenbreasted Bunting ☐
885 **Cape Bunting** ☐
886 Rock Bunting ☐
☐
☐
☐
☐
☐

ORIBI GORGE NATURE RESERVE

approximately 226 species recorded to date

This locality, about half an hour's drive inland of Port Shepstone on the main road to Harding, is arguably the finest birding spot on the lower Natal south coast because it is accessible to the public, and the birder with limited time gains access to the most productive parts of the gorge by tarred road. The gorge is huge: the area covered here is limited to that which is administered by the Natal Parks Board. As is typical in a gorge, the plant habitats are thrilling. Descending you will go from grassland on the cliff tops to cliffs (both moist and dry), then to wooded cliff bases and thick riverine forest that will make way for thick valley bushveld that is Acacia dominated. Oribi has a hutted camp which may be booked through the Natal Parks Board.

ALSO RECORDED

Unusual records include Greenbacked Heron, Cape Vulture, Wahlberg's Eagle, Redbacked Shrike and Brownthroated Martin.

Geoff Nichols

SPECIAL AND INTERESTING SPECIES

The camp gardens have a stunning array of plant species which in turn attract many of the avian specials to the reserve. Look out for **Brown Robin**, **Grey**, **Olive**, **Collared** and **Lesser Doublecollared Sunbirds**. These species always seem to be around the huts, especially in the winter months when the aloes and erythrinas are in flower. If one walks on the cliff edge in front of the huts and sits quietly the area suddenly becomes filled with birds like **Striped Pipit** and **Cape Rock Thrush** on the rocks and **Grey Cuckooshrike** in

From Port Shepstone travel 20 km on the Harding road, then turn right to the hutted camp. The road is well sign-posted.

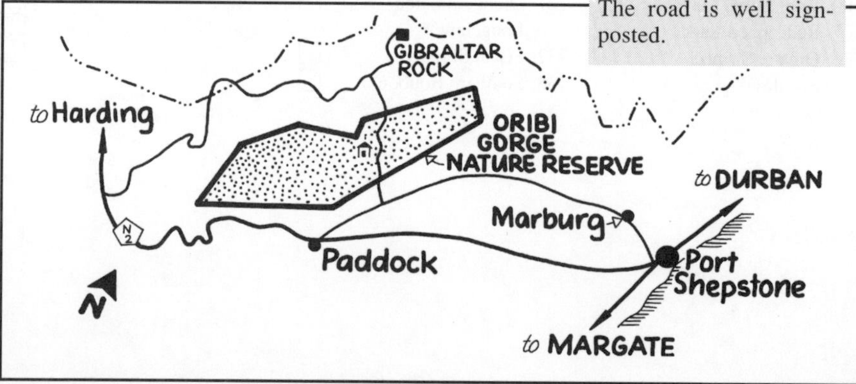

the forest below the cliffs, where one also sees samango monkeys. Raptors are the feature of this vantage point: **Crowned Eagle**, **Cuckoo Hawk**, **Black Sparrowhawk** and **African Goshawk** can be seen. **Crowned** and **Trumpeter Hornbills** and **Knysna Louries** are usually seen flying below into the fruiting trees. The best time to find birds in this reserve is at dawn and a walk down the tarred road will give you some of the most exciting birding in Natal. Leave the camp and take the road down into the gorge proper: notice how the vegetation changes all the way down to the Umzimkulwana River. The **Narina Trogon** can be enticed out of its forest shelter by mimicking its hooting call. In the drier parts of the gorge, which face west and north, look out for bird parties. Among these mixed groups **Knysna Woodpecker** is the find of the day in Natal. This bird may be located by its call, a very high-pitched "heeee". If found, it is quite accommodating and will allow itself to be observed from close quarters. At the bottom of the valley look out for **African Black Duck**, **Longtailed Wagtail** and **Halfcollared Kingfisher** along the river. When you work your way up the other side of the valley towards the plains near the top, you will cross a short bridge, set diagonally to the road, which spans a boulder-strewn stream. In this extremely productive area **Spotted Thrush**, **Cinnamon Dove** and **African Broadbill** are recorded. From this road, the forest seedeaters that may be seen include **Swee** and **Grey Waxbill**, **Green Twinspot** and **Bluebilled Firefinch**. **Bluemantled Flycatcher** and **Yellowthroated Warbler** are often found if you search through the creepers at the edge of the forest. In the evening just after dark, take a stroll up the Horseman's Point Trail which leads off to the left of the road at the bottom of the valley if one is facing west. Go up this trail for about 500 m and listen for **Scops Owl**. On the rocky outcrops in the reserve you might be lucky to find a **Freckled Nightjar** blending in with the lichen-covered rocks. During the breeding season its puppy-like yapping call can be heard.

65% OF SPECIES

No.	Species	☐	No.	Species	☐	No.	Species	☐
094	Hadeda Ibis	☐	158	**Black Sparrowhawk**	☐	229	African Finfoot	☐
105	**African Black Duck**	☐	160	**African Goshawk**	☐	349	Rock Pigeon	☐
126a	Yellowbilled Kite	☐	169	Gymnogene	☐	350	Rameron Pigeon	☐
128	**Cuckoo Hawk**	☐	172	Lanner Falcon	☐	352	Redeyed Dove	☐
141	**Crowned Eagle**	☐	181	Rock Kestrel	☐	354	Cape Turtle Dove	☐
149	Steppe Buzzard	☐	196	Natal Francolin*	☐	355	Laughing Dove	☐
152	Jackal Buzzard**	☐	203	Helmeted Guineafowl	☐	358	Greenspotted Dove	☐
157	Little Sparrowhawk	☐	218	Buffspotted Flufftail	☐	359	Tambourine Dove	☐

360 **Cinnamon Dove** ☐
361 Green Pigeon ☐
370 **Knysna Lourie**** ☐
377 Redchested Cuckoo ☐
378 Black Cuckoo ☐
384 Emerald Cuckoo ☐
385 Klaas's Cuckoo ☐
386 Diederik Cuckoo ☐
391 Burchell's Coucal* ☐
394 Wood Owl ☐
396 **Scops Owl** ☐
405 Fierynecked Nightjar ☐
408 **Freckled Nightjar** ☐
415 Whiterumped Swift ☐
417 Little Swift ☐
424 Speckled Mousebird ☐
427 **Narina Trogon** ☐
428 Pied Kingfisher ☐
429 Giant Kingfisher ☐
430 **Halfcollared Kingfisher** ☐
431 Malachite Kingfisher ☐
432 Pygmy Kingfisher ☐
435 Brownhooded Kingfisher ☐
444 Little Bee-eater ☐
451 Hoopoe ☐
452 Redbilled Woodhoopoe ☐
455 **Trumpeter Hornbill** ☐
460 **Crowned Hornbill** ☐
464 Blackcollared Barbet ☐
469 Redfronted Tinker Barbet ☐
471 Goldenrumped Tinker Barbet ☐
475 Scalythroated Honeyguide ☐
476 Lesser Honeyguide ☐
484 **Knysna Woodpecker**** ☐
486 Cardinal Woodpecker ☐
488 Olive Woodpecker ☐
490 **African Broadbill** ☐
494 Rufousnaped Lark ☐
518 European Swallow ☐
520 Whitethroated Swallow ☐
527 Lesser Striped Swallow ☐
529 Rock Martin ☐
536 Black Sawwing Swallow ☐
538 Black Cuckooshrike ☐
540 **Grey Cuckooshrike** ☐
541 Forktailed Drongo ☐
542 Squaretailed Drongo ☐
545 Blackheaded Oriole ☐
548 Pied Crow ☐
550 Whitenecked Raven ☐
554 Southern Black Tit* ☐
568 Blackeyed Bulbul ☐
569 Terrestrial Bulbul ☐
572 Sombre Bulbul ☐
574 Yellowbellied Bulbul ☐
576 Kurrichane Thrush ☐
577 Olive Thrush ☐
578 **Spotted Thrush** ☐
581 **Cape Rock Thrush**** ☐
589 Familiar Chat ☐
593 Mocking Chat ☐
596 Stonechat ☐
598 Chorister Robin** ☐
600 Natal Robin ☐
601 Cape Robin ☐
606 Starred Robin ☐
613 Whitebrowed Robin ☐
616 **Brown Robin**** ☐
639 Barratt's Warbler** ☐
643 Willow Warbler ☐
644 **Yellowthroated Warbler** ☐
645 Barthroated Apalis ☐
648 Yellowbreasted Apalis ☐
657 Bleating Warbler ☐
661 Grassbird** ☐
672 Rattling Cisticola ☐
674 Redfaced Cisticola ☐
678 Croaking Cisticola ☐
679 Lazy Cisticola ☐
681 Neddicky ☐
683 Tawnyflanked Prinia ☐
690 Dusky Flycatcher ☐
691 Bluegrey Flycatcher ☐
694 Black Flycatcher ☐
700 Cape Batis** ☐
701 Chinspot Batis ☐
708 **Bluemantled Flycatcher** ☐
712 **Longtailed Wagtail** ☐
720 **Striped Pipit** ☐
732 Fiscal Shrike ☐
736 Southern Boubou** ☐
740 Puffback ☐
742 Southern Tchagra** ☐
747 Gorgeous Bush Shrike ☐
750 Olive Bush Shrike* ☐
761 Plumcoloured Starling ☐
764 Glossy Starling* ☐
768 Blackbellied Starling ☐
769 Redwinged Starling ☐
783 **Lesser Double-collared Sunbird**** ☐
787 Whitebellied Sunbird ☐
789 **Grey Sunbird** ☐
790 **Olive Sunbird** ☐
792 Black Sunbird ☐
793 **Collared Sunbird** ☐
796 Cape White-eye** ☐
804 Greyheaded Sparrow ☐
807 Thickbilled Weaver ☐
808 Forest Weaver ☐
810 Spectacled Weaver ☐
811 Spottedbacked Weaver ☐
817 Yellow Weaver ☐
824 Red Bishop ☐
835 **Green Twinspot** ☐
840 **Bluebilled Firefinch** ☐
848 **Grey Waxbill** ☐
850 **Swee Waxbill*** ☐
857 Bronze Mannikin ☐
858 Redbacked Mannikin ☐
864 Black Widowfinch ☐
869 Yelloweyed Canary ☐
873 Forest Canary** ☐
877 Bully Canary ☐
881 Streakyheaded Canary ☐
☐

OTHER BIRDING SPOTS WORTH VISITING

Albert Falls Dam Nature Reserve
This reserve lies 20 km north of Pietermaritzburg on the Greytown road and provides excellent birding. Accommodation and camping can be booked through the Natal Parks Board.

Bona Manzi Game Farm
This privately owned reserve, which has treehouse and luxury chalet accommodation, lies south-east of Hluhluwe village. Advance booking is normally necessary for this popular reserve which rates as one of the best birding spots in Natal.

Bushlands Game Lodge
A small luxury lodge with good birding in pleasant surroundings not far from Hluhluwe village.

Goudhoek Farm
The farm is 16 km from Babanango, is privately owned and offers accommodation in the form of a luxury lodge. This popular birding spot is situated in Natal valley bushveld, where African Hawk Eagles have successfully bred for many years.

Harold Johnson Nature Reserve
The 104 ha reserve on the south bank of the Tugela River is administered by the Natal Parks Board. This spot is worth visiting for woodland, valley, bushveld and riverine bird species.

Josini Dam and Surrounding Woodland
The campsite region on the edge of the dam north of Mkuze offers excellent birding.

Kosi Bay Nature Reserve
Run by the KwaZulu Bureau of Natural Resources, this reseve offers both luxury accommodation and camping. Excellent coastal birding can be had on the lake and its surroundings.

Pigeon Valley
A small patch of coastal bush below the University of Natal in Durban, offering exciting species such as Spotted Thrush in winter. From the tollgate offramp take South Ridge Road towards the University, turn left into King George V Avenue, then right into Princess Alice Avenue: the entrance gate is on the right.

Royal Natal National Park
This 8 094 ha reserve, controlled by the Natal Parks Board, is a productive birding spot, set in one of the most beautiful parts of the Natal Drakensberg.

Roosfontein
Take the Westville turnoff (Spine Road) from the N3 leading out of Durban towards Pietermaritzburg and travel south to the entrance gate on the left. This small reserve is predominantly grassland with riverine and valley bottom woodland.

Stainbank Nature Reserve
Situated within suburban Durban, south of the city centre. The reserve is predominantly coastal evergreen forest and open grassland.

Wesa Forest
Lies between Harding and Kokstad and offers forest species such as Cape Parrot, Barratt's Warbler and Yellowthroated Warbler.

Windy Ridge Game Park
Dominated by Acacia thickets and riverine woodland. The park is 28 km west of Empangeni, is privately owned and has an impressive bird list. Both luxury and basic hutted accommodation is available.

USEFUL TELEPHONE NUMBERS

Beachwood Mangroves
(031) 25-1271/84-0815

Bushlands Game Lodge
(03562) 144

Bona Manzi
(03562) 3530

Giant's Castle (Warden)
(0363) 2-4616

Goudhoek Farm – Nonpareil Lodge
(03872) 1303

Harold Johnson Nature Reserve
(0324) 6-1574

Ian Sinclair (private pelagic organiser)
(031) 28-3209

Isle of Capri (deep-sea fishing trawler)
(031) 37-7751

KwaZulu Bureau of Natural Resources
(0331) 94-6698

Mtunzini Chalets (Mlalazi Nature Reserve)
(0353) 40-1953

Natal Parks Board Reservations
(0331) 47-1981

Umgeni Valley Nature Reserve
(0332) 30-3931

Windy Ridge Game Park
(0351) 2-3465

9 Eastern Cape

Co-ordinator Dave Brown

1 Rhodes and Naudesnek Pass
2 Graaff-Reinet
3 Mountain Zebra National Park
4 Hogsback
5 Bosberg Nature Reserve
6 Kei Mouth and Surroundings
7 East London and Gonubie
8 Amalinda Fish Station and Nature Reserve
9 Baviaanskloof
10 Addo Elephant National Park
11 Mondplaas Ponds
12 Swartkops Estuary
13 Plettenberg Bay
14 Knysna

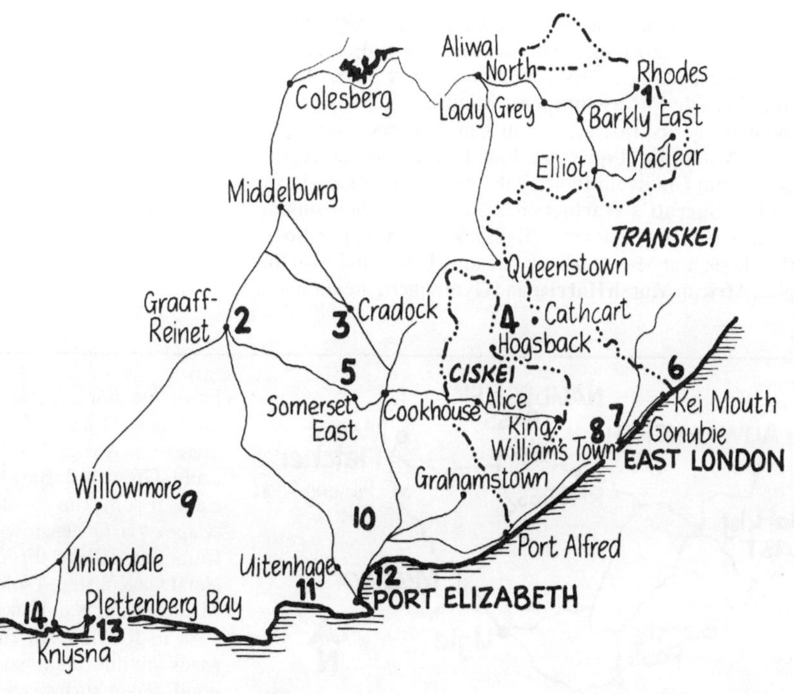

RHODES AND NAUDESNEK PASS

approximately 123 species recorded to date

Rhodes lies in the north-eastern corner of the Cape Province bordered by Lesotho and Transkei. The Naudesnek Pass, at 2 740 m, is the highest mountain pass in South Africa, providing a link over the Drakensberg Mountains between Rhodes in the eastern Cape and Maclear. This area has spectacular mountain scenery, sandstone formations, Bushman paintings, unspoilt valleys, waving grassland and air crisper and cleaner than you'll find anywhere else in the country. Most of the area is privately owned – if you want to walk off the roads, ask permission from the Rhodes Hotel where permits are issued.

SPECIAL AND INTERESTING SPECIES

Cape and **Bearded Vultures** are common and may be seen anywhere in the area, especially on the pass and other high areas. The Naudesnek Pass is one of the best places to see **Orangebreasted Rockjumpers**, **Wailing Cisticolas** and **Drakensberg Siskins**. Here you can also see eight chat species. **Mountain Pipits** are found here and are distinguished from Grassveld Pipit by the pink, not yellow, lower mandible. **Barratt's Warblers** deafen one with their singing in summer in the thickets all along the Kloppershoek, Carlislehoek and Maartenshoek streams. **Black** and **Martial Eagles, African Marsh Harrier** and **Gymnogene** are common.

ALSO RECORDED

A few records exist for Yellowbreasted Pipit from the eastern side of Naudesnek Pass and down towards Maclear.

Libby McGill

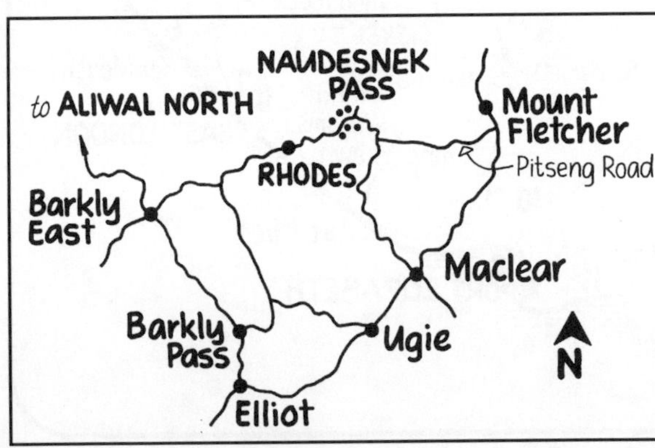

From the north (Transvaal and Orange Free State) via Aliwal North, Lady Grey and Barkly East. From the south (Cape) via Queenstown, Cala and Elliot. From Natal via Kokstad, Tsolo, Maclear and Naudesnek Pass to Rhodes. All the roads in this area have good gravel surfaces.

Expend a bit of energy and walk up the track through Carlislehoek onto the high plateau. Here you will find the highest peak in the Cape: Ben Macdhui (3 001 m). **Greywing Francolin** are common, as are **Ground Woodpeckers**. A very rewarding scenic day drive, during which you will see most of the specials for the area, is the Bastervoetpad circuit. Take the road westwards out of Rhodes and after about 15 km turn south on the Bokspruit-Sterkspruit road to Barkly Pass. Some 35 km on you will see the signpost for the Bastervoetpad to the left. This brings you back to Rhodes via Ugie, Maclear and the Naudesnek Pass. On this circuit you should see plenty of **Crowned Cranes**.

90% OF SPECIES

- 008 Dabchick ☐
- 055 Whitebreasted Cormorant ☐
- 058 Reed Cormorant ☐
- 060 Darter ☐
- 062 Grey Heron ☐
- 063 Blackheaded Heron ☐
- 071 Cattle Egret ☐
- 076 Blackcrowned Night Heron ☐
- 081 Hamerkop ☐
- 083 White Stork ☐
- 084 Black Stork ☐
- 091 Sacred Ibis ☐
- 094 Hadeda Ibis ☐
- 095 African Spoonbill ☐
- 102 Egyptian Goose ☐
- 103 South African Shelduck** ☐
- 104 Yellowbilled Duck ☐
- 105 African Black Duck ☐
- 118 Secretarybird ☐
- 119 **Bearded Vulture** ☐
- 122 **Cape Vulture**** ☐
- 127 Blackshouldered Kite ☐
- 131 **Black Eagle** ☐
- 140 **Martial Eagle** ☐
- 149 Steppe Buzzard ☐
- 152 Jackal Buzzard** ☐
- 160 African Goshawk ☐
- 165 **African Marsh Harrier** ☐
- 169 **Gymnogene** ☐
- 172 Lanner Falcon ☐
- 181 Rock Kestrel ☐
- 190 **Greywing Francolin**** ☐
- 203 Helmeted Guineafowl ☐
- 208 Blue Crane** ☐
- 209 **Crowned Crane** ☐
- 228 Redknobbed Coot ☐
- 249 Threebanded Plover ☐
- 258 Blacksmith Plover ☐
- 297 Spotted Dikkop ☐
- 348 Feral Pigeon ☐
- 349 Rock Pigeon ☐
- 352 Redeyed Dove ☐
- 354 Cape Turtle Dove ☐
- 355 Laughing Dove ☐
- 377 Redchested Cuckoo ☐
- 401 Spotted Eagle Owl ☐
- 412 Black Swift ☐
- 415 Whiterumped Swift ☐
- 416 Horus Swift ☐
- 417 Little Swift ☐
- 418 Alpine Swift ☐
- 424 Speckled Mousebird ☐
- 429 Giant Kingfisher ☐
- 438 European Bee-eater ☐
- 451 Hoopoe ☐
- 480 **Ground Woodpecker**** ☐
- 507 Redcapped Lark ☐
- 518 European Swallow ☐
- 520 Whitethroated Swallow ☐
- 526 Greater Striped Swallow* ☐
- 529 Rock Martin ☐
- 530 House Martin ☐
- 534 Banded Martin ☐
- 547 Black Crow ☐
- 548 Pied Crow ☐
- 550 Whitenecked Raven ☐
- 567 Redeyed Bulbul* ☐
- 577 Olive Thrush ☐
- 581 Cape Rock Thrush** ☐
- 582 Sentinel Rock Thrush** ☐
- 586 Mountain Chat* ☐
- 588 Buffstreaked Chat** ☐
- 589 Familiar Chat ☐
- 591 Sicklewinged Chat** ☐
- 592 Karoo Chat* ☐
- 593 Mocking Chat ☐
- 595 Anteating Chat** ☐
- 596 Stonechat ☐
- 601 Cape Robin ☐
- 612 **Orangebreasted Rockjumper**** ☐
- 639 **Barratt's Warbler**** ☐
- 643 Willow Warbler ☐
- 661 Grassbird** ☐
- 664 Fantailed Cisticola ☐
- 665 Desert Cisticola ☐
- 667 Ayres' Cisticola ☐

669 Greybacked Cisticola* ☐
670 **Wailing Cisticola** ☐
677 Levaillant's Cisticola ☐
681 Neddicky ☐
686a Spotted Prinia** ☐
706 Fairy Flycatcher** ☐
713 Cape Wagtail ☐
716 Grassveld Pipit ☐
901 **Mountain Pipit*** ☐
718 Plainbacked Pipit ☐
721 Rock Pipit** ☐
725 Yellowbreasted Pipit** ☐
727 Orangethroated Longclaw** ☐
732 Fiscal Shrike ☐
746 Bokmakierie* ☐
759 Pied Starling** ☐
769 Redwinged Starling ☐
775 Malachite Sunbird ☐
796 Cape White-eye** ☐
801 House Sparrow ☐
803 Cape Sparrow* ☐
804 Greyheaded Sparrow ☐
813 Cape Weaver** ☐
814 Masked Weaver ☐
824 Red Bishop ☐
826 Golden Bishop ☐
827 Yellowrumped Widow ☐
846 Common Waxbill ☐
852 Quail Finch ☐
860 Pintailed Whydah ☐
869 Yelloweyed Canary ☐
872 Cape Canary ☐
875 **Drakensberg Siskin**** ☐
878 Yellow Canary* ☐
881 Streakyheaded Canary ☐
885 Cape Bunting ☐
886 Rock Bunting ☐

GRAAFF-REINET

approximately 209 species recorded to date

Graaff-Reinet, known as the gem of the Karoo, is situated in the heart of the Great Karoo. The southern part of the district, known as the plains of Camdeboo, is flat while the northern parts are mountainous. The Sundays River, the largest in the district, runs more or less north/south and is fed by water from the Verwoed Dam on the Orange River. The Karoo Nature Reserve forms a horseshoe around the west, north and east of the town and includes the Van Ryneveld's Pass Dam.

The town itself lies on the R57, the main route from the north to the southern Cape. A wide variety of accommodation, from hotels to guest farms, is available. The Karoo Nature Reserve falls under the control of the Cape Department of Nature and Environmental Conservation. To reach both the game viewing area and the Valley of Desolation leave the town on the Murraysburg road (R63). The turnoff to the Valley of Desolation is 4 km from the town and that to the game viewing area 8 km.

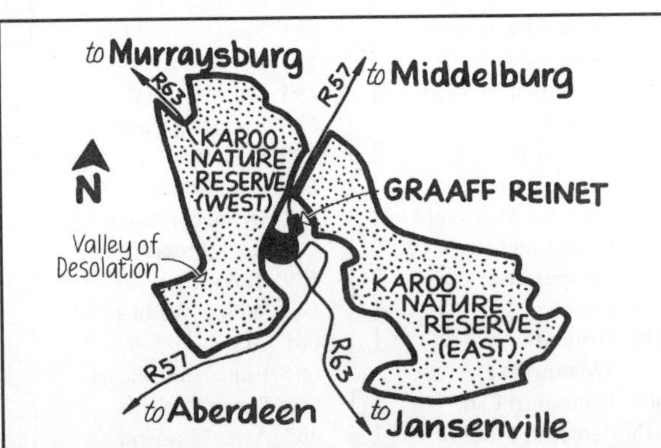

SPECIAL AND INTERESTING SPECIES

Roadside birdwatching can be very rewarding in this area. In the flat country to the south of the town both **Kori** and **Ludwig's Bustards** are fairly easily seen, along with **Sicklewinged Chat**, **Rufouseared Warbler**, **Sabota** and **Spikeheeled Larks**. **Chat Flycatchers** are also found here. Watch telephone and power lines for **Rock** and **Greater Kestrels**. In summer **Lesser Kestrels** are commonly seen. Riverside vegetation, as along the Sundays River, supports an interesting assemblage of birds such as **Namaqua Prinia**, **Titbabbler**, **Pririt Batis** and **Southern Tchagra**. **Great Spotted Cuckoos** are also found in this habitat, particularly close to nesting areas of **Pied Starling**. Bushy watercourses on the way up to the lookout over the Valley of Desolation are the preferred habitat of **Layard's Titbabbler**, though it is not common nor easily seen unless calling. At the lookout point watch for **Black Eagle**, **Black** and **Alpine Swifts** and **Palewinged Starling**. Now that water is a permanent feature thanks to the Van Rynevelds Pass Dam, birds such as **Great Crested Grebe** have established themselves here. Also to be seen are **Greater** and **Lesser Flamingos**, **Southern Pochard** and **Greyheaded Gull**. Elsewhere, small dams and stock drinking troughs attract a variety of birds. Time spent near such places, particularly in the morning, may produce **Larklike Bunting**, **Namaqua Sandgrouse**, **Yellow** and **Whitethroated Canaries** and **Redheaded Finch**. **Ground Woodpecker**, **Rock Bunting** and **Rock Pipit** should be looked for in the mountains and hills of the district, the first particularly near road cuttings. **Karoo** and **Black Korhaans** are found throughout in areas of low scrub, while **Whitebacked Mousebird** prefers riverine vegetation and gardens.

ALSO RECORDED

Van Rynevelds Pass Dam has attracted Blacknecked Grebe and Yellowbilled Stork and, doubtless, other rarities will be recorded there in future, now that there is water permanently. Cape Eagle Owl has been recorded from the north-eastern part of the district. Both Fiery-necked and Rufouscheeked Nightjars along with Barn Owl have been heard.

Dave Brown

72% OF SPECIES

006 **Great Crested Grebe** ☐
008 Dabchick ☐
055 Whitebreasted Cormorant ☐
058 Reed Cormorant ☐
062 Grey Heron ☐
063 Blackheaded Heron ☐
067 Little Egret ☐
071 Cattle Egret ☐
081 Hamerkop ☐
083 White Stork ☐
091 Sacred Ibis ☐
094 Hadeda Ibis ☐
095 African Spoonbill ☐
096 **Greater Flamingo** ☐
097 **Lesser Flamingo** ☐
102 Egyptian Goose ☐
103 South African Shelduck** ☐
104 Yellowbilled Duck ☐
108 Redbilled Teal ☐
113 **Southern Pochard** ☐
127 Blackshouldered Kite ☐
131 **Black Eagle** ☐
149 Steppe Buzzard ☐
152 Jackal Buzzard** ☐
162 Pale Chanting Goshawk* ☐
181 **Rock Kestrel** ☐
182 **Greater Kestrel** ☐
183 **Lesser Kestrel** ☐
200 Common Quail ☐
203 Helmeted Guineafowl ☐
208 Blue Crane** ☐
228 Redknobbed Coot ☐
230 **Kori Bustard** ☐
232 **Ludwig's Bustard*** ☐
235 **Karoo Korhaan**** ☐
239 **Black Korhaan**** ☐

Eastern Cape

- 249 Threebanded Plover
- 255 Crowned Plover
- 258 Blacksmith Plover
- 264 Common Sandpiper
- 294 Avocet
- 295 Blackwinged Stilt
- 297 Spotted Dikkop
- 315 **Greyheaded Gull**
- 344 **Namaqua Sandgrouse***
- 348 Feral Pigeon
- 349 Rock Pigeon
- 352 Redeyed Dove
- 354 Cape Turtle Dove
- 355 Laughing Dove
- 356 Namaqua Dove
- 380 **Great Spotted Cuckoo**
- 382 Jacobin Cuckoo
- 386 Diederik Cuckoo
- 401 Spotted Eagle Owl
- 412 **Black Swift**
- 415 Whiterumped Swift
- 417 Little Swift
- 418 **Alpine Swift**
- 424 Speckled Mousebird
- 425 **Whitebacked Mousebird****
- 426 Redfaced Mousebird
- 431 Malachite Kingfisher
- 435 Brownhooded Kingfisher
- 438 European Bee-eater
- 451 Hoopoe
- 465 Pied Barbet*
- 480 **Ground Woodpecker****
- 486 Cardinal Woodpecker
- 495 Clapper Lark**
- 498 **Sabota Lark***
- 500 Longbilled Lark*
- 502 Karoo Lark**
- 506 **Spikeheeled Lark***
- 512 Thickbilled Lark**
- 518 European Swallow
- 520 Whitethroated Swallow
- 523 Pearlbreasted Swallow
- 526 Greater Striped Swallow*
- 529 Rock Martin
- 533 Brownthroated Martin
- 541 Forktailed Drongo
- 547 Black Crow
- 548 Pied Crow
- 551 Southern Grey Tit**
- 557 Cape Penduline Tit*
- 567 Redeyed Bulbul*
- 577 Olive Thrush
- 586 Mountain Chat*
- 589 Familiar Chat
- 591 **Sicklewinged Chat****
- 592 Karoo Chat*
- 595 Anteating Chat**
- 601 Cape Robin
- 614 Karoo Robin**
- 621 **Titbabbler***
- 622 **Layard's Titbabbler****
- 631 African Marsh Warbler
- 643 Willow Warbler
- 645 Barthroated Apalis
- 651 Longbilled Crombec
- 653 Yellowbellied Eremomela
- 664 Fantailed Cisticola
- 669 Greybacked Cisticola*
- 681 Neddicky
- 686a Karoo Prinia**
- 687 **Namaqua Prinia****
- 688 **Rufouseared Warbler****
- 697 **Chat Flycatcher***
- 698 Fiscal Flycatcher**
- 703 **Pririt Batis***
- 706 Fairy Flycatcher**
- 710 Paradise Flycatcher
- 713 Cape Wagtail
- 716 Grassveld Pipit
- 721 **Rock Pipit****
- 732 Fiscal Shrike
- 733 Redbacked Shrike
- 736 Southern Boubou**
- 742 **Southern Tchagra****
- 746 Bokmakierie*
- 757 European Starling
- 759 **Pied Starling****
- 760 Wattled Starling
- 769 Redwinged Starling
- 770 **Palewinged Starling***
- 775 Malachite Sunbird
- 783 Lesser Double-collared Sunbird**
- 788 Dusky Sunbird*
- 796 Cape White-eye**
- 801 House Sparrow
- 803 Cape Sparrow*
- 805 Yellowthroated Sparrow
- 814 Masked Weaver
- 821 Redbilled Quelea
- 824 Red Bishop
- 846 Common Waxbill
- 856 **Redheaded Finch***
- 860 Pintailed Whydah
- 869 Yelloweyed Canary
- 870 Blackthroated Canary
- 872 Cape Canary
- 876 Blackheaded Canary
- 878 **Yellow Canary***
- 879 **Whitethroated Canary***
- 881 Streakyheaded Canary
- 884 Goldenbreasted Bunting
- 885 Cape Bunting
- 886 **Rock Bunting**
- 887 **Larklike Bunting***

MOUNTAIN ZEBRA NATIONAL PARK

approximately 199 species recorded to date

The Mountain Zebra National Park, situated 27 km west of Cradock, was proclaimed in 1937 to ensure the survival of the Cape Mountain Zebra, and is now 6 536 ha in extent. It consists mainly of the spectacular scenery of the northern slopes of the Bankberg with the valleys running up into it, and a plateau, Rooiplaat, on the northern side of the park. Bird habitats include mountain grassveld, hillside scrub, valley Acacia and open mixed karoo or grassveld. The only dam of any size is on the Wilgerboom River. The total road length within the park is 42 km. There is a 25,6 km three-day hiking trail on the Bankberg and a shorter walk near the rest camp. Some species on the list are unlikely to be seen unless these trails are walked. The usual National Parks Board reservations, accommodation, regulations and facilities (including a swimming pool) apply. Walking the three-day trail may not be possible during strong cold fronts in winter.

SPECIAL AND INTERESTING SPECIES

The park is ideal habitat for **Black** and **Booted Eagles** and **Cape Eagle Owl**, which all breed here. Seeing or hearing the eagle owl will probably only happen from the trail huts. **Orangebreasted Rockjumper** has been seen on the middle section of the trail. **Ground Woodpecker**, **Palewinged Starling**, **Cape Rock Thrush** and **Rock Pipit** are other rock-

ALSO RECORDED

Buffstreaked Chat has been recorded on the stony slopes; Black Cuckooshrike, Knysna Woodpecker, Redthroated Wryneck, Olive Bush Shrike, Little Sparrowhawk and Scalythroated Honeyguide in the bush; Stanley's Bustard, Temminck's Courser and Blue Korhaan in the open veld. Redbreasted Sparrowhawk used to breed in stands of exotic poplar and pines which have now been removed. Unusual waterbirds recorded are Goliath and Greenbacked Herons, Blackcrowned Night Heron, Southern Pochard and Whitebacked Duck. Also recorded in the past are Mocking Chat and Cape Sugarbird.

Joan Collett

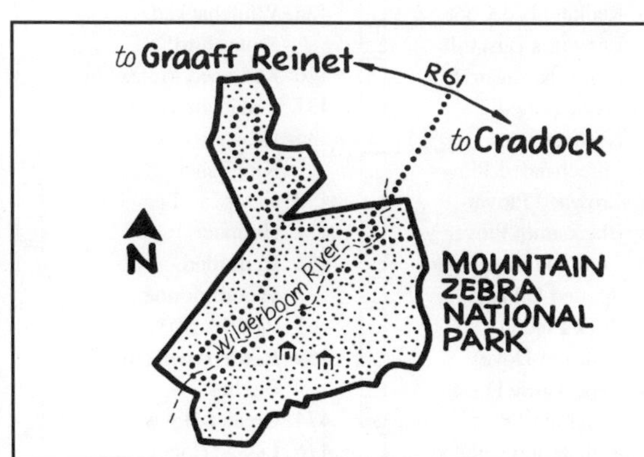

The park is approached from the tarred Cradock-Graaff Reinet road (R61). A signposted gravel road turns off the R61 in a south-westerly direction.

loving birds to watch for. The Rock Pipit may be identified by its far-carrying call. **Layard's Titbabbler**, **Dusky Sunbird** and **Blackheaded Canary** should be looked for in hillside shrubs. In the thick Acacia woodland in the valleys the calls of **Redfronted Tinker Barbet** and **Redchested Cuckoo** (summer) may be heard. One of the interesting features of the park is the presence of these species as well as **Sombre Bulbul**, **Redbilled Woodhoopoe**, **Tambourine Dove** and others that do not normally occur in the Cradock district. The other three cuckoos listed are common summer migrants to the district. Specials of the open mixed veld are **Rufouseared Warbler**, **Sicklewinged Chat** and three species of lark, **Clapper**, **Thickbilled** and **Spikeheeled**, all resident breeders. **Longbilled Lark** and **Longbilled Pipit** favour stony slopes and may be identified with the aid of a tape, which is also the best way of making sure of some of the LBJs, such as **Greybacked Cisticola** (mountain slopes) and **Namaqua Prinia** (bushy undergrowth).

74% OF SPECIES

001 Ostrich ☐
008 Dabchick ☐
055 Whitebreasted Cormorant ☐
058 Reed Cormorant ☐
062 Grey Heron ☐
063 Blackheaded Heron ☐
071 Cattle Egret ☐
081 Hamerkop ☐
083 White Stork ☐
084 Black Stork ☐
091 Sacred Ibis ☐
094 Hadeda Ibis ☐
095 African Spoonbill ☐
102 Egyptian Goose ☐
103 South African Shelduck** ☐
104 Yellowbilled Duck ☐
105 African Black Duck ☐
108 Redbilled Teal ☐
118 Secretarybird ☐
127 Blackshouldered Kite ☐
131 **Black Eagle** ☐
136 **Booted Eagle** ☐
149 Steppe Buzzard ☐
152 Jackal Buzzard** ☐
160 African Goshawk ☐
162 Pale Chanting Goshawk* ☐
169 Gymnogene ☐
181 Rock Kestrel ☐
183 Lesser Kestrel ☐
190 Greywing Francolin** ☐
200 Common Quail ☐
203 Helmeted Guineafowl ☐
208 Blue Crane** ☐
228 Redknobbed Coot ☐
232 Ludwig's Bustard* ☐
235 Karoo Korhaan** ☐
239a Whitequilled Korhaan** ☐
249 Threebanded Plover ☐
255 Crowned Plover ☐
258 Blacksmith Plover ☐
264 Common Sandpiper ☐
297 Spotted Dikkop ☐
349 Rock Pigeon ☐
352 Redeyed Dove ☐
354 Cape Turtle Dove ☐
355 Laughing Dove ☐
377 Redchested Cuckoo ☐
380 Great Spotted Cuckoo ☐
382 Jacobin Cuckoo ☐
386 Diederik Cuckoo ☐
400 **Cape Eagle Owl** ☐
401 Spotted Eagle Owl ☐
405 Fierynecked Nightjar ☐
412 Black Swift ☐
415 Whiterumped Swift ☐
417 Little Swift ☐
418 Alpine Swift ☐
424 Speckled Mousebird ☐
425 Whitebacked Mousebird** ☐
426 Redfaced Mousebird ☐
431 Malachite Kingfisher ☐
435 Brownhooded Kingfisher ☐
438 European Bee-eater ☐
451 Hoopoe ☐
452 **Redbilled Woodhoopoe** ☐
465 Pied Barbet* ☐
469 **Redfronted Tinker Barbet** ☐
474 Greater Honeyguide ☐
476 Lesser Honeyguide ☐

480 **Ground Woodpecker**** ☐
486 Cardinal Woodpecker ☐
495 **Clapper Lark**** ☐
500 **Longbilled Lark*** ☐
506 **Spikeheeled Lark*** ☐
512 **Thickbilled Lark**** ☐
518 European Swallow ☐
520 Whitethroated Swallow ☐
526 Greater Striped Swallow* ☐
529 Rock Martin ☐
533 Brownthroated Martin ☐
541 Forktailed Drongo ☐
548 Pied Crow ☐
550 Whitenecked Raven ☐
551 Southern Grey Tit** ☐
557 Cape Penduline Tit* ☐
567 Redeyed Bulbul* ☐
572 **Sombre Bulbul** ☐
577 Olive Thrush ☐
581 **Cape Rock Thrush**** ☐
586 Mountain Chat* ☐
589 Familiar Chat ☐
591 **Sicklewinged Chat**** ☐
595 Anteating Chat** ☐
596 Stonechat ☐
601 Cape Robin ☐
612 **Orangebreasted Rockjumper**** ☐
614 Karoo Robin** ☐
621 Titbabbler* ☐
622 **Layard's Titbabbler**** ☐
643 Willow Warbler ☐
645 Barthroated Apalis ☐
651 Longbilled Crombec ☐
669 **Greybacked Cisticola*** ☐
677 Levaillant's Cisticola ☐
681 Neddicky ☐
686a Karoo Prinia** ☐
687 **Namaqua Prinia**** ☐
688 **Rufouseared Warbler**** ☐
698 Fiscal Flycatcher** ☐
701 Chinspot Batis ☐
706 Fairy Flycatcher** ☐
710 Paradise Flycatcher ☐
713 Cape Wagtail ☐
716 Grassveld Pipit ☐
717 **Longbilled Pipit** ☐
721 **Rock Pipit**** ☐
727 Orangethroated Longclaw** ☐
732 Fiscal Shrike ☐
736 Southern Boubou** ☐
742 Southern Tchagra** ☐
750 **Olive Bush Shrike*** ☐
759 Pied S arling** ☐
760 Wattled Starling ☐
769 Redwinged Starling ☐
770 **Palewinged Starling*** ☐
775 Malachite Sunbird ☐
783 Lesser Double-collared Sunbird** ☐
788 **Dusky Sunbird*** ☐
796 Cape White-eye** ☐
801 House Sparrow ☐
803 Cape Sparrow* ☐
804 Greyheaded Sparrow ☐
805 Yellowthroated Sparrow ☐
813 Cape Weaver** ☐
814 Masked Weaver ☐
821 Redbilled Quelea ☐
824 Red Bishop ☐
846 Common Waxbill ☐
860 Pintailed Whydah ☐
869 **Yelloweyed Canary** ☐
870 **Blackthroated Canary** ☐
872 Cape Canary ☐
876 **Blackheaded Canary** ☐
877 **Bully Canary** ☐
879 **Whitethroated Canary*** ☐
881 **Streakyheaded Canary** ☐
885 Cape Bunting ☐
886 Rock Bunting ☐
☐
☐
☐
☐
☐

HOGSBACK

approximately 221 species recorded to date

The village of Hogsback in the Amatola Mountains is bordered by indigenous forest and exotic plantations. Hotels, caravan and camping sites as well as holiday cottages are available. There are many well marked trails in the area, details of which can be obtained from the hotels and at the local store.

SPECIAL AND INTERESTING SPECIES

During summer **Emerald, Black**, **Klaas's**, **Diederik** and **Redchested Cuckoos** can be seen throughout the network of forest and verge trails. The beautiful **Narina Trogon** is more often heard than seen and patience is needed to locate it in the canopy. In summer it may respond to the low hooting sound made by cupping one's hands and blowing past the thumbs. Birding is much easier in the forest on sunny days when more light filters through the canopy. **Grey Cuckooshrike**, **Knysna Lourie**, **Bush Blackcap**, **Yellowthroated** and **Barratt's Warblers**, **Blackheaded Oriole**, **Starred** and **Brown Robins** and **Orange Thrush** can all be seen or heard in the forest. **Knysna** and **Olive Woodpeckers** are easy to locate once you know their calls. Flocks of **Cape Parrots**, sometimes as many as 30, screech their way to and fro, mostly in the early morning and late afternoon. **Rameron Pigeons** can be seen in the canopy and **Terrestrial Bulbuls** usually forage in dead leaves on the forest floor. You may flush a **Cinnamon Dove** which will take off at the last moment to fly a short distance

ALSO RECORDED

Cuckoo Hawk occurs but is easily overlooked. Sentinel Rock Thrush, Mountain and Sicklewinged Chats, Ground Woodpecker and Orange-breasted Rockjumper have been recorded and are well worth watching for.

Wendy Perks

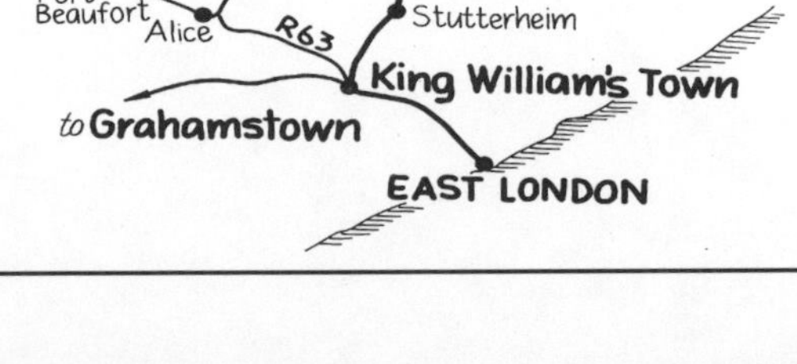

Hogsback is about 160 km inland of East London. Take the road to King Williams Town, then through the Ciskei; turn right 5 km before reaching Alice. To reach Coolin and Gaika's Kop, continue through Hogsback to a T-junction and turn right towards Cathcart. Along this route stops at fields, small dams and rivers may be rewarding.

away. Look out for **Forest Buzzard**, which can be found on the edges of both exotic and indigenous forest. Other raptors to be seen include **Crowned Eagle**, **Jackal** and **Steppe Buzzards**, **African Goshawk** and **Black Sparrowhawk**. The Coolin/ Gaika's Kop area has a variety of LBJs such as **Ayres' Cisticola**, **Grassbird** and **Plainbacked Pipit**. **Pied Starling** and **Yellowrumped Widow** can be seen in the fields and near small dams. **Buffstreaked Chats** are usually seen in the rockier areas. **Malachite**, **Lesser** (mainly forest) and **Greater Doublecollared Sunbirds** are not uncommon. Both **Gurney's** and **Cape Sugarbirds** have been recorded in the proteas.

65% OF SPECIES

008 Dabchick ☐
058 Reed Cormorant ☐
060 Darter ☐
063 Blackheaded Heron ☐
067 Little Egret ☐
071 Cattle Egret ☐
081 Hamerkop ☐
083 White Stork ☐
091 Sacred Ibis ☐
094 Hadeda Ibis ☐
095 African Spoonbill ☐
102 Egyptian Goose ☐
104 Yellowbilled Duck ☐
105 African Black Duck ☐
116 Spurwinged Goose ☐
126a Yellowbilled Kite ☐
127 Blackshouldered Kite ☐
140 Martial Eagle ☐
141 **Crowned Eagle** ☐
149 **Steppe Buzzard** ☐
150 **Forest Buzzard**** ☐
152 **Jackal Buzzard**** ☐
158 **Black Sparrowhawk** ☐
160 **African Goshawk** ☐
169 Gymnogene ☐
172 Lanner Falcon ☐
181 Rock Kestrel ☐
183 Lesser Kestrel ☐
190 Greywing Francolin** ☐
192 Redwing Francolin ☐
198 Rednecked Francolin ☐
200 Common Quail ☐
209 Crowned Crane ☐
218 Buffspotted Flufftail ☐
228 Redknobbed Coot ☐
231 Stanley's Bustard ☐
349 Rock Pigeon ☐
350 **Rameron Pigeon** ☐
352 Redeyed Dove ☐
355 Laughing Dove ☐
360 **Cinnamon Dove** ☐
362 **Cape Parrot** ☐
370 **Knysna Lourie**** ☐
377 **Redchested Cuckoo** ☐
378 **Black Cuckoo** ☐
384 **Emerald Cuckoo** ☐
385 **Klaas's Cuckoo** ☐
386 **Diederik Cuckoo** ☐
394 Wood Owl ☐
396 Scops Owl ☐
400 Cape Eagle Owl ☐
412 Black Swift ☐
418 Alpine Swift ☐
424 Speckled Mousebird ☐
427 **Narina Trogon** ☐
451 Hoopoe ☐
455 Trumpeter Hornbill ☐
460 Crowned Hornbill ☐
469 Redfronted Tinker Barbet ☐
480 Ground Woodpecker** ☐
484 **Knysna Woodpecker**** ☐
488 **Olive Woodpecker** ☐
494 Rufousnaped Lark ☐
518 European Swallow ☐
520 Whitethroated Swallow ☐
523 Pearlbreasted Swallow ☐
526 Greater Striped Swallow* ☐
527 Lesser Striped Swallow ☐
529 Rock Martin ☐
530 House Martin ☐
540 **Grey Cuckooshrike** ☐
531 Forktailed Drongo ☐
545 **Blackheaded Oriole** ☐
547 Black Crow ☐
548 Pied Crow ☐
550 Whitenecked Raven ☐
554 Southern Black Tit* ☐
565 **Bush Blackcap**** ☐
568 Blackeyed Bulbul ☐
569 **Terrestrial Bulbul** ☐
572 Sombre Bulbul ☐
577 Olive Thrush ☐
579 **Orange Thrush** ☐
588 **Buffstreaked Chat**** ☐
596 Stonechat ☐
598 Chorister Robin** ☐
601 Cape Robin ☐
606 **Starred Robin** ☐
616 **Brown Robin**** ☐

639 **Barratt's Warbler**** ☐
643 Willow Warbler ☐
644 **Yellowthroated Warbler** ☐
645 Barthroated Apalis ☐
648 Yellowbreasted Apalis ☐
657 Bleating Warbler ☐
661 **Grassbird**** ☐
667 **Ayres' Cisticola** ☐
670 Wailing Cisticola ☐
677 Levaillant's Cisticola ☐
679 Lazy Cisticola ☐
681 Neddicky ☐
686 Karoo Prinia** ☐
690 Dusky Flycatcher ☐
694 Black Flycatcher ☐
700 Cape Batis** ☐
708 Bluemantled Flycatcher ☐
710 Paradise Flycatcher ☐
711 African Pied Wagtail ☐
712 Longtailed Wagtail ☐
713 Cape Wagtail ☐
716 Grassveld Pipit ☐
718 **Plainbacked Pipit** ☐
727 Orangethroated Longclaw** ☐
732 Fiscal Shrike ☐
736 Southern Boubou** ☐
740 Puffback ☐
746 Bokmakierie* ☐
750 Olive Bush Shrike* ☐
757 European Starling ☐
759 **Pied Starling**** ☐
764 Glossy Starling* ☐
769 Redwinged Starling ☐
773 **Cape Sugarbird**** ☐
774 **Gurney's Sugarbird**** ☐
775 **Malachite Sunbird** ☐
783 **Lesser Double-collared Sunbird**** ☐
785 **Greater Double-collared Sunbird**** ☐
792 Black Sunbird ☐
796 Cape White-eye** ☐
808 Forest Weaver ☐
813 Cape Weaver** ☐
824 Red Bishop ☐
827 **Yellowrumped Widow** ☐
831 Redcollared Widow ☐
846 Common Waxbill ☐
850 Swee Waxbill* ☐
852 Quail Finch ☐
857 Bronze Mannikin ☐
860 Pintailed Whydah ☐
869 Yelloweyed Canary ☐
872 Cape Canary ☐
873 Forest Canary** ☐
877 Bully Canary ☐
881 Streakyheaded Canary ☐
884 Goldenbreasted Bunting ☐
885 Cape Bunting ☐

Swee Waxbills

BOSBERG NATURE RESERVE

approximately 150 species recorded to date

The recently proclaimed Bosberg Nature Reserve, controlled by the Town Council of Somerset East, is situated immediately to the north of the town. Its 2 050 ha comprise a wide variety of habitats. The south-facing slopes of the Bosberg range enjoy high rainfall which supports the evergreen forest found there. Wild olive grows in profusion; Cape chestnut, yellowwood, kiepersol and sneezewood are well represented. The game camp, at a lower altitude, consists of mixed bushveld with a substantial Acacia (sweet thorn) component interspersed with both grass and Karoo vegetation. The mountain plateau, at an altitude of over 1 500 m, is undulating grassland with occasional ironstone outcrops. Within several hundred metres of the mountain's summit, a mountain dam can be reached by following the nature trail. The upper section of the drive in the game camp can only be negotiated by four-wheel drive vehicles. Caravan and camping sites are available, as is nearby guest farm accommodation and a hotel at Somerset East.

SPECIAL AND INTERESTING SPECIES

Black Stork, **Cape Vulture**, **Crowned Eagle** and **Forest Buzzard**, although uncommon, may be seen. The game camp is the most likely area for **Black Harrier**, **Titbabbler** and **Southern Tchagra**. **Rameron Pigeon** and **Knysna Lourie** are frequently found feeding on berries in yellowwood, wild

ALSO RECORDED

Eastern and Western Red-footed Kestrels may be found in the company of Lesser Kestrels on fences and telephone lines. Giant Eagle and Scops Owl, as well as Redthroated Wryneck, have been sighted on private farmland adjoining the reserve. Two Peregrine Falcons were seen in the vicinity of Rooikrans during March 1990.

Brian von Holdt

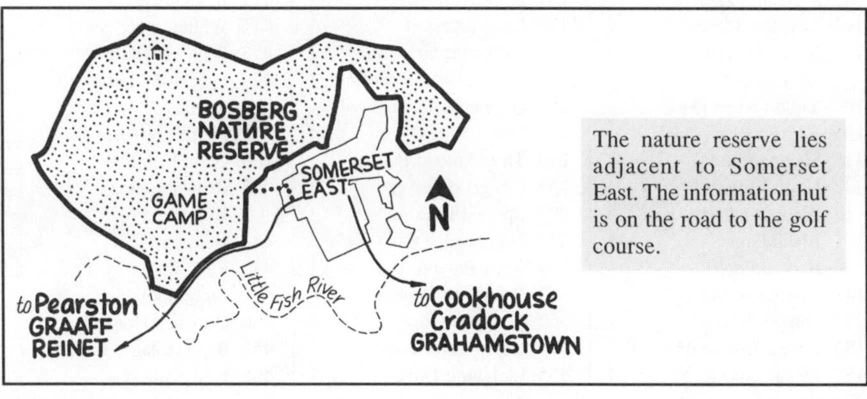

The nature reserve lies adjacent to Somerset East. The information hut is on the road to the golf course.

olive and white stinkwood trees. **Grey Cuckooshrike** favours the olive groves on the mountain slopes. Shy **Cinnamon Doves** may be flushed from the ground in the gloom of the tall forest in the kloofs. The camper or caravanner spending the night in the picnic area will almost certainly hear the calls of **Cape Eagle Owl** and **Wood Owl**. **Knysna** and **Olive Woodpeckers** give their presence away by their call or tell-tale tapping on the tree trunks. **Bush Blackcaps** are fond of a prominent perch on top of trees in the early morning. The ironstone outcrops on the top of the mountain are home to **Buffstreaked Chat**. The picnic area in the early morning is a good place to find robins, batises and flycatchers. It is here that **Yellowthroated Warbler**, **Bluemantled Flycatcher** and **Forest Canary** are frequently seen. **Swee Waxbill** may be sought at the fringes of the forest, wherever grass and other seedbearing plants are found.

100% OF SPECIES

008 Dabchick
055 Whitebreasted Cormorant
058 Reed Cormorant
060 Darter
062 Grey Heron
063 Blackheaded Heron
081 Hamerkop
083 White Stork
084 **Black Stork**
091 Sacred Ibis
094 Hadeda Ibis
095 African Spoonbill
102 Egyptian Goose
103 South African Shelduck**
104 Yellowbilled Duck
105 African Black Duck
118 Secretarybird
122 **Cape Vulture****
127 Blackshouldered Kite
131 Black Eagle
136 Booted Eagle
141 **Crowned Eagle**
149 Steppe Buzzard
150 **Forest Buzzard****
152 Jackal Buzzard**
155 Redbreasted Sparrowhawk
157 Little Sparrowhawk
158 Black Sparrowhawk
160 African Goshawk
168 **Black Harrier****
169 Gymnogene
171 Peregrine Falcon
179 Western Redfooted Kestrel
180 Eastern Redfooted Kestrel
181 Rock Kestrel
183 Lesser Kestrel
190 Greywing Francolin**
198 Rednecked Francolin
203 Helmeted Guineafowl
208 Blue Crane**
249 Threebanded Plover
255 Crowned Plover
297 Spotted Dikkop
315 Greyheaded Gull
349 Rock Pigeon
350 **Rameron Pigeon**
352 Redeyed Dove
354 Cape Turtle Dove
355 Laughing Dove
359 Tambourine Dove
360 **Cinnamon Dove**
370 **Knysna Lourie****
377 Redchested Cuckoo
378 Black Cuckoo
382 Jacobin Cuckoo
385 Klaas's Cuckoo
386 Diederik Cuckoo
394 **Wood Owl**
400 **Cape Eagle Owl**
401 Spotted Eagle Owl
405 Fierynecked Nightjar
412 Black Swift
415 Whiterumped Swift
418 Alpine Swift
424 Speckled Mousebird
426 Redfaced Mousebird
428 Pied Kingfisher
429 Giant Kingfisher
435 Brownhooded Kingfisher
451 Hoopoe
452 Redbilled Woodhoopoe
460 Crowned Hornbill
464 Blackcollared Barbet
465 Pied Barbet*

469 Redfronted Tinker Barbet ☐
476 Lesser Honeyguide ☐
484 **Knysna Woodpecker**** ☐
486 Cardinal Woodpecker ☐
488 **Olive Woodpecker** ☐
518 European Swallow ☐
520 Whitethroated Swallow ☐
526 Greater Striped Swallow* ☐
527 Lesser Striped Swallow ☐
529 Rock Martin ☐
538 Black Cuckooshrike ☐
540 **Grey Cuckooshrike** ☐
541 Forktailed Drongo ☐
545 Blackheaded Oriole ☐
547 Black Crow ☐
550 Whitenecked Raven ☐
554 Southern Black Tit* ☐
565 **Bush Blackcap**** ☐
567 Redeyed Bulbul* ☐
568 Blackeyed Bulbul ☐
569 Terrestrial Bulbul ☐
572 Sombre Bulbul ☐
577 Olive Thrush ☐
581 Cape Rock Thrush** ☐
586 Mountain Chat* ☐
588 **Buffstreaked Chat**** ☐
589 Familiar Chat ☐
596 Stonechat ☐
598 Chorister Robin** ☐
601 Cape Robin ☐
613 Whitebrowed Robin ☐
621 **Titbabbler*** ☐
643 Willow Warbler ☐
644 **Yellowthroated Warbler** ☐
645 Barthroated Apalis ☐
648 Yellowbreasted Apalis ☐
657 Bleating Warbler ☐
670 Wailing Cisticola ☐
681 Neddicky ☐
686 Karoo Prinia** ☐
689 Spotted Flycatcher ☐
690 Dusky Flycatcher ☐
698 Fiscal Flycatcher** ☐
700 Cape Batis** ☐
701 Chinspot Batis ☐
708 **Bluemantled Flycatcher** ☐
710 Paradise Flycatcher ☐
713 Cape Wagtail ☐
727 Orangethroated Longclaw** ☐
732 Fiscal Shrike ☐
736 Southern Boubou** ☐
740 Puffback ☐
742 **Southern Tchagra**** ☐
746 Bokmakierie* ☐
750 Olive Bush Shrike* ☐
764 Glossy Starling* ☐
769 Redwinged Starling ☐
775 Malachite Sunbird ☐
783 Lesser Double-collared Sunbird** ☐
785 Greater Double-collared Sunbird** ☐
789 Grey Sunbird ☐
792 Black Sunbird ☐
796 Cape White-eye** ☐
803 Cape Sparrow* ☐
804 Greyheaded Sparrow ☐
805 Yellowthroated Sparrow ☐
813 Cape Weaver** ☐
840 Bluebilled Firefinch ☐
846 Common Waxbill ☐
850 **Swee Waxbill*** ☐
860 Pintailed Whydah ☐
864 Black Widowfinch ☐
869 Yelloweyed Canary ☐
872 Cape Canary ☐
873 **Forest Canary**** ☐
877 Bully Canary ☐
881 Streakyheaded Canary ☐
884 Goldenbreasted Bunting ☐
☐
☐

KEI MOUTH AND SURROUNDINGS

approximately 265 species recorded to date

The village of Kei Mouth on the southern bank of the Kei River, together with Morgan's Bay and Double Mouth, is a popular holiday resort. The area covered here includes the farmlands from Mpetu Kop to the coast. The varied farming activities create a mosaic of habitats: from indigenous coastal forest, through to bushveld and grasslands (natural and cultivated) down to the seashore. The privately owned Ocean View Guest Farm is a registered natural heritage site with approximately 60 ha of natural forest.

SPECIAL AND INTERESTING SPECIES

The forest on Ocean View Guest Farm is home to **Narina Trogon**, **Starred** and **Brown Robins** and **Buffspotted Flufftail**. There is also a resident pair of **Crowned Eagles** and, on occasion, **Forest Buzzard** may be seen. **Longtailed Wagtails** occur sparingly on the forest streams. While **Cardinal Woodpecker** is to be found in open woodland, both **Knysna** and **Olive Woodpeckers** occur in dense woodland or forest. **Longcrested Eagle** is most often seen perched on telephone poles where the road to Kei Mouth crosses the Cwili River. **Cape Vultures** are regular visitors to the area and can be seen circling overhead. Grasslands support a wide variety of species including **Stanley's Bustard**, **Blackwinged Plover**, **Ayres' Cisticola** and **Quail Finch**. **Croaking**

ALSO RECORDED

This area is the southernmost range of a number of species. Squaretailed Drongo, Pygmy Kingfisher, Bluegrey Flycatcher and Natal Robin have been recorded. Occasional seabird visitors include Jackass Penguin, Cape Cormorant and Little Tern. Terek Sandpiper has been recorded on the Kei estuary.

Dave Brown

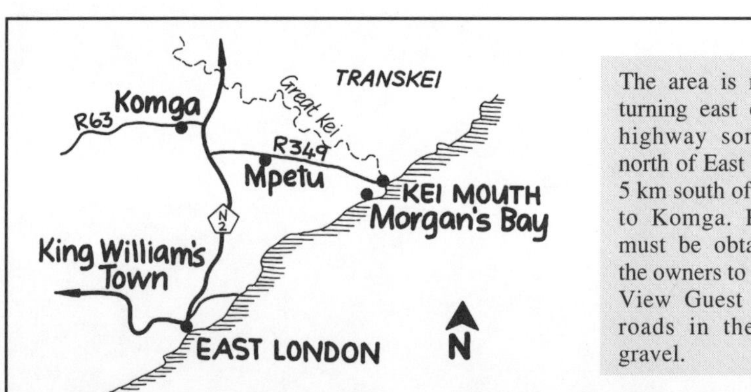

The area is reached by turning east off the N2 highway some 60 km north of East London, or 5 km south of the turnoff to Komga. Permission must be obtained from the owners to visit Ocean View Guest Farm. All roads in the area are gravel.

Cisticola prefers moist grassy slopes such as at Double Mouth. Woodlands provide a number of interesting species including **Olive**, **Orangebreasted** and **Greyheaded Bush Shrikes**. **Green Pigeons** move around the area, concentrating at food sources such as wild figs (*Ficus spp.*). Of interest is the large tern roost on the estuary at Kei Mouth. **Caspian**, **Swift**, **Sandwich** and **Common Terns** may be found together. For a closer look, it may be necessary to take the ferry to the Transkei side of the river. **Wood Owl** and **Fierynecked Nightjar** are often heard.

60% OF SPECIES

058 Reed Cormorant ☐
062 Grey Heron ☐
063 Blackheaded Heron ☐
067 Little Egret ☐
071 Cattle Egret ☐
094 Hadeda Ibis ☐
104 Yellowbilled Duck ☐
116 Spurwinged Goose ☐
122 **Cape Vulture**** ☐
126a Yellowbilled Kite ☐
127 Blackshouldered Kite ☐
139 **Longcrested Eagle** ☐
141 **Crowned Eagle** ☐
149 Steppe Buzzard ☐
150 **Forest Buzzard**** ☐
160 African Goshawk ☐
198 Rednecked Francolin ☐
203 Helmeted Guineafowl ☐
209 Crowned Crane ☐
218 **Buffspotted Flufftail** ☐
228 Redknobbed Coot ☐
231 **Stanley's Bustard** ☐
244 African Black Oystercatcher** ☐
246 Whitefronted Plover ☐
249 Threebanded Plover ☐
254 Grey Plover ☐
255 Crowned Plover ☐
257 **Blackwinged Plover** ☐
258 Blacksmith Plover ☐
264 Common Sandpiper ☐
266 Wood Sandpiper ☐
270 Greenshank ☐
272 Curlew Sandpiper ☐
274 Little Stint ☐
281 Sanderling ☐
290 Whimbrel ☐
297 Spotted Dikkop ☐
312 Kelp Gull ☐
322 **Caspian Tern** ☐
324 **Swift Tern** ☐
326 **Sandwich Tern** ☐
327 **Common Tern** ☐
352 Redeyed Dove ☐
354 Cape Turtle Dove ☐
355 Laughing Dove ☐
358 Greenspotted Dove ☐
359 Tambourine Dove ☐
361 **Green Pigeon** ☐
378 Black Cuckoo ☐
385 Klaas's Cuckoo ☐
386 Diederik Cuckoo ☐
415 Whiterumped Swift ☐
418 Alpine Swift ☐
424 Speckled Mousebird ☐
427 **Narina Trogon** ☐
428 Pied Kingfisher ☐
435 Brownhooded Kingfisher ☐
451 Hoopoe ☐
452 Redbilled Woodhoopoe ☐
455 Trumpeter Hornbill ☐
460 Crowned Hornbill ☐
464 Blackcollared Barbet ☐
469 Redfronted Tinker Barbet ☐
484 **Knysna Woodpecker**** ☐
486 **Cardinal Woodpecker** ☐
488 **Olive Woodpecker** ☐
494 Rufousnaped Lark ☐
507 Redcapped Lark ☐
518 European Swallow ☐
520 Whitethroated Swallow ☐
527 Lesser Striped Swallow ☐
533 Brownthroated Martin ☐
536 Black Sawwing Swallow ☐
538 Black Cuckooshrike ☐
540 Grey Cuckooshrike ☐
541 Forktailed Drongo ☐
545 Blackheaded Oriole ☐
547 Black Crow ☐
550 Whitenecked Raven ☐
554 Southern Black Tit* ☐
568 Blackeyed Bulbul ☐
569 Terrestrial Bulbul ☐
572 Sombre Bulbul ☐
577 Olive Thrush ☐
581 Cape Rock Thrush** ☐
596 Stonechat ☐
598 Chorister Robin** ☐
601 Cape Robin ☐
606 **Starred Robin** ☐
613 Whitebrowed Robin ☐
616 **Brown Robin**** ☐

631 African Marsh Warbler ☐
635 Cape Reed Warbler ☐
643 Willow Warbler ☐
644 Yellowthroated Warbler ☐
645 Barthroated Apalis ☐
648 Yellowbreasted Apalis ☐
657 Bleating Warbler ☐
664 Fantailed Cisticola ☐
667 **Ayres' Cisticola** ☐
677 Levaillant's Cisticola ☐
678 **Croaking Cisticola** ☐
679 Lazy Cisticola ☐
681 Neddicky ☐
683 Tawnyflanked Prinia ☐
686a Spotted Prinia** ☐
690 Dusky Flycatcher ☐
694 Black Flycatcher ☐
700 Cape Batis** ☐
701 Chinspot Batis ☐
708 Bluemantled Flycatcher ☐
710 Paradise Flycatcher ☐
712 **Longtailed Wagtail** ☐
713 Cape Wagtail ☐
716 Grassveld Pipit ☐
727 Orangethroated Longclaw** ☐
732 Fiscal Shrike ☐
733 Redbacked Shrike ☐
736 Southern Boubou** ☐
740 Puffback ☐
742 Southern Tchagra** ☐
744 Blackcrowned Tchagra ☐
746 Bokmakierie* ☐
748 **Orangebreasted Bush Shrike** ☐
750 **Olive Bush Shrike*** ☐
751 **Greyheaded Bush Shrike** ☐
757 European Starling ☐
764 Glossy Starling* ☐
768 Blackbellied Starling ☐
769 Redwinged Starling ☐
783 Lesser Double-collared Sunbird** ☐
785 Greater Double-collared Sunbird** ☐
789 Grey Sunbird ☐
792 Black Sunbird ☐
793 Collared Sunbird ☐
796 Cape White-eye** ☐
801 House Sparrow ☐
804 Greyheaded Sparrow ☐
808 Forest Weaver ☐
810 Spectacled Weaver ☐
811 Spottedbacked Weaver ☐
813 Cape Weaver** ☐
817 Yellow Weaver ☐
828 Redshouldered Widow ☐
832 Longtailed Widow ☐
846 Common Waxbill ☐
850 Swee Waxbill ☐
852 **Quail Finch** ☐
860 Pintailed Whydah ☐
869 Yelloweyed Canary ☐
872 Cape Canary ☐
873 Forest Canary** ☐
877 Bully Canary ☐
881 Streakyheaded Canary ☐
884 Goldenbreasted Bunting ☐
☐
☐

Black Egret

EAST LONDON AND GONUBIE

approximately 376 species recorded to date

GONUBIE RESERVE

There are two vlei areas with an abundance of reed coverage and a small area of clear water. The reserve is locked but there are two observation stands outside the fence, one on each side of the reserve, which afford good views of the water.

ALSO RECORDED

A Masked Weaver, way out of range, has been present for several years. Wattle-eyed Flycatcher, Marsh Harrier and Barn Owl have been recorded. Whitebacked Night Herons have bred on the Gonubie River. Sooty Tern has also been recorded.

SPECIAL AND INTERESTING SPECIES

Crowned Cranes have bred in the reserve for several years with varied success. In the water area look out for **Ethiopian Snipe**, **Cape Shoveller**, **African Jacana** and **Wood Sandpiper**. A patient wait at the stand near the main gate should produce **Baillon's Crake** and **Little Bittern**, with **African Rail** showing itself once in a while. **Purple Gallinule** and **Malachite Kingfisher** stay close to the edge of the reeds. Dead trees on the little island are used for perching by herons and kingfishers: **Little Egrets** and **Giant Kingfishers** can be seen on them.

Travel along the main tarred road into Gonubie until you reach 7th Avenue. Just in front of the municipal offices (where a key can be obtained during business hours if you wish to enter the reserve) turn right and travel down 7th Avenue to a T-junction, then turn right again. The reserve entrance is about 100 m ahead.

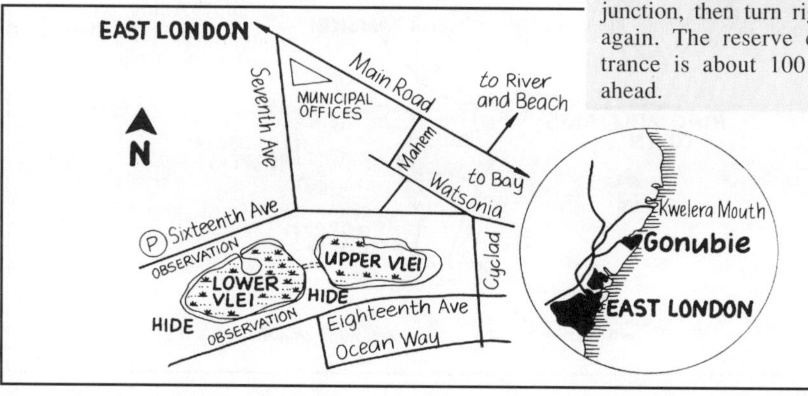

NAHOON ESTUARY

Apart from the mud flats, the riverbanks are heavily vegetated and there are open cliff faces in places. The area is well worth visiting in summer when the migrant waders and terns are present.

SPECIAL AND INTERESTING SPECIES

Up to 20 **Water Dikkop** can be seen on the far bank. On the mud flats waders such as **Terek Sandpiper**, **Ringed Plover**, **Greenshank**, **Wood Sandpiper**, the occasional **Whimbrel** and even **Curlew** can be seen. **Threebanded** and **White-fronted Plovers** are present year round. **Little Egrets** feed in tidal pools and **Cape Cormorant** can be seen on buoys. The cliffs and forest are home to **Trumpeter Hornbill**, **Little Sparrowhawk** and **Rock Kestrel**. Even **Crowned Eagle** can be seen in and over the forest. **Giant**, **Pied**, **Halfcollared**, **Malachite** and **Pygmy Kingfishers** occur, the latter usually found on the forest edge. At high tide **Sanderling**, **Turnstone** and **African Black Oystercatcher** roost on the flats.

Two other spots near East London worth a visit are Umtiza Forest Reserve (indigenous forest) and the Cove Rock area. Both lie to the south-west of the city. The latter is excellent for seabirds and waders. Access details can be obtained from the East London Publicity Association. Around East London look out for European Roller, Redbacked Mannikin and the European Nightjar that spends each summer in the same fig tree at the museum, arriving in late November and departing in March.

ALSO RECORDED

Palmnut Vulture and Red-tailed Tropicbird have occurred. African Finfoot has been seen higher up the Nahoon River.

Wendy Perks

Take the Beacon Bay offramp from the highway going north from East London and cross Batting Bridge over the Nahoon River. Turn right into Beaconhurst Drive, pass the sports club then turn right again into Blue Bend Road. Just past the Bluewaters sign, the road changes from tar to gravel. Continue on this road to the parking area. A path leads through the bush to the estuary itself.

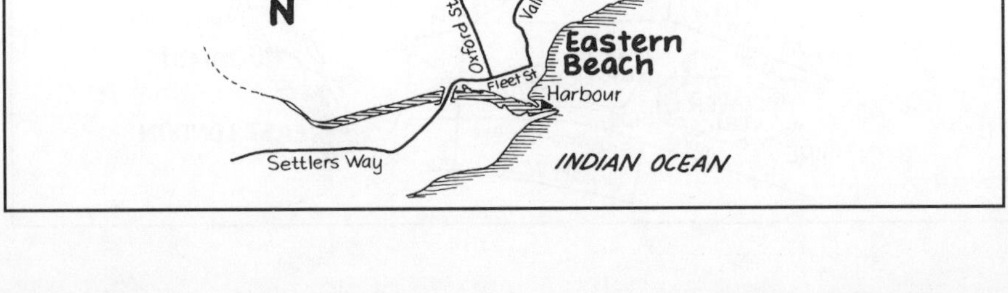

40% OF SPECIES

008 Dabchick ☐
055 Whitebreasted Cormorant ☐
056 **Cape Cormorant*** ☐
058 Reed Cormorant ☐
060 Darter ☐
062 Grey Heron ☐
063 Blackheaded Heron ☐
065 Purple Heron ☐
067 **Little Egret** ☐
071 Cattle Egret ☐
078 **Little Bittern** ☐
081 Hamerkop ☐
091 **Sacred Ibis** ☐
094 Hadeda Ibis ☐
095 African Spoonbill ☐
102 Egyptian Goose ☐
103 South African Shelduck** ☐
104 Yellowbilled Duck ☐
105 African Black Duck ☐
108 Redbilled Teal ☐
112 **Cape Shoveller*** ☐
116 Spurwinged Goose ☐
126a Yellowbilled Kite ☐
127 Blackshouldered Kite ☐
139 Longcrested Eagle ☐
141 **Crowned Eagle** ☐
148 African Fish Eagle ☐
149 Steppe Buzzard ☐
152 Jackal Buzzard** ☐
157 **Little Sparrowhawk** ☐
160 African Goshawk ☐
181 **Rock Kestrel** ☐
203 Helmeted Guineafowl ☐
209 **Crowned Crane** ☐
210 **African Rail** ☐
215 **Baillon's Crake** ☐
223 **Purple Gallinule** ☐
226 Moorhen ☐
228 Redknobbed Coot ☐
229 African Finfoot ☐
240 **African Jacana** ☐
244 **African Black Oystercatcher**** ☐
245 **Ringed Plover** ☐
246 **Whitefronted Plover** ☐
249 **Threebanded Plover** ☐
255 Crowned Plover ☐
257 Blackwinged Plover ☐
258 Blacksmith Plover ☐
262 **Turnstone** ☐
263 **Terek Sandpiper** ☐
264 Common Sandpiper ☐
266 **Wood Sandpiper** ☐
270 **Greenshank** ☐
281 **Sanderling** ☐
286 **Ethiopian Snipe** ☐
289 **Curlew** ☐
290 **Whimbrel** ☐
297 Spotted Dikkop ☐
298 **Water Dikkop** ☐
312 Kelp Gull ☐
324 Swift Tern ☐
326 Sandwich Tern ☐
327 Common Tern ☐
328 Arctic Tern ☐
348 Feral Pigeon ☐
352 Redeyed Dove ☐
354 Cape Turtle Dove ☐
355 Laughing Dove ☐
360 Cinnamon Dove ☐
361 Green Pigeon ☐
362 Cape Parrot ☐
370 Knysna Lourie** ☐
378 Black Cuckoo ☐
382 Jacobin Cuckoo ☐
385 Klaas's Cuckoo ☐
386 Diederik Cuckoo ☐
391 Burchell's Coucal* ☐
424 Speckled Mousebird ☐
427 Narina Trogon ☐
428 **Pied Kingfisher** ☐
429 **Giant Kingfisher** ☐
430 **Halfcollared Kingfisher** ☐
431 **Malachite Kingfisher** ☐
432 **Pygmy Kingfisher** ☐
451 Hoopoe ☐
455 **Trumpeter Hornbill** ☐
460 Crowned Hornbill ☐
464 Blackcollared Barbet ☐
469 Redfronted Tinker Barbet ☐
484 Knysna Woodpecker** ☐
488 Olive Woodpecker ☐
494 Rufousnaped Lark ☐
518 European Swallow ☐
520 Whitethroated Swallow ☐
527 Lesser Striped Swallow ☐
541 Forktailed Drongo ☐
545 Blackheaded Oriole ☐
548 Pied Crow ☐
550 Whitenecked Raven ☐
554 Southern Black Tit* ☐
568 Blackeyed Bulbul ☐
569 Terrestrial Bulbul ☐
572 Sombre Bulbul ☐
577 Olive Thrush ☐
613 Whitebrowed Robin ☐
635 Cape Reed Warbler ☐
638 African Sedge Warbler ☐
643 Willow Warbler ☐
645 Barthroated Apalis ☐
657 Bleating Warbler ☐
677 Levaillant's Cisticola ☐
681 Neddicky ☐
683 Tawnyflanked Prinia ☐
686a Spotted Prinia** ☐
690 Dusky Flycatcher ☐
691 Bluegrey Flycatcher ☐
700 Cape Batis** ☐
701 Chinspot Batis ☐
710 Paradise Flycatcher ☐
713 Cape Wagtail ☐
716 Grassveld Pipit ☐
718 Plainbacked Pipit ☐
727 Orangethroated Longclaw** ☐
736 Southern Boubou** ☐
742 Southern Tchagra** ☐
744 Blackcrowned Tchagra ☐
746 Bokmakierie* ☐

750 Olive Bush Shrike* ☐
764 Glossy Starling* ☐
769 Redwinged Starling ☐
783 Lesser Double-collared Sunbird** ☐
792 Black Sunbird ☐
796 Cape White-eye** ☐
804 Greyheaded Sparrow ☐
807 Thickbilled Weaver ☐
810 Spectacled Weaver ☐
811 Spottedbacked Weaver ☐
813 Cape Weaver** ☐
817 Yellow Weaver ☐
824 Red Bishop ☐
828 Redshouldered Widow ☐
831 Redcollared Widow ☐
840 Bluebilled Firefinch ☐
846 Common Waxbill ☐
857 Bronze Mannikin ☐
860 Pintailed Whydah ☐
869 Yelloweyed Canary ☐
877 Bully Canary ☐
881 Streakyheaded Canary ☐
884 Goldenbreasted Bunting ☐

☐

AMALINDA FISH STATION AND NATURE RESERVE

approximately 150 species recorded to date

The main dam or reservoir of this 134 ha reserve surrounded by industrial and residential areas of East London is over a century old. There are 73 ponds for the hatchery, which can be visited during normal office hours with permission from the office. The main dam and circular walks, through bush and grasslands, are accessible throughout the year, with picnic and braai facilities at the parking area. Waterbirds and reed-loving birds abound in summer; the trails give access to the grassland and woodland species.

SPECIAL AND INTERESTING SPECIES

Walk up the side of the wall of the main dam on the path. At the top you can start along the wall or go left over a small

ALSO RECORDED

For several months four Swallowtailed Bee-Eaters were present in the reserve. Occasionally Cape Shoveller has been seen in the main dam and Whiskered Tern has also visited. A Spotted Eagle Owl may sometimes be flushed from its daylight resting place in the thick bush.

Wendy Perks

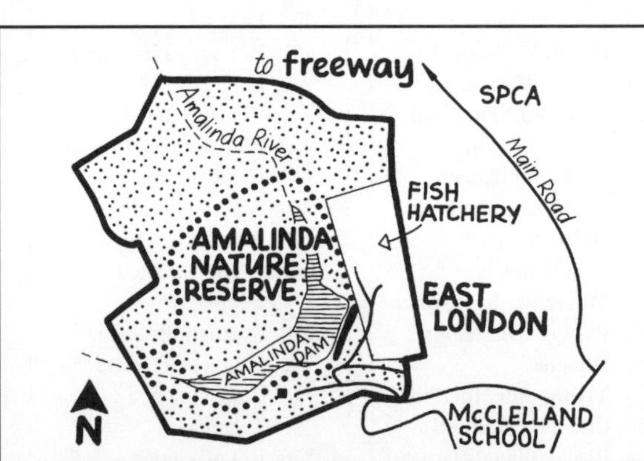

From the traffic lights at the museum turn into Connaught Avenue, past the Frere Hospital, past the Amalinda shopping areas and Crewe Primary School (4,6 km). Turn left at the signpost for the fish station and right at the McClelland School – the gravel road is 2,8 km to the picnic site.

bridge. **South African Shelduck**, **Spurwinged Goose**, **African Spoonbill**, **Yellowbilled Duck** and **Redbilled Teal**, and along the edges **Greenshank** and **African Jacana** are all usually present. **Thickbilled**, **Yellow** and **Cape Weavers** always build in the reeds in summer as do **Red Bishop** and **Redshouldered Widow**. **African Sedge Warbler**, with its "train picking up speed on slippery rails" sound, **Cape Reed Warbler**, with its beautiful, bubbling rich call and **Levaillant's Cisticola** are not uncommon. **Water Dikkop** and **Cape** and **African Pied Wagtails** can be found on the inside edge of the dam wall. **Grassveld Pipit**, **Orangethroated Longclaw** and **Stonechat** keep to the grasslands on the far side of the dam. **Jackal Buzzard**, **Longcrested Eagle**, **African Goshawk** and **Yellowbilled Kite** may fly over these areas and an **African Fish Eagle** normally perches on a bush overlooking the dam. The **Whitebrowed Robin's** voice usually accompanies you on the entire walk in spring and summer! **Goliath Heron** and **Great White Egret** usually visit during summer.

67% OF SPECIES

008 Dabchick ☐
055 Whitebreasted Cormorant ☐
058 Reed Cormorant ☐
060 Darter ☐
062 Grey Heron ☐
063 Blackheaded Heron ☐
064 **Goliath Heron** ☐
066 **Great White Egret** ☐
067 Little Egret ☐
071 Cattle Egret ☐
081 Hamerkop ☐
091 Sacred Ibis ☐
094 Hadeda Ibis ☐
095 **African Spoonbill** ☐
102 Egyptian Goose ☐
103 **South African Shelduck**** ☐
104 **Yellowbilled Duck** ☐
105 African Black Duck ☐
108 **Redbilled Teal** ☐
112 Cape Shoveller* ☐
116 **Spurwinged Goose** ☐
126a **Yellowbilled Kite** ☐
127 Blackshouldered Kite ☐
139 **Longcrested Eagle** ☐
148 **African Fish Eagle** ☐
152 **Jackal Buzzard**** ☐
157 Little Sparrowhawk ☐
160 **African Goshawk** ☐
203 Helmeted Guineafowl ☐
209 Crowned Crane ☐
226 Moorhen ☐
228 Redknobbed Coot ☐
240 **African Jacana** ☐
249 Threebanded Plover ☐
257 Blackwinged Plover ☐
258 Blacksmith Plover ☐
264 Common Sandpiper ☐
266 Wood Sandpiper ☐
270 **Greenshank** ☐
297 Spotted Dikkop ☐
298 **Water Dikkop** ☐
352 Redeyed Dove ☐
354 Cape Turtle Dove ☐
355 Laughing Dove ☐
358 Greenspotted Dove ☐
359 Tambourine Dove ☐
361 Green Pigeon ☐
370 Knysna Lourie** ☐
391 Burchell's Coucal* ☐
424 Speckled Mousebird ☐
428 Pied Kingfisher ☐
429 Giant Kingfisher ☐
430 Halfcollared Kingfisher ☐
431 Malachite Kingfisher ☐
432 Pygmy Kingfisher ☐
435 Brownhooded Kingfisher ☐
484 Knysna Woodpecker** ☐
486 Cardinal Woodpecker ☐
488 Olive Woodpecker ☐
489 Redthroated Wryneck ☐
520 Whitethroated Swallow ☐
527 Lesser Striped Swallow ☐
536 Black Sawwing Swallow ☐
538 Black Cuckooshrike ☐
541 Forktailed Drongo ☐
545 Blackheaded Oriole ☐
554 Southern Black Tit* ☐

569 Terrestrial Bulbul ☐
577 Olive Thrush ☐
596 **Stonechat** ☐
613 **Whitebrowed Robin** ☐
635 **Cape Reed Warbler** ☐
638 **African Sedge Warbler** ☐
645 Barthroated Apalis ☐
657 Bleating Warbler ☐
677 **Levaillant's Cisticola** ☐
690 Dusky Flycatcher ☐
700 Cape Batis** ☐
701 Chinspot Batis ☐
710 Paradise Flycatcher ☐
711 **African Pied Wagtail** ☐
713 **Cape Wagtail** ☐
716 **Grassveld Pipit** ☐
727 **Orangethroated Longclaw**** ☐
744 Blackcrowned Tchagra ☐
746 Bokmakierie* ☐
748 Orangebreasted Bush Shrike ☐
750 Olive Bush Shrike* ☐
789 Grey Sunbird ☐
793 Collared Sunbird ☐
796 Cape White-eye** ☐
804 Greyheaded Sparrow ☐
805 Yellowthroated Sparrow ☐
807 **Thickbilled Weaver** ☐
813 **Cape Weaver**** ☐
817 **Yellow Weaver** ☐
824 **Red Bishop** ☐
828 **Redshouldered Widow** ☐
872 Cape Canary ☐
877 Bully Canary ☐

BAVIAANSKLOOF

approximately 215 species recorded to date

The Baviaanskloof, 120 km west of Port Elizabeth on the road to Willowmore via Patensie, stretches for about 120 km along the valley between the Kouga and the Baviaanskloof mountains. This land is owned and administered by the Department of Nature and Environmental Conservation and forms one of the largest and most pristine wilderness areas in South Africa. The wilderness area itself covers 70 000 ha, while the whole area owned by Nature Conservation covers 270 000 ha. Nature Conservation has a camp with six-bedded huts to rent at Geelhoutbos in the heart of the Baviaanskloof. The Baviaanskloof Wilderness Area is of interest and

From Willowmore take the road to Uniondale; 3 km outside Willowmore turn left at the Baviaanskloof sign. You will enter the Baviaanskloof at Nuwekloof about 20 km further. From Port Elizabeth follow the N2 freeway towards Cape Town and take the turnoff to Loerie. The entrance gate is about 100 km from the N2. An entrance fee is charged and a permit is required, obtainable from the office of the Department of Nature Conservation in Port Elizabeth.

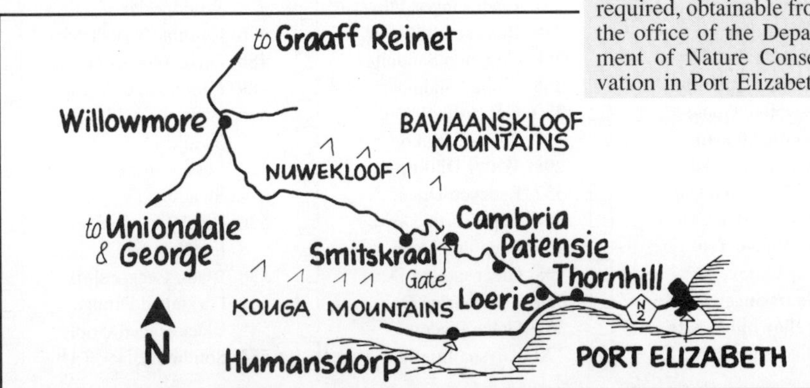

importance because within its boundaries are six diverse veld types, namely fynbos, valley bushveld, spekboomveld, grassland, Karoo shrubland and remnants of evergreen coastal forest in moist and protected kloofs. Three large rivers run through the area: the Baviaans, the Groot and the Kouga.

SPECIAL AND INTERESTING SPECIES

Beyond the gate lies Poortjies, where the winding road crosses the river many times, while overhead the forest canopy forms a green ceiling. Here one may see **Halfcollared Kingfisher**, **Paradise Flycatcher** and **Forest Canary**. Climbing up to Bergplaats on a narrow and spectacular pass one comes out of the forest into the fynbos where **Victorin's Warbler**, **Orangebreasted Sunbird** and **Protea Canary** can be seen. Pause a moment beyond Bergplaats before descending into the kloof and enjoy the view: the conical hill Langkop dominates the foreground and one sees glimpses of the Kouga River and the Paul Sauer Dam beyond. Once down at the river level watch out for **Black** and **Booted Eagles**. **African Fish Eagles** will be found in the vicinity of the dam. Continue along the road, which is lined with drought-resistant thornscrub interspersed with taller, more luxuriant vegetation. **Longbilled Crombec**, **Yellowbellied Eremomela**, **Greenspotted Dove** and **Yellowthroated Sparrow** may be heard, with **African Black Duck** in pairs on quiet stretches of river, which is also home to the Cape Clawless Otter. In summer the calls of six species of cuckoo echo throughout the kloof. Continue past Doornkraal, drive over another narrow pass and pause at Geelhoutbos. This camp is situated in a secluded kloof in the midst of a mini forest of yellowwood and wild fig trees alive with louries, batises, apalises, robins, thrushes and warblers. **Knysna**, **Cardinal** and **Olive Woodpeckers** may be recorded in the camp, while **Black Storks** are regulars. Have a look at the artesian springs at Studtis and drive on to Nuwekloof at the Willowmore end of the Baviaanskloof. Here you may see **Layard's Titbabbler**, **Palewinged Starling** and **Namaqua Prinia**. Up on the Willowmore plateau watch out for **Rufouseared Warbler** and **Karoo Chat**.

ALSO RECORDED

Longtailed Wagtails have been seen along the south-flowing streams of the Baviaanskloof Mountains in the Poortjies area. Purple and Blackcrowned Night Herons may be seen along the rivers. Greater, Scalythroated and Lesser Honeyguides betray their presence by their calls.

Libby McGill

70% OF SPECIES

055 Whitebreasted Cormorant ☐
058 Reed Cormorant ☐
063 Blackheaded Heron ☐
081 Hamerkop ☐
084 **Black Stork** ☐
094 Hadeda Ibis ☐
102 Egyptian Goose ☐
104 Yellowbilled Duck ☐
105 **African Black Duck** ☐
131 **Black Eagle** ☐
136 **Booted Eagle** ☐
148 **African Fish Eagle** ☐
149 Steppe Buzzard ☐
152 Jackal Buzzard** ☐
160 African Goshawk ☐
169 Gymnogene ☐
172 Lanner Falcon ☐
181 Rock Kestrel ☐
190 Greywing Francolin** ☐
198 Rednecked Francolin ☐
203 Helmeted Guineafowl ☐
208 Blue Crane** ☐
255 Crowned Plover ☐
258 Blacksmith Plover ☐
264 Common Sandpiper ☐
297 Spotted Dikkop ☐
349 Rock Pigeon ☐
350 Rameron Pigeon ☐
352 Redeyed Dove ☐
354 Cape Turtle Dove ☐
355 Laughing Dove ☐
358 **Greenspotted Dove** ☐
359 Tambourine Dove ☐
370 Knysna Lourie** ☐
377 Redchested Cuckoo ☐
378 Black Cuckoo ☐
382 Jacobin Cuckoo ☐
384 Emerald Cuckoo ☐
385 Klaas's Cuckoo ☐
386 Diederik Cuckoo ☐
394 Wood Owl ☐
401 Spotted Eagle Owl ☐
405 Fierynecked Nightjar ☐
415 Whiterumped Swift ☐
417 Little Swift ☐
418 Alpine Swift ☐
424 Speckled Mousebird ☐
425 Whitebacked Mousebird** ☐
426 Redfaced Mousebird ☐
428 Pied Kingfisher ☐
429 Giant Kingfisher ☐
430 **Halfcollared Kingfisher** ☐
431 Malachite Kingfisher ☐
435 Brownhooded Kingfisher ☐
451 Hoopoe ☐
452 Redbilled Woodhoopoe ☐
469 Redfronted Tinker Barbet ☐
474 Greater Honeyguide ☐
480 Ground Woodpecker** ☐
484 **Knysna Woodpecker**** ☐
486 **Cardinal Woodpecker** ☐
488 **Olive Woodpecker** ☐
518 European Swallow ☐
520 Whitethroated Swallow ☐
523 Pearlbreasted Swallow ☐
526 Greater Striped Swallow* ☐
527 Lesser Striped Swallow ☐
529 Rock Martin ☐
530 House Martin ☐
533 Brownthroated Martin ☐
536 Black Sawwing Swallow ☐
538 Black Cuckooshrike ☐
541 Forktailed Drongo ☐
545 Blackheaded Oriole ☐
547 Black Crow ☐
548 Pied Crow ☐
550 Whitenecked Raven ☐
566 Cape Bulbul** ☐
567 Redeyed Bulbul* ☐
572 Sombre Bulbul ☐
577 Olive Thrush ☐
581 Cape Rock Thrush** ☐
586 Mountain Chat* ☐
589 Familiar Chat ☐
592 **Karoo Chat*** ☐
596 Stonechat ☐
601 Cape Robin ☐
614 Karoo Robin** ☐
621 Titbabbler* ☐
622 **Layard's Titbabbler**** ☐
635 Cape Reed Warbler ☐
638 African Sedge Warbler ☐
641 **Victorin's Warbler**** ☐
643 Willow Warbler ☐
645 Barthroated Apalis ☐
648 Yellowbreasted Apalis ☐
651 **Longbilled Crombec** ☐
653 **Yellowbellied Eremomela** ☐
657 Bleating Warbler ☐
664 Fantailed Cisticola ☐
669 Greybacked Cisticola* ☐
677 Levaillant's Cisticola ☐
681 Neddicky ☐
686 Karoo Prinia** ☐
687 **Namaqua Prinia**** ☐
688 **Rufouseared Warbler**** ☐
690 Dusky Flycatcher ☐
698 Fiscal Flycatcher** ☐
700 Cape Batis** ☐
703 Pririt Batis* ☐
706 Fairy Flycatcher** ☐
710 **Paradise Flycatcher** ☐
713 Cape Wagtail ☐
716 Grassveld Pipit ☐
732 Fiscal Shrike ☐
736 Southern Boubou** ☐
740 Puffback ☐
742 Southern Tchagra** ☐

746 Bokmakierie* ☐
750 Olive Bush Shrike* ☐
759 Pied Starling** ☐
764 Glossy Starling* ☐
769 Redwinged Starling ☐
770 **Palewinged Starling*** ☐
775 Malachite Sunbird ☐
777 **Orangebreasted Sunbird**** ☐
783 Lesser Double-collared Sunbird** ☐
785 Greater Double-collared Sunbird ☐
789 Grey Sunbird ☐
792 Black Sunbird ☐
796 Cape White-eye** ☐
801 House Sparrow ☐
803 Cape Sparrow ☐
804 Greyheaded Sparrow ☐
805 **Yellowthroated Sparrow** ☐
813 Cape Weaver** ☐
814 Masked Weaver ☐
824 Red Bishop ☐
840 Bluebilled Firefinch ☐
846 Common Waxbill ☐
850 Swee Waxbill* ☐
860 Pintailed Whydah ☐
873 **Forest Canary**** ☐
874 Cape Siskin** ☐
877 Bully Canary ☐
879 Whitethroated Canary* ☐
880 **Protea Canary**** ☐
881 Streakyheaded Canary ☐
884 Goldenbreasted Bunting ☐
885 Cape Bunting ☐
☐
☐
☐

ADDO ELEPHANT NATIONAL PARK

approximately 133 species recorded to date

In July 1931 the Addo Elephant National Park was proclaimed to protect the remnants of a herd of elephant that was being exterminated. Today the park covers an area of more than 7 500 ha between the Zuurberg Mountains and the Sundays River near the village of Addo. The vegetation is principally Addo bush, a dense vegetation type suited to dry conditions and characterised by spekboom (*Portulacaria afra*) and various thorn trees. Canopy height is approximately 3 m. There is very little open water and only the pond at the rest camp has waterside vegetation.

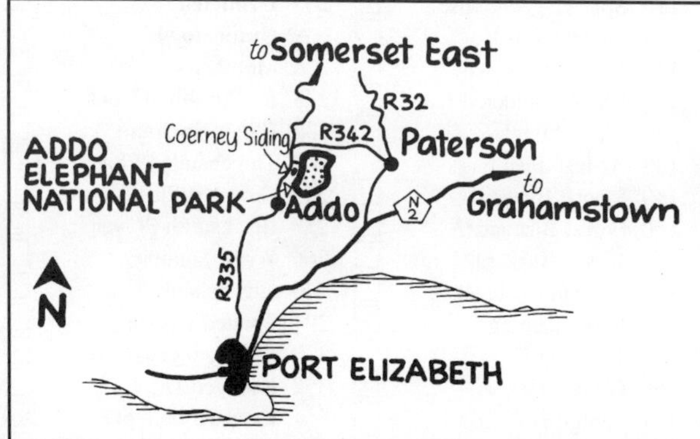

The park is 72 km from Port Elizabeth. To reach it, leave Port Elizabeth on the N2 towards Grahamstown. A short way beyond Bluewater Bay, turn westwards at the offramp to Markman township and continue along the road, passing through Markman township and Addo as far as Coerney siding, where the turnoff to the park is signposted.

SPECIAL AND INTERESTING SPECIES

The reedbed in the pond at the rest camp is home to **Dabchick**, **Blackcrowned Night Heron**, **Cape Weaver**, **Red Bishop** and **Cape Reed Warbler**. The trees in the rest camp have created a suitable habitat for **Dusky Flycatcher** and the buildings provide nesting sites for **Lesser Striped Swallows**. Some of the nests are taken over by **Whiterumped Swifts**. The vegetation in the north-eastern part of the park, formerly known as the antelope camp, consists of low scrub with scattered clumps of bush. Here **Black Korhaan**, **Helmeted Guineafowl**, **Cape Penduline Tit** and **Longbilled Crombec** can be seen. **Pearlbreasted Swallows** also occur over this habitat, with numbers varying from year to year. **South African Shelduck** can usually be found at the earth dam in the area. A bird characteristic of this area is the **Greybacked Cisticola**. In the thick Addo bush, birds are not easily seen unless attracted to an abundant food source. When flowering, *Schotia spp*. attract up to four species of sunbird including **Greater** and **Lesser Doublecollared Sunbirds**. Another species pair, **Whitethroated** and **Streakyheaded Canaries**, occur in the park and provide an opportunity to learn to tell them apart. Areas of seeding grass attract species such as **Bluebilled Firefinch**, **Swee** and **Common Waxbills**. **Karoo Robins** are often seen flashing across the roads in the park while **Greenspotted Doves** feed on the road verges in the late afternoon. More often heard than seen are species such as **Southern Tchagra**, **Southern Boubou**, **Olive Bush Shrike** and **Whitebrowed Robin**.

ALSO RECORDED

A number of birds wander across from the nearby Zuurberg Mountains including Forest Buzzard, Redbilled Woodhoopoe, Bleating Warbler, Crowned Hornbill and Puffback. European Roller, European Golden Oriole and House Martin, along with Whitewinged Tern, are migrants which have made an unexpected appearance. Namaqua Doves are seen sporadically. Wattled Starling, Black Sawwing Swallow and Alpine Swift have been recorded. Of the owls, only Spotted Eagle Owl has been recorded. The Ostrich has been introduced into the park.

Dave Brown

100% OF SPECIES

001 Ostrich ☐
008 **Dabchick** ☐
058 Reed Cormorant ☐
062 Grey Heron ☐
063 Blackheaded Heron ☐
071 Cattle Egret ☐
076 **Blackcrowned Night Heron** ☐
078 Little Bittern ☐
081 Hamerkop ☐
083 White Stork ☐
090 Yellowbilled Stork ☐
094 Hadeda Ibis ☐
102 Egyptian Goose ☐
103 **South African Shelduck**** ☐
104 Yellowbilled Duck ☐
116 Spurwinged Goose ☐
118 Secretarybird ☐
126a Yellowbilled Kite ☐
127 Blackshouldered Kite ☐
140 Martial Eagle ☐
148 African Fish Eagle ☐
149 Steppe Buzzard ☐
150 Forest Buzzard** ☐
152 Jackal Buzzard** ☐
160 African Goshawk ☐
162 Pale Chanting Goshawk* ☐
169 Gymnogene ☐
171 Peregrine Falcon ☐
181 Rock Kestrel ☐
198 Rednecked Francolin ☐
203 **Helmeted Guineafowl** ☐
226 Moorhen ☐
228 **Redknobbed Coot** ☐
239 **Black Korhaan**** ☐
249 Threebanded Plover ☐
255 Crowned Plover ☐
258 Blacksmith Plover ☐
266 Wood Sandpiper ☐
270 Greenshank ☐
297 Spotted Dikkop ☐
339 Whitewinged Tern ☐
352 Redeyed Dove ☐
354 Cape Turtle Dove ☐
355 Laughing Dove ☐

356 Namaqua Dove ☐
358 **Greenspotted Dove** ☐
382 Jacobin Cuckoo ☐
385 Klaas's Cuckoo ☐
386 Diederik Cuckoo ☐
401 Spotted Eagle Owl ☐
415 **Whiterumped Swift** ☐
417 Little Swift ☐
418 Alpine Swift ☐
424 Speckled Mousebird ☐
426 Redfaced Mousebird ☐
435 Brownhooded Kingfisher ☐
438 European Bee-eater ☐
446 European Roller ☐
451 Hoopoe ☐
452 Redbilled Woodhoopoe ☐
460 Crowned Hornbill ☐
465 Pied Barbet* ☐
469 Redfronted Tinker Barbet ☐
474 Greater Honeyguide ☐
476 Lesser Honeyguide ☐
486 Cardinal Woodpecker ☐
489 Redthroated Wryneck ☐
518 European Swallow ☐
520 Whitethroated Swallow ☐
523 **Pearlbreasted Swallow** ☐
526 Greater Striped Swallow* ☐
527 **Lesser Striped Swallow** ☐
529 Rock Martin ☐
530 House Martin ☐
533 Brownthroated Martin ☐
536 Black Sawwing Swallow ☐
541 Forktailed Drongo ☐
543 European Golden Oriole ☐
545 Blackheaded Oriole ☐
547 Black Crow ☐
557 **Cape Penduline Tit*** ☐
566 Cape Bulbul** ☐
572 Sombre Bulbul ☐
577 Olive Thrush ☐
601 Cape Robin ☐
613 **Whitebrowed Robin** ☐
614 **Karoo Robin**** ☐
621 Titbabbler* ☐
635 **Cape Reed Warbler** ☐
645 Barthroated Apalis ☐
651 **Longbilled Crombec** ☐
657 Bleating Warbler ☐
669 **Greybacked Cisticola*** ☐
681 Neddicky ☐
686 Karoo Prinia** ☐
690 **Dusky Flycatcher** ☐
698 Fiscal Flycatcher** ☐
700 Cape Batis** ☐
713 Cape Wagtail ☐
716 Grassveld Pipit ☐
717 Longbilled Pipit ☐
718 Plainbacked Pipit ☐
732 Fiscal Shrike ☐
736 **Southern Boubou**** ☐
740 Puffback ☐
742 **Southern Tchagra**** ☐
746 Bokmakierie* ☐
750 **Olive Bush Shrike*** ☐
757 European Starling ☐
759 Pied Starling** ☐
760 Wattled Starling ☐
764 Glossy Starling* ☐
775 Malachite Sunbird ☐
783 **Lesser Double-collared Sunbird**** ☐
785 **Greater Double-collared Sunbird**** ☐
792 Black Sunbird ☐
796 Cape White-eye** ☐
801 House Sparrow ☐
803 Cape Sparrow* ☐
810 Spectacled Weaver ☐
813 **Cape Weaver**** ☐
814 Masked Weaver ☐
824 **Red Bishop** ☐
840 **Bluebilled Firefinch** ☐
846 **Common Waxbill** ☐
850 **Swee Waxbill*** ☐
860 Pintailed Whydah ☐
869 Yelloweyed Canary ☐
873 Forest Canary** ☐
877 Bully Canary ☐
879 **Whitethroated Canary*** ☐
881 **Streakyheaded Canary** ☐
884 Goldenbreasted Bunting ☐

☐
☐
☐

MONDPLAAS PONDS

approximately 137 species recorded to date

Mondplaas ponds lie about 50 km west of Port Elizabeth just off the N2 highway to Cape Town. A series of pans and dams (some reed-fringed) lie along the course of an old meander loop on the Gamtoos River. Cultivated and fallow lands and lush grasslands surround the ponds, which are used for irrigation, thus the water level fluctuates. The property is privately owned, but the ponds may be viewed from the road.

SPECIAL AND INTERESTING SPECIES

A small colony of **Blackcrowned Night Herons** may be found on the lower ponds. The westernmost breeding population of **African Jacanas** in South Africa occur at Mondplaas. Numerous species of duck are to be seen, including **Cape** and **Redbilled Teal**, **Maccoa Duck**, **Spurwinged Goose**, **Cape Shoveller** and **Southern Pochard**. **Purple Gallinule** and **Black Crake** are common, and **African Rail** is present. Sit down on the edge of the bank and spend a quiet half hour watching the reeds on the far side, in and out of which is a continual coming and going of waterbirds. With patience you will be rewarded with good sightings of **Baillon's Crake**, which has been recorded at Mondplaas in all months of the year. Waders are well represented, while gulls and terns, including **Whitewinged** and **Whiskered Terns**, are frequently seen. Raptors recorded include **Booted Eagle**, **African Fish Eagle**, **African Marsh Harrier**, **Lanner Falcon**

ALSO RECORDED

Hottentot Teal may be recorded on occasion, as well as Squacco Heron and Little Bittern. Blacknecked Grebes and Whitebacked Ducks make an occasional appearance. A few records exist of Glossy Ibis at Mondplaas – perhaps en route to the southwest Cape region. For the first time ever a Spotted Crake spent the summer months of 1990/91 at Mondplaas.

Libby McGill

Take the N2 westwards to Cape Town; 50 km from Port Elizabeth the freeway crosses the Gamtoos River and 1,5 km further take the turnoff to Mondplaas. Turn right under the freeway and after 1 km park where the barrier ends. The lower ponds are visible on your right. To reach the upper ponds, continue for 1,3 km (the tar road changes to gravel after 800 m). Exactly 500 m after the end of the tar you will see an insignificant crossroad. The left-hand road leads to farm buildings. Take the right-hand road for 100 m and park just before the raised causeway. There are ponds on both sides of the causeways.

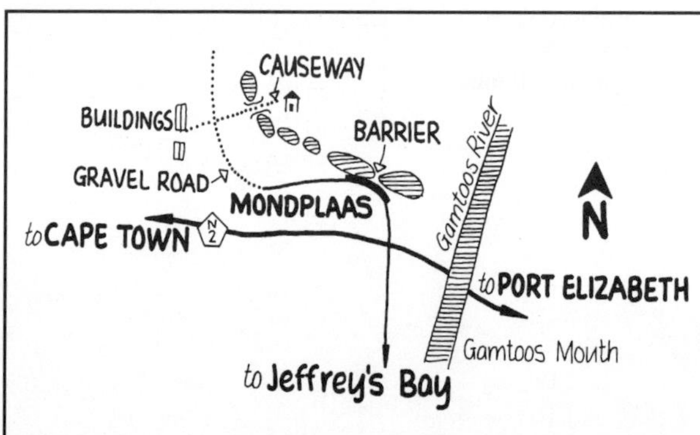

and **Redbreasted Sparrowhawk**. The full range of bush and grassland birds is represented in suitable habitat alongside the pans, and may include **White Stork** in summer, as well as various cisticolas, and **Redcapped** and **Rufousnaped Larks**. Don't forget to watch for swallows, swifts and martins (nine species) as they swoop over the water.

100% OF SPECIES

No.	Species	
007	Blacknecked Grebe	☐
008	Dabchick	☐
055	Whitebreasted Cormorant	☐
058	Reed Cormorant	☐
060	Darter	☐
062	Grey Heron	☐
063	Blackheaded Heron	☐
065	Purple Heron	☐
067	Little Egret	☐
071	Cattle Egret	☐
072	Squacco Heron	☐
076	**Blackcrowned Night Heron**	☐
078	Little Bittern	☐
081	Hamerkop	☐
083	**White Stork**	☐
091	Sacred Ibis	☐
093	Glossy Ibis	☐
094	Hadeda Ibis	☐
095	African Spoonbill	☐
101	Whitebacked Duck	☐
102	Egyptian Goose	☐
103	South African Shelduck**	☐
104	Yellowbilled Duck	☐
106	**Cape Teal**	☐
107	Hottentot Teal	☐
108	**Redbilled Teal**	☐
112	**Cape Shoveller***	☐
113	**Southern Pochard**	☐
116	**Spurwinged Goose**	☐
117	**Maccoa Duck**	☐
118	Secretarybird	☐
126a	Yellowbilled Kite	☐
127	Blackshouldered Kite	☐
136	**Booted Eagle**	☐
148	**African Fish Eagle**	☐
149	Steppe Buzzard	☐
152	Jackal Buzzard	☐
155	**Redbreasted Sparrowhawk**	☐
165	**African Marsh Harrier**	☐
172	**Lanner Falcon**	☐
181	Rock Kestrel	☐
198	Rednecked Francolin	☐
200	Common Quail	☐
203	Helmeted Guineafowl	☐
210	**African Rail**	☐
213	**Black Crake**	☐
214	Spotted Crake	☐
215	**Baillon's Crake**	☐
223	**Purple Gallinule**	☐
226	Moorhen	☐
228	Redknobbed Coot	☐
240	**African Jacana**	☐
246	Whitefronted Plover	☐
248	Kittlitz's Plover	☐
249	Threebanded Plover	☐
255	Crowned Plover	☐
258	Blacksmith Plover	☐
264	Common Sandpiper	☐
266	Wood Sandpiper	☐
269	Marsh Sandpiper	☐
270	Greenshank	☐
271	Knot	☐
274	Little Stint	☐
281	Sanderling	☐
284	Ruff	☐
286	Ethiopian Snipe	☐
294	Avocet	☐
295	Blackwinged Stilt	☐
297	Spotted Dikkop	☐
298	Water Dikkop	☐
312	Kelp Gull	☐
338	**Whiskered Tern**	☐
339	**Whitewinged Tern**	☐
348	Feral Pigeon	☐
352	Redeyed Dove	☐
354	Cape Turtle Dove	☐
355	Laughing Dove	☐
382	Jacobin Cuckoo	☐
386	Diederik Cuckoo	☐
391	Burchell's Coucal*	☐
415	Whiterumped Swift	☐
417	Little Swift	☐
424	Speckled Mousebird	☐
428	Pied Kingfisher	☐
429	Giant Kingfisher	☐
431	Malachite Kingfisher	☐
435	Brownhooded Kingfisher	☐
438	European Bee-eater	☐
451	Hoopoe	☐
494	**Rufousnaped Lark**	☐
507	**Redcapped Lark**	☐
518	European Swallow	☐
520	Whitethroated Swallow	☐
523	Pearlbreasted Swallow	☐
526	Greater Striped Swallow*	☐
527	Lesser Striped Swallow	☐
529	Rock Martin	☐
533	Brownthroated Martin	☐
541	Forktailed Drongo	☐
547	Black Crow	☐
566	Cape Bulbul**	☐
572	Sombre Bulbul	☐
577	Olive Thrush	☐
589	Familiar Chat	☐

596 Stonechat ☐
601 Cape Robin ☐
635 Cape Reed Warbler ☐
638 African Sedge Warbler ☐
645 Barthroated Apalis ☐
664 Fantailed Cisticola ☐
666 Cloud Cisticola ☐
677 Levaillant's Cisticola ☐
681 Neddicky ☐
686 Karoo Prinia** ☐
698 Fiscal Flycatcher** ☐
713 Cape Wagtail ☐
716 Grassveld Pipit ☐
718 Plainbacked Pipit ☐
727 Orangethroated Longclaw** ☐
732 Fiscal Shrike ☐
736 Southern Boubou** ☐
746 Bokmakierie* ☐
757 European Starling ☐
759 Pied Starling** ☐
760 Wattled Starling ☐
764 Glossy Starling* ☐
775 Malachite Sunbird ☐
801 House Sparrow ☐
803 Cape Sparrow* ☐
813 Cape Weaver** ☐
824 Red Bishop ☐
827 Yellowrumped Widow ☐
846 Common Waxbill ☐
860 Pintailed Whydah ☐
872 Cape Canary ☐
877 Bully Canary ☐
881 Streakyheaded Canary ☐

SWARTKOPS ESTUARY

approximately 223 species recorded to date

The Swartkops estuary, 15 km north of Port Elizabeth harbour, is tidal for 16 km, with extensive intertidal banks and salt marshes near the mouth and saltpans near Redhouse. The northern escarpment supports dense valley bushveld vegetation.

SPECIAL AND INTERESTING SPECIES

Most of the estuarine species can be seen on the mud bank in front of Swartkops village. In addition to the common waders and terns, **Terek Sandpiper**, **Bartailed Godwit**, **Cur-**

Swartkops village is signposted from the N2. Any turn right in the village will lead to the river. Intertidal areas can also be viewed from Amsterdamhoek (cross the Wylde Bridge – see map). The most extensive intertidal banks are accessible only by boat or by walking down the riverbank opposite Swartkops. To see estuarine birds it is essential to go at low tide and a telescope is desirable. To walk in the Aloe Reserve take the road from Amsterdamhoek to Bluewater Bay and use the gate at the top of the hill or at the garden refuse site next to the church. The saltpan opposite Redhouse is reached by turning left a few hundred metres after driving under the rail bridge next to the police station, crossing the main road and continuing past the

lew and **Little Tern** are often seen, especially in summer. **Sand Plovers** are best seen on the main mud banks between Swartkops and Amsterdamhoek. **African Black Oystercatcher** and **Caspian Tern** are common and **Great White Egret** and **Goliath Heron** can often be seen on the salt marsh. On the saltpans are many **Greater** and a few **Lesser Flamingos**. Waterfowl include **South African Shelduck** and **Cape Teal** and on the Chatty Saltpans many **Blacknecked Grebes**. Cormorants, egrets and **African Spoonbills** are abundant on the saltpan opposite Redhouse in winter and waders are numerous when the water level is low in summer. **Greybacked Cisticolas** inhabit the low bushes next to the saltpans. Birds can be difficult to see in the thick valley bushveld but a calm, early morning may produce **Greywing Francolin**, **Southern Grey** and **Cape Penduline Tits**, **Southern Tchagra** and **Whitethroated Canary**. Sunbirds are particularly common when the aloes flower in July.

60% OF SPECIES

007	**Blacknecked Grebe**	☐	149	Steppe Buzzard	☐
008	Dabchick	☐	152	Jackal Buzzard**	☐
055	Whitebreasted Cormorant	☐	172	Lanner Falcon	☐
			181	Rock Kestrel	☐
056	Cape Cormorant*	☐	190	**Greywing Francolin****	☐
058	Reed Cormorant	☐			
062	Grey Heron	☐	228	Redknobbed Coot	☐
063	Blackheaded Heron	☐	239	Black Korhaan**	☐
064	**Goliath Heron**	☐	244	**African Black Oystercatcher****	☐
066	**Great White Egret**	☐			
067	Little Egret	☐	245	Ringed Plover	☐
071	Cattle Egret	☐	246	Whitefronted Plover	☐
076	Blackcrowned Night Heron	☐	248	Kittlitz's Plover	☐
			249	Threebanded Plover	☐
091	Sacred Ibis	☐	251	**Sand Plover**	☐
094	Hadeda Ibis	☐	254	Grey Plover	☐
095	**African Spoonbill**	☐	255	Crowned Plover	☐
096	**Greater Flamingo**	☐	258	Blacksmith Plover	☐
097	**Lesser Flamingo**	☐	262	Turnstone	☐
102	Egyptian Goose	☐	263	**Terek Sandpiper**	☐
103	**South African Shelduck****	☐	264	Common Sandpiper	☐
			266	Wood Sandpiper	☐
104	Yellowbilled Duck	☐	269	Marsh Sandpiper	☐
106	**Cape Teal**	☐	270	Greenshank	☐
108	Redbilled Teal	☐	272	Curlew Sandpiper	☐
112	Cape Shoveller*	☐	274	Little Stint	☐
127	Blackshouldered Kite	☐	281	Sanderling	☐

brickfields on a poor dirt road. To view the Chatty Saltpans turn at the traffic lights in Swartkops and stop where the road crosses a stream halfway to Redhouse.

ALSO RECORDED

Rarities sometimes turn up on the estuary and saltpans. Some of the most recent include European Oystercatcher, Redshank, Blacktailed Godwit and Hudsonian Godwit (first southern African record). Terns have included Lesser Crested, Roseate and Damara. Knysna Woodpecker can be heard, but rarely seen, in dense valley bushveld opposite Redhouse.

Paul Martin

Eastern Cape

284 Ruff ☐
288 **Bartailed Godwit** ☐
289 **Curlew** ☐
290 Whimbrel ☐
294 Avocet ☐
295 Blackwinged Stilt ☐
297 Spotted Dikkop ☐
312 Kelp Gull ☐
315 Greyheaded Gull ☐
322 **Caspian Tern** ☐
324 Swift Tern ☐
326 Sandwich Tern ☐
327 Common Tern ☐
335 **Little Tern** ☐
339 Whitewinged Tern ☐
348 Feral Pigeon ☐
349 Rock Pigeon ☐
352 Redeyed Dove ☐
354 Cape Turtle Dove ☐
355 Laughing Dove ☐
358 Greenspotted Dove ☐
385 Klaas's Cuckoo ☐
386 Diederik Cuckoo ☐
415 Whiterumped Swift ☐
417 Little Swift ☐
424 Speckled Mousebird ☐
426 Redfaced Mousebird ☐
428 Pied Kingfisher ☐
429 Giant Kingfisher ☐
451 Hoopoe ☐
465 Pied Barbet* ☐
486 Cardinal Woodpecker ☐
507 Redcapped Lark ☐
518 European Swallow ☐
520 Whitethroated Swallow ☐
526 Greater Striped Swallow* ☐
527 Lesser Striped Swallow ☐
529 Rock Martin ☐
533 Brownthroated Martin ☐
541 Forktailed Drongo ☐
548 Pied Crow ☐
551 **Southern Grey Tit**** ☐
557 **Cape Penduline Tit*** ☐
566 Cape Bulbul** ☐
572 Sombre Bulbul ☐
589 Familiar Chat ☐
601 Cape Robin ☐
614 Karoo Robin** ☐
621 Titbabbler* ☐
645 Barthroated Apalis ☐
651 Longbilled Crombec ☐
664 Fantailed Cisticola ☐
669 **Greybacked Cisticola*** ☐
677 Levaillant's Cisticola ☐
681 Neddicky ☐
686 Karoo Prinia** ☐
690 Dusky Flycatcher ☐
698 Fiscal Flycatcher** ☐
700 Cape Batis** ☐
713 Cape Wagtail ☐
716 Grassveld Pipit ☐
727 Orangethroated Longclaw** ☐
732 Fiscal Shrike ☐
736 Southern Boubou** ☐
742 **Southern Tchagra**** ☐
746 Bokmakierie* ☐
757 European Starling ☐
759 Pied Starling** ☐
760 Wattled Starling ☐
769 Redwinged Starling ☐
775 Malachite Sunbird ☐
783 Lesser Double-collared Sunbird** ☐
792 Black Sunbird ☐
796 Cape White-eye** ☐
801 House Sparrow ☐
803 Cape Sparrow* ☐
810 Spectacled Weaver ☐
813 Cape Weaver** ☐
814 Masked Weaver ☐
824 Red Bishop ☐
846 Common Waxbill ☐
860 Pintailed Whydah ☐
877 Bully Canary ☐
879 **Whitethroated Canary*** ☐
881 Streakyheaded Canary ☐
☐

PLETTENBERG BAY

approximately 278 species recorded to date

This includes the estuary of the Keurbooms River with its tidal mud flats and lagoon, the Bitou River, mud banks and pans, forest on the Piesang Nature Trail and the macchia-covered first section of the Robberg Peninsula.

SPECIAL AND INTERESTING SPECIES

Bartailed Godwits visit the lagoon in summer and feed with the **Whimbrels** and **Grey Plovers**. **Swift** and **Sandwich Terns** rest at low tide on the mud banks. The scrub at the side of the lagoon is home to **Southern Tchagra**. **Purple Heron** is usually present. The Bitou River is excellent for waterbirds and waders. They are easily sighted all along the road to the Wittedrift turnoff. **Yellowbilled Egret**, **African Spoonbill**, **Curlew**, **Avocet**, **Ruff**, **Ringed Plover** and **Hottentot Teal** feed here. **Blue Crane** may be seen in the fields adjoining the river. The Piesang River Nature Trail, which winds down the cliffs through forest and ferns, affords views of **Knysna Lourie**, parties of **Terrestrial Bulbul**, **Puffback** and other forest birds. At Robberg **Victorin's Warbler** sings on the southern macchia-covered slopes. On the northern slopes look for **Cape Siskin**. **Orangebreasted Sunbird** may also be found.

Four localities are included:

- ***The Bitou River.*** From Plettenberg Bay take the N2 towards Port Elizabeth, turn left where the signpost indicates Wittedrift and Avontuur. The Bitou River is on your left.
- ***The Keurbooms estuary and lagoon.***
- ***Piesang River Nature Trail.*** Off Marine Way at the fire station turn into Cuttyspark Avenue and continue to the waterworks. The trail starts here and winds down through forest to the Piesang River.
- ***Robberg Peninsula.*** From the Piesang Valley road take the Robberg road to the airport. Robberg is signposted.

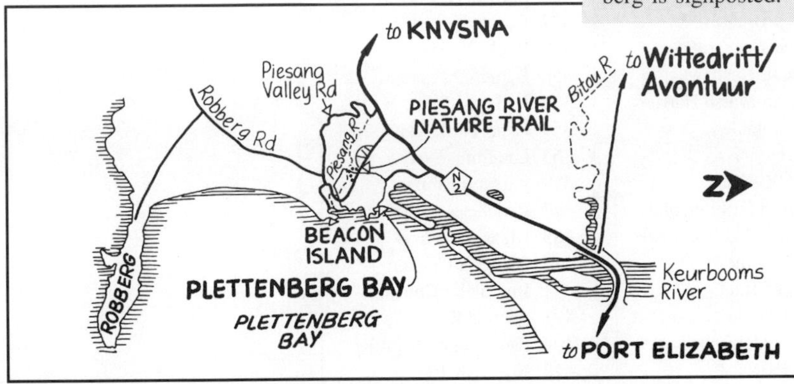

57% OF SPECIES

053 Cape Gannet*
055 Whitebreasted Cormorant
056 Cape Cormorant*
058 Reed Cormorant
060 Darter
062 Grey Heron
063 Blackheaded Heron
065 **Purple Heron**
067 Little Egret
068 **Yellowbilled Egret**
071 Cattle Egret
076 Blackcrowned Night Heron
081 Hamerkop
083 White Stork
091 Sacred Ibis
094 Hadeda Ibis
095 **African Spoonbill**
102 Egyptian Goose
103 South African Shelduck**
104 Yellowbilled Duck
106 Cape Teal
107 **Hottentot Teal**
108 Redbilled Teal
112 Cape Shoveller*
116 Spurwinged Goose
127 Blackshouldered Kite
148 African Fish Eagle
149 Steppe Buzzard
150 Forest Buzzard**
152 Jackal Buzzard**
160 African Goshawk
165 African Marsh Harrier
169 Gymnogene
170 Osprey
181 Rock Kestrel
198 Rednecked Francolin
203 Helmeted Guineafowl
208 **Blue Crane****
210 African Rail
213 Black Crake
223 Purple Gallinule
226 Moorhen
228 Redknobbed Coot
244 African Black Oystercatcher**
245 **Ringed Plover**
246 Whitefronted Plover
248 Kittlitz's Plover
249 Threebanded Plover
254 **Grey Plover**
255 Crowned Plover
257 Blackwinged Plover
258 Blacksmith Plover
263 Terek Sandpiper
264 Common Sandpiper
266 Wood Sandpiper
269 Marsh Sandpiper
270 Greenshank
272 Curlew Sandpiper
274 Little Stint
284 **Ruff**
286 Ethiopian Snipe
288 **Bartailed Godwit**
289 **Curlew**
290 **Whimbrel**
294 **Avocet**
295 Blackwinged Stilt
297 Spotted Dikkop
298 Water Dikkop
312 Kelp Gull
322 Caspian Tern
324 **Swift Tern**
326 **Sandwich Tern**
327 Common Tern
349 Rock Pigeon
350 Rameron Pigeon
352 Redeyed Dove
354 Cape Turtle Dove
355 Laughing Dove
370 **Knysna Lourie****
377 Redchested Cuckoo
385 Klaas's Cuckoo
386 Diederik Cuckoo
391 Burchell's Coucal*
401 Spotted Eagle Owl
405 Fierynecked Nightjar
412 Black Swift

ALSO RECORDED

Baillon's Crake has been recorded at Rietvlei and White-backed Duck on the Bitou River. Crab Plover has been seen three years in succession near the Bitou bridge. Maccoa Duck has been seen at the Derbyshire Brick-works Dam just off the main road before you get to the Bitou bridge. Little Bittern in the reeds on the lagoon, Chestnutbanded Plover, Turnstone, Greyheaded Gull, Little, Whiskered and White-winged Terns have all been recorded. Wattled Starling has been seen feeding at the side of the lagoon together with the flocks of European Starling.

Anne Brash

415 Whiterumped Swift ☐
417 Little Swift ☐
418 Alpine Swift ☐
424 Speckled Mousebird ☐
428 Pied Kingfisher ☐
429 Giant Kingfisher ☐
430 Halfcollared Kingfisher ☐
431 Malachite Kingfisher ☐
435 Brownhooded Kingfisher ☐
451 Hoopoe ☐
488 Olive Woodpecker ☐
518 European Swallow ☐
520 Whitethroated Swallow ☐
526 Greater Striped Swallow* ☐
527 Lesser Striped Swallow ☐
529 Rock Martin ☐
533 Brownthroated Martin ☐
536 Black Sawwing Swallow ☐
540 Grey Cuckooshrike ☐
541 Forktailed Drongo ☐
545 Blackheaded Oriole ☐
550 Whitenecked Raven ☐
566 Cape Bulbul** ☐
569 **Terrestrial Bulbul** ☐
572 Sombre Bulbul ☐
577 Olive Thrush ☐
596 Stonechat ☐
598 Chorister Robin** ☐
601 Cape Robin ☐
635 Cape Reed Warbler ☐
638 African Sedge Warbler ☐
641 **Victorin's Warbler**** ☐
645 Barthroated Apalis ☐
657 Bleating Warbler ☐
661 Grassbird** ☐
677 Levaillant's Cisticola ☐
681 Neddicky ☐
686 Karoo Prinia** ☐
690 Dusky Flycatcher ☐
698 Fiscal Flycatcher** ☐
700 Cape Batis** ☐
710 Paradise Flycatcher ☐
713 Cape Wagtail ☐
716 Grassveld Pipit ☐
718 Plainbacked Pipit ☐
727 Orangethroated Longclaw** ☐
732 Fiscal Shrike ☐
736 Southern Boubou** ☐
740 **Puffback** ☐
742 **Southern Tchagra**** ☐
746 Bokmakierie* ☐
750 Olive Bush Shrike* ☐
757 European Starling ☐
769 Redwinged Starling ☐
773 Cape Sugarbird** ☐
775 Malachite Sunbird ☐
777 **Orangebreasted Sunbird**** ☐
783 Lesser Double-collared Sunbird** ☐
785 Greater Doublecollared Sunbird** ☐
792 Black Sunbird ☐
796 Cape White-eye** ☐
801 House Sparrow ☐
813 Cape Weaver** ☐
827 Yellowrumped Widow ☐
846 Common Waxbill ☐
850 Swee Waxbill* ☐
860 Pintailed Whydah ☐
872 Cape Canary ☐
873 Forest Canary** ☐
874 **Cape Siskin**** ☐
877 Bully Canary ☐
881 Streakyheaded Canary ☐
☐
☐
☐
☐

Crab Plovers

KNYSNA

approximately 233 species recorded to date

Knysna is situated on the shores of one of the country's largest permanent estuaries, which boasts sand banks, mud banks, salt marshes and reed banks, hillsides of fynbos and pockets of surviving forest. Close by is the largest temperate forest in southern Africa.

SPECIAL AND INTERESTING SPECIES

The **Knysna Warbler** can be found in the coastal scrub at the Heads: the best place is on the road down to the rocks at Coney Glen. The Woodbourne Lagoon is excellent for waders and waterbirds: **African Spoonbill**, **Avocet**, **Little Stint**, **Ruff**, **Ringed Plover** and **African Rail** feed here while **Blackcrowned Night Herons** perch in the thickets on the water's edge. **Osprey** is present all year and often perches on poles at low tide south of Thesen's Island. The sewage works has **Black Crake**, warblers, waders and waterbirds. **African Marsh Harrier** has also been recorded in this vicinity. In the Pledge Nature Reserve (turn up Grey Street) are **Forest Canary**, **Olive Bush Shrike** and **Chorister Robin**. **Yellowthroated Warbler** is present in pockets of forest near town (take Short Street on the west side of town). Watch for **Tambourine Dove** and **Bluemantled Flycatcher**. On the fynbos-covered southern slopes of the Brenton hills look for **Victorin's Warbler** and **Orangebreasted Sunbird**. As with most warblers one needs to know the song of Victorin's: the notes ascend and descend with increased rapidity

ALSO RECORDED

Whitebacked Night Heron can occasionally be seen up the Knysna River and there is a record of African Finfoot. Buffspotted Flufftail has been heard on the outskirts of the forest above town. There are records of Redshank, Turnstone, Whitewinged, Whiskered and Little Tern.

Anne Brash

See the map for areas surrounding the lagoon and ask the Knysna Publicity Association for details of forest walks.

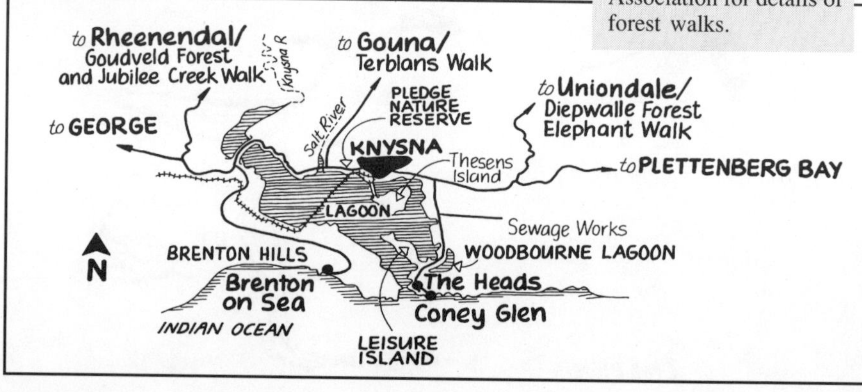

"mississippippippippi." Having located it by song is the first step, the second is trying to see the bird, which may surprise you by suddenly hopping into the open when you will be able to see its russet brown chest and orange eye. However, this warbler usually keeps to the undergrowth. **Bartailed Godwit**, **Terek Sandpiper** and **Curlew** are present in summer on the mud banks and reed banks in the middle of the lagoon towards the point, but one needs to be on the water at mid-tide to see them – a canoe is ideal. **Scalythroated Honeyguide** can be heard along the Knysna River. **Knysna Woodpecker** and five different kingfishers can be seen. Although bird species are not numerous in the forests the **Narina Trogon** is vocal in summer. **Grey Cuckooshrike** is common, often in pairs frequenting the tree canopies. The **Emerald Cuckoo** calls and the lower to mid-stratum are home to **Starred** and **Chorister Robins** and **Bleating Warbler**. In the Goudveld Forest there is a walk from Jubilee Creek and halfway between Knysna and Plettenberg Bay at Harkerville is the Kranshoek Walk, where **Cape Sugarbird** and **Orangebreasted Sunbird** are found in the fynbos at the top of the cliffs.

70% OF SPECIES

008 Dabchick
055 Whitebreasted Cormorant
058 Reed Cormorant
060 Darter
062 Grey Heron
063 Blackheaded Heron
065 Purple Heron
067 Little Egret
071 Cattle Egret
076 **Blackcrowned Night Heron**
081 Hamerkop
083 White Stork
091 Sacred Ibis
094 Hadeda Ibis
095 **African Spoonbill**
102 Egyptian Goose
104 Yellowbilled Duck
106 Cape Teal
108 Redbilled Teal
112 Cape Shoveller*
127 Blackshouldered Kite
148 African Fish Eagle
149 Steppe Buzzard
150 Forest Buzzard**
152 Jackal Buzzard**
157 Little Sparrowhawk
160 African Goshawk
165 **African Marsh Harrier**
169 Gymnogene
170 **Osprey**
181 Rock Kestrel
198 Rednecked Francolin
203 Helmeted Guineafowl
210 **African Rail**
213 **Black Crake**
226 Moorhen
228 Redknobbed Coot
244 African Black Oystercatcher**
245 **Ringed Plover**
246 Whitefronted Plover
248 Kittlitz's Plover
249 Threebanded Plover
254 Grey Plover
255 Crowned Plover
257 Blackwinged Plover
258 Blacksmith Plover
263 **Terek Sandpiper**
264 Common Sandpiper
266 Wood Sandpiper
269 Marsh Sandpiper
270 Greenshank
272 Curlew Sandpiper
274 **Little Stint**
284 **Ruff**
286 Ethiopian Snipe
288 **Bartailed Godwit**
289 **Curlew**
290 Whimbrel
294 **Avocet**
295 Blackwinged Stilt
297 Spotted Dikkop
298 Water Dikkop
312 Kelp Gull
322 Caspian Tern
326 Sandwich Tern

Eastern Cape

327 Common Tern ☐
349 Rock Pigeon ☐
350 Rameron Pigeon ☐
352 Redeyed Dove ☐
354 Cape Turtle Dove ☐
355 Laughing Dove ☐
359 **Tambourine Dove** ☐
360 Cinnamon Dove ☐
370 Knysna Lourie** ☐
377 Redchested Cuckoo ☐
384 **Emerald Cuckoo** ☐
385 Klaas's Cuckoo ☐
386 Diederik Cuckoo ☐
391 Burchell's Coucal* ☐
394 Wood Owl ☐
401 Spotted Eagle Owl ☐
405 Fierynecked Nightjar ☐
412 Black Swift ☐
415 Whiterumped Swift ☐
416 Horus Swift ☐
417 Little Swift ☐
418 Alpine Swift ☐
424 Speckled Mousebird ☐
427 **Narina Trogon** ☐
428 Pied Kingfisher ☐
429 Giant Kingfisher ☐
430 Halfcollared Kingfisher ☐
431 Malachite Kingfisher ☐
435 Brownhooded Kingfisher ☐
451 Hoopoe ☐
452 Redbilled Woodhoopoe ☐
475 **Scalythroated Honeyguide** ☐
484 **Knysna Woodpecker**** ☐
488 Olive Woodpecker ☐
518 European Swallow ☐
520 Whitethroated Swallow ☐
526 Greater Striped Swallow* ☐
529 Rock Martin ☐
533 Brownthroated Martin ☐
536 Black Sawwing Swallow ☐
538 Black Cuckooshrike ☐
540 **Grey Cuckooshrike** ☐
541 Forktailed Drongo ☐
545 Blackheaded Oriole ☐
550 Whitenecked Raven ☐
566 Cape Bulbul** ☐
569 Terrestrial Bulbul ☐
572 Sombre Bulbul ☐
577 Olive Thrush ☐
596 Stonechat ☐
598 **Chorister Robin**** ☐
601 Cape Robin ☐
606 **Starred Robin** ☐
635 Cape Reed Warbler ☐
638 African Sedge Warbler ☐
640 **Knysna Warbler**** ☐
641 **Victorin's Warbler**** ☐
644 **Yellowthroated Warbler** ☐
645 Barthroated Apalis ☐
657 **Bleating Warbler** ☐
661 Grassbird** ☐
677 Levaillant's Cisticola ☐
681 Neddicky ☐
686 Karoo Prinia** ☐
690 Dusky Flycatcher ☐
698 Fiscal Flycatcher** ☐
700 Cape Batis** ☐
708 **Bluemantled Flycatcher** ☐
710 Paradise Flycatcher ☐
713 Cape Wagtail ☐
716 Grassveld Pipit ☐
718 Plainbacked Pipit ☐
727 Orangethroated Longclaw** ☐
732 Fiscal Shrike ☐
736 Southern Boubou** ☐
740 Puffback ☐
746 Bokmakierie* ☐
750 **Olive Bush Shrike*** ☐
757 European Starling ☐
768 Blackbellied Starling ☐
769 Redwinged Starling ☐
773 **Cape Sugarbird**** ☐
775 Malachite Sunbird ☐
777 **Orangebreasted Sunbird**** ☐
783 Lesser Double-collared Sunbird** ☐
785 Greater Double-collared Sunbird** ☐
792 Black Sunbird ☐
796 Cape White-eye** ☐
801 House Sparrow ☐
813 Cape Weaver** ☐
827 Yellowrunped Widow ☐
846 Common Waxbill ☐
850 Swee Waxbill ☐
860 Pintailed Whydah ☐
872 Cape Canary ☐
873 **Forest Canary**** ☐
877 Bully Canary ☐
881 Streakyheaded Canary ☐
☐
☐

OTHER BIRDING SPOTS WORTH VISITING

Dweza Nature Reserve
This coastal forest reserve lies between Port St Johns and East London. Mangrove Kingfishers have bred here and Yellowstreaked Bulbul and Spotted Thrush are some of the many forest species that can be seen.

Alexandria Forest Reserve
An excellent area to see Chorister and Brown Robins and possibly even Cuckoo Hawk. Permits obtainable from the Forestry Office at the southern entrance to the forest. A public road passes through to the north.

Cape Receife Nature Reserve and Sewage Works (Port Elizabeth)
A good area for waterfowl and seabirds. To enter the sewage works request permission at the office. Permits to enter the reserve are obtainable at the Beach Manager's office at Happy Valley.

Kabeljous River Estuary and Seekoei River Nature Reserve
Situated to the east and west of Jeffrey's Bay respectively. These are good areas for waders, terns, etc. There are no specific requirements for entrance at present.

Van Stadens Wildflower Reserve
Entrance free during the day. Well known for Cape Sugarbird; Orangebreasted Sunbird also occurs. The adjoining Van Stadens Pass has produced Forest Buzzard and Peregrine Falcon.

Tsitsikamma Coastal National Park
Access is subject to the usual National Parks Board regulations. The usual forest birds of the southern Cape can be seen. A very good area for Forest Buzzard. The well-known Otter Trail is in the park.

USEFUL TELEPHONE NUMBERS

Addo Elephant National Park
(0426) 40-0556

Baviaanskloof
(04232) 3-0270

Bosberg (Somerset East Municipality)
(0424) 3-1333

Cape Department of Environmental Conservation (Port Elizabeth)
(041) 390-2179

Ocean View Guest Farm
(04372) 2603

10 South-Western Cape

Co-ordinator Philip A.R. Hockey

1 Akkerendam Nature Reserve
2 Karoo National Park
3 Lower Berg River and Estuary
4 West Coast National Park
5 Gamkapoort Nature Reserve
6 Anysberg Nature Reserve
7 Pelagic
8 Vrolijkheid Nature Reserve
9 Grootvadersbos
10 Bontebok National Park
11 Helderberg Nature Reserve
12 Strandfontein Sewage Works
13 Rondevlei Nature Reserve
14 Cape of Good Hope Nature Reserve
15 De Hoop Nature Reserve
16 Salmonsdam Nature Reserve

AKKERENDAM NATURE RESERVE

80 species recorded on two visits

This 2 750 ha reserve controlled by the Calvinia municipality was established in 1962. Situated on the slopes of the Hantamsberg, a northern outlier of the Great Escarpment, the stark flat-topped cliffs and boulder-strewn hillsides are strongly reminiscent of parts of the Karoo National Park at Beaufort West. The highest point is 1 672 m above sea level and the mean annual rainfall is approximately 250 mm. The reserve falls within the transitional zone between the winter rainfall and summer rainfall regions. The vegetation is classified as western mountain Karoo and mountain renosterbosveld and on the plains there are areas of dwarf succulent shrubland. In some years, after above average winter rains, the spring flowers turn the veld into a blaze of colour, although, sadly, the condition of the veld within the reserve is not as good as it should be, because of gross over-stocking in past years. The birds listed are those recorded on two brief visits – many other species will undoubtedly be added to the list in time.

SPECIAL AND INTERESTING SPECIES

This semi-arid reserve, which has not been adequately explored for birds, is included here as it is a good place to see the elusive **Cinnamonbreasted Warbler**. Follow the road from the entrance gate which, after a few kilometres, crosses

ALSO RECORDED

Ludwig's Bustards have been seen flying over the reserve and are reasonably common in the Calvinia district.

Rob Martin

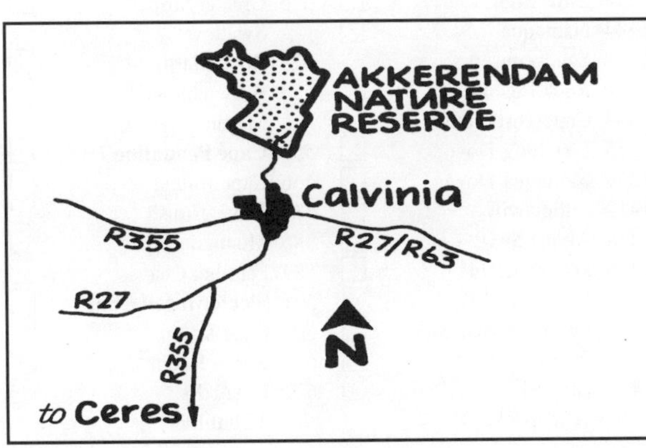

The reserve is 2 km north of Calvinia and is inadequately signposted – take the road out of the town (on the Brandvlei side) which skirts the prominent grain silos or ask locally for directions. The reserve is open daily and there is no entry charge. Several hiking trails have been laid out but there are no other facilities.

a small stream and shortly after that passes a dam. Beyond the dam the condition of the road soon deteriorates and it is advisable to walk from there. Follow the rough track past the windmill and enter the kloof on the right-hand side (below the prominent radio tower). The rocky ridge along the left of the kloof supports several pairs of warblers: some days they are very vocal, at other times they utter not a sound and can then be difficult to find, particularly as they hop between the rocks rather like miniature rockjumpers. They have also been heard calling in the left-hand kloof and are probably fairly widespread in the reserve. This is typical **Booted Eagle** habitat and two pairs are present from August to March. **Black Harriers** are most likely to be seen in the spring. The streamside cover supports **Cape Penduline Tit** and **Fairy Flycatcher** and the hillside bush is the favoured habitat of **Layard's Titbabbler**. In the more open areas look for **Whitethroated** and **Blackheaded Canaries** and, after rain, **Larklike Buntings**. The cliffs of the escarpment provide ideal nesting sites for **Palewinged Starling**. The scrub near the entrance gate is a good place to look for **Sicklewinged Chat** and **Karoo Lark**. **Namaqua Prinia** occurs along the stream especially where there are reeds.

100% OF SPECIES

- 007 Blacknecked Grebe ☐
- 008 Dabchick ☐
- 063 Blackheaded Heron ☐
- 071 Cattle Egret ☐
- 091 Sacred Ibis ☐
- 094 Hadeda Ibis ☐
- 095 African Spoonbill ☐
- 102 Egyptian Goose ☐
- 103 South African Shelduck** ☐
- 104 Yellowbilled Duck ☐
- 105 African Black Duck ☐
- 113 Southern Pochard ☐
- 127 Blackshouldered Kite ☐
- 131 Black Eagle ☐
- 136 **Booted Eagle** ☐
- 162 Pale Chanting Goshawk* ☐
- 168 **Black Harrier**** ☐
- 172 Lanner Falcon ☐
- 181 Rock Kestrel ☐
- 195 Cape Francolin* ☐
- 228 Redknobbed Coot ☐
- 232 Ludwig's Bustard* ☐
- 249 Threebanded Plover ☐
- 258 Blacksmith Plover ☐
- 270 Greenshank ☐
- 274 Little Stint ☐
- 344 Namaqua Sandgrouse* ☐
- 349 Rock Pigeon ☐
- 354 Cape Turtle Dove ☐
- 355 Laughing Dove ☐
- 356 Namaqua Dove ☐
- 417 Little Swift ☐
- 418 Alpine Swift ☐
- 425 Whitebacked Mousebird** ☐
- 438 European Bee-eater ☐
- 465 Pied Barbet* ☐
- 480 Ground Woodpecker** ☐
- 500 Longbilled Lark* ☐
- 502 **Karoo Lark**** ☐
- 507 Redcapped Lark ☐
- 518 European Swallow ☐
- 520 Whitethroated Swallow ☐
- 526 Greater Striped Swallow* ☐
- 529 Rock Martin ☐
- 533 Brownthroated Martin ☐
- 557 **Cape Penduline Tit*** ☐
- 566 Cape Bulbul** ☐
- 577 Olive Thrush ☐
- 586 Mountain Chat* ☐
- 589 Familiar Chat ☐
- 591 **Sicklewinged Chat**** ☐
- 601 Cape Robin ☐
- 614 Karoo Robin** ☐
- 622 **Layard's Titbabbler**** ☐

631 African Marsh Warbler ☐
638 African Sedge Warbler ☐
651 Longbilled Crombec ☐
660 **Cinnamonbreasted Warbler**** ☐
669 Greybacked Cisticola* ☐
677 Levaillant's Cisticola ☐
686 Karoo Prinia** ☐
687 **Namaqua Prinia**** ☐
706 **Fairy Flycatcher**** ☐
713 Cape Wagtail ☐
732 Fiscal Shrike ☐
746 Bokmakierie* ☐
770 **Palewinged Starling*** ☐
775 Malachite Sunbird ☐
783 Lesser Double-collared Sunbird** ☐
796 Cape White-eye** ☐
803 Cape Sparrow* ☐
814 Masked Weaver ☐
824 Red Bishop ☐
846 Common Waxbill ☐
872 Cape Canary ☐
876 **Blackheaded Canary** ☐
878 Yellow Canary* ☐
879 **Whitethroated Canary*** ☐
885 Cape Bunting ☐
887 **Larklike Bunting*** ☐
☐
☐

KAROO NATIONAL PARK

approximately 166 species recorded to date

The Karoo National Park, controlled by the National Parks Board, was purchased with the financial assistance of the South African Nature Foundation and was proclaimed in 1976. At present it is 32 795 ha in size but it is hoped to increase this to 100 000 ha in the coming years. The climate it typical of the Great Karoo with sunny but cold winters and hot summers with infrequent thunderstorms. The Great Escarpment transects the park and, with peaks of over 1 800 m, is the dominant geographical feature. The main habitats are the scrub-covered plains, the Acacia thornveld along the usually dry stream beds, the Danthonia grassveld on the plateau and the cliffs and rocky gorges at the base of the

ALSO RECORDED

Decades ago Cape Vultures used to roost on the cliffs of the Great Escarpment but sadly they are no longer to be seen here. A Black Sparrowhawk was once observed circling over one of the alien poplar stands – one wonders if they will eventually establish themselves in the Great Karoo as Redbreasted Sparrowhawks have done. Short-toed Rock Thrush, at the southern limit of its range, is occasionally seen around the

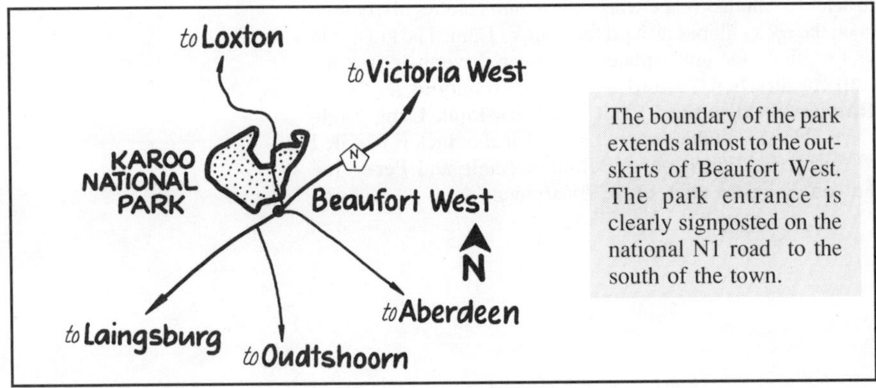

The boundary of the park extends almost to the outskirts of Beaufort West. The park entrance is clearly signposted on the national N1 road to the south of the town.

escarpment. The bird life in the park, as in all semi-arid regions, fluctuates markedly according to climatic conditions: there are times when many species are hard to find. The park is perhaps at its best after good summer rains. Until recently visitors were permitted to walk about quite freely within the park. However, with the sudden influx of visitors following the opening of a rest camp plus an increase in game, this may no longer be allowed – check with members of the staff.

SPECIAL AND INTERESTING SPECIES

The plains support **Ludwig's Bustard**, **Karoo Korhaan**, **Karoo Chat**, **Rufouseared Warbler**, **Yellowbellied** and **Karoo Eremomelas** and **Larklike Bunting**. After substantial summer rains **Blackeared Finchlark**, together with the more common **Greybacked Finchlark**, move into grassy areas to breed. In places where scattered tall bushes and stunted thorn trees occur look for **Sabota Lark** (at the southern limit of its distribution), **Southern Grey Tit**, **Cape Penduline Tit**, **Chat Flycatcher** and **Dusky Sunbird**. The Acacia thickets are often the most productive habitat and hold **Namaqua Prinia**, **Pririt Batis**, **Fairy Flycatcher**, **Southern Tchagra** and (irregularly) **Redbilled Firefinch**. One of the most elusive of the Karoo endemics is the **Cinnamonbreasted Warbler**. It is very much more common than is generally realised but, like the **Rock Pipit**, is extremely difficult to track down unless the call is known. Its usual habitat in the park is the boulder-covered hills at the base of the escarpment and these are most easily reached from the Springbok Trail – ask for directions. The two kloofs beyond the overnight hut nearest to the camp are a good area to search. Another place where these birds are regularly seen is on the rocky slopes around the Gamka Dam. The grassveld and scrub on the upper plateau (one can drive there, ask the staff for directions) afford a good opportunity to see **Black Harrier**, **Sicklewinged Chat** and Rock Pipit. **Cape Eagle Owls** also inhabit this area but a good deal of luck is required to flush one. Watch out for **Booted Eagle** and **Peregrine Falcon** along the edge of the escarpment.

headquarters of the park, mainly in the colder months. European Golden Orioles on migration have been seen in the tall trees around the headquarters of the park and flocks of European Swifts are not infrequently seen after summer rains.

Rob Martin

100% OF SPECIES

001 Ostrich ☐
008 Dabchick ☐
055 Whitebreasted Cormorant ☐
058 Reed Cormorant ☐
060 Darter ☐
062 Grey Heron ☐
063 Blackheaded Heron ☐
076 Blackcrowned Night Heron ☐
081 Hamerkop ☐
083 White Stork ☐
084 Black Stork ☐
094 Hadeda Ibis ☐
095 African Spoonbill ☐
102 Egyptian Goose ☐
103 South African Shelduck** ☐
104 Yellowbilled Duck ☐
105 African Black Duck ☐
116 Spurwinged Goose ☐
118 Secretarybird ☐
126a Yellowbilled Kite ☐
127 Blackshouldered Kite ☐
131 Black Eagle ☐
136 **Booted Eagle** ☐
140 Martial Eagle ☐
148 African Fish Eagle ☐
149 Steppe Buzzard ☐
152 Jackal Buzzard** ☐
155 Redbreasted Sparrowhawk ☐
158 Black Sparrowhawk ☐
162 Pale Chanting Goshawk* ☐
168 **Black Harrier**** ☐
169 Gymnogene ☐
171 **Peregrine Falcon** ☐
172 Lanner Falcon ☐
181 Rock Kestrel ☐
182 Greater Kestrel ☐
183 Lesser Kestrel ☐
190 Greywing Francolin** ☐
200 Common Quail ☐
203 Helmeted Guineafowl ☐
208 Blue Crane** ☐
228 Redknobbed Coot ☐
232 **Ludwig's Bustard*** ☐
235 **Karoo Korhaan**** ☐
249 Threebanded Plover ☐
255 Crowned Plover ☐
258 Blacksmith Plover ☐
270 Greenshank ☐
297 Spotted Dikkop ☐
301 Doublebanded Courser ☐
344 Namaqua Sandgrouse* ☐
349 Rock Pigeon ☐
352 Redeyed Dove ☐
354 Cape Turtle Dove ☐
355 Laughing Dove ☐
356 Namaqua Dove ☐
382 Jacobin Cuckoo ☐
386 Diederik Cuckoo ☐
392 Barn Owl ☐
400 **Cape Eagle Owl** ☐
401 Spotted Eagle Owl ☐
406 Rufouscheeked Nightjar ☐
408 Freckled Nightjar ☐
411 European Swift ☐
415 Whiterumped Swift ☐
417 Little Swift ☐
418 Alpine Swift ☐
424 Speckled Mousebird ☐
425 Whitebacked Mousebird** ☐
426 Redfaced Mousebird ☐
428 Pied Kingfisher ☐
431 Malachite Kingfisher ☐
435 Brownhooded Kingfisher ☐
438 European Bee-eater ☐
451 Hoopoe ☐
465 Pied Barbet* ☐
474 Greater Honeyguide ☐
476 Lesser Honeyguide ☐
480 Ground Woodpecker** ☐
486 Cardinal Woodpecker ☐
677 Levaillant's Cisticola ☐
686 Karoo Prinia** ☐
687 **Namaqua Prinia**** ☐
688 **Rufouseared Warbler**** ☐
689 Spotted Flycatcher ☐
697 **Chat Flycatcher*** ☐
698 Fiscal Flycatcher** ☐
703 **Pririt Batis*** ☐
706 **Fairy Flycatcher**** ☐
710 Paradise Flycatcher ☐
713 Cape Wagtail ☐
716 Grassveld Pipit ☐
717 Longbilled Pipit ☐
718 Plainbacked Pipit ☐
721 **Rock Pipit**** ☐
732 Fiscal Shrike ☐
733 Redbacked Shrike ☐
742 **Southern Tchagra**** ☐
746 Bokmakierie* ☐
757 European Starling ☐
759 Pied Starling** ☐
760 Wattled Starling ☐
769 Redwinged Starling ☐
770 Palewinged Starling* ☐
775 Malachite Sunbird ☐
783 Lesser Double-collared Sunbird** ☐
788 **Dusky Sunbird*** ☐
796 Cape White-eye** ☐
801 House Sparrow ☐
803 Cape Sparrow* ☐
804 Greyheaded Sparrow ☐
813 Cape Weaver** ☐
814 Masked Weaver ☐
821 Redbilled Quelea ☐
824 Red Bishop ☐
842 **Redbilled Firefinch** ☐
846 Common Waxbill ☐
856 Redheaded Finch* ☐
860 Pintailed Whydah ☐
872 Cape Canary ☐
876 Blackheaded Canary ☐
878 Yellow Canary* ☐
879 Whitethroated Canary* ☐
881 Streakyheaded Canary ☐
885 Cape Bunting ☐
887 **Larklike Bunting*** ☐
☐
☐
☐
☐

LOWER BERG RIVER AND ESTUARY

approximately 239 species recorded to date

Between the farm Kersefontein and the village of Laaiplek, the Berg River and its immediate surrounds form one of the most exciting birdwatching areas in the south-western Cape. In the non-tidal reaches of the river, riparian vegetation includes woodland, strandveld, reedbeds and agricultural lands, and in the lower reaches there are extensive tidal mud and sand flats, as well as large reedbeds, salt marshes and a series of commercial saltpans. The river flows into St Helena Bay, where the coastline is mainly sandy with some rocky reefs and dense offshore kelp beds.

SPECIAL AND INTERESTING SPECIES

The intertidal mud flats support the highest density of migrant shorebirds found anywhere along the entire east Atlantic seaboard. The diversity of species is high, and good numbers of **Marsh Sandpipers** can be seen in front of the Riviera Hotel in early summer. The waders are regularly harried by **Lanner Falcons** and sometimes by **Peregrine Falcons**. In late summer several hundred **White Pelicans** gather in the river, sometimes feeding at sea in St Helena Bay. Terns are well represented, and this is the best area locally to see **Caspian** (up to 200) and **Little Terns**. When watching terns at the river mouth, keep an eye open for **Arctic Skuas**.

Although there is a road that runs parallel to the south bank of the river between Velddrif and Kersefontein, most of the land between the road and the river is private, and access here is difficult. However, a bridge crosses the river at Kersefontein and a good variety of birds can be seen at this point. There is access to large intertidal mud flats in front of the Riviera Hotel at Velddrif and at Die Plaat. For access to the latter turn right off the Velddrif-Piketberg road onto a sand road at the point where the main road veers away from the river. There is a large salt marsh adjacent to the main road just east of Velddrif. Access to the commercial saltpans is possible *only by prior arrangement* with the works manager. The harbour at Laaiplek is well worth a visit for gulls, terns and cormorants. A small cruise boat runs up the river from the Port Owen marina between Velddrif and Laaiplek. There are inexpensive hotels at Velddrif and Laaiplek, and there is a campsite adjacent to the beach just north of Laaiplek harbour.

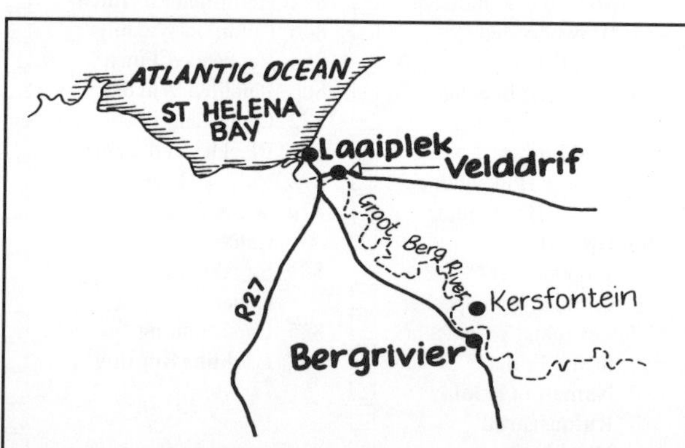

Greater and **Lesser Flamingos** are common in the saltpans, and both species have attempted to breed in recent years. In the most easterly saltpans **Chestnutbanded Plovers** are fairly common and, when the water level is low, these saltpans are important high-tide roosts for waders that feed on the mud flats. All three species of grebe may be seen. Adjacent to the river look out for **Namaqua Sandgrouse**, **Karoo** and **Thickbilled Larks**, **Banded Martin** and **Layard's Titbabbler**.

ALSO RECORDED

The estuary boasts an impressive list of rare waders, and the keen wader-watcher should always be aware of the possibility of something unusual. In recent years rarities have included European Oystercatcher, Mongolian and Caspian Plovers, Redshank, Lesser Yellowlegs, Rednecked Stint, Pectoral and Broadbilled Sandpipers (the latter is regular), Blacktailed and Hudsonian Godwits, and Rednecked and Wilson's Phalaropes. Franklin's Gull was recorded recently and could be expected again in the future.

Philip A.R. Hockey

63% OF SPECIES

006 Great Crested Grebe ☐
007 Blacknecked Grebe ☐
008 Dabchick ☐
049 **White Pelican** ☐
053 Cape Gannet* ☐
055 Whitebreasted Cormorant ☐
056 Cape Cormorant* ☐
058 Reed Cormorant ☐
060 Darter ☐
062 Grey Heron ☐
063 Blackheaded Heron ☐
065 Purple Heron ☐
067 Little Egret ☐
071 Cattle Egret ☐
076 Blackcrowned Night Heron ☐
091 Sacred Ibis ☐
093 Glossy Ibis ☐
095 African Spoonbill ☐
096 **Greater Flamingo** ☐
097 **Lesser Flamingo** ☐
102 Egyptian Goose ☐
103 South African Shelduck** ☐
104 Yellowbilled Duck ☐
106 Cape Teal ☐
108 Redbilled Teal ☐
112 Cape Shoveller* ☐
116 Spurwinged Goose ☐
126a Yellowbilled Kite ☐
127 Blackshouldered Kite ☐
148 African Fish Eagle ☐
149 Steppe Buzzard ☐
165 African Marsh Harrier ☐
171 **Peregrine Falcon** ☐
172 **Lanner Falcon** ☐
181 Rock Kestrel ☐
190 Greywing Francolin** ☐
195 Cape Francolin** ☐
200 Common Quail ☐
203 Helmeted Guineafowl ☐
223 Purple Gallinule ☐
226 Moorhen ☐
228 Redknobbed Coot ☐
239 Black Korhaan** ☐
242 Painted Snipe ☐
244 African Black Oystercatcher** ☐
245 Ringed Plover ☐
246 Whitefronted Plover ☐
247 **Chestnutbanded Plover** ☐
248 Kittlitz's Plover ☐
249 Threebanded Plover ☐
254 Grey Plover ☐
255 Crowned Plover ☐
258 Blacksmith Plover ☐
262 Turnstone ☐
264 Common Sandpiper ☐
269 **Marsh Sandpiper** ☐
270 Greenshank ☐
271 Knot ☐
272 Curlew Sandpiper ☐
274 Little Stint ☐
281 Sanderling ☐

284 Ruff ☐
288 Bartailed Godwit ☐
289 Curlew ☐
290 Whimbrel ☐
294 Avocet ☐
295 Blackwinged Stilt ☐
297 Spotted Dikkop ☐
307 **Arctic Skua** ☐
312 Kelp Gull ☐
315 Greyheaded Gull ☐
316 Hartlaub's Gull** ☐
322 **Caspian Tern** ☐
324 Swift Tern ☐
326 Sandwich Tern ☐
327 Common Tern ☐
335 **Little Tern** ☐
339 Whitewinged Tern ☐
344 **Namaqua Sandgrouse*** ☐
349 Rock Pigeon ☐
352 Redeyed Dove ☐
354 Cape Turtle Dove ☐
355 Laughing Dove ☐
356 Namaqua Dove ☐
385 Klaas's Cuckoo ☐
401 Spotted Eagle Owl ☐
412 Black Swift ☐
415 Whiterumped Swift ☐
417 Little Swift ☐
424 Speckled Mousebird ☐
425 Whitebacked Mousebird** ☐
426 Redfaced Mousebird ☐
428 Pied Kingfisher ☐
431 Malachite Kingfisher ☐
438 European Bee-eater ☐
451 Hoopoe ☐
465 Pied Barbet* ☐
500 Longbilled Lark* ☐
502 **Karoo Lark**** ☐
507 Redcapped Lark ☐
512 **Thickbilled Lark**** ☐
516 Greybacked Finchlark* ☐
518 European Swallow ☐
520 Whitethroated Swallow ☐
523 Pearlbreasted Swallow ☐
526 Greater Striped Swallow* ☐
529 Rock Martin ☐
533 **Brownthroated Martin** ☐
534 Banded Martin ☐
548 Pied Crow ☐
551 Southern Grey Tit** ☐
566 Cape Bulbul** ☐
587 Capped Wheatear ☐
595 Anteating Chat** ☐
596 Stonechat ☐
601 Cape Robin ☐
614 Karoo Robin** ☐
621 Titbabbler* ☐
622 **Layard's Titbabbler**** ☐
631 African Marsh Warbler ☐
635 Cape Reed Warbler ☐
638 African Sedge Warbler ☐
645 Barthroated Apalis ☐
651 Longbilled Crombec ☐
669 Greybacked Cisticola* ☐
677 Levaillant's Cisticola ☐
686 Karoo Prinia** ☐
698 Fiscal Flycatcher** ☐
703 Pririt Batis* ☐
716 Grassveld Pipit ☐
727 Orangethroated Longclaw** ☐
732 Fiscal Shrike ☐
746 Bokmakierie* ☐
757 European Starling ☐
759 Pied Starling** ☐
760 Wattled Starling ☐
775 Malachite Sunbird ☐
783 Lesser Double-collared Sunbird** ☐
796 Cape White-eye** ☐
801 House Sparrow ☐
803 Cape Sparrow* ☐
813 Cape Weaver** ☐
814 Masked Weaver ☐
824 Red Bishop ☐
827 Yellowrumped Widow ☐
846 Common Waxbill ☐
860 Pintailed Whydah ☐
872 Cape Canary ☐
☐
☐
☐

WEST COAST NATIONAL PARK

approximately 251 species recorded to date

The West Coast National Park (18 700 ha) was proclaimed in 1985 and currently comprises much of the land adjoining Langebaan Lagoon, a substantial section of the adjacent beach and four of the five seabird islands in Saldanha Bay. The park is under the control of the National Parks Board, which is planning further land acquisition in the area. The park contains an excellent cross-section of west coast habitat types, including strandveld, mud flats, reedbeds, salt marshes and saltpans, open shoreline and granitic seabird islands. There is a particularly high diversity of habitats at the southern end of the lagoon.

SPECIAL AND INTERESTING SPECIES

The West Coast National Park is famous for its populations of seabirds and shorebirds, but also supports a rich diversity of terrestrial species. **Jackass Penguins**, **Cape Gannets** and all four marine cormorants breed on islands in Saldanha Bay and may be seen from the shore in the Postberg section of the park. **Swift Terns** breed on the islands in the summer, and **Caspian Terns** regularly forage in the southern reaches of the lagoon. In winter there is a roost of **Antarctic Terns** on the beach south of Klein Island. Saldanha Bay supports 12 per cent of the world population of **African Black Oystercatchers**. Among the migrant waders there are noteworthy populations of **Bartailed Godwit**, **Curlew**, **Knot** and **Terek Sandpiper**: all four species may be seen at the southern end

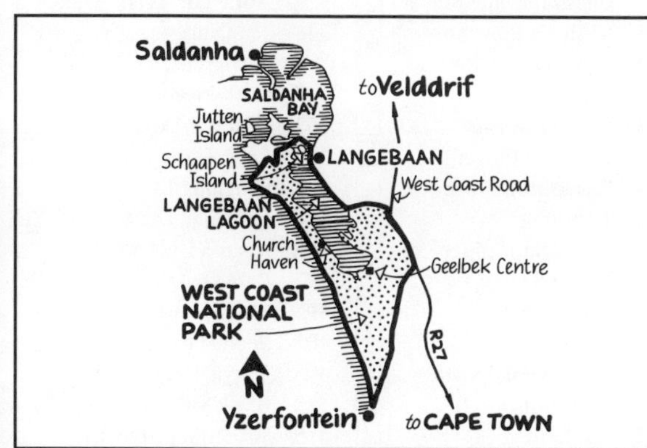

The park headquarters and Langebaan Lodge are situated at the southern end of Langebaan village, which is 110 km north of Cape Town and provides the best access point to the park. Several information brochures are available at the lodge, and there is excellent overnight accommodation. At Geelbek there is an information centre, and this is the starting point for self-guided day and overnight trails. Information about courses and trails can be obtained telephonically from Geelbek. At present there is *no public access to seabird islands*, but this is likely to change in the near future. Two viewing hides have been completed and others are under construction. Phone for general information about the park and the current state of access to different areas. Bookings for accommodation at Langebaan Lodge can be made at National Parks Board offices in Cape Town, George and Pretoria.

of the lagoon. **African Marsh** and **Black Harriers** are fairly common and are conspicuous when hunting over reedbeds and adjacent bush. They are most easily seen from the road running south of Langebaan village. This is also the best area to see **Marsh Owl** (at dawn and dusk). **Redchested Flufftails** are common in mixed reeds and bush between Bottelary and Geelbek, but are rarely seen. There are several breeding colonies of **European Bee-eater** in the park, and in the well developed bush look out for **Southern Grey** and **Cape Penduline Tits**, **Titbabbler**, **Layard's Titbabbler** and **Longbilled Crombec**.

ALSO RECORDED

Many rare species have been seen in the park. Notable among these in recent years are Redtailed Tropicbird, Australian Gannet, Montagu's Harrier, European Oystercatcher, Caspian Plover, Broadbilled Sandpiper, Hudsonian Godwit, Redshank, Franklin's Gull and Common Noddy.

Philip A.R. Hockey

59% OF SPECIES

001 Ostrich
002 **Jackass Penguin**
017 Southern Giant Petrel
032 Whitechinned Petrel
037 Sooty Shearwater
049 White Pelican
053 **Cape Gannet***
055 Whitebreasted Cormorant
056 Cape Cormorant*
057 Bank Cormorant**
058 Reed Cormorant
059 Crowned Cormorant*
062 Grey Heron
063 Blackheaded Heron
065 Purple Heron
067 Little Egret
071 Cattle Egret
091 Sacred Ibis
095 African Spoonbill
096 Greater Flamingo
097 Lesser Flamingo
102 Egyptian Goose
103 South African Shelduck**
104 Yellowbilled Duck
106 Cape Teal
126a Yellowbilled Kite
127 Blackshouldered Kite
131 Black Eagle
149 Steppe Buzzard
165 **African Marsh Harrier**
168 **Black Harrier****
172 Lanner Falcon
181 Rock Kestrel
190 Greywing Francolin**
195 Cape Francolin**
203 Helmeted Guineafowl
217 **Redchested Flufftail**
239 Black Korhaan**
244 **African Black Oystercatcher****
245 Ringed Plover
246 Whitefronted Plover
247 Chestnutbanded Plover
248 Kittlitz's Plover
249 Threebanded Plover
251 Sand Plover
254 Grey Plover
255 Crowned Plover
258 Blacksmith Plover
262 Turnstone
263 **Terek Sandpiper**
269 Marsh Sandpiper
270 Greenshank
271 **Knot**
272 Curlew Sandpiper
274 Little Stint
281 Sanderling
284 Ruff
286 Ethiopian Snipe
288 **Bartailed Godwit**
289 **Curlew**
290 Whimbrel
294 Avocet
295 Blackwinged Stilt
297 Spotted Dikkop
312 Kelp Gull
315 Greyheaded Gull
316 Hartlaub's Gull**
322 **Caspian Tern**
324 **Swift Tern**
326 Sandwich Tern
327 Common Tern
329 **Antarctic Tern**
344 Namaqua Sandgrouse*
349 Rock Pigeon
352 Redeyed Dove
354 Cape Turtle Dove
355 Laughing Dove
356 Namaqua Dove
385 Klaas's Cuckoo
392 Barn Owl
395 **Marsh Owl**
401 Spotted Eagle Owl
405 Fierynecked Nightjar
412 Black Swift
415 Whiterumped Swift

417 Little Swift ☐
424 Speckled Mousebird ☐
425 Whitebacked Mousebird** ☐
426 Redfaced Mousebird ☐
428 Pied Kingfisher ☐
438 **European Bee-eater** ☐
451 Hoopoe ☐
465 Pied Barbet* ☐
500 Longbilled Lark* ☐
502 Karoo Lark** ☐
507 Redcapped Lark ☐
512 Thickbilled Lark** ☐
518 European Swallow ☐
520 Whitethroated Swallow ☐
526 Greater Striped Swallow* ☐
529 Rock Martin ☐
533 Brownthroated Martin ☐
534 Banded Martin ☐
548 Pied Crow ☐
551 **Southern Grey Tit**** ☐
557 **Cape Penduline Tit*** ☐
566 Cape Bulbul** ☐
587 Capped Wheatear ☐
589 Familiar Chat ☐
595 Anteating Chat** ☐
596 Stonechat ☐
601 Cape Robin ☐
614 Karoo Robin** ☐
621 **Titbabbler*** ☐
622 **Layard's Titbabbler**** ☐
631 African Marsh Warbler ☐
635 Cape Reed Warbler ☐
638 African Sedge Warbler ☐
645 Barthroated Apalis ☐
651 **Longbilled Crombec** ☐
669 Greybacked Cisticola* ☐
677 Levaillant's Cisticola ☐
686 Karoo Prinia** ☐
698 Fiscal Flycatcher** ☐
713 Cape Wagtail ☐
716 Grassveld Pipit ☐
727 Orangethroated Longclaw** ☐
732 Fiscal Shrike ☐
746 Bokmakierie* ☐
757 European Starling ☐
759 Pied Starling** ☐
760 Wattled Starling ☐
775 Malachite Sunbird ☐
783 Lesser Double-collared Sunbird** ☐
796 Cape White-eye** ☐
801 House Sparrow ☐
803 Cape Sparrow* ☐
813 Cape Weaver** ☐
814 Masked Weaver ☐
824 Red Bishop ☐
827 Yellowrumped Widow ☐
846 Common Waxbill ☐
860 Pintailed Whydah ☐
872 Cape Canary ☐
877 Bully Canary ☐
878 Yellow Canary* ☐
879 Whitethroated Canary* ☐
885 Cape Bunting ☐

Whitequilled Korhaan

GAMKAPOORT NATURE RESERVE

approximately 155 species recorded to date

This 9 000 ha reserve controlled by the Directorate of Nature and Environmental Conservation was established in 1980. The Gamkapoort Dam accounts for about 1 000 ha of the total surface area. The reserve is situated 35 km west of the village of Prince Albert in the southern Great Karoo. The Swartberge, with peaks of over 2 000 m, form the southern boundary and as a result of the blocking effect that these mountains have on the winter rain storms, the mean annual rainfall is a mere 150 mm. The summers are excessively hot with shade temperatures frequently exceeding 40° C. The reserve affords protection to some fine riverine Acacia thornveld. Other habitats include the dam and its associated reedbeds, the scrub-covered plains and succulent mountain scrub.

SPECIAL AND INTERESTING SPECIES

The most easily accessible Acacia thornveld is just within the entrance gate, below the foreman's house. A short walk has been laid out through the otherwise impenetrable thickets and this enhances one's chances of seeing the more skulking species – ask for directions to the starting point. Typical Great Karoo species found here include **Southern Grey Tit**, **Cape Penduline Tit**, **Namaqua Prinia** (particularly common), **Fairy Flycatcher** and **Whitethroated Canary**. **Redbilled Firefinch**, uncommon so far south, is regularly present. There is a resident

ALSO RECORDED

Goliath Heron, Dwarf Bittern and European Swift are three of the species seen in recent years that are uncommon in the region.

Rob Martin

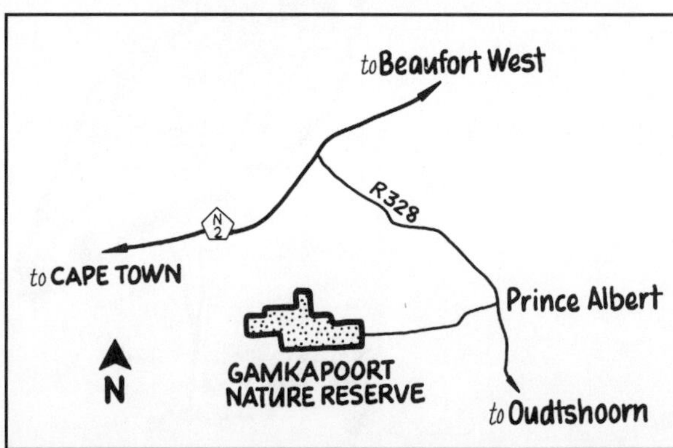

Look for the reserve signpost on the southern side of Prince Albert on the main road through the village. The road to the reserve is not tarred but it is usually in good condition. It is advisable to arrange visits in advance with the reserve foreman.

pair of **Gabar Goshawks** but they are surprisingly unobtrusive. **Southern Tchagra** is common but skulking and most easily seen in spring when the males are displaying. **Redeyed Bulbul**, here at the southern limit of its range, occurs in approximately equal numbers with the **Cape Bulbul**, a most unusual situation. The occurrence of **Pririt Batis** and **Cape Batis** together in the same habitat is also worth mentioning. **Dusky Sunbirds** are most likely to be found after substantial rains. **Booted Eagles** hunt over the more open areas and **Peregrine Falcons** from the mountains further south are irregularly recorded. The road from the foreman's house to the dam and to the most productive of the plains is often in appalling condition and it is advisable to use an alternate northern sector of the reserve, then swing southwards through a shallow kloof before emerging near the dam. In the kloof look for **Layard's Titbabbler**, **Rock Pipit** (almost impossible to find when not calling), **Palewinged Starling** and, after rain, **Larklike Bunting**. The plains on this northern side of the reserve support **Ludwig's Bustard**, **Karoo Korhaan**, **Tractrac** and **Karoo Chats**, **Yellowbellied** and **Karoo Eremomelas**, **Rufouseared Warbler** and **Blackheaded Canary**. **Rufouscheeked Nightjars** nest on exposed patches of gravel.

100% OF SPECIES

006	Great Crested Grebe	☐	095	African Spoonbill	☐	226	Moorhen	☐
008	Dabchick	☐	102	Egyptian Goose	☐	228	Redknobbed Coot	☐
055	Whitebreasted Cormorant	☐	103	South African Shelduck**	☐	230	Kori Bustard	☐
						232	**Ludwig's Bustard***	☐
058	Reed Cormorant	☐	104	Yellowbilled Duck	☐	235	**Karoo Korhaan****	☐
060	Darter	☐	105	African Black Duck	☐	249	Threebanded Plover	☐
062	Grey Heron	☐	127	Blackshouldered Kite	☐	258	Blacksmith Plover	☐
063	Blackheaded Heron	☐	131	Black Eagle	☐	264	Common Sandpiper	☐
064	Goliath Heron	☐	136	**Booted Eagle**	☐	270	Greenshank	☐
067	Little Egret	☐	148	African Fish Eagle	☐	297	Spotted Dikkop	☐
068	Yellowbilled Egret	☐	149	Steppe Buzzard	☐	298	Water Dikkop	☐
071	Cattle Egret	☐	161	**Gabar Goshawk**	☐	315	Greyheaded Gull	☐
076	Blackcrowned Night Heron	☐	162	Pale Chanting Goshawk*	☐	344	Namaqua Sandgrouse*	☐
078	Little Bittern	☐	168	Black Harrier**	☐	349	Rock Pigeon	☐
079	Dwarf Bittern	☐	169	Gymnogene	☐	352	Redeyed Dove	☐
081	Hamerkop	☐	171	**Peregrine Falcon**	☐	354	Cape Turtle Dove	☐
083	White Stork	☐	172	Lanner Falcon	☐	355	Laughing Dove	☐
084	Black Stork	☐	181	Rock Kestrel	☐	356	Namaqua Dove	☐
091	Sacred Ibis	☐	195	Cape Francolin**	☐	382	Jacobin Cuckoo	☐
094	Hadeda Ibis	☐	203	Helmeted Guineafowl	☐	385	Klaas's Cuckoo	☐

386 Diederik Cuckoo ☐
401 Spotted Eagle Owl ☐
406 **Rufouscheeked Nightjar** ☐
411 European Swift ☐
415 Whiterumped Swift ☐
417 Little Swift ☐
418 Alpine Swift ☐
424 Speckled Mousebird ☐
425 Whitebacked Mousebird** ☐
426 Redfaced Mousebird ☐
428 Pied Kingfisher ☐
429 Giant Kingfisher ☐
431 Malachite Kingfisher ☐
435 Brownhooded Kingfisher ☐
438 European Bee-eater ☐
451 Hoopoe ☐
465 Pied Barbet* ☐
474 Greater Honeyguide ☐
476 Lesser Honeyguide ☐
480 Ground Woodpecker** ☐
486 Cardinal Woodpecker ☐
500 Longbilled Lark* ☐
518 European Swallow ☐
520 Whitethroated Swallow ☐
523 Pearlbreasted Swallow ☐
526 Greater Striped Swallow* ☐
529 Rock Martin ☐
530 House Martin ☐
533 Brownthroated Martin ☐
538 Black Cuckooshrike ☐
541 Forktailed Drongo ☐
551 **Southern Grey Tit**** ☐
557 **Cape Penduline Tit*** ☐
566 **Cape Bulbul**** ☐
567 **Redeyed Bulbul*** ☐
572 Sombre Bulbul ☐
577 Olive Thrush ☐
586 Mountain Chat* ☐
589 Familiar Chat ☐
590 **Tractrac Chat*** ☐
592 **Karoo Chat*** ☐
601 Cape Robin ☐
614 Karoo Robin** ☐
621 Titbabbler* ☐
622 **Layard's Titbabbler**** ☐
631 African Marsh Warbler ☐
635 Cape Reed Warbler ☐
645 Barthroated Apalis ☐
651 Longbilled Crombec ☐
653 **Yellowbellied Eremomela** ☐
654 **Karoo Eremomela**** ☐
669 Greybacked Cisticola* ☐
677 Levaillant's Cisticola ☐
686 Karoo Prinia** ☐
687 **Namaqua Prinia**** ☐
688 **Rufouseared Warbler**** ☐
697 Chat Flycatcher* ☐
698 Fiscal Flycatcher** ☐
700 Cape Batis** ☐
703 **Pririt Batis*** ☐
706 **Fairy Flycatcher**** ☐
713 Cape Wagtail ☐
716 Grassveld Pipit ☐
717 Longbilled Pipit ☐
721 **Rock Pipit**** ☐
732 Fiscal Shrike ☐
736 Southern Boubou** ☐
742 **Southern Tchagra**** ☐
746 Bokmakierie* ☐
757 European Starling ☐
759 Pied Starling** ☐
760 Wattled Starling ☐
769 Redwinged Starling ☐
770 **Palewinged Starling*** ☐
775 Malachite Sunbird ☐
777 Orangebreasted Sunbird** ☐
783 Lesser Double-collared Sunbird** ☐
788 **Dusky Sunbird*** ☐
796 Cape White-eye** ☐
801 House Sparrow ☐
803 Cape Sparrow* ☐
804 Greyheaded Sparrow ☐
813 Cape Weaver** ☐
814 Masked Weaver ☐
824 Red Bishop ☐
842 **Redbilled Firefinch** ☐
846 Common Waxbill ☐
850 Swee Waxbill* ☐
872 Cape Canary ☐
874 Cape Siskin ☐
876 **Blackheaded Canary** ☐
877 Bully Canary ☐
878 Yellow Canary* ☐
879 **Whitethroated Canary*** ☐
881 Streakyheaded Canary ☐
885 Cape Bunting ☐
887 **Larklike Bunting*** ☐

ANYSBERG NATURE RESERVE

approximately 161 species recorded to date

Anysberg Nature Reserve is controlled by the Directorate of Nature and Environmental Conservation. At 34 015 ha it is one of the largest reserves in the Cape Province. Established in 1988, it is situated on the western fringe of the Little Karoo in the broad transitional zone between the fynbos vegetation of the winter rainfall area and the Karoo. All the endemic fynbos species are present on the mountains, and the plains support many Karoo specials. As in all Karoo areas, visits after substantial rains are likely to be the most successful. The two most important habitats are the scrub-covered plains and the belts of Acacia thorn trees along the usually dry stream beds. Both habitats are accessible from the gravel road that traverses the reserve.

SPECIAL AND INTERESTING SPECIES

The plains support **Karoo Korhaan**, **Namaqua Sandgrouse**, **Longbilled** and **Karoo Larks**, **Karoo Chat**, **Yellowbellied Eremomela** (especially where there are scattered bushes), **Karoo Eremomela**, **Greybacked Cisticola**, **Rufouseared Warbler** (responds well to tapes), **Blackheaded Canary** and **Larklike Bunting** (mainly in spring). This bleak habitat can be disappointing and calm, early mornings are the most productive. In the Acacia trees and tall riverine thickets look for **Whitebacked Mousebird**, **Cardinal Woodpecker**, **Southern Grey Tit**, **Cape Penduline Tit**, **Namaqua Prinia**,

ALSO RECORDED

Cape Eagle Owls occur on the mountains but are not easily found. Rufouscheeked Nightjars are frequently flushed from the roads at night but to find them by day is difficult. Chat Flycatchers are of irregular occurrence and are most often seen in the taller scrub on the plains. They are easily overlooked.

Rob Martin

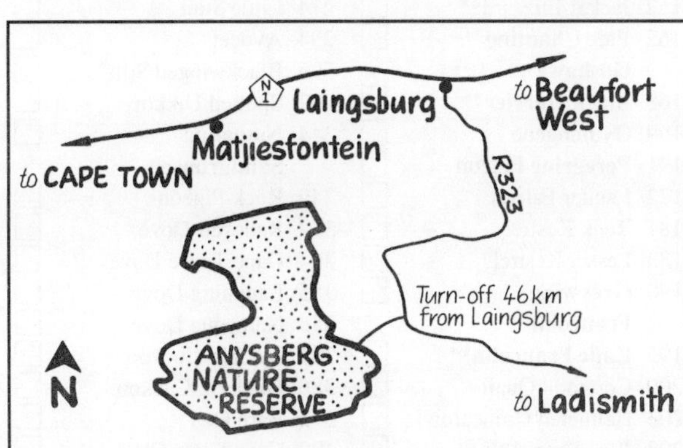

From Laingsburg take the Ladismith road (it is easy to overlook the unexpected turnoff to the town after 22 km) and watch for the reserve sign 46 km from Laingsburg. It is advisable to arrange all visits in advance with the officer in charge as heavy rains can make the roads impassable. No accommodation is available at present.

Pririt Batis, **Fairy Flycatcher**, **Southern Tchagra**, **Dusky Sunbird** (after good rains) and **Whitethroated Canary**. **Cape Francolins** are widespread. Access to the higher mountain slopes is restricted to owners of four-wheel drive vehicles or to those who are prepared to walk up the steep track. Here the fynbos supports **Greywing Francolin**, **Ground Woodpecker**, **Cape** and **Sentinel Rock Thrushes**, **Cape Rockjumper**, **Victorin's Warbler**, **Cape Sugarbird**, **Orangebreasted Sunbird**, **Cape Siskin** and **Protea Canary**. Without exception these species can be seen more readily elsewhere and, unless time allows, it is better to concentrate on the karroid areas. **Rock Pipits** occur on the lower slopes of the north face of the main range (listen for their far-carrying whistle). **Layard's Titbabblers** and **Palewinged Starlings** are common in the kloofs, the latter often wandering onto the plains. **Booted Eagles** and **Black Harriers** are most easily seen in the spring and early summer, **Pale Chanting Goshawks** at any time. **Peregrine Falcons** are to be found in some of the deeper kloofs but are not seen without a considerable effort. Several pairs of **Pearlbreasted Swallows** breed on the buildings.

100% OF SPECIES

001 Ostrich ☐
008 Dabchick ☐
055 Whitebreasted Cormorant ☐
058 Reed Cormorant ☐
062 Grey Heron ☐
063 Blackheaded Heron ☐
067 Little Egret ☐
071 Cattle Egret ☐
076 Blackcrowned Night Heron ☐
081 Hamerkop ☐
083 White Stork ☐
084 Black Stork ☐
091 Sacred Ibis ☐
094 Hadeda Ibis ☐
095 African Spoonbill ☐
102 Egyptian Goose ☐
103 South African Shelduck** ☐
104 Yellowbilled Duck ☐
105 African Black Duck ☐
106 Cape Teal ☐
108 Redbilled Teal ☐
116 Spurwinged Goose ☐
126a Yellowbilled Kite ☐
127 Blackshouldered Kite ☐
131 Black Eagle ☐
136 **Booted Eagle** ☐
140 Martial Eagle ☐
149 Steppe Buzzard ☐
152 Jackal Buzzard** ☐
162 **Pale Chanting Goshawk*** ☐
168 **Black Harrier**** ☐
169 Gymnogene ☐
171 **Peregrine Falcon** ☐
172 Lanner Falcon ☐
181 Rock Kestrel ☐
183 Lesser Kestrel ☐
190 **Greywing Francolin**** ☐
195 **Cape Francolin**** ☐
200 Common Quail ☐
203 Helmeted Guineafowl ☐
208 Blue Crane** ☐
226 Moorhen ☐
228 Redknobbed Coot ☐
235 **Karoo Korhaan**** ☐
239 Black Korhaan** ☐
249 Threebanded Plover ☐
255 Crowned Plover ☐
258 Blacksmith Plover ☐
270 Greenshank ☐
274 Little Stint ☐
294 Avocet ☐
295 Blackwinged Stilt ☐
297 Spotted Dikkop ☐
344 **Namaqua Sandgrouse*** ☐
349 Rock Pigeon ☐
352 Redeyed Dove ☐
354 Cape Turtle Dove ☐
355 Laughing Dove ☐
356 Namaqua Dove ☐
382 Jacobin Cuckoo ☐
386 Diederik Cuckoo ☐
392 Barn Owl ☐
400 Cape Eagle Owl ☐

401 Spotted Eagle Owl ☐
405 Fierynecked Nightjar ☐
406 Rufouscheeked Nightjar ☐
412 Black Swift ☐
415 Whiterumped Swift ☐
417 Little Swift ☐
418 Alpine Swift ☐
425 **Whitebacked Mousebird**** ☐
426 Redfaced Mousebird ☐
429 Giant Kingfisher ☐
438 European Bee-eater ☐
451 Hoopoe ☐
465 Pied Barbet* ☐
474 Greater Honeyguide ☐
480 **Ground Woodpecker**** ☐
486 **Cardinal Woodpecker** ☐
495 Clapper Lark** ☐
500 **Longbilled Lark*** ☐
502 **Karoo Lark**** ☐
506 Spikeheeled Lark* ☐
507 Redcapped Lark ☐
512 Thickbilled Lark** ☐
518 European Swallow ☐
523 **Pearlbreasted Swallow** ☐
526 Greater Striped Swallow* ☐
529 Rock Martin ☐
530 House Martin ☐
533 Brownthroated Martin ☐
541 Forktailed Drongo ☐
548 Pied Crow ☐
550 Whitenecked Raven ☐
551 **Southern Grey Tit**** ☐
557 **Cape Penduline Tit*** ☐
566 Cape Bulbul** ☐
577 Olive Thrush ☐
581 **Cape Rock Thrush**** ☐
582 **Sentinel Rock Thrush**** ☐
586 Mountain Chat* ☐
589 Familiar Chat ☐
592 **Karoo Chat*** ☐
601 Cape Robin ☐
611 **Cape Rockjumper**** ☐
614 Karoo Robin** ☐
621 Titbabbler* ☐
622 **Layard's Titbabbler**** ☐
631 African Marsh Warbler ☐
641 **Victorin's Warbler**** ☐
643 Willow Warbler ☐
645 Barthroated Apalis ☐
651 Longbilled Crombec ☐
653 **Yellowbellied Eremomela** ☐
654 **Karoo Eremomela**** ☐
661 Grassbird** ☐
669 **Greybacked Cisticola*** ☐
677 Levaillant's Cisticola ☐
686 Karoo Prinia** ☐
687 **Namaqua Prinia**** ☐
688 **Rufouseared Warbler**** ☐
697 Chat Flycatcher* ☐
698 Fiscal Flycatcher** ☐
703 **Pririt Batis*** ☐
706 **Fairy Flycatcher**** ☐
713 Cape Wagtail ☐
716 Grassveld Pipit ☐
717 Longbilled Pipit ☐
721 **Rock Pipit**** ☐
732 Fiscal Shrike ☐
733 Redbacked Shrike ☐
742 **Southern Tchagra**** ☐
746 Bokmakierie* ☐
757 European Starling ☐
759 Pied Starling** ☐
760 Wattled Starling ☐
769 Redwinged Starling ☐
770 **Palewinged Starling*** ☐
773 **Cape Sugarbird**** ☐
775 Malachite Sunbird ☐
777 **Orangebreasted Sunbird**** ☐
783 Lesser Double-collared Sunbird** ☐
788 **Dusky Sunbird*** ☐
796 Cape White-eye** ☐
801 House Sparrow ☐
803 Cape Sparrow* ☐
813 Cape Weaver** ☐
814 Masked Weaver ☐
824 Red Bishop ☐
827 Yellowrumped Widow ☐
846 Common Waxbill ☐
860 Pintailed Whydah ☐
872 Cape Canary ☐
874 **Cape Siskin**** ☐
876 **Blackheaded Canary** ☐
878 Yellow Canary* ☐
879 **Whitethroated Canary*** ☐
880 **Protea Canary**** ☐
881 Streakyheaded Canary ☐
885 Cape Bunting ☐
887 **Larklike Bunting*** ☐
☐
☐
☐

PELAGIC

The south-western Cape is regarded by many specialists as one of the best pelagic birding spots in the world. An average day at sea usually produces over 20 seabird species. Although a number of large and small harbours are dotted around the coast only Hout Bay is ideally situated for pelagic birding trips. If one is to make the most of a day's sea birding then it is necessary to visit the outer edge of the continental shelf, 30 to 40 nautical miles offshore. The tuna fleet regularly visits this area and if you are lucky enough to get aboard one of these vessels then a truly spectacular birding experience awaits you. It is, however, not always easy to arrange a trip on one of these vessels and those interested should either take part in a bird club charter or should use one of the contact telephone numbers.

SPECIAL AND INTERESTING SPECIES

Unlike other birding spots in southern Africa this area has its best migrant visitors and highest bird densities in winter when seabirds breeding in the southern oceans move northwards to avoid the harsh winter. During winter **Blackbrowed**, **Shy** and **Yellownosed Albatrosses** are common, but one can see them all year. **Pintado Petrel**, **Broadbilled Prion** and **Sooty Shearwater** often occur in large flocks. If one is lucky enough to locate a deep-sea demersal trawler one is guaranteed the awesome sight of up to 5 000 seabirds, mainly albatrosses but comprising up to 15 species, following the

ALSO RECORDED

Each year a few of the following winter vagrants are seen: Royal and Greyheaded Albatrosses, Blue, Grey, Kerguelen and Atlantic Petrels, Little Shearwaters and South Polar Skuas. Each foray out into the deep waters west of the Cape Peninsula during winter could potentially produce one or more of these birds.

Barrie Rose

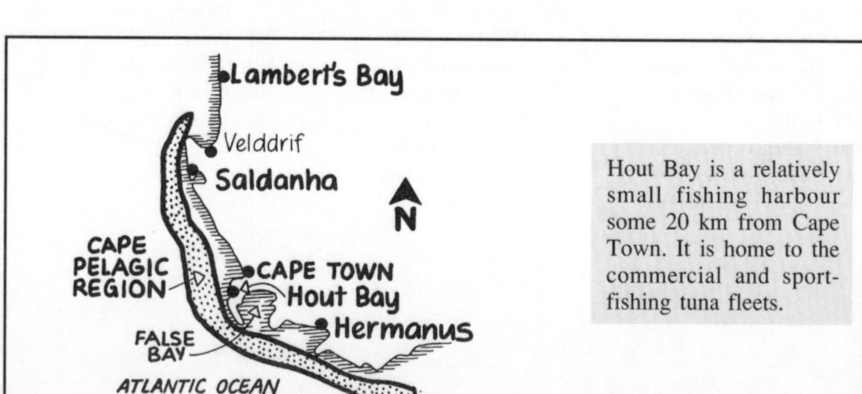

Hout Bay is a relatively small fishing harbour some 20 km from Cape Town. It is home to the commercial and sport-fishing tuna fleets.

vessel. Once the initial excitement is over then one has to sift carefully through the flock in search of the less common species. **Wandering Albatrosses** are large, impressive and easily identified; not so with some of the smaller species and one has to keep a careful watch for **Softplumaged Petrels**, **Antarctic Fulmars** and other less common birds. Both **Southern** and **Northern Petrels**, **Whitechinned Petrel**, **Sooty Shearwater**, **Wilson's Storm Petrel** and all the resident coastal birds can be seen throughout the year. **Great Shearwaters** and **Blackbellied Storm Petrels** are most likely to be seen in spring and autumn. Summer visitors from the northern hemisphere are **Cory's** and **Manx Shearwaters**, **Grey Phalarope** and the three northern skuas, **Arctic**, **Longtailed** and **Pomarine**. The winter-breeding **Greatwinged Petrel** is also regular in offshore waters during summer.

010 **Wandering Albatross** ☐
011 **Shy Albatross** ☐
012 **Blackbrowed Albatross** ☐
014 **Yellownosed Albatross** ☐
017 **Southern Giant Petrel** ☐
018 **Northern Giant Petrel** ☐
019 **Antarctic Fulmar** ☐
021 **Pintado Petrel** ☐
023 **Greatwinged Petrel** ☐
024 **Softplumaged Petrel** ☐
029 **Broadbilled Prion** ☐
032 **Whitechinned Petrel** ☐
034 **Cory's Shearwater** ☐
035 **Great Shearwater** ☐
036 Fleshfooted Shearwater ☐
037 **Sooty Shearwater** ☐
038 **Manx Shearwater** ☐
042 European Storm Petrel ☐
043 Leach's Storm Petrel ☐
044 **Wilson's Storm Petrel** ☐
046 **Blackbellied Storm Petrel** ☐
053 Cape Gannet* ☐
055 Whitebreasted Cormorant ☐
056 Cape Cormorant* ☐
291 **Grey Phalarope** ☐
307 **Arctic Skua** ☐
308 **Longtailed Skua** ☐
309 **Pomarine Skua** ☐
310 Subantarctic Skua ☐
312 Kelp Gull ☐
316 Hartlaub's Gull** ☐
318 Sabine's Gull ☐
324 Swift Tern ☐
326 Sandwich Tern ☐
327 Common Tern ☐
328 Arctic Tern ☐
329 Antarctic Tern ☐

VROLIJKHEID NATURE RESERVE

approximately 183 species recorded to date

This reserve is 15 km south of Robertson, in the Breede River valley. At 1 827 ha it is one of the smaller reserves under the control of the Directorate of Nature and Environmental Conservation. It was established in the late 1950s as a training centre for those involved in the control of problem animals. In 1985 the training centre was discontinued and the management has since concentrated on the rehabilitation of the natural vegetation and the indigenous fauna. The rainfall, largely confined to the winter months, is low at 250 mm per annum. The winters are mild and the summers can be hot with temperatures sometimes reaching 40°C. The reserve is at its best from July to October and is especially good in years of above average rainfall. The most important habitats are the low scrub interspersed with bush-clumps, a few stands of Acacia thorn trees and the reedbeds around one of the three small dams. No accommodation is available in the reserve at present.

SPECIAL AND INTERESTING SPECIES

The low scrub supports **Clapper**, **Longbilled** and **Thickbilled Larks**, **Karoo Chat** and **Rufouseared Warbler**. In the taller vegetation look for **Whitebacked Mousebird**, **Southern Grey Tit**, **Cape Penduline Tit**, **Yellowbellied Eremomela**, **Fairy Flycatcher**, **Whitethroated** and **Blackheaded Ca-**

ALSO RECORDED

In spring Longbilled Pipits move into the reserve where they breed in the low scrub, especially where there are scattered Acacia trees. Capped Wheatears are occasionally seen on old agricultural lands. Doublebanded Courser and Namaqua Sandgrouse are irregular visitors. Rufouscheeked Nightjars, uncommon in the region, are sometimes heard calling at night but are only flushed by chance during the day. Booted Eagles and Black Harriers are by no means uncommon in the district and may sometimes be seen flying overhead. Larklike Buntings occur after exceptional rains.

Rob Martin

From Robertson take the McGregor road, which crosses the railway line to the south of the town, for 15 km. The reserve headquarters, to the right of the road, are well signposted. A network of roads gives access to most parts of the reserve and visitors are allowed to drive along these but those who choose to walk will certainly see more birds. A hiking trail has also recently been opened. It is advisable to arrange all visits in advance with the officer in charge.

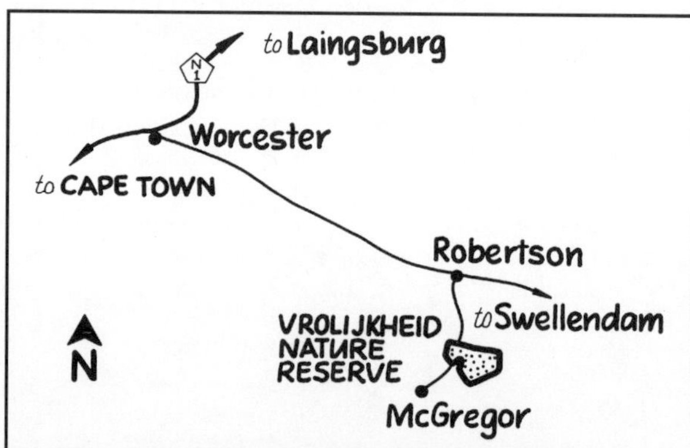

naries (after the winter rains). **Rock Pipits** are to be found on the tops of the hills – this is perhaps the best place to look for them in the region but unless the bird's call is heard this is a particularly difficult species to locate. These hills also support a few pairs of **Ground Woodpecker**. The thicker hillside scrub is where **Layard's Titbabbler** is most often encountered. The Acacia thickets are the habitat of **Namaqua Prinia** and **Southern Tchagra**, both easily called up with tapes. A hide has recently been built at one of the dams. On the approach to this there is a patch of marshy ground (dry towards the end of summer) where **African Rail** and **Redchested Flufftail** are frequently heard but less often seen. **Pearlbreasted Swallows** nest around the buildings.

82% OF SPECIES

006 Great Crested Grebe
008 Dabchick
055 Whitebreasted Cormorant
058 Reed Cormorant
060 Darter
062 Grey Heron
063 Blackheaded Heron
067 Little Egret
068 Yellowbilled Egret
071 Cattle Egret
076 Blackcrowned Night Heron
081 Hamerkop
091 Sacred Ibis
094 Hadeda Ibis
095 African Spoonbill
102 Egyptian Goose
103 South African Shelduck**
104 Yellowbilled Duck
105 African Black Duck
112 Cape Shoveller*
113 Southern Pochard
116 Spurwinged Goose
127 Blackshouldered Kite
136 Booted Eagle
148 African Fish Eagle
149 Steppe Buzzard
152 Jackal Buzzard**
155 Redbreasted Sparrowhawk
162 Pale Chanting Goshawk*
165 African Marsh Harrier
168 Black Harrier**
172 Lanner Falcon
181 Rock Kestrel
190 Greywing Francolin**
195 Cape Francolin**
200 Common Quail
203 Helmeted Guineafowl
210 **African Rail**
213 Black Crake
217 **Redchested Flufftail**
226 Moorhen
228 Redknobbed Coot
239 Black Korhaan**
249 Threebanded Plover
255 Crowned Plover
258 Blacksmith Plover
270 Greenshank
286 Ethiopian Snipe
295 Blackwinged Stilt
297 Spotted Dikkop
301 Doublebanded Courser
339 Whitewinged Tern
344 Namaqua Sandgrouse*
349 Rock Pigeon
352 Redeyed Dove
354 Cape Turtle Dove
355 Laughing Dove
356 Namaqua Dove
385 Klaas's Cuckoo
386 Diederik Cuckoo
391 Burchell's Coucal*
401 Spotted Eagle Owl
405 Fierynecked Nightjar
406 Rufouscheeked Nightjar
412 Black Swift
415 Whiterumped Swift
417 Little Swift
418 Alpine Swift
424 Speckled Mousebird
425 **Whitebacked Mousebird****
426 Redfaced Mousebird
428 Pied Kingfisher
429 Giant Kingfisher
431 Malachite Kingfisher
435 Brownhooded Kingfisher
451 Hoopoe
465 Pied Barbet*
474 Greater Honeyguide
480 **Ground Woodpecker****

486 Cardinal Woodpecker ☐
495 **Clapper Lark**** ☐
500 **Longbilled Lark*** ☐
507 Redcapped Lark ☐
512 **Thickbilled Lark**** ☐
518 European Swallow ☐
520 Whitethroated Swallow ☐
523 **Pearlbreasted Swallow** ☐
526 Greater Striped Swallow* ☐
529 Rock Martin ☐
533 Brownthroated Martin ☐
541 Forktailed Drongo ☐
548 Pied Crow ☐
550 Whitenecked Raven ☐
551 **Southern Grey Tit**** ☐
557 **Cape Penduline Tit*** ☐
566 Cape Bulbul** ☐
577 Olive Thrush ☐
586 Mountain Chat* ☐
587 Capped Wheatear ☐
589 Familiar Chat ☐
592 **Karoo Chat*** ☐
596 Stonechat ☐
601 Cape Robin ☐
614 Karoo Robin** ☐
621 Titbabbler* ☐
622 **Layard's Titbabbler**** ☐
631 African Marsh Warbler ☐
635 Cape Reed Warbler ☐
638 African Sedge Warbler ☐
645 Barthroated Apalis ☐
651 Longbilled Crombec ☐
653 **Yellowbellied Eremomela** ☐
661 Grassbird** ☐
664 Fantailed Cisticola ☐
669 Greybacked Cisticola* ☐
677 Levaillant's Cisticola ☐
686 Karoo Prinia** ☐
687 **Namaqua Prinia**** ☐
688 **Rufouseared Warbler**** ☐
698 Fiscal Flycatcher** ☐
706 **Fairy Flycatcher**** ☐
713 Cape Wagtail ☐
716 Grassveld Pipit ☐
717 Longbilled Pipit ☐
721 **Rock Pipit**** ☐
727 Orangethroated Longclaw** ☐
732 Fiscal Shrike ☐
736 Southern Boubou** ☐
742 **Southern Tchagra**** ☐
746 Bokmakierie* ☐
757 European Starling ☐
759 Pied Starling** ☐
769 Redwinged Starling ☐
775 Malachite Sunbird ☐
783 Lesser Double-collared Sunbird** ☐
796 Cape White-eye ☐
803 Cape Sparrow* ☐
813 Cape Weaver** ☐
814 Masked Weaver ☐
824 Red Bishop ☐
827 Yellowrumped Widow ☐
846 Common Waxbill ☐
850 Swee Waxbill* ☐
872 Cape Canary ☐
876 **Blackheaded Canary** ☐
878 Yellow Canary* ☐
879 **Whitethroated Canary*** ☐
881 Streakyheaded Canary ☐
885 Cape Bunting ☐
887 Larklike Bunting* ☐

Little Egrets

GROOTVADERSBOS

approximately 46 species recorded to date

This temperate forest is situated in a depression in the southern foothills of the Langeberg, 20 km north-west of Heidelberg and 40 km east of Swellendam. At 251 ha the largest indigenous forest west of the Knysna forest complex, it is controlled by the Directorate of Nature and Environmental Conservation and forms part of the Boosmansbos Widerness Area. The birds listed were all seen in the forest, or on the forest fringe, and many other species occur in the adjoining wilderness area. The forest is most productive from September to November.

SPECIAL AND INTERESTING SPECIES

There are three resident pairs of **Forest Buzzard** in the forest or in the adjacent pine woods and they are most readily seen in spring and early summer when the males display above the canopy. **Knysna Woodpecker** is most likely to be found on the forest fringe and is a difficult species to locate. Listen for its call: it is the only woodpecker in the region that "screams". **Olive Woodpecker** is very much more common and a number of occupied nest-holes have been found. There is at least one pair of **Narina Trogons** present – this is the farthest west that the species normally occurs. **Knysna Warbler**, perhaps more readily seen at Kirstenbosch, inhabits the riverine scrub between the two forest sectors and is not easily found unless the males are in song. A pair of **Martial Eagles** nested in an alien Eucalyptus tree in the forest a decade ago

From Swellendam take the national N2 road to the small settlement of Buffeljags (about 11 km), turn left at the Barrydale-Suurberg signpost and follow this road, ignoring the Barrydale turnoff, for about 26 km. Look for the rather inconspicuous Boosmansbos Wilderness Area signposts which guide one to the forest. The forest is divided into an eastern and western sector with a circular drive passing through a small tract of forest between the two sectors. The smaller eastern sector is the most readily accessible. There are no footpaths and care should be taken as the sloping forest floor can be slippery after rain. All visits should be arranged in advance with the officer in charge.

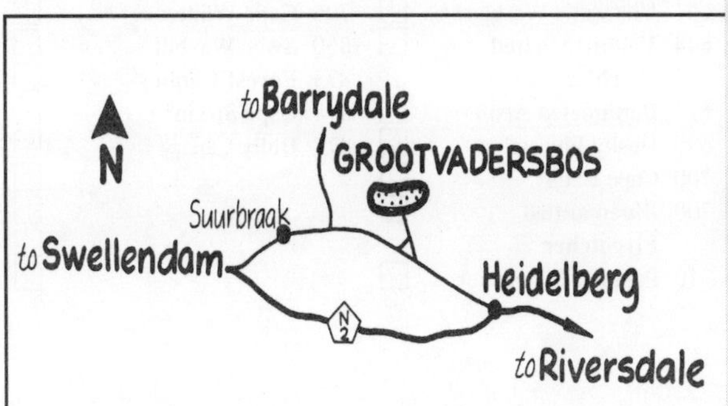

and, although they do not breed in the forest now, they are often seen. **Black Sparrowhawks** are resident in the forest and are sometimes seen chasing prey along the forest fringe or in the adjacent alien pine trees. **Yellowthroated Warbler** and **Olive Bush Shrike** are two resident species but both are most easily found in spring and early summer when they are particularly vocal. **Bluemantled Flycatcher** is a common resident and, as it tends to be vocal throughout the year, is not difficult to locate. Less conspicuous are the **Terrestrial Bulbuls** and the **Grey Cuckooshrikes**, the latter keeping well hidden in the canopy. **Forest Canaries** are most often seen on the forest fringe or in clearings in the forest. **Cinnamon Doves** are quite common and are sometimes flushed from the forest floor.

ALSO RECORDED

Rednecked Francolins reach the western limit of their range at Grootvadersbos and are more often heard than seen. Victorin's Warblers, Orangebreasted Sunbirds and Cape Siskins can be seen on the forest fringe where this adjoins the fynbos. Wood Owls are occasionally seen and, as with many nocturnal species, their numbers are difficult to assess. Black Sunbird, uncommon this far west, is an irregular visitor.

Rob Martin

100% OF SPECIES

094 Hadeda Ibis
105 African Black Duck
140 **Martial Eagle**
150 **Forest Buzzard****
158 **Black Sparrowhawk**
160 African Goshawk
169 Gymnogene
198 Rednecked Francolin
350 Rameron Pigeon
352 Redeyed Dove
360 **Cinnamon Dove**
377 Redchested Cuckoo
385 Klaas's Cuckoo
394 Wood Owl
424 Speckled Mousebird
427 **Narina Trogon**
474 Greater Honeyguide
484 **Knysna Woodpecker****
488 **Olive Woodpecker**
536 Black Sawwing Swallow
540 **Grey Cuckooshrike**
541 Forktailed Drongo
569 **Terrestrial Bulbul**
572 Sombre Bulbul
577 Olive Thrush
601 Cape Robin
640 **Knysna Warbler****
641 Victorin's Warbler**
644 **Yellowthroated Warbler**
645 Barthroated Apalis
690 Dusky Flycatcher
700 Cape Batis**
708 **Bluemantled Flycatcher**
710 Paradise Flycatcher
736 Southern Boubou**
750 **Olive Bush Shrike***
775 Malachite Sunbird
777 Orangebreasted Sunbird**
783 Lesser Double-collared Sunbird**
785 Greater Double-collared Sunbird**
792 Black Sunbird
796 Cape White-eye**
850 Swee Waxbill*
873 **Forest Canary****
874 Cape Siskin**
877 Bully Canary

BONTEBOK NATIONAL PARK

approximately 191 species recorded to date

This 3 000 ha park controlled by the National Parks Board was proclaimed in 1960 to protect the Bontebok, which was then in danger of extinction. It is situated just south of Swellendam, the Breede River representing the southern boundary of the park. The most important habitats are renosterbosveld, coastal fynbos and dense riverine thickets. In very wet years the flooded veld attracts many waterbirds that would not otherwise be present. There is a caravan and camping site in the park.

SPECIAL AND INTERESTING SPECIES

The park is one of the best places to see **Stanley's Bustard**: carefully scan the open plains as they can be surprisingly difficult to spot. Look for **Cape** and **Greywing Francolins** on the road, especially in the early morning. **Thickbilled**, **Longbilled** and **Clapper Larks** are all resident but the Clapper is unobtrusive when not calling. The two common cisticolas are **Cloud** and **Greybacked Cisticola**, the latter being one of the dominant birds in the park. Cloud Cisticola is most easily found in spring and early summer when the males perform their aerial call. The tall trees beside the river support a resident pair of **Black Sparrowhawks** but one is lucky to catch even tantalising glimpses of them. The thickest riverine growth provides ideal habitat for **Tambourine Dove**, this being one of only a few localities in the south-western

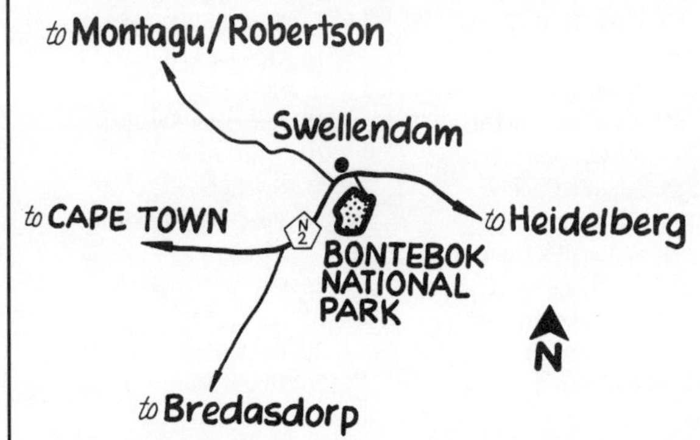

ALSO RECORDED

Martial and Booted Eagles and Black Harriers are irregular visitors, the harrier being a fairly common bird in the Swellendam district. Cape Vultures from the nearby Potberg breeding colony are occasionally seen soaring overhead. Black-rumped Buttonquails have been recorded on the plains but vehicle-bound visitors have little chance of adding this elusive species to their lists.

Rob Martin

The access road to the park turns off the national N2 road just opposite the eastern entrance to Swellendam. A few kilometres of gravel road, sometimes flooded after heavy rains, bring one to the park gates. There is a good system of roads in the park and although visitors may not alight from their vehicles, the vegetation is low enough to make viewing easy. Starting at the camping site there are three short trails through a variety of vegetation types. One meanders through Acacia thornveld, another along the banks of the river and the third through dense hillside bush dominated by aloes.

Cape where it can be seen. During the breeding season tapes can be used to good effect to obtain better views of this otherwise shy species. A breeding pair of **African Black Ducks** are often seen in the vicinity of the picnic area. A pair of **Pearlbreasted Swallows**, absent from April to July, have nested for many years in one of the ablution blocks in the caravan park. The hillside trail affords the best chance of seeing **Southern Grey Tit** and **Southern Tchagra**, the latter easily called up by means of tapes. **Fairy Flycatchers** can also be seen here, mainly during the winter months. **Whitethroated Canary** can be seen throughout the year.

100% OF SPECIES

No.	Species	
058	Reed Cormorant	☐
062	Grey Heron	☐
063	Blackheaded Heron	☐
065	Purple Heron	☐
068	Yellowbilled Egret	☐
071	Cattle Egret	☐
081	Hamerkop	☐
083	White Stork	☐
094	Hadeda Ibis	☐
102	Egyptian Goose	☐
104	Yellowbilled Duck	☐
105	**African Black Duck**	☐
116	Spurwinged Goose	☐
118	Secretarybird	☐
122	Cape Vulture**	☐
127	Blackshouldered Kite	☐
131	Black Eagle	☐
136	Booted Eagle	☐
140	Martial Eagle	☐
148	African Fish Eagle	☐
149	Steppe Buzzard	☐
152	Jackal Buzzard**	☐
158	**Black Sparrowhawk**	☐
160	African Goshawk	☐
165	African Marsh Harrier	☐
168	Black Harrier**	☐
172	Lanner Falcon	☐
181	Rock Kestrel	☐
183	Lesser Kestrel	☐
190	**Greywing Francolin****	☐
195	**Cape Francolin****	☐
200	Common Quail	☐
203	Helmeted Guineafowl	☐
206	Blackrumped Buttonquail	☐
208	Blue Crane**	☐
231	**Stanley's Bustard**	☐
239	Black Korhaan**	☐
249	Threebanded Plover	☐
255	Crowned Plover	☐
258	Blacksmith Plover	☐
264	Common Sandpiper	☐
270	Greenshank	☐
295	Blackwinged Stilt	☐
297	Spotted Dikkop	☐
298	Water Dikkop	☐
344	Namaqua Sandgrouse*	☐
349	Rock Pigeon	☐
350	Rameron Pigeon	☐
352	Redeyed Dove	☐
354	Cape Turtle Dove	☐
355	Laughing Dove	☐
356	Namaqua Dove	☐
359	**Tambourine Dove**	☐
377	Redchested Cuckoo	☐
385	Klaas's Cuckoo	☐
386	Diederik Cuckoo	☐
391	Burchell's Coucal*	☐
401	Spotted Eagle Owl	☐
405	Fierynecked Nightjar	☐
412	Black Swift	☐
415	Whiterumped Swift	☐
417	Little Swift	☐
418	Alpine Swift	☐
424	Speckled Mousebird	☐
425	Whitebacked Mousebird**	☐
426	Redfaced Mousebird	☐
428	Pied Kingfisher	☐
429	Giant Kingfisher	☐
431	Malachite Kingfisher	☐
435	Brownhooded Kingfisher	☐
438	European Bee-eater	☐
451	Hoopoe	☐
465	Pied Barbet*	☐
474	Greater Honeyguide	☐
476	Lesser Honeyguide	☐
486	Cardinal Woodpecker	☐
488	Olive Woodpecker	☐
495	**Clapper Lark****	☐
500	**Longbilled Lark***	☐
507	Redcapped Lark	☐
512	Thickbilled Lark**	☐
516	Greybacked Finchlark*	☐
518	European Swallow	☐
520	Whitethroated Swallow	☐
523	**Pearlbreasted Swallow**	☐
526	Greater Striped Swallow*	☐
529	Rock Martin	☐
530	House Martin	☐
533	Brownthroated Martin	☐

536 Black Sawwing Swallow ☐
541 Forktailed Drongo ☐
547 Black Crow ☐
548 Pied Crow ☐
550 Whitenecked Raven ☐
551 **Southern Grey Tit**** ☐
566 Cape Bulbul** ☐
572 Sombre Bulbul ☐
589 Familiar Chat ☐
596 Stonechat ☐
601 Cape Robin ☐
614 Karoo Robin** ☐
621 Titbabbler* ☐
631 African Marsh Warbler ☐
638 African Sedge Warbler ☐
643 Willow Warbler ☐
645 Barthroated Apalis ☐
651 Longbilled Crombec ☐
661 Grassbird** ☐
666 **Cloud Cisticola** ☐
669 **Greybacked Cisticola*** ☐
677 Levaillant's Cisticola ☐
681 Neddicky ☐
686 Karoo Prinia** ☐
689 Spotted Flycatcher ☐
698 Fiscal Flycatcher** ☐
700 Cape Batis** ☐
706 **Fairy Flycatcher**** ☐
713 Cape Wagtail ☐
716 Grassveld Pipit ☐
717 Longbilled Pipit ☐
718 Plainbacked Pipit ☐
727 Orangethroated Longclaw** ☐
732 Fiscal Shrike ☐
736 Southern Boubou** ☐
742 **Southern Tchagra**** ☐
746 Bokmakierie* ☐
757 European Starling ☐
759 Pied Starling** ☐
769 Redwinged Starling ☐
773 Cape Sugarbird** ☐
775 Malachite Sunbird ☐
777 Orangebreasted Sunbird** ☐
783 Lesser Double-collared Sunbird** ☐
796 Cape White-eye** ☐
801 House Sparrow ☐
803 Cape Sparrow* ☐
813 Cape Weaver** ☐
814 Masked Weaver ☐
824 Red Bishop ☐
827 Yellowrumped Widow ☐
846 Common Waxbill ☐
852 Quail Finch ☐
860 Pintailed Whydah ☐
872 Cape Canary ☐
877 Bully Canary ☐
878 Yellow Canary* ☐
879 **Whitethroated Canary*** ☐
881 Streakyheaded Canary ☐
885 Cape Bunting ☐
887 Larklike Bunting* ☐

Halfcollared Kingfishers

HELDERBERG NATURE RESERVE

approximately 139 species recorded to date

This 385 ha reserve controlled by the Somerset West municipality is situated on the slopes of the Helderberg, which provides an impressive backdrop. The lower section of the reserve is a botanical garden planted largely with various fynbos species from all over the region. The upper section, extending well up the slopes of the Helderberg, is covered with montane fynbos and is prone to the ravages of fire. When the area is burnt, as happened in March 1990, the vegetation takes quite some time to recover to the stage when birding can be considered to be back to normal. The reserve is hemmed in by alien pine plantations, not a welcome sight to many perhaps, but providing suitable habitat for a number of raptor species that would not otherwise be present. There is a remnant patch of indigenous forest in Disa Gorge just below the cliffs. Although there are roads up the mountain slopes, these are very steep and impassable when wet. Visitors are obliged to walk at all times. A number of trails have been laid out, one of them to the very base of the mountain cliffs and returning via Disa Gorge.

SPECIAL AND INTERESTING SPECIES

All five fynbos endemics are present. **Cape Sugarbirds** occur in abundance in the garden and are most conspicuous during the winter breeding season (April-August) but can be

ALSO RECORDED

Horus Swifts have attempted to breed in the road cuttings in the past but are not regularly present. Cape Eagle Owls are resident but only found with considerable difficulty. Black Harriers have bred in the past but have not done so in recent years. Peregrine Falcons occasionally hunt over the reserve. Both Redchested and Striped Flufftails are present, the latter being a most difficult species to find. Sharpbilled Honeyguides, not a species normally found in the region, have been observed many times over the last few years. European Golden Orioles, in spite of their bright plumage, are not readily seen but occasionally enter the alien pines during the summer months.

Rob Martin

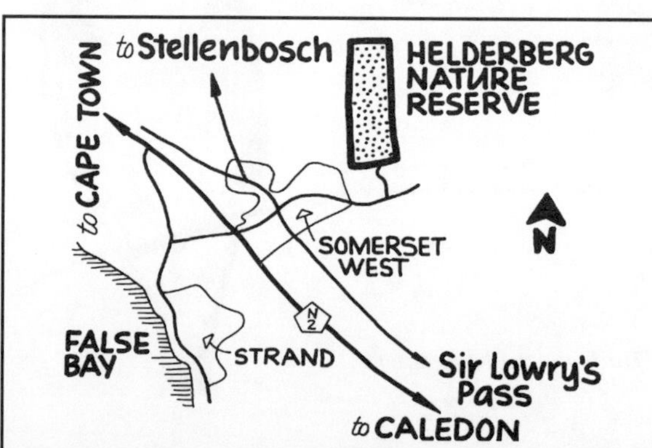

From Cape Town, on the national N2 road, take the first signpost marked "Somerset West". Follow the signs into the town and at the first set of traffic lights (at the Main Street/Lourensford Road intersection) turn left. Follow the reserve signs from there for 4,5 km to the entrance gate. The reserve is open daily and there is an entry charge at weekends.

seen all year. During the height of summer they tend to move into local gardens but many return to the reserve in the evenings. Follow one of the trails into the natural vegetation on the slopes. Here the four other endemics can be seen. **Victorin's Warblers**, most easily located in late winter and spring when they are particularly vocal, are found in the dense growth along the small streams but they also wander into the drier adjacent vegetation. A tape recorder is invaluable in enticing them closer but even then they seldom show themselves for more than a few seconds and many a birder has had to be satisfied with but a fleeting glance. **Orangebreasted Sunbird** is vocal and conspicuous when the various Ericas are in flower (mainly late autumn and winter) but can also be reasonably easily found at other times. **Cape Siskin**, usually encountered in small parties, is most frequently seen flying overhead with its characteristic undulating flight. They feed on grass seeds between the taller bushes and, strangely, also frequent the alien pines. **Protea Canary**, contrary to popular opinion, is a common and widespread bird in the mountains of the south-western Cape and is usually not difficult to find. In the reserve it is best searched for in the taller patches of fynbos along the small streams. For a canary, though, it is inconspicuous and unless the call is known a fair amount of luck is required. During the August to November breeding season the males perch prominently while in full song, a song that incorporates some fine mimicry. **Cape Rockjumpers**, more common nearer the summit of the Helderberg, can also be seen on the rocky slopes below the cliffs. Listen for their far-carrying piping call. **Black Sawwing Swallows** nest in the road banks and are largely absent during the wettest months. **Black Sparrowhawk** and **Forest Buzzard** are two inconspicuous species at the alien plantations.

100% OF SPECIES

055 Whitebreasted Cormorant ☐
058 Reed Cormorant ☐
060 Darter ☐
062 Grey Heron ☐
063 Blackheaded Heron ☐
071 Cattle Egret ☐
081 Hamerkop ☐
094 Hadeda Ibis ☐
102 Egyptian Goose ☐
103 South African Shelduck** ☐
104 Yellowbilled Duck ☐
105 African Black Duck ☐
106 Cape Teal ☐
108 Redbilled Teal ☐
112 Cape Shoveller* ☐
113 Southern Pochard ☐
116 Spurwinged Goose ☐
126a Yellowbilled Kite ☐
127 Blackshouldered Kite ☐
131 Black Eagle ☐
136 Booted Eagle ☐
140 Martial Eagle ☐
148 African Fish Eagle ☐
149 Steppe Buzzard ☐
150 **Forest Buzzard**** ☐

152 Jackal Buzzard** ☐
155 Redbreasted Sparrowhawk ☐
158 **Black Sparrowhawk** ☐
160 African Goshawk ☐
168 Black Harrier** ☐
169 Gymnogene ☐
171 Peregrine Falcon ☐
172 Lanner Falcon ☐
181 Rock Kestrel ☐
190 Greywing Francolin** ☐
195 Cape Francolin** ☐
200 Common Quail ☐
203 Helmeted Guineafowl ☐
213 Black Crake ☐
217 Redchested Flufftail ☐
221 Striped Flufftail ☐
226 Moorhen ☐
255 Crowned Plover ☐
258 Blacksmith Plover ☐
286 Ethiopian Snipe ☐
297 Spotted Dikkop ☐
298 Water Dikkop ☐
349 Rock Pigeon ☐
350 Rameron Pigeon ☐
352 Redeyed Dove ☐
354 Cape Turtle Dove ☐
356 Namaqua Dove ☐
377 Redchested Cuckoo ☐
378 Black Cuckoo ☐
385 Klaas's Cuckoo ☐
386 Diederik Cuckoo ☐
391 Burchell's Coucal* ☐
394 Wood Owl ☐
400 Cape Eagle Owl ☐
401 Spotted Eagle Owl ☐
405 Fierynecked Nightjar ☐
412 Black Swift ☐
415 Whiterumped Swift ☐
417 Little Swift ☐
418 Alpine Swift ☐
424 Speckled Mousebird ☐
425 Whitebacked Mousebird** ☐
426 Redfaced Mousebird ☐
428 Pied Kingfisher ☐
429 Giant Kingfisher ☐
431 Malachite Kingfisher ☐
451 Hoopoe ☐
474 Greater Honeyguide ☐
476 Lesser Honeyguide ☐
478 Sharpbilled Honeyguide ☐
480 Ground Woodpecker ☐
486 Cardinal Woodpecker ☐
488 Olive Woodpecker ☐
518 European Swallow ☐
520 Whitethroated Swallow ☐
523 Pearlbreasted Swallow ☐
526 Greater Striped Swallow* ☐
529 Rock Martin ☐
530 House Martin ☐
533 Brownthroated Martin ☐
536 **Black Sawwing Swallow** ☐
543 European Golden Oriole ☐
548 Pied Crow ☐
550 Whitenecked Raven ☐
566 Cape Bulbul** ☐
577 Olive Thrush ☐
581 Cape Rock Thrush** ☐
582 Sentinel Rock Thrush** ☐
589 Familiar Chat ☐
596 Stonechat ☐
601 Cape Robin ☐
611 **Cape Rockjumper**** ☐
614 Karoo Robin** ☐
638 African Sedge Warbler ☐
641 **Victorin's Warbler**** ☐
643 Willow Warbler ☐
645 Barthroated Apalis ☐
661 Grassbird** ☐
669 Greybacked Cisticola* ☐
677 Levaillant's Cisticola ☐
681 Neddicky ☐
686 Karoo Prinia** ☐
689 Spotted Flycatcher ☐
690 Dusky Flycatcher ☐
698 Fiscal Flycatcher** ☐
700 Cape Batis** ☐
710 Paradise Flycatcher ☐
713 Cape Wagtail ☐
717 Longbilled Pipit ☐
727 Orangethroated Longclaw** ☐
732 Fiscal Shrike ☐
736 Southern Boubou** ☐
746 Bokmakierie* ☐
757 European Starling ☐
760 Wattled Starling ☐
769 Redwinged Starling ☐
773 **Cape Sugarbird**** ☐
775 Malachite Sunbird ☐
777 **Orangebreasted Sunbird**** ☐
783 Lesser Double-collared Sunbird** ☐
796 Cape White-eye** ☐
801 House Sparrow ☐
803 Cape Sparrow* ☐
813 Cape Weaver** ☐
814 Masked Weaver ☐
824 Red Bishop ☐
827 Yellowrumped Widow ☐
846 Common Waxbill ☐
860 Pintailed Whydah ☐
872 Cape Canary ☐
874 **Cape Siskin**** ☐
877 Bully Canary ☐
880 **Protea Canary**** ☐
885 Cape Bunting ☐

STRANDFONTEIN SEWAGE WORKS

approximately 182 species recorded to date

Strandfontein sewage works is a large complex of settling ponds on the False Bay coastline between Muizenberg and Strandfontein, Cape Town. Administered by the Cape Town City Council, the ponds are no longer used to treat sewage, and do not support as many birds as they did when sewage was passed through the ponds. However, a large variety of birds still can be seen in the area during a short visit. The ponds are separated by well-grassed banks, but the adjacent dunes support strandveld vegetation that has been invaded in places by alien Acacias (Port Jackson and Rooikrantz). North of the complex are seasonally inundated fields that are earmarked for housing developments.

SPECIAL AND INTERESTING SPECIES

There are no birds especially restricted to Strandfontein sewage works, but the ponds support a large number of waterbirds, including marine species that enter the complex from False Bay to roost and breed. All three species of grebe are common on the ponds, as are most duck species found in the south-western Cape. **Maccoa Ducks** occur, but are much more scarce than when the ponds were used to treat sewage. Scan for them on the larger ponds or lurking near the reeds in sheltered spots. In summer, when pan levels drop, fairly large flocks of waders are present, and these can be readily

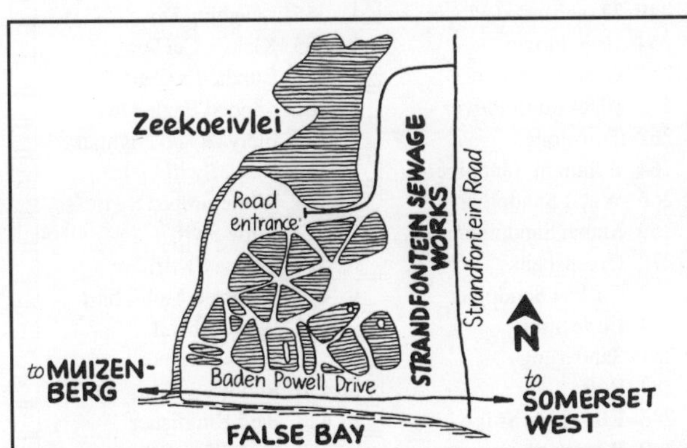

ALSO RECORDED

Frequent visits by birdwatchers to Strandfontein have resulted in several rare species being recorded. Most are waterbirds such as Whiterumped Sandpiper (first southern African record), American Purple Gallinule, European Oystercatcher and Pectoral Sandpiper. Rednecked Phalarope was a regular summer visitor until recently. Rare seabirds such as Redtailed Tropicbird and Pomarine Skua have also occurred, as have regional vagrants including Fulvous Duck, Bluecheeked Bee-eater and Yellow Wagtail.

Peter Ryan

The complex can be entered only with a permit, which is obtained from the Sewerage Branch, 19th Floor, Civic Centre, Cape Town. There is a small fee for daily or annual permits. Access by car is via Strandfontein Road, with the entrance gate at the end of the road along the eastern shore of Zeekoeivlei. The area can also be entered on foot from Baden Powell Drive, the coastal road east of Muizenberg.

examined from the car window. **Glossy Ibis** have become common during the last few years, particularly in the narrow canals and smaller ponds. **Greater Flamingos** remain throughout the year in small numbers. **Lesser Flamingos** occur sporadically, primarily in summer, but the flocks of up to 10 000 flamingos have disappeared with cessation of sewage treatment. **Whitewinged Terns** are abundant in summer and perform spectacular aerial displays prior to departing in autumn. Up to 20 000 **Cape Cormorants** roost on the roads and islands near the sea, and roosting **White Pelicans** can be approached to within metres by car. The adjacent dune scrub supports a variety of strandveld birds, and **Ethiopian Snipes** breed in the seasonally inundated fields.

73% OF SPECIES

- 006 Great Crested Grebe ☐
- 007 Blacknecked Grebe ☐
- 008 Dabchick ☐
- 049 **White Pelican** ☐
- 055 Whitebreasted Cormorant ☐
- 056 **Cape Cormorant*** ☐
- 058 Reed Cormorant ☐
- 060 Darter ☐
- 062 Grey Heron ☐
- 063 Blackheaded Heron ☐
- 065 Purple Heron ☐
- 067 Little Egret ☐
- 068 Yellowbilled Egret ☐
- 071 Cattle Egret ☐
- 076 Blackcrowned Night Heron ☐
- 091 Sacred Ibis ☐
- 093 **Glossy Ibis** ☐
- 096 **Greater Flamingo** ☐
- 097 **Lesser Flamingo** ☐
- 102 Egyptian Goose ☐
- 103 South African Shelduck** ☐
- 104 Yellowbilled Duck ☐
- 106 Cape Teal ☐
- 108 Redbilled Teal ☐
- 112 Cape Shoveller* ☐
- 113 Southern Pochard ☐
- 116 Spurwinged Goose ☐
- 117 **Maccoa Duck** ☐
- 127 Blackshouldered Kite ☐
- 149 Steppe Buzzard ☐
- 165 African Marsh Harrier ☐
- 195 Cape Francolin** ☐
- 203 Helmeted Guineafowl ☐
- 213 Black Crake ☐
- 223 Purple Gallinule ☐
- 226 Moorhen ☐
- 228 Redknobbed Coot ☐
- 244 African Black Oystercatcher** ☐
- 245 Ringed Plover ☐
- 246 Whitefronted Plover ☐
- 248 Kittlitz's Plover ☐
- 249 Threebanded Plover ☐
- 254 Grey Plover ☐
- 255 Crowned Plover ☐
- 258 Blacksmith Plover ☐
- 262 Turnstone ☐
- 264 Common Sandpiper ☐
- 266 Wood Sandpiper ☐
- 269 Marsh Sandpiper ☐
- 270 Greenshank ☐
- 272 Curlew Sandpiper ☐
- 274 Little Stint ☐
- 281 Sanderling ☐
- 284 Ruff ☐
- 286 **Ethiopian Snipe** ☐
- 290 Whimbrel ☐
- 294 Avocet ☐
- 295 Blackwinged Stilt ☐
- 297 Spotted Dikkop ☐
- 312 Kelp Gull ☐
- 315 Greyheaded Gull ☐
- 316 Hartlaub's Gull** ☐
- 322 Caspian Tern ☐
- 324 Swift Tern ☐
- 326 Sandwich Tern ☐
- 327 Common Tern ☐
- 339 **Whitewinged Tern** ☐
- 348 Feral Pigeon ☐
- 349 Rock Pigeon ☐
- 352 Redeyed Dove ☐
- 354 Cape Turtle Dove ☐
- 355 Laughing Dove ☐
- 385 Klaas's Cuckoo ☐
- 391 Burchell's Coucal* ☐
- 401 Spotted Eagle Owl ☐
- 405 Fierynecked Nightjar ☐
- 412 Black Swift ☐
- 415 Whiterumped Swift ☐
- 417 Little Swift ☐
- 418 Alpine Swift ☐
- 424 Speckled Mousebird ☐
- 425 Whitebacked Mousebird** ☐
- 426 Redfaced Mousebird ☐
- 428 Pied Kingfisher ☐
- 429 Giant Kingfisher ☐

431 Malachite Kingfisher ☐
451 Hoopoe ☐
465 Pied Barbet* ☐
507 Redcapped Lark ☐
518 European Swallow ☐
520 Whitethroated Swallow ☐
526 Greater Striped Swallow* ☐
529 Rock Martin ☐
533 Brownthroated Martin ☐
548 Pied Crow ☐
566 Cape Bulbul** ☐
596 Stonechat ☐
601 Cape Robin ☐
614 Karoo Robin** ☐
631 African Marsh Warbler ☐
635 Cape Reed Warbler ☐
638 African Sedge Warbler ☐
645 Barthroated Apalis ☐
651 Longbilled Crombec ☐
661 Grassbird** ☐
664 Fantailed Cisticola ☐
669 Greybacked Cisticola* ☐
677 Levaillant's Cisticola ☐
686 Karoo Prinia** ☐
713 Cape Wagtail ☐
716 Grassveld Pipit ☐
727 Orangethroated Longclaw** ☐
732 Fiscal Shrike ☐
736 Southern Boubou** ☐
746 Bokmakierie* ☐
757 European Starling ☐
769 Redwinged Starling ☐
775 Malachite Sunbird ☐
783 Lesser Double-collared Sunbird** ☐
796 Cape White-eye** ☐
801 House Sparrow ☐
803 Cape Sparrow* ☐
813 Cape Weaver** ☐
814 Masked Weaver ☐
827 Yellowrumped Widow ☐
846 Common Waxbill ☐
860 Pintailed Whydah ☐
872 Cape Canary ☐
877 Bully Canary ☐
878 Yellow Canary* ☐
885 Cape Bunting ☐

RONDEVLEI NATURE RESERVE

approximately 218 species recorded to date

Rondevlei Nature Reserve, administered by the Western Cape Regional Services Council, occupies an area of 217 ha, of which 50 ha is under water when the vlei is full. The land surrounding the vlei consists of Acacia thickets on the northern and eastern sides, while the southern sections consist of indigenous dune and marsh vegetation. The vlei's

The reserve is situated on the Cape flats next to Zeekoevlei about 24 km south of Cape Town. It is reached via the M5 from Cape Town or Prince George Drive (extension of the M5) from Muizenberg. Visitor access is from Fisherman's Walk off Victoria Road every

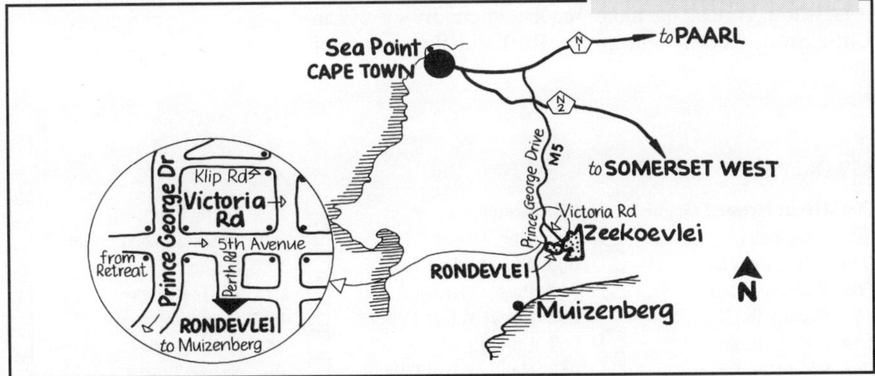

level fluctuates throughout the year, exposing a sandy shore during summer which attracts numerous migratory and local waders. Hippos, which occurred in the area 300 years ago, were returned to the vlei in 1981 and have successfully eradicated the dense mats of grass that were overgrowing the shoreline. There are a number of islands and large reedbeds in the vlei which are used for nesting and roosting purposes. Visitors are restricted to a 1 km waterside trail in the north-eastern portion of the reserve. Along this winding path there are two viewing towers with telescopes, five hides for quiet observation and photography, benches and a small informal picnic area (no fires). At the beginning of the trail, there is an environmental education centre consisting of a field museum depicting the flora and fauna of the area, a 50 seat lecture theatre and a resource centre. No overnight accommodation or refreshments are available.

day from 08h00 to17h00. A small entrance fee is payable at the gate. Educational groups of up to 50 are catered for on weekday mornings with slide shows and a guide. These must be booked well in advance.

SPECIAL AND INTERESTING SPECIES

Of the 218 species recorded in the reserve, 84 are resident. In the bush thickets, **Southern Boubou**, **Pied Barbet** and **Burchell's Coucal** are usually heard before they are seen. **Hottentot Teal**, **Painted Snipe** and **Great White Egret** are sometimes found in front of the hides. **Little Bittern** and **Black Crake** are residents that can regularly be seen in and around reedbeds, while **African Marsh Harriers**, which breed here, frequently hunt over these reeds. Rondevlei is perhaps the best locality in the area for watching **Purple Gallinules** feeding in the open at close range. **African Fish Eagle** is a regular visitor, often seen circling overhead, but seldom comes down to roost. Rondevlei also offers sanctuary to **White Pelican**, **Great Crested Grebe** and **Caspian Tern**. **Greater** and **Lesser Flamingos** can be seen when the water level is low. Among the more frequent migratory species are **Little Stint**, **Curlew Sandpiper**, **Ruff** and **Wood Sandpiper**.

ALSO RECORDED

Some rare species seen in the reserve have been Osprey, Peregrine Falcon, Dunlin, Pectoral Sandpiper, Bartailed Godwit and Blue-cheeked Bee-eater.

Gill Wheeler

68% OF SPECIES

006 **Great Crested Grebe** ☐
008 Dabchick ☐
049 **White Pelican** ☐
055 Whitebreasted Cormorant ☐
056 Cape Cormorant* ☐
058 Reed Cormorant ☐
060 Darter ☐
062 Grey Heron ☐
063 Blackheaded Heron ☐
065 Purple Heron ☐
066 **Great White Egret** ☐
067 Little Egret ☐
068 Yellowbilled Egret ☐
071 Cattle Egret ☐
076 Blackcrowned Night Heron ☐
078 **Little Bittern** ☐
081 Hamerkop ☐
084 Black Stork ☐
091 Sacred Ibis ☐

093 Glossy Ibis ☐
095 **African Spoonbill** ☐
096 **Greater Flamingo** ☐
097 **Lesser Flamingo** ☐
102 Egyptian Goose ☐
103 South African Shelduck** ☐
104 Yellowbilled Duck ☐
106 Cape Teal ☐
107 **Hottentot Teal** ☐
108 Redbilled Teal ☐
112 Cape Shoveller* ☐
113 Southern Pochard ☐
116 Spurwinged Goose ☐
117 Maccoa Duck ☐
126a Yellowbilled Kite ☐
127 Blackshouldered Kite ☐
148 African Fish Eagle ☐
149 Steppe Buzzard ☐
155 Redbreasted Sparrowhawk ☐
165 **African Marsh Harrier** ☐
172 Lanner Falcon ☐
181 Rock Kestrel ☐
190 Greywing Francolin** ☐
195 Cape Francolin** ☐
203 Helmeted Guineafowl ☐
210 African Rail ☐
213 **Black Crake** ☐
223 **Purple Gallinule** ☐
226 Moorhen ☐
228 Redknobbed Coot ☐
242 **Painted Snipe** ☐
245 Ringed Plover ☐
248 Kittlitz's Plover ☐
249 Threebanded Plover ☐
255 Crowned Plover ☐
258 Blacksmith Plover ☐
264 Common Sandpiper ☐
266 **Wood Sandpiper** ☐
269 Marsh Sandpiper ☐
270 Greenshank ☐
272 **Curlew Sandpiper** ☐
274 **Little Stint** ☐
284 **Ruff** ☐
286 Ethiopian Snipe ☐

294 Avocet ☐
295 Blackwinged Stilt ☐
297 Spotted Dikkop ☐
298 Water Dikkop ☐
312 Kelp Gull ☐
315 Greyheaded Gull ☐
316 Hartlaub's Gull** ☐
322 **Caspian Tern** ☐
324 Swift Tern ☐
327 Common Tern ☐
339 Whitewinged Tern ☐
348 Feral Pigeon ☐
349 Rock Pigeon ☐
350 Rameron Pigeon ☐
352 Redeyed Dove ☐
354 Cape Turtle Dove ☐
355 Laughing Dove ☐
385 Klaas's Cuckoo ☐
386 Diederik Cuckoo ☐
391 **Burchell's Coucal*** ☐
392 Barn Owl ☐
395 Marsh Owl ☐
401 Spotted Eagle Owl ☐
405 Fierynecked Nightjar ☐
412 Black Swift ☐
415 Whiterumped Swift ☐
417 Little Swift ☐
418 Alpine Swift ☐
424 Speckled Mousebird ☐
425 Whitebacked Mousebird** ☐
426 Redfaced Mousebird ☐
428 Pied Kingfisher ☐
429 Giant Kingfisher ☐
431 Malachite Kingfisher ☐
451 Hoopoe ☐
465 **Pied Barbet*** ☐
518 European Swallow ☐
520 Whitethroated Swallow ☐
526 Greater Striped Swallow* ☐
529 Rock Martin ☐
533 Brownthroated Martin ☐
548 Pied Crow ☐
566 Cape Bulbul** ☐
577 Olive Thrush ☐

601 Cape Robin ☐
614 Karoo Robin** ☐
631 African Marsh Warbler ☐
635 Cape Reed Warbler ☐
638 African Sedge Warbler ☐
645 Barthroated Apalis ☐
651 Longbilled Crombec ☐
661 Grassbird** ☐
664 Fantailed Cisticola ☐
669 Greybacked Cisticola* ☐
677 Levaillant's Cisticola ☐
686 Karoo Prinia** ☐
690 Dusky Flycatcher ☐
698 Fiscal Flycatcher** ☐
700 Cape Batis** ☐
710 Paradise Flycatcher ☐
713 Cape Wagtail ☐
716 Grassveld Pipit ☐
727 Orangethroated Longclaw** ☐
732 Fiscal Shrike ☐
736 **Southern Boubou**** ☐
746 Bokmakierie* ☐
757 European Starling ☐
769 Redwinged Starling ☐
773 Cape Sugarbird** ☐
775 Malachite Sunbird ☐
783 Lesser Double-collared Sunbird** ☐
796 Cape White-eye** ☐
801 House Sparrow ☐
803 Cape Sparrow* ☐
813 Cape Weaver** ☐
814 Masked Weaver ☐
824 Red Bishop ☐
827 Yellowrumped Widow ☐
846 Common Waxbill ☐
860 Pintailed Whydah ☐
872 Cape Canary ☐
877 Bully Canary ☐
878 Yellow Canary* ☐
879 Whitethroated Canary* ☐
885 Cape Bunting ☐
☐
☐

CAPE OF GOOD HOPE NATURE RESERVE

approximately 240 species recorded to date

The Cape of Good Hope Nature Reserve, administered by the Western Cape Regional Services Council, occupies the southern tip of the Cape Peninsula, some 40 km south of Cape Town. The major terrestrial habitat is mountain fynbos. Small patches of strandveld (broad-leaved coastal thicket) and infestations of alien plants (notably Rooikrantz *Acacia cyclops*) occur. A varied coastline supports rocky- and sandy-shore species. Cormorants nest on the spectacular cliffs at Cape Point and Cape Maclear. Take the Cape of Good Hope road for seawatching and the Olifantsbos road for shore and strandveld birds.

SPECIAL AND INTERESTING SPECIES

Winter is by far the best season for seawatching, but the Cape of Good Hope in summer can produce **Blackbrowed** and **Shy Albatrosses**, **Whitechinned Petrel** and **Sooty Shearwater**. Here and in False Bay, **Arctic Skuas** harry feeding terns (mainly Common) and the occasional **Sabine's Gull**. Sandy beaches support resident **Black Oystercatcher** and **Whitefronted Plover** with **Sanderling** and **Curlew Sandpiper** in summer. **Grey Plover**, **Turnstone**, **Greenshank** and **Whimbrel** frequent rocky shores. Mountain fynbos is generally poor for bush birds, but **Grassbird**, **Greybacked Cisticola** and **Yellowrumped Widow** are common. A small popula-

ALSO RECORDED

The reserve boasts a fairly impressive list of rarities and has tremendous potential for many more (notably seabirds and American vagrants). Rarities include Rockhopper and Macaroni Penguins, American (Snowy) Sheathbill, Baird's Sandpiper (second African record, first since 1863) and White-rumped Sandpiper. Light-mantled Sooty Albatross and Little Shearwater have been seen from the shore, plus more regular pelagic species such as Yellownosed Albatross, Softplumaged and Greatwinged Petrels and Pomarine Skua. Out-of-range species recorded are Temminck's Courser, Greyheaded Kingfisher, Scimitarbilled Woodhoopoe, Icterine Warbler and Redbacked and Lesser Grey Shrikes.

Mike Fraser

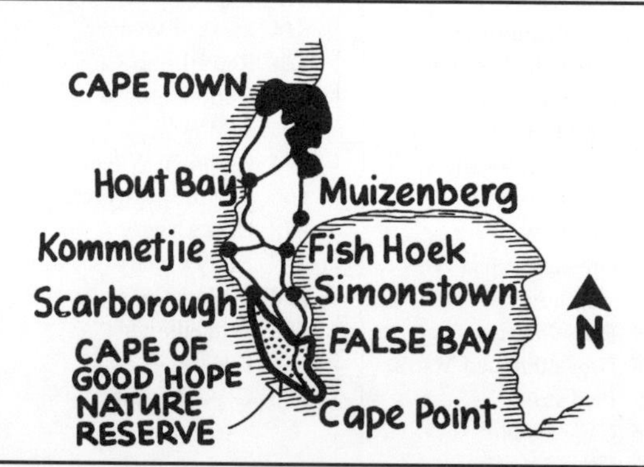

From Cape Town via Chapman's Peak scenic drive or via Simonstown. Open daily from one hour after sunrise until one hour before sunset. A fee is charged and maps are distributed at the entrance. Visitors may walk on existing tracks and access is available to all parts except those indicated on the map.

tion of **Cloud Cisticolas** may be found along Circular Drive. In old fynbos, flowering proteas and ericas (notably, in summer, the yellow pincushion *Leucospermum conocarpodendron* and *Erica gilva*) attract large numbers of nectarivores, particularly two fynbos specials, **Cape Sugarbird** and **Orangebreasted Sunbird**. These can be watched at close range from your car where their foodplants flower at the roadside. Young or recently burned veld holds **Crowned Plover**, **Plainbacked Pipit** and **Orangethroated Longclaw**. Rocky areas with sparse vegetation support **Ground Woodpecker** (most easily located by their high, ringing call), **Sentinel Rock Thrush** and **Cape Siskin** (also regularly seen around the viewing spots overlooking Cape Point). Strandveld supports more species and numbers of birds than fynbos and there is less seasonal variation in density. **Cape Robin**, **Southern Boubou** and **Karoo Prinia** are common in this habitat. The wild dagga *(Leonotis oxymifolia)* patch, which flowers November-April, at Olifantsbos may attract hundreds of **Malachite** and **Lesser Double-collared Sunbirds**.

34% OF SPECIES

001 Ostrich ☐
011 **Shy Albatross** ☐
012 **Blackbrowed Albatross** ☐
032 **Whitechinned Petrel** ☐
034 Cory's Shearwater ☐
037 **Sooty Shearwater** ☐
053 Cape Gannet* ☐
055 Whitebreasted Cormorant ☐
056 Cape Cormorant* ☐
057 Bank Cormorant** ☐
059 Crowned Cormorant* ☐
067 Little Egret ☐
076 Blackcrowned Night Heron ☐
102 Egyptian Goose ☐
127 Blackshouldered Kite ☐
131 Black Eagle ☐
148 African Fish Eagle ☐
149 Steppe Buzzard ☐
152 Jackal Buzzard** ☐
171 Peregrine Falcon ☐
181 Rock Kestrel ☐
190 Greywing Francolin** ☐
244 **African Black Oystercatcher**** ☐
245 Ringed Plover ☐
246 **Whitefronted Plover** ☐
254 **Grey Plover** ☐
255 **Crowned Plover** ☐
258 Blacksmith Plover ☐
262 **Turnstone** ☐
264 Common Sandpiper ☐
270 **Greenshank** ☐
272 **Curlew Sandpiper** ☐
281 **Sanderling** ☐
290 **Whimbrel** ☐
294 Avocet ☐
297 Spotted Dikkop ☐
307 **Arctic Skua** ☐
312 Kelp Gull ☐
316 Hartlaub's Gull** ☐
318 **Sabine's Gull** ☐
324 Swift Tern ☐
326 Sandwich Tern ☐
327 Common Tern ☐
349 Rock Pigeon ☐
354 Cape Turtle Dove ☐
412 Black Swift ☐
418 Alpine Swift ☐
424 Speckled Mousebird ☐
428 Pied Kingfisher ☐
465 Pied Barbet* ☐
480 **Ground Woodpecker**** ☐
529 Rock Martin ☐
550 Whitenecked Raven ☐
566 Cape Bulbul** ☐
581 Cape Rock Thrush** ☐
582 **Sentinel Rock Thrush**** ☐
589 Familiar Chat ☐
596 Stonechat ☐
601 **Cape Robin** ☐
661 **Grassbird**** ☐
666 **Cloud Cisticola** ☐
669 **Greybacked Cisticola*** ☐
677 Levaillant's Cisticola ☐
686 **Karoo Prinia**** ☐
698 Fiscal Flycatcher** ☐

713	Cape Wagtail	775	**Malachite Sunbird**	846	Common Waxbill
718	**Plainbacked Pipit**	777	**Orangebreasted Sunbird****	872	Cape Canary
727	**Orangethroated Longclaw****	783	**Lesser Double-collared Sunbird****	874	**Cape Siskin****
732	Fiscal Shrike	796	Cape White-eye**	877	Bully Canary
736	**Southern Boubou****	827	**Yellowrumped Widow**	885	Cape Bunting
746	Bokmakierie*				
773	**Cape Sugarbird****				

DE HOOP NATURE RESERVE

approximately 246 species recorded to date

This reserve, approximately 50 km east of Cape Agulhas and 25 km west of the Breede River mouth, was purchased in 1956 by the Cape Provincial Administration and placed under the control of the Directorate of Nature and Environmental Conservation. It is 18 000 ha in extent and comprises four distinct habitats. First there is the Potberg, an inselberg of Table Mountain sandstone, with its own endemic fynbos plant types which are acidic-soil dependent. Second there is approximately 12 500 ha of coastal fynbos, which overlies limestone and has its own distinctive plant populations dependent on alkaline soil. Third, the heart of the area is De Hoop Vlei, a landlocked brackish expanse of water running from north to south (15 km by 0,5 km), with sparse flanking sedge and reedbeds. And, last, there is coastline of alternating rocky outcrops and sandy beaches. The average annual rainfall of 450 mm falls mainly between March and October. The best months for birds are from August to December.

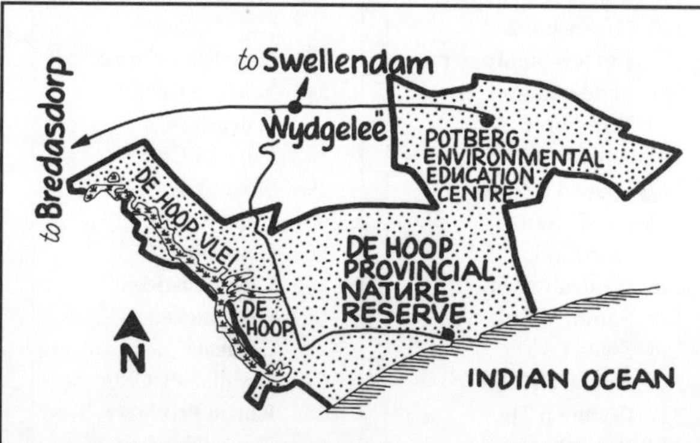

From Bredasdorp take the Swellendam road. At 7 km turn right to Wydgelee (Ouplaas), 29 km further turn right to De Hoop Reserve, and the entrance gate is 10 km further. From Swellendam, 1,4 km north of the Breede River bridge turn left off the N2 towards Malgas. At 22 km turn right to Wydgelee and 2 km beyond the village turn left to the reserve. Accommodation is available and advance booking is essential.

SPECIAL AND INTERESTING SPECIES

The water level of the vlei varies greatly from year to year. Under optimal conditions one of the highlights is the vast flocks of waterfowl, up to several thousand strong, including **Redknobbed Coot**, **Cape Shoveller** and **Southern Pochard**. **Greater Flamingos** are invariably noted in large flocks. Indeed, it is here that the first mass breeding of this species was recorded in South Africa in the early 1960s: there were approximately 800 nests. The vlei is well known for the numbers of grebes that occur there, all three species being well represented in most years. On the vlei shores **Water Dikkop** are frequent as are **Yellowbilled** and **Little Egrets**. Several pairs of resident **African Fish Eagles** regularly breed here. In the flanking riverine bush **Fierynecked Nightjar**, **Southern Tchagra**, **Southern Boubou**, **Olive Woodpecker** and **Rameron Pigeon** are common. In the coastal fynbos good populations of **Stanley's Bustard** are constantly present. Here too **Wattled Starling**, **Blue Crane**, **Longbilled** and **Thickbilled Larks**, **Capped Wheatear** and **Namaqua Sandgrouse** abound. **Black Harrier** is resident. Several breeding pairs of **Secretarybird** still occur in this area. Along the coastline a notable special is **Damara Tern** which also nests here, and there are healthy populations of **African Black Oystercatcher**. The Potberg is well known for its nesting colony of **Cape Vultures**, constituting the only extant colony in the southern and western Cape.

ALSO RECORDED

A pair of Palmnut Vultures have recently been spotted. Blackrumped Buttonquail may be flushed in the mountain and coastal fynbos. A notable recent arrival to establish itself is Black Sparrowhawk. Greyheaded Gulls frequent the vlei on and off, and De Hoop is probably the most eastern limit for Hartlaub's Gull. Occasional unusual visitors are Corncrake, African Jacana and Rufouscheeked Nightjar.

C. J. Uys

61% OF SPECIES

- 001 Ostrich ☐
- 006 **Great Crested Grebe** ☐
- 007 **Blacknecked Grebe** ☐
- 008 **Dabchick** ☐
- 055 Whitebreasted Cormorant ☐
- 058 Reed Cormorant ☐
- 060 Darter ☐
- 062 Grey Heron ☐
- 063 Blackheaded Heron ☐
- 065 Purple Heron ☐
- 067 **Little Egret** ☐
- 068 **Yellowbilled Egret** ☐
- 071 Cattle Egret ☐
- 076 Blackcrowned Night Heron ☐
- 091 Sacred Ibis ☐
- 095 African Spoonbill ☐
- 096 **Greater Flamingo** ☐
- 097 Lesser Flamingo ☐
- 102 Egyptian Goose ☐
- 103 South African Shelduck** ☐
- 104 Yellowbilled Duck ☐
- 106 Cape Teal ☐
- 108 Redbilled Teal ☐
- 112 **Cape Shoveller*** ☐
- 113 **Southern Pochard** ☐
- 116 Spurwinged Goose ☐
- 117 Maccoa Duck ☐
- 118 **Secretarybird** ☐
- 122 **Cape Vulture**** ☐
- 127 Blackshouldered Kite ☐
- 131 Black Eagle ☐
- 148 **African Fish Eagle** ☐
- 149 Steppe Buzzard ☐
- 152 Jackal Buzzard** ☐
- 165 African Marsh Harrier ☐
- 168 **Black Harrier**** ☐
- 172 Lanner Falcon ☐
- 181 Rock Kestrel ☐
- 190 Greywing Francolin** ☐
- 195 Cape Francolin** ☐
- 200 Common Quail ☐
- 203 Helmeted Guineafowl ☐
- 208 **Blue Crane**** ☐
- 226 Moorhen ☐
- 228 **Redknobbed Coot** ☐
- 231 **Stanley's Bustard** ☐
- 239 Black Korhaan** ☐
- 244 **African Black Oystercatcher**** ☐
- 245 Ringed Plover ☐

South-Western Cape

246 Whitefronted Plover
247 Chestnutbanded Plover
248 Kittlitz's Plover
249 Threebanded Plover
255 Crowned Plover
258 Blacksmith Plover
266 Wood Sandpiper
270 Greenshank
272 Curlew Sandpiper
274 Little Stint
284 Ruff
290 Whimbrel
294 Avocet
295 Blackwinged Stilt
297 Spotted Dikkop
298 **Water Dikkop**
312 Kelp Gull
315 Greyheaded Gull
322 Caspian Tern
324 Swift Tern
327 Common Tern
334 **Damara Tern***
338 Whiskered Tern
339 Whitewinged Tern
344 **Namaqua Sandgrouse***
349 Rock Pigeon
350 **Rameron Pigeon**
352 Redeyed Dove
354 Cape Turtle Dove
355 Laughing Dove
356 Namaqua Dove
385 Klaas's Cuckoo
392 Barn Owl
401 Spotted Eagle Owl
405 **Fierynecked Nightjar**
412 Black Swift
415 Whiterumped Swift
417 Little Swift
418 Alpine Swift
424 Speckled Mousebird
425 Whitebacked Mousebird**
428 Pied Kingfisher
429 Giant Kingfisher
451 Hoopoe
465 Pied Barbet*
486 Cardinal Woodpecker
488 **Olive Woodpecker**
495 Clapper Lark**
500 **Longbilled Lark**
507 Redcapped Lark
512 **Thickbilled Lark****
518 European Swallow
520 Whitethroated Swallow
523 Pearlbreasted Swallow
526 Greater Striped Swallow*
529 Rock Martin
533 Brownthroated Martin
541 Forktailed Drongo
547 Black Crow
550 Whitenecked Raven
566 Cape Bulbul**
572 Sombre Bulbul
587 **Capped Wheatear**
589 Familiar Chat
601 Cape Robin
614 Karoo Robin**
635 Cape Reed Warbler
645 Barthroated Apalis
651 Longbilled Crombec
661 Grassbird**
669 Greybacked Cisticola*
677 Levaillant's Cisticola
686 Karoo Prinia**
698 Fiscal Flycatcher**
700 Cape Batis**
713 Cape Wagtail
716 Grassveld Pipit
727 Orangethroated Longclaw**
732 Fiscal Shrike
736 **Southern Boubou****
742 **Southern Tchagra****
746 Bokmakierie*
757 European Starling
759 Pied Starling**
760 **Wattled Starling**
769 Redwinged Starling
773 Cape Sugarbird**
775 Malachite Sunbird
777 Orangebreasted Sunbird**
783 Lesser Double-collared Sunbird**
796 Cape White-eye**
801 House Sparrow
803 Cape Sparrow*
813 Cape Weaver**
824 Red Bishop
827 Yellowrumped Widow
846 Common Waxbill
877 Bully Canary
878 Yellow Canary*
879 Whitethroated Canary*
885 Cape Bunting

SALMONSDAM NATURE RESERVE

approximately 130 species recorded to date

This small reserve (846 ha) established in 1962 was originally owned by the Caledon Divisional Council but since 1982 has been under the control of the Directorate of Nature and Environmental Conservation. The mean annual rainfall is 550 mm and the highest point in the reserve is 638 m above sea level. The dominant vegetation is fynbos, there are a few small tracts of indigenous forest along the two streams and there is a marsh in the low-lying area. The name of the reserve is misleading as there are no dams worth mentioning. Vehicles may only be used on the road between the entrance gate and the camp but there is a good network of hiking trails, mostly in very hilly terrain – consult the information brochure available at the unmanned entrance kiosk.

SPECIAL AND INTERESTING SPECIES

The reserve is a good place to see **Cape Rockjumper**. Follow the steep track climbing out of the camp until this joins another track. Turn right, cross the small stream and then turn left onto a disused track which enters a shallow valley. The rocky slopes on either side of the valley provide ideal conditions for rockjumpers – listen for their distinctive and far-carrying piping call. These birds, almost invariably found in small parties, show little tendency to wander and remain attached to the same hillside throughout the year, so one

ALSO RECORDED

Black Sparrowhawks utilise the poplar stands outside the reserve and can occasionally be seen overhead. Cape Eagle Owls occur along the stream valleys but they are not easily flushed and few will be lucky enough to see them. Southern Tchagras are present in small numbers but are much more easily seen elsewhere.

Rob Martin

From Stanford take the tarred road (R326) which is clearly marked "Salmonsdam"; 4 km from the village turn right onto a gravel road and after 7 km turn left at the small signpost onto a narrower gravel road and follow this for 5 km to the entrance gate. The reserve is open daily and at present there is no entry charge. Basic accommodation in the form of huts and cottages is available and there is a caravan and camping site. All bookings must be made, and paid for, in advance.

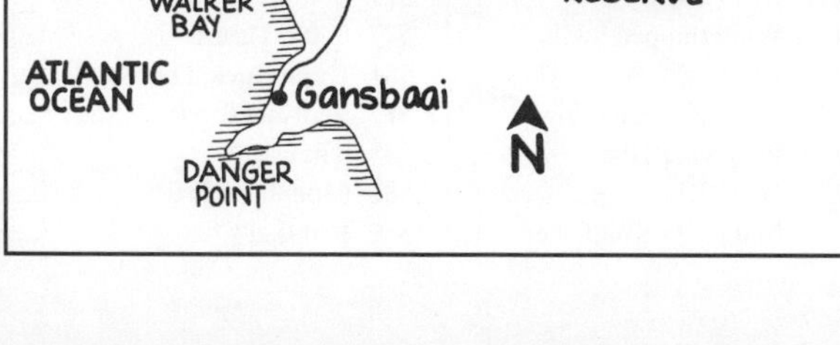

stands a good chance of finding them. **Sentinel Rock Thrushes** are also regularly present but, as they are less vocal than the rockjumpers, one can easily overlook them. **Cape Rock Thrushes** also occur on these hills and any rock thrush seen should be carefully examined. **Cape Sugarbirds** and **Orangebreasted Sunbirds** are most likely to be seen in the taller fynbos on the lower slopes but both are common and widespread in the reserve. **Cape Siskin** is a wanderer and is likely to be seen anywhere in the reserve but the stream valleys afford one the best chance. The marsh supports a small population of **Redchested Flufftails** – with a tape one can easily induce them to call but it is not so easy to entice them into view. **Black Harriers** are most likely to be seen in spring and early summer.

100% OF SPECIES

058 Reed Cormorant ☐
062 Grey Heron ☐
063 Blackheaded Heron ☐
065 Purple Heron ☐
071 Cattle Egret ☐
081 Hamerkop ☐
102 Egyptian Goose ☐
104 Yellowbilled Duck ☐
108 Redbilled Teal ☐
116 Spurwinged Goose ☐
118 Secretarybird ☐
122 Cape Vulture** ☐
127 Blackshouldered Kite ☐
131 Black Eagle ☐
140 Martial Eagle ☐
148 African Fish Eagle ☐
149 Steppe Buzzard ☐
152 Jackal Buzzard** ☐
155 Redbreasted Sparrowhawk ☐
158 Black Sparrowhawk ☐
160 African Goshawk ☐
161 Gabar Goshawk ☐
165 African Marsh Harrier ☐
168 **Black Harrier**** ☐
169 Gymnogene ☐
171 Peregrine Falcon ☐
172 Lanner Falcon ☐
181 Rock Kestrel ☐
183 Lesser Kestrel ☐
190 Greywing Francolin** ☐
195 Cape Francolin** ☐
203 Helmeted Guineafowl ☐
208 Blue Crane** ☐
213 Black Crake ☐
217 **Redchested Flufftail** ☐
255 Crowned Plover ☐
258 Blacksmith Plover ☐
286 Ethiopian Snipe ☐
297 Spotted Dikkop ☐
349 Rock Pigeon ☐
350 Rameron Pigeon ☐
352 Redeyed Dove ☐
354 Cape Turtle Dove ☐
355 Laughing Dove ☐
356 Namaqua Dove ☐
377 Redchested Cuckoo ☐
385 Klaas's Cuckoo ☐
391 Burchell's Coucal* ☐
392 Barn Owl ☐
400 Cape Eagle Owl ☐
401 Spotted Eagle Owl ☐
405 Fierynecked Nightjar ☐
412 Black Swift ☐
415 Whiterumped Swift ☐
418 Alpine Swift ☐
424 Speckled Mousebird ☐
428 Pied Kingfisher ☐
429 Giant Kingfisher ☐
431 Malachite Kingfisher ☐
435 Brownhooded Kingfisher ☐
446 European Roller ☐
451 Hoopoe ☐
474 Greater Honeyguide ☐
480 Ground Woodpecker** ☐
486 Cardinal Woodpecker ☐
488 Olive Woodpecker ☐
507 Redcapped Lark ☐
512 Thickbilled Lark** ☐
518 European Swallow ☐
523 Pearlbreasted Swallow ☐
526 Greater Striped Swallow* ☐
529 Rock Martin ☐
536 Black Sawwing Swallow ☐
541 Forktailed Drongo ☐
547 Black Crow ☐
550 Whitenecked Raven ☐
566 Cape Bulbul** ☐
572 Sombre Bulbul ☐
577 Olive Thrush ☐
581 **Cape Rock Thrush**** ☐
582 **Sentinel Rock Thrush**** ☐
586 Mountain Chat* ☐
589 Familiar Chat ☐

596 Stonechat ☐
601 Cape Robin ☐
611 **Cape Rockjumper**** ☐
614 Karoo Robin** ☐
638 African Sedge Warbler ☐
645 Barthroated Apalis ☐
651 Longbilled Crombec ☐
661 Grassbird** ☐
664 Fantailed Cisticola ☐
669 Greybacked Cisticola* ☐
677 Levaillant's Cisticola ☐
681 Neddicky ☐
686 Karoo Prinia** ☐
689 Spotted Flycatcher ☐
690 Dusky Flycatcher ☐
698 Fiscal Flycatcher** ☐
700 Cape Batis** ☐
710 Paradise Flycatcher ☐
713 Cape Wagtail ☐
716 Grassveld Pipit ☐
718 Plainbacked Pipit ☐
727 Orangethroated Longclaw** ☐
732 Fiscal Shrike ☐
736 Southern Boubou** ☐
742 Southern Tchagra** ☐
746 Bokmakierie* ☐
757 European Starling ☐
759 Pied Starling** ☐
760 Wattled Starling ☐
769 Redwinged Starling ☐
773 **Cape Sugarbird**** ☐
775 Malachite Sunbird ☐
777 **Orangebreasted Sunbird**** ☐
783 Lesser Double-collared Sunbird** ☐
796 Cape White-eye** ☐
801 House Sparrow ☐
803 Cape Sparrow* ☐
813 Cape Weaver** ☐
824 Red Bishop ☐
827 Yellowrumped Widow ☐
846 Common Waxbill ☐
860 Pintailed Whydah ☐
872 Cape Canary ☐
874 **Cape Siskin**** ☐
877 Bully Canary ☐
879 Whitethroated Canary* ☐
885 Cape Bunting ☐
☐
☐
☐
☐
☐

Black Sparrowhawk

OTHER BIRDING SPOTS WORTH VISITING

Bird Island, Lamberts Bay
This island is open to the public throughout the year. There are large Cape Gannet and cormorant colonies and small numbers of Jackass Penguins breed on the island. While at Lamberts Bay, visit Jakkalsriviervlei immediately north of the village.

Verlorenvlei
This is a large open body of water immediately south of Elands Bay. It can be viewed from the road on both sides and there are bridges across the vlei at Elands Bay and Redelinghuys. The latter bridge is well worth a stop for rails and crakes.

Rocher Pan Nature Reserve
This reserve on the west coast between Dwarskersbos and Elands Bay is controlled by the Cape Chief Directorate of Nature and Environmental Conservation. It contains a series of ephemeral saline pans abutting arid coastal strandveld where a good variety of waterbirds can be seen.

Paarl Mountain Reserve
This reserve, bordering the town of Paarl and controlled by the Paarl Municipality, is a good locality for fynbos birds, with easy access. Open daily, with a weekend admission fee charged per car.

Swellendam State Forest
This forest is controlled by the Cape Chief Directorate of Environmental Conservation, and is open to the public daily. It is situated immediately above Swellendam on the southern slopes of the Langeberg. There are well laid out paths and easy access to indigenous forest patches.

Kirstenbosch Botanical Gardens
Situated between the suburbs of Newlands and Bishopscourt in Cape Town. Good diversity of fynbos and forest birds, and probably the best place in the south-western Cape to see Knysna Warbler.

Kommetjie
This section of the Cape Peninsula contains rocky and sandy shorelines. Seabird-watching is excellent from below the lighthouse in winter, especially early in the morning with a westerly wind. There is a tern roost used in most months, with many Antarctic Terns at the roost during winter.

USEFUL TELEPHONE NUMBERS

Anysberg: Officer in charge
(02372) 1913

Gamkapoort Research Office
(04436) 905

Geelbek (Langebaan Lagoon)
(02287) 2-2798

Grootvadersbos: Officer in charge
(02962) 1812

Lower Berg River
(Commercial Saltpans) Works Manager
(02288) 3-1133

National Parks Board (Cape Town)
(021) 419-5365

National Parks Board (George)
(0441) 74-6924/5

Port Owen Marina
(Lower Berg River)
(02288) 3-1144

Private Pelagic Organiser (a/h)
(021) 75-7318

Rondevlei Nature Sanctuary (mornings)
(021) 706-2404

Salmonsdam Nature Reserve
(0283) 30-0789

Vrolijkheid Nature Reserve
(02353) 621

West Coast National Park
(02287) 2-2144

Checklists

001 Ostrich ☐
002 King Penguin ☐
003 Jackass Penguin* ☐
004 Rockhopper Penguin ☐
005 Macaroni Penguin ☐
006 Great Crested Grebe ☐
007 Blacknecked Grebe ☐
008 Dabchick ☐
009 Royal Albatross ☐
010 Wandering Albatross ☐
011 Shy Albatross ☐
012 Blackbrowed Albatross ☐
013 Greyheaded Albatross ☐
014 Yellownosed Albatross ☐
015 Darkmantled Sooty Albatross ☐
016 Lightmantled Sooty Albatross ☐
017 Southern Giant Petrel ☐
018 Northern Giant Petrel ☐
019 Antarctic Fulmar ☐
020 Antarctic Petrel ☐
021 Pintado Petrel ☐
022 Bulwer's Petrel ☐
023 Greatwinged Petrel ☐
024 Softplumaged Petrel ☐
025 Whiteheaded Petrel ☐
026 Atlantic Petrel ☐
027 Kerguelen Petrel ☐
028 Blue Petrel ☐
029 Broadbilled Prion ☐
030 Slenderbilled Prion ☐
031 Fairy Prion ☐
032 Whitechinned Petrel ☐
033 Grey Shearwater ☐
034 Cory's Shearwater ☐
035 Great Shearwater ☐
036 Fleshfooted Shearwater ☐
037 Sooty Shearwater ☐
038 Manx Shearwater ☐
039 Little Shearwater ☐
040 Audubon's Shearwater ☐
041 Wedgetailed Shearwater ☐
042 European Storm Petrel ☐
043 Leach's Storm Petrel ☐
044 Wilson's Storm Petrel ☐
045 Whitebellied Storm Petrel ☐
046 Blackbellied Storm Petrel ☐
047 Redtailed Tropicbird ☐
048 Whitetailed Tropicbird ☐
049 White Pelican ☐
050 Pinkbacked Pelican ☐
051 Masked Booby ☐
052 Brown Booby ☐
053 Cape Gannet* ☐
054 Australian Gannet ☐
055 Whitebreasted Cormorant ☐
056 Cape Cormorant* ☐
057 Bank Cormorant** ☐
058 Reed Cormorant ☐
059 Crowned Cormorant* ☐
060 Darter ☐
061 Greater Frigatebird ☐
062 Grey Heron ☐
063 Blackheaded Heron ☐
064 Goliath Heron ☐
065 Purple Heron ☐
066 Great White Egret ☐
067 Little Egret ☐
068 Yellowbilled Egret ☐
069 Black Egret ☐
070 Slaty Egret* ☐
071 Cattle Egret ☐
072 Squacco Heron ☐
073 Madagascar Squacco Heron ☐
074 Greenbacked Heron ☐
075 Rufousbellied Heron ☐
076 Blackcrowned Night Heron ☐
077 Whitebacked Night Heron ☐
078 Little Bittern ☐
079 Dwarf Bittern ☐
080 Bittern ☐
081 Hamerkop ☐
082 Shoebill ☐
083 White Stork ☐
084 Black Stork ☐
085 Abdim's Stork ☐
086 Woollynecked Stork ☐
087 Openbilled Stork ☐
088 Saddlebilled Stork ☐
089 Marabou Stork ☐
090 Yellowbilled Stork ☐
091 Sacred Ibis ☐
092 Bald Ibis** ☐
093 Glossy Ibis ☐
094 Hadeda Ibis ☐
095 African Spoonbill ☐
096 Greater Flamingo ☐
097 Lesser Flamingo ☐
098 Mute Swan ☐
099 Whitefaced Duck ☐
100 Fulvous Duck ☐
101 Whitebacked Duck ☐
102 Egyptian Goose ☐
103 South African Shelduck** ☐
104 Yellowbilled Duck ☐
105 African Black Duck ☐
106 Cape Teal ☐
107 Hottentot Teal ☐
108 Redbilled Teal ☐
109 Pintail ☐
110 Garganey ☐
111 European Shoveller ☐
112 Cape Shoveller* ☐
113 Southern Pochard ☐
114 Pygmy Goose ☐
115 Knobbilled Duck ☐
116 Spurwinged Goose ☐
117 Maccoa Duck ☐
118 Secretarybird ☐
119 Bearded Vulture ☐
120 Egyptian Vulture ☐
121 Hooded Vulture ☐
122 Cape Vulture** ☐
123 Whitebacked Vulture ☐
124 Lappetfaced Vulture ☐
125 Whiteheaded Vulture ☐
126 Black Kite ☐
126a Yellowbilled Kite ☐
127 Blackshouldered Kite ☐
128 Cuckoo Hawk ☐
129 Bat Hawk ☐

130 Honey Buzzard ☐
131 Black Eagle ☐
132 Tawny Eagle ☐
133 Steppe Eagle ☐
134 Lesser Spotted Eagle ☐
135 Wahlberg's Eagle ☐
136 Booted Eagle ☐
137 African Hawk Eagle ☐
138 Ayres' Eagle ☐
139 Longcrested Eagle ☐
140 Martial Eagle ☐
141 Crowned Eagle ☐
142 Brown Snake Eagle ☐
143 Blackbreasted Snake Eagle ☐
144 Southern Banded Snake Eagle ☐
145 Western Banded Snake Eagle ☐
146 Bateleur ☐
147 Palmnut Vulture ☐
148 African Fish Eagle ☐
149 Steppe Buzzard ☐
150 Forest Buzzard** ☐
151 Longlegged Buzzard ☐
152 Jackal Buzzard** ☐
153 Augur Buzzard ☐
154 Lizard Buzzard ☐
155 Redbreasted Sparrowhawk ☐
156 Ovambo Sparrowhawk ☐
157 Little Sparrowhawk ☐
158 Black Sparrowhawk ☐
159 Little Banded Goshawk ☐
160 African Goshawk ☐
161 Gabar Goshawk ☐
162 Pale Chanting Goshawk* ☐
163 Dark Chanting Goshawk ☐
164 European Marsh Harrier ☐
165 African Marsh Harrier ☐
166 Montagu's Harrier ☐
167 Pallid Harrier ☐
168 Black Harrier** ☐
169 Gymnogene ☐
170 Osprey ☐
171 Peregrine Falcon ☐
172 Lanner Falcon ☐
173 Hobby Falcon ☐
174 African Hobby Falcon ☐
175 Sooty Falcon ☐
176 Taita Falcon ☐
177 Eleonora's Falcon ☐
178 Rednecked Falcon ☐
179 Western Redfooted Kestrel ☐
180 Eastern Redfooted Kestrel ☐
181 Rock Kestrel ☐
182 Greater Kestrel ☐
183 Lesser Kestrel ☐
184 Grey Kestrel ☐
185 Dickinson's Kestrel ☐
186 Pygmy Falcon ☐
187 Chukar Partridge ☐
188 Coqui Francolin ☐
189 Crested Francolin ☐
190 Greywing Francolin** ☐
191 Shelley's Francolin ☐
192 Redwing Francolin ☐
193 Orange River Francolin* ☐
194 Redbilled Francolin* ☐
195 Cape Francolin** ☐
196 Natal Francolin* ☐
197 Hartlaub's Francolin* ☐
198 Rednecked Francolin ☐
199 Swainson's Francolin* ☐
200 Common Quail ☐
201 Harlequin Quail ☐
202 Blue Quail ☐
203 Helmeted Guineafowl ☐
204 Crested Guineafowl ☐
205 Kurrichane Buttonquail ☐
206 Blackrumped Button-quail ☐
207 Wattled Crane ☐
208 Blue Crane** ☐
209 Crowned Crane ☐
210 African Rail ☐
211 Corncrake ☐
212 African Crake ☐
213 Black Crake ☐
214 Spotted Crake ☐
215 Baillon's Crake ☐
216 Striped Crake ☐
217 Redchested Flufftail ☐
218 Buffspotted Flufftail ☐
219 Streakybreasted Flufftail ☐
220 Longtoed Flufftail ☐
221 Striped Flufftail ☐
222 Whitewinged Flufftail ☐
223 Purple Gallinule ☐
224 Lesser Gallinule ☐
225 American Purple Gallinule ☐
226 Moorhen ☐
227 Lesser Moorhen ☐
228 Redknobbed Coot ☐
229 African Finfoot ☐
230 Kori Bustard ☐
231 Stanley's Bustard ☐
232 Ludwig's Bustard* ☐
233 Whitebellied Korhaan ☐
234 Blue Korhaan** ☐
235 Karoo Korhaan** ☐
236 Rüppell's Korhaan* ☐
237 Redcrested Korhaan* ☐
238 Blackbellied Korhaan ☐
239 Black Korhaan** ☐
239a Whitequilled Korhaan** ☐
240 African Jacana ☐
241 Lesser Jacana ☐
242 Painted Snipe ☐
243 European Oystercatcher ☐
244 African Black Oystercatcher** ☐
245 Ringed Plover ☐
246 Whitefronted Plover ☐
247 Chestnutbanded Plover ☐
248 Kittlitz's Plover ☐
249 Threebanded Plover ☐
250 Mongolian Plover ☐
251 Sand Plover ☐
252 Caspian Plover ☐
253 Lesser Golden Plover ☐

254 Grey Plover ☐
255 Crowned Plover ☐
256 Lesser Blackwinged Plover ☐
257 Blackwinged Plover ☐
258 Blacksmith Plover ☐
259 Whitecrowned Plover ☐
260 Wattled Plover ☐
261 Longtoed Plover ☐
262 Turnstone ☐
263 Terek Sandpiper ☐
264 Common Sandpiper ☐
265 Green Sandpiper ☐
266 Wood Sandpiper ☐
267 Spotted Redshank ☐
268 Redshank ☐
269 Marsh Sandpiper ☐
270 Greenshank ☐
271 Knot ☐
272 Curlew Sandpiper ☐
273 Dunlin ☐
274 Little Stint ☐
275 Longtoed Stint ☐
276 Rednecked Stint ☐
277 Whiterumped Sandpiper ☐
278 Baird's Sandpiper ☐
279 Pectoral Sandpiper ☐
280 Temminck's Stint ☐
281 Sanderling ☐
282 Buffbreasted Sandpiper ☐
283 Broadbilled Sandpiper ☐
284 Ruff ☐
285 Great Snipe ☐
286 Ethiopian Snipe ☐
287 Blacktailed Godwit ☐
288 Bartailed Godwit ☐
289 Curlew ☐
290 Whimbrel ☐
291 Grey Phalarope ☐
292 Rednecked Phalarope ☐
293 Wilson's Phalarope ☐
294 Avocet ☐
295 Blackwinged Stilt ☐
296 Crab Plover ☐
297 Spotted Dikkop ☐
298 Water Dikkop ☐
299 Burchell's Courser* ☐
300 Temminck's Courser ☐
301 Doublebanded Courser ☐
302 Threebanded Courser ☐
303 Bronzewinged Courser ☐
304 Redwinged Pratincole ☐
305 Blackwinged Pratincole ☐
306 Rock Pratincole ☐
307 Arctic Skua ☐
308 Longtailed Skua ☐
309 Pomarine Skua ☐
310 Subantarctic Skua ☐
311 South Polar Skua ☐
312 Kelp Gull ☐
313 Lesser Blackbacked Gull ☐
314 Herring Gull ☐
315 Greyheaded Gull ☐
316 Hartlaub's Gull** ☐
317 Franklin's Gull ☐
318 Sabine's Gull ☐
319 Blackheaded Gull ☐
320 Blacklegged Kittiwake ☐
321 Gullbilled Tern ☐
322 Caspian Tern ☐
323 Royal Tern ☐
324 Swift Tern ☐
325 Lesser Crested Tern ☐
326 Sandwich Tern ☐
327 Common Tern ☐
328 Arctic Tern ☐
329 Antarctic Tern ☐
330 Roseate Tern ☐
331 Blacknaped Tern ☐
332 Sooty Tern ☐
333 Bridled Tern ☐
334 Damara Tern* ☐
335 Little Tern ☐
336 Whitecheeked Tern ☐
337 Black Tern ☐
338 Whiskered Tern ☐
339 Whitewinged Tern ☐
340 Common Noddy ☐
341 Lesser Noddy ☐
342 Fairy Tern ☐
343 African Skimmer ☐
344 Namaqua Sandgrouse* ☐
345 Burchell's Sandgrouse* ☐
346 Yellowthroated Sandgrouse ☐
347 Doublebanded Sandgrouse* ☐
348 Feral Pigeon ☐
349 Rock Pigeon ☐
350 Rameron Pigeon ☐
351 Delegorgue's Pigeon ☐
352 Redeyed Dove ☐
353 Mourning Dove ☐
354 Cape Turtle Dove ☐
355 Laughing Dove ☐
356 Namaqua Dove ☐
357 Bluespotted Dove ☐
358 Greenspotted Dove ☐
359 Tambourine Dove ☐
360 Cinnamon Dove ☐
361 Green Pigeon ☐
362 Cape Parrot ☐
363 Brownheaded Parrot ☐
364 Meyer's Parrot ☐
365 Rüppell's Parrot* ☐
366 Roseringed Parakeet ☐
367 Rosyfaced Lovebird* ☐
368 Lilian's Lovebird ☐
369 Bluecheeked Lovebird* ☐
370 Knysna Lourie** ☐
370a Livingstone's Lourie ☐
371 Purplecrested Lourie ☐
372 Ross's Lourie ☐
373 Grey Lourie ☐
374 European Cuckoo ☐
375 African Cuckoo ☐
376 Lesser Cuckoo ☐
377 Redchested Cuckoo ☐
378 Black Cuckoo ☐
379 Barred Cuckoo ☐
380 Great Spotted Cuckoo ☐
381 Striped Cuckoo ☐
382 Jacobin Cuckoo ☐
383 Thickbilled Cuckoo ☐
384 Emerald Cuckoo ☐

385 Klaas's Cuckoo ☐
386 Diederik Cuckoo ☐
387 Green Coucal ☐
388 Black Coucal ☐
389 Copperytailed Coucal ☐
390 Senegal Coucal ☐
391 Burchell's Coucal* ☐
391a Whitebrowed Coucal ☐
392 Barn Owl ☐
393 Grass Owl ☐
394 Wood Owl ☐
395 Marsh Owl ☐
396 Scops Owl ☐
397 Whitefaced Owl ☐
398 Pearlspotted Owl ☐
399 Barred Owl ☐
400 Cape Eagle Owl ☐
401 Spotted Eagle Owl ☐
402 Giant Eagle Owl ☐
403 Pel's Fishing Owl ☐
404 European Nightjar ☐
405 Fierynecked Nightjar ☐
406 Rufouscheeked Nightjar ☐
407 Natal Nightjar ☐
408 Freckled Nightjar ☐
409 Mozambique Nightjar ☐
410 Pennantwinged Nightjar ☐
411 European Swift ☐
412 Black Swift ☐
413 Bradfield's Swift* ☐
414 Pallid Swift ☐
415 Whiterumped Swift ☐
416 Horus Swift ☐
417 Little Swift ☐
418 Alpine Swift ☐
419 Mottled Swift ☐
420 Scarce Swift ☐
421 Palm Swift ☐
422 Mottled Spinetail ☐
423 Böhm's Spinetail ☐
424 Speckled Mousebird ☐
425 Whitebacked Mousebird** ☐
426 Redfaced Mousebird ☐
427 Narina Trogon ☐
428 Pied Kingfisher ☐
429 Giant Kingfisher ☐
430 Halfcollared Kingfisher ☐
431 Malachite Kingfisher ☐
432 Pygmy Kingfisher ☐
433 Woodland Kingfisher ☐
434 Mangrove Kingfisher ☐
435 Brownhooded Kingfisher ☐
436 Greyhooded Kingfisher ☐
437 Striped Kingfisher ☐
438 European Bee-eater ☐
439 Olive Bee-eater ☐
440 Bluecheeked Bee-eater ☐
441 Carmine Bee-eater ☐
442 Böhm's Bee-eater ☐
443 Whitefronted Bee-eater ☐
444 Little Bee-eater ☐
445 Swallowtailed Bee-eater ☐
446 European Roller ☐
447 Lilacbreasted Roller ☐
448 Rackettailed Roller ☐
449 Purple Roller ☐
450 Broadbilled Roller ☐
451 Hoopoe ☐
452 Redbilled Woodhoopoe ☐
453 Violet Woodhoopoe* ☐
454 Scimitarbilled Woodhoopoe ☐
455 Trumpeter Hornbill ☐
456 Silverycheeked Hornbill ☐
457 Grey Hornbill ☐
458 Redbilled Hornbill ☐
459 Southern Yellowbilled Hornbill* ☐
460 Crowned Hornbill ☐
461 Bradfield's Hornbill* ☐
462 Monteiro's Hornbill* ☐
463 Ground Hornbill ☐
464 Blackcollared Barbet ☐
465 Pied Barbet* ☐
466 White-eared Barbet ☐
467 Whyte's Barbet ☐
468 Green Barbet ☐
469 Redfronted Tinker Barbet ☐
470 Yellowfronted Tinker Barbet ☐
471 Goldenrumped Tinker Barbet ☐
472 Green Tinker Barbet ☐
473 Crested Barbet ☐
474 Greater Honeyguide ☐
475 Scalythroated Honeyguide ☐
476 Lesser Honeyguide ☐
477 Eastern Honeyguide ☐
478 Sharpbilled Honeyguide ☐
479 Slenderbilled Honeyguide ☐
480 Ground Woodpecker** ☐
481 Bennett's Woodpecker ☐
482 Specklethroated Woodpecker ☐
483 Goldentailed Woodpecker ☐
484 Knysna Woodpecker** ☐
485 Little Spotted Woodpecker ☐
486 Cardinal Woodpecker ☐
487 Bearded Woodpecker ☐
488 Olive Woodpecker ☐
489 Redthroated Wryneck ☐
490 African Broadbill ☐
491 Angola Pitta ☐
492 Melodious Lark** ☐
493 Monotonous Lark* ☐
494 Rufousnaped Lark ☐
495 Clapper Lark** ☐
496 Flappet Lark ☐
497 Fawncoloured Lark ☐
498 Sabota Lark* ☐
499 Rudd's Lark** ☐
500 Longbilled Lark* ☐
501 Shortclawed Lark** ☐
502 Karoo Lark** ☐

503 Dune Lark** ☐
504 Red Lark** ☐
505 Dusky Lark ☐
506 Spikeheeled Lark* ☐
507 Redcapped Lark ☐
508 Pinkbilled Lark* ☐
509 Botha's Lark** ☐
510 Sclater's Lark** ☐
511 Stark's Lark* ☐
512 Thickbilled Lark** ☐
513 Bimaculated Lark ☐
514 Gray's Lark* ☐
515 Chestnutbacked Finchlark ☐
516 Greybacked Finchlark* ☐
517 Blackeared Finchlark** ☐
518 European Swallow ☐
519 Angola Swallow ☐
520 Whitethroated Swallow ☐
521 Blue Swallow ☐
522 Wiretailed Swallow ☐
523 Pearlbreasted Swallow ☐
524 Redbreasted Swallow ☐
525 Mosque Swallow ☐
526 Greater Striped Swallow* ☐
527 Lesser Striped Swallow ☐
528 South African Cliff Swallow** ☐
529 Rock Martin ☐
530 House Martin ☐
531 Greyrumped Swallow ☐
532 Sand Martin ☐
533 Brownthroated Martin ☐
534 Banded Martin ☐
535 Mascarene Martin ☐
536 Black Sawwing Swallow ☐
537 Eastern Sawwing Swallow ☐
538 Black Cuckooshrike ☐
539 Whitebreasted Cuckooshrike ☐
540 Grey Cuckooshrike ☐
541 Forktailed Drongo ☐
542 Squaretailed Drongo ☐
543 European Golden Oriole ☐
544 African Golden Oriole ☐
545 Blackheaded Oriole ☐
546 Greenheaded Oriole ☐
547 Black Crow ☐
548 Pied Crow ☐
549 House Crow ☐
550 Whitenecked Raven ☐
551 Southern Grey Tit** ☐
552 Ashy Tit* ☐
553 Northern Grey Tit ☐
554 Southern Black Tit* ☐
555 Carp's Black Tit* ☐
556 Rufousbellied Tit ☐
557 Cape Penduline Tit* ☐
558 Grey Penduline Tit ☐
559 Spotted Creeper ☐
560 Arrowmarked Babbler ☐
561 Blackfaced Babbler* ☐
562 Whiterumped Babbler ☐
563 Pied Babbler** ☐
564 Barecheeked Babbler* ☐
565 Bush Blackcap** ☐
566 Cape Bulbul** ☐
567 Redeyed Bulbul* ☐
568 Blackeyed Bulbul ☐
569 Terrestrial Bulbul ☐
570 Yellowstreaked Bulbul ☐
571 Slender Bulbul ☐
572 Sombre Bulbul ☐
573 Stripecheeked Bulbul ☐
574 Yellowbellied Bulbul ☐
575 Yellowspotted Nicator ☐
576 Kurrichane Thrush ☐
577 Olive Thrush ☐
578 Spotted Thrush ☐
579 Orange Thrush ☐
580 Groundscraper Thrush ☐
581 Cape Rock Thrush** ☐
582 Sentinel Rock Thrush** ☐
583 Shorttoed Rock Thrush* ☐
584 Miombo Rock Thrush ☐
585 European Wheatear ☐
586 Mountain Chat* ☐
587 Capped Wheatear ☐
588 Buffstreaked Chat** ☐
589 Familiar Chat ☐
590 Tractrac Chat* ☐
591 Sicklewinged Chat** ☐
592 Karoo Chat* ☐
593 Mocking Chat ☐
594 Arnot's Chat ☐
595 Anteating Chat** ☐
596 Stonechat ☐
597 Whinchat ☐
598 Chorister Robin** ☐
599 Heuglin's Robin ☐
600 Natal Robin ☐
601 Cape Robin ☐
602 Whitethroated Robin** ☐
603 Collared Palm Thrush ☐
604 Rufoustailed Palm Thrush ☐
605 Whitebreasted Alethe ☐
606 Starred Robin ☐
607 Swynnerton's Robin ☐
608 Gunning's Robin ☐
609 Thrush Nightingale ☐
610 Boulder Chat* ☐
611 Cape Rockjumper** ☐
612 Orangebreasted Rockjumper** ☐
613 Whitebrowed Robin ☐
614 Karoo Robin** ☐
615 Kalahari Robin* ☐
616 Brown Robin** ☐
617 Bearded Robin ☐
618 Herero Chat* ☐
619 Garden Warbler ☐
620 Whitethroat ☐
621 Titbabbler* ☐
622 Layard's Titbabbler** ☐
623 Yellowbreasted Hyliota ☐
624 Mashona Hyliota ☐
625 Icterine Warbler ☐
626 Olivetree Warbler ☐
627 River Warbler ☐
628 Great Reed Warbler ☐
629 Basra Reed Warbler ☐

630 European Reed Warbler ☐
631 African Marsh Warbler ☐
632 Cinnamon Reed Warbler ☐
633 European Marsh Warbler ☐
634 European Sedge Warbler ☐
635 Cape Reed Warbler ☐
636 Greater Swamp Warbler ☐
637 Yellow Warbler ☐
638 African Sedge Warbler ☐
639 Barratt's Warbler** ☐
640 Knysna Warbler** ☐
641 Victorin's Warbler** ☐
642 Broadtailed Warbler ☐
643 Willow Warbler ☐
644 Yellowthroated Warbler ☐
645 Barthroated Apalis ☐
646 Chirinda Apalis** ☐
647 Blackheaded Apalis ☐
648 Yellowbreasted Apalis ☐
649 Rudd's Apalis* ☐
650 Redfaced Crombec ☐
651 Longbilled Crombec ☐
652 Redcapped Crombec ☐
653 Yellowbellied Eremomela ☐
654 Karoo Eremomela** ☐
655 Greencapped Eremomela ☐
656 Burntnecked Eremomela ☐
657 Bleating Warbler ☐
657a Greybacked Bleating Warbler ☐
658 Barred Warbler* ☐
659 Stierling's Barred Warbler ☐
660 Cinnamonbreasted Warbler** ☐
661 Grassbird** ☐
662 Rockrunner* ☐
663 Moustached Warbler ☐
664 Fantailed Cisticola ☐
665 Desert Cisticola ☐
666 Cloud Cisticola ☐
667 Ayres' Cisticola ☐
668 Palecrowned Cisticola ☐
669 Greybacked Cisticola* ☐
670 Wailing Cisticola ☐
671 Tinkling Cisticola ☐
672 Rattling Cisticola ☐
673 Singing Cisticola ☐
674 Redfaced Cisticola ☐
675 Blackbacked Cisticola ☐
676 Chirping Cisticola ☐
677 Levaillant's Cisticola ☐
678 Croaking Cisticola ☐
679 Lazy Cisticola ☐
680 Shortwinged Cisticola ☐
681 Neddicky ☐
682 Redwinged Warbler ☐
683 Tawnyflanked Prinia ☐
684 Roberts's Prinia** ☐
685 Blackchested Prinia* ☐
686 Karoo Prinia** ☐
686a Spotted Prinia** ☐
687 Namaqua Prinia** ☐
688 Rufouseared Warbler** ☐
689 Spotted Flycatcher ☐
690 Dusky Flycatcher ☐
691 Bluegrey Flycatcher ☐
692 Collared Flycatcher ☐
693 Fantailed Flycatcher ☐
694 Black Flycatcher ☐
695 Marico Flycatcher* ☐
696 Mousecoloured Flycatcher ☐
697 Chat Flycatcher* ☐
698 Fiscal Flycatcher** ☐
699 Vanga Flycatcher ☐
700 Cape Batis** ☐
701 Chinspot Batis ☐
702 Mozambique Batis ☐
703 Pririt Batis* ☐
704 Woodwards' Batis* ☐
705 Wattle-eyed Flycatcher ☐
706 Fairy Flycatcher** ☐
707 Livingstone's Flycatcher ☐
708 Bluemantled Flycatcher ☐
709 Whitetailed Flycatcher ☐
710 Paradise Flycatcher ☐
711 African Pied Wagtail ☐
712 Longtailed Wagtail ☐
713 Cape Wagtail ☐
714 Yellow Wagtail ☐
715 Grey Wagtail ☐
716 Grassveld Pipit ☐
717 Longbilled Pipit ☐
718 Plainbacked Pipit ☐
719 Buffy Pipit ☐
720 Striped Pipit ☐
721 Rock Pipit** ☐
722 Tree Pipit ☐
723 Bushveld Pipit ☐
724 Shorttailed Pipit ☐
725 Yellowbreasted Pipit** ☐
726 Golden Pipit ☐
727 Orangethroated Longclaw** ☐
728 Yellowthroated Longclaw ☐
729 Fülleborn's Longclaw ☐
730 Pinkthroated Longclaw ☐
731 Lesser Grey Shrike ☐
732 Fiscal Shrike ☐
733 Redbacked Shrike ☐
734 Sousa's Shrike ☐
735 Longtailed Shrike ☐
736 Southern Boubou** ☐
737 Tropical Boubou ☐
738 Swamp Boubou ☐
739 Crimsonbreasted Boubou* ☐
740 Puffback ☐
741 Brubru ☐
742 Southern Tchagra** ☐
743 Threestreaked Tchagra ☐
744 Blackcrowned Tchagra ☐
745 Marsh Tchagra ☐
746 Bokmakierie* ☐
747 Gorgeous Bush Shrike ☐
748 Orangebreasted Bush Shrike ☐

749 Blackfronted Bush Shrike ☐
750 Olive Bush Shrike* ☐
751 Greyheaded Bush Shrike ☐
752 Whitetailed Shrike* ☐
753 White Helmetshrike ☐
754 Redbilled Helmetshrike ☐
755 Chestnutfronted Helmetshrike ☐
756 Whitecrowned Shrike* ☐
757 European Starling ☐
758 Indian Myna ☐
759 Pied Starling** ☐
760 Wattled Starling ☐
761 Plumcoloured Starling ☐
762 Burchell's Starling* ☐
763 Longtailed Starling* ☐
764 Glossy Starling* ☐
765 Greater Blue-eared Starling ☐
766 Lesser Blue-eared Starling ☐
767 Sharptailed Starling ☐
768 Blackbellied Starling ☐
769 Redwinged Starling ☐
770 Palewinged Starling* ☐
771 Yellowbilled Oxpecker ☐
772 Redbilled Oxpecker ☐
773 Cape Sugarbird** ☐
774 Gurney's Sugarbird** ☐
775 Malachite Sunbird ☐
776 Bronze Sunbird ☐
777 Orangebreasted Sunbird** ☐
778 Coppery Sunbird ☐
779 Marico Sunbird ☐
780 Purplebanded Sunbird ☐
781 Shelley's Sunbird ☐
782 Neergaard's Sunbird** ☐
783 Lesser Double-collared Sunbird** ☐
784 Miombo Double-collared Sunbird ☐
785 Greater Doublecollared Sunbird** ☐
786 Yellowbellied Sunbird ☐
787 Whitebellied Sunbird ☐
788 Dusky Sunbird* ☐
789 Grey Sunbird ☐
790 Olive Sunbird ☐
791 Scarletchested Sunbird ☐
792 Black Sunbird ☐
793 Collared Sunbird ☐
794 Bluethroated Sunbird ☐
795 Violetbacked Sunbird ☐
796 Cape White-eye** ☐
797 Yellow White-eye ☐
798 Redbilled Buffalo Weaver ☐
799 Whitebrowed Sparrowweaver ☐
800 Sociable Weaver** ☐
801 House Sparrow ☐
802 Great Sparrow* ☐
803 Cape Sparrow* ☐
804 Greyheaded Sparrow ☐
805 Yellowthroated Sparrow ☐
806 Scalyfeathered Finch* ☐
807 Thickbilled Weaver ☐
808 Forest Weaver ☐
809 Oliveheaded Weaver ☐
810 Spectacled Weaver ☐
811 Spottedbacked Weaver ☐
812 Chestnut Weaver ☐
813 Cape Weaver** ☐
814 Masked Weaver ☐
815 Lesser Masked Weaver ☐
816 Golden Weaver ☐
817 Yellow Weaver ☐
818 Brownthroated Weaver ☐
819 Redheaded Weaver ☐
820 Cuckoo Finch ☐
821 Redbilled Quelea ☐
822 Redheaded Quelea ☐
823 Cardinal Quelea ☐
824 Red Bishop ☐
825 Firecrowned Bishop ☐
826 Golden Bishop ☐
827 Yellowrumped Widow ☐
828 Redshouldered Widow ☐
829 Whitewinged Widow ☐
830 Yellowbacked Widow ☐
831 Redcollared Widow ☐
832 Longtailed Widow ☐
833 Goldenbacked Pytilia ☐
834 Melba Finch ☐
835 Green Twinspot ☐
836 Redfaced Crimsonwing ☐
837 Nyasa Seedcracker ☐
838 Pinkthroated Twinspot** ☐
839 Redthroated Twinspot ☐
840 Bluebilled Firefinch ☐
841 Jameson's Firefinch ☐
842 Redbilled Firefinch ☐
843 Brown Firefinch ☐
844 Blue Waxbill ☐
845 Violeteared Waxbill* ☐
846 Common Waxbill ☐
847 Blackcheeked Waxbill ☐
848 Grey Waxbill ☐
849 Cinderella Waxbill* ☐
850 Swee Waxbill* ☐
851 East African Swee ☐
852 Quail Finch ☐
853 Locust Finch ☐
854 Orangebreasted Waxbill ☐
855 Cutthroat Finch ☐
856 Redheaded Finch* ☐
857 Bronze Mannikin ☐
858 Redbacked Mannikin ☐
859 Pied Mannikin ☐
860 Pintailed Whydah ☐
861 Shafttailed Whydah* ☐
862 Paradise Whydah ☐
863 Broadtailed Paradise Whydah ☐
864 Black Widowfinch ☐
865 Purple Widowfinch ☐
866 Violet Widowfinch ☐
867 Steelblue Widowfinch ☐
868 Chaffinch ☐

869 Yelloweyed Canary ☐
870 Blackthroated Canary ☐
871 Lemonbreasted Canary* ☐
872 Cape Canary ☐
873 Forest Canary** ☐
874 Cape Siskin** ☐
875 Drakensberg Siskin** ☐
876 Blackheaded Canary ☐
877 Bully Canary ☐
878 Yellow Canary* ☐
879 Whitethroated Canary* ☐
880 Protea Canary** ☐
881 Streakyheaded Canary ☐
882 Blackeared Canary** ☐
883 Cabanis's Bunting ☐
884 Goldenbreasted Bunting ☐
885 Cape Bunting ☐
886 Rock Bunting ☐
887 Larklike Bunting* ☐
901 Mountain Pipit ☐
902 Lesser Yellowlegs ☐
903 Redthroated Pipit ☐
904 Redrumped Swallow ☐
905 Laysan Albatross ☐
906 Greater Yellowlegs ☐
907 Pied Wheatear ☐
908 Kentish Plover ☐
909 Wood Pipit ☐
910 Redbilled Tropicbird ☐
911 European Blackcap ☐
912 Snowy Sheathbill ☐
913 Whiteheaded Sawwing Swallow ☐
914 Hudsonian Godwit ☐
915 Isabelline Wheatear ☐
916 European Redstart ☐
917 Whitethroated Bee-eater ☐
918 Matsudaira's Storm Petrel ☐
919 (European) Turtle Dove ☐

Recent Changes to the Southern African Checklist

Black Korhaan

239 Black Korhaan *Eupodotis afra*: southern and western Cape

239a Whitequilled Korhaan *Eupodotis afraoides*: central Cape northwards to Kunene and Zambezi rivers

Knysna Lourie

370 Knysna Lourie *Tauraco corythaix*: southern Cape to the Transvaal Drakensberg and Soutpansberg ranges

370a Livingstone's Lourie *Tauraco livingstonii*: Zululand coast, Mozambique, eastern Zimbabwean highlands and the Zambezi river northwards

Burchell's Coucal

391 Burchell's Coucal *Centropus burchellii:* eastern southern Africa

391a Whitebrowed Coucal *Centropus superciliosus:* northern Namibia, Botswana and Zimbabwe northwards

Bleating Warbler

657 Bleating Warbler *Camaroptera brachyura*: greenbacked forms in eastern southern Africa, ranging from the southern Cape to the Zambezi and adjacent Mozambique

657a Greybacked Bleating Warbler *Camaroptera brevicaudata:* greybacked forms ranging northwards from central Transvaal and central Namibia

Spotted Prinia

686 Karoo Prinia *Prinia maculosa*: southern, central and western Cape to southern Namibia

686a Spotted Prinia *Prinia hypoxantha*: north from East London through the eastern grasslands and Drakensberg region

Southern African Endemics

(86 species)

057 Bank Cormorant** ☐
092 Bald Ibis** ☐
103 South African Shelduck** ☐
122 Cape Vulture** ☐
150 Forest Buzzard** ☐
152 Jackal Buzzard** ☐
168 Black Harrier** ☐
190 Greywing Francolin** ☐
195 Cape Francolin** ☐
208 Blue Crane** ☐
234 Blue Korhaan** ☐
235 Karoo Koraan** ☐
239 Black Korhaan** ☐
239a Whitequilled Korhaan** ☐
244 African Black Oystercatcher** ☐
316 Hartlaub's Gull** ☐
370 Knysna Lourie** ☐
425 Whitebacked Mousebird** ☐
480 Ground Woodpecker** ☐
484 Knysna Woodpecker** ☐
492 Melodious Lark** ☐
495 Clapper Lark** ☐
499 Rudd's Lark** ☐
501 Shortclawed Lark** ☐
502 Karoo Lark** ☐
503 Dune Lark** ☐
504 Red Lark** ☐
509 Botha's Lark** ☐
510 Sclater's Lark** ☐
512 Thickbilled Lark** ☐
517 Blackeared Finchlark** ☐
528 South African Cliff Swallow** ☐
551 Southern Grey Tit** ☐
563 Pied Babbler** ☐
565 Bush Blackcap** ☐
566 Cape Bulbul** ☐
581 Cape Rock Thrush** ☐
582 Sentinel Rock Thrush** ☐
588 Buffstreaked Chat** ☐
591 Sicklewinged Chat** ☐
595 Anteating Chat** ☐
598 Chorister Robin** ☐
602 Whitethroated Robin** ☐
611 Cape Rockjumper** ☐
612 Orangebreasted Rockjumper** ☐
614 Karoo Robin** ☐
616 Brown Robin** ☐
622 Layard's Titbabbler** ☐
639 Barratt's Warbler** ☐
640 Knysna Warbler** ☐
641 Victorin's Warbler** ☐
646 Chirinda Apalis** ☐
654 Karoo Eremomela** ☐
660 Cinnamonbreasted Warbler** ☐
661 Grassbird** ☐
684 Roberts's Prinia** ☐
686 Karoo Prinia** ☐
686a Spotted Prinia** ☐
687 Namaqua Prinia** ☐
688 Rufouseared Warbler** ☐
698 Fiscal Flycatcher** ☐
700 Cape Batis** ☐
706 Fairy Flycatcher** ☐
721 Rock Pipit** ☐
725 Yellowbreasted Pipit** ☐
727 Orangethroated Longclaw** ☐
736 Southern Boubou** ☐
742 Southern Tchagra** ☐
759 Pied Starling** ☐
773 Cape Sugarbird** ☐
774 Gurney's Sugarbird** ☐
777 Orangebreasted Sunbird** ☐
782 Neergaard's Sunbird** ☐
783 Lesser Double-collared Sunbird** ☐
785 Greater Double-collared Sunbird** ☐
796 Cape White-eye** ☐
800 Sociable Weaver** ☐
813 Cape Weaver** ☐
838 Pinkthroated Twinspot** ☐
873 Forest Canary** ☐
874 Cape Siskin** ☐
875 Drakensberg Siskin** ☐
880 Protea Canary** ☐
882 Blackeared Canary** ☐

Southern African Near Endemics

(84 species)

003 Jackass Penguin* ☐
053 Cape Gannet* ☐
056 Cape Cormorant* ☐
059 Crowned Cormorant* ☐
070 Slaty Egret* ☐
112 Cape Shoveller* ☐
162 Pale Chanting Goshawk* ☐
193 Orange River Francolin* ☐
194 Redbilled Francolin* ☐
196 Natal Francolin* ☐
197 Hartlaub's Francolin* ☐
199 Swainson's Francolin* ☐
232 Ludwig's Bustard* ☐
236 Rüppell's Korhaan* ☐
237 Redcrested Korhaan* ☐
299 Burchell's Courser* ☐
334 Damara Tern* ☐
344 Namaqua Sandgrouse* ☐
345 Burchell's Sandgrouse* ☐
347 Doublebanded Sandgrouse* ☐
365 Rüppell's Parrot* ☐
367 Rosyfaced Lovebird* ☐
369 Blackcheeked ☐ Lovebird* ☐
391 Burchell's Coucal* ☐
413 Bradfield's Swift* ☐
453 Violet Woodhoopoe* ☐
459 Southern Yellowbilled Hornbill* ☐
461 Bradfield's Hornbill* ☐
462 Monteiro's Hornbill* ☐
465 Pied Barbet* ☐
493 Monotonous Lark* ☐
498 Sabota Lark* ☐
500 Longbilled Lark* ☐
506 Spikeheeled Lark* ☐
508 Pinkbilled Lark* ☐
511 Stark's Lark* ☐
514 Gray's Lark* ☐
516 Greybacked Finchlark* ☐
526 Greater Striped Swallow* ☐
552 Ashy Tit* ☐
554 Southern Black Tit* ☐
555 Carp's Black Tit* ☐
557 Cape Penduline Tit* ☐
561 Blackfaced Babbler* ☐
564 Barecheeked Babbler* ☐
567 Redeyed Bulbul* ☐
583 Shorttoed Rock Thrush* ☐
586 Mountain Chat* ☐
590 Tractrac Chat* ☐
592 Karoo Chat* ☐
610 Boulder Chat* ☐
615 Kalahari Robin* ☐
618 Herero Chat* ☐
621 Titbabbler* ☐
649 Rudd's Apalis* ☐
658 Barred Warbler* ☐
662 Rockrunner* ☐
669 Greybacked Cisticola* ☐
685 Blackchested Prinia* ☐
695 Marico Flycatcher* ☐
697 Chat Flycatcher* ☐
703 Pririt Batis* ☐
704 Woodwards' Batis* ☐
739 Crimsonbreasted Boubou* ☐
746 Bokmakierie* ☐
750 Olive Bush Shrike* ☐
752 Whitetailed Shrike* ☐
756 Whitecrowned Shrike* ☐
762 Burchell's Starling* ☐
763 Longtailed Starling* ☐
764 Glossy Starling* ☐
770 Palewinged Starling* ☐
788 Dusky Sunbird* ☐
802 Great Sparrow* ☐
803 Cape Sparrow* ☐
806 Scalyfeathered Finch* ☐
845 Violeteared Waxbill* ☐
849 Cinderella Waxbill* ☐
850 Swee Waxbill* ☐
856 Redheaded Finch* ☐
861 Shafttailed Whydah* ☐
871 Lemonbreasted Canary* ☐
878 Yellow Canary* ☐
879 Whitethroated Canary* ☐
887 Larklike Bunting* ☐
901 Mountain Pipit* ☐

Index to localities